Pers .... *ture*

A Crit .... *Theory*

in .... *gy*

PEARSON
Prentice
Hall

Upper Saddle River, New Jersey 07458

Library of Congress Cataloging-in-Publication Data

Sidky, H.

   Perspectives on culture : a critical introduction to theory in cultural anthropology / H. Sidky.
      p. cm.
Includes bibliographical references and index.
   ISBN 0-13-093134-9
   1. Ethnology—Philosophy.   2. Ethnology—History.   I. Title.
   GN345.S554 2004
   306'.01—dc22

                                  2003022460

Publisher: Nancy Roberts
Editorial Assistant: Lee Peterson
Senior Marketing Manager: Marissa Feliberty
Marketing Assistant: Adam Laitman
Production Liaison: Joanne Hakim
Manufacturing Buyer: Ben Smith
Cover Art Director: Jayne Conte
Cover Design: Bruce Kenselaar

Illustrator (Interior): Mirella Signoretto
Photo Researcher: Elaine Soares
Image Permission Coordinator: Carolyn Gauntt
Composition/Full-Service Project Management: Karen Berry/Pine Tree Composition
Printer/Binder: Phoenix Color Book Technology

For permission to use copyrighted material, grateful acknowledgment is made to the copyright holders on pages 502 to 509, which are hereby made part of this copyright page.

Pearson Education LTD., London
Pearson Education Singapore, Pte. Ltd
Pearson Education, Canada, Ltd
Pearson Education–Japan
Pearson Education Australia PTY, Limited

Pearson Education North Asia Ltd
Pearson Educación de Mexico, S.A. de C.V.
Pearson Education Malaysia, Pte. Ltd
Pearson Education, Upper Saddle River, New Jersey

10 9 8 7 6 5 4 3 2 1
ISBN: 0-13-093134-9

Contents

Chapter 4

Lewis Henry Morgan and the Evolution of Society

Chapter 5

The Diffusionists: Unbridled Imagination and the History of Culture

Chapter 14
Scientific, Materialist, and Marxist Anthropology   334

Chapter 15
Postmodern Anthropology and Cultural Constructionism   394

Chapter 16
Conclusions: Anthropology in the Twenty-First Century   413

Preface

This book provides a critical introduction to theory in cultural anthropology from the perspective of the philosophy of science. Anthropological paradigms are assessed in terms of their central assumptions, the kind of knowledge or understanding they yield, and how closely those understandings approach the anthropological goal of obtaining reliable, objectively valid knowledge about humankind, human behavior, and the evolution and operation of sociocultural systems.

In my discussion of anthropological theory I take an historical approach. This is indispensable because new theoretical perspectives often continue to utilize ideas, concepts, and analytical categories that were part of the paradigms that were displaced (cf. Orlove 1980: 237). New paradigms are molded by a dialectical relationship with earlier paradigms that affect the manner in which their epistemological and theoretical principles are expressed (cf. Barrett 1984; Erickson and Murphy 2001: xi; McGee and Warms 2000: 2). A continual dialogue exists between past and present perspectives and often what seems new, upon close scrutiny, turns out to be a reformulation of previously worked out ideas and approaches. For this reason, rejecting "disciplinary origins and traditions" (Marcus 1992: viii–ix), as some anthropologists have done, is a

particularly egregious blunder. Those who do so are condemned to repeat past errors.

There is much that we can learn from the efforts of the anthropologists who lived and worked over the course of the last one hundred years. Their works were full of flaws, but they do not deserve blanket condemnation. These works require critical analysis, not sweeping denigration and dismissal. We can learn from our predecessors' ideas, debates, mistakes, and successes, and insights may be gained from the problems and cultural puzzles they chose to tackle.

Numerous examples of such anthropological puzzles are presented throughout this book in order to illustrate the various theoretical operations associated with particular research strategies and to familiarize the reader with key anthropological concepts and ideas. One learns how to assess different claims to knowledge by systematically working through them. Present-day anthropological findings that have a bearing upon the problems that engaged earlier researchers are included at various points in the discussion. This will allow the reader to gain familiarity with contemporary anthropological thinking on the topics and issues that preoccupied our predecessors.

The primary objectives of this book are threefold:

1. To familiarize the reader with anthropological knowledge and a range of theoretical perspectives developed over the course of the last one hundred and twenty years
2. To introduce readers to epistemology, the branch of inquiry that deals with the nature and the sources of knowledge
3. To enable readers to develop the analytical skills necessary to assess competing theoretical perspectives, to critically evaluate different claims to knowledge, and to be able to distinguish between scientific, pseudoscientific, and nonscientific accounts of sociocultural phenomena

Without the ability to evaluate different kinds of knowledge, students of anthropology are ill equipped in their efforts to assess the often contradictory claims and conflicting accounts of the world that they will encounter in the course of their studies. Such an understanding is especially needed at the present when American anthropology is in a state of disarray as a result of the "culture wars" between exponents of scientific anthropology, who are striving to build increasingly more accurate empirical understandings of the world, and cultural constructionists, otherwise glossed as postmodern interpretive anthropologists, who are absorbed with thick descriptions and the pursuit of discourses immune to appraisal or validation.

This book teaches students the valuable lesson that "the problem of knowledge" is not insoluble. The critical conceptual tools are already there for anyone who wishes to use them. Obtaining reliable understandings of the world is not easy, but it can be done.

I would like to thank the following colleagues who reviewed this work in manuscript form for their thoughtful comments and suggestions: E. Paul Durrenberger, Pennsylvania State University; Ratimaya Bush, Wright State University; Barry A. Kass, Orange County Community College, State University of New York; Charles Harper, Creighton University; James G. Flanagan, University of Southern Mississippi; Mark Moberg, University of Southern Alabama; and Geraldine Gamburd, University of Massachusetts, Dartmouth.

H. Sidky
Miami University

Chapter 1

The Nature of Anthropology and Anthropological Knowledge

Anthropology (from two Greek words, *anthropos* for "human" and *logos* for "study") is the scientific study of humanity in the broadest sense of the term. Modern anthropology may be described as the comparative and holistic study of humans, human biology, human behavior, and human societies. Since its inception as a university-based field of study, anthropology has aspired to be a scientific discipline. This means that anthropologists are committed to a particular set of epistemological premises about the nature of sociocultural reality and how best to generate meaningful generalizations about humans and human nature. As a science anthropology has made unparalleled advances in our knowledge of humankind and the human condition.

Anthropology's scientific orientation accounts for the scope of its subject matter. A sense of this is evident from a quick glance at some introductory anthropological texts. As the cultural anthropologists James Peoples and Garrick Bailey (1994: 3) have put it,

> Anthropologists are interested in almost everything about people. We want to know when and where

the human species originated, how and why we evolved into our present form, and the ways in which this biological evolution continues to affect us today. Anthropologists want to know about the technological, economic, political, and intellectual development of humanity. We want to know the extent to which different human populations vary in their biological and social characteristics and to understand why these differences exist.[1]

The anthropological archeologist David Hurst Thomas (1998: 30) shares a similar view:

> What all anthropologists share is a perspective, an outlook. Anthropologists believe that the best understanding of the human condition can arise only from a global and comparative approach. It is not enough to look at any single group—Americans, Chinese, Balinese, or *Australopithecines*—to find the keys to human existence. Neither is it enough to look at just one part of the human condition. . . . Looking at part of the picture only gives you just that—part of the picture. . . . What holds anthropology together is its dogmatic insistence that every aspect of human society, extant or extinct, counts. For a century, anthropologists have tried to arrive at the fullest possible understanding of human similarities and diversity. Because of this

1

broad-brush approach, anthropology is uniquely qualified to understand what makes humankind distinct from the rest of the animal world.[2]

The physical anthropologist John Relethford (1990: 8) expresses the same objectives:

In a general sense, anthropology is concerned with determining what humans are, how they evolved, and how they differ from one another. Where other disciplines focus on specific issues of humanity, anthropology is unique in dealing simultaneously with questions of origins, evolution, variation, and adaptation.[3]

Linguistic anthropologists hold a comparable viewpoint on the discipline. As Zdenek Salzmann (1993: 2) writes,

The one commitment that anthropologists profess regardless of their specialization is the holistic approach. The term **holistic** refers to concern with a system as a whole rather than with only cultural, social, and biological.[4]

These passages capture the distinguishing feature of the discipline that sets it apart from all the other fields that study humans and human behavior. Anthropology alone has sought to present a holistic, evolutionary, and pan-human/comparative understanding of humans and human behavior in which the biological and cultural aspects of humankind are both deemed to be relevant and important. This unique holistic perspective is embedded in the four-field organization of American anthropology (Figure 1.1), the central intellectual aspiration of which has been and remains

the exchange of data and theories among different fields and subfields concerned with the global, comparative, diachronic, and synchronic study of humankind: the origin of the hominids, the emergence of language and culture, the evolution of cultural differences and similarities, and the ways in which biocultural, mental, behavioral, demographic, and environmental and other nomothetic processes have shaped and continue to shape the human world (Harris 1994: 62).[5]

All anthropologists, despite the fact that they may be engaged in quite different intellectual pursuits, share, or until recently shared, this focus. The unity of a discipline with such a diverse subject matter is based upon a set of shared theoretical ideas among its practitioners regarding biological evolution and human behavior (McGee and Warms 2000: 1).

CULTURAL ANTHROPOLOGY

This book deals primarily with theoretical perspectives in cultural anthropology, the subfield of the discipline concerned with the first-hand scientific study and comparison of contemporary or recently extant human populations/societies. In this chapter I shall discuss the manner in which cultural anthropologists generate knowledge and formulate statements or generalizations about humans and human behavior. I shall argue that scientific anthropological knowledge represents a special and novel way of understanding humanity. As such, anthropological knowledge is vastly different from the knowledge or understandings of any given culture, including the culture to which anthropologists themselves belong.

Cultural anthropology has two interconnected components, **ethnography** and **ethnology.** Ethnography (derived from Greek) entails the systematic description of a particular people/culture through fieldwork. The word *ethnography* denotes both the research process and the end product of that research, which is usually in the form of a written monograph (Angrosino 2002: 1). Ethnology refers to the systematic comparison of cultures around the globe in order to answer particular questions and produce useful generalizations about humankind and human behavior.

The basic data of cultural anthropology comes from fieldwork. Fieldwork comprises one of the "outstanding" characteristics of the discipline, and practitioners in all four fields of the

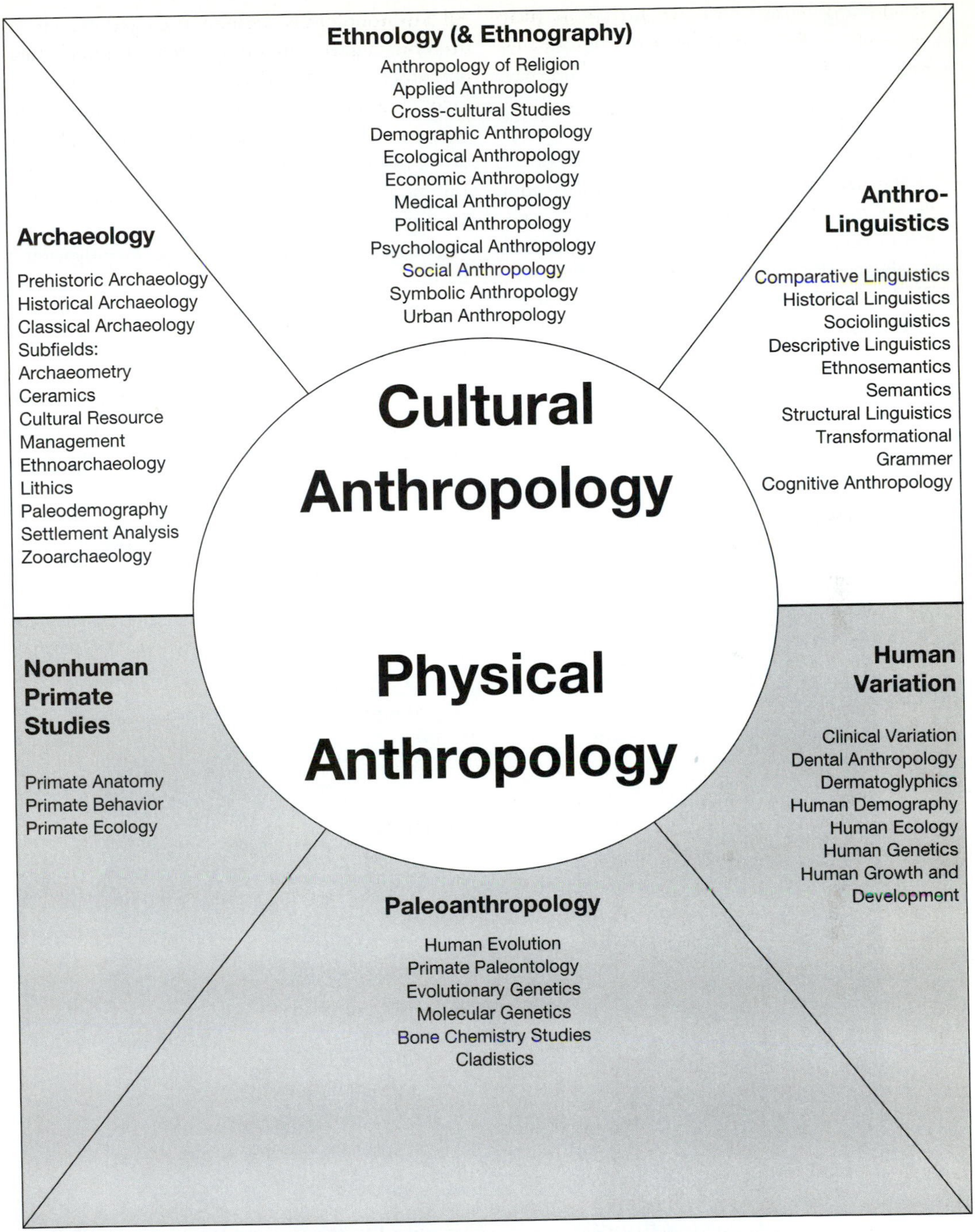

Ethnology (& Ethnography)
Anthropology of Religion
Applied Anthropology
Cross-cultural Studies
Demographic Anthropology
Ecological Anthropology
Economic Anthropology
Medical Anthropology
Political Anthropology
Psychological Anthropology
Social Anthropology
Symbolic Anthropology
Urban Anthropology

Anthro-Linguistics

Comparative Linguistics
Historical Linguistics
Sociolinguistics
Descriptive Linguistics
Ethnosemantics
Semantics
Structural Linguistics
Transformational
Grammer
Cognitive Anthropology

Archaeology

Prehistoric Archaeology
Historical Archaeology
Classical Archaeology
Subfields:
Archaeometry
Ceramics
Cultural Resource
Management
Ethnoarchaeology
Lithics
Paleodemography
Settlement Analysis
Zooarchaeology

Cultural Anthropology

Physical Anthropology

Nonhuman Primate Studies

Primate Anatomy
Primate Behavior
Primate Ecology

Human Variation

Clinical Variation
Dental Anthropology
Dermatoglyphics
Human Demography
Human Ecology
Human Genetics
Human Growth and
Development

Paleoanthropology

Human Evolution
Primate Paleontology
Evolutionary Genetics
Molecular Genetics
Bone Chemistry Studies
Cladistics

Figure 1.1 The subdisciplines of anthropology. *After Gross (1992); Scupin (1992).*

discipline engage in field research (Barrett 1991: 2). The most significant advances in our understanding of humans and humankind have emerged through anthropological fieldwork.

Ethnographic field research involves developing a close relationship with the people one is studying, learning their language, living among them, taking part to some extent in their day-to-day routines, and observing and recording various aspects of their society through first-hand experience. This procedure has been called **participant observation,** a research technique developed and refined during the last century (Howard and Dunaif-Hattis 1992: 377; see Angrosino 2002; Ellen 1984; Spradley 1980; Wolcott 1995).

Anthropologists are not interested merely in studying a particular custom or describing a single aspect of a certain culture, but rather they seek to understand the various aspects of a culture in terms of the larger system of which they are a part. Cultures are treated as being made up of distinct but interrelated components. Cultures, in other words, are thought to be **integrated.** Therefore, even when investigating a particular question (for example, whether or not large-scale irrigation works contribute to the rise of political complexity or why certain areas experience periodic or chronic outbreaks of witchcraft accusations and witch-hunting), the anthropologist must take into account the complete cultural context. This focus on the total

The anthropologist Napoleon Chagnon conducting fieldwork among the Yanomamö. Scientific anthropologists gather empirical data about the cultures they study by living and participating in the daily activities of the members of the culture.

way of life of a people is an aspect of the holistic perspective.

During the course of their field research, anthropologists constantly ask questions, collect historical information and **life histories** (details of the life of particular individuals as a cultural profile of their experiences from their point of view), take photographs, and videotape rituals. In addition, the fieldworker will draw maps of settlement patterns and investigate subsistence strategies, division of labor, and types of tools and technology being used. The field researcher will also study social and political organization, kinship terminologies, courtship, marriage patterns, residence rules, child rearing, funeral rites, food taboos, religious ceremonies, and the numerous other elements that altogether constitute culture (cf. Murdock 1945: 124).

Beyond the treatment of the systemic or integrated nature of cultures, anthropologists are also interested in the broader ecological settings within which cultural systems operate. The field-worker may collect information on the physical environment and investigate the **adaptive strategies** of the people he or she is studying. This approach, which examines human-environmental interactions, focuses upon the ecological context and the patterns of human **adaptation** in that context (Bates 1998: 24–25; Moran 2000).

In addition to the preceding, the fieldworker may collect information relevant to his or her own theoretical focus or specialization, such as psychological anthropology, economic anthropology, political anthropology, urban anthropology, and medical anthropology, among others (see Figure 1.1).

The fieldwork tradition through participant observation first began out of the need for reliable data given the poor quality, paucity, or absence of accounts about the cultures anthropologist were keen to understand. The solution to this problem was for anthropologists to go out and gather firsthand data themselves through extended field research (Barrett 1991: 4). In the

past, the focused was upon small-scale, faraway peoples and places that to Europeans appeared "exotic." Today, anthropologists have broadened their scope to include cultures of all scales and pursue a diversity of topics ranging from studies of globalization and underdevelopment to homelessness in America and many other socially significant questions (see Fowler and Hardesty 1994 for an overview).

The reason for this shift is simply that the world has changed drastically from the circumstances in which the pioneering anthropologists such as Bronislaw Malinowski, E. Evans-Pritchard, or Margaret Mead found themselves. The world in which we live today, and the world anthropologists engage, is in the grips of an ever-increasing process of globalization. As a result, large-scale and small-scale societies are becoming incorporated into one large homogenous system, with vast social, political, and economic inequalities. Transnational corporations, along with modern communication, such as radios, television, movies, digital and satellite telephones, computers, and the Internet, among other things, have transformed the world into a "global village" (Washburn 1998: 6). This global village reflects the late stages of capitalism. It is also a world of cultural fragmentation, of "deterritorialization," where war, ethnic cleansing, warlords, terror networks, famine, and poverty have driven "Third World" populations into "First World" nations (Appadurai 1991: 192).

Despite these new circumstances and regardless of whether anthropologists are working at home or abroad, they have not abandoned the fieldwork tradition based on participant observation. As Richard Barrett (1991: 4–5) explains,

Anthropologists have learned that by living with the people themselves, they can achieve a level of understanding that would be impossible by any other means. People tend to develop relationships of trust and confidence with someone who shares their life and becomes a familiar presence. They will open up with such a person in ways that they would never do with strangers. It is also a means by which anthropologists discover aspects of the society that remain concealed to all but those who live there.[6]

Fieldwork through participant observation offers the potential that the anthropologist can gain the "insider's perspective," an intimate understanding of a culture from the point of view of its participants (Barrett 1991: 28).

The length of time anthropologists spend in the field (usually at least a year, but preferably longer) allows them to establish friendships, learn the local language or dialect, as well as gain an understanding of local customs and traditions. Being situated in this way the anthropologist is also able to observe people in a variety of situations.

The nature of ethnographic fieldwork raises important and thorny ethical questions pertaining to the relationship between the ethnographer and the people he or she is studying (Fluehr-Lobban 1991). The Statements on Ethics adopted by the American Anthropological Association (1971) clearly stipulates the ethnographer's obligations:

> In research, an anthropologist's paramount responsibility is to those he studies. When there is a conflict of interest, these individuals must come first. The anthropologist must do everything within his power to protect their physical, social, and psychological welfare and to honor their dignity and privacy. . . . Every effort should be exerted to cooperate with members of the host society in the planning and execution of research projects.

The amount of time a researcher spends in the field is important because different cultural activities occur at different times during a particular season or annual cycle and thus remain hidden from the casual visitor during a short stay (Barrett 1991: 30–32). Extended field research through participant observation has yet another value. Anthropologists have long noted that there is often a difference between "what people say" and "what they actually do." Discovering this difference in the context of a particular cul-

tural setting may easily elude the casual visitor. It is for these reason, therefore, that modern anthropologists see participant observation as "an indispensable tool for penetrating beyond what people say—and often believe—about their own culture" (Barrett 1991: 32).

Given the important difference between what people say and what is the case, anthropologists have made a distinction between **emic** and **etic** perspectives. I shall discuss the emic/etic distinction at length later on. For now it suffices to note that emic denotes the "insider's/native's point of view," or the folk model, and etic refers to the point of view of the outside observer, or the analytical model (Harris 2001: 32).

It is well known among anthropologists that our observations are influenced by implicit or explicit interpretive frameworks, subjective predispositions, cultural filters, theoretical orientations, biases, prejudices, individual personality, cultural and linguistic backgrounds, authorial skills, as well as political and historical contingencies that affect where we look, what we see, and what we ignore. One means of dealing with the problem of bias is for the fieldworker to adopt the axiom of **cultural relativism.**

Cultural relativism holds that each culture must be evaluated in its own terms, and not in terms of the standards and values of the anthropologist's own society (see Hatch 1983). All anthropologists endeavor to promulgate the basic lesson of cultural relativism by pointing out that each culture is valid and valuable in its own way and represents one solution to the problems which humans face everywhere.

While cultural relativism enabled the correction of many of the gross misrepresentations of so-called primitive people in nineteenth-century ethnology, as we shall see, the concept has resulted in innumerable theoretical difficulties in contemporary anthropological thinking.

Aside from the axiom of cultural relativism, another strategy anthropologists have relied upon to overcome observer bias, one to which I alluded earlier, is to attempt to get the "insider's view" of another culture. This requires that one become familiar with "native" values, logic, and beliefs to the degree that one can understand the world from the point of view of the participants of the culture being studied. This type of familiarity with another culture is known as "subjective understanding" (Barrett 1991: 8). How does the ethnographer achieve this? As Evans-Pritchard (1962: 148) put it long ago,

> He goes to live for some months or years among a people. He lives among them as intimately as he can, *and he learns to speak their language, to think in their concepts and to feel in the values. He then lives the experiences over again critically and interpretively in the conceptual categories and values of his own culture and in terms of the general body of knowledge in his discipline.* In other words, he translates from one culture into another (emphasis added).

One way of determining if the anthropologist has obtained a degree of understanding is whether he or she can account for cultural phenomena in terms of both emic and etic perspectives—that is, from the insider's point of view and the analytical/outsiders' point of view (Wagner 1999: 93). For example, Evans-Pritchard was able to grasp the different ways in which an Azande tribesman and an Englishman would answer the question: Why did the granary collapse and kill a man sleeping in its shade? The European would attribute it to the action of carpenter ants and coincidence, or accident. The Azande man would state the question differently and query: Why this granary on this man's head? His answer would be: carpenter ants and witchcraft (Wagner 1999: 93).

As part of field research, modern anthropologists usually rely upon **informants,** now referred to as "consultants." Consultants are individuals who have been raised, or have been **enculturated,** in the culture being studied. As such, when asked the appropriate questions, such individuals can offer important details that could lead to significant insights into their beliefs, values, and social norms that would normally escape

the outsider's attention. Sometimes certain individuals are selected as informants, either because of differences in age, social status, gender, or occupation—factors that effect or influence individual points of view—or because they possess special skills or cultural knowledge (cf. Barrett 1991: 33–36; see Spradley 1979 for a discussion of modern ethnographic interview techniques).

When conducting ethnographic field research, anthropologists may come to rely on specific individuals as their **key informants,** but they never depend upon the "voices" or opinions of one or two individuals. It is common practice for the fieldworker to crosscheck information gathered from one individual with accounts provided by many others. This is necessary in order to ensure the reliability of the data and to determine whether the information obtained is widely shared by members of the group or whether it reflects the viewpoints of marginal or atypical individuals.

Such crosschecking is also indispensable in order for the ethnographer to avoid being hoaxed. The anthropologist Napoleon Chagnon (1992: 10–11) describes encountering just such a problem during his fieldwork among the Yąnomamö:

> With respect to collecting the data I sought, there was a very frustrating problem. . . . to understand the Yąnomamö way of life I had to collect extensive genealogies. I could not have deliberately picked a more difficult group to work with in this regard: They have very stringent name taboos. . . . I tried to use kinship terms to collect genealogies at first, but the kinship terms were so ambiguous that I ultimately had to resort to names. They were quick to grasp that I was bound to learn everybody's name and reacted . . . by inventing false names. . . . They enjoyed watching me learn these names. I assumed, wrongly, that I would get the truth to each question and that I would get the best information by working in public. This set the stage for converting a serious project into a farce. Each informant tried to outdo his peers by inventing a name even more ridiculous than what I had been given earlier, or by asserting that the

individual about whom I inquired was married to his mother or daughter, and the like.

After spending five months collecting such data, Chagnon realized that he had been subjected to a hoax. He thus had to change his research strategy.

> I was forced to do my genealogy work in private because of the horseplay and nonsense. Once I did so, my informants began to agree with each other and I managed to learn a few new names, real names. I could then test any new informant by collecting a genealogy from him that I knew to be accurate. I was able to weed out the more mischievous informants this way. Little by little I extended the genealogies and learned the real names (Chagnon 1992: 11).[7]

Anthropologists are interested only in ideas, values, beliefs, norms, and behaviors shared by members of a society, and not with idiosyncratic beliefs and behaviors of particular individuals. As Barrett (1991: 37–38) points out,

> the possibility of distortion is ever-present when working with informants. All individuals have specific interests and points of view that they communicate to the fieldworker, many of which do not accurately reflect the culture at large. The individuals themselves may be atypical a paranoiac, misogynist. . . . Even in a small peasant community the divergence of opinion on almost any matter between Catholic priest, anarchist, blacksmith, and village prostitute might be so great as to constitute radically different interpretations of local society. It would be simplistic in the extreme if anthropologists were merely to adopt one of these perspectives as the "correct" one, since each is likely to be biased in a particular fashion. They instead view each as part of the multifaceted reality that they must struggle to interpret. . . . *Nothing could be more mistaken, therefore, than to believe that the anthropologist merely sits down with informants and is "told what the culture is."* This would be quite impossible, since informants—even the most detached and analytical—can give only their version of their culture. A priest is disposed to emphasize certain aspects of the society, and a prostitute, or a

drunk, will emphasize quite different aspects. *But it is precisely here that anthropologists have an advantage because they are not members of the local society, they can view it with some detachment; no socially conditioned role predisposes them to emphasize one reality at the expense of another.* An additional advantage is that they work with many members of the community and gain specialized knowledge and a particular point of view from each. By so doing they hope to attain a more comprehensive perspective on the culture than is available to any single member of society (emphasis added).[8]

The requirement that ethnographic findings must be gauged against the perspectives of many different individuals in a community is one of the most powerful and distinctive features of the modern ethnography.

Holistic ethnographic studies of particular cultures have traditionally been valued for a number of reasons. First, such works are considered to be important because they filled in voids in the **ethnographic record,** the sum total of information gathered by anthropologists over the last century or more, documenting the range of human possibilities and cultural variations. Second, holistic ethnographies are deemed valuable as starting points for more "in-depth" and focused studies of the specific details of these cultures. Such focused investigations could include, for example, political authority, the ritual use of hallucinogenic drugs, the effects of cash markets on local subsistence economies, or the impact of broader regional and global economic or political events at the local level (cf. Howard and Dunaif-Hattis 1992: 379).

ETHNOLOGY: THE SCIENCE OF CULTURE

Documenting cultural similarities and differences through empirical field research is a component of the anthropological agenda of building and enhancing our knowledge of the world. However, producing descriptive accounts is not an end in itself. Such accounts are necessary for the systematic comparison of historically related and unrelated cultures around the globe and throughout time in order to arrive at scientific generalizations about human behavior and the operation of sociocultural systems (see Bernard 1995; Ember and Ember 2001; Ferraro 1992: 7; Goodenough 1970: Wolcott 1995).

Ethnological research and the comparative perspective constitute the central distinguishing feature that sets anthropology apart from all other fields of study that focus upon humans and human behavior (Barrett 1991: 11). Ethnological analysis encompasses the whole range of sociocultural similarities and differences through time and space. The scientific status of theoretical generalizations depends upon taking this range of diversity into account. Anthropologists insist that all generalizations about humans and human behavior must be appraised in this way, from a comparative, cross-cultural perspective.

In other words, anthropologists insist that any statement we make about any aspect of human life and human behavior must be based upon empirical evidence from many historically unrelated societies, both similar and different, and not just on evidence from one culture or one group. Hence the pan-human dimension of anthropology. Anthropologists have good reasons for adopting this point of view. As Ember and Ember (1990: 2) note,

> What induces the anthropologist to choose so broad a subject for study? In part, he or she is motivated by the belief that any suggested generalization about human beings, any possible explanation of some characteristic of human culture and biology, should be shown to apply to many times and places of human existence. If a generalization or explanation does not prove to apply widely, we are entitled or even obliged to be skeptical about it. The skeptical attitude, in the absence of persuasive evidence, is our best protection against accepting ideas about humans that are wrong.[9]

The requirement that all generalizations about humankind must demonstrably apply to many places and many times has great epistemological significance. For the lack of something better, this offers our only safeguard against our embracing erroneous ideas about people and cultures.

THE NATURE OF ANTHROPOLOGICAL KNOWLEDGE

The way in which anthropological knowledge is generated sets it apart from other kinds of knowledge or understandings. Every society, including the ones to which anthropologists belong, have bodies of knowledge that explain human life, the world, the universe and everything in it. Such knowledge may be referred to as folk knowledge. Anthropological knowledge differs from folk knowledge and other kinds of knowledge about humankind, whether mystical, poetic, intuitive, allegorical, and so forth. This is because anthropological knowledge is empirical and is obtained systematically by means of first-hand fieldwork and because such knowledge strives to be holistic, pan-human, evolutionary, and diachronic. To conflate anthropological knowledge with these other types of knowledge is to commit an epistemological blunder. Scientific anthropological knowledge can help us formulate generalizations capable of explaining cross-cultural similarities and differences everywhere and has the potential of generating a reliable understanding of the complex and conflicting cultural systems that exist today (cf. Bodley 1994: 1; Spiro 1986: 278).

In this chapter I have outlined the nature of anthropology and the manner in which cultural anthropologists generate knowledge and formulate generalizations about humans and human behavior. I have argued that scientific anthropological knowledge comprises a special and novel way of understanding humanity. As such, anthropological knowledge is qualitatively different from the knowledge or understandings of any given culture, including the culture to which anthropologists themselves belong (for a more elaborate treatment of these topics and those covered in subsequent chapters, see Sidky 2003). In the next chapter I shall examine the epistemological foundations of science and scientific anthropology and develop a set of criteria for the assessment of anthropological theories of culture that have been developed over the last one hundred and thirty years.

Chapter 2

Science and Anthropology: Epistemological Questions

Anthropologists who seek a scientific understanding of humankind subscribe to a particular set of epistemological premises. This choice is dictated by the fact that there are many different ways of knowing or understandings about the world, universe, and everything in them—including mystical, poetic, intuitive, and allegorical, among others. Not all of these are of equal use if our goal it to obtain reliable, objectively valid knowledge about humankind, human origins, human behavior and cognition, and the evolution and operation of sociocultural systems.

Epistemology is the area of study that is concerned with the investigation of the nature and sources of knowledge and whether claims to knowledge are justified (Hospers 1988: 10; see Creel 2001; Greco and Sosa 1999; Hales 2002; Williams 2001). A consideration of epistemology is central to any discussion of theory and anthropological claims to knowledge. Those who neglect epistemology risk falling prey to fallacious arguments, deceptive rhetoric, and obscurantism and mystification (cf. Reyna 1994).

The present discussion is also necessitated by the fact that many epistemological questions of central relevance to anthropology have been overlooked or irresponsibly ignored by practitioners in the field, some of whom assert that "epistemology is dead," logic and rationality are cultural prejudices, and call for the abandonment of science and reason in the study of culture, and advocate a free-for-all in the pursuit of knowledge (e.g., Herzfeld 2001: x, 2, 5, 9, 10, 22; Rabinow 1986: 236; Tedlock 1991; Toulmin 1982; Tyler 1986a: 37).

The aims of this chapter are as follows: (1) to describe the different foundations upon which claims to knowledge are based; (2) to stipulate the reasons why not all ways of knowing are equally valuable if our objective is to obtain consistently reliable knowledge about the world; (3) to clarify some of the basic issues in the contemporary debate between scientific anthropologists and those advocating nonscientific, intuitive, subjective, and interpretive approaches; and (4) to establish a set of criteria by means of which various theoretical perspectives may be assessed.

EPISTEMOLOGY AND THE FOUNDATIONS OF KNOWLEDGE

Ultimately, all claims to knowledge, whether about people, cultures, the world, or the universe, are epistemological questions. There are innumerable, often contradictory, claims to knowledge about the world, people, and cultures. Therefore, if our goal is the acquisition of objectively valid knowledge about the world, it is necessary to find ways of making distinctions between different ways of knowing (Gellner 1992: 38). This is where epistemology comes in.

Epistemology addresses the questions: How do we know what we know? How do we know what or whom to believe? How do we differentiate between what is reasonable and what is not? Prudent thinkers who wish to avoid accepting positions guided by fallacious and unfounded arguments must ask these questions, whether they are discussing medicine, religion, anthropology, or any other topic (Feder 1990: 12). Epistemology requires accountability by forcing us to expose and evaluate the sources or foundations of what we claim to know (Brook and Stainton 2000: 1–3; Lett 1987: 15, 20).

Knowledge can be based on various foundations. There is knowledge based upon sense experience, logic, authority, popular consensus, intuition, revelation, and faith (Hospers 1988; Lett 1987). Each of these foundations generates a very different form of knowledge or understanding. The critical evaluation of the diverse ways of knowing, including theoretical positions in anthropology, hinges upon grasping this key epistemological point.

Many people think that first-hand knowledge through our senses is reliable. Hence the adage, "seeing is believing." However, things are not a straightforward as they may seem (Brook and Stainton 2000: 15–31). It is well known that our observations are influenced by implicit or explicit interpretive frameworks, subjective predispositions, cultural filters, theoretical orientations, biases, prejudices, individual personality, cultural and linguistic backgrounds, authorial skills, as well as political and historical contingencies that affect where we look, what we see, and what we ignore.

Moreover, humans have the notorious proclivity to maintain their convictions in the face of overwhelming evidence to the contrary, to foist their wishes and desires upon the universe, to create fantasies, to believe that their beliefs are true, and even to deny that an external reality exists (D'Andrade 1995: 1; Johnson 1995: 8; Sagan 1993: 63). The effect of our beliefs on our perceptions is so powerful that one could almost say, "not seeing is believing, but believing is seeing" (Abel 1976: 39).

Sense experience is a powerful foundation of knowledge. However, because of the nature of our sensory and cognitive apparatus, our senses can lead us into error. As Thomas Gilovich has pointed out in his book *How We Know What Isn't So* (1991),

> Evolution has given us powerful intellectual tools for processing vast amounts of information with accuracy and dispatch, and our questionable beliefs derive primarily from our misapplication or overutilization of generally valid and effective strategies for knowing. Just as we are subject to perceptual illusions in spite of, and largely because of, our extraordinary perceptual capacities, so too are many of our cognitive shortcomings closely related to, or even an unavoidable cost of, our greatest strengths (Gilovich 1991: 2).[1]

We may say, therefore, that while sense experience is probably the most significant source of knowledge, it is subject to a wide range of biases and distortions and is hence problematic.

Another foundation of knowledge to which people frequently appeal is logic. "Logic is the study of valid reasoning, and it attempts to show why some types of argument are valid and others are not" (Hospers 1988: 129). What is often misunderstood, however, is that logic can tell us only whether a conclusion is justified by its premises, not whether the premises themselves are correct.

As Hospers (1988: 129) points out, "In a valid argument, the premises need not be true: It is only required that conclusion follows logically from the premises—that is, if the premises are true, then the conclusion must be true." Take the following syllogism: All cows are green; I am a cow; therefore, I am green (Hospers 1988: 129). The argument is valid, although the premises are false. To establish the truth of a premise requires that we resort to empirical evidence, or empirical facts. This is why the scientific enterprise requires that our formulations must be assessed *both* on logical grounds and empirical ones.

Logic is a prerequisite of rational inquiry (Lett 1997: 98). Scientific reasoning must adhere to formal rules of logic. To disregard valid reasoning and rationality, or to make the relinquishment of rationality a prerequisite for anthropological research, as some interpretive anthropologists have done (e.g., Herzfeld 2001: x, 2, 5, 9, 10, 22), opens the door to our accepting fallacious, self-contradictory positions (cf. Lett 1997: 18).

A self-contradictory position is epistemologically meaningless. As Dawes (2001: 3) has put it, "*The conclusions it generates are . . . always false, because conclusions about the world that are self-contradictory cannot be accurate ones. . . . what is logically impossible cannot exist*" (emphasis added). It is for this reason that sound thinking is so crucial to science. One way to think soundly is to be aware of fallacious thinking and faulty logic in anthropological discourse.

The following are some examples of logical fallacies that frequently appear in cultural constructionist, antiscience perspectives glossed as interpretive or postmodern anthropology. These examples show the problematic nature of perspectives that rejection the rules of rational inquiry.

Begging the Question *(petitio principii):* The truth of the conclusion is assumed in the premises. "Begging the question" entails "circular reasoning." There is no conclusion to be deduced from the premise because the conclusion is already there to begin with. For example, the cultural determinist position, which posits that cultures are different because cultures are different entail this fallacy. Postmodernists commit this fallacy when they make statements such as: Science is degraded because it is (cf. Reyna 1994: 561).

Ad Hominem (against the person): Discrediting a position or rejecting an argument by attacking the character of the person forwarding the proposition rather than the argument itself. Such attacks appear to be addressing the proposition in question, but instead focus upon the personal characteristic of its exponent that seldom have a bearing on the truth or falsity of the proposition. For example, postmodern writers often commit this fallacy when they state that scientific knowledge is worthless because scientists are simple-minded minions of neo-colonial powers. Also, this fallacy is committed when postmodernists label colleagues down the hall neocolonialists because they conduct empirical field research and are concerned with testing hypotheses and believe that that anthropological claims to knowledge must be supported by compelling evidence (Sidky 2003: 5). This is also a form of the **red herring** fallacy, in which the actual issue is avoided by diverting attention toward issues that are irrelevant to the proposition in question.

Appeal to Mockery: The substitution of ridicule in the place of evidence. For example, the postmodern anthropologist Stephen Tyler (1987: 207) attempts to discredit science and scientific knowledge by offering such words as "degraded," "a game," "empty," "ridiculous," "simple-minded," "absurdity," and so forth, in support of his opinion that science and scientific knowledge are a big joke and a sham and a fraud.

Confusing Cause and Effect: Concluding without justification that variable A is the cause of variable B, because A and B occur together.

For example, anthropologists have noted the close relationship between language and culture. The linguists Edward Sapir and Benjamin Whorf offered the following causal relationship: Language and culture occur together; therefore, language causes/determines culture. Causality is a complex issue. A may be the cause of B if whenever A occurs B occurs, and whenever A does not occur B does not occur. Effects must come after their causes. But it is easy to mistake the direction of causality. Also, there may be a common cause for both variables. Alternatively, the cause may be one component of a larger causal effect.

Genetic Fallacy: The origins of a perspective are treated as evidence for refuting that perspective. For example, postmodernists commit this fallacy when they claim that science is a product of Western culture; therefore, scientific knowledge cannot have universal validity.

The Fallacy of Composition: What is true of the parts must be true of the whole. For example, an individual elephant consumes more food than an individual human; therefore, elephants as a group eat more food than humans as a group. Or, anthropologist X was a racist who supported the Western colonial domination of indigenous people; therefore, all anthropologists are racists who support colonialism and the oppression of non-Western people. This is fallacious thinking if it follows without justification, because the whole may not necessarily have the properties of its individual components.

Postmodernists commit this fallacy when they take the fact that some aspects of reality are agreed-upon things, or are culturally constructed, to the absurd conclusion that everything is so constructed, or that reality is a cultural construct and an objective reality does not exist.

Relativist Fallacy (Subjectivist Fallacy): Truth is relative to a particular culture, time, or indi-

vidual. Take, for example, the assertion that for the members of culture X the earth is flat. For those who commit the relativist fallacy, this does not mean simply that beliefs are relative to cultures, but rather that truth is relative. Hence the members of culture X live in a world that is ontologically different from the one occupied by the rest of humankind. Such assertions frequently appear in the discourse of cultural constructionist, antiscience anthropologists.

Another example of this logical fallacy is the cultural constructionists' rejection of logic and rational inquiry and their claim that logical contradictions may be problematic for those deluded by the logo-centric, repressive Euro-American worldview but are perfectly up to standard for their position.

Slippery Slope *(reductio ad absurdum):* To demonstrate the unacceptability of a proposition by positing a chain of progressively more objectionable events that would follow from it. Employed correctly pushing an argument to its logical limits can demonstrate the absurdity of the position and the flaw in the argument. However, in fallacious reasoning it involves taking a position to a presumed inevitable and absurd outcome without providing evidence or specifying the reasons for the inevitability of the conclusion. It involves the incorrect use of the IF–THEN operator. For example, "legalize marijuana and next we will legalize crack cocaine and heroin." Or, "legalize abortion and next we will legalize the killing of the old and the physically and mentally handicapped." Or, "if we allow the banning of pornography, next it will be other literature, and soon they will be burning all books."

Special Pleading: Applying rules and principles upon others, while declaring oneself exempt without providing evidence to justify the exemption. For example, postmodern anthropologists relegate everyone to the prison of language, yet they themselves claim the privilege of alone being free from the mysterious fetters of linguistic templates and therefore have access to special truths.

Straw Man Fallacy: Intentional misrepresentation of the opponent's position to make it appear weak or untenable and then arguing against this distorted version of the position. For example, postmodern anthropologists are guilty of this fallacy when they describe scientific anthropology as "laws-and-causes social physics" based upon "Newtonian models," or assert that science is about transcendental and absolute objectivity and universal timeless truths.

Another straw man argument is the postmodernists' depiction of scientific knowledge as dependent upon the rhetorical and figurative devices and tropes rather than the factual and theoretical formulations—the real basis of such knowledge. Through this kind of deception, texts are privileged over facts and the crucial empirical dimension of science is masked. Through such cleverness, science is transmuted into another narrative or story that is then subjected to attack. This is also an example of the fallacy of **style over substance.**

Appeal to Emotion: Attempting to establish the validity of a proposition by appealing to peoples' emotions in the absence of evidence. Politicians and advertising firms often engaged in this kind of fallacy. This is fallacious because inciting emotions is substituted for evidence. *Ad hominem* arguments often operate by inciting emotional responses. For example, postmodern writers often commit this fallacy when they project eco-apocalyptic scenarios caused by the dehumanizing technocratic scientific establishment as evidence that science must be rejected.

Another example of this fallacy is when postmodern writers describe science in such terms as degraded, a game, empty, ridiculous, simpleminded, absurdity, and so on to convey the idea that science is rotten, a cadaver that must be discarded (Reyna 1994: 561).

Appeal to Popularity *(argumentum ad populum):* Since a lot of people agree with position A, then position A is true. This is an effective technique used by the advertising industry and politicians. This is fallacious because it substitutes approval by people for evidence. Lots of people believe in lots of things that are totally false. At one time lots of people believed that the sun revolved around the earth, or that the human body could not sustain travel at speeds exceeding 25 miles per hour (see below under popular consensus as a foundation of knowledge).

Argument from Ignorance *(argumentum ad ignorantiam):* Absence of proof is taken as proof. No one can prove that the premise is false therefore it is true. No one can prove that UFOs do not exist therefore UFOs exist. This is a fallacy because there may be no evidence for a proposition, but that is insufficient to prove that it is true. A proposition also requires evidence for it. The postmodernist writer Tyler (1986a: 37) commits this fallacy when he says "no one has ever demonstrated the independence of reason, or logic and mathematics, from the discourses that constitute them." There is an overwhelming amount of pragmatic evidence for the objective independence of reason, logic, and mathematics (Lett 1997: 67).

Appeal to Authority *(argumentum ad verecundiam):* Citing prestigious individuals such as rock stars as experts, even though they do not have the appropriate qualifications, citing individuals whose expertise is in a different field, citing authorities out of context, or citing authorities in issues over which experts in the discipline disagree. Postmodernists commit this fallacy when they cite individuals, such as the postmodern writers Michel Foucault and Jacques Derrida, individuals with little or no background, training, or grasp of even the basics of scientific research, as authorities in order to discredit science.

Style over Substance: The manner in which the argument is presented determines the truth of the propositions. Postmodernists commit this fallacy when they assert that authorial skills have more to do with the acceptance of ethnographic accounts or scientific texts than "factual substantiality or conceptual elegance" (Geertz 1988: 8) This is a fallacy because the truth or falsity of premises depends upon factual evidence, not rhetoric.

Non Sequitur (from the Latin for "it does not follow"): A conclusion that does not follow from the premises. For example, "the sky is blue; therefore, God exists." Postmodern discourse is rife with non sequiturs. Consider the following: The way ethnographic knowledge is obtained must be scrutinized. This is linked to the fact that there is much inequality in the world. From this the conclusion is reached that the way knowledge of the world is obtained and how ethnographies are written create the inequalities that exist in the world (Gellner 1992: 39). Or, traditional ethnographies are laden with the subjective biases and oppressive language that make them instruments of domination. Therefore, to create social justice we must jettison all standards and adopt subjectivism. In other words, political liberation is contingent upon cognitive subjectivism. All of this is passed off pretentiously as morally driven political radicalism.

Non sequiturs include the following invalid arguments:

Affirming the Consequent: If X then Y: Y therefore X. For example, I am in Los Angeles, then I am in California. I am in California; therefore, I am in Los Angeles.

Denying the Antecedent: If X then Y: Y therefore X. For example, I am in Los Angeles then I am in California. I am not in Los Angeles; therefore, I am not in California.

Equivocation: Using the same term in two different senses. This ambiguity results in erroneous conclusions. For example, "something that is odd disturbs people. The number five is odd. Therefore, the number five disturbs people." Or, homicide is a criminal action that is illegal, tribunals are criminal actions; therefore, tribunals are illegal. Irrationalist philosophers such as Thomas Kuhn commit this fallacy when they phrase their argument to suggest that scientific knowledge does advance and grow and at the same time that it does not advance.

Appeal to Complexity: The assertion that the phenomenon in question is too complex for anyone to comprehend, therefore the opinion of the one making this argument is as valid as any other opinion. Postmodernists commit this fallacy when they argue that the world is too complicated for comprehension, everything is relative, cultures are incommensurable, everything is interpretation. This being so, postmodern narratives developed through subjective approaches are presented as being equally valid as scientific knowledge.

Least Plausible Hypothesis: A perspective that disregards a probable scenario and opts for an improbable one. For example, culture X possesses detailed astronomically correct information about the solar system on par with what is known in Western science. Therefore, members of culture X must have acquired such knowledge from extraterrestrial beings, rather than contact with Europeans (see Chapter 5).

There are many other logical fallacies aside from the ones mentioned here. The point is that anthropologists can ill afford to disregard rationality and logical standards. Those who have done so have pushed the discipline towards self-contradictory positions that are epistemologically meaningless.

Returning to the foundations of knowledge, aside from sense experience and logic, people also appeal to authority as a foundation of knowledge. The problem here is that lots of authorities, or "experts," have been in error lots of times (Sagan 1993: 73). The validity and reliability of the authority's claim to knowledge depends not on their credentials, reputation, social status, or office in an academic hierarchy, but upon the epistemological foundations of his/her knowledge (Lett 1987: 17). As such, knowledge based upon this foundation can be highly problematic. It entails the logical fallacy of *argumentum ad verecundiam,* noted previously.

Another foundation of knowledge is popular consensus, common knowledge, folk knowledge, or, in the jargon of 1960s anthropology, "ethnoscience." This is what anthropologists refer to as the "insider's point of view," the "native's voice," "the local frame of reference." It refers to shared and culturally specific context dependent knowledge and folk wisdom. People accept such beliefs to be true because everyone else believes them to be true. For example, many in the United States believe that "lightning never strikes the same place twice," or that "tobacco is not addicting," or that "poor people are poor because they are lazy," or that "hard work and perseverance are a guarantee of economic success in the United States" (Lett 1987: 17). None of these is true.

Also, there are lots of people who believe in ancient extraterrestrial astronauts, astrology, ESP, UFOs, Atlantis, and a global deluge. However, these things are not made real simply because lots of people sincerely believe in these things (cf. Lett 1987: 42). Such beliefs are held in spite of overwhelming contrary evidence and seem to fulfill a yearning for security and simplicity (Futuyma 1982: 163). Or they may satisfy unfulfilled religious needs or simply make life more interesting for some (Sagan 2001: 384). As a foundation of knowledge popular consensus is therefore very problematic. It entails the logical fallacy of *argumentum ad populum,* discussed previously.

Another foundation of knowledge is intuition. Intuitions are subjective feelings of certitude, the reasons for which elude us (Sperber 1996: 89). People often have contradictory intuitions and deciding between them on the basis of intuition alone is impossible. "Intuition itself provides no way of deciding which of two conflicting intuitions is correct. . . . not all intuitions can be true, since they sometimes contradict one another; and there is no criterion to be found in intuition itself that will distinguish between true claims and false ones" (Hospers 1988: 137). To accept the validity of an interpretation based on intuition simply because it was arrived at intuitively involves deplorable circular reasoning (Spiro 1986: 275). Intuition is therefore problematic as the basis for establishing the truth of a proposition.

Intuition has an important place in science during the process of formulating novel hypotheses. However, science adheres to an **externalist** means of epistemic evaluation. This perspective holds that we live in an external world/universe/reality that exists independently of any beliefs we may have about that reality and that this external reality comprises the conditions of knowledge (Williams 2001: 32, 138). This is why in science intuition is an insufficient means of validating hypotheses arrived at through intuitions (Spiro 1986: 274). In contrast, perspectives that are based solely upon the ethnographer's own intuition, empathy, and subjectivism (cf. Spiro 1986: 263) are **internalist** and are founded upon the premise that intuition and reflection alone can tell us whether our beliefs are justified (Greco 1999: 10–11).

Aside from intuition, people also frequently appeal to revelation as a foundation of knowledge. This constitutes information received through dreams, visions, and visitations from the supernatural world (Lett 1987: 18). The problem is that the revelation received by one person is merely hearsay to another (Hospers 1988: 139). When a person accepts the truth of a "revelation" from vatic (A), as opposed to the revelatory knowledge of visionaries (B), (C), or (D), he or she does so because of emotionally appealing forceful persuasive arguments, not on the basis of any kind of evidence.

The foundation of faith is based on the axiom that "strength of the belief guarantees the truth of the belief" (Lett 1987: 18). Strength of belief alone cannot alter the relationship between energy and matter, which affect the physical universe and which are grounded in nature and subject to physical laws. As Hospers (1988: 140–141) observes, "Faith has been defined as 'a firm belief in something for which there it no evidence' . . . *faith is an attitude—an attitude of belief in something in the absence of evidence.*' Therefore faith cannot be a source of knowledge."

From the preceding discussion, it should be clear that there are many foundations that, alone or in combination with others, underlie various kinds of knowing, or claims to knowledge. All of these are in one way or another problematic. Moreover, it should be evident that the foundation of sense experience must be distinguished from all others. Our sensory apparatus, the common evolutionary heritage of humankind, is the means through which we know and navigate the external world. But our senses are prone to distortions, as noted previously, on account of our habitual modes of thought, implicit or explicit interpretive or theoretical frameworks, subjective predispositions, cultural filters, political and historical contingencies, and so forth, which greatly influence where we look and what we see. Herein lies the crux of the problem of knowledge.

Does this undermine our efforts to acquire objective knowledge of the world? Should we resign to the fact that everything, after all, is interpretation, that reality is culturally constructed, and efforts to apprehend reality are misplaced? This is the position taken by many interpretive anthropologists who subscribe to the **cultural constructionist** view of reality. Philosophically, the constructionist view is a form of ultra-idealism based on the doctrine that "thought and reality are really one and the same" (Williams 2001: 138).

Taking the cultural constructionist point of view to its logical conclusion (reduction to ab-

surdity), as it has been by some writers, results in uncompromising radical **epistemological relativism,** namely, that it is impossible for us to acquire any reliable knowledge about the external world, and the belief that there is nothing real "outside the discourses that constitute them" (e.g., Fabian 1989; Tedlock 1991; Tyler 1986a: 37; Veeser 1989). One might note at this point that this position is based upon the logically contradictory assertion that relativism is absolute (Sidky 2003: 45).

Cultural constructionists treat all knowledge as being equally uncertain (the logical fallacy of appeal to complexity): Everything is interpretation, one as good/true/valid as another, and what is considered to be true or real is defined by the human observer, rather than with reference to an external objective reality (the relativist fallacy). This position is called **truth by coherence,** a kind of truth based upon sets of ideas that are internally consistent and mutually reinforcing, but with no external points of reference. Knowledge/truth therefore becomes relative.

Science recognizes that some truths are so constituted. For example, there are different systems of geometry that consist of coherent and internally consistent propositions. While these systems are true by coherence, they are not "true of the world" (Hospers 1988: 117). For those who subscribe to the truth by coherence position, searching for what is "true of the world" is a misplaced enterprise. Epistemological relativists therefore resort to subjective, intuitive foundations of knowledge—these produce "understandings" based upon logically fallacious reasoning and foundations that are proof exempt and beyond validation by any objective standards.

Scientific anthropologists find the cultural constructionist option problematic because it converts reasonable doubt into uncompromising epistemological skepticism (Lett 1987: 19; Sokal and Bricmont 1998: 191). While we cannot really be sure that we are not in the midst of a grand illusion, not with absolute certainty, neither can we reasonably doubt that there is a real knowable world out there of people, cultures, objects, things, processes, forces, and so forth (Lett 1997: 42; Sosa 1999: 145). We survive and act more or less successfully in the world by assuming that an objective reality exists. Our senses do not systematically mislead us all of the time. Otherwise, we would not have survived as a species. Therefore, while all epistemological stances ultimately depend upon certain assumptions that cannot be proven, there are pragmatic grounds why all epistemological positions are not equally useful if our objective is to figure out how the world works. As Sagan (1993: 19) observed in this regard,

> The universe forces those who live in it to understand it. Those creatures who find everyday experience a muddled jumble of events with no predictability, no regularity, are in grave peril. The universe belongs to those who, at least to some degree, have figured it out.[2]

There are lots of good reasons why scientists take it for granted that our sensations persist and have coherence because they are caused by phenomena external to our consciousness (Sokal and Bricmont 1998: 53). We act successfully in the world by continuously making decisions about our perceptions according to the principle of hypothesis testing and refutation, a principle encapsulated in the scientific method (Fox 1997: 341).

Put another way, although our senses may fool us some of the time, this does not mean that we must resort to something above and beyond our senses; it means that we must use our senses more critically, pay heed to their shortcomings and limitations and attend to the logical principles of valid reasoning (Abel 1976: 30; Hospers 1988: 123).

This is one of the central features of the scientific enterprise. Science commences by acknowledging the problems of knowledge, but does not treat them as insurmountable or insoluble. Science is based upon the idea that it is possible to compensate for the distorting effects of our perceptions by systematically testing our findings through further sense experience against empirical data and candidly and constantly exposing our theoretical formulations to challenge on logical and empirical grounds. An integral part of scientific research is that one must meet the criteria of replication and validation. This might not be the best approach, but it has proven to be far better than perspectives based upon subjectivism, intuition, mysticism, and the like, if the goal is obtaining reliable information about the world.

SCIENCE AND THE IRRATIONAL PHILOSOPHERS: THOMAS KUHN AND PAUL FEYERABEND

Cultural constructionists draw considerable inspiration from the irrationalist philosophers Thomas Kuhn (1922–1996) and Paul Feyerabend (1924–1994). For this reason, the works of these writers require a brief consideration in the context of the present discussion. Kuhn and Feyerabend stress the idea that scientific knowledge is simply another set of agreed upon conventions and negotiated meanings/assumptions, powerfully shaped by irrational, historical, sociopolitical factors, including leaps of faith, rather than being based upon logic, reason, and empirical evidence. In other words, dialogue, negotiation, and agreement among scientists rather than "the nature of nature" (i.e., the way the world is) are the defining condition of scientific knowledge (Kuhn 1970: 168–169).

If science operates as these writers suggest, then there could not be any growth or accumulation of scientific knowledge. This position, however, is highly implausible for the simple fact that more is known today than was known ten years ago, fifty years ago, a century ago, and so forth. As the Australian philosopher David Stove (1982: 3–4) pointed out in his devastating critique,

> Much more is known now than was known fifty years ago, and much was known then than in 1580. So there has been a great accumulation or

growth of knowledge in the last four hundred years. . . . But if a philosopher of science takes a position which obliges him, on pain of inconsistency, to be reluctant to admit *this*, then his position can be rightly described as irrationalism.

Irrationalist writers such as Kuhn, Feyerabend, and their followers begin with the reasonable idea that knowledge is problematic and that cultural and linguistic factors intrude upon knowledge and make the unjustifiable generalization that *all* knowledge (the fallacy of composition) is culturally constructed (at least this is one reading of their works). Because Kuhn and Feyerabend seem to downplay or dismiss the role of empirical evidence and logical operations in the generation of scientific knowledge, their works confer an aura of credibility or legitimacy to proponents of irrational, subjective perspectives who feel empowered by these writers to forward whatever they please as being equal to scientific knowledge, if not better (the relativist fallacy and fallacy of special pleading).

Thomas S. Kuhn, twentieth-century irrationalist philosopher, whose book The Structure of Scientific Revolutions *(1970) has inspired relativists of all kinds.*

Kuhn's principal work is *The Structure of Scientific Revolutions* (1970 [1962]). In this book he characterizes scientific research in terms of "paradigms," sets of agreed upon conventions and negotiated meanings/assumptions that guide research and define questions to be answered (Kuhn 1970: 43). Kuhn emphasizes the irrational historical and sociopolitical factors that impinge upon scientific knowledge and account for why new paradigms are accepted (Kuhn 1970: 168–169).

The problem with Kuhn's work is that it is fraught with ambiguities (Lakatos and Musgrave 1970). He employs equivocation in order to lend plausibility to his irrationalist depiction of science and scientific knowledge. As Stove (1982: 6; 2001: 21–50) has pointed out, Kuhn's strategy is "leave them guessing what it is you really believe, the irrationalist bits, or the other ones."

As noted previously, equivocation is a logical fallacy that involves employing the same word in several different senses in the context of a single argument (Lett 1997: 64). As Masterman (1970) has pointed out, Kuhn employs the word *paradigm* alone in over twenty different ways. More than this, equivocation characterizes the whole of his work. On account of such ambiguities, Kuhn's views on science lend themselves both to a rational interpretation as well as an irrational one (cf. Bell 1994: 206–208). Epistemological relativists have highlighted the irrational angle in Kuhn's work in order to support their assertion that "science is no different than any other type of knowledge."

According to Kuhn's view of the development of knowledge, irrational factors determine the establishment of new paradigms and affect the questions that fall under the purview of paradigmatic research. A new paradigm is viable for a while and directs research. This constitutes a period Kuhn calls "normal science." Over time, the paradigm encounters new facts/phenomena, or anomalies, that it fails to solve. These anomalies eventually grow to a point where they cannot be ignored. This is when a "scientific revolution" occurs and ultimately results in the establishment of an entirely new paradigm (Kuhn 1970: 68, 167–169).

From the irrationalist angle, Kuhn's argument is that paradigms are incommensurable, each one is a new beginning, there is no growth of knowledge, and advances in science do not result in further scientific breakthroughs and better understandings about the world (Kuhn 1970: 206). But Kuhn (1970: 149) also says that dislodged paradigms are not totally abandoned and therefore knowledge is built upon previous discoveries. He writes, for instance, that Newtonian dynamics is "a special case of" and is "derivable from Einsteinian theory" (Kuhn 1970: 99).

Although his discussion of Newtonian dynamics is tied to his effort to show the irrational nature of the growth of scientific knowledge, it is actually a demonstration that paradigms are commensurable and knowledge is cumulative (Kuznar 1997: 57). The new paradigms explain what the previous paradigm could explain, as well as being able to explain anomalies that the latter failed to accommodate (Kuznar 1997: 57). As Stove (1982: 6) points out,

> Kuhn would admit that normal science has solved a great many problems since 1580. Well, if it has solved those problems, then those problems have been solved, haven't they? We know Kuhn says that a new paradigm "replaces", "destroys", and old one. But he never says that every solution of a particular problem, achieved under the old paradigm, somehow is "destroyed" or becomes an un-solution under the new. If a problem has been solved then it really has been solved. But if this tautology is not denied, then solutions of problems (unless they were, for example, forgotten) would accumulate through successive paradigms. But what then becomes of Kuhn's famous rejection of the cumulative view of the history of science?[3]

Kuhn acknowledges throughout his book that scientific knowledge about the nature of reality has grown immensely over the last four centuries, in spite of paradigm shifts. The cumulative nature of scientific knowledge is obvious and Kuhn is wise not to contest the issue (Stove 1982: 6). However, Kuhn's strategy of equivocation allows him to also maintain that such is not the case and that "the world is somehow plastic to our paradigms," or "that what constitutes the solution of a problem is relative to the paradigm, the group, and the time" (Stove 1982: 6). Kuhn is able to uphold his irrationalist arguments by means of clever inconsistencies built into his case.

Turning to Feyerabend's views, for him science is merely an ideology and scientific truths are socially constructed with no connection to objective reality. For this reason there are no objective rational standards or criteria transcending cultural standards for assessing the validity of theories (cf. Tiles and Tiles 1993: 162–163).

Paul Feyerabend, twentieth-century irrationalist philosopher, who advocated the "anything goes" approach to knowledge.

Truth is the result of political and sociological factors, and methods and rationality are invented to justify theories rather than to discover truth. Practically any belief, irrespective of evidence, flaws in reasoning, and so on can be accepted as true in the appropriate sociopolitical climate, according to Feyerabend. Method is really an afterthought to lend credibility to what is considered to be true or false in terms of other factors. Method therefore hinders the growth of knowledge and must be discarded (Gross and Levitt 1994: 47).

Feyerabend therefore advocated the "anything goes" approach to knowledge now popular among one group of interpretive anthropologists. Orans (1996: 137) has described the anthropological incarnation of Feyerabend's "against method" position as follows:

> The ambiguous notion of multiple truths has become a charter for the idea that "anything goes," that you have your truth and I have mine, and ultimately for a rejection of empirical verification. In its most egregious form this approach holds truth to be merely a label employed by competing interest groups to sanctify beliefs useful for furthering their ends. From this perspective, evidence for propositions is of little interest; competing claims are seen simply as furthering competing ends, and the demand that propositions be stated in a manner capable of verification is vilified as ethnocentric positivism and doubtless the tool of some ruling class.[4]

Feyerabend saw science as no different than religious ideology or supernatural beliefs and argued that in the modern world science is an analogue of theology in medieval times. For example, in one of his papers Feyerabend (1963: 32) argued that the "theory" of witchcraft during the fifteenth and sixteenth centuries in Europe was based upon sound empirical evidence and that this theory was no less valid than our scientific theories. In his book *Against Method* (1975), he makes use of Galileo's heliocentric view to demonstrate that theories are established irrespective of scientific standards. Galileo's views were accepted, he argues, not because he

was able to bring to bear overwhelming evidence, but because Galileo was a clever orator, adept at using tropes, "rhetorical strategies," and "figurative devices." The heliocentric view triumphed because it was convenient to the political interests of powerful groups.

Feyerabend's rejection of rational or logical standards in the context of justification is highly problematic. He makes a blunder in treating the theory of witchcraft current in Europe during the fifteenth and sixteenth centuries as an analogue of science because the way anti-witchcraft experts built their "theory" violated all the logical and empirical standards fundamental to science. The witch hunters themselves often fabricated in the torture chambers the so-called "empirical evidence" on the basis of which people were convicted. Astute contemporary thinkers were not only cognizant of the flawed reasoning in the discourse of the witch hunters, but they also knew that deception was rampant and much of the evidence was false (see Sidky 1997: 117–154).

In the case of Galileo, even if we grant that his telescope was not good enough to demonstrate to others as to what was the case and that his heliocentric model might have at first been accepted because it suited someone's political interests, what Feyerabend overlooks is that the theory survived because it was corroborated by evidence (Bell 1994: 245–246). Evidence matters a lot, and in the long run theories stand or fall according to how well they are supported by the facts.

It is for these reasons that scientific knowledge is distinct from ways of knowing based upon the foundations of intuition, empathy, faith, and authority. The latter comprise nonobjective, nonrational ways of knowing that are proof exempt. Knowledge based upon these foundations is immune to public verification and testability, the defining features of science.

To say that scientific knowledge is no different than understandings based upon the folk knowledge of any other culture or to maintain that science is simply another set of beliefs/narratives accepted on faith is an egregious episte- mological blunder and misrepresentation. Irra- tionalists such as Kuhn and Feyerabend, as Stove (1982: 12) reminds us, "not only exercise but more or less openly claim the right to talk non- sense." These writers have only succeeded in making a case that science is no different than any other ways of knowing on the basis of equivocation. But their case is weak. As Stove (1982: 45) has remarked on this point, "they have succeeded in making irrationalist philoso- phy of science acceptable to many readers who would reject it out of hand if it were presented to them without equivocation and consistently."

Many contemporary cultural constructionists consider science as merely another narrative, no different from any other story. As Barrett (1996: 155) has stated, "Science now is regarded as just another type of story, no better than, and indeed possibly inferior to, the indigenous explanatory systems in other cultures." Some anthropologists have adopted Feyerabend's (1975: 298) construal of science as merely an accretion of stories or myths. The science-as-myth analogy would be plausible if anyone could cite examples of myths that have been altered because experiments con- tradicted them, or produce myths that postulate experimental procedures to discriminate be- tween earlier and later versions of the myth (Sokal and Bricmont 1992: 82). Such myths do not exist. This is the fundamental difference be- tween science and myth.

There are therefore considerable grounds for being skeptical about the views on science es- poused by Kuhn, Feyerabend, and their follow- ers. As Gross and Levitt (1994: 58) have observed with respect to the idea that negotiation and agreement among scientists rather than "the na- ture of nature" are the defining condition of sci- entific knowledge,

> to read this as it applies to a concrete situation, we must believe that William Harvey's views of the circulation of the blood prevailed over that of his critics not because blood flows from the heart through a series of arteries and returns to the heart through the veins, but because Harvey was able to

construct a "representation" and wheedle a place for it among the accepted conventions of the sa- vants! In other words, it is not to be admitted that nature might provide a template in conformity to which these "representations" are tightly molded.

To illustrate their point Gross and Levitt (1994: 58) offer the following example:

> Imagine that a few of us are cooped up in a win- dowless office, wondering whether or not it's rain- ing. Opinions vary. We decide to settle the issue by stepping outside, where we note that the streets are beginning to fill up with puddles, that cars are kicking up rooster-tails of spray, and thunder and lightning fill the air, and, most significantly, that we are being pelted incessantly by drops of water falling from the sky. We retreat into the office and say to each other, "Wow, it's really coming down!" We are now all in agreement that it's raining. Inso- far as we are [cultural constructionists], we can never explain our agreement on this point by the simple fact that it is raining. Rain, remember, is the outcome of our "settlement," not its cause![5]

The problematic nature of the assertion that sci- entific knowledge of the world does not accord with the reality of the world is evident in these examples.

Some anthropologists have raised similar is- sues with respect to the cultural constructionist view in anthropology. Some things are culturally constituted it is true. This is an important point of which we must not lose sight. These con- structed things, however, do not constitute everything cultural. As D'Andrade (1999: 88) points out,

> In my experience as a cognitive anthropologist, I have found that many cultural models are simply descriptive and are strongly shaped by the ordinary world of normal perception. . . . Folk taxonomies in botany and zoology, the folk model of the mind, the categorizations of color, and numerous other cultural classification schemes seem to be strongly influenced by the structure of the world as normally perceived. So the statement that reality is culturally constructed is another of these partial truth arguments, in which a claim is made as if "culture is everything," and only on closer in- spection does one find that the claim is much

exaggerated—one part of culture is made to stand for the whole. I believe that people in other cultures most of the time inhabit the same reality as you or I do. Cultural reality is more often reality-shaped than culturally constituted.

D'Andrade makes an important point by observing that cultural constructionists have taken a partial truth (i.e., that certain aspects of culture are "agreed upon things") and have converted it into an absolute truth, namely that all of culture is so constituted (the logical fallacy of composition).

WHAT IS SCIENCE AND WHAT ISN'T SCIENCE?

Having treated some of the epistemological issues relating to the generation of knowledge, I shall now focus specifically upon science as a way of knowing. Science is a distinct and systematic means of generating knowledge about the world, universe, and everything in them. Science is based upon a specific set of epistemological assumptions. As Bernard (1994: 168) points out,

> The assumptions are: (1) There is a reality "out there" (or "in there" in the case of ideas and emotions); (2) it can be apprehended, more or less, by human beings through direct experience (or through some proxy for experience); (3) all natural phenomena can be explained without recourse to mysterious forces beyond investigation; and (4) though the truth about phenomena is never known, we do better and better as old explanations are knocked down and are replaced by better ones.[6]

Put differently, science is founded upon the assumption that there is an objective reality that exists independently of the imperfect perceptions, interpretations, motivations, feelings, wishes, and desires of individual human beings and moreover that this reality is amenable to rational inquiry (Lett 1997: 42). The problem of knowledge arises from the fact that different hu-

mans perceive this reality differently. The crucial question in science is, How can we determine which of the various interpretations generated by the same common reality is the correct one or the one that comes closest to rendering that reality?

For the cultural constructionists distinguishing between the different interpretations is impossible. Truth testing and facts are not relevant. Ethnography becomes analogous to "fiction" and "objects," "facts," "verification," "truth," and the like become "empty evocations" for these writers (Tyler 1986b: 130). Their alternative is to embrace a multiplicity of different views/opinions/subjective musings and consider all of them to be equally valid. What is not addressed is the following question: When it comes to the serious task of trying to understand cultural phenomena is it not necessary to at least have some of the facts right?

Moreover, if we do not strive to differentiate between what is factual and reasonable and what is not, nothing can prevent us from falling prey to our tendency of "believing that our beliefs are true" (D'Andrade 1995: 1). Anthropological knowledge based upon foundations that do not make such distinctions becomes indistinguishable from **pseduoscience** and pseudoscientific "theories" about unicorns, UFOs, extraterrestrial visitations, extrasensory perception, astrology, ghost, goblins, fairies, and so forth. I maintain that such an enterprise is not only intellectually irresponsible, but irrelevant, and spurious as well.

The physicist Rory Coker (2001) has listed some of the distinguishing characteristics of pseudoscience. What I find remarkable is that Coker's description of pseudoscience could very well be a description of the cultural constructionist perspective in American anthropology today being taught in many anthropology departments (see Chapter 15).

The distinguishing features of pseudoscience, according to Coker (2001), are indifference to facts, sloppy research techniques, lack of interest in rules of valid evidence, reliance on subjective validation, and dependence upon arbitrary cultural conventions rather than regularities in nature. Also, pseudoscience possesses its own large, pretentious, but imprecise and ambiguous jargon terms that are used to generate an aura of authority and validity equal to that of science.

Pseudoscientists avoid submitting their premises to meaningful tests. Extraordinary claims are forwarded in the absence of the extraordinary evidence that such claims require. Pseudoscience is therefore different from "erroneous science" because it frames hypotheses that are proof-exempt, while a requisite of science is that hypotheses must be capable of disproof (Sagan 1995: 21). Pseudoscientific knowledge does not grow or expand, new information is seldom produced, and nothing concrete is ever learned (Coker 2001).

Pseudoscience appeals to emotion and sentiment and encourages a distrust of established facts and scholarly traditions. Skeptical scrutiny and rejection by scientists is attributed to the scholarly establishment's vested interest in the subject matter and their conspiracy to suppress the truth (Sagan 1995: 21). Pseudoscientists frequently appeal to what Coker calls the "Galileo Argument." This entails drawing parallels between the rejection of their own outlandish claims and the rejection of Galileo's ideas by the "establishment" terrified of being proven wrong. This, Coker points out, entails a non sequitur, the logical fallacy in which the conclusion does not follow. It was the ecclesiastical establishment that persecuted Galileo—the scientists of the time accepted his findings. The reply to those who assert that "they laughed at Galileo, they mocked Columbus" is to say, "But they also laughed at Bozo the Clown" (Sagan 1993: 79). A distinction must be made here between legitimate skepticism and dogmatic close-mindedness—Galileo's persecutors refused to examine the evidence (Gilovich 1991: 51). Scientists look at the evidence.

Another characteristic of pseudoscience is that it strives to persuade through rhetoric,

propaganda, deliberate omissions of crucial data, and misrepresentation, rather than valid evidence. Explanations are by "scenario," or stories, and narratives, and nothing else (Coker 2001).

Finally, pseudoscience eschews rational standards and argues from logical fallacies, such as non sequiturs, argument from ignorance, reduction to absurdity, appeal to authority, special appeal, and least plausible hypothesis, among others. Pseudoscience operates on the basis of irrational, unobjective modes of thought that predate science by millennia and that have generated all sorts of fanciful and patently false superstitious beliefs about humans and humankind (Sagan 2001: 385). As Coker (2001) puts it, "Pseudoscience encourages people to believe anything they want. It supplies specious 'arguments' for fooling yourself into thinking that any and all beliefs are equally valid."

While some anthropologists might feel that dabbling in epistemological free-for-alls and treating all beliefs as equally valid is a good thing, "cutting edge" research, and so forth, there are grave consequences associated with such undertakings. Prudent thinkers reject flawed thinking of this sort for good reasons. As Gilovich (1991: 6) has put it,

There is . . . [a] price we pay when we tolerate flawed thinking and superstitious beliefs. It is the familiar problem of the slippery slope: How do we prevent the occasional acceptance of faulty reasoning and erroneous beliefs from influencing our habits of thought more generally? Thinking straight about the world is a precious and difficult process that must be carefully nurtured. By attempting to turn our critical intelligence off and on at will, we risk losing it altogether, and thus jeopardize our ability to see the world clearly. Furthermore, by failing to develop our critical faculties, we become susceptible to the arguments and exhortations of those with other than benign intentions. . . . As individuals and as a society, we should be less accepting of superstition and sloppy thinking, and should strive to develop those "habits of mind" that promote a more accurate view of the world.[7]

Those who are content to do without truth testing, facts and rational standards and consider ethnography as a genre of fiction writing overlook the serious implications of their position. As Appell (1989: 197) has pointed out,

> While the concept of error at first seems strangely missing in [the cultural constructionists'] discourse, it is missing because it is not appropriate to the appreciation of fiction. And under the concept of ethnography as fiction or interpretation all sorts of errors can be perpetuated. Yet error and correction of error are the means whereby we human beings, as well as other animals, navigate in dealing with the world. And we communicate our knowledge of the discovered objective world to others so that they do not have to go through the same error-correcting exercise. The perpetuation of errors and follies means in the long run impaired adaptation to the complex social and physical environment in which we live.[8]

This is why scientific anthropologists are wary of perspectives based upon subjectivism, reflection, intuition, empathy, imagination, as advocated by interpretive anthropological writers, because these render us prone to creating fantasies.

So how does science approach the issue of contending claims to knowledge based upon the various interpretations generated by the same common reality? Kuznar (1997: 6) explains:

> Science is a method of generating knowledge about the experienced world based on the evaluation of logical theories with empirical data. There are many other important details, but the notion of testing an idea against data and the requirement that theories must adhere to the rule of logic are indispensable and distinctive elements of scientific practice.[9]

D'Andrade (1995: 1) has put it as follows:

> Science is: (1) trying to find out about the world by making observations, (2) checking to see if these observations are reliable, (3) developing a general model or account that explains these observations, (4) checking this model or account against new observations and (5) comparing it to other models or accounts to see which model fits the observation best.

"Science entails the demand for clarity of thought, coherence of theories, and the necessity of validating theories with empirical evidence" (Sokal and Bricmont 1998: 193). The hallmark of science, Futuyma (1982: 163) has written,

> is not the question: "Do I wish to believe this?" but the question "What is the evidence?" It is this demand for evidence, this habit of cultivated skepticism, that is most characteristic of the scientific way of thought. It is not limited to science, but it isn't universal either. Many people still cling to traditional beliefs in the face of contrary evidence, out of wishful thinking, or desire for security and simplicity. . . . science challenges not only nonscientific views but established scientific views as well. . . . Our knowledge can progress only if we can find errors and learn from them. Thus, much of the history of science consists of a rejection or modification of views that were once widely held. . . . currently accepted beliefs are provisional.[10]

From among the various ways of knowing, science alone focuses critical judgment upon itself. As Harris (2001: 27) put it,

> In the entire course of prehistory and history only one way of knowing has encouraged its own practitioners to doubt their own premises and to systematically expose their own conclusions to the hostile scrutiny of nonbelievers.[11]

Despite rhetorical putdowns about science being an instrument of Western domination, a cultural construct no more valid than the myths of any other culture, science works. It works not because the scientific approach guarantees that our accounts of the world will automatically be true. Rather it works because it entails the systematic and critical evaluation of competing claims to knowledge by means of a unique combination of logical analysis and appraisal of empirical evidence and the detection and correction of errors.

Science thrives on errors, cutting them away one by one. False conclusions are drawn all the time, but they are drawn tentatively. Hypotheses are framed so they are capable of being disproved. A succession of alternative hypotheses is confronted by experiment and observation. Science gropes and staggers toward improved understanding. Proprietary feelings are of course offended when a scientific hypothesis is disproved, but such disproofs are recognized as central to the scientific enterprise (Sagan 1995: 20–21).[12]

Science is therefore a systematic "self-correcting" mode of generating knowledge about the world (Kuznar 1997: 6; Lett 1987: 21). It is for these reasons that scientific knowledge grows and changes over time. This is also why science has been so successful and why it surpasses all other ways of knowing if the objective is to obtain factual knowledge about the world. And, as Bernard (1995: 17) has pointed out,

> we're getting more and more accurate all the time. Since the eighteenth century, every phenomenon (including human thought and behavior) to which the scientific method has been systematically applied, over a sustained period of time, by a large number of researchers, has yielded its secrets, and the knowledge has been turned into more effective human control of events.[13]

Science generates objective knowledge. Objectivity has a specific meaning here. It does not mean absolute transcendental, and "value-free" knowledge (the straw man argument), as opponents of scientific approaches erroneously assert (e.g., Abu-Lughod 1991: 150–151; Rosaldo 1991: 21; Tyler 1986b: 127). It is indeed true, as Wagner (1999: 88) has put it, that "a value-free social scientist has a fool for a philosopher." However, scientific anthropologists do not espouse the idea of value-free knowledge.

Scientifically objective knowledge is generated through critical operations designed to help us decide which among a multiplicity of views more accurately reflects what is the case. Logically it is impossible for all claims to knowledge about objective reality to be correct. They can all be false, but only one can be correct. In order to determine which claim to knowledge is the most accurate representation of reality science employs particular epistemological operations. The criteria for scientifically objective knowledge are verification and testability.

First, the validity of propositions must be assessed independently of the biases, prejudices, and office of researcher proposing it. This requires that propositions "be capable of test by reference to publicly ascertainable evidence," with the added stipulation that all propositions so tested are to be only provisionally accepted and are subject to review, modification, and even rejection (Hempel 1965: 334). There are no absolute truths and absolutely accurate predictions here. Rather, science "claims provisional certainty based upon a process of unrelenting skeptical inquiry in which no premise or assumption is ever considered to be beyond question" (Lett 1997: 42). As Kuznar (1997: 42) has noted, "a basic axiom of science is that all knowledge is provisional, tentative, and never absolute."

Scientifically objective knowledge then is knowledge that is obtainable independently by different investigators employing the same set of procedures and observations (Futuyma 1982: 167). The check that the scientific community thus exerts is one way through which errors are found and corrected (Futuyma 1982: 164). Public verifiability "means that claims about the nature of nature can be measured against the evidence" (Lett 1997: 56). Here the "ultimate arbiters" are the data (Kuznar 1997: 25).

This position may be referred to as **truth by correspondence.** It contrasts with the truth by coherence view of the cultural constructionists by holding that the truth of propositions depends upon correspondence to the way the world is (Williams 2001: 139). In other words, the external world/universe that exists independently of the beliefs people have about them comprises the defining conditions of knowledge (Williams 2001: 32, 138).

Public verification alone, however, does not rule out the likelihood of collective misperceptions or mass hallucinations. The second criterion that must be met is that propositions have to be tested against what is outside of collective subjectivity or the unfounded prejudices of the subculture of scientists (Lett 1997: 48, 56). Science is concerned only with propositional statements, statements that can be demonstrated to be either true or false (Bernard 1995: 13; Lett 1997: 23, 1999: 105). This necessitates that the conditions under which propositions would be refuted need to be specified. If these conditions cannot be stated, the proposition is not falsifiable.

To give one example, take the following assertion: Capricious invisible evil spirits are the cause of disease. This proposition cannot be falsified because by definition evil spirits cannot be detected and they afflict their victims randomly. It is not possible to specify conditions, which if detected would disprove the assertion. In contrast, we can specify such conditions in the case of the germ theory of disease: Germs could not cause disease if people who fall ill have not come into contact with infected materials (Futuyma 1982: 168).

Lett (1997: 54) has noted the implications of the requirements of validation and testability:

If the epistemological procedures employed were not publicly verifiable, then they would be ultimately subjective, and there would be no limits (other than the limits of the human imagination) upon what could be claimed as knowledge. Without the rule of verifiability, any dream, any fantasy, any hallucination could be regarded as real and true. It is logically possible, of course, that everyone in a given community of observers could share the same illusion at the same time. For that reason, it is not sufficient that a claim to knowledge be verifiable; objectivity demands that it be testable as well. If the claim to knowledge were not testable, then it would not be propositional, and any and all evidence would be irrelevant to the truth or falsity of the claim. Without the rule of testability, propositionally meaningless

statements could be regarded as significant and substantive.[14]

THE SCIENTIFIC CYCLE

Science is a way of representing reality (experiences/observations, i.e., facts). Its goals are explanation and validation of explanation (Reyna 1994: 556). An explanation is a proposition made up of sets of related concepts that is a representation of "how and why reality is constituted as it is" (Reyna 1994: 556). Highly abstract propositions are called theories; less abstract ones are referred to as empirical generalizations or hypotheses.

Validation refers to the assessment of how accurate the representations of reality are. Valid conceptual representations are parsimonious and have higher correspondence (i.e., predictive power). This means that their conceptual representations fit the facts by correctly stating that something does, will, or did occur in reality, relative to competing explanations (Reyna 1994: 557). An explanation that fits more facts and has stumbled upon fewer instances of counterfactual observations is considered to have a greater degree of validity, but never in an absolute sense (Reyna 1994: 557). Science is not concerned with absolutes or universals, but rather with approximate truths (Reyna 1994: 557).

Scientific research begins in the realm of facts, which means observations and experiences of what occurs or has occurred (Reyna 1994: 556). The facts are scrutinized through induction (see Figure 2.1). In **inductive reasoning** one begins by identifying common characteristics (called pattern recognition), and developing generalizations. Simple generalizations are descriptive rather than explanatory in nature and scientifically uninteresting (Kuznar 1997: 46). Explanatory theories are logically constructed models or representations of "how and why reality is constituted as it is" that are based upon empirical data and are meant to account for a wider, and as yet unobserved phenomena.

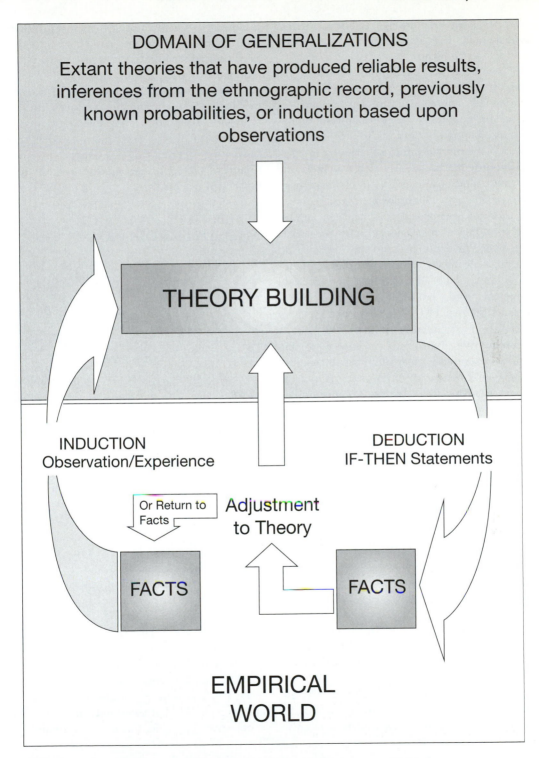

Figure 2.1 Stages in the scientific cycle. *After Thomas (1998); Kuznar (1997).*

Theories posit relationships and linkages that contribute to new understandings that further research can confirm.

Theories are generated on the basis of several sources: extant theories that have produced reliable results, inferences from the ethnographic record, previously known probabilities, or induction based upon observations. To determine how accurate the representation of reality is, the theory must be validated. This is achieved by testing it against additional independent observations to determine how well it holds up.

Theories are general statements or models and their logical consequences must be worked out before they can be tested. In order to do this, logically valid propositions, called hypotheses, must be deduced from the theory to yield statements with predictable empirical consequences (Kuznar 1997: 46). These take the form of IF-THEN statements (Thomas 1998: 47).

Deductive reasoning is central to the process of testing or confirming hypotheses. Deductive arguments are comprised of two or more assertions from which a conclusion is drawn. They may be stated in syllogistic form:

Premise: All men are mortal.
Premise: Socrates was a man.
Conclusion: Socrates was mortal.

If the premises are true, then the conclusion will be valid.

The IF-THEN statements deduced from the theory are tested in the realm of facts through further empirical investigation in order to determine if they can be falsified. If the IF-THEN statement corresponds with the facts it is to some extent corroborated. The validity of a hypothesis increases the more times it is corroborated in this manner, although no hypothesis is ever validated absolutely. Replication of the research findings is required to establish the reliability of the results.

Falsification is somewhat tricky because errors in measurement, skewed samples, and the nature of the data used can lead to a negative finding. It is for this reason that hypotheses require repeated testing. This ensures that the theory is not falsified on the basis of errors and unrepresentative data (Kuznar 1997: 47).

If the hypothesis is refuted, then adjustments may be made so that the theory more accurately represents reality. But if the hypotheses generated by a theory are consistently falsified, then alternative theories that are better representations of reality are proposed and the whole process repeats itself.

SCIENTIFIC PRACTICE AND ANTHROPOLOGY

A question that one might raise at this point is, How relevant are the aforementioned procedures in anthropology? The postmodern anthropological writer Crapanzano objects to the relevance of science in anthropology. Conceding that perhaps science works in other fields, he asserts that anthropologists seldom meet the criteria of replication.

> We cannot buy into irrelevant or only partially relevant models of science that have clout because they have been successful in other domains. It seems obvious that most but by no means all of anthropological research precludes correction through replication. Are we to dismiss all but the replicable? Better that we accept it, acknowledging self-critically its limitations and acknowledging the limitations, the determinants, of our self-criticism (Crapanzano 1995: 421).[15]

Crapanzano overlooks the fact that the defining condition of science is acknowledging self-critically the limitations of knowledge. Scientific anthropologists have also acknowledged that certain domains of anthropological knowledge are not amenable to analysis by scientific procedures. This is why, through most of its existence as a discipline, anthropology has embraced both scientific and humanistic perspectives (Johnson 1995: 10). The issue is not about dismissing all but the replicable, but about not conflating what is objective, replicable, and sound anthropological knowledge with subjective, impressionistic, and idiosyncratic musings, clever stories, and self-contradictory, irrational beliefs.

Assessments of science in anthropology must take into account that many practitioners who have attached the label "scientific" to their work have been negligent in adhering to scientific standards (Sidky 2003). Rather than indicating the flaws in the scientific approach or its irrelevance in anthropological research, this failing may be traced to the lack of commitment on the part of many researchers to support generalizations with evidence, such as, for example, statements about land tenure being supported by detailed maps and evidence of inheritance of specific tracts of land (cf. Fox 1997: 341). Ethnographers routinely treat estimates and guesses of their informants as actual empirical observations and measurements and then proceed to develop empirical generalizations on the basis of such information. There is sufficient justification for us to be extremely skeptical about the scientific status of any anthropological account that presents peoples' "customs" but neglects to supply such empirical evidentiary support (Fox 1997: 341).

It should be noted also that Crapanzano's assertion that scientific anthropologists fail to meet scientific standards is false. Those who correctly employ a scientific approach frequently satisfy the requirements of reliability, testability, and falsifiability. Moreover, there is also the intense scrutiny and criticism that anthropological theories and findings are subjected to by the community of anthropologists in the principle anthropological journals (Harris 1994: 64).

It is because such scrutiny takes place that scientific anthropology is self-correcting and has also made unparalleled advances in our knowledge of humankind. As Fox (1992: 48–49) has pointed out,

> We resisted the nineteenth-century notion that differences are qualitative on a scale from "lowest savagery to advanced civilization." They are just different strategies adapted to different circumstances by people capable of managing any strategy from the most elementary to the most advanced. . . . We reduced the myriad kinship systems of the world to a manageable order even mathematical analyzability. We found common and universal elements in myths and rituals. We understood non-monetary economic systems as operating on principles of exchange and reciprocity. We interpreted the workings of political systems that had no sovereigns or central monopolies on force, but which did work. We invented objective phonetic systems for recording all the diversities of languages, and semantic analyses whereby we could compare them and even reconstruct their histories. We even found formulas that linked all these together as expressions of basic mental structures. . . . Structuralism was shrugged off too early and graph theory is taking up where it left of anyway. What is more, we combined all this with the even more daring excursion into the Other of the past and the very remote past. We literally dug up the ancient origins of our civilizations and their precursors; our Others in time not just space. And this we related to our even more ancient origins in pre-human primate society, to discover the common heritage from which we all sprang, how we got here, and what we are doing now. We even know a bit about why. There is a long way to go, but knowledge expands all the time and even ten years ago we would not have predicted that we would have today the scientific tools we have to carry on these explorations into areas previously denied to our puny science. This is not a bad record.[16]

Scientific anthropological knowledge has corrected itself over time. Kuznar's (1997: 67–90) analysis of the anthropological investigations of the role of hunting in foraging cultures and his examination of archaeological research on the Hopewell burial mounds are two examples of the self-correcting nature of scientific work in anthropology. He observes that

> despite the real-life human interests [ideological/sociological], in both cases a basic scientific commitment to generating more objective knowledge resulted in theories that better account for the empirical data (Kuznar 1997: 68).[17]

"Science," as D'Andrade (1995: 4) has put it, "is a public activity in which people check on each other's observations and reasoning, and it is this that gives science a chance at the truth. Science is the best bias destroyer we have."

Not only is science our best bias buster; there is considerable evidence that scientific perspectives have and continue to contribute to the growth of knowledge about sociocultural phenomena. There is therefore no justification for anthropologists to discard science in favor of subjectivism and storytelling. As Reyna (1994: 557) has pointed out,

> Prudent thinkers might be persuaded to reject science provided that two questions had been answered. The first of these is whether criticisms of science are compelling. The second is whether there is another, more powerful mode of knowing than science, so that investigators might turn to a replacement that would help them address reality more adequately than science has. If the criticisms of science are valid, there is reason to be dubious about scientific metanarratives, and if there is a more powerful epistemology, then it is appropriate to abandon science.[18]

Not only are compelling reasons against science lacking, but the nonobjective approaches and epistemological free-for-all provided as better alternatives by some anthropologists are the least suitable means of dealing with bias. On the contrary, such approaches only ensure that subjective biases and ideological intrusions will multiply and remain forever obscured from critical scrutiny of any kind (cf. Spiro 1986: 276). It is for these reasons that those engaged in the effort to expunge science from anthropology and replace it with nonobjective, proof-exempt alternatives are doing a great disservice to the discipline and to the lives and cultures of the peoples they write about. There is little one can say

about the intellectual merits of a scholarly enterprise that is indistinguishable in its methods, premises, and orientation from the pseudoscientific nonsense produced by popular presses.

CRITERIA FOR THE ASSESSMENT OF ANTHROPOLOGICAL THEORY

In the following chapters I shall examine some of the major theoretical perspectives, research strategies, or paradigms in anthropology during the last one hundred years or so in terms of their epistemological assumptions and their respective attempts at increasing our understanding of sociocultural phenomena. I assess anthropological paradigms from the perspective of the philosophy of science. This assessment is based upon the key epistemological point discussed in this chapter, which is that *although the world abounds with meanings, claims to knowledge, and ways of knowing, not all of these are equally useful if our goal is to obtain reliable, objectively valid knowledge about humankind, human origins, human behavior and cognition, and the evolution and operation of sociocultural systems.*

The minimal standard upon which my evaluation is based is whether a theoretical perspective in question is systematic, logically consistent, and adheres to the principle of validation of explanations against empirical data. In other words, theories will be assessed in terms of the minimal criteria for responsible scientific inquiry.

Those who advocate research programs without adhering to these basic and minimal criteria, for whatever reasons, are merely making excuses for engaging in proof-exempt discourses and subjective, idiosyncratic shoddy work and storytelling. That brings us back to the familiar problem of the slippery slope.

Chapter 3

Evolutionism and the Beginnings of Anthropology During the Nineteenth Century

Anthropology as a formal discipline is a little over a century old. Anthropological thinking, however, probably goes back to when humans first began to reflect upon themselves and speculate about human origins, the nature of society, the relationship between culture and nature, and the customs of other people.

In the West, such ideas can be traced back to ancient and classical writers such as Xenophon, Herodotus, and Tacitus, among others (see Gruber 1973). Also, there is a body of western literature spanning the period between the fourteenth to the eighteenth centuries that is clearly anthropological in nature (see Slotkin 1965).

During the medieval period there are the works of the Spanish Muslim theologian Averroës and the Arab geographer Ibn Khaldûn (see Honigmann 1976). There are, of course, many other accounts with an anthropological focus. The existence of such accounts poses a problem for the historian of anthropology because, as Bohannan and Glazer (1988: xii) have put it: "There is no event, no person, before which there was no anthropology and after which there was."

Up to a hundred years ago anthropological topics were the domain of historians, philosophers, theologians, and antiquarians (Honigmann 1976: 1). It is not until the latter part of the 1800s that we find the first group of scholars who called themselves anthropologists and who set forth a corpus of anthropological theories focusing upon pan-human cross-cultural similarities and differences.

The latter part of the nineteenth century was the formative period of anthropology, when the discipline became organized and institutionalized. Moreover, some of the major theoretical issues and controversies that carried well into the twentieth century were formulated during this period (Service 1985: x). I begin my discussion of anthropological theory here.

NINETEENTH-CENTURY EVOLUTIONISM

The anthropologists writing during the nineteenth century did not comprise a single theoretical school of thought (Stocking 1974: 416). These included Edward Burnett Tylor (1832–1917),

Lewis Henry Morgan (1818–1881), John Lubbock/Lord Avebury (1834–1913), Herbert Spencer (1820–1903), James Frazer (1854–1941), Johann Bachofen (1815–1887), Henry Main (1822–1888), and John McLennan (1827–1881), among others. These men were all British, with the exception of Morgan, who was American, and Bachofen, who was German.

What united these major anthropological thinkers was the shared belief in the idea of evolution and progress and the certainty that humankind had arisen from primitive and lowly beginnings and had evolved toward a more "advanced" state. They also shared in common the commitment to a naturalistic theory of causation and a naturalistic analytical framework for the study of culture. The many problematic aspects of nineteenth-century ethnology do not detract from its most important contributions to the discipline of anthropology, the commitment to a naturalistic perspective, the effort to produce parsimonious scientific understandings of sociocultural evolution, and the elimination of supernaturalism from anthropological discourse.

The gross ethnocentrism of many of the nineteenth-century anthropologists usually shrouds for present-day readers the overall intellectual implication of their enterprise. Franz Boas and his students in United States took it upon themselves to highlight, with various degrees of justification, the naivety, bias, racism, and ethnocentrism of their nineteenth-century predecessors. The Boasians, however, had their own ideological agenda and not all of the sins they attributed to the nineteenth-century pioneers are justifiable.

A more useful perspective on the work of nineteenth-century anthropologists is to uncover the reasons why they made the assumptions they made and adopted the methods they did to pursue the study of cultural phenomena. One must also bear in mind the limitations under which people like Tylor and Morgan were operating, such as the quality of ethnographic data available, as well as social and ideological constraints of the time.

The primary objective of nineteenth-century ethnology was not to denigrate indigenous peoples and their traditions, but rather to show how Western customs and institutions, from the family to government and religion, arose from humble primitive beginnings, rather than being divinely ordained (Harris 2001: 210). These achievements, as Morgan (1887: 29–45, 554) put it, arose from the "struggles, the sufferings, the heroic exertions and the patient toil" of savage and barbarous ancestors. It is from this perspective that I shall approach nineteenth-century evolutionary thought.

EDWARD B. TYLOR AND THE DEVELOPMENT OF ANTHROPOLOGY

Edward Burnett Tylor (1832–1917) is credited with transforming anthropology into a formal scientific discipline (see Leopold 1980; Stocking 1987: 156–164). Tylor established anthropology at the University of Oxford, where he was appointed reader (lecturer) in 1875 and Professor of Anthropology in 1896. He was without a doubt one of the giants of nineteenth-century ethnology. Tylor adopted the words *anthropology* and *culture* from German and made them part of his disciplinary vocabulary and referred to himself as an anthropologist. So influential was Tylor in his field that some of his contemporaries dubbed anthropology in England "Mr. Tylor's Science."

Tylor's interest in anthropology developed when as a young man in his early twenties he developed symptoms of tuberculosis, forcing him to seek the warmer climates of Cuba (see Hays 1964: 56–83). There he met the British archaeologist Henry Christy and the two set off on an extended visit to Mexico. Their journeys took the two men from cities to villages, plantations, and archaeological sites and ancient ruins, such as Teotihuacan and Cholula. Tylor's keen and careful observations during his excursion led to the publication of his first work, a travel book entitled *Anahuac: Or Modern Mexico and Mexicans*

Edward Burnett Tylor, one of the principal nineteenth-century evolutionists in Britain. Tylor was responsible for making anthropology into a university-based discipline.

(1861). As a result of his experiences in the Americas, Tylor's career as an anthropologist had been launched.

During his professional career Tylor did not conduct any ethnographic fieldwork, as we understand the enterprise today, but instead relied mainly upon information collected by others. As such, strictly speaking, he may be classified as an **"armchair anthropologist."** However, Tylor did pursue ethnographic knowledge in his own fashion. In his book *The History of Ethnological Theory* (1959), the anthropologists Robert Lowie describes Tylor's approach:

> Tylor was not technically a field worker, yet he was the very opposite of an armchair anthropologist. That he saw Mexican natives in his early manhood and later (1884) paid a brief visit to Pueblo villages counts for something, but more important is his unremitting tendency to study culture in the very heart of a metropolis. He receives a Tasmanian skin-scraper and forthwith has it tested by his butcher;

he peers into shop windows for a parallel of the Oceanian pump-drill; in Somersetshire he watches a weaver throw her shuttle from hand to hand and discerning a problem in aboriginal gesture language, he learns hundreds of signs in the Berlin Deaf and Dumb Institution (Lowie 1959: 69).

In addition to being dubbed "the father of modern anthropology" by some, Tylor has been given the distinction of having provided the first definition of the discipline's key concept, culture, in "its modern technical or anthropological meaning" (Kroeber and Kluckhohn 1963: 11). This is the definition, as Bohannan and Glazer (1988: 62) point out, that anthropologists "fall back on when others prove too cumbersome." Tylor's definition of culture appears on the first page of his masterpiece, *Primitive Culture* (1871):

> Culture, or Civilization, taken in its widest ethnographic sense, is that complex whole which includes knowledge, belief, art, morals, laws, custom, and any other capabilities and habits acquired by man as a member of society.

The anthropologists Alfred Kroeber and Clyde Kluckhohn (1963: 295) maintained that Tylor "possessed unusual insight and wisdom" and that he established the science of anthropology "by defining its subject matter." This at least is the reading of the passage by American anthropologist for whom the concept of culture was of central theoretical concern (see Stocking 1968: 73; 1987: 300–301).

Tylor's major works include *Researches into the Early History of Mankind* (1865), *Primitive Culture* (1871), the first chapter of which frequently appears in many modern readers on the history of anthropology, and *Anthropology* (1881), the first "textbook" or "proto-textbook" in the field. The noted British anthropologist A. C. Haddon (1910: 159) described Tylor's works as follows:

> replete with vast erudition [they] are so suggestive and graced by such quiet humour that they have become "classics," and have profoundly influenced modern thought. From their first appearance it was recognized that a mastermind was guiding the destinies of the nascent science.

Tylor was principally interested in the investigation of the history of mankind and the development of civilization, as the full title of his first major anthropological work suggests. As Tylor (1929 [1871]: 20–21) put it,

> In carrying on the great task of rational ethnography, the investigation of the causes which have produced the phenomena of culture, and the laws to which they are subordinate, it is desirable to work out as systematically as possible a scheme of evolution of this culture along its many lines.

Tylor was working in a climate of great intellectual change. Archaeological and geological research had demonstrated the great age of the earth and the existence of ancient and "primitive cultures" that once flourished in Europe and elsewhere. Moreover, it was by then clear that there were at least three successive stages of cultural development, as suggested by the **Three-Age-System** (stone-bronze-iron) chronological framework developed by Christian Jurgensen Thomsen (1788–1865), curator of the Danish National Museum (Fagan 1972: 27–28). As Tylor noted,

> It has been especially the evidence of prehistoric archaeology which, within the last few years, has given to the natural development theory of civilisation a predominance hardly disputed on anthropological grounds. . . . The finding of ancient stone implements buried in the ground in almost every habitable district of the world, including the great ancient civilisations, such as Egypt, Assyria, India, China, Greece, etc., may be adduced to show that the inhabitants at that time belonged to the stone age (Tylor 1878; in Harris 2001: 149).

In addition to the evidence of archaeology, there was also the ethnographic data on the contemporary, "nonliterate peoples" across the globe that had been steadily accumulating since the voyages of discovery. The problem was how to utilize the available information in order to build a scientific picture of the cultural transformations suggested by the archaeological evidence. Here the cultural evolutionists benefited from the Darwinian milieu and the deep commitment to a naturalistic model of causality and the scientific perspective. As Murphree (1961: 267) noted,

> The anthropology of Tylor, Lubbock, and Morgan represents a convergence of ideas which had successively enveloped geology, biology, and archaeology. The interchange among these sciences was like a cross-fertilization, and discoveries and theories in one field were not easily contained within narrow limits. By the time the evolutionary idea in its nineteenth-century dress was firmly entrenched in all of them, geologists and biologists presented a common front with paleontologists, archaeologists, and students of culture.[1]

Parenthetically, it might be noted that some of our most important insights into the human condition have stemmed from the type of cross-fertilization noted by Murphree and was built into the four-field approach in American anthropology.

For nineteenth-century ethnologists, archaeology had shown that the roots of "mankind," or human origins, stretched far back in antiquity. Darwin had shown the continuity between past and present life forms. Continuity in nature extended to culture, which was considered to be equally a part of nature. As Tylor (1929: 2) brilliantly put it, "the history of mankind is part and parcel of the history of nature with laws as definite as those which govern the motion of waves, the combination of acids and bases, and the growth of plants and animals."

Geology suggested a principle that had been so effective in that field, namely that the present is the key to the past. If there was continuity in cultures, and if the present could be used as the key to understanding the past, then the study of extant "primitive" peoples could shed light on the history of mankind as a whole. Nineteenth-century cultural evolutionary thought may best be characterized as the working out and application of these assumptions.

Charles Darwin, author of The Origin of Species *(1859) and expositor of the theory of evolution through natural selection. Anthropological thought of the period was influenced heavily by the intellectual milieu and the deep commitment to a naturalistic model of causality and the scientific perspective inspired by Darwin's ideas.*

EVOLUTIONISM AND THE DEFENDERS OF SUPERNATURALISM

Another factor impinged upon the anthropological thought of the time that we must bear in mind was religion and **supernaturalism.** The evolutionists had to contend with the theological perspective on the origin and antiquity of "mankind" and civilization. Thus evolutionists such as Tylor, Lubbock, and Morgan, who struggled to establish anthropology as a scientific discipline were, as Murphree (1961: 267) observed, "embattled men straining to take the curse of Adam from their primeval ancestors." Or as

Stocking (1965: 141) has put it with respect to Tylor, his problem was "to fill the gap between Brixham Cave and European Civilization without introducing the hand of God."

The theory of cultural evolution therefore was in part shaped by the disputation between anthropologists and the ardent proponents of theological views of "man," or the defenders of supernaturalism. At issue was the question of the origins of "primitive," nonliterate societies and their relationship to European culture. The controversy of the period was between the **progressionists,** a camp to which the majority of ethnologists belonged, and the **degenerationists,** the theological camp.

The religious orthodoxy, challenged and vexed by the new scientific developments, reacted to the idea that humans had evolved from a primitive state similar to "savages" living in the present. Rabid ethnocentrism and religious conceit made unbearable the idea that the "naked," "immoral," "pagan savages" represented mankind's glorious beginning and God's perfect creation.

The godly folks presented their own scheme as an alternative. Known as **degenerationism,** this view held that humans were created in a high state of morality and civilization (a point of view espoused in present-day pseudoscientific accounts regarding Atlantis or other long lost advanced civilizations). The primitive savages, according to this view, were merely the "outcasts of the human race," degenerates who had fallen from a state of "grace" (cf. Kardiner and Preble 1962: 59–60). Moreover, the degenerationists held that primitive people were incapable of progressing without some form of outside intervention.

This view is exemplified in the works of men such as Richard Whately (1787–1863), the Archbishop of Dublin. He observed that "we have no reason to believe that any community ever did, or ever can, emerge, unassisted by external helps, from a state of utter barbarism into any thing that can be called civilization" (Whately 1832:

106). The external helps to which Whately was referring involved the miraculous intervention by the hand of god (Whately 1832: 120).

Degeneration was popular because it was highly compatible with the biblical notions of the Fall and the divine origins of culture (Murphree 1961: 277). Moreover, construing subjugated peoples as less than human, as the degenerationists depicted non-European peoples, had conscious-saving value for the citizens of imperial nations, such as Britain, France, Germany, and the United States. Genocide, ethnocide, slavery, and exploitation became less distasteful if those suffering these outrages were made out to be not quite human. One might note that it was the theological/supernaturalist perspective that expressed European colonial and imperial conceit, not the point of view of the anthropologists of the period who bitterly opposed the theological viewpoint.

The progressionists maintained that culture was the product of a gradual but cumulative and lawful natural progressive development and that the course of cultural evolution was in general upward from a primitive condition of savagery and barbarism. Among those who entered this debate was Charles Lyell (1797–1875), expositor of the **principle of uniformitarianism** (that the past must be explained by the present) and author of *Principles of Geology* (1830–1833), which provided extensive geological evidence for the great antiquity of the earth. Lyell finally committed himself to the evolutionary view in his book *The Geological Evidences of the Antiquity of Man* (1863), having been convinced by the overwhelming weight of the evidence before him. In *Geological Evidences* he brought geological, archaeological, paleontological, and ethnological facts to bear in support of the position that culture had evolved from earlier primitive stages (A. White 1955: 241).

Lyell argued that had early man attained an advanced stage anywhere close to modern civilization, the archaeologists would be uncovering

lines of buried railways or electric telegraphs, from which the best engineers of our day might gain invaluable hints; astronomical instruments and microscopes of more advanced construction than any known in Europe, and other indications of perfection in the arts and sciences, such as the nineteenth century has not yet witnessed. . . . Vainly should we be straining our imaginations to guess the possible uses and meanings of such relics—machines, perhaps, for navigating the air or exploring the depths of the ocean, or for calculating arithmetical problems, beyond the wants or even the conception of living mathematicians (Lyell 1863: 379).

Tylor objected to the degenerationist perspective on numerous grounds. That perspective, he wrote,

has practically resolved itself into two assumptions, first, that the history of culture began with the appearance on earth of a semi-civilized races of men, and second, that from this stage culture has proceeded in two ways, backward to produce savages, and forward to produce civilized men. . . . It must be borne in mind, however, that the grounds upon which this theory has been held is theological with no ethnographic evidence to support it (Tylor 1929, I: 35, 36).

Tylor also brought to bear archeological and ethnographic evidence, citing evidence from prehistoric archaeology that humans in "remotely ancient ages were in the savage state, as attested by the discovery of his relics side by side with extinct animals." Tylor pointed out that

against the idea that tribes now ignorant of metallurgy and pottery formerly possessed but have since lost these arts [we] . . . assert, on a general proposition, that no weapons or instruments of metal have ever been found in any country inhabited by savages wholly ignorant of metallurgy (Tylor 1929, I: 57).

Tylor added,

The examination of district after district of the world has now all but established a universal rule that the Stone Age (bone or shell being the occasional substitutes for stone) underlies the Metal Age everywhere (Tylor 1929, I: 60).

Another line of argument against the degeneration view was based on the evidence of independent inventions and evidence for an order of progression in an unbroken chain of cumulative technological innovations. This chain links the most ancient stone tools to the latest industrial, technological innovations in which no shortcuts or deviations can be detected:

[The] appearance of an art in a particular locality where it is hard to account for it as borrowed from elsewhere, and especially if it concerns some special native product, is evidence of its being a native invention. . . . As the isolated possession of an art goes to prove its invention where it is found, so the absence of an art goes to prove that it was never present (Tylor 1929, I: 63).

Fire-making, cooking, pottery, the textile arts, are to be traced along lines of gradual improvement. Music begins with the rattle and the drum, which in one way or another hold their places from end to end of civilization, while pipes and stringed instruments represent an advanced musical art which is still developing. So with architecture and agriculture (Tylor 1929, I: 67–68).

Finally, Tylor confronted the degenerationist claim that evidence of technological advances, such as stone tools following metal ones, had no relevance because man's moral or spiritual progress and his material progress were distinct, and that spiritual progress was not subject to natural laws nor was it amenable to scientific enquiry. Tylor took up the challenge in his book *Primitive Cultures* (1871), which was written to answer precisely these arguments by bringing religious beliefs into the progressivist model (Stocking 1968: 82).

Tylor argued that not only religious beliefs, but also other aspects of mental life, such as mythology and other "spontaneous" traits (i.e., things unconnected to practical matters) are the products of evolutionary development and subject to the same natural laws as the material dimensions of culture:

Rudimentary as the science of culture still is, the symptoms are becoming very strong that even what seem its most spontaneous and motiveless phenomena will, nevertheless, be shown to come within the range of distinct cause and effect as certainly as the facts of mechanics. What could be popularly though more indefinite and uncontrolled than the products of the imagination in myths and fables? Yet any systematic investigation of mythology, on the basis of a wide collection of evidence, will show plainly enough in such efforts of fancy at once a development from stage to stage, and a production of uniformity of result from uniformity of cause (Tylor 1929, I: 18).

As for religion, Tylor wrote,

Nowhere, perhaps, are broad views of historical development more needed than in the study of religion. . . . Few who will give their minds to master the general principles of savage religion will ever again think it ridiculous, or the knowledge superfluous to the rest of mankind. Far from its beliefs and practices being a rubbish-heap of miscellaneous folly, they are consistent and logical in so high a degree as to being, as soon as even roughly classified, to display the principles of their formation and development; and these principles prove to be essentially rational, though working in a mental condition of intense and inveterate ignorance (Tylor 1929, I: 22).

I shall turn to Tylor's explanation for the origins of religion later in this chapter.

EVOLUTION AND DIFFUSION

It was in part the disputation with the proponents of theological views that led the evolutionists into conceptual difficulties. For example, to combat the orthodoxy, John Lubbock stressed that savages were perfectly capable of developing a civilized culture without outside intervention (Murphree 1961: 273). Lubbock attributed all cultural development to the indigenous creativity and inventiveness of people and resorted to the concept of **psychic unity of mankind** (i.e., that all human minds are fundamentally the same) to explain all cultural similarities (Murphree 1961: 273, 280).

Lubbock de-emphasized the diffusionist perspective because it cast doubt upon the mental aptitude of "primitive" people and ascribed creativity and inventiveness to a small and select group of cultures, or a single culture, such as that of ancient Egypt (see Chapter 5). The view that most cultures had developed as a result of borrowing of traits invented by a more ingenious race elsewhere accorded well with the degenerationist perspective.

In his rejoinder to Whately, Lubbock overstated the case of indigenous efflorescence and de-emphasized or dismissed altogether the effects of **diffusion** (borrowing of cultural traits as a result of contact, imitation, or migration) in culture change. This delivered a lethal weapon into the hands of later critics such as Franz Boas and his students, as we shall see in Chapter 6.

However, diffusion is only de-emphasized in Lubbock's book *The Origin of Civilization* (1870) and not in his other principle work, *Pre-Historic Times* (1865). In fact, the evolutionary ethnologists recognized the significance of diffusion and its implications, as their various views on this issue suggests. Indeed, as Tylor put it, not only was diffusion important, but it was the mechanism that ensured that once something was invented it would not be lost, contrary to degenerationist opinion, even if the culture that produced it was swept away:

> What is produced in some limited district is diffused over a wider and wider area, where the process of effectual "stamping-out" becomes more and more difficult. Thus it is even possible for the habits and inventions of races long extinct to remain as the common property of surviving nations; and the destructive actions which make such havoc with the civilizations of particular districts fail to destroy the civilization of the world (Tylor 1929, I: 39).

Morgan, whose work I shall examine in the next chapter, also stresses the importance of diffusion in his evolutionary scheme. He wrote, for example,

> The most advanced portion of the human races were halted, so to express it, at certain stages of progress, until some great invention or discovery, such as the domestication of animals or the smelting of iron ore, gave a new and powerful impulse forward. While thus restrained, the ruder tribes, continually advancing, approached in different degrees of nearness to the same status; for wherever a continental connection existed, all the tribes must have shared in some measure in each other's progress. All great inventions and discoveries propagated themselves but the inferior tribes must have appreciated their values before they could appropriate them. In the continental areas certain tribes would lead; but the leadership would be apt to shift a number of times in the course of an ethnical period [evolutionary stage] (Morgan 1877: 39–40).

Thus the claim by the subsequent generation of anthropologists that the evolutionists overlooked the effects of diffusion is patently false (see L. White 1987).

EVOLUTIONISM AND POLYGENISM

Another challenge to the evolutionary theory of culture was the polygenist argument. During the eighteenth century, two views of human origins had developed. The first was **monogenism,** which held that all humans arose from a common stock and that the perceptible variations between contemporary human groups were due to environmental factors that had developed following a single act of creation. Associated with this perspective was the idea of the psychic unity of humankind, namely that the human mind is the same everywhere.

The other view was **polygenism,** which held that the different races of humankind arose as a consequence of separate acts of creation and each race belonged to a separate species. Parenthetically, monogenism and polygenism are not to be confused with **the single origin theory** for the origins of *sapiens* populations (Cavalli-Sforza et al., 1994; Horai et al., 1995: Klein 1989) and **the multiple origin theory** (Clark and Lindley 1989; Wolpoff 1989), which deal with the evolution of modern humans and the relationships between modern and archaic *sapiens*.

Monogenists tended to be advocates of racial equality, while the polygenists were committed racial determinists who ardently believed in a racial hierarchy in which Europeans were considered to represent the highest strata. Polygenism was especially popular in the United States among the fervid defenders of slavery. Eventually, however, racialists managed to also reconcile monogenism with the extreme folk racism of the kind that flourished in the Bible belt of the United States (Harris 2001: 84). Both views carried well into the nineteenth century and were part of the intellectual debates engaged in by anthropologists.

DEVELOPING A SCIENCE OF CULTURE

In their quest to establish a science of culture, Tylor, Morgan, Lubbock, and others sought to replace theological explanations based upon spontaneous, supernatural interventions with a naturalistic model of cultural progress. This was no easy task as opposition came from all corners, from theologically oriented thinkers and other defenders of supernaturalism. In this context Tylor's remarks are of significance in light of the present-day antiscience view in anthropology:

> Our modern investigators in the sciences of inorganic nature are foremost to recognize, both within and without their special fields of work, the unity of nature, the fixity of its laws, the definite sequence of cause and effect through which every fact depends on what has gone before it, and acts upon what is to come after it. They grasp firmly

the Pythagorean doctrine of pervading order in the universal Kosmos. They affirm, with Aristotle, that nature is not full of incoherent episodes, like a bad tragedy. They agree with Leibnitz in what he calls "my axiom, that nature never acts by leaps" . . . as well as his "great principle, commonly little employed, that nothing happens without sufficient reason." Nor again, in studying the structure and habits of plants and animals, or in investigating the lower functions even of man, are these leading ideas unacknowledged. But when we talk of the higher processes of human feeling and action, or thought and language, knowledge and art, a change appears in the prevalent tone of opinion. The world at large is scarce prepared to accept the general study of human life as a branch of natural science. . . . To many educated minds there seems something presumptuous and repulsive in the view that the history of mankind is part and parcel of the history of nature with laws as definite as those which govern the motion of waves, the combination of acids and bases, and the growth of plants and animals (1929: 2).

During the nineteenth century those who attempted to develop scientific theories of culture were confronted with the contention that "fact" and "social" were incommensurable (Murphree 1961: 272). In recent years, as we shall see in subsequent chapters, cultural constructionists have dredged up this two hundred years' old debate and have made it the foundations of their new anthropological perspective.

Establishing what Tyler called "The Science of Culture" hinged upon a demonstration that human cultural development was subject to uniform processes, rather than being the effect of capricious supernatural interventions or historical accidents. According to Tylor (1929, I: 19),

> It is only when men fail to see the line of connexion in events, that they are prone to fall upon the notions of arbitrary impulses, causeless freaks, chance and nonsense and indefinite unaccountability.

What Tylor could never have foreseen is that the subsequent generation of anthropologists, namely Franz Boas and his disciples in the

United States, did in fact lose sight of all lines of connection in cultural events. They became proponents of a position that was guided precisely by what Tylor noted, "arbitrary impulses," "causeless freaks," and all the rest. In turn, few Boasians could have imagined that in yet another generation or two, their interpretive/postmodern heirs would take the idea of "causeless freaks" and nonsense to new heights of absurdity (but more on that in later chapters).

The evolutionist premise was that culture was cumulative and had developed gradually along an even and unbroken line that preserved continuity between the present and past, and that each stage grew out of the previous one. The idea of uniformity and cumulative nature of cultural development was an important aspect of nineteenth-century anthropological thought and the foundation of its scientific aspiration. As Murphree (1961: 278) put it,

> The concept of culture as a cumulative social agency was the central idea upon which the new anthropology depended. The geology of Hutton and Lyell, the biology of Darwin and Wallace, and the ethnology of Tylor, Lubbock, and Morgan formed a universe of discourse around evolution and the unity of nature.[2]

According to Tylor (1929, I: 1),

> The condition of culture among the various societies of mankind, in so far as it is capable of being investigated on general principles, is a subject apt for the study of laws of human thought and action. On the one hand, the uniformity which so largely pervades civilization may be ascribed, in great measure, to the uniform action of uniform causes: while on the other hand its various grades may be regarded as stages of development or evolution, each the outcome of previous history, and about to do its proper part in shaping the history of the future.

Thus the evolution of culture was determined by invariant laws comparable to the laws at work in other natural domains, such as biology, physics, and geology. This view finds it most explicit statement in the works of Herbert Spencer

who placed everything organic, biological, and cultural, within a single cosmic framework that he posited to operate solely according to the universal law of evolution (Magli 2001: 66).

EVOLUTION AS PROGRESS

The effort to create a science of culture in which Tylor, Morgan, and others were engaged is best seen as part of a broader intellectual climate during the second half of the nineteenth century. This was a time of change and progress and it is not surprising that the theory of cultural evolution was coupled with the notion of progress. The idea of progress, which was central to Enlightenment thought during the eighteenth century, was taken up anew during the latter part of the nineteenth century (see Adams 1998: 39–63).

It was a sign of the times. Progress was a corollary of the rapid and breathtaking advances in technology and industry, achieved through the scientific method. Many European intellectuals, including the greatest anthropologists of the age, shared the conviction that progress was inevitable, that "mankind" was advancing and that Western cultures had attained the pinnacle in the ladder of progress surpassing all others. The faith in progress coupled with the uniformitarian principle that the present is the key to the past, became integral parts of Tylor's approach for explaining culture.

Progress, however, was not considered to be an automatic process or outcome but was linked to important associated environmental factors. Nor was every aspect of cultural progress considered as positive in nature.

> To have learnt to give poison secretly and effectually, to have raised corrupt literature to pestilent perfection, to have organized a successful scheme to arrest free enquiry and proscribe free expression, are works of knowledge and skill whose progress toward their goal has hardly conduced to the general good. . . . [Still], on the whole the civilized man is not only wiser and more capable than

the savage, but also better and happier, and the barbarian stands in between (Tylor 1929, I: 28, 31).

But how does one measure progress? Tylor wrote,

[the] standard of reckoning progress and decline is not that of ideal good and evil, but movement along a measured line from grade to grade of actual savagery, barbarism, and civilization. The thesis which I venture to sustain, within limits, is simply this, that the savage state in some measure represents an early condition of mankind, out of which the higher culture has gradually been developed or evolved, by processes still in regular operation as of old, the result showing that, on the whole, progress has far prevailed over relapse. . . . On this proposition, the main tendency of human society during its long term of existence has been to pass from a savage to a civilized state. . . . Referred to direct history, a great section of it proves to belong not to the domain of speculation, but to that of positive knowledge. It is mere matter of chronicles that modern civilization is a development of mediæval civilization, which again is a development from civilization of the order represented in Greece, Assyria, or Egypt. Thus the higher culture being clearly traced back to what may be called the middle culture, the question which remains is whether this middle culture may be traced back to the lower culture, that is, to savagery. To affirm this, is merely to assert that the same kind of development in culture which has gone on inside our range of knowledge has also gone on outside it, its course of proceeding being unaffected by our having or not having reporters present. If any one holds that human thought and action were worked out in primæval times according to laws essentially other than those of the modern world, it is for him to prove by valid evidence this anomalous state of things, otherwise the doctrine of permanent principle will hold good, as in astronomy or geology. That the tendency of culture has been similar throughout the existence of human society, and that we may fairly judge from its known historic course what its prehistoric course may have been, is a theory clearly entitled to precedence as a fundamental principle of ethnographic research (Tylor 1929, I: 32–33).

The idea of progress meant that evolution had a definite direction. As Tylor pointed out,

development in Culture is recognized by our most familiar knowledge. Mechanical invention supplies apt examples of the kind of development which affects civilizations at large. . . . Such examples of progression are known to us as direct history, but so thoroughly is this notion of development at home in our minds, that by means of it we reconstruct lost history without scruple, trusting to general knowledge of principles of human thought and action as a guide in putting the facts in their proper order. Whether chronicles speaks or is silent on the point, no one comparing a long-bow and a cross-bow would doubt that the cross-bow was a development arising from the simpler instrument. So among the fire-drills for igniting by friction, it seems clear on the face of the matter that the drill worked by a cord or bow is a later improvement on the clumsier primitive instrument twirled between the hands. . . . And thus, in the other branches of our history, there will come again and again into view series of facts which may be consistently arranged as having followed one another in a particular order of development, but which will hardly bear being turned round and made to follow in reverse order. . . . Such . . . are the facts . . . which tend to prove that as to this point of culture at least, savage tribes reached their position by learning and not by unlearning, by elevation from a lower rather than by degradation from a higher state (Tylor 1929, I: 15–16).

Directionality of evolution entails transformations from form X to form Y, with the latter form treated as a more progressive stage. However, the measure of progress (i.e., that Y represents progress, improvement, etc., over X) is difficult to determine. What criteria should one use? The nineteenth-century anthropologists used criteria that were based upon their own European values and ethnocentric assumptions, such as patrilineal organization representing progressive evolutionary development over matrilineal organization, monogamy over polygyny, and so on (Rambo 1991: 41).

In nineteenth-century ethnological thought, evolutionary progress was treated as immanent and teleological, and change was merely the unfolding of latent potential (Sanderson 1990: 17, 46). The idea of the directionality of evolution, although not of immanent, teleological, change as unfolding of latent potential, reoccurs in the work of twentieth-century evolutionists, expressed in transformations from small-scale, internally undifferentiated, sociocultural systems toward large-scale, internally differentiated, or more complex systems.

The idea of simple forms evolving into more complex ones is evident in Tylor's discussion of technological change, cited previously. It is central to Herbert Spencer's formulations regarding the course of evolution within the cosmic framework in which he placed all evolutionary events. Many twentieth-century anthropologists have used complexity as their criterion for directionality of evolutionary development (e.g., Carneiro 1967b; Dole 1973).

The treatment of evolution as progress rather than as progression was one of the major errors of nineteenth-century evolutionism. This is because the corollary of equating progress with evolution is a construal of evolutionary change as something immanent and necessary, directional, and teleological involving betterment (Sanderson 1990: 17, 46). This error is more common in the works of Morgan and Spencer rather than in that of Tylor, who seems not to have adhered to the epistemology of immanent change (Sanderson 1990: 20–21).

THE COMPARATIVE METHOD

From the perspective of nineteenth-century evolutionism, modern culture was the outcome of evolutionary progress, a natural development from savage and barbaric cultures, as indicated by the comparison of extant cultures at different stages of evolutionary elaboration. Therefore, the degenerationist view that savages had reverted from a higher to a lower stage of cultural development was simply wrong. As Tylor (1929, I: 21) stressed,

By comparing the various stages of civilization among races known to history, with the aid of archaeological inference from the remains of prehistoric tribes, it seems possible to judge in a rough way of an early general condition of man, which from our point of view is to be regarded as a primitive condition, whatever yet earlier state many in reality have lain behind it. This hypothetical primitive condition corresponds to a considerable degree to that of modern savage tribes, who, in spite of their difference and distance, have in common certain elements . . . which seem remains of an early state of the human race at large. If this hypothesis be true, then, notwithstanding the continual interference of degeneration, the main tendency of culture from primæval up to modern times has been from savagery towards civilization.

Modern civilization was construed to be one end of a long chain that linked it to the barbarian and savage stages from which it presumably arose. The savage and the civilized were thus part of the same ongoing evolutionary process. Therefore, present-day cultures could be used to understand the past.

The rational behind this was the idea that traits and customs that are similar to one another have evolutionary connections and similar points of origin that could be revealed through systematic comparisons. This procedure was known as **the comparative method.** It had proven highly successful to paleontologists who employed it to classify and assign taxonomic places to fossil forms by comparing them with extant species. The comparative method had also produced significant results in the field of linguistics, where the comparison of known languages, such as Sanskrit, enabled the reconstruction of a proto-Indo-European language, thereby shedding light on the historical development of the Indo-European languages.

The comparative method was already known and widely used before the nineteenth century. However, it found new utility for anthropologists attempting to sort out the accumulating body of archaeological data and ethnographic information. The remarkable success with which the comparative method had been put to use in other fields was the reason that Tylor and other evolutionists felt confident that this method would yield sound knowledge (for the philosophical antecedents of the comparative approach see Adams 1998: 34–38).

The usefulness of the comparative method for ethnologists was clear, as John Lubbock (1865: 416) put it:

> [T]he archaeologist is free to follow the methods which have been so successful in geology—the rude bone and stone implements of bygone ages being to the one what the remains of extinct animals are to the other. The analogy may be pursued even further than this. Many mammalia which are extinct in Europe have representatives still living in other countries. Our fossil pachyderms, for instance, would be almost unintelligible but for the species which still inhabit some parts of Asia and Africa; the secondary marsupials are illustrated by their existing representatives in Australia and South America; and in the same manner, if we wish to clearly understand the antiquities of Europe, we must compare them with the rude implements and weapons still, or until lately, used by the savage races in other parts of the world.

Morgan subscribed to the same belief regarding the present as the key to understanding the past evolutionary history of culture.

> Since mankind were one in origin, their career has been essentially one, running in different but uniform channels upon all continents, and very similarly in all the tribes and nations of mankind down to the same status and advancements. It follows that the history and experience of the American Indian tribes represent, more or less nearly, the history and experience of our own remote ancestors when in corresponding conditions. Forming a part of the human record, their institutions, arts, inventions and practical experiences possess a high and special value reaching far beyond the Indian race itself (Morgan 1877: vii).

The comparative method associated with nineteenth-century ethnology is one among a number of approaches employed by modern anthropologists, and the differences between these need to be pointed out so as to avoid confusion. For the nineteenth-century ethnologists the comparative method entailed the assumption that contemporary "primitive" cultures around the world represented earlier stages of evolutionary development and that primitive cultures could therefore be used to reconstruct past evolutionary histories.

The principle upon which the nineteenth-century comparative approach is based is sound (Harris 2001: 155). Where nineteenth-century ethnologists went astray was in the manner in which they applied the method. They attempted to use the comparative method to sort out an evolutionary picture on the basis of meager and faulty information at their disposal and they abused it in order to forward their own racist and ethnocentric opinions or agendas.

The principle is sound because contemporary small-scale, nonindustrial cultures can be used to help us formulate ideas about prehistoric cultural forms in the same way that knowledge of extant bioforms can help us interpret the characteristics of extinct fossil species. The anthropologist Elman Service (1971: 6–7) has expressed this view as follows:

> There has long been an injunction in anthropology against using data from contemporary primitive people to characterize ancient cultural forms. "Their history is as long as ours," goes the argument that is supposed to make this an unwarranted procedure. The rebuttal to this is not, of course, "No, it isn't: it's shorter." Certainly aboriginal Arunta culture is not younger than Western civilization: it is obviously a great deal older, and precisely therein lays one of the virtues of studying that kind of culture.... But if the aboriginal culture of the Arunta of Australia is not a form of adaptation to a particular kind of (total) environment made long, long ago and preserved into modern times because of its isolation, then what is it? Does a people have whatever kind of culture it might dream up at any given time? Obviously not. Do the Arunta have a rudimentary technology and simple social life because that is as far as their mental powers would take them? No. Anthropolo-

gists would deny that these people have such a limited mental capacity. What else can explain such a culture, then, but that there have been survivals into the present of ancient cultural forms which because of relative isolation have maintained a relatively stable adaptation. Many primitive societies have changed greatly in modern times and ultimately all will be changed, assimilated, or obliterated, but that only makes the point clear.[3]

In other words, if a cultural pattern that evolved long ago has persisted relatively unchanged into the present, then there is every reason to assume that we can gain insights about sociocultural processes by studying such a culture.

Modern anthropologists employ the comparative method in two ways, conducting **controlled comparisons** and **statistical cross-cultural comparisons.** Cross-cultural comparisons are undertaken in order to discover what things go together, or display **covariation,** in a range of societies.

Controlled comparisons (Eggan 1954; Nadel 1952; Radcliffe-Brown 1977: 53–69) involve the comparison of particular cases/societies that share certain factors in common (for example subsistence, economy, group size, sociopolitical organization, religious beliefs, and ecological setting). Selecting societies that have many things in common makes it easier to detect the factors that differ between them. This is because the factors that are constant between them can be ruled out, or "controlled," as explanations for what is different between the two societies.

Statistical cross-cultural comparison refers to a method designed to test the validity of hypotheses against data drawn from cultures around the world. The pioneering work in this direction was Tylor's paper "On a Method of Investigating the Development of Institutions: Applied to Laws of Marriage and Descent" (1889). This represents one of the first studies to use statistical analysis of correlations, or what Tylor called "adhesions," between specific variables, such as postmarital residence, descent, **teknonymy,** and **couvade.** It is for this reason that

Harris (2001: 158) considers Tylor to be the founder of the modern statistical cross-cultural research commonly associated with the work of Murdock.

Tylor's objective was to infer the evolutionary development of sociocultural institutions, rather than seeking generalizations about culture. The objective of modern anthropologists is to develop broad generalizations about culture. What these investigator look for are statistical correlations between specific variables and they attempt to show that the **covariations** in question entail cause and effect relationships.

For the data required to test hypotheses in this manner investigators once had to turn directly to the ethnographic accounts provided by anthropologists during the course of the last one hundred years or so. This demanded a survey of the ethnographic literature that was both grueling and time consuming. The problem of plowing through books and papers containing relevant ethnographic data for statistical cross-cultural comparisons led George Peter Murdock (1897–1985) to undertake the classification, cross-referencing, and cataloging of available descriptive information in ethnographic sources.

The result of this effort was the **Human Relations Area Files** or **HRAF.** Murdock's influential book *Social Structure* (1949), in which he examines the correlation between kinship classification and such variables as forms of marriage and postmarital residence rules, was based upon the database he created. (For a discussion of cross-cultural comparisons and associate methodological problems, see Bernard 1995: 343–347; Naroll 1973; Pelto and Pelto 1979: 257–268).

RECONSTRUCTING EVOLUTIONARY STAGES AND THE CONCEPT OF SURVIVALS

Given the belief by nineteenth-century evolutionists that civilization developed along an unbroken chain of connection that tied the present with the past, Euro–American culture was seen as the end result or the most recent product of a developmental sequence that stretched far back into antiquity. In the minds of the evolutionists, the civilized could thus legitimately be used as a gauge to mark the most advanced segment of the evolutionary continuum.

What other starting point could there be but to begin with what was known and work backward (Murphree 1961: 279)? As Tylor observed,

> In taking up the problem of the development of culture as a branch of ethnological research, a first proceeding is to obtain a means of measurement. Seeking something like a definite line along which to reckon progression and retrogression in civilization, we may apparently find it best in the classification of real tribes and nations, past and present. Civilization actually existing among mankind in different grades, we are enabled to estimate and compare it by positive examples. The educated world of Europe and America practically settles a standard by simply placing its own nations at one end of the social series and the savage tribes at the other, arranging the rest of mankind between these limits according as they correspond more closely to savage or to cultured life. The principle criteria of classification are the absence or presence, high or low development, of the industrial arts, especially metal-working, manufacturing of implements and vessels, agriculture, architecture, &c., the extent of scientific knowledge, the definiteness of moral principles, the condition of religious belief and ceremony, the degree of social and political organization, and so forth (Tylor 1929, I: 26–27).

From the assumption that western European societies represented the most advanced stage of cultural evolution, namely civilization, it followed that the other societies around the globe had to occupy lower stages in the ladder of progress. The basic evolutionary schemes presented had cultures passing through three stages: "savagery," "barbarism," and "civilization" (see Figure 3.1). These stages were construed to be sequential, not temporal, because contemporary

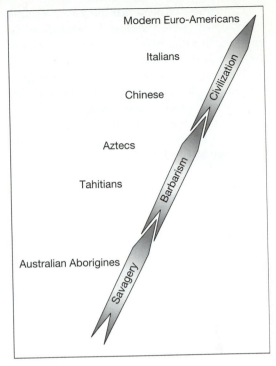

Figure 3.1   Tylor's sequential stages of cultural evolution.

cultures in different parts of the globe were to be found at different stages (Salzman 2001: 92).

The three stages represented a movement from simple to more complex forms.

> Thus, on the definite basis of compared facts, ethnographers are able to set up at least a rough scale of civilization. Few would dispute that the following races are arranged rightly in order of culture:—Australian, Tahitian, Aztec, Chinese, Italian. By treating the development of civilization on this plain ethnographic basis, many difficulties may be avoided which have embarrassed its discussion. This may be seen by a glance at the relation which theoretical principles of civilization bear to the transitions to be observed as matter of fact between the extremes of savage and cultured life (Tylor 1929, I: 27).

Critics have charged that nineteenth-century ethnologists were **unilineal evolutionists,** meaning that they suggested that all cultures follow the same sequence of evolutionary stages without skipping or bypassing a particular stage. Present-day defenders argue that Tylor and Morgan, among others, noted exceptions in their discussion of the general line of development (Carneiro 1967a, 1973). However, I concur with Sanderson (1990: 43), who has cogently pointed out that the "conception of evolutionary transformation as a predetermined unfolding of immanences automatically presupposes a unilinear conception of change, and in such a view divergence can only be regarded as a deviation from the typical path."

Most present-day readers will find such a ranking of cultures and peoples into stages extremely objectionable and an example of European ethnocentrism and conceit. For nineteenth-century ethnologists, however, this approach had immense possibilities. The taxonomic relationship between different cultures could be established through comparison. Once the taxonomic relationships had been worked out, it would be possible to explain similarities and differences among contemporary cultures. Thus, if two cultures are similar in certain respects, it is either because of diffusion (contact/borrowing), independent invention, or because they occupy the same evolutionary stage; if they are different, it is because they occupy different evolutionary stages.

Another utility of the approach was that it could shed light on what contemporary cultures must have been like in the past. It was posited, for example, that European societies at the civilization stage must have passed through the preceding stages of barbarism and savagery. Thus, in order to find out how the ancestors of present-day Europeans were like, one could look at contemporary cultures occupying those stages.

It is here that the comparative approach was much abused by nineteenth-century ethnolo-

gists. Traits and institutions thought to have evolved at different periods in evolutionary history were selected from among the extant inventory of cultures around the world thought to represent those earlier stages and arranged in chronological order to reconstruct the history of humankind. Such schemes were formulated on the basis of preconceived assumptions about how things must have developed, without any consideration of the unique historical trajectories in the development of particular cultures.

To be fair, however, it was in part the quality of the data available to writers such as Tylor that led them to misjudge the range of diversity among contemporary and prehistoric societies. Poor data also led these writers to ignore the adaptive adjustments cultures make to their varied and particular environments.

Given the paucity of solid data, Tylor employed another line of evidence as proof that culture has passed through evolutionary stages. He called this type of evidence **survivals,** by which he meant traits and customs that had persisted but which were anachronistic and represented elements from a previous evolutionary stage. Tylor (1929, I: 71) writes,

> When in the process of time there has come general change in the condition of a people, it is usual, notwithstanding, to find much that manifestly had not its origin in the new state of things, but has simply lasted on into it. On the strength of these survivals, it becomes possible to declare that the civilization of the people they are observed among must have been derived from an earlier state, in which the proper home and meaning of such facts are to be worked as mines of historical knowledge. . . . Among the evidence aiding us to trace the course which the civilizations of the world has actually followed, is that great class of facts to denote which I have found convenient to introduce the term "survivals." These are processes, customs, opinions, and so forth, which have been carried on by force of habit into a new state of society different from that in which they had their original home, and they thus remain as proofs and exam-

ples of an older condition of culture out of which a newer has been evolved.

Tylor (1929, I: 16) provides the following examples:

> Thus, I know an old Somersetshire woman whose hand-loom dates from the time before the introduction of the "flying shuttle," which new-fangled appliance she has never even learnt to use, and I have seen her throw her shuttle from hand to hand in true classic fashion; this old woman is not a century behind her times, but she is a case of survival. Such examples often lead us back to the habits of hundreds and even thousands of years age. The ordeal of the Key is a survival; the Briton peasant's All Souls' supper for the spirits of the dead is a survival. The simple keeping up of ancient habits is only one part of the transition from old into new and changing times. The serious business of ancient society may be seen to sink into the sport of later generations, and its serious beliefs to linger on in nursery folk-lore, while superseded habits of old-world life may be modified into new-world forms still powerful for good and evil.

Survivals are customs that have lost their former utility and meaning and persist only in ceremonies or in games children play and in the superstitions of peasants. The notion of survivals enabled Tylor to explain the presence of cultural traits and customs that were incongruous with the posited stages of progress, such as, for example, the presence of beliefs in ghosts or luck superstitions assigned to a bygone stage among "civilized" Europeans.

For Tylor survivals proved the action of "processes still in regular operation as of old, the result showing that, on the whole, progress has far prevailed" (Tylor 1929, I: 32). Thus, just as individual traits persisted into the present, so too have entire societies possessing features belonging to earlier stages have persisted into modern times. Survivals therefore offered clear evidence that cultures evolved from lower stages, and that evidence for this process can be found in the present.

CROSS-CULTURAL SIMILARITIES AND THE UNITY OF HUMANKIND

The nineteenth-century evolutionists fully subscribed to the principle of uniformitarianism, the comparative method, a conviction in the psychological and biological unity of humankind, and the belief that cultural evolution was essentially progressive (Murphree 1961: 279). The evolutionist perspective was based on the following assumptions: (1) that similar customs and practices found among cultures widely separate in time and space were due to similar causes, and (2) the belief in the "mental uniformity" of humankind. Tylor put it forcefully:

> It is no more reasonable to suppose the laws of mind differently constituted in Australia and in England, in the time of the cave-dwellers and in the time of the builders of sheet-iron houses, than to suppose that the laws of chemical combination were of one sort in the time of the coal-measures, and are of another now. The thing that has been will be; and we are to study savages and old nations to learn the laws that under new circumstances are working for good or ill in our own development (Tylor 1929, I: 158–159).

In the conclusion to his book *Researches into the Early History of Mankind* (1865), Tylor called attention to cross-cultural regularities as the result of like minds and rejects the idea fashionable in our day that each culture is unique, that cultures produce an essential "otherness," and that cultures are therefore incommensurable:

> The foregoing chapters treating the history of some early arts, of the practice of sorcery, of curious customs and superstitions, are indeed full of instances of recurrence of like phenomena in the remotest regions of the world. We might reasonably expect that men of like minds, when placed under widely different circumstances of country, climate, vegetable and animal life, and so forth, should develop very various phenomena of civilization, and we even know by evidence that they actually do so; but nevertheless it strikingly

illustrates the extent of mental uniformity among mankind to notice that it is really difficult to find, among a list of twenty items of art or knowledge, custom or superstition, taken at random from a description of any uncivilized race, a single one to which something closely analogous may not be found elsewhere among some other race, unlike the first in physical characters, and living thousands of miles off (Tylor 1964: 233).[4]

In connection with the notion of psychic unity, Tylor made an important comment during a review of Spencer's *Principles of Sociology* in 1877 that is of significant interest in light of current anthropological opinions regarding rationality and the Other. Tylor writes that it is the "besetting sin" of all who have studied primitive man "to treat the savage mind according to the needs of our argument, sometimes as extremely ignorant and inconsequent, at other times as extremely observant and logical" (in Stocking 1987: 187). While this recognition of the inconsistency in evolutionary formulations may be interpreted as indicative of the poor ethnographic grounding of anthropological thought of the period (Adams 1998: 57), it is also recognition of ideological/political bias in theoretical formulations regarding the mentality of the Other.

Tylor himself adhered to the principle of the unity of "mankind" and sought to demonstrate that common rationality in the thought processes of all human minds. The notion of unity was one of the principles that prevented writers such as Tylor from making recourse to racialist explanations.

For modern anthropologists the notion of psychic unity remains an important concept. The idea that all minds work alike (i.e., psychic unity) was developed by the German ethnologist Adolf Bastian (1826–1905). Bastian used the term *Elementargedanken* to denote a basic set of elementary thought patterns which indicate that all human minds are alike and produced similar responses to similar stimuli, although expressed with differing permutations in differing contexts (Bastian 1895; see Koepping 1982).

It follows from this, therefore, that under the appropriate environmental circumstances any human population could attain cultural complexity or civilization. For Bastian such phenomena as independent inventions and parallel cultural developments are attributable entirely to similar innate mental processes possessed by all humans, rather than due to diffusion through contact, migration, or borrowing. According to Bastian, only when fully documented are cultural similarities to be explained in terms of diffusion.

A number of evolutionists used Bastian's notion of psychic unity to account for crosscultural similarities rather than by recourse to innate biopsychological differences between people, as I have already noted. As Tylor (1929, I: 7) put it,

> For the present purpose it appears both possible and desirable to eliminate considerations of hereditary varieties of races of man, and to treat mankind as homogeneous in nature, though placed in different grades of civilization. The details of the enquiry will, I think, prove that stages of culture may be compared without taking into account how far tribes who use the same implement, follow the same custom, or believe the same myth, may differ in their bodily configuration and the colour of their skin and hair.

Like Bastian, the evolutionists also maintain that members of different groups possessed the same potential for progress. Morgan wrote,

> Progress has been found to be substantially the same in kind in tribes and nations inhabiting different and even disconnected continents, while in the same status, with deviations from uniformity in particular instances produced by special causes (Morgan 1877: 18).

The axiom of "mankind's" psychic unity had a number of implications for nineteenth-century evolutionary thinkers. First, it justified the use of the comparative method and the search for universal laws of culture (Murphree 1961: 281). This is because all sociocultural phenomena were viewed to be the expression of the same evolutionary processes sharing the same underlying unity. Second, the axiom was incompatible with the differential treatment of human populations on the basis of race.

Racism, as Murphree points out, "was not only generally absent from the evolutionary school; it was tacitly forbidden." Leacock (1963: ix) renders a similar verdict with respect to Morgan. It is correct that in principle, the search for universal laws of evolution was incompatible with beliefs in white supremacy. Yet as we shall see in our discussion of Morgan's work in Chapter 4, there are sufficient indications in the writings of the nineteenth-century evolutionists to indicate that they were men of their time who espoused various forms of racist and white supremacists views (see Harris 2001: 137–141; Kahn 1995: 11).

TYLOR AND THE EVOLUTION OF RELIGION: AN EXAMPLE OF NINETEENTH-CENTURY EVOLUTIONARY ANALYSIS

Tylor's *Primitive Culture* has been described as "one of the most detailed accounts of the development of religions every published" (Honigmann 1976: 125). Tylor's study of religion illustrates the two distinctive epistemological foundations of his work. First, he treats the evolution of religion not in terms of inevitable progressive development or fixed stages but rather as a pattern suggested by the evidence, a feature that sets his work apart from those of his contemporaries, such as Spencer (Morris 1988: 99).

Second, Tylor's study of religion illustrates the idealist/cognitive thrust of his anthropology, which, as Adams (1998: 56) observes, places him within the ranks of **culturologists** (i.e., those who place causality in the domain of culture defined entirely in cognitive/symbolic terms).

The epistemological orientation of Tylor's evolutionism entails a construal of historical change in terms of intellectual progression.

Moreover, his approach, as illustrated in his study of religion, focuses upon historical development of particular aspects of culture in terms of general principles of human thought. Unlike Morgan and Spencer, Tylor did not construe evolutionary change as immanent, necessary, directional, and teleological, involving the unfolding of "latent potentialities" present from the start of existence. (Sanderson 1990: 17).

Tylor begins his study by addressing the question of whether or not "primitive" people and early humans did or did not have religion.

Are there, or have there been, tribes of men so low in culture as to have no religious conceptions whatever? This is practically the question of the universality of religion, which for so many centuries had been affirmed or denied, with a confidence in striking contrast to the imperfect evidence on which both affirmation and denial have been based. Ethnographer, if looking to a theory of development to explain civilization, and regarding its successive stages as arising one from another, would receive with peculiar interest accounts of tribes devoid of all religion. Here, they would naturally say, are men who have no religion because their forefathers had none, men who represent a præ-religious condition of the human race, out of which in the course of time religious conditions have arisen. It does not, however, seem advisable to start from this ground in an investigation of religious development. . . . The case is in some degree similar to that of the tribes asserted to exist without language or without fire; nothing in the nature of things seems to forbid the possibility of such existence, but as a matter of fact the tribes have not been found. Thus the assertion that rude non-religious tribes have been known in actual existence, though in theory possible, and perhaps in fact true, does not at present rest on that sufficient proof which, for an exceptional state of things, we are entitled to demand (Tylor 1929, I: 417–418).

Tylor noted that such attitudes stem from the general tendency of Europeans to define doctrines that differed from their own as being irreligious. Tylor not only criticized such views as ethnocentric or due to poor reporting or faulty observations but also went on to point out the abundance of ethnographic accounts that support the idea that primitive peoples do indeed hold various religious beliefs. Throughout his study, Tylor employs a vast number of ethnographic examples to illustrate his case.

True to the naturalistic perspective, Tylor (1929, I: 427) approaches the study of religion as "theological systems devised by human reason, without supernatural aid or revelation," and he is interested in demonstrating the connection between the religions of "the savage and civilized world." Tylor would thus attempt to demonstrate that European notions of religion are human creations that had their start in the primitive mind of savages and barbarians.

Anticipating the findings of modern anthropologists based on firsthand ethnographic research, Tylor (1929 1: 22) rejected the idea that savage religion is ridiculous or that its knowledge is superfluous to the rest of humankind. This view contrasts with those of other nineteenth-century anthropologists, such as Morgan (1877: 5–6), who considered primitive religions incomprehensible because of their absurd and grotesque nature.

The study of primitive religion, Tylor argued, is necessary for the understanding of civilized religion. Moreover, he maintained that savage religion is not only consistent and logical, but that its development is rational "though working in a mental condition of intense and inveterate ignorance." Tylor's approach has been referred to as the rationalist or intellectualist approach, as opposed to the irrationalist approach of Lévy-Bruhl and the emotionalist approach of Malinowski, discussed in Chapter 8 (cf. Morris 1988: 145–147). Tylor's views also differ from those espoused by Freud and Durkheim, who maintain that religious beliefs contain deep, encrypted symbolic and psychological meanings and cannot be taken literally or at face value (Hicks 2002: 15).

The initial step in the anthropological study of religion, Tylor argued, is to define what is meant by the term *religion*. He provided what may be called the minimum definition of *religion*.

> The first requisite in a systematic study of the religions of the lower races is to lay down a rudimentary definition of religion. By requiring in this definition the belief in a supreme deity or of a judgment after death, the adoration of idols or the practice of sacrifice, or other partially-diffused doctrines or rites, no doubt many tribes may be excluded from the category of religious. But such narrow definition has the fault of identifying religion rather with particular developments than with the deeper motive which underlies them. It seems best to fall back at once on this essential sources, and simply to claim, as a minimum definition of Religion, the belief in Spiritual Beings (1929, I: 424).

Tylor calls this belief in spiritual beings **animism,** or the theory of souls. The cautious application of this definition, Tylor observes, suggests that none of the cultures that have been adequately described can be said to lack a religious belief system. Hence Tylor proposes that religion is a cultural universal, a point with which most present-day anthropologists would agree (Morris 1988: 1).

Tylor considered animism to be the basis of the "Philosophy of Religion," meaning all religions, which is both ancient and worldwide:

> Animism characterizes tribes very low in the scale of humanity, and thence ascends, deeply modified in its transmission, but from first to last preserving an unbroken continuity, into the midst of high modern culture. . . .
>
> Animism divides into two great dogmas, forming part of one consistent doctrine; first, concerning souls of individuals creatures, capable of continued existence after the death or destruction of the body; second, concerning other spirits upward to the rank of powerful deities. Spiritual beings are held to affect or control the events of the material world and man's life here and hereafter; and it being considered that they hold intercourse with men, and receive pleasure or displeasure from human actions, the belief in their existence leads naturally, and it might almost be said inevitably,

sooner or later to active reverence and propitiation. Thus Animism in its full development, includes the belief in souls and in a future state, in controlling deities and subordinate spirits, these doctrines practically resulting in some kind of active worship (Tylor 1929, I: 426–427).

Tylor goes on to consider how the doctrine of souls developed. His approach is to grasp savage reasoning by "rethinking" the steps leading to the formulation of the idea through "subjective understanding" (Hatch 1973: 28). Tylor is therefore interested only in the cognitive aspects of religion and does not incorporate the institutional aspects or sociological context of religion into his analysis.

Tylor proceeds to describe the logical processes that led primitive man to formulate the assumptions upon which religious beliefs are constructed:

It seems as though thinking men, as yet at a low level of culture, were deeply impressed by two groups of biological problems. In the first place, what is it that makes the difference between a living body and a dead one; what causes waking, sleep, trance, disease, death? In the second place, what are those human shapes which appear in dreams and visions? Looking at these two groups of phenomena, the ancient savage philosophers probably made their first step by the obvious inference that every man had two things belonging to him, namely, a life and a phantom. These two are evidently in close connexion with the body, the life as enabling it to feel and think and act, the phantom as being its image or second self; both, also, are perceived to be things separable from the body, the life as able to go away and leave it insensible or dead, the phantom as appearing to people at a distance from it. The second step would seem also easy for savages to make, seeing how extremely difficult civilized men have found it to unmake. It is merely to combine the life and the phantom. As both belong to the body, why should they not also belong to one another, and be manifestations of one and the same soul? Let them then be considered as united, and the result is that well-known conception which may be described as an apparition-soul, a ghost-soul (Tylor 1929, I: 429).

The belief in spirits and the idea of the survival of souls after death, according to Tylor, derived from the things primitive people saw and experienced in dreams, visions, and trances. But the belief in spirits and the psychology and logic behind it, Tylor noted, were not confined to savages only:

We know well how in civilized countries a current rumour of some one having seen a phantom is enough to bring a sign of it to others whose minds are in a properly receptive state. The condition of the modern ghost-seer, whose imagination passes on such slight excitement into positive hallucination is rather the rule than the exception among uncultured and intensely imaginative tribes, whose minds may be thrown off their balance by a touch, a word, a gestures, an unaccustomed noise. Among savage tribes, however, as among civilized races who have inherited remains of early philosophy formed under similar conditions, the doctrine of visibility or invisibility of phantoms has been obviously shaped with reference to actual experience. To declare that souls or ghosts are necessarily either visible or invisible, would directly contradict the evidence of men's senses. But to assert or to imply, as the lower races do, that they are visible sometimes and to some persons, but not always or to every one, is to lay down an explanation of the facts which is not indeed our usual modern explanation, but which is perfectly rational and intelligible product of early science (Tylor 1929, I: 446–447).

The ancient "savage philosophers," observing the difference between someone who is living and someone who is dead, tried to understand the difference, according to Tylor, and came to the conclusion that people have a spiritual as well as a material body. After death, the spirit leaves permanently, becoming a soul. This is how primitive man explained death and this is the principle underlying all religions. The body dies: The soul continues to exist. The reasoning is logical and rational:

That [the] soul should be looked on as surviving beyond death is a matter scarcely needing elaborate argument. Plain experience is there to teach it to every savage; his friend or his enemy is dead, yet still in dream or open vision he sees the spectral form which is to his philosophy a real objective being, carrying personality as it carries likeness (Tylor 1929, II: 24).

Tylor (1929, I: 429) observed that the belief in the soul is based on "the plain evidence of men's senses, as interpreted by a fairly consistent and rational primitive philosophy." Part of the reason why primitive man came to believe in the reality of spiritual beings, Tylor argued, was his propensity to conflate subjective and objective experiences:

> The evidence of visions corresponds with the evidence of dreams in their bearing on primitive theories of the soul, and the two classes of phenomena substantiate and supplement one another. Even in healthy waking life, the savage or barbarian has never learnt to make that rigid distinction between subjective and objective, between imagination and reality, to enforce which is one of the main results of scientific education. Still less, when disordered in body and mind he sees around him phantom human forms, can he distrust the evidence of his very senses. Thus it comes to pass that throughout the lower civilization men believe, with the most vivid and intense belief, in the objective reality of the human spectres which they see in sickness, exhaustion, or excitement. As will be hereafter noticed, one main reason of the practices of fasting, penance, narcotising by drugs, and other means of bringing on morbid exaltation, is that the patients may obtain the sight of spectral beings, from whom they look to gain spiritual knowledge and even worldly power (Tylor 1929, I: 445–446).

Tylor makes the remarkable observation that the belief in spirits that is extended to cover a wide range of phenomena in savage philosophy was a theory of causation, or a form of explanation for experience:

> It was no spontaneous fancy, but the reasonable inference that effects are due to causes, which led rude men of old days to people with such ethereal phantoms their own homes and haunts, and the vast earth and sky beyond. *Spirits are simply personified causes.* As men's ordinary life and actions were

held to be caused by souls, so the happy or disastrous events which affect mankind, as well as the manifold physical operations of the outer-world, were accounted for as caused by soul-like beings, spirits whose essential similarity of origin is evident through all their wondrous variety of power and function. (Tylor 1929, II: 108–109).

The belief in the soul, according to Tylor, therefore underlies a vast range of other ideas, such as the belief in an afterlife, heaven and hell, the notion of rewards or punishment after death for deeds done in life, and so forth (Figure 3.2).

This thought of the soul's continued existence is, however, but the gateway into a complex region of belief. The doctrines which, separate or compounded, make up the scheme of future existence among particular tribes are principally these: the theories of lingering, wandering, and returning ghosts, and of souls dwelling on or below or above the earth in a spirit-world, where existence is

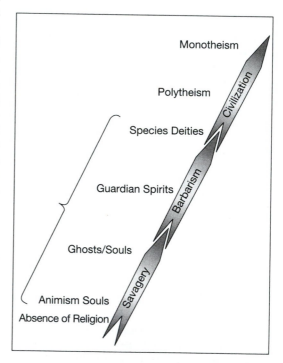

Figure 3.2   Sequential stages of the evolution of religion.   *After Langness (1993).*

modelled upon the earthly life, or raised to higher glory, or placed under reversed conditions, and lastly, the belief in a division between happiness and misery of departed souls, by a retribution for deeds done in life, determined in a judgement after death (Tylor 1929, II: 24).

Tylor's savage philosophers attributed different powers to the soul, hovering about as it does, believing it able to influence the world of people. Offerings and sacrifices were made to them. Spirits of dead ancestors were worshipped as guardians of lineages and clans. Thus ancestor worship developed. The belief in the soul naturally led to beliefs in places where such entities must dwell, leading to the idea of an afterlife, heaven, Elysian Fields, paradise, Hades, hell, and so forth.

Souls were believed to be able to occupy objects and enter the bodies of living humans, leading to the idea of charms, amulets, and effigies. Shrines are erected as places for the spirits to occupy. The idea of intrusion into or departure from the body of spirits explained physical or mental illnesses. Associated with this are the idea of spirit possession and the development of rites of exorcism. Attempts to harness souls, Tylor surmised, led to the practice of human sacrifice, or "slaying men in order to liberate their souls for ghostly uses" such as in funeral human sacrifice for the service of the dead (Tylor 1929, I: 458).

Some souls were associated with evil, leading to the development of beliefs in demons. The belief in spirits residing inside objects, which thereby acquired supernatural qualities, led to the development of **fetishes.** At some point fetishes were fashioned to resemble idols, giving rise to idolatry, and spirits became deities, each with its own sphere of influence over the world of humans.

Similarly, the idea of souls attributed to natural objects, such as trees in a forest, led, through abstraction, to the idea of a single forest deity. Eventually, the idea of single deities of different sorts led to the development of polytheism.

Finally, multiple deities were hierarchically arranged, eventually leading to the elevation of one god over all others, and thus the idea of monotheism developed.

Thus for Tylor, animism, or "the doctrine of spirits," is the foundation for a wide range of spiritual beliefs. These include "the idea of souls, demons, deities, and any other classes of spiritual beings, are conceptions of similar nature throughout, the conceptions of souls being the original ones of the series" (Tylor 1929, II: 109). Therefore, Tylor notes,

the doctrine of souls, founded on the natural perceptions of primitive man, gave rise to the doctrine of spirits, which extends and modifies its general theory for new purposes, but in developments less authenticated and consistent, more fanciful and far-fetched. It seems as though the conception of a human soul, when once attained by man, served as a type or model on which he framed not only his ideas of other souls of lower grade, but also his ideas of spiritual beings in general, from the tiniest elf that sports in the long grass up to the heavenly Creator and Ruler of the world, the Great Spirit (Tylor 1929, II: 110).

Tylor traces the evolution of religion through a sequence of stages, from animism to the idea of a supreme deity associated with monotheistic religions without proposing a rigid set of stages for religious evolution.

Tylor's theory of the origins of religion may be summarized as follows. Religion developed on the basis of essentially rational principles. It was an attempt to explain sensory evidence, or "the plain evidence of men's senses," deriving from two sources, observed differences between living and dead humans and images seen in dreams and visions. The attempt to explain these phenomena gave rise to the notion of ghost-soul. This led to animistic thought, which attributes life and personality to biological species and material objects. This simple idea then evolved "upwards" leading eventually to the concept of a Supreme Being. In Tylor's work we therefore find that primitive man in an attempt to create science, accidentally creates religion (Stocking 1987: 192).

Tylor views magic in a similar way. Magic is based upon a set of rational ideas and genuine observations. It entails a belief in impersonal power (versus religion, which involves personalized power) and a classificatory knowledge of phenomena linked on the basis of subjective and symbolic associations, in contrast to science, in which phenomena are linked on the basis of objective and experimentally proven connections. For Tylor, magic is really defective science, a science that does not work (Morris 1988: 102).

The major influence of Tylor's work has been upon scholars interested in the history of religion. Among these are such writers as Sir James Frazer (1854–1941), author of the massive study, *The Golden Bough* (1919–1927), which traces the origins and development of religion. Other writers influenced by Tylor include his student,

James Frazer, a leading evolutionary anthropologist and author of the influential The Golden Bough *(1919–1927).*

Robert R. Marett (1866–1943), who formulated the concept of **animatism** to refer to an unpersonalized life force or vitalism in inanimate objects (e.g., **Mana, Baraka**), and wrote a number of books on religion. Tylor also influenced Robertson Smith (1846–1894), author of *Lectures on the Religion of the Semites* (1889), whose comparative work on religion influenced both Durkheim and Freud.

TYLOR'S INTELLECTUALIST APPROACH AND HIS CRITICS

The shortcomings of Tylor's analysis of religion are those characterizing all approaches that focus exclusively on the mental or cognitive dimensions and which attempt to come to grips with cultural phenomena through various forms of subjective understanding. Tylor's approach, one might add, is as problematic but no less reasonable than the procedures used by present-day interpretive anthropological writers, ranging from Clifford Geertz to the nihilist postmodernists, who also employ various subjective approaches to grasp cultural phenomena.

Subsequent writers have criticized Tylor's theory of religion for a variety of reasons, ranging from his treatment of primitive man as a rationalist philosopher to errors in ethnographic detail (for a summary, see Lowie 1952: 106–133). Some have faulted Tylor for seeking origins for what would never be known. For writers such as Radcliffe-Brown what Tylor was engaged in was conjectural history and as such it was intellectually worthless.

The German diffusionist Wilhelm Schmidt rejected the entire evolutionary sequence of animism-polytheism-monotheism and proposed a degenerationist scheme that begins with monotheism as the first and original religion among ancient primitive people that subsequently degraded into polytheistic conceptions (see Chapter 5). Durkheim criticized Tylor from the point of view of his own theory of totemistic origins of religion, which I discuss in Chapter 11.

It is Tylor's intellectualist approach that has been subjected to the greatest criticisms. The British anthropologist Edward Evans-Pritchard (1965: 25) chastises him for imposing a logical structure in his own mind upon "the primitive" and treats his explanation for the origins of religion as a "just-so-story" like "how the leopard got his spots." Evans-Pritchard adds that religion might have arisen in the way Tylor suggested but that there is no evidence that it did. Moreover, Evans-Pritchard criticized Tylor's evolutionary sequences on the grounds that animistic and magical beliefs along with ancestral cults coexist, sometimes in institutional contexts, alongside beliefs in a Supreme Being (Bowie 2000: 16).

Murphy (1989: 189–190) has pointed out that Tylor "overintellectualized" religion and committed the error of assuming that the main function of religion is to explain things. Moreover, Tylor has been faulted for treating religion as if it consists only of belief devoid of emotional and psychological dimensions and for assuming that his own line of reasoning is the same as that of prehistoric peoples (Murphy 1989: 189–190).

Robin Horton (2002) has outlined the reasons why anthropologists dealing with "preliterate" peoples from other cultures have rejected the intellectualist approach. According to Horton, the anti-intellectualist position is based upon five main arguments, none of which he feels has much justification on the basis of ethnographic evidence:

1. Preliterate people could not have thought in rational ways because they do not possess an objective understanding of the world or an explanatory system such as that found associated with the Western scientific perspective.
2. Preliterate peoples are practice- rather than theory-oriented, and any approach that construes the religious ideas of such societies as explanatory theories is superfluous.
3. Ideas and beliefs of preliterate people are not logically consistent, and therefore approaches such as Tylor's that seek logical consistency are wrong.
4. Religion as understood in the European context is about other things, it does not actually provide explanations, and therefore preliterate religions must be about other things as well.
5. If we construe preliterate religious beliefs as explanations, then we must concede that they are wrong, and consequently those who hold such beliefs are construed as ignorant savages, which is a racist perspective.

Anyone familiar with the ethnographic evidence will realize that there is little support for suggestions that preliterate people are irrational, lack explanatory accounts of the world, universe, and so are incapable of developing conceptual explanatory systems apart from practical application, or that non-European religions are about other things, not explanations. As for the objection that an intellectualist approach leads to racist judgments about preliterate people, Horton points out that holding wrong ideas also characterizes science and this does not entail the idea that scientists are ignorant. One could argue that it is the new moral anthropologists, the postmodernist and their ilk, who attribute non-rational modes of thought and an essential otherness to people from non-European cultures, who verge upon ethnocentrism and racism.

ASSESSMENT

Tylor's anthropology, as Adams (1998: 57) has correctly put it, was the product "much more of imagination and retrodiction than of ethnography." One of the major problems with Tylor's anthropological theories was that they were developed on the basis of inaccurate, fragmentary second- and third-hand reports furnished by travelers, missionaries, traders, civil servants, and the like. The notion that the anthropologists should themselves gather first-hand ethnographic data was not contemplated. This is well illustrated by the attitude of the evolutionary anthropologist James Frazer, who, when William James asked if he had ever encountered any of the primitives whose cultures were the subjects of his books, made the now famous reply, "But Heaven forbid!" (Beattie 1964: 7; Washburn 1998: 5).

Indeed, there was a sort of division of labor between the ethnologist who stayed at home in his study, eruditely propounding questions, and the man in the field, knowledgeable in the ways of the local tribesmen but unschooled in theory, who gathered the raw facts (cf. Kuper 1999: 32). Fact and theory, as we have seen, are intimately connected to one another and herein lay one of the major epistemological weaknesses of nineteenth-century anthropology.

The poor quality of ethnographic data led to blatant and gross blunders on the part of many nineteenth-century evolutionists. For example, Lubbock, who is lauded as one of the prominent prehistorians of his age, wrote that what savages believe and do is based upon "absurd reasons." The minds of savages, he said, "rock to and fro out of mere weakness," and they tell lies and talk nonsense. Savages, Lubbock believed, lack marriage institutions and that they do not know love (Langness 1993: 35). The Boasian anthropologist Robert Lowie (1959: 24) listed other of Lubbock's mistaken assertions regarding primitive people:

> The Andamanese have "no sense of shame"; "many of their habits are like those of beasts." The Greenlanders have no religion, no worship, no ceremonies; The Iroquois have no religion, no word for God. The Fuegians not the least spark of religion . . . there can be no doubt that, as an almost universal rule, savages are cruel.

Morgan (1877: 5–6) wrote that "all primitive religions are grotesque and to some extent unintelligible," a position that stands in stark contrast to that of Tylor. Other errors of this sort included assumptions that people who did not have knowledge of metallurgy lacked social stratification, or that **matrilineality** preceded **patrilineal** social organization (Harris 2001: 155).

The dilemma encountered by Tylor and the other evolutionists was to reconstruct "the early history of mankind" by working backward in time from fragmentary and uneven information about "primitive" peoples in the present. This is not to say that they were altogether oblivious of the problem of data quality and that all nineteenth-century ethnologists used the sources uncritically. Tylor clearly states the problem and prescribes remedies:

> How can a statement as to customs, myths, beliefs &c., of a savage tribe be treated as evidence where it depends on the testimony of some traveller or missionary, who may be a superficial observer, more or less ignorant of the natives language, a careless retailer of unsifted talk, a man prejudiced or even wilfully deceitful? This question is, indeed, one which every ethnographer ought to keep clearly and constantly before his mind. Of course he is bound to use his best judgment as to the trustworthiness of all authors he quotes, and if possible to obtain several accounts certify each point in each locality. But it is over and above these measures of precaution that the test of recurrence comes in. If two independent visitors to different countries say a mediaeval Mohammedan in Tartary and a modern Englishman in Dahome, or a Jesuit missionary in Brazil and a Wesleyan in the Fiji Islands, agree in describing some analogous art or rite or myth among the people they have visited, it becomes difficult or impossible to set down such correspondence to accident or wilful fraud. A story by a bushranger in Australia may, perhaps, be objected to as a mistake or an invention, but did a Methodist minister in Guinea conspire with him to cheat the public by telling the same story there? The possibility of intentional or unintentional mystification is often barred by such a state of things as that a similar statement is made in two remote lands, by two witnesses, of whom A lived a century before B, and B appears never to have heard of A. . . . Experience leads the student after a while to expect and find that the phenomena of culture, as resulting from widely-acting similar causes, should recur again and again in the world. He even mistrusts isolated statements to which he knows no parallel elsewhere, and waits for their genuineness to be shown by corresponding accounts from the other side of the earth, or the other end of history. So strong, indeed, is this means of authentication, that the ethnographer in his library may sometimes presume to decide, not only whether a particular explorer is a shrewd,

honest observer, but also whether what he reports is conformable to the general rules of civilization (Tylor 1929, I: 9–10).

The evolutionists of the period were never able to solve the problem of poor ethnographic information. The solution would not come until the next century, when the anthropologist Bronislaw Malinowski established an intensive fieldwork tradition in anthropology based on participant observation (see Chapter 8).

In nineteenth-century evolutionary thought, where data were lacking logical inferences and creative thinking were brought to bear in order to arrange contemporary groups into a chrono-logical sequence representing the successive stages of cultural evolution. This is not to say that these procedures are disallowed in scientific reasoning. The mistake nineteenth-century evolutionists made, as Kaplan and Manners (1972: 40) observe, was to assume "that the empirical world was under some obligation to conform to their logical reconstructions."

Finally, aside from a host of empirical mistakes, nineteenth-century evolutionists also made the epistemological error of equating evolution with progress and adopting teleological, developmental, directional evolutionist models (Sanderson 1990: 46).

Chapter 4

Lewis Henry Morgan and the Evolution of Society

Lewis Henry Morgan (1818–1881) was among the leading evolutionists of the nineteenth century. Although most of Morgan's ethnological formulations have been refuted by subsequent ethnographic research, his work has had a significant impact upon anthropology and anthropological thought. This is because many of the subjects he chose to tackle, such as the evolution of the family, the incest taboo, and the rise of the state, generated questions that have occupied anthropologists for well over a century (Magli 2001: 69; Service 1985). Morgan's work also had a significant effect upon the ideas of Karl Marx and Friedrich Engels, whose own sociological formulations had a considerable influence in various ways upon much of twentieth-century social thought (see Chapters 10 and 14). In this chapter I shall evaluate Morgan's work and situate his contributions to evolutionary theory in the context of modern anthropological thought.

MORGAN: FROM LAWYER TO ETHNOGRAPHER

Morgan was trained in law at Union College in Albany. In 1844 he settled to practice his trade in Rochester, New York. Morgan's career as an anthropologist began as a result of his interest in the Seneca Iroquois Indians who lived on the Tonawanda reservation near Rochester. Keen to learn as much about the Iroquois as he could, Morgan paid them numerous visits. During one of these visits members of the tribe brought a legal case to his attention. The Ogden Land Company was attempting to take possession of a large portion of the reservation and have the Seneca removed to the West. Morgan, appalled by the tactics of the land speculators, took up the case and successfully thwarted the efforts to dispossess the Seneca of their landholdings. This earned him the friendship of the Seneca, who adopted him into the tribe (see Hays 1964: 14–24, 41–49).

Lewis Henry Morgan, one of the principal nineteenth-century evolutionists in the United States. Morgan was among the few evolutionary theorists to have conducted extensive ethnographic fieldwork.

Passing over his fervent career as a Whig and Republican politician, other scholars have thought him a spokesman of socialism. Some cite his magnum opus as a defense of American capitalism, although it contains the severest censures of the profit motive. A few view Morgan as an apologist for imperialism. But he supplied the strongest single argument against the white man's burden philosophy. His mind, in short, cannot be pinned down nicely without being divested of its rich and many-sided character (Resek 1960: vii).[1]

MORGAN AND THE PEOPLING OF THE NEW WORLD: FROM ETHNOGRAPHER TO EVOLUTIONIST

Morgan spent considerable time among the Iroquois and it is clear from his writings that he had great admiration for them. His writings also reveal that he was a keen observer of ethnographic detail. Thus, unlike many other nineteenth-century ethnologists, who could rightly be described as "armchair philosophers," Morgan was unique in the depth and extent of his fieldwork. As his modern admirer Leslie White (1951: 11) put it, Morgan was not only a major theoretician, but he was also "an industrious, critical, versatile and productive field worker."

During the litigation against the land speculators, a young Seneca law student named Ely Parker (later Commissioner of Indian Affairs) befriended Morgan. Parker would assist Morgan in his ethnological studies. Morgan thus embarked on a career in anthropology, but a career quite unlike that of any other anthropologist then or since. As his biographer Carl Resek has noted,

> Morgan's story . . . is one of the strangest in American intellectual history. It is that. No other American in his own time or since has looked at human society in quite the manner that Morgan did, and few have wandered down the path of scholarship that he charted. He fits no customary interpretation of the nineteenth-century mind and will not allow any tidy explanation of his views and motives. Some writers have called him a conservative Social Darwinist, though he deeply suspected that body of doctrine and only partially understood it.

Morgan's anthropological efforts led to the publication of *The League of Ho-dé-no-sau-nee, or Iroquois* in 1851, in which he describes Iroquois religion, language, social and political structure, family organization, marriage, kinship terminology, descent rules, as well as material culture. John Wesley Powell (1834–1902), the noted scholar of Native American cultures, praised Morgan's work as the "first scientific account of an Indian tribe ever given to the world" (in White 1948: 139).

Morgan's career as an anthropologist may have been a result of his interests in the Iroquois, but his career as an evolutionary anthropologist started when he delved further into the investigation of Native American "systems of consanguinity" or **kinship terminology systems** (naming of relatives).

Morgan was especially intrigued by the discovery of what he called a **classificatory kinship terminology.** In this system, members of an individual's nuclear family (lineal relatives) are classified along with more distant collateral kinfolk in each generation. The Iroquois child refers to his mother's sister with the term Morgan glossed as "mother," his father's brother as "father," mother's sister's sons and daughters and father's brother's sons and daughters are called by the same terms as brothers and sisters, and mother's brother's sons and daughters and father's sister's sons and daughters are called cousins. Morgan contrasted this system with the **descriptive kinship terminology system,** such as that in English in which collateral and lineal kin are kept separate (Figure 4.1). Father and father's brother are referred to by different terms, as are mother and mother's sister. The children of these categories of relatives (the off-spring of uncles and aunts) are referred to by different terms (i.e., cousins) than those used to refer to ego's siblings (brothers/sisters).

In 1858 Morgan obtained kinship data from the Ojibway wife of a fur trader in Marquette, Wisconsin and discovered to his surprise that the Ojibway also used a classificatory kinship terminology system. Having discovered a terminology system he at first thought to be unusual and unique to the Iroquois among another Native American group, Morgan began to consider the possibility that both systems had a common source or origin. A review of the literature on the Dakotas suggested to Morgan the possibility that the Creek Indians also possessed a similar system.

These findings opened up a new possibility. If Morgan could show that all Native Americans used a classificatory kinship system, and further,

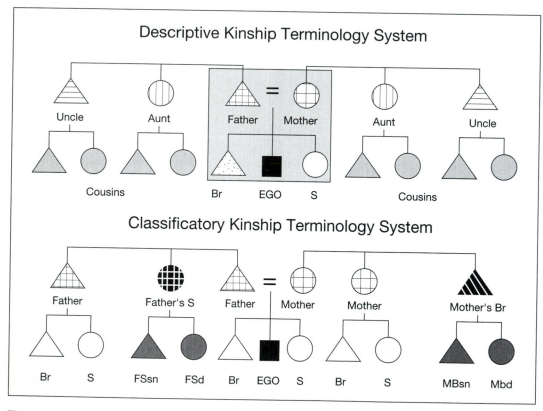

Figure 4.1   Descriptive and classificatory kinship terminologies.

if he could find evidence of this system in Asia, he could settle one of the pressing ethnological debates of the time, namely the Asiatic origins of the American Indians.

The peopling of the Americas has been the subject of ongoing research among anthropologists and archaeologists since Morgan's days. Today, we know that the **Paleoindians** (the most ancient inhabitants of the Western Hemisphere) arrived by way of a now submerged land bridge called **Beringia** (Figure 4.2) that linked Siberia and Alaska sometime around 12,000 years ago during the last Ice Age (Harris 1997: 156; Hoffecker et al. 1993). The land bridge was uncovered because a large quantity of water was locked in the form of ice, resulting in a drop in sea levels. Beringia was actually partially exposed

during the interval between 60,000 to 12,000 years ago (Hoffecker et al. 1993), but the undisputed archaeological evidence suggests that humans were in Americas by 12,000 years ago. There is also some evidence to suggest the presence of humans in the Americas as early as 20,000 to 50,000 years ago, although these dates are not widely accepted.

Archeological evidence has revealed similarities in the stone tools found in Siberia and Alaska (Kunza and Reanier 1994). In addition, there are the **phenotypical** similarities between Native Americans and East Asians, such as epicanthic eye folds, straight black hair, and certain dental features (Harris 1997: 156). In other words, the question of the Asiatic origins of Native Americans, which was a highly debated

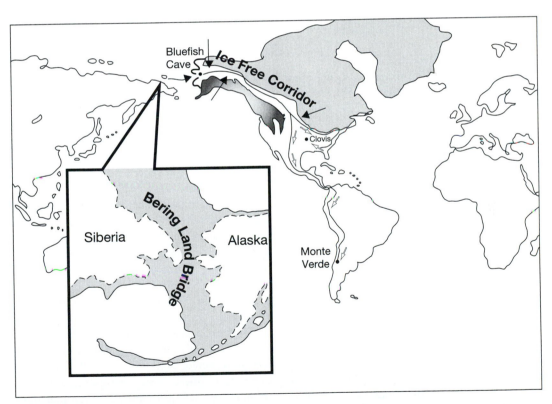

Figure 4.2   Beringia and the peopling of the Americas. In Morgan's time the ancestry of Native Americans was a major ethnological puzzle. Morgan attempted to solve this puzzle and conclusively demonstrate the Asiatic origins of Native Americans by contrasting kinship terminology systems.

problem in Morgan's day, has been laid to rest. Today the problem is not from *where* did the ancestors of Native Americans come, but rather *when* they first arrive in the Americas.

The possibility of solving the great anthropological puzzle of the day led Morgan into the direction of a comparative study of kinship systems. He visited a number of Native American groups during extensive travels. His objective was to gather information on kinship systems from as many groups as possible. Between 1859 and 1862, Morgan made trips to Kansas and Nebraska, visited Fort Gary, near Winnipeg Lake, and finally traveled up the Missouri River, past Yellowstone, to Fort Benton (White 1951: 12).

During this time Morgan became increasingly aware of the rapid disappearance of traditional Native American cultures and he appealed to scholars to collect as much information about these cultures before it was too late. Morgan wrote,

> The ethnic life of the Indian tribes is declining under the influence of American civilization, their arts and languages are disappearing and their institutions are dissolving. After a few more years, facts that may now be gathered with ease will become impossible of discovery. These circumstances appeal strongly to Americans to enter this great field and gather abundant harvest (Morgan 1877: viii).

The importance of recording information on disappearing groups, what present-day science critics call "salvage ethnography," has been a long standing concern among ethnographers and was undertaken with great vigor by the next generation of American anthropologists under the tutelage of Franz Boas. This was no imperialistic butterfly collecting exercise, as the postmodern interpretivists wish people to think (e.g., Marcus and Fischer 1986: 24), but an attempt to address a genuine and pressing issue, the loss of information about humankind's cultural heritage. Such efforts should be lauded and even encouraged, especially in our own time when cultural forms are undergoing rapid transformations. The reason for this is simple: The more we learn about

the range of variability and human possibilities, the closer we come to understanding the nature of sociocultural phenomena.

Morgan sought to supplement his own data with information solicited from Indian Agents and missionaries across the United States. Moreover, with assistance from the Smithsonian Institute Morgan expanded his field of inquiry by providing a seven-page questionnaire with over two hundred questions to United States government personnel overseas. The results of his surveys revealed that several additional Native American groups (aside from the ones for which he already possessed information) used the classificatory system as well. Moreover, it became apparent that the classificatory system of designating kin was also found among groups in Asia and Polynesia.

Based on the data he obtained, Morgan was able to identify three permutations of the classificatory system and three permutations of the descriptive system. The classificatory system included: *Malayan* (Hawaiians, Maoris, and other groups in Oceania); *Ganowanian* (native North Americans); and *Turanian* (Chinese, Japanese, Hindu, and other groups in the Indian subcontinent). The descriptive system included: *Aryan* (all speakers of Indo-European languages, such as Persian and Sanskrit); *Semitic* (Arabs, Hebrews, and Armenians); and *Uralian* (Turks, Magyar, Finn, and Estonians). In present-day anthropological terms the Malayan system corresponds to what is called the **Hawaiian kinship terminology system,** and the Ganowanian-Turanian to **Iroquois kinship terminology system.** The Aryan-Semitic-Uralian grouping corresponds to the **Eskimo kinship terminology system** (see Figure 4.3).

The presence of the classificatory kinship system in Polynesia and among Australian aborigines (discovered later) convinced Morgan that there was no merit in the attempt to use kinship terminology systems to link American Indians to Asia (Malefijt 1974: 148–149). However, what appeared more intriguing were the broader

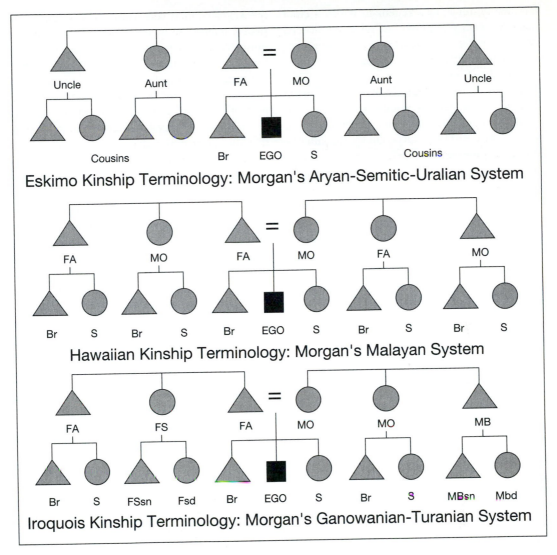

Eskimo Kinship Terminology: Morgan's Aryan-Semitic-Uralian System

Hawaiian Kinship Terminology: Morgan's Malayan System

Iroquois Kinship Terminology: Morgan's Ganowanian-Turanian System

Figure 4.3 Morgan's kinship terminology systems.

questions about the evolution of different forms of social organization that were raised by the data. Thus, while Morgan began his research in order to gather proof for the Asian origins of the American Indians, he ended up pursuing an altogether different avenue of research.

Morgan's friend Joshua McIlvaine, a Calvinist minister and scholar of Sanskrit guided his thoughts in this direction. McIlvaine noted that philologists had shown that linguistic forms tend to persist long after they have lost their function, the same, he argued, could be assumed of kinship terms. Kin terms were **survivals,** the residues of ancient patterns of social organization. If true, this would have enormous intellectual implications because kinship nomenclature could be used to reconstruct the history of humankind. The assumption behind this idea was that, for example, in a system in which a child used the term for "father" to refer to collateral kin in the ascending (parents') generation, one could deduce that those individuals were indistinguishable from the child's actual father. This, according to McIlvaine's thinking, could mean that the system had its origins in "promiscuous sex involving the cohabitation of brothers and sisters" (Morgan 1871: 481). Under the circumstances of promiscuity, according to McIlvaine, it would have been impossible for a child to identify which man was his father, and so all potential fathers of the ascending generation were referred to by the same term. Similarly, women in the ascending generation, being either mother or potential stepmothers, were referred to by the same term.

The idea of a previous stage of promiscuous sex was not new, however. Johan Bachofen had already forwarded the idea of an original state of promiscuity in 1861 in his book *Das Mutterrecht* ("Mother Right"). Working primarily with Greek and Roman sources, Bachofen also argued that the family had evolved through matriarchy and matrilineal descent to patriarchy and patrilineal descent. However, McIlvaine and Morgan were unaware of Bachofen's work at the time (Service 1985: 45). So the idea was not new, what was new was the manner in which McIlvaine and Morgan would use kinship term systems, construed as survivals in Tylor's sense of the term, to reconstruct past stages of evolutionary development.

For the Reverend McIlvaine the implication of all this was satisfyingly clear: a concrete demonstration of the superiority over all others of the Aryan and Semitic systems based on the monogamous family and the moral code behind it (Resek 1960: 96).

Needless to say, McIlvaine's hypothesis was based on several erroneous assumptions. These errors were incorporated into Morgan's work. First, he assumed incorrectly that kinship terms denoted actual or true biological ("consanguinal") relationships rather than serving as signifiers of social statuses (cf., Service 1985:

30–31). Second, it was erroneous to assume that people referred to by the same label are indistinguishable. In other words, just because the word for "father" extends to many others, does not mean that those others have the same sexual rights over "mother" as the actual father. This aspect of Morgan's work, as Bloch (1983: 69) has pointed out, is based on an "illusion." Third, there is no evidence that there is a lag of the magnitude required by Morgan's scheme between kinship terminological systems and marriage systems or that terminology systems correspond with systems of marriage with the precision that Morgan attributed to them. Modern anthropologists have found that marriage and kinship terminology systems are both highly variable (Bloch 1983: 97).

Morgan wrestled with McIlvaine's suggestion for three years before adopting it. He then recast his materials in evolutionary terms. This is an astonishing case of tailoring the data to suit the one's needs. This marked Morgan's conversion to the evolutionary perspective. He described the shift in his thinking as follows:

> When Darwin's great work on the origin of species first appeared I resisted his theory and was inclined to adopt Agassiz' view of the permanence of species. For some years I stood in this position. After working up the results from consanguinity I was compelled to change them and to adopt the conclusion that man commenced at the bottom of the scale from which he worked himself up to his present status (in Resek 1960: 99).[2]

Morgan's acceptance of cultural evolution did not mean that he also embraced the Darwinian position on the biological evolution of human beings from "animals" (Service 1985: 47). Nor did Morgan embrace the materialist/naturalistic point of view. Indeed, Morgan ends his *Ancient Society* (1877), in which he expounded his ideas of the evolution of culture, by thanking God for granting the Aryans civilization:

> It may well serve to remind us that we owe our present condition, with its multiplied means of safety and happiness, to the struggles, the suffer-

ings, the heroic exertions and the patient toil of our barbarous, and more remotely, of our savage ancestors. Their labors, their trials and their successes were a part of the plan of the Supreme Intelligence to develop a barbarian out of a savage, and a civilized man out of this barbarian (Morgan 1877: 554).

Thus, it would seem that although Morgan may have been among the embattled men fighting to lift the curse of Adam from his primitive ancestors (cf. Murphree 1961: 267), he was not quite willing to lift "the hand of God" from his ancestor's affairs.

Having adopted the evolutionary perspective and McIlvaine's hypothesis, Morgan reached the following conclusion:

> Upon one side are the Aryan, Semitic, and Uralian, and upon the other the Ganowanian, the Turanian, and Malayan, which gives nearly the line of demarcation between civilized and uncivilized nations (Morgan 1871: 469).

In other words, kinship terminology systems were the basis for evaluating cultural evolution, in which societies that possessed classificatory kinship systems were lower on an evolutionary scale than those with descriptive kinship terminology systems.

From the kinship terminology systems, Morgan inferred corresponding marriage and family types, or domestic structures. He then attempted to classify these arrangements along an evolutionary scale, a theme he would develop more fully in his book *Ancient Society* (1877), which we shall examine later.

Morgan first traced out the evolutionary development of the family from sexual promiscuity to the nuclear type based on monogamous marriage in a paper entitled "A Conjectural Solution to the Origin of the Classificatory System of Relationships." He presented the paper before the Academy of Arts and Sciences in Boston in 1867 (Morgan 1868). Morgan, like McIlvaine, argued that the monogamous family was the most advanced evolutionary form and the principle he thought he had discovered was that the

number of licit sexual partners decreases chronologically from the stage of savagery to civilization, moving from promiscuity to monogamy. The paper received positive reception.

This success led to the publication of Morgan's *Systems of Consanguinity and Affinity of the Human Family* (1871). Despite its shortcomings, this work was important in the development of anthropological thought because it represented the first attempt at the systematic analysis of kinship systems that explored the implications of kin classification and highlighted their sociological correlates. As such, the work opened up an entirely new direction in anthropological research, as subsequent anthropologists have acknowledged (W. Adams 1998: 56; Fortes 1969: 19; Magli 2001: 70; Rivers 1914: 5–6).

MORGAN AS EVOLUTIONIST

In his *Ancient Society* (1877) Morgan elaborated upon the ideas presented in *Systems of Consanguinity* and turned his attention to the reconstruction of the evolutionary history of humankind as a whole. The scheme Morgan proposed entails a construal of evolution as progress and evolutionary change as immanent, necessary, directional, and teleological, involving the unfolding of latent potentialities present from the start of existence (cf. Sanderson 1990: 17). In other words, all of the major elements for which nineteenth-century evolutionism has been criticized appear in Morgan's formulations. He begins his study as follows:

> The latest investigations respecting the early condition of the human race, are tending to the conclusion that mankind commenced their career at the bottom of the scale and worked their way up from savagery to civilization through the slow accumulation of experimental knowledge. . . . As it is undeniable that portions of the human family have existed in a state of savagery, other portions in a state of barbarism, and still other portions in the state of civilization, it seems equally so that these three distinct conditions are connected to each other in a natural as well as necessary sequence of

progress. Moreover, that this sequence has been historically true of the entire human family, up to the status attained by each branch respectively, is rendered probable by the conditions under which all progress occurs, and by the known advancement of several branches of the family through two or more of these conditions (Morgan 1877: 61).

The scheme Morgan proposed was similar to that of Tylor (1871 [1929]: I: 32–33) involving three successive stages: Savagery, Barbarism, and Civilization. "The principle institutions of mankind," according to Morgan (1877: vi), "originated in savagery, were developed in barbarism, and are maturing in civilization." The stages are construed to be sequential, not temporal, because various existing cultures around the world were to be found at various stages of evolutionary development (Salzman 2001: 92).

Each stage, as Morgan saw it, contains the "germ" of thought that would emerge and blossom in the succeeding stage. For Morgan, germs of thought produced kinship terminology systems and other cultural arrangements. The question Morgan did not ask is why should such thoughts occur in the first place (Harris 2001: 231). The reason, as Sanderson (1990: 20, 22) has pointed out, is that Morgan, like many of his contemporaries, had no clear model of causation and because he saw evolution as the unfolding of inherent potentialities, which to his mind made evolution self-explanatory.

This is what separates Morgan's work from modern materialist evolutionary research strategies. The materialist would ask, If cultural elements such as kinship terminologies are the product of someone's spontaneous flights of fancy, what compels others to adopt and incorporate them in their culture? People do not simply think up things like kinship systems and postmarital residence rules at will and then whimsically adopt them as they wish (Harris 2001: 231). And if people capriciously adopt any new idea that strikes their fancy, then why are there not as many kinship terminology systems as there are cultures? Why have people culturally

and technologically as far apart as the Euro-Americans and the Inuit use essentially the same kinship terminology system? Morgan does not take into account that germs of thought are actualized under particular socioeconomic, political, demographic and ecological circumstances (Harris 2001: 231). He does not consider these questions because he attributes cultural development to self-propelling mental processes.

There are, therefore, central theoretical differences between Morgan's mentalist perspective and the materialist evolutionary models used by modern anthropologists. It requires more than "nimble terminological adjustments," motivated by political correctness to substitute categories such as "savages" with "hunter-gatherers," contra Barrett (1996: 51), to make Morgan's scheme compatible with modern evolutionism.

Morgan's evolutionism is based on a thorough commitment to an ideational or mentalist perspective and his model is directional and teleological, which entails the idea of evolution as the unfolding of latent potentialities present from the start of existence, as noted previously. As Morgan (1877: 61) observes,

> *Out of a few germs of thought, conceived in the early age have been evolved all the principle institutions of mankind.* Beginning their growth in the period of savagery, fermenting through the period of barbarism, they have continued their advancement through the period of civilization. *The evolution of these germs of thought have been guided by a natural logic which formed an essential attribute of the brain itself.* So unerringly has this principle performed its functions in all conditions of experience, and in all periods of time, that its results are uniform, coherent and traceable in their courses. These results alone will in time yield convincing proofs of the unity of origin of mankind. The mental history of the human race, which is revealed in institutions, inventions, and discoveries, is presumptively the history of a single species, perpetuated through individuals, and developed through experience (Morgan 1877: 61, emphasis added).

Morgan's idealism also extends to his construal of the mechanism of evolutionary development in terms of the inherent self-expansion of ideas that give rise to new sociocultural transformations (Sanderson 1999: 11, 35). Again, this makes his scheme incompatible with modern evolutionary thought with its materialist mechanisms for sociocultural transformation.

The reason why there is confusion over Morgan's precise theoretical stance stems from numerous interspersed statements throughout *Ancient Society* that can be interpreted to mean that he was committed to a materialist theory of causation, stressing the primacy of technological or economic variables (Harris 2001: 213–214). For instance, Morgan (1877: 39–40) writes that

the most advanced portion of the human race were halted . . . at certain stages of progress, until some great invention or discovery, such as the domestication of animals or the smelting of iron ore, gave a new and powerful impulse forward.

Or with respect to the evolution of cultures in the Americas, Morgan (1877: 460) states that

improvement in subsistence, which followed the cultivation of maize and plants among the American aborigines, must have favored the general advancement of the family. It led to localization, to the use of additional arts, to an improved house architecture, and to a more intelligent life.

Despite such statements, Morgan's (1877: 37) deep commitment to a mentalist view is unquestionable. However, biology plays a major role in his thinking. For example, he writes that "with the production of inventions and discoveries, and with the growth of institutions, the human brain necessarily grew and expanded; and we are led to recognize a gradual enlargement of the brain itself, particularly of the cerebral portion."

Other factors that "gave a remarkable impulse to society" were changes in marriage practices that decreased inbreeding because they "brought unrelated persons into marriage relations," creating "a more vigorous stock physically and mentally" (Morgan 1877: 459). When two advanced tribes were brought together and blended "the

new skull and brain would widen and lengthen to the sum of the capabilities of both." This would then give the new "stock" superiority asserted in an increase of intelligence and numbers (Morgan 1877: 459). Morgan thus sees strong links between social and biological evolution, which not only sets him apart from Tylor, but also accounts for his racism, discussed later (Kahn 1995: 11).

MORGAN, PSYCHIC UNITY, AND RACISM

Many of Morgan's passages give the impression that he shares the central assumptions of the evolutionists of his time regarding human cultural diversity, the uniformitarian perspective, and humankind's biopsychological unity:

It may be remarked finally that the experience of mankind has run in nearly uniform channels; the human necessities in similar conditions have been substantially the same; and that the operations of the mental principle have been uniform in virtue of the specific identity of the brain of all the races of mankind (Morgan 1877: 8).

This would put Morgan squarely on the side of those arguing for the racial unity of humankind. However, these statements are made in reference to the polygenesis theory (see Chapter 3), not necessarily as an advocacy of the unity of the human race.

It is true that Morgan had great admiration for the American Indians, especially the Seneca; it is also true that he was a blatant racist and white supremacist. Racism did not conflict with Morgan's acknowledgement of the idea of the unity of mankind. This is because an argument could be made that while it is true that there are no biopsychological differences between people of different races; however, this does not hold true for those races occupying different stages on the ladder of evolutionary progress. Primitive people who are at the lower stages are inferior to Euro-Americans because their mental powers, brain size, and so on have as yet not reached their fullest potential. Thus unity meant there was unity for those in the same evolutionary stage, but not for others. The idea of the unity of mankind was therefore fully compatible with racist explanations of cultural similarities and difference.

It is not surprising then to find that Morgan had a special hatred of people of African ancestry. As his biographer Resek (1960: 63, n. 1) has pointed out,

> During the debate in the Congress over the Compromise of 1850, Morgan expressed the not uncommon sentiment of Negrophobia, based partially on the belief that the Negro was a separate species. He urged Seward to limit the expansion of slavery because "it is time to fix some limits to the reproduction of this black race among us. It is limited in the north by the traits of the whites. The black population has no independent vitality among us. In the south while the blacks are property, there can be no assignable limit to their reproduction. It is too thin a race intellectually to be fit to propagate and I am perfectly satisfied from reflection that the feeling towards this race is one of hostility throughout the north. We have no respect for them whatsoever."[3]

Moreover, while Morgan may have affirmed that all the races of mankind were making their way upward "from savagery to civilization through the slow accumulation of experimental knowledge," "in nearly uniform channels," for Morgan God, or the "Supreme Intelligence," favored one particular group above all others:

> The Aryan family represents the central stream of human progress, because it produced the highest type of mankind, and because it has proved its intrinsic superiority by gradually assuming the control of the earth (Morgan 1877: 553).

It was, in the final analysis, the Aryan and Semitic families, which from the Middle Period of Barbarism assumed the central trends of evolutionary progress; they were the first to emerge from Barbarism and "were substantially the founders of civilization" (Morgan 1877: 39). Ultimately, it was the Aryan family alone that came

to embody progress (Morgan 1877: 40). Only one conclusion can follow from these statements: While there may be some confusion regarding Morgan's materialist leanings, there can be no doubts about his racism and devotion to the stance of white supremacy.

MORGAN'S EVOLUTIONARY SCHEME

As noted previously, Morgan saw the evolution of culture as the working out and realization of "a few primary germs of thought" (Morgan 1877: 4). Among the lines of development Morgan focused upon are technological innovations, changing forms of the family, the development of property rights, and the evolution of political complexity and the rise of the state.

Morgan set forth a three-stage evolutionary scale of progress that he called **ethnical periods:** Savagery, Barbarism, and Civilization. He subdivided the first two stages into subperiods: lower, middle, and upper. Each stage of evolutionary progress was defined in terms of particular technological developments (Morgan 1877: 10–12). Morgan's scheme is summarized as follows in Figure 4.4.

Morgan described the evolutionary stages set forth in Figure 4.4 as follows:

> Each of these periods has a distinct culture and exhibits a mode of life more or less special and peculiar to itself. This specialization of ethnical periods renders it possible to treat a particular society according to its conditions of relative advancement, and to make it a subject of independent study and discussion. It does not affect the main result that different tribes and nations on the same continent, and even the same linguistic family, are in different conditions at the same time, since for our purpose the *condition* of each is the material fact, the *time* being immaterial (Morgan 1877: 13).

Morgan associated the stages of evolution with the evolution of social organization, going from a stage of promiscuous marriage to the development of the monogamous family, which

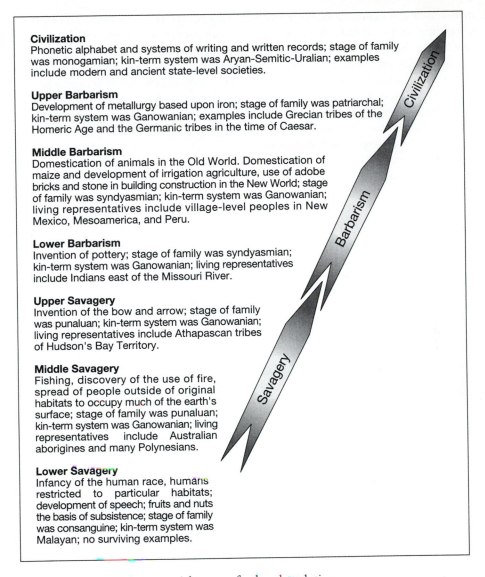

Civilization
Phonetic alphabet and systems of writing and written records; stage of family was monogamian; kin-term system was Aryan-Semitic-Uralian; examples include modern and ancient state-level societies.

Upper Barbarism
Development of metallurgy based upon iron; stage of family was patriarchal; kin-term system was Ganowanian; examples include Grecian tribes of the Homeric Age and the Germanic tribes in the time of Caesar.

Middle Barbarism
Domestication of animals in the Old World. Domestication of maize and development of irrigation agriculture, use of adobe bricks and stone in building construction in the New World; stage of family was syndyasmian; kin-term system was Ganowanian; living representatives include village-level peoples in New Mexico, Mesoamerica, and Peru.

Lower Barbarism
Invention of pottery; stage of family was syndyasmian; kin-term system was Ganowanian; living representatives include Indians east of the Missouri River.

Upper Savagery
Invention of the bow and arrow; stage of family was punaluan; kin-term system was Ganowanian; living representatives include Athapascan tribes of Hudson's Bay Territory.

Middle Savagery
Fishing, discovery of the use of fire, spread of people outside of original habitats to occupy much of the earth's surface; stage of family was punaluan; kin-term system was Ganowanian; living representatives include Australian aborigines and many Polynesians.

Lower Savagery
Infancy of the human race, humans restricted to particular habitats; development of speech; fruits and nuts the basis of subsistence; stage of family was consanguine; kin-term system was Malayan; no surviving examples.

Figure 4.4   Morgan's sequential stages of cultural evolution.

we shall examine later. Morgan, however, did not recognize any sort of logical or causal articulation between the technological and economic innovations by means of which he differentiated evolutionary stages and substages and associated forms of family types of social organization.

Such obscurities in Morgan's work have led him to be classified as a materialist by some, as an idealist by others, and as an eclectic theoretician by still others (Sanderson 1990: 25). The lack of articulation between the technological traits Morgan used to demarcate evolutionary stages and other features of culture have rendered his typology difficult to use (Rambo 1991: 30).

Again, contra Barrett (1996: 51), more than "nimble terminological adjustments" have been necessary to make what has not been discarded in Morgan's work compatible with modern evolutionary thought, as evident in Service's (1971) band-tribe-chiefdom-state typology. Morgan's use of subsistence strategies and techno-economic factors to distinguish different types of cultures is still a viable idea, and as Leacock (1963: xi) points out, "his general sequence of stages has been written into our understanding of prehistory and interpretation of archaeological remains." This is true, but only because of substantial modifications to Morgan's original typology (Rambo 1991: 30–32).

It is only in the context of Morgan's discussion of the transition from descent-based to territorially and politically based polities or **state-level societies** that an articulation between the technological traits and other cultural features becomes evident, and even this is problematic. This aspect of Morgan's work was emphasized in Marx and Engels' reworking of his scheme (see Bloch 1983: 47–48; Harris 2001: 248–249; Magli 2001: 70–76).

Morgan's evolutionary scheme as a whole is fraught with errors (Harris 2001: 184–185). For example, Morgan's association of Lower Savagery with a fruit and nut subsistence is contrary to archaeological evidence, which has shown that Paleolithic people were hunters and gatherers. Similarly, there is an overlap if not synchronization between the domestication of plants and animals (Bar-Yosef and Valla 1990; Harris 1997: 143–144; Zohary and Hopf 1988), which Morgan places into two separate stages, with **pastoralism** preceding agriculture. Also, Morgan's assumption that the manufacture of pottery, which "presupposes village life," came before domestication of animals and cereal cultivation is false.

Morgan's other errors include placing the agricultural and highly stratified aboriginal Hawaiians, who possessed a complex government (see Kirch 1984, 1988), in the level of Middle Savagery because they lacked the bow and arrow. Similarly he failed to recognize the tremendous complexity achieved by the Aztecs, who possessed a highly developed state-level society, simply because they did not use iron tools. Finally, using writing as a criterion for "civilization" has led Morgan to underestimate the nature of the Inca society, which had become a super-state, or empire, without a system of writing (on the Aztec and Inca states, see Fiedel 1987). Another error is assigning the bronze-age people of the Homeric age to the stage of iron tools.

THE EVOLUTION OF THE FAMILY AND THE INCEST TABOO

Morgan's analysis, as noted previously, is based upon the assumption that kinship terminology systems are static and tend to endure for long periods of time after the social arrangements that gave rise to them have vanished. Morgan's acceptance of this idea and the logic underlying it is clear in his *Ancient Society* (1877):

> Systems of consanguinity are neither adopted, modified, nor laid aside at pleasure. They are identified in their origin with organic movement of society which produced a great change of condition. When a particular form had come into general use, with its nomenclature invented and its methods settled, it would, from the nature of the case, be very slow to change. Every human being is the center of a group of kindred, and therefore every person is compelled to use and to understand the prevailing system. A change in any one of these relationships would be extremely difficult. This tendency to permanence is increased by the fact that these systems exist by custom rather than legal enactment, as growth rather than artificial creations, and therefore a motive to change must be as universal as the usage. While every person is a party to the system, the channel of its transmission is blood. Powerful influences thus existed to per-

petuate the system long after the conditions under which each originated had been modified or had altogether disappeared. *This element of permanence gives certainty to conclusions drawn from the facts, and preserved and brought forward a record of ancient society which otherwise would have been entirely lost to human knowledge* (1877: 398, emphasis added).

Morgan's reconstruction of the evolution of the family is as follows: In the beginning there was the promiscuous **horde.** This is "the bottom of the scale—the lowest conceivable stage of savagery" a time when people "possessed feeble intellect and feebler moral sense" (Morgan 1877: 500). The next stage is the development of the consanguine family. This was characterized by a rule restricting sexual intercourse within the group consisting of males who cooperate in food acquisition and defense and who share a group of women. For this reason the membership of the group consists of brothers and sisters. Morgan (1877: 388, 401) notes that the consanguine family disappeared altogether with no present-day groups conforming to this pattern.

There is, however, no tangible evidence for the existence of this presumed stage of evolutionary development, other than what Morgan supplies from his imagination. We must remember that there is a lot more of imaginative speculations and retrodiction than of ethnography in the works of nineteenth-century writers such as Morgan, as Adams (1998: 57) has correctly pointed out. Morgan maintained, however, that the evidence in question has been preserved in the Malayan system (now known as the Hawaiian kinship terminology system), in which the same terms used to refer to parents apply to their siblings and the same terms used to refer to siblings also apply to cousins. Thus, from a set of kin terms presumed to be survivals from a period long gone, Morgan inferred a set of social relationships and domestic arrangements that, he argued, gave rise to those terms. The inferences as to the possible family types associated with particular terminology systems were based entirely on Morgan's own imaginative reconstruction.

In the next phase of Morgan's scheme, the consanguine family evolves into a form called the punaluan family. This is the conjectural type that Morgan inferred from the Ganowanian kinship terminology, as exemplified by the Iroquois system. According to the Iroquois kinship terminology, ego refers to mother and mother's sister by the same term, and father and father's brother are denoted by the same term. Mother's sister's children and father's brother's children are referred to by the same terms ego uses to refer to brother and sister. However, mother's brother's children and father's sister's children are referred to as cousin. The system (Figure 4.5) distinguishes between cross cousins (children of mother's brother and father's sister) and parallel cousins (children of mother's sister and father's brother). Again, Morgan takes this to indicate social relations that held true in the past, rather than sets of social relationships observable among the Iroquois during the nineteenth century.

Morgan saw in the Iroquois system evidence of a previous evolutionary stage in which marriage rules became more restricted, producing a system in which a group of brothers shared each others' wives and sisters shared each others' husbands. The significant development here, as Morgan sees it, was the prohibition on brother-sister marriages. At this stage, according to Morgan, the kinship terminology system underwent a significant transformation. If brothers and sisters were no longer mates, then their children could no longer be referred to as brothers and sisters by ego. Because brothers belonged to the same marriage group, children of brothers would still address one another as brother/sister. Similarly, since sisters belonged to the same marriage group, their children continued to address one another as brother/sister.

Morgan considered the prohibition of brother-sister marriages to have had important evolutionary consequences. Such marriages, he argued, eliminated the deleterious genetic effects of inbreeding. This led to increased intelligence

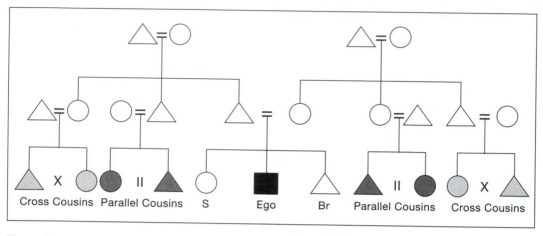

Figure 4.5   Parallel and cross cousins.

that, in turn, led to technological progress. Morgan viewed such progress as evidence of "natural selection" at work (Morgan 1877: 421).

This evolutionary stage led to the development of what Morgan refers to as the **gens** (singular, plural = **gentes**), a group of consanguinally related individuals descended from a common ancestor. The gens had a particular name and its members observed the rule of exogamy; they were forbidden to marry anyone descended from the same common ancestor. Thus recognizing the "evils of consanguine marriages," according to Morgan, people sought marriage partners from other clans. At first descent was traced through the female line because prevailing mating practices made it impossible to identify the biological father of any child (Morgan 1877: 67–68). The rule of **exogamy** led to the production of "a stock of savages superior to any then existing on earth," who then spread because of their superior powers (Morgan 1877: 378).

Morgan thus offers an explanation for the **incest taboo,** a topic that not only attracted the attention of nineteenth-century ethnologists

such as McLennan, Lubbock, Tylor, Spencer, and Durkheim, among others, but also of twentieth-century anthropologists. Morgan's inbreeding explanation holds that the incest taboo arose because of the biological advantages it conferred upon those who adopted this practice. This idea stands in contrast to Tylor's (1889) position, which stresses that the explanation for the incest taboo lies in the survival advantages it confers in terms of the establishment and maintenance of alliances with other groups. Both perspectives have advocates among present-day anthropologists (see Kang 1979; Leavitt 1989, 1990, 1992; Ottenheimer 1996; Thornhill 1993; see also the discussion in Chapter 11).

What is most problematic about Morgan's assumption that the offspring of outbreeding were biologically superior to others is that exogamy excludes only certain categories of relatives as mates and is associated with "inbreeding" with other types of relatives (Murphy 1989: 221; see the discussion in Chapter 11). Finally, Morgan's idea of biologically superior offspring is based on Lamarckian conceptions of heredity, rather than a Mendelian one, as one is first led to believe. This makes his ideas incompatible with Darwinian explanations for the incest taboo.

Overall, the problems in Morgan's work on kinship and family forms are legion. As noted previously, there is no evidence that kinship terminological systems persist unchanged through time. Moreover, there is no evidence for the assumption that the kinship terminology in use in the present reflects a past stage and that people in the present are employing marriage rules belonging to the next stage of evolutionary development. However, there is evidence that shows other kinds of kinship systems changing into the Hawaiian kind over time, which is the reverse of Morgan's developmental sequence (Murphy 1989: 131).

Morgan's reconstruction of the evolution of the family is for the most part an artifact of his imagination. Validation against empirical evidence necessary in order to determine the accuracy of such representations is absent in his work.

Morgan's errors illustrates some of the dangers of relying upon free reigning imagination without empirical verification of propositions. To call Morgan's work scientific, despite the fact that he uses that honorific to describe his own studies, is therefore entirely unjustified.

EVOLUTION OF THE STATE

Morgan stressed the importance of the gentes, and their larger groupings, **phratries** and **tribes,** in the evolution of society (Morgan 1877: 62). He contrasted "gentile" societies (*societas*) based upon gentes with the type of polities we call the state (*civitas*) and attempted to explain the transition of the one to the other, beginning a line of inquiry that eventually led to his conception of the rise of the state. Morgan felt that the manner in which the changeover took place from a kinship-based society to a territorially based "civil society" was crucial to the understanding of social evolution. On this subject we find Morgan's legal mind at work in top form as he teases out issues of marriage rights, property rights, inheritance rules, and their social and legal implications.

Before we proceed with a discussion of Morgan's theory for the rise of the state, it might be useful to define what anthropologists mean by "state-level societies" and examine some of the theories presented to explain the rise of states. In the context of my own study of state formation in the former kingdom of Hunza, in what is now northern Pakistan, I have defined the state as follows:

> [The state is] an autonomous political body, controlling a defined territory incorporating many communities, possessing a centralized government and administrative bureaucracy, with powers to issue and enforce legislation, extract taxes, conscript labor, and draft men for military service. State level polities are also characterized by a degree of social stratification and differential access on the part of higher and lower social strata to necessary resources and means of production (Sidky 1996: 27).[4]

I have also noted the criterion of scale, which sets states apart from other political entities. To this definition one might add the following criteria suggested by Sanderson (1999: 56): "a state [may be defined as] a form of sociopolitical organization that has achieved a monopoly over the means of violence within a specified territory." Also, another feature that sets states apart from other political entities, such as for example, chiefdoms, is the separation of their specialized institutions from systems of kinship (Sanderson 1999: 57), a characteristic central to Morgan's scheme.

The state evolved in six and up to eight places independently of one another about 5,000 years ago in the Old World, and somewhat later in the Americas (for an overview, see Sanderson 1999: 68–86). Thereafter the state as a form of sociopolitical organization has dominated the face of the earth. For this reason, many anthropologists see the rise of the state as perhaps one of the most significant events in human history (Gross 1992: 430). The evolutionary process contributing to the rise of the state, which is now seen as a case of worldwide parallelism, has been the focus of a number of studies by cultural and archaeological anthropologists (Figure 4.6). These represent a line of research the initiation of which has been credited to Morgan (R. Adams 1966; Blanton et al. 1981; Carniero 1970, 1987; Fried 1967; Johnson and Earle 1987; Krader 1968: 2; Service 1975; Sidky 1996; Spencer 1990; see Steward 1955).

Morgan's distinction between societies based upon kinship organization and those based upon state organization is central to his conceptualization of how the state emerged. According to his scheme, in "gentile" societies (*societas*), social and political relationships were based upon kinship

and operated through personal relations in the gens and its larger groupings, phratries, and tribes (Morgan 1877: 62, 66). Under the state (*civitas*), a political society developed in which the government dealt with people through territorial organization, such as township, county, and the state. This is an important distinction that modern anthropologists have accepted as one of the defining features of state level societies, as noted previously.

According to Morgan (1877: 67), gentile societies, which were founded upon the principles of gens, phratry, and tribe, were communal and democratic in nature. Such societies continued to be the dominant form through the stage of Barbarism. However, "the germs of thought" for the evolutionary developments to follow were contained in the gens. Thus, although Morgan talks about associated technological innovations,

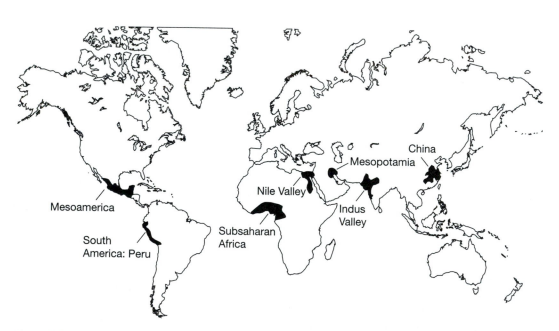

Figure 4.6   Early state–level societies thought to have evolved independently of one another about 5000 years ago in the Old World, and somewhat later in the Americas. The evolutionary processes contributing to the rise of the state are now seen as a case of worldwide parallelism.

ultimately the engines of evolutionary development in his scheme are "the germs of thought." As Morgan (1877: 64) put it,

> The gens has passed through successive stages of development in its transition from its archaic to its final form with the progress of mankind. These changes were limited, in the main, to two: firstly, changing descent from the female line, which was the archaic rule, as among the Iroquois, to the males, which was the final rule, as among the Grecian and Roman gentes; and, secondly, changing the inheritance of the property of a deceased member of the gens from his gentiles who took it in the archaic period, first to his agnatic kindred, and finally to his children. These changes, slight as they may seem, indicate very great changes of condition as well as a large degree of progressive development.

The evolutionarily significant changes described here are tied in Morgan's view to technological innovations associated with an economy based upon herding and agriculture, the latter being an expression of the growth of ideas. The new technology of production entailed the use of arable land, tools, livestock, and slaves and was operated by males and slowly became the private property of men. Thus, with an agrarian plow economy based upon the intensive use of land arose the notion of private property and with private property came socioeconomic and political differences. This resulted in an elevation of the economic status of men in the family, who emerged as the first group in human history to possess private property.

Although critics at the time argued that private land ownership was common among some hunting-gathering peoples in Canada, thereby refuting Morgan's scheme, modern anthropological research has proven that these patterns were a postcontact phenomenon (Murphy 1989: 159–160). Moreover, it is now clear that nowhere are hunting territories, fishing areas, or places for the collection of nuts owned by individuals in hunting-gathering societies (Murphy 1989: 159–160).

In Morgan's scheme it is the appearance of private property, and the associated disparities in wealth, that marked the beginnings of classes and class exploitation. This, along with Morgan's seeming materialism, as evidenced by his focus upon technology and economy (he in fact viewed these as expressions of the growth of ideas), attracted the attention of Karl Marx and Friedrich Engels (Bloch 1983: 57). It has been said that Marx held Morgan in such admiration that he wanted to dedicate his book, *Capital,* to him. However, Morgan being "a highly conservative lawyer" was appalled by this and refused the honor (Barrett 1996: 50).

For Morgan the changes he describes had other ramifications. Associated with this shift in the economic powers of men and private ownership came a shift in clan descent rules from matrilineality to patrilineality. A new form of marriage and new inheritance rules favoring men accompanied this shift. To put it in a Marxist vein, as the new technology and relations of production developed they became incongruous with the prevailing pattern of social organization and form of inheritance. This resulted in a radical transformation from a system based upon matrilineal descent to one based on patrilineal descent and to inheritance along the male line.

To Marx and Engels this appeared to substantiate their own theory of social transformation in which change was seen as a result of incompatibilities between the relations of production and the forces of production (Bloch 1983: 10). Morgan's work was therefore seen as evidence that the same principles that created capitalism operated in the early history of humankind as well.

According to Morgan, the new form of marriage that emerged was monogamy. The monogamous family is linked in Morgan's scheme to the stage of Civilization. "It was founded upon marriage between single pairs, with exclusive cohabitation" (Morgan 1877: 384). This meant that men now had exclusive sexual monopoly over particular women. This ensured that men could identify the children they sired and to whom they could pass on their property. Along with the new form of family a different system of kinship terms appeared as well, marking a shift from the classificatory system to the descriptive one.

Morgan's explanation for the shift from a classificatory system to a descriptive one centers upon "rights of property and succession to estates."

> There is one powerful motive which might under certain circumstances tend to overthrow the classificatory form and the substitution of the descriptive, but it would arise after the attainment of civilization. This is the inheritance of estates. Hence the growth of property and settlement of its distribution might be expected to lead to a more precise discrimination of consanguinity (Morgan 1871: 14).

Here the lag time that Morgan posits to exist in kinship terminology systems and actual practices, something upon which he bases his entire method of evolutionary reconstruction, seems to disappear completely. At this point Morgan is also inconsistent and oscillates between mentalism and materialism. On the one hand, he says the idea of property resulted in changes in the way the family was defined and organized, and then he points out that the idea of property was a consequence of the development of a particular form of family. For example, he writes that

> the growth of the idea of property in the human mind, through its creation and enjoyment, and especially through the settlement of legal rights with respect to its inheritance, are intimately connected with the establishment of this form [monogamous] of the family (Morgan 1877: 389).

Morgan (1871: 492) maintains that the development of private ownership of property and the issue of its transmission to lineal descendants radically transformed the structure of the family and the kinship terminology system. Morgan's formulations, it must be noted, were based upon the assumption that "noncivilized" people lacked

any conceptions of inheritance, which, of course, is simply not true. Morgan summed up his views on these evolutionary developments as follows:

> Two forms of the family have now been explained in their origin by two parallel systems of consanguinity. The proofs seem conclusive. It gives the starting point of human society after mankind had emerged from a still lower condition and entered the organism of the consanguine family. From this first form to the second the transition was natural; a development from lower into a higher social condition through observation and experience. It was a result of the improvable mental and moral qualities which belong to the human species. The consanguine and the punaluan families represent the substance of human progress through the greater part of the period of savagery. Although the second was a great improvement upon the first, it was still very distant from the monogamian. An impression may be formed by a comparison of the several forms of the family, or the slow rate of progress in savagery, where the means of advancement were slight, and the obstacles were formidable. Age upon age of substantially stationary life, with advance and decline, undoubtedly marked the course of events but the general movement of society was from a lower to a higher condition, otherwise mankind would have remained in savagery. It is something to find an assured initial point from which mankind started on their great and marvelous career of progress, even though so near the bottom of the scale, and though limited to a form of the family so peculiar as the consanguine (Morgan 1877: 447).

Like his other formulations, this aspect of Morgan's work is fraught with numerous errors. First, there is no concrete ethnographic evidence showing that corporate descent is associated with matrilineal systems as opposed to patrilineal systems (Bloch 1983: 75–76). Second, the postulated correlation between kinship terminology and sociopolitical organization finds no ethnographic confirmation. For example, the Eskimo kinship terminology system is used not only by foraging peoples, but also by Euro-Americans, two groups that would fall on opposite ends of Morgan's evolutionary scale (Bloch 1983: 71). Third, there is no evidence to suggest that matrilineality preceded patrilineality on the grounds that promiscuous marriages prevented the identification of a child's biological father. Fourth, as for the issue of promiscuous marriages, Morgan was working purely from his imagination, rather than on the basis of any kind of empirical evidence. His reasoning was simply that if monogamy represented the most advanced or "civilized" form, then the other end of the scale had to be characterized by promiscuity. Again, there is much imaginative speculation here and very little ethnography.

MORGAN AND MARXISM

Leslie White (1948: 138) lauded Morgan as one of the greatest sociologists of the nineteenth century who devised "the most impressive system of institutional evolution in that century." Whether we are willing to accept White's appraisal or hold an opposite view, it is nevertheless true that Morgan's work and the topics he wrote about generated some of the lasting and significant controversies in sociocultural theory during the twentieth century (see Service 1985). One of these controversies is the relationship between the works of Morgan and Marx.

Morgan's writings, as noted at the beginning of this chapter, had a notable impact upon social theory as a result of the endorsement given to it by Marx and Engels (Service 1985: 4, 24). The latter found Morgan's work appealing because, unlike most of the other anthropologists of the period, Morgan not only provides an evolutionary scheme but also seems to describe the mechanisms for evolutionary transformations in which new forms emerged out of older ones, which they overthrow and replace. This, however, is an illusion because Morgan really has no coherent causal mechanism other than the idea that evolutionary change is immanent.

Morgan's construal of evolutionary change seems similar to Marx's analysis of the rise of capitalism and the internal contradictions that bring about its demise (Bloch 1983: 8–9). Also, Marx saw in Morgan's idea of gens, which Morgan deems the most ancient form of social existence, proof for his own view on the forms of family and property rights. Morgan's work supported Marx's argument that the monogamous family and private property are features of particular historical stages and are not eternal phenomena inseparable from human nature, as evolutionists such as McLennan and Maine would have it (Bloch 1983: 74).

More important, Marx and Engels believed erroneously that Morgan had independently discovered the materialistic conception of history that Marx had formulated forty years earlier (Bloch 1983: 48). They accordingly modified their own ideas regarding the early history of humankind in view of Morgan's seemingly vast erudition regarding primitive cultures. Marx and Engels were willing to accommodate the most up-to-date scientific developments in relevant fields, anthropology, and Morgan's work were among them (Godelier 1977: 102).

Engels's book, *The Origins of the Family, Private Property and the State* (1884), is basically an exposition of Morgan's anthropology. It is for this reason that Hallpike (1988: 283) rejects Engel's work as "an entirely obsolete account of social evolution" and Marxist theory in general as irrelevant and "comprehensively refuted by events."

Marx and Engels were wrong in treating Morgan as a fellow materialist. The incorporation of Morgan's formulations into Marxism presented it with an irresolvable conceptual dilemma. If all class societies developed from original classless societies, and if the evolutionary dynamics of Marxist theory is contradiction or struggle between classes, then what propelled classless societies toward classes? What Morgan proposed as the mechanism of evolutionary development, the inherent self-expansion of ideas (Sanderson 1999: 11, 35), is not only unmaterialist, it is decidedly un-Marxist.

What our discussion has shown is that Morgan tied sociocultural evolution to "the germs of thought" in the human mind, "guided by a natural logic which formed an essential attribute of the brain itself," rather than to environmental, demographic, technological, or economic factors. The development of the human mind, in turn, according to Morgan, was linked to the inheritance of acquired characteristics through "experience," which led to larger brains. Morgan's evolutionism was therefore not Darwinian (contra Opler 1964) but rather of the Lamarckian variety (Service 1985: 49).

Jean-Baptiste Lamarck's (1744–1892) theory of **inheritance of acquired characteristics** was based upon the assumption that species evolved and changed through time as a result of adjustments to the direct effects of the environment in which they lived and that the characteristics acquired in life by parents could be passed on to the next generation. Engels' adopted the Lamarckian perspective as a result of the influence Morgan. It figured prominently in Engels's book, *The Dialectics of Nature* (1876), the source through which Lamarckian ideas and Morgan's evolutionary ideas made their way into the party-linked Marxist ideology and into Soviet agronomy under Trofim D. Lysenko (1898–1976). Lysenko devised a Marxist science of genetic based upon Lamarckian ideas that devastated Soviet agronomy (Futuyma 1982: 162).

In addition to this, until the second quarter of the twentieth century, Morgan's evolutionary scheme served as the standard source of ethnological wisdom for Marxists (Harris 2001: 246). When the anthropologist Leslie White visited the Soviet Union in 1929, he encountered Morgan's evolutionary ideas, which had been fully integrated into Marxist doctrine by Soviet theoreticians (Orlove 1980: 238). White's work, in turn, was instrumental in reincorporating a number of Morgan's ideas back into American cultural anthropology during the twentieth century (see Chapter 10).

The association of Morgan with Marxist doctrine had other ironic consequences with respect to American anthropology. The linkage with Communist ideology was responsible for a massive assault upon Morgan's evolutionary model. American anthropologists denounced Morgan and his work was rejected. Along with them went the comparative method and all efforts to develop a science of culture based upon the search for generalizations (Harris 2001: 249).

ASSESSMENT

The problems of nineteenth-century evolutionary approaches had several sources. First, schemes such as Morgan's entail a construal of evolution as progress and evolutionary change as immanent, necessary, directional, and teleological, involving the "unfolding of latent potentialities" present from the start of existence (cf. Sanderson 1990: 17). As such, evolution was thought to be rooted entirely in mysterious metaphysical internal dynamics of sociocultural systems. It is evolutionism without material causation, and as such it is incompatible with scientific materialist evolutionary models.

Second, their construal of evolution in terms of "the unfolding of latent potentialities" led to other problems because rather than starting their research by looking for governing principles, they proposed principles as explanations without attempting to verify whether those principles did indeed hold true in the empirical world (Honigmann 1976: 116). In other words, instead of seeking to discover scientific laws governing evolutionary growth, cognitive principles underlying customs, or generalizations about the determining factors of kinship terminologies, writers such as Morgan took these laws as given (Honigmann 1976: 116). Despite lip service to science, much of what passed for evolutionary theory in the nineteenth century was basically an exercise in free reigning imagination, as I noted earlier.

Third, as noted in the previous chapter, nineteenth-century ethnologists were working with extremely low quality, secondhand ethnographic data. Their empirical errors were countless.

Finally, there was the abuse of the comparative method in which postulated stages were filled in by culling bits and pieces of data, a custom from here, an institution from there, an invention from yet somewhere else, which best illustrates the unscientific nature of anthropological theories of the period.

The accumulated errors of nineteenth-century evolutionism, in turn, cast a dark shadow upon scientific research in anthropology, which became associated with the groundless formulations of evolutionists such as Morgan. The quest for a science of culture came to a halt in the twentieth century thanks to the endeavors of Franz Boas, who made the refutation of evolutionary anthropology and the formulation of any and all types of generalizations about culture one of his primary prerogatives and career objectives, as we shall see in Chapter 6.

Chapter 5

The Diffusionists: Unbridled Imagination and the History of Culture

Toward the latter part of the nineteenth century, several research strategies based upon the principle of diffusion were forwarded in Britain, Germany, and the United States. These perspectives attempted to account for cultural similarities and differences in terms of the transmission of traits between groups through direct/indirect contact. In its heyday, diffusionism was considered to be one of the most powerful theoretical perspectives in anthropology. Today it is defunct as a theoretical approach. Harris (2001: 373) called it a "nonprinciple" and diffusionism is hardly ever mentioned in books on anthropological theory, except in passing or in footnotes (Barrett 1996: 53; Erickson and Murphy 1998: 53; McGee and Warms 2000: 45).

Nevertheless, a discussion of diffusionism is highly instructive for a number of reasons. First, modern American anthropology began as a diffusionist enterprise that went together with a particular set of epistemological assumptions about the nature of sociocultural phenomena that have left an indelible mark upon anthropological thought.

Second, diffusionism, especially in the hands of the extreme British writers, is a testament to the follies that can ensue when anthropologists disregard established conventions of scholarship and rules of evidence. There are lessons to be learned here for anyone who disregards method, scholarly conventions, and rules of evidence.

Third, diffusionist theories that trace all human cultural development to long lost civilizations, or to extraterrestrial sources, abound in the popular literature and students of anthropology, who nowadays are getting less and less training in scientific thinking, are often unable to judge the merits of these pseudoscientific accounts.

Pseudoscience and alternative histories have gained great popularity in the present-day antiscience intellectual climate of unreason, irrationalism, and epistemological relativism. Having adopted an "anything goes" approach to knowledge, expositors of nonscientific and antiscientific viewpoints insist that they be absolved of all scholarly standards of validation and rules of evidence so that they may have a free hand to present the "truth" (cf. Fagan and Hale 2001). These writers dismissed scholarly criticisms and demands for supporting evidence as attempts by academic communities with vested interests in false orthodox views to suppress the truth (the "Galileo argument" discussed in Chapter 2).

Pseudoscience capitalizes upon the gullibility of a public lacking a basic understanding of scientific standards and incapable of appraising the disingenuous, uninformed, and tendentious methods and the irrational beliefs upon which the "alternative views" are based (Fagan and Hale 2001). Unsuspecting readers are thus bamboozled into accepting mythologized history and a host of other irrational beliefs as forms of knowledge having equal if not greater validity than scientific knowledge.

DIFFUSION AND DIFFUSIONISM

Diffusionist perspectives emerged around the turn of the twentieth century as a rival paradigm to sociocultural evolutionism. Diffusionist writers asserted that the process of borrowing/imitation negated the notion of evolutionary stages, as noted in Chapter 3. Two major diffusionist schools emerged in Europe, one in Britain and the other in Germany/Austria. A diffusionist perspective known as the American Historical Tradition associated with the "culture area" concept developed in the United States under the influence of Franz Boas, Alfred Kroeber, and other Boasian anthropologists. In this chapter I shall examine the European diffusionist schools, leaving the treatment of American diffusionism to the chapters dealing with Boas and his students.

To begin with, it is necessary to distinguish between diffusion as a sociocultural process and diffusionism as a causal explanatory model. Anthropologists have long noted that cultures situated far apart from one another share many elements in common and researchers employing different theoretical perspectives have attempted to account for these cross-cultural similarities. The

nineteenth-century evolutionists, for example, sought to account for cross-cultural similarities and differences in terms of regular, uniform, and recurring processes. As we have seen in the previous two chapters, the evolutionists maintained that if two unconnected cultures have similar institutions and customs, the similarities could be due to the fact of psychic unity, namely that all minds work alike. People who have never been in contact with each other think and behave in the same way and arrive at similar innovations under similar environmental circumstances.

But there was yet another possibility to consider—one that was familiar to Tylor, Morgan, and many other evolutionists—the process of diffusion. Cultural similarities could be accounted for in terms of the spread of traits (or **acculturation**) resulting from contact and imitation or through the actual movement of personnel, or migration.

Diffusion entails the process whereby cultural items from one group are incorporated into the repertoire of another group. Among the most scholarly investigations of the diffusion of an elaborate cultural trait is James Mooney's study *The Ghost-Dance Religion and Wounded Knee* (1896), which documents the development and spread of the Ghost Dance movement.

Patterns of diffusion include **direct contact, intermediate contact,** and **stimulus diffusion** (Ember and Ember 2002: 272–273). A good example of direct contact is the spread of the manufacture of paper from China, where it is was invented in A.D. 105. The method of manufacturing paper is thought to have spread from China to the Arab world, and then to Europe by Arab traders, reaching France by 1189, Italy by 1276, Germany around 1391, and England in 1494 (Ember and Ember 2002: 272).

Diffusion by means of intermediate contact occurs through the agency of traders, soldiers, missionaries, and so on. The role of Phoenician traders, who brought the alphabet, invented by another Semitic group, to Greece is an example of intermediate contact. Stimulus diffusion entails the invention of a local equivalent of a trait associated with another culture. Cherokee syllabic system of writing developed in this way as a consequence of contact with Europeans (Ember and Ember 2002: 272). The rise of **secondary states,** where local chiefdoms acquired greater political complexity as a result of contact with **primary states** that first evolved independently out of local conditions, is another example of stimulus diffusion.

Ralph Linton (1893–1953), a noted anthropologist from the Boasian era saw diffusion as a major factor in cultural development. He maintained that "if every human group had been left to climb upward by its own unaided efforts, progress would have been so slow that it is doubtful whether any society by now would have advanced beyond the level of the Old Stone Age" (Linton 1936: 324). To illustrate the powerful role of diffusion in the growth of Euro-American culture, Linton wrote the following now classic passage looking at the start of an "average" American man's day:

> Our solid American citizen awakens in a bed built on a pattern which originated in the Near East but which was modified in northern Europe before it was transmitted to America. He throws back covers made from cotton, domesticated in India, or linen, domesticated in the Near East, or wool from sheep also domesticated in the Near East, or silk, the use of which was discovered in China. All of these materials have been spun and woven by processes invented in the Near East. . . . He takes off his pajamas, a garment invented in India and washes with soap invented by the ancient Gauls. He then shaves, a masochistic rite which seems to have derived from either Sumer or ancient Egypt.
>
> Returning to the bedroom, he removes his clothes from a chair of southern European type and proceeds to dress. He puts on garments whose form originally derived from the skin clothing of the nomads of the Asiatic steppes, puts on shoes made from skins tanned by a process invented in ancient Egypt and cut to a pattern derived from the classical civilizations of the Mediterranean, and ties around his neck a strip of bright-colored cloth which is a vestigial survival of the shoulder shawls worn by the seventeenth-century Croatians. Before going out for breakfast he glances through the window, made of glass invented in Egypt, and if it is raining puts on overshoes made of rubber discovered by the Central American Indians and takes an umbrella, invented in southeastern Asia. Upon his head he puts a hat made of felt a material invented in the Asiatic steppes.
>
> On his way to breakfast he stops to buy a paper paying for it with coins, an ancient Lydian invention. At the restaurant a new series of borrowed elements confront him. His plate is made of a form of pottery invented in China. His knife is of a steel alloy first made in southern India, his fork a medieval Italian invention, and his spoon a derivative of a Roman original. He begins breakfast with an orange, from the eastern Mediterranean, a cantaloupe from Persia, or perhaps a piece of African watermelon. With this he has coffee, an Abyssinian plant, with cream and sugar. Both the domestication of cows and the idea of milking them originated in the Near East, while sugar was first made in India. After his fruit and coffee he goes on to waffles, cakes made by a Scandinavian technique from wheat domesticated in Asia Minor. Over these he pours maple syrup, invented by the Indians of the Eastern woodlands. As a side dish he may have the egg of a species of bird domesticated in Indo-China, or thin strips of the flesh of an animal domesticated in Eastern Asia which have been salted and smoked by a process developed in northern Europe.
>
> When our friend has finished eating he settles back to smoke, an American Indian habit, consuming a plant domesticated in Brazil in either a pipe, derived from the Indians of Virginia, or a cigarette, derived from Mexico. If he is hardy enough he may even attempt a cigar, transmitted to us from the Antilles by way of Spain. While smoking he reads the news of the day, imprinted in characters invented by the ancient Semites upon a material invented in China by a process invented in Germany. As he absorbs the accounts of foreign troubles he will, if he is a good conservative citizen, thank a Hebrew deity in an Indo-European language that he is 100 percent American.[1]

There is no denying that diffusion takes place; there is also evidence that contact stimulates innovation through the process of stimulus diffusion (Ember and Ember 2002: 272–273). However, the significant question is what part does diffusion play as a mechanism for producing cultural similarities and differences? As Murphy (1989: 223) pointed out,

> It would be safe to say that over 90 percent of the content of almost all cultures was derived from in the first place through diffusion. Nonetheless, there are important examples of independent and parallel inventions, which show that cultural innovations are made possible by the culture matrix from which they arise.[2]

In other words, while the transmission of artifacts, customs, and beliefs is not only fully documented but is experienced by people everywhere today in the massive process of globalization, the real question is whether it is warranted to treat diffusion as the sole universal mechanism for cultural development and change. The writers whose works I shall discuss in this chapter felt that diffusion was indeed such a universal mechanism.

CENTRAL PREMISES OF DIFFUSIONIST PERSPECTIVES

One of the central epistemological assumptions upon which diffusionist explanatory schemes were based was the premise that primitive people lack the ingenuity to develop innovative ideas on their own. Independent inventions were assumed to be extremely rare and the majority of the cultural features around the world were thought to have arisen in one or a few places and then spread outwards to other cultures. Those who espouse this position are really saying that the ancestors of indigenous people around the world were incapable of any achievements on their own, thereby divesting them of their rightful cultural heritage (Fagan and Hale 2001: 85).

MODERATE BRITISH DIFFUSIONISM: W. H. R. RIVERS

Among those who adopted the diffusionist position was W. H. R. Rivers (1864–1922), a prominent British anthropologist and a noted scholar. Rivers was a member of the pioneering 1898 multidisciplinary anthropological expedition to the Torres Straits islands. He is credited for having developed the widely used **Genealogical Method,** a technique for collecting and organizing genealogical data for the analysis of descent based societies. Rivers is also known for his

Step Pyramid of Saqqara (Djoser/Zoser) in Egypt compared to the Pyramid of the Sun, Teotihuacan, Mexico. Diffusionists mistakenly attributed such remarkable parallel evolutionary developments in the ancient monuments of Egypt and the Americas to contact and borrowing.

superb ethnographic research among the Toda in India (Rivers 1906).

Rivers adopted the diffusionist perspective late in his career, while he was attempting to explain the similarities and differences among the cultures of Melanesia and Polynesia. In his book *The History of Melanesian Society* (1914), Rivers attempted to account for regional cultural patterns and variations by inferring contact with groups elsewhere. He did this by postulating a series of migrations between islands. Wherever the ethnographic evidence did not support a presumed sequence or pattern of diffusion, Rivers relied upon auxiliary mechanisms to explain them.

For example, Rivers explained the absence of canoes on some islands as a trait originally present but subsequently lost by the dying out of the island's canoe making guild. Wherever items such as pottery, the bow and arrow, or sturdy seagoing vessels were absent, it was posited that these must have at one time existed but were subsequently lost as the culture degenerated. Thus the idea that traits become diluted or are lost as they spread from one place to another is transformed in Rivers's work from singular historical events to a general rule (Malefijt 1974: 166). To account for traits in places they were not expected, Rivers posited separate arrival of groups of migrants who brought the traits with them to some areas, but not others.

Errors and Problems

Some of the difficulties of Rivers' diffusionism are illustrated in his explanation of the presence of different **mortuary rituals** among the Australian aborigines (e.g., burial, placement on platforms, embalming, cremation), a people that he construed to be an otherwise homogeneous population. Since Rivers's epistemological assumptions prevented him from treating different mortuary practices as local innovations, he had to explain them in terms of migrations by a number of culturally and technologically supe-

rior groups of outsiders. Being small in numbers, Rivers conjectured, these newcomers settled down, married local women, and were totally assimilated, so that they left no "racial" traces, evidence of their technologies, or even traces of their languages, which they presumably gave up when they learned the local dialects.

Once the newcomers settled down among the culturally less sophisticated indigenous people, according to Rivers, their own cultural inventories degenerated and were lost. The only practices these men refused to give up were their burial rites to which they had strong emotional attachments. Rivers posited that the local groups that had accepted the newcomers subsequently took up their alien mortuary rites. Why local people gave up their own burial practices and adopted alien rituals is not explained (Lowie 1959: 174–175; Malefijt 1974: 166). The line of reasoning Rivers used to support his conjectural history is an analogue of the **multiple outs** that occur in the works of proponents of paranormal phenomena, conspiracy theorists, UFO cultists, and New Atlantis pseudohistorians, which enables expositors of such views to use the absence of evidence as evidence.

EXTREME DIFFUSIONISM: THE HELIOCENTRIC (PAN-EGYPTIAN) SCHOOL OF SMITH AND PERRY

In contrast to Rivers's moderate approach, the proponents of the perspective known as the Heliocentric School espoused an extreme form of diffusionism. The principal architects of this perspective were Grafton Elliot Smith (1871–1937), an eminent anatomist and surgeon, and William J. Perry (1887–1949), a school headmaster. Although less enduring and influential than the diffusionism of the German and American groups, the Heliocentric view is highly instructive in revealing the problems that arise when unbridled imagination, irrationalism, and unrea-

Grafton Elliot Smith, leader of the British Heliocentric diffusionist school.

son are substituted for methodological rigor and empirical evidence.

Unlike Rivers, whose formulations were restricted to **Oceania,** Smith and Perry presented a diffusionist scheme that was global in scale in which the nexus of all cultural innovations and creativity was considered to be ancient Egypt. In comparison to Rivers's work, the formulations of Smith and Perry are remarkably naive, implausible, illogical, inconsistent, and marred with glaring empirical errors, as well as being highly ethnocentric. What these writers proposed and the methods they adopted in order to demonstrate their assertions went against all the established conventions of science, historiography, and even common sense. Indifference to rules and conventions of scholarship leads to fiction writing, mythologized history, and fantasy in the

truest sense of those terms. It might make for fun reading, but it certainly cannot be accepted as knowledge.

Assumptions about Culture

Smith was launched on a career in Heliocentric anthropology during a visit to Egypt to study the anatomy of mummies. The complexity of mummification procedures used by the ancient Egyptians convinced him that the technique could have only been invented once. Moreover, he was greatly impressed by the stunning cultural achievements of the ancient Egyptians, especially their pyramids and other large stone monuments. Reminded of megalithic structures such as Stonehenge back home in England, Smith became convinced that the megalithic structures in Europe must have been modeled after Egyptian prototypes.

Smith soon formulated a view of ancient Egypt as the nexus of a vast cultural complex centered upon a sun worshipping religion and the construction of large stone monuments. To support his hypothesis he then began looking for elements of this sun-centered complex in other parts of the world. For this reason British diffusionism under Smith and Perry became known as the **Heliocentric school.**

Smith pointed to the worldwide recurrence of an assemblage of traits, which he associated with Egypt to prove his **pan-Egyptian theory.** This assemblage, according to Smith, included pyramids and other megalithic structures, sun worship, tattooing, and circumcision, none of which inherently belong with one another but are similar to Egyptian cultural patterns.

Sadly, the combination of traits that Smith associate with Egypt is an artifact of his own imagination, made possible by the widest latitude in the interpretation of the evidence. It is the same with the present-day practitioners of this kind of pseudohistory, who cleverly reveal bogus architectural star maps or encoded

Temple of Abu Simbel, Egypt, built by Ramesses II (c. 1290–1224 B.C.) whose colossal statues flank the entrance. Impressed by the magnificent monumental architecture of the ancient Egyptians, British diffusionists erroneously assumed that Egypt was the source of all cultural innovations.

mathematical formulas in ancient monuments on earth, the "face on Mars," and so on (Fagan and Hale 2001; Sagan 1995: 41–60).

Enthralled by the Egyptian connection, Smith soon found evidence everywhere that he looked. Playing fast and loose with the interpretation of archeological and ethnographic evidence he later went on to link all **monumental architecture** around the world, from Mayan pyramids and Native North American earthworks, to Cambodian temples and the like, to

Egyptian designs (Figure 5.1). He went on to postulate routes along which traits could have spread from Egypt to the farthest corners of the world.

Egyptians or bearers of Egyptian cultural elements, according to Smith, reached the Americas via Oceania and Polynesia:

In Central America, Mexico, and Peru civilization made its appearance in a fully developed form. . . . it conformed in almost every respect to the distinctive type of civilizations (admittedly a very pe-

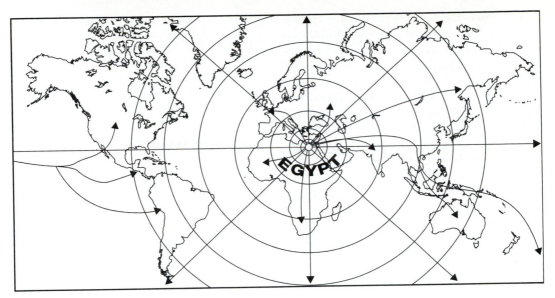

Figure 5.1   The Conjectural Heliocentric diffusionist model proposed by Grafton Elliot Smith and William J. Perry, in which all cultural innovations were traced to Egypt.

culiar one) that was flourishing in the southeastern corner of Asia at the time when it made its appearance in Central America. The type of pyramid found in America was also the dominant feature of the architecture of Cambodia and Java during the same centuries. The same system of beliefs and customs, the same distinctive features of its architecture, in fact a whole series of arts and crafts, customs and beliefs, were suddenly introduced into the New World, which seem to bear unmistakable evidence of their Asiatic origin. Moreover, the only additions that were made to these customs in their transit across the Pacific were features distinctive of Melanesian and Polynesian practices. Instead of detracting from the cogency of the identity, these trivial additions afford striking corroboration, not only of the original source of the inspiration, but also of the road taken by the ancient mariners who were responsible for the introduction into the New World of the germs of its distinctive civilization. It is an altogether incredible supposition that the Polynesian sailors who searched many thousands of miles in the Pacific with such thoroughness as not to miss even the minutest

islets were not repeatedly landing on the shores of America for ten centuries or more. How could people who found Hawaii, Easter Island, and New Zealand have failed to discover the vast continent stretching from pole to pole? (Smith 1927: 22–24).

Smith's questions regarding cultural contact between the groups he mentions are not all that unreasonable given the evidence available at the time. It was perhaps in part for this reason that he completely misjudged the range of diversity among ancient cultures and totally ignored the adaptive adjustments cultures make to their varied and particular environments. Also, he was unaware of what anthropologists today know about the remarkable worldwide parallelism in the transition from foraging to agricultural modes of production and the rise of complex societies (see Sanderson 1999: 31–34, 58–68).

With independent parallel inventions excluded from their explanatory repertoire, it is easy to see how diffusionist writers such as Smith could have treated the worldwide cross-cultural similarities in terms of common origins. Smith should not be criticized too harshly on these points. However, Smith and his followers were guilty of proposing explanatory schemes and principles, which were taken as a given, without ever attempting to determine in a systematic way whether those schemes or principles did indeed hold true against an independent body of ethnographic or archeological data. More so than the nineteenth-century evolutionists, the British diffusionists took great liberties in what they accepted as evidence. Their anthropology was therefore basically an exercise in free reigning imagination. It made for wonderful tall tales, which take the reader to the far corners of the world, with images of daring ocean voyages, the arrival of civilized men among primitive savages, and the subsequent cultural transformations, all ultimately linked to the mysterious and ancient culture of Egypt. But it is fiction.

The notion of the uninventiveness of primitive people underlies Smith's position that the development of civilization was a singular occurrence and his travels convinced him the cradle of "civilization" was Egypt. As Smith put it,

> One might take up one after another of the thousands of ingredients that go to the making of civilization, ancient and modern, and show in each case the complexity of the set of circumstances, in which chance played an obtrusive part, involved in every invention. Each of them originated in one place and from there became diffused abroad, the complex tissue of civilization itself no less than the individual threads of which it is woven (Smith 1927: 9–10).

Inventiveness was thus denied to everyone who ever lived except for the ancient Egyptians. Thus, as Malefijt (1974: 164) observes, "Multiple origins, independent invention, multiple diffusions, psychic unity, progress, evolution, and survivals were all abolished in one mighty stroke." Smith's (1928: 20, 25) ethnocentric views of "primitive" people, whom he considered to be "wholly devoid of any thing worthy of the name of culture," illustrates this point:

Those field-workers who have acquired an intimate acquaintance with relatively uncultured people have repeatedly called attention to the lack of that inventiveness which the theorists are so fond of taking for granted, or rather to their failure to appreciate the need for inventing devices that we regard as obvious and essential in character.

Historical Reconstruction

Smith's version of the unfolding of events in human cultural history is as follows. In the beginning, the world was populated by "Natural Man," who lacked clothing, social organization, chiefs, laws, religion, and rituals for marriage or burials. Natural Man had no inclinations to build buildings or make implements other than a few items needed for hunting (Smith 1927: 22). In fact, Natural Man "lived like apes," according to Smith (1928: 31). Then miraculously in one place and one time only, in the Nile Valley around 4000 B.C., people attained civilization. Smith attributed the rise of Egyptian civilization to a unique set of circumstances produced by the Nile River with its inundations, which created rich silt-laden banks that promoted the growth of wild barley. Learning from the example set by nature, the early Egyptians settled down, began planting barley, imitated the Nile's inundations by developing irrigation techniques, and soon developed an agricultural economy.

This is a kind of "eureka" explanation for the domestication of plants (i.e., a sudden accidental realization that plants can be cultivated by gazing upon the fertile banks of the Nile) that is not supported by ethnographic and archeological evidence. That evidence suggests that **Paleolithic** and **Mesolithic** peoples were thoroughly familiar with the characteristics of plants and animals upon the hunting and gathering of which their livelihoods depended (Harlan 1978; Henry 1985; Moore 1988; Wright 1994).

Moreover, there is considerable evidence that the shift from hunting-gathering to reliance upon domesticated plants and animals was a gradual one which took place in many places as a case of worldwide parallel development, not a sudden revolutionary breakthrough in one location (Sanderson 1999: 20–52). In Smith's view, however,

> The creation of civilization was due not so much to persons endowed with intellectual pre-eminence or exceptional initiative so much as the existence of a particular set of natural conditions that forced upon men's attention the possibility of embarking upon a certain course of action and the immediate benefit of doing so (Smith 1928: 26).

In Smith's scheme the discovery of agriculture in the Nile Valley was followed by a series of other startling inventions, such as pottery, granaries which later became houses, the wheel, the plough, metallurgy, the calendar, and writing, all necessary for the operation of the new agricultural economy. Cattle were soon domesticated as well. The erection of towns and cities, large-scale monuments, and the development of a centralized government followed shortly.

Kings, whose role it was to predict the timing of the Nile's flooding, became the embodiments of the sun and an elaborate religion centered upon sun worship emerged around these divine beings. Deified in life, the kings were made immortal after death by means of elaborate funerary rituals and mummification. These practices, in Smith's view, led to the development of elaborate ceremonies and rites, dancing, music, and pyramid building.

The invention of seaworthy boats and development of navigation techniques by the industrious Egyptians soon enabled them to venture forth around the world in search of raw materials and precious metals. Wherever these daring Egyptians went they took with them the gift of civilization and their religion of sun worship.

Proof of an Egyptian connection for Smith lay in the worldwide recurrence of irrigation agriculture, sun worship, pyramid construction, and mummification, along with other items such as stone monuments and ear piercing. Even the economic significance attached to gold was taken as evidence of an Egyptian link, where the metal, Smith maintained, had acquired a magical reputation as the incorruptible substance of immortality and divinity (Smith 1928: 49):

> The fact that almost every early civilization did assign to this soft and relatively useless metal a fantastic and irrelevant value is surly the strongest possible evidence of Egypt, in which a peculiar set of fortuitous circumstances was responsible for creating the fictitious attributes assigned to this metal (Smith 1927: 14).

Errors and Problems

A central diffusionist axiom to which Smith subscribed was that as items spread outwards they became more and more diluted, resulting in progressively cruder imitations of the prototypes in the cultural center. This enabled him to interpret practically any large structure that had the faintest resemblance to a pyramid as a degraded form of the Egyptian original. It did not matter whether the structures in question were temples, tombs, or shrines. The slightest resemblance was sufficient to infer historical contact. Similarly, any burial practice that entailed preservation of parts of a deceased's body could be counted as evidence in the form of a degraded imitation of Egyptian mummification (Malefijt 1974: 166).

Even the mortuary practices and other customs of the Australian aborigines were shown through this type of reasoning to have derived from Egyptian prototypes, but in degenerated form. As Smith put it,

> There is also evidence to establish the fact that such elements of culture as are possessed by the aboriginal Australians—their mummification of the dead, their social organization and totemism, their methods of initiation, et cetera—are degraded and otherwise modified results of the adoption of alien [meaning Egyptian] practices and beliefs (Smith 1928: 25).

Similar generalizations enabled Smith to identify nearly all other customs or traits from around the world as deriving from Egyptian originals.

Using Smith's approach, it might be noted, one could make an equal case that it was in fact Sumeria or Babylonia that was the cradle of all civilization. Indeed, the Boasian anthropologist Robert Lowie (1959: 161) chided Smith by suggesting that "had he tarried on the Euphrates, we may reasonably surmise him to have fathered a pan-Babylonian theory."

Smith used the idea that traits become diluted as they spread further from their point of origin to explain why none of the supposed imitators were ever able to develop exact replicas of Egyptian prototypes. Also, he argued that during the process of transmission some traits could disappear and others could be picked up along the way, resulting in new permutations. This offered a convenient explanation for the absence of certain cultural items in places where they ought to have been found and the presence of others where they were not expected.

Smith reasoned falsely that the Egyptians were the first and earliest people to develop agriculture, which gave them an evolutionary head start. Contra Smith, the earliest archaeological sites indicating a sedentary lifestyle and reliance upon the cultivation of cereals date between eight to twelve thousand years ago and are located in the **Near East** (Jordan, Syria and Iraq), not Egypt (Bar-Yosef and Valla 1990; Fagan 1997; Harlan 1978; Henry 1985; Moore 1988; Wright 1994). Moreover, we now know that there was not just one, but rather several centers

Stonehenge (c. 3000 to 1200 B.C.). The idea that as items spread outwards they became more and more diluted, resulting in progressively cruder imitations of the prototypes in the cultural center, enabled British diffusionists to attribute all sorts of monumental architecture from unrelated cultures to Egypt, including Stonehenge (Photo by H. Sidky).

YEARS AGO	SW Asia	S. Asia	E. Asia	South Europe	Africa	North America	Meso-America	South America
1000								Potatoes
2000								
3000					Cats (Egypt) Yam Oil-palm	Sunflower, squash		
4000				Horse (Eurasia)				
5000	Camels							Llamas, alpacas, cotton, gourds, lima beans, guinea pigs, manioc, squash
6000		Chicken Cotton	Pigs, water-buffalo, millet	Sheep, goat, pigs, wheat, barley, cattle	Millet, sorghum, sheep, goat, donkey		Maize, beans, pepper, gourds	
7000	Cattle, sheep, goat, pigs, wheat, barley	Cattle	Rice					
8000								
9000							Squash	
10,000				Dogs				
11,000	Dogs					Dogs		
12,000								

Figure 5.2 Schematic chronology of approximate dates for domestication of plants and animals in various parts of the world. *(After Bogucki 1999; Jolly and White 1995; Schultz and Lavenda 1995).*

where the transition to farming took place, more or less, independently of one another (Figure 5.2).

Smith's view on the evolution of ancient societies was based upon another erroneous assumption. He believed that the rise of "civilization" was such a unique event that it could not have occurred more than once. As Smith (1928: 25–26) put it,

It is one of the fashionable fallacies of modern speculation that civilization itself and the various ingredients, material, social and spiritual, which go to its making, are such obvious and inevitable things for man to invent, that almost instinctively he sets about doing so. If there were any truth in this opinion, why did men wait all those thousands, perhaps millions, of years before any of them took such a so-called obvious and inevitable step? Or, if it is suggested in reply that man's mental powers were slowly developing, why should the momentous achievement of creating civilization have been reserved for on particular group of people to accomplish?

The questions Smith raises are important ones. Why, if humans have been around for some three millions of years, did the development of agriculture and the rise of complex societies take place only in the last 10,000 years? This is a valid question, and anthropologists have developed a range of theories to address the issue (see

Bogucki 1999: 192–198; Cohen 1977; Harris 1977; McCorriston and Hole 1991; Wenke 1990).

Smith was wrong, however, to assume that an event such as the rise of complex societies was a singular occurrence. Archaeological evidence, some of which was available in Smith's time, suggests that primary states, or pristine states (polities that evolved out of local conditions independently of one another), arose in at least six or seven places. These centers of state formation were located in **Mesopotamia,** Egypt (North Africa), Subsaharan Africa, India, China, Mesoamerica, and South America (Bodley 1994: 170; Gross 1992: 43; see Carneiro 1970, 1987, 1988). The more conservative writers exclude Africa from the list, while others (e.g., Sanderson 1999: 69, 95) include Europe in addition to Africa as centers for state formation (for Mesopotamia see Wenke 1990; for Egypt see Trigger 1982; for Africa see Connah 1987; McIntosh and McIntosh 1988; for the Indus Valley see Possehl 1990; Miller 1985; for China see Chang 1986; for Mesoamerica and Peru see R. Adams 1991 and Fiedel 1987).

Smith was also in error to assume that Egyptian civilization was the earliest. Archeological evidence has revealed that the first state level societies developed in Mesopotamia, before Egyptian civilization (see Johnson 1973; Trigger 1982; Wenke 1990).

Smith and Perry were not anthropologists and the primary impact of their work was upon popular audiences. The popularity of the Heliocentric view was short lived, and most anthropologists now dismiss this perspective.

DIFFUSIONISM: THE GERMAN/AUSTRIAN SCHOOL

An intellectually more sophisticated version of diffusionism was developed by the German scholars. Chief among these were Fredrick Ratzel (1844–1904), Fritz Graebner (1877–1934), and Father Wilhelm Schmidt (1868–1954). The German perspective came to be known variously as the cultural historical school, the *Kulturkreise* (culture circle) school, or historical ethnology.

These writers were less extreme in their views and more attentive to methodological problems than were the British diffusionists. Also, the German historical school was fieldwork based and the ethnographies produced by proponents of this school are still useful, despite being wedded to a diffusionist theoretical perspective (Adams 1998: 381).

The German historical ethnologists, like their British counterparts, held the view that humans are generally uninventive and that new cultural developments were due nearly always to the spread of traits from elsewhere and their recombination into new patterns and permutations. For the expositors of *Kulturkreise* the diffusion of traits was attributed not to the spread of ideas but rather to actual migration of people from one place to another. Moreover, German diffusionism was guided by the religious ideological agenda of its proponents, such as Father Schmidt. This was an example of an anthropological paradigm wedded to theology and as such was harnessed to the cause of supernaturalism.

Father Schmidt, one of the principle expositors of historical ethnology, described the methods and objectives of this school:

> [These are] not only to understand the conditions existing among the primitive peoples today, but also to recognize in them witnesses and survivals of the oldest development of mankind and thus to reach back over the epochs of written history, far back into those distant millennia of mankind's past history, and with their help to construct the objective succession of events and thereby the actual genesis of culture among different peoples (Schmidt 1939: 13).

Assumptions about Culture

Like the evolutionists of the period, the diffusionists were also seeking to reconstruct the history of cultural development. Similarly, for the

German ethnologists the study of extant primitive cultures was not an end in itself but rather as a key to understanding the past.

> For to concern ourselves only with conditions we find among the primitives today in order to "explain" them on the basis of present-day circumstances is a matter of little interest considering the insignificant role the modern primitives play in the history of mankind. Besides, such an "explanation" on the basis of present-day conditions could not be a true explanation, as it remains too much on the surface; time and again it must be the cause of misinterpretations and could not even satisfy the needs of colonial administrations, for whose "practical" purposes such "explanations" might allegedly be perfectly satisfactory. . . . However . . . if these primitives . . . be taken as precious documents of mankind, as living witnesses representing the oldest phases of development, through which also the most highly developed culture peoples have passed, so that in these primitives we can study the stages of past development in religion, law, custom, morality, and art. If the culture historical school gives us the means to determine the deepest meaning of those ancient times from their correct sequence, then it shall have made ethnol*ogy* into what its name implies, to ethno*logy* which is not mere ethno*graphy*, or description of peoples spread out spatially, but penetration into the *ratio* . . . of the elements and events of culture (Schmidt 1939: 13–14).

Reconstructing the sequence of cultural development through time, and arranging cultures "into a succession of strata" using evidence from extant societies involved the comparative method, which was also part of the methodological tool kit of the nineteenth-century evolutionists.

The main point of departure between the German diffusionists and the evolutionists was in their construal of the mechanisms of culture change. The diffusionists maintained that development "does not always proceed from the lower to the higher" (Schmidt 1939: 11). Moreover, they maintained that degeneration of cultures leading from high to low forms confounds attempts to assign greater age to the simpler cul-

tural forms. Finally, they de-emphasized the role of independent inventions, making the familiar argument that humans are inherently uninventive, new inventions are relatively rare, and much, if not all of cultural developments occurs as a result of the fusion of different cultural complexes resulting in various permutations.

The Germans focused upon the spread not just of individual cultural traits, but of whole cultural complexes. A **culture complex** was defined as a cluster of interlocked traits, such as beliefs, practices, and arrangements associated with, for example, **totemism,** or a system of matrilineal descent. Traits were thought to spread individually by borrowing, but the diffusion of cultural complexes usually meant the actual movement of people, or migration.

The Germans, unlike the British diffusionists, posited several centers of creativity, rather than a single place, such as on the banks of the Nile. In this scheme, migration and contact were the primary if not the only mechanism for cultural development. History consisted almost entirely of migrations. As Schmidt (1939: 25) put it,

> During these migrations peoples and cultures came into contact with each other and thus mutually influenced each other. . . . this mutual influence has been exercised to a greater extent than had hitherto been admitted. It has also been the cause of new creations and modifications of culture, and wherever positively established, it makes the assumption of independent origin untenable and superfluous.

Unless it could be conclusively demonstrated that contact has not taken place, similarities between cultural elements, no matter how far apart they were situated, were to be accounted for in terms of diffusion or historical contact. The principle of diffusion was thus held as a given, more or less on faith. This line of argument involves the logical fallacy of appeal to ignorance, which entails the assertion that whatever that has not be been proven to be false is therefore true. Proponents of extraterrestrial visitations and conjectural histories regarding long forgotten advanced civilizations often resort to this fallacy to make their case.

Having ruled out the possibility of independent inventions in the majority of instances, the German diffusionists focused primarily on cultural complexes and the intricate ways in which one was superimposed upon another and how traits were combined or fused to produce new complexes. For this reason, it was essential for methods to be developed that would enable the ethnologist to determine the relationships between different cultural elements, to discover whether there were historical connections between them, and to discern how they were related chronologically.

The Methodology of the Cultural Historical School

One methodological problem to be solved was how to distinguish similarities based on purely functional reasons from similarities due to historical contact. For example, all arrows must have points and all bows must have strings, and these similarities do not indicate historical connections. However, such a connection may be established through the use of the criterion of "form," proposed by Friedrich Ratzel, a cultural geographer and founder of German historical ethnology.

In 1891 Ratzel called attention to the remarkable similarities between the bow and arrow used in West Africa and the bow and arrow in Oceania (Honigmann 1976: 167; Schmidt 1939: 26). Ratzel focused on features such as the cross section of the bow shaft, the manner in which bowstrings are fastened, and the material from which they are made, and the way feathers are attached to arrows, traits that do not have a necessary functional relationship. In other words, one could make an equally functional bow and arrow without including any of these characteristics. Ratzel identified the same features associated with the bow and arrow in Oceania.

For him the explanation for the parallelism was not independent invention, or similar minds operating the same way, as the principle of psychic unity would have it, but historical connection between the West Africa and Oceania. Ratzel's criterion of "form" led to the axiom that if similarities between traits cannot be explained in terms of function or the material from which they are made, then the similarities are due to diffusion no matter how far apart the cultures may be (Schmidt 1939: 143).

Ratzel concluded that the most important factor in the development of culture throughout human history was the ceaseless movement of people. He envisioned an unending series of migrations that brought alien peoples and their cultural inventories into contact, resulting in new cultural patterns. Thus, the ancient world conceived by Ratzel was much like the "postmodern world," a world in flux, with people on the move, and the blurring and crumbling of boundaries. Understanding the cultural development of mankind therefore required the reconstruction of the waves of migrations in space and time.

Ratzel set forth one of the main principles of historical ethnology, which entailed the reconstruction of human cultural history by mapping the culture areas, or *Kulturkreise* (culture circles), around the world and sketching the lines of passage linking them and over which cultures had spread (Honigmann 1976: 168)

Leo Frobenius (1873–1938), a pupil of Ratzel, introduced the criterion of "quantity." He argued that since cultural traits diffuse as complexes, historical contact might be inferred if one finds multiple elements that show similarities. Thus in the case of the Africa-Oceania connection, Frobenius pointed out that not only does the West African bow and arrow resemble the bow and arrow in Oceania but that there were also similarities in the two regions among house types, shields, masks, clothing, and drums.

Parenthetically, to date these similarities remain unexplained (Adams 1998: 380). For Frobenius the explanation was fairly clear. He concluded that the two areas had formed the fringes of a single continuous culture circle, the central portion of which had been altered by successive migrations (Adams 1998: 380).

In the hands of Graebner and Father Schmidt, the criteria of "quality" and "quantity" became the guiding methodological axioms of the German diffusionist school (Malefijt 1974: 169). In his book *Die Methode der Ethnologie* (1911), Graebner attempted to develop his own methodological principles that would enable the ethnologist to identify diffusion by examining the geographical distribution of cultural elements. Schmidt (1939) attempted to refine these principles and applied them to reconstruct human cultural history.

The German diffusionists were interested in reconstructing how cultures had been physically transmitted both through time and space, producing all the extant cultures in the world. Here they relied upon the concept of *kulturkreis,* or culture circle. According to Schmidt, a culture circle, as a totality

is by definition a living organism like the life itself which it serves. That means that its individual spheres, economics, material culture, social life, custom, religion, do not stand disconnected alongside one another in a merely accidental connection, but rather that they are organically connected with one another, so that one can often infer from the nature of one sphere to that of another (Schmidt 1939: 177–178).

Schmidt's notion of integration pertains to the linkages between traits forming trait complexes. It should not be mistaken for the notion of culture as a functionally integrated organic whole, which appears in association with twentieth-century functional perspectives in anthropology (see Chapters 8 and 9). This idea was important for Schmidt because if the components of trait complexes are integrated then they must spread as wholes, or as more-or-less closed systems.

One of the facts which has been established by culture history beyond all preadventure of doubt is that not only discrete culture elements or small groups of elements migrate and exert an influence, but also whole compact culture complexes. If such a culture complex embraces all the essential and necessary categories of human culture, material culture, economic life, social life, custom, religion, then we call it a "culture circle," because returning into itself, like a circle, it is sufficient unto itself and, hence, also assures its independent existence. Should it neglect or fail to satisfy one of the more important human needs, then a substitute for this must be called from another culture—the greater the number of such substitutes that are required, the more it would cease to be an independent culture circle (Schmidt 1939: 176).

Thus, as a culture complex spreads, because it is a system of integrated elements it picks up those elements it lacks to meet certain vital human needs from other cultures with which it comes into contact.

Historical Reconstruction

Using the conceptual tools described here, the German historical ethnologists devised the following reconstruction of human cultural history. In the beginning there was primitive man who lived in small isolated groups somewhere in Asia. Being small in number and lacking effective means of transport, these groups lived in isolation, detached from one another. Over time each one of these groups developed its own unique culture, or *Kreise*. Once their numbers grew and methods of transportation were developed, members of these primeval culture complexes began to radiate outward.

At first cultures spread by land bridges connecting different continents; later on, with the development of watercrafts, cultures spread to Oceania, Polynesia, and other formerly inaccessible places. Contact led either to fusion, destruction, or displacement. Each wave of migration led to primitive groups being pushed further and further into barren and infertile regions of the world where today they survive as peripheral populations.

Today, we know that such movements or migrations did take place. Humans first populated the earth from Africa, not Asia. Also, the flow of people and cultural elements was not a continuous, multidirectional process that the German diffusionists envisioned. For example, it is clear that immigrants from Siberia, who crossed Beringia, a land bridge connecting East Asia to Alaska, populated the Americas.

At present Beringia is submerged, but sometime around 12,000 years ago, when humans are thought to have crossed over, the land bridge was uncovered because a large quantity of water was locked up as ice, causing sea levels to drop (Harris 1997: 157; Hoffecker et al. 1993). As noted in Chapter 4, Beringia was actually partially uncovered between 60,000 to 12,000 years ago; however, undisputed archaeological evidence for the presence of humans in the Americas suggests that movement took place only around 12,000 years ago (Lynch 1990). There are some archaeologists, however, who maintain that humans arrived at a much earlier date (Bryan 1987; Guidon and Delibrias 1986).

In contrast to the Americas, human populations moved into and inhabited other regions of the earth much earlier. For example, Australia (Figure 5.3) was populated sometime between 50,000 to 40,000 years ago by groups who possessed watercrafts (Harris 1997: 156; Jones 1989). Thus, there were long intervals between the times when humans moved into and inhabited different parts of the earth, rather than a continuous movement of people in time and space.

As for evidence for the diffusion of cultural complexes, the best and among the most significant examples was once thought to be the spread of the Neolithic mode of production based upon domesticated plants and animals. It was thought that the Neolithic complex originated in the Middle East and then spread to Europe, Asia, and Africa through a process of diffusion. However, the more recent view is that the Neolithic was essentially a worldwide case of

parallelisms, comprising a series of independent inventions, based upon adaptive responses to local ecological and demographic conditions (Chang 1986; Harlan 1978; Harris 1997: 150; Higham 1988; Howell 1987; Phillipson 1985; Rowley-Conwy 1995). In other words, the development of the Neolithic was more or less an independent phenomenon in Southwest Asia, China, Southeast Asia, Europe, and Africa (Sanderson 1999). Thus, here again, evidence does not support the idea that diffusion alone was the crucial evolutionary mechanism.

According to the German diffusionist reconstruction, the cultures of the world represent a massive jumble of different culture circles, one overlapping another, to produce unique cultural permutations through the variegated combination or fusion of different complexes and traits.

> . . . now this, now that culture trait, now single, now several culture elements spread over the boundary of their original culture region and thereby come into contact with alien culture traits. In fact, even the entire culture complex in its full extension can thus come into contact with another culture complex. If the contact occurs essentially only on the boundaries of the two culture regions, then we have "contact action." The time depths in this case are naturally smaller, since the contact on the narrow border regions is more quickly accomplished. It is also quite possible that we are dealing with local forms which have quite recently originated in the peripheral region and found their way across the boundary into the region of the alien culture. . . . But if a culture has displaced a seemingly great part of the alien culture region and stays there, we then have "mixture," which is nothing else than a more or less mutual blending between culture elements of two cultures covering a large district. Exactly this circumstance enables us to gain greater time depths here, since such an overlay and mixing require a longer time (Schmidt 1939: 167–168).

A culture circle originating in one part of the world could spread and become established in another area, while its point of origin may be taken over by a different complex. Sometimes contact leads to the development of compound

Figure 5.3   Peopling of Australia 50,000 years ago. The arrows mark the possible entry points, through island hoping by boats during times when sea-levels were low. Sites named are 20,000 years or older.   *After Gowlett (1984: 136).*

cultures, cultures composed out of the fusion of several other cultures.

Compound cultures might of themselves be recognizable here and there from the fact that single functional elements contain two different concurring forms; for instance, several house forms (each one of which goes back to its own culture). When, on the contrary, the heterogeneous elements are not of a concurring nature (a house form of one culture circle, a form of navigation from another, etc.), then the compound character of the culture is only recognizable by comparison with related conditions, but in which the different elements ap-

pear still separated in the different complexes (Graebner in Schmidt 1939: 148).

Each culture circle had to be identified through the careful analysis of the distribution of traits over various geographical regions and then chronological relationships had to be established between each culture circle. For the German diffusionists, ethnology was concerned not only with time relations, but also with spatial relations (Schmidt 1939: 8–9). One way to work out chronological relationships was by looking at spatial distribution. It was assumed that the more widely distributed complexes were older than those that were geographically more confined (Schmidt 1939: 165). Schmidt described another way of establishing chronological relationships:

> In case one or several culture circles as a whole have migrated into a continent, an important possibility for the objective establishment of the (relative) date of this immigration results from the way in which Africa, Oceania, and America are situated with regard to the largest and central continent, that of Asia. . . . The continents most important for the history of the preliterates, Africa, Oceania and America, are joined to Asia with such narrow connections that, at least for land diffusion cultures, there remain but very restricted possibilities of immigration, Hence, we necessarily get a kind of stratification of the complexes following one after the other, so that the youngest complexes lie near the gate of entry and the oldest seem to be pushed into the most distant districts of the respective continents (Schmidt 1939: 196–197).

Thus on the basis of this approach, one could establish which culture is the most ancient by examining the distance it occupies from a point of entry. Applying this approach to North America, Schmidt wrote:

> Here the present-day chain of islands of the Bering Strait, which was a continuous strip of land at the end of the Miolithicum [Mesolithic] and Neolithicum [Neolithic], forms the one narrow entrance to the extensive continent of America during those ancient times. Besides, South America is separated from Asia by the whole breadth of the Pacific and the tribes living farthest from the *porta invasionis* [point of entery] the Fuegians [inhabitants of Tierra del Fuego], belong to the oldest tribes of the whole American hemisphere (Schmidt 1939: 197).

The German diffusionists identified several original culture circles and arranged them in a chronological order or grades. This was basically an evolutionary scheme in which each grade was purported to have given rise to cultures in the succeeding grades. However, change was not unidirectional, and there were no necessary

stages of development in this scheme. The four grades were Primitive Cultures, Primary Cultures, Secondary Cultures, and Tertiary Cultures.

In Schmidt's (1939: 223, 350–351) scheme, the earliest or "first grade," the Primitive Cultures, or hunting and foraging peoples, consisted of three contemporaneous culture circles (Figure 5.4). The first was a Central Circle comprising the Pygmies of Africa and Asia, who were identified as being exogamous and practicing monogamy. The second was an Antarctic Circle, made up of the Southeastern Australians, Bushmen, and Tasmanians, who were exogamous and had sex totems. The third was the Arctic Circle, made up of the Samoyeds, Eskimos, and Algonkians, who were exogamous and egalitarian.

Schmidt's interest in the origins of religion led him to pay considerable attention to the cultures in the primitive grade, which he considered the most ancient of the three primitive circles, for clues regarding the original form of religion. Monotheism based upon the belief in a personal Supreme Being, the first and pristine form of religion, according to Schmidt, was associated with cultures in this grade.

The "second grade" included Primary Cultures. The diffusionists maintained that domestication of plants and animals as well as the development of unilineal descent took place in this cultural grade. Nomadic pastoralism, the mode of subsistence based on the herding of cattle, in which men controlled economic activity, was posited to have led to patrilineal descent. Horticulture, in which women predominate in economic activities, was said to have led to matrilineal descent and village life. What is important to note is that in Schmidt's scheme patrilineal and matrilineal forms of social organization exist side by side, rather than developing in succession as in the evolutionary formulations of Morgan and Bachofen. Ideologically this grade was characterized by the dilution of monotheism and the belief in a personal Supreme Being, which was slowly displaced by magical beliefs and practices.

The "third grade" represented Secondary Cultures, which developed out of Primary

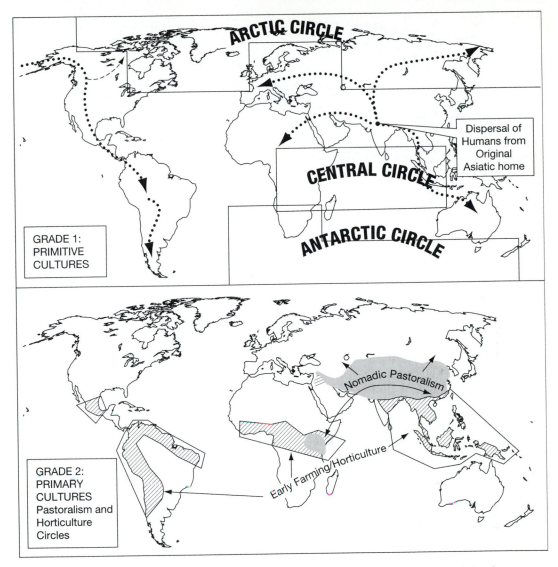

Figure 5.4 The cultural historical school (*Kulturkreise*) time-space model of cultural development.

Grade 1—Primitive Cultures: Hunting and foraging peoples. These consisted of three contemporaneous culture circles: the Central Circle (Pygmies of Africa and Asia); an Antarctic Circle (southeastern Australians, Bushmen, and Tasmanians); the Arctic Circle (Samoyeds, Eskimos and Algonkians). **Grade 2—Primary Cultures:** Nomadic pastoralism and horticulture.

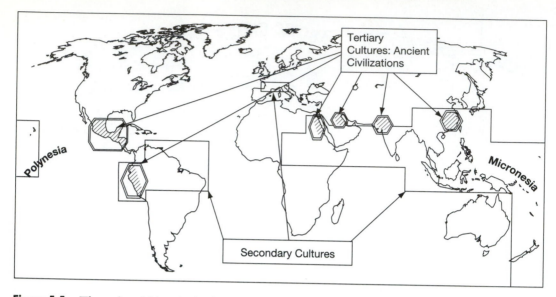

Figure 5.5 The cultural historical school (*Kulturkreise*) time-space model of cultural development.

Grade 3—Secondary Cultures: Intensive agriculture, pantheon of deities, deified kings. Includes the cultures of Polynesia, the Sudan, India, western Asia, southern Europe/the matrilineal cultures of southern China, Indo-China, Melanesia, and northeastern South America.

Grade 4—Tertiary Cultures: The oldest civilizations of Asia, Europe, and America.

Cultural forms with elements of the Primitive grade included (Figure 5.5). Intensive agriculture became the main mode of subsistence. At this stage people developed a pantheon of deities as well as the idea of deified kings. Secondary Cultures included the patrilineal cultures of Polynesia, the Sudan, India, western Asia, and southern Europe, as well as the matrilineal cultures of southern China, Indo-China, Melanesia, and northeastern South America. From this stage the "fourth grade" or Tertiary Cultures emerged, which included the oldest civilizations of Asia, Europe, and America.

The chronological transformations leading to the emergence of one grade from another were construed as singular events, rather than stages through which different cultures pass, unlike the schemes of the nineteenth-century evolutionists. German ethnology had no room for lawlike regularities or processes because it was in the hands of priests such as Schmidt. Writers such as

Schmidt were guided by the metaphysical assumptions of the Roman Catholic Church and were determined to force the facts of anthropology to fit scriptural truths and miraculous origins and to demonstrate that human affairs were not amenable to naturalistic explanations. Parenthetically, this is analogous to kind of supernaturalism that the so-called scientific creationists are trying to pawn off upon an ill-informed and gullible public in America today.

In his massive twelve-volume study of the origin of the idea of God, *Der Ursprung der Gottesidee* (1926–1955), Schmidt used ethnographic data from extant "primitive" peoples to prove that all religions developed from monotheism and beliefs in a personal Supreme Being, the original form of religion. The origins of religion, according to Schmidt, date back to the time when God personally appeared before primitive people, thereby convincing them of the truth of the "true religion." For Schmidt, subsequent religious elaborations, such as the development of pantheons of deities, were the result of deterioration in religious ideas. This is a variant of the degenerationist point of view professed by writers such as Whately (1832: 106), which I discussed in Chapter 3.

Errors and Problems

The works of German diffusionists were fraught with problems. The downfall of their paradigm was diffusion itself, which, according to their own formulations, produced such an incredible jumble of traits and elements so as to make it impossible to sort through the entanglements. In other words, the problem they faced was irresolvable given their epistemological assumption that cultural complexes combine in numerous ways during which some traits are dropped, some picked up, and others altered by combination with other traits as a result of adjustments to local cultural configurations. Thus the number of grades, circles, subcircles, superimpositions, and overlaps and marginal areas had to be increased in order to resolve the complex cultural puzzle facing these diffusionists. As Malefijt (1974: 170) put it,

> To accommodate these and other complications, a very elaborate vocabulary was constructed: there were primitive, secondary, and tertiary *Kreise*, each of which consisted of sub-circles, and those that did not fit anywhere were either marginal, peripheral, or overlapping *Kreise*. In other words, the system did not work and in fact all it proved was that cultural spread and development did *not* take place in the way posited by the *Kulturekreis* scholars.

The demise of the German diffusionist paradigm was due both to its central epistemological assumptions regarding the development of culture and the methods employed in the study of diffusion. There is no justification to assume that all or most cross-cultural similarities are due to historical contact; some are others are not. Moreover, positing that all the cultures of the world derived from a handful of primeval cultures is

pure speculation on par with the view that earthly cultures have extraterrestrial origins.

Methodologically, the German diffusionists had no explicitly stated criteria with which various traits could be selected as belonging to different *Kreise* or to different grades. The choice of elements associated with particular culture circles was mostly subjective and arbitrary. The culture circles themselves were nothing more than an artifact of creative imagination, rather than being dictated by the evidence in hand. Finally, and perhaps most damaging of all, was the fact that despite the seemingly sophisticated methods employed, the German diffusionists failed to identify most of the centers of invention upon which their reconstruction of world cultural history was based. As Schmidt (1939: 213) put it, "the secondary and tertiary culture circles will form a particularly important subject for future research."

German anthropology, although no longer diffusionist, remains curiously idealist/mentalist, historical, and narrowly particularistic in orientation with theoretical formulations sparse and closely tied to ethnographic data. This is not the place one would look for parsimonious theory building. The epistemological roots of present-day German ethnology remain grounded in the ideas of nineteenth-century philosophers (Adams 1998: 378).

THE DOGON SIRIUS MYTHOLOGY: ANTHROPOLOGY, DIFFUSIONISM, AND PSEUDOSCIENCE

As an anthropological paradigm diffusionism is now defunct. However, there are an abundance of diffusionist theses based upon the assumption that indigenous or ancient peoples could not on their own have achieved institutional complexity, or invented mathematics, writing, astronomy, and monumental architecture. These hypotheses range from the late Thor Heyerdahl's (1952,

1989) far-fetched but scholarly theories of contact between the Americas and the cultures of Polynesia to the totally incredulous hypotheses of writers such as Erich von Däniken (1968), who attribute the rise of earthly "civilizations" to extraterrestrial intervention and visitations.

There is a particular account grounded upon solid ethnographic research by a reputable anthropologist that should be included in the present discussion as a modern example of diffusionism. It concerns the remarkable mythology about the star Sirius held by the Dogon of Mali (former French Sudan), in West Africa. The ethnographic data in question come from the field studies of the French anthropologist Marcel Griaule (1898–1956), who worked in West Africa during the 1930s and 1940s (see Griaule 1965a, 1965b). Much of what is known about Dogon folk beliefs comes from Griaule's work, and there are no earlier European accounts on the subject (Sagan 1993: 81).

The Dogon live in the territory south of the ancient city of Timbuktu, on the southern edge of the Sahara Desert (see Hollyman 2001). Unlike the oral traditions of other non-industrial, "prescientific" societies, Dogon folk beliefs contain remarkably accurate astronomical descriptions. The Dogon hold a heliocentric view of our solar system and also believe that the earth and all the planets rotate about their axes. They also believe that Jupiter has four moons and that Saturn has a ring around it. Moreover, they hold that the planets have elliptical orbits rather than circular ones. It was during the Renaissance that Johan Kepler (1571–1630) discovered that the planets revolve around the Sun in an elliptical path. The accuracy of Dogon astronomical ideas is remarkable. Griaule himself was puzzled by the startling scientific precision of Dogon astronomical lore concerning the stars and planets.

How do we account for this finding? One could argue that given the fact that thousands of cultures have existed on earth, each one possessing its own cosmology, there is the likelihood

that every so often one of these may formulate concepts entirely by chance that are both accurate and unexpected (Sagan 1993: 82). But when we consider Dogon cosmology we find too many details that are difficult to be accounted for by mere chance.

Dogon beliefs about the star Sirius are even more astonishing than their knowledge of Saturn and Jupiter or the orbits of the planets. Sirius is the brightest star in the heavens and is clearly visible to the naked eye. The Dogon say that Sirius has an invisible dark companion, which orbits it every fifty years. This dark star is said to be very small and is made of a very heavy metal that does not exist on earth (Griaule and Dieterlen 1976: 44).

This is an extraordinary piece of information. As the renowned astronomer Carl Sagan (1993: 82–83) has observed,

> The remarkable fact is that the visible star, Sirius A, does have an extraordinary dark companion, Sirius B, which orbits it in an elliptical orbit once each 50.4 [plus/minus 0.09] years. Sirius B is the first example of a white dwarf star discovered by modern astrophysics. Its matter is in a state called "relativistically degenerate," which does not exist on Earth, and since the electrons are not bound to the nuclei in such degenerate matter, it can properly be described as metallic.[3]

How do we assess Dogon mythology about Sirius? Intrigued by this information, the British author Robert Temple suggests in his book *The Sirius Mystery* (1976) that Dogon mythology, which he traces back to ancient Egypt, is a concrete piece of evidence of past contact between humans and an advanced extraterrestrial civilization with the technology for interstellar travel. As such, this account, which is considered by UFO buffs to be incontrovertible, challenges anthropology and anthropological knowledge.

Temple has proposed a somewhat unorthodox version of a "diffusionist" explanation that is in principle similar to explanations proposed by British and German anthropologists discussed previously. Whereas the latter traced the source of all cultural creativity and inventiveness to a few advanced centers of civilizations on earth, such as Egypt, Temple goes on an interstellar excursion for his source of diffusion. Temple (1976: 5) writes that

[Dogon traditions] seem to reveal a contact in the distant past between our planet Earth and an advanced race of intelligent beings from another planetary system several light years away in space. If there is another answer to the Sirius mystery it may be even more surprising rather than less so. It certainly will not be trivial.[4]

The answer is indeed surprising, but not in the way Temple thinks.

A claim such as the one made by Temple has enormous implications for anthropology. If true, it would require that we discard much and radically revise the remainder of our existing knowledge on the evolution of culture, the development of technology, world history, and so on. The claim, however, is an extraordinary one, and prudent thinkers would agree that "extraordinary claims require extraordinary evidence" (Sagan 1993: 73). The important question then becomes whether there is extraordinary evidence to support Temple's hypothesis.

When confronted with works such as *The Sirius Mystery*, it is important to distinguish between what is reasonable and what is not, to assess the evidence with care, and to ask whether there are plausible and more parsimonious alternative explanations. We must avoid "the least plausible hypothesis." This is where epistemology becomes important. Our questions must be, How do we know what we know? How do we know what or whom to believe?

In the example under consideration, we must take into consideration, for example, that the Dogon Sirius story is embedded in a larger corpus of mythology, which is rich and complex but not very different from myths among other preindustrial cultures (Sagan 1993: 84). There is nothing in the larger corpus of Dogon mythology that corresponds to modern astronomical knowledge. Also, we might consider the fact that twins play a role in many of these stories, and it is plausible that this is the source of the idea about the existence of Sirius' companion. The elliptical orbit might be accounted for by the Dogon's preference to place an ellipse around pictures they draw and that this was mistakenly interpreted by Temple as signifying an elliptical orbit (Sagan 1993: 83).

Yet the details about Sirius and its companion are too accurate to be easily dismissed in these terms. One possibility we might consider is that the Dogon or their ancestors based their stories upon observational empirical evidence. This would be plausible if at some point in the past Sirius B had been visible to the naked eye. Since white dwarfs evolve from red giants, which are extremely bright, some astrophysicists have suggested that Sirius B and its orbit around Sirius A might have been visible in historic times.

Ancient writers in the first centuries A.D., for example Horace, described Sirius as a "red dog star," a description unlike the star's appearance today (Sagan 1993: 85). Is it possible that Sirius B was visible when it was a red giant? It is plausible, but not probable. If Sirius was a red giant in Horace's days, then there is not enough time for it to have evolved into its form today (Sagan 1993: 85). Also, it is puzzling why despite the presence of several sophisticated schools of observational astronomy in Mesopotamia, Alexandria (Egypt), China and Korea, only the ancestors of the Dogon were able to spot Sirius B (Sagan 1993: 85).

Direct observational evidence can therefore be ruled out. But this does not alter the fact that the Dogon possess information that would be impossible without the use of powerful telescopes. One may therefore conclude that since they did not have the appropriate instrumentality, they must have had contact with a technologically advanced society that possessed such instrumentation. The issue, however, is which technologically advanced society—an extraterrestrial or European one?

Temple has opted to locate this technologically advanced society in outer space, at a location many light years away. Sagan opts for the latter:

> Far more credible than an ancient extraterrestrial foray among the Dogon might be a comparatively recent contact with scientifically literate Europeans who conveyed to the Dogon the remarkable European myth of Sirius and its white dwarf companion, a myth that has all the superficial earmarks of a splendidly inventive tall story. Perhaps the contact came from a European visitor to Africa, or from the local French schools, or perhaps from contact in Europe by West Africans inducted to fight for the French in World War I. . . . The likelihood that these stories arise from contact with Europeans rather than extraterrestrials has been increased by a recent astronomical finding: a Cornell University research team led by James Elliot, employing a high-altitude airborne observatory over the Indian Ocean, discovered in 1977 that the plant Uranus is surrounded by rings—a finding never hinted at by ground-based observations. Advanced extraterrestrial beings viewing our solar system upon approach to Earth would have little difficulty discovering the rings of Uranus. But European astronomers in the nineteenth and early twentieth centuries would have had nothing to say in this regard. The fact that the Dogon do not talk of another planet beyond Saturn with rings suggests to me that their informants were European, not extraterrestrial (Sagan 1993: 85–86).[5]

But was European astronomical knowledge about Sirius known widely enough to have made its way to the Dogon? Sagan goes on to point out that the German astronomer F. W. Bessel discovered the existence of Sirius B, Sirius A's dark companion in 1844. He deduced the existence of a companion star on the basis of the long-term motion of Sirius A, which was not straight but wavy in relation to the background of distant stars. Bessel inferred that Sirius had a dark companion whose gravitational influence was responsible for the observable motion of Sirius A. Because the period of wobbliness was fifty years, Bessel concluded that the dark com-

panion had a period of equal length in the joint motion of Sirius A and B around their common center of mass (Sagan 1993: 86).

The dark companion was visually detected in 1862. By 1915 it had been established that Sirius B was very small, and that it had a higher density than the larger and brighter Sirius A. The idea that Sirius B was a very dense star, a white dwarf, was thus generally accepted and widely reported during the early twentieth century. In his popular book *The Nature of the Physical World* (1928), Sir Arthur Stanley Eddington (1882–1944) wrote that

> [a]stronomical evidence seems to leave practically no doubt that in the so-called *white dwarf* stars the density of matter far transcends anything of which we have terrestrial experience; in the Companion of Sirius, for example, the density is about a ton to the cubic inch. This condition is explained by the fact that the high temperature and correspondingly intense agitation of the material breaks up (ionises) the outer electron system of the atoms, so that the fragments can be packed much more closely together (in Sagan 1993: 87).[6]

Eddington's book, Sagan points out, was reprinted ten times in English and was translated into several languages, including French. The information about the binary star system was therefore widely available. In 1925, R. H. Fowler suggested that white dwarfs were made of electron degenerate matter. Between 1934 and 1937, sometime just prior to Griaul's recording of the Dogon Sirius legend, a major debate was taking place regarding the composition of the white dwarf, making sensational scientific headlines and was being disseminated among popular audiences. Sagan therefore offers a more parsimonious explanation of the Dogon Sirius myth in comparison with Temple's hypothesis, as a case of the diffusion of ideas, not from outer space, but from a European source.

An explanation is parsimonious in relation to a competing account if it has fewer concepts and the relationships between the concepts are less complex (Hempel 1965: 40–41). Sagan's account is more parsimonious than that of Temple, whose position requires that we assume the possibility of a series of conditions. These include the existence of intelligent extraterrestrial beings, human and extraterrestrial contact and communication, faster than the speed of light space travel, the existence of extraterrestrial beings possessing advanced space travel capabilities but ignorant of the existence of the rings of Uranus, the preservation of a highly detailed oral account for over five thousand years in one specific place, and so forth. Sagan's explanation is as follows:

> I can picture a Gallic visitor to the Dogon people, in what was then French West Africa, in the early part of this century. He may have been a diplomat, an explorer, an adventurer or an early anthropologist. Such people—for example, Richard Francis Burton—were in West Africa many decades earlier. The conversation turns to astronomical lore. Sirius is the brightest star in the sky. The Dogon regale the visitor with their Sirius mythology. Then, smiling politely, expectantly, they inquire of their visitor what *his* Sirius myth might be. Perhaps he refers before answering to a well-worn book in his baggage. The white dwarf companion of Sirius being a current astronomical sensation, the traveler exchanges a spectacular myth for a routine one. After he leaves, his account is remembered, retold, and eventually incorporated into the corpus of Dogon mythology— or at least into a collateral branch (perhaps filed under "Sirius myths, bleached peoples' account"). When Marcel Griaule makes mythological inquiries in the 1930s and 1940s, he has his own European Sirius myth played back to him (Sagan 1993: 87–88).[7]

This is what Sagan refers to as the "full-cycle return" of a myth to its culture of origin by way of the unwary ethnographer. This is indicative of the predicament of the anthropologist conducting field research in a world grown small.

There are many examples to suggest that such full-cycle returns have taken place frequently. The cultural constructionist anthropological writer James Clifford (1986: 116) provides the following "true story":

A student of African ethno-history is conducting field research in Gabon. He is concerned with the Mpongwé, a coastal group who, in the nineteenth century, were active in contacts with European traders and colonists. The "tribe" still exists, in the region of Libreville, and the ethno-historian has arranged to interview the current Mpongwé chief about traditional life, religious ritual, and so on. In preparation for his interview the researcher consults a compendium of local customs compiled in the early twentieth century by a Gabonese Christian. Before meeting the Mpongwé chief the ethnographer copies out a list of religious terms, institutions and concepts, recorded and defined by Raponda-Walker. The interview will follow this list, checking whether the customs persist, and if so, with what innovations. At first things go smoothly, with the Mpongwé authority providing descriptions and interpretations of the terms suggested; however, when the researcher asks about a particular word, the chief seems uncertain, knits his brows. "Just a moment," he says cheerfully, and disappears into his house to return with a copy of Raponda-Walker's compendium. For the rest of the interview the book lies open in his lap.[8]

A similar story has been reported about an ethnographer conducting research among Native Americans. There is also the case of Dr. Carleton Gajdusek, the Nobel Prize–winning researcher who studied the transmission of a viral disease called *kuru* among the Fore people of New Guinea. During a rainstorm, when Gajdusek and his team of researchers were in a Fore village and confined indoors, their Fore hosts entertained them by singing songs. Gajdusek reciprocated by singing Russian songs, including "*Otchi Chornye.*" The villagers were pleased and asked him to sing the song many times. A few years later, while Gajdusek was gathering examples of local music in another part of Fore territory, he asked a group of young men to go through their repertoire of songs. One of the songs turned out to be "*Otchi Chornye*" (Sagan 1993: 90–91). The local people considered it a traditional song and had no knowledge of its source. Gajdusek recounts several other examples of such diffusion among the Fore.

A naive ethnomusicologist, working on the assumption that this part of New Guinea has been unaffected by outside influences (an assumption once commonly held by Western writers about many parts of the world), would be confronted by a great mystery indeed upon finding that a song sung by an isolated "primitive people" resembles the famous Russian folk song (Sagan 1993: 90–91). A similar situation may have confronted Griaule on his visit to Dogon territory.

These examples illustrate just some of the tricky problems one can encounter when attempting to learn the "ancient legends" of contemporary "primitive peoples." Not knowing who has visited an area before, it is difficult to know just what one is recording, pristine local myths, if such things even exist, or tall tales obtained from a previous traveler. As Sagan (1993: 94) observes,

> I wonder if the Dogon, having heard from a Westerner an extraordinarily inventive myth about the star Sirius—a star already important in their own mythology—did not carefully play it back to the visiting French anthropologist. Is this not more likely than a visit by extraterrestrial spacefarers to ancient Egypt, with one cluster of hard scientific knowledge, in striking contradiction to common sense, preserved by oral tradition, over the millennia, and only in West Africa? . . . There are too many loopholes, too many alternative explanations for such a myth to provide reliable evidence of past extraterrestrial contact.[9]

Clifford (1988: 10–17) has noted that cases such as the one he describes in Gabon occur frequently and are an indication that our postmodern world is one of multivocal exchanges that are part of a pervasive global process erasing and creating new traditions. Under the new circumstances (although this process seem to go back to the early decades of the twentieth-century and ultimately centuries prior to that) cultural data does not move from oral account to written

one, Clifford points out, but from "text to text" and "inscription becomes transcription" (Clifford 1986: 116). For Clifford these full-circle returns are important because they reveal the complex circumstances ethnographers confront and how traditional ethnographic approaches are no longer appropriate under such changed circumstances.

Writers who disregard method, scholarly conventions, and rules of evidence are ill equipped to deal with accounts such as the Dogon Sirius myth. Would they treat it as a fiction? One interpretation among many? A local truth? Equally valid as modern astrophysics? It is unwise and intellectually irresponsible to abandon rules of evidence and the requirements of science when dealing with paranormal and UFO phenomena. The paranormal, which includes extraterrestrial visitations as well as astrology, clairvoyance, faith healing, pyramid power, and so on, poses a challenge to anthropological knowledge. If such claims could be proven, they would demonstrate that anthropological understanding is a sham and a delusion (cf. Lett 1997: 68). However, such accounts have always either been falsified, or are not falsifiable at all, and are thus unscientific.

Those embracing subjective methods devoid of procedures and rules of evidence with which claims to knowledge could be assessed are at a great disadvantage (Lett 1997: 71–72). Some of these cultural constructionist anthropologists seriously entertain the possibility that paranormal hypotheses may indeed explain certain phenomena, such as spirits breaking objects, shape-shifting (i.e., humans transforming themselves into animals), and so forth that they have supposedly encountered during fieldwork (e.g., Jackson 1989: 13; Stoller 1986: 55). Yet a casual glance at the massive available literature encompassing over a century of rigorous scholarship would show paranormal hypotheses have been decisively falsified (Lett 1999: 113).

This is a lapse into a kind of gullibility that is inexcusable for anthropologists, whose job is to advance our understanding of the world rather than promulgate nonsense and thus contribute to its mystification (Lett 1999: 113). Such scholarship, moreover, undermines the credibility of anthropology as a discipline. If anthropologists are incapable of judging the epistemological status of ludicrous claims such as shape-shifting, then it is rather unreasonable to expect or assume that anyone would believe what they have to say about any significant matters, such as racism, war, poverty, overpopulation, and terrorism (cf. Lett 1997: 72).

Adopting the cultural constructionist approach, we must grant Temple's extraterrestrial hypotheses equal validity as Sagan's account, and moreover, we must consider Dogon mythology as a whole to be as valid as Euro-American astrophysics. It would not matter, whether the Dogon developed their Sirius myth independently, or if they acquired their knowledge of astrophysics from ancient Egyptians, who in turn obtained it from the crew of the Starship Enterprise or a European traveler.

However, the source of such knowledge is important. As already pointed out, evidence of extraterrestrial contact would have revolutionary implications and must therefore be put to close and rigorous epistemological inspection. Those who maintain otherwise, declaring epistemology dead, irrelevant, or both, undermine the credibility of the discipline of anthropology.

DIFFUSIONISM AND PSEUDOSCIENTIFIC THEORIES OF CULTURE

Alternative histories, as exemplified by the works of Temple and Von Däniken, have recently been revived following the publication of Graham Hancock's *Fingerprints of the Gods* (1995). Works of this sort attempt to explain the origins of "civilization" by postulating contact with some forgotten ancient culture, such as Atlantis or some other lost Golden Age civilization (Oppenheimer 1999). These works are saturated with mind boggling unrestrained speculations, flawed reasoning, and disregard of established facts and rules of evidence (all the errors of pseudoscience as discussed in Chapter 2). They are cleverly written to feed the cravings of popular audiences disaffected by conventional wisdom and science but possessed with a yearning for the fantastic and the implausible.

Proponents of such bogus "theories" capitalize upon the gullibility of a public, eager to hear about the spiritual and mystical forces shaping human history, the evidence of which is allegedly locked inside the Pyramid of Giza, or the Sphinx, or some other ancient architectural wonder. Such accounts have far more emotional appeal than the mundane scholarly accounts, which seem to take the fun and mystery out of things.

The pseudohistorians, conspiracy theorists, and UFO writers also capitalize upon their readers' lack of a basic comprehension of science and scientific standards as well as upon the present widespread antiscience, irrationalist, anti-intellectual climate. Sagan's (1995: 6) observation on this point is worth noting: "If it were widely understood that claims to knowledge require adequate evidence before they can be accepted, there would be no room for pseudoscience." Pseudoscience is popular because it exploits our emotional "awestruck responses to ancient monuments" (Fagan and Hale 2001). "The lure of the marvelous blunts our critical faculties" (Sagan 1995: 50).

Like Rivers, Smith, Perry, and the German diffusionists, writers such as Däniken and Hancock also subscribe to the assumption that "primitive" (i.e., indigenous) people are uninventive or too stupid to have achieved anything on their own. This view not only divests indigenous people of their rightful cultural heritage, as noted previously, but it is also erroneous. As Sagan (1993: 63) has pointed out, all of the evidence and artifacts used to support "spaceman theories" have "plausible and simpler explanations." The same is true of the New Atlantis beliefs. Sagan adds that Däniken and writers like him overlook an important fact:

> Our ancestors were no dummies. They may have lacked high technology, but they were as smart as we, and they sometimes combined dedication, intelligence and hard work to produce results that impress even us (Sagan 1993: 63).[10]

Diffusionist theories, such as the ones proposed by Schmidt concerning the evolution of religion, or those proposed by Däniken and Hancock, appear to fulfill deep emotional needs and ideological agendas, and this seems to be the reason for their popularity. As Stiebing (1984: 171) has pointed out,

> These are people who want to believe, regardless of the evidence. For such individuals it would seem that the unscientific, quasi-religious, and anti-establishment nature of the theories is important. . . . In some ways, popular theories function in the way myths do in primitive cultures. They resolve psychological dilemmas and provide answers for the unknown and unknowable.

Alternate histories engendered by epistemological relativism and the idea that everything is interpretation, one interpretation is as good as another, and that facts, rules of evidence and validation are irrelevant have a dangerous side. As Fagan and Hale (2001: 85) have pointed out,

> When history is decoupled from rational analysis, and careful scrutiny of evidence is superseded by speculation and bald assertion, history is transformed into myth. People whose sense of history has become mythologized can be very dangerous. A striking example of this is the role Atlantis played in Nazi ideology. It was considered the original home of the Aryans, the first great civilization from which all others had arisen. . . . there are striking parallels between the New Atlantis and the ideas expressed by the numerous *volkisch* ("people's") groups in Germany after the First World War. There is the same fascination with "original" cultures and even an obsession with arcane astronomy. Heinrich Himmler was an enthusiast for many of these ideas and founded the Ahnenerbe as a branch of the SS to promote this

alternative archaeology and anthropology in the service of the Third Reich's racial ideology. The dire consequences of that ideology are obvious.[11]

ASSESSMENT

Diffusionist anthropologists failed to answer a number of important questions regarding culture change. For example, why, despite long periods of contact, have some groups maintained their own distinctive ways of life, while others have adopted customs, practices, and technologies of cultures with which they have come into contact? Such evidence suggests that diffusion is not an automatic outcome of contact in every case and in every place. Also, cultures borrow selectively, rather than incorporating every trait with which they come into contact. The British and German anthropologists ignored the selective nature of diffusion (Ember and Ember 2002: 273).

Moreover, diffusion cannot account for the fact that societies that did not have contact have demonstrated extraordinary parallels in their evolutionary development on nearly every continent on earth. Parallel evolution refers to the development of similar adaptations by two or more sociocultural systems in response to similar causal forces (cf. Harris 1997: 431). Good examples of this are the rise of pristine states, which evolved independently in at least six or seven places, as discussed previously, and the transition from hunting-gathering to farming modes of production.

The diffusionists attempted to bypass the problem of parallel evolution by assuming that human history was characterized by free, continuous, multidirectional contact between cultures, whether empirical evidence was present or not. In other words, cross-cultural similarities were explained in terms of diffusion even though no evidence of contact could be found. Diffusion was treated as a given. However, archeological and ethnographic evidence does not support this position. Because diffusionists treated historical contact as the only force in cultural development, they neglected to pay attention to ecological and demographic factors that could have resulted in similar developments. They did not consider that similarities between two cultures could be the result of their occupying similar environments.

Another shortcoming of the diffusionist perspective was that it downplayed the role of independent inventions. Someone somewhere had to have invented a trait that has diffused. It is therefore necessary to know the conditions that lead to the development of new customs and practices in the first place. Citing miraculous intervention, such as God physically appearing on earth (or in the modern variants, singular extraterrestrial visitations), or suggesting unique, singular circumstances, such as the inundation of the Nile, are scientifically unacceptable, at least not without overwhelming evidence.

Chapter 6

Historical Particularism: The Anthropology of Franz Boas and the Demise of Theory

One of the central figures in American anthropology was Franz Boas (1858–1942). He has been hailed as the father of modern anthropology in the United States. Boas did not invent anthropology; there was already a strong ethnological tradition in the United States associated with such individuals as Henry Schoolcraft (1793–1864), James Mooney (1861–1921), Frank Hamilton Cushing (1857–1900), and Lewis Henry Morgan, among others. What Boas did was to reconfigure the discipline along entirely different epistemological assumptions and methodological premises. He also set forth a new intellectual agenda for the discipline.

The Boasian paradigm, called Historical Particularism or the American Historical School, was built around the concept of culture and the principle of cultural relativism. It continues to exert considerable effects upon anthropological thought in the United States (cf. Adams 1998: 298–316; Cerroni-Long 1999: 2; Stocking 1974: 1). Boas and the cadre of students trained by him put into place the foundation upon which "modern" American anthropology was

built (cf. Rohner and Rohner 1969: xxx; Stocking 1974: 1).

Boas sought to transform anthropology into an empirically grounded scientific enterprise. Although Boas and his students expended considerable effort toward this goal, the Boasian paradigm contained within it elements that were fundamentally incompatible with the establishment of a scientific anthropology. Ever since, American anthropology has been struggling with this paradoxical situation or internal contradiction. The predicament of contemporary anthropology and the "culture wars" plaguing the field are in part rooted in the inherently antiscientific elements of the Boasian paradigm.

When the anthropologist Marvin Harris wrote his book *Cultural Materialism* (2001a [1979]), he excluded Boasian anthropology from detailed consideration. Harris (2001a: 117) had reasonable justification for doing so, considering that his work focused upon the viable and most influential theoretical strategies in anthropology at the time. In the present study, Boasian anthro-

Franz Boas, expositor of cultural determinism who established the foundations of modern anthropology in the United States by defining its subject matter, instituting rigorous standards for empirical data collection, and stressing the primacy of culture over biology. Boas is shown here posing as a Kwakiutle hamatsa dancer for a museum display.

pology is treated in great detail for a number of reasons. First, the inherent and long-standing interpretive, relativistic, idiosyncratic, and theory-phobic trend in American cultural anthropology that embodies the cultural constructionist approaches that emerged during the 1980s is in part derived from Boasian anthropology.

Second, a discussion of the Boasian paradigm illustrates the futility of research programs that lack the essential elements of a viable scientific approach, regardless of how rigorous and empiricist they are in their methodology. These elements include a parsimonious, generalizing perspective, material causation, and evolutionary holism, all of which are absent from Boas's perspective. As Sanderson (1990: 47) has said of Boasian anthropology, "It was rigorously scientific in its deep respect for empirical documentation of assertions, it was profoundly antiscientific in its focus on the particular rather than the general." Those who usually rise to the defense of Boas "the scientists" hold the erroneous idea that empiricism and science are one and the same.

Having said all of this, it is also necessary to point out that the problems noted here do not detract from Boas's overall contributions to the discipline. These include defining its subject matter, insisting on field research as the primary means of data collection, establishing rigorous standards of empirical accuracy, and extricating anthropology from racialist premises by separating the concept of culture from biology (Magli 2001: 78).

In this chapter I shall examine the key concepts, central premises, and the intellectual agenda of Boas's anthropology. I leave the treatment of the works of the cadre of students trained by Boas to the following chapter.

BOAS: FROM PHYSICS TO ANTHROPOLOGY

Boas was born and raised in Germany, where he received training in physics, mathematics, and geography. He earned his doctorate in 1881 upon the completion of his dissertation, which was entitled "Contributions to the Understanding of the Color of Water." Boas's interest in anthropology began in earnest in 1883 when he visited Baffin Island in the Northwest Territories of Canada (see Stocking 1968: 133–160). His experiences among the **Inuit** (Eskimo) confirmed his beliefs in the importance of first-hand data collection through fieldwork and launched him on a career in anthropology.

Boas returned home to Germany soon after his Baffinland expedition. But by 1886 he was back in America to conduct field research in British Columbia, among the Kwakiutl of the Northwest Coast (see Boas 1966; Rohner and Rohner 1970) and would devote the next sixty years of his life to the study of Northwest Coast peoples and cultures (Rohner and Rohner 1969: xii).

Following his 1886 expedition, Boas accepted the position of assistant editor of the journal *Science,* married, became an American citizen, and took up residence in the United States. Here his academic career flourished, and over the coming years Boas began to dominate the field of anthropology (Langness 1993: 54).

Boas's overall accomplishments in the field are staggering. Aside from Baffinland and the Northwest Coast work, he also conducted fieldwork in New Mexico, Mexico, and Puerto Rico. His other achievements included founding the American Folk-Lore Society (1888), revamping the journal *American Anthropologist* (1898), providing impetus for the establishment of the American Anthropological Association (1902), reviving the American Ethnological Society (1900), and launching the *International Journal of American Linguistics* (1917). In addition, he published 700 articles and a half dozen books and trained an entire generation of anthropologists (see Rohner and Rohner 1969: 309–313).

Finally, to Boas goes the honor of having supervised the first Ph.D. in anthropology in the United States. This was granted to Alexander Chamberlain (1865–1914), in 1892, at Clark University in Worcester, Massachusetts, where Boas taught from 1889 to 1892 (Rohner and Rohner 1969: 310). As Harris (2001b: 252) has put it,

Boas' accomplishments as a teacher, administrator, researcher, founder and president of societies, editor, lecturer, and traveler are exhausting to behold. To anyone who has ever worried about publishing or perishing, the fact that all of this activity was accompanied by the publication of a torrent of books and articles is well-nigh terrifying.[1]

It was Boas and his students who transformed anthropology into a university-based academic profession. During this time Columbia University became the epicenter of American anthropology. There Boas trained some of the most distinguished anthropologists of the twentieth century: Alfred Kroeber, Ruth Benedict, Margaret Mead, Robert Lowie, Edward Sapir, Melville Herskovits, Alexander Goldenweiser, Paul Radin, Clark Wissler, Ashley Montagu, and many others. They, in turn, joined or created departments of anthropology throughout the United States, where Boas's perspective was taught to a new generation of anthropologists. As a group, the Boasians dominated the discipline during most of the first half of the century.

Boas was primarily a cultural anthropologist, although his interests and expertise extended into physical anthropology, linguistics, and archaeology. The influence of Boas's model of multifaceted research program and his holistic conception of the field upon his students gave American anthropology its unique four-field perspective. This is something that did not develop in Britain or on the Continent, where the fields of physical anthropology and archaeology remained separate from cultural anthropology (cf. Lesser 1981: 3; Stocking 1974: 14).

BOAS AND ANTHROPOLOGY IN AMERICA

When Boas arrived upon the anthropological scene in the United States, unilineal evolutionism and Social Darwinism, associated with the ideas of writers such as Lewis Henry Morgan and Herbert Spencer, were the dominant theoretical perspectives (Harris 2001b: 254). Social

Darwinism was a racist ideological perspective that emerged out of the merger of nineteenth-century evolutionary anthropological thought and the idea that cultural evolution is linked to biological evolution.

Social Darwinists posited the existence of innate biological differences linked to differences in intelligence, the capacity for language, and modes of behavior. Biological evolution and cultural evolution were thus fused into a single explanatory scheme. This position is known as **biological determinism** (see Kennedy 1973; see Gould 1996 for a critique of present-day biological determinism). According to this view, cultural differences denoted racial or biological differences. It followed therefore that the reason Euro-Americans occupied the top of the evolutionary ladder of progress, while other groups were at lower levels of the evolutionary scale, was because Euro-Americans were biologically superior to all other people.

For Social Darwinists the driving force of evolutionary change was the law of "survival of the fittest" (see Carneiro 1967: ix–lvii; Sanderson 1990: 28). Herbert Spencer (1820–1903) postulated it on the basis of his interpretation of Thomas Malthus's (1766–1834) idea that populations grow faster than their food supplies and this leads to a "struggle for survival." Cultural evolution was thus construed as struggle of all against all from which only the fittest or racially superior emerged victorious.

Put in these terms, Social Darwinism was a dogma that justified white supremacy, slavery, colonialism, imperialism, the political domination of indigenous people, and genocide as natural and preordained, the working out of the "laws" of evolutionary development. Social Darwinism was highly compatible with right wing politics and offered a convenient theory to justify capitalism and free enterprise and the rational for attacking government intercession, socialism, and communism (S. Barrett 1996: 52).

Writers such as Spencer went as far as to advocate that efforts had to be made to avoid in-

Herbert Spencer, a major nineteenth-century evolutionist and key exponent of the racist doctrine of Social Darwinism.

terference with evolutionary development. He recommended a halt to charity and assistance to the impoverished classes and "inferior races," as these would only prolonged their wretchedness and delayed the inevitable (Harris 1983: 321).

Boas entered into the intellectual arena, bringing with him the intimacy of focus acquired through his own ethnographic field experiences. It was clear to him that the evolutionist had grossly misrepresented indigenous peoples and their intellectual capabilities. What was being touted as scientific anthropology was, for Boas, nothing more than the racist, prejudicial, and ethnocentric beliefs of the expositors of such views.

Boas formulated his anthropological position in response to the prevailing ideas and assumptions about the nature of sociocultural phenomena and the meaning of cultural diversity (Stocking 1974: 17). This illustrates a point noted earlier, that new paradigms are shaped by a dialectical relationship with preceding paradigms that affect the manner in which their epistemological and theoretical principles are expressed (cf. Barrett 1984; Erickson and Murphy 2001: xi; McGee and Warms 2000: 2).

REJECTION OF EVOLUTIONARY THEORY

Boas attacked his evolutionary foes on empirical, theoretical, and methodological grounds. He also challenged the idea that culture and biology (i.e., race) are connected. While doing so, Boas offered an alternative approach for anthropological inquire. I shall discuss Boas's rejoinder to evolutionism in each of these areas.

Empirical Issues

Boas challenged the evolutionists for forwarding speculative models that lacked adequate empirical foundations. The majority of nineteenth-century evolutionists, we might recall, relied upon information gathered from material furnished by travelers, traders, colonial officers, and missionaries. Boas asserted that a science of anthropology could not rest upon such flimsy foundations and he accused his rivals of being "armchair" anthropologists.

In place of the kinds of unrestraint speculations that characterized much of the ethnological works of the time Boas suggested firsthand empirical fieldwork and systematic collection of information on the cultures around the world. In absence of concrete empirical evidence on a range of cultures to back up models and schemes, Boas argued, theories and schemes were worthless. As he put it,

> Unless we know how the culture of each group of man came to be what it is we cannot expect to reach any conclusions in regard to the conditions controlling the general history of culture (Boas 1940: 230).[2]

Boas thus set a new agenda for anthropology as he envisioned it, the systematic empirical documentation and description of cultural diversity.

Theoretical Issues

Boas also attacked the evolutionary perspective on theoretical grounds. First, he questioned the process of cultural evolution itself. His rejoinder to the idea of all cultures passing through the same fixed stages of evolutionary progress was to point out that the theory was wrong because diffusion interferes with any such process. Boas cited cases that involving cultures that had skipped the presumably fixed stages of evolutionary development. For example, he pointed out that as a result of contact, certain African tribes had gone directly from the use of stone technology to iron technology, bypassing the evolutionists' fixed stages of stone–bronze–iron (White 1987a [1959]: 139). This example became part of the Boasians' antievolutionary arsenal, which they often cited as a demonstration that diffusion negates evolution.

Second, Boas questioned the idea of progress so central to the work of nineteenth-century evolutionists. Many of the evolutionary schemes of Boas's time were devised through the random selection of traits without reference to historical or geographic contexts and the arbitrary arrangement of cultures along a hierarchy of stages of progress and complexity based upon criteria derived from European culture. In its crudest rendition, nineteenth-century evolutionism held that all cultures evolve through the same stages, from simple forms to more complex ones, as they progressed from the stage of "savagery" to "barbarism" to "civilization."

Boas objected to these schemes and maintained that evaluating other cultures in terms of Western concepts such as "progress" or "complexity" was impossible and ethnocentric. As he pointed out,

> We may recognize progress in a definite direction in the development of invention and knowledge. . . .

It is not easy to define progress in any phase of social life other than in knowledge and control of nature. . . . It is difficult to define progress in ethical ideas. It is still more difficult to discern universally valid progress in social organization, for what we choose to call progress depends upon standards chosen. The extreme individualist might consider anarchy his ideal. Others may believe in extreme voluntary regimentation (in White 1987b [1947]: 71–72).[3]

Alluding to the situatedness of cultural standards and the need for the anthropologist to adopt a relativistic perspective, Boas added further that

[t]he question of development in a definite direction is closely connected to our concept of progress. The very concept of progress presupposes a standard toward which a culture advances, and a decision cannot be avoided what this standard is to be. It seems almost unavoidable that this standard will be based on our own experience, on our own civilization. It is clear that this is an arbitrary standard and it is perhaps the greatest value of anthropology that makes us acquainted with a great variety of such standards. Before the question can be decided as to what progress is, we must know whether general human values exist by which we may measure progress (Boas 1938: 676).[4]

The evolutionists, Boas observed, were working on the basis of unproven assumptions. Their models did not derive from ethnographic data but were inventions that they imposed upon what flimsy information they did have. For example, one could arguable say that a flintlock rifle is more complex than the bow and arrow. But how, Boas queried, can we say that European religions, forms of marriage, family types, or landholding and property rights are at a higher evolutionary level than those of other cultures? How can we say that patrilinieal organization evolved from matrilinial kinship systems? On what grounds can one say that monogamous marriage is more advanced or more complex than polygynous or polyandrous marriage patterns?

Similarly, Boas asked, on what ethnographic basis can one say that monotheism is at a higher evolutionary stage than animism or polytheism or that the latter two preceded the former? According to what ethnographic criteria could one say that private ownership of property somehow represented progress over communal or corporate forms of land tenure? Various institutions differ from one culture to another, Boas argued, and there are no scientific criteria on the basis of which we can determine that one pattern is more advance than another (Peoples and Bailey 1994: 71–72).

Boas's answer to the problems he noted was to advocate ethnographic particularism and a relativistic approach that placed and focused attention on each culture's unique historical and geographical contexts.

Methodological Issues

Boas also challenged nineteenth-century evolutionism on methodological grounds. He questioned the idea that "similar cultural developments were due to similar causes." In doing so, Boas launched anthropology on a trajectory that was incompatible with all efforts at developing scientific anthropology. As Boas put it,

Anthropological research which compares similar cultural phenomena from various parts of the world, in order to discover the uniform history of their development, makes the assumption that the same ethnological phenomenon has everywhere developed in the same manner. Here lies the flaw in the argument of [this] method, for no such proof can be given. Even the most cursory review shows that the same phenomena may develop in a multitude of ways (Boas 1940: 273).[5]

Moreover, Boas noted,

The evolutionary point of view presupposes that the course of historical change in the cultural life of mankind follows definite laws which are applicable everywhere, and which bring about cultural development is, in its main lines, the same among all races and all peoples. . . . As soon as we admit that the hypothesis of a uniform evolution has to be proved before it can be accepted, the whole structure loses its foundations (1940: 281).[6]

Boas argued that efforts at cross-cultural comparisons and efforts to produce generalizations had to wait until the detailed ethnographic evidence was in hand:

> We cannot say that *the occurrence of the same phenomenon is always due to the same causes,* and that thus it is proved that the human mind obeys the same laws everywhere. We must demand that the causes from which it developed be investigated and that comparisons be restricted to those phenomena which have been proved to be effects of the same causes. We must insist that this investigation be made a preliminary to all extended comparative studies (Boas 1940: 275).[7]

Boas's reply was that "unlike causes produce like effects" (Boas 1887: 485). This shift of emphasis upon ethnographic particularism would become the basis for subsequent antiscience, antigeneralizing approaches in American anthropology.

By rejecting the idea that "like causes will have like effects" Boas in effect dismissed the axiom upon which are founded scientific generalizations and theory-construction (cf. Gellner 1982: 188). It was a rejection of the nomothetic or generalizing approach in favor of an idiographic, or particularizing, approach. What Boas proposed as a remedy for the evolutionists' bad science was, in other words, a rejection of science itself. Although incompatible with science, Boas's stance was highly compatible with interpretive, idiographic orientations that have since dominated mainstream American cultural anthropology.

Boas did not start out with the intention of eradicating science from American anthropology. On the contrary, he was striving for a more rigorous and empirically grounded scientific discipline. Initially, he was also open to the possibility that "laws of culture" would someday be discovered through cross-cultural comparisons. He saw such developments as contingent upon an accurate database (Boas 1940: 276). Without this

it would be impossible to determine whether the "things" being compared belonged to the same class or only resembled one another superficially. Thus, as Boas saw it, only after the "facts were in" would the laws of culture be laid bare. In other words, what Boas did was to call for a moratorium on theorizing until such an ethnographic database was completed. His big mistake was to treat data collection as if it was a separate activity from theoretical frameworks that guide field research.

Wittingly or unwittingly, Boas committed himself to an antiscience stance. His moratorium on generalizations and theory construction became a permanent state of affairs and Boas himself spent the remainder of his career happily refuting anthropological generalizations of all kinds. The anthropologist Murray Wax (1956: 63) captures in the following passage the essence of Boas's intellectual enterprise:

> The form of a typical ethnological study by Franz Boas was as follows: A general hypothesis about culture or about cultural processes had been advanced by some scholar. Boas would then collect a considerable mass of data of the most objective kind—material objects or texts. He would then describe these succinctly and with little or no interpretation. The data, so presented, would speak for themselves: they were an exception to the general hypothesis and it was therefore refuted. Then Boas would present his own point of view: the situation was a complex one; the refuted hypothesis had ignored the complexities; a full analysis, if humanly possible, would reveal many factors in operation. . . . The logic of his argument was simple and potent. The hypothesis advanced could be framed in the from, "All *A* is B." Boas would then present an entity that was clearly an *A* and yet equally not B. Accordingly the hypothesis was false.

In Chapter 2, it was noted that science is about finding errors and eliminating false conclusions again and again. What Boas did was incompatible with science because his objective was not to eliminate untenable hypotheses so as to make room for better hypotheses, but rather to altogether discredit this mode of inquiry. As Wax (1956: 63) adds,

> This logic was and is frequently utilized by natural scientists. But the aim there is usually not to discredit completely but to test the limits, to discover the region where the hypothesis applies and where it fails. Then the scientists attempt to reformulate the hypothesis so that in its revised form it fits both regions. But Boas was not interested in the partial truth that might be implicit in the refuted generalization; as a *generalization* it was wholly false and should no longer receive any respect whatsoever from the scientist. He would, therefore, attack it over and over again in his publications and in his classes.

The Biology and Culture Issue

Boas also set out to purge anthropology of the evolutionists' biological determinism, or to de-biologize culture (Harris 1999: 67–77). He did this by bringing to bear a large body of ethnographic data to show the degree to which the evolutionists had distorted indigenous people's ingenuity, linguistic sophistication, intelligence, and sociocultural accomplishments. Boas attacked the biological determinism of his rivals by calling into question the validity of racial typologies and the suggested linkages between biology and language/culture/modes of thought/behavior.

With respect to racial categories, Boas argued that biological determinists had grossly underestimated the degree of variability in each human population. The racial category into which evolutionists assigned different groups, he wrote, "contains so many individuals of different hereditary make-up that the average differences between races freed of elements determined by history cannot readily be ascertained, but appear as insignificant" (Boas 1940: 248).

As for the linkages biological determinists postulated between race and language/culture/modes of thought, Boas (1938 [1911]: 151) wrote that

anatomical type, language and culture have not necessarily the same fates; that a people may remain constant in type and language, and change in culture; that it may remain constant in type, but change in language; or it may remain constant in language, and change in type and culture.[8]

From this, Boas (1911: 146) concluded, "We are led to the conclusion that that [biological] type, language, and type of culture are not closely and permanently connected."

With respect to the idea that race and modes of thought/behavior are somehow linked, Boas noted that "in the few cases in which the influence of culture upon mental reaction of populations has been investigated it can be shown that culture is a much more important determinant than bodily build" (Boas 1940: 230). He added,

> A critical investigation shows that forms of thought and action which we are inclined to consider as based on human nature are not generally valid, but characteristic of our specific culture (Boas 1940: 258).[9]

Boas (1911: 143) went on to point out that

> [o]ur brief consideration of some of the mental activities of man in civilized and in primitive society has led us to the conclusion that the functions of the human mind are common to the whole of humanity.

It was Boas's position that although all human minds work alike—a perspective akin to the notion of "psychic unity of mankind" of the evolutionists—he suggested diversity and infinite expression in modes of thought due to the effects of individual cultures (Boas 1901: 1). The roots of ideas such as the radical plurality and incommensurability of cultures, which are central postulates of today's cultural constructionist perspectives, are to be found here.

Another means of undermining the idea of fixed racial typologies for Boas was to demonstrate that the variables upon which those typologies were based were plastic and subject to change. One such variable was the **cephalix index,** the ratio of the length and breadth of the head, which was considered fixed genetically and was believed to be an indicator of intelligence. Biological determinists used such measures to demonstrate the superiority of Euro-Americans over other populations.

Based on statistical analysis using a sample of some 17,000 subjects, Boas was able to show changes in the cephalix index of American-born children of immigrants within a single generation due to better nutrition and other cultural factors (Boas 1911: 74–98; see Sparks and Jantz 2002 for a reanalysis of this data). The demonstrable effects of environment and culture upon a measure that the biological determinists had treated as a fixed racial trait greatly undermined racial classifications.

Boas's case for the separation of biology and culture, which was compiled in his book *The Mind of Primitive Man* (1911), has been nicely summarized by Peoples and Bailey (1994: 34):

1. Members of any race of physical type are equally capable of learning any culture. For instance, the United States now contains people whose biological ancestors came from all parts of the world. Yet modern-day African-, Chinese-, Indian-, Irish-, Hispanic-, and Italian-Americans have far more in common in their thoughts and actions than any of them have with the peoples of their ancestral homelands.

2. An enormous range of cultural diversity occurs among members of a single race. The cultures of Africa, the Americas, Asia, the Pacific, and Europe were and are quite diverse—far too much cultural diversity is found within a single race that can be accounted for biologically.

3. Hugely different cultural systems succeed one another in time within the same race and indeed within the same society. Cultures can and regularly do undergo changes within a single human generation; these changes cannot be due to genetic changes in the population, which usually take many generations to be noticeable.[10]

THE BOASIAN PARADIGM

In answer to the prevailing anthropological theories, Boas proposed his own formulation, a paradigm built around the concept of culture and

the principle of cultural relativism. Here I shall describe Boas's paradigm and its implications with respect to anthropological thought in the United States during part of the twentieth century.

By demonstrating that culture, language, modes of thought, and biology were unrelated, Boas proposed cultural determinism and ethnographic particularism as an answer to the evolutionary models. He reformulated the concept of culture to mean distinct traditions and ways of life particular to each society. There were many different cultures, each one unique and understandable in its own terms, rather than a single culture, as the evolutionists employed the term. For the latter culture was interchangeable with "civilization," something that some societies possessed and others were progressing toward.

For Boas, it was the task of anthropology to document and describe the range of cultural variation around the globe (Cerroni-Long 1999: 2). His call for attention to context and history led him to focus upon the complexity of culture and to take notice of the innumerable factors impinging upon each culture (Boas 1940: 257). As Boas (1940: 285–286) put it,

> We . . . see that each cultural group has its own unique history, dependent partly upon the peculiar inner development of the social group, and partly upon the foreign influences to which it has been subjected. There have been processes of gradual differentiation as well as processes of leveling down differences between neighboring cultural centers.[11]

For Boas (1940: 277), the processes of historical contact and diffusion (i.e., "foreign influences" and "leveling down of differences between neighboring cultural centers") was another reason to doubt the viability of the evolutionary stages and the cultural analogies and parallels and convergences that were central to the evolutionist schemes.

Diffusion, the process of the transfer of innovations, artifacts, and other traits from one culture to another through contact and borrowing or migration was a conspicuous feature of Historical Particularism (cf. S. Barrett 1996: 52). As discussed in Chapter 5, at the time, diffusionism was the basis of two anthropological paradigms, one in Britain and the other in Germany. The British and German schools subscribed to the idea of universal diffusionism. Boas's approach was much narrower because he cautioned that the concept of diffusion was useful in charting the distribution of elements only "through a limited area." The Boasians' concept of **culture area** developed from such a construal of diffusion (see Chapter 7).

The idea of culture areas was hinted at in Boas's debate with the ethnologists Otis Mason (1838–1905) of the National Museum over the issue of arranging ethnological artifacts for display. Boas argued that artifacts should be displayed according to where they originated, while Mason wanted to display them according to their position in the evolutionary typologies. Boas's interest in the geographical diffusion and distribution of traits was one of the many ideas that would later be developed by his students (see Chapter 7).

Boas treated every culture as unique, each with its own distinctive flavor or texture, "genius," and inner dynamic, shaped by its particular historical, psychological, and social forces. Although Boas stressed the idea that cultures are wholes, he was unclear about how elements were related to the wholes. He saw culture not as an "organic growth" but rather as the result of the accretion of elements brought together by diffusion. This was very similar to the way the German historical diffusionists viewed culture.

Boas believed that elements were integrated into the whole "according to the genius of the people who borrowed it." In other words, traits were accepted or rejected because of psychological reasons. Cultural integration was psychological in nature [Hegel's *Geist* or spirit of a people], being based on a layer of unconscious categories and dominant ideas (Stocking 1974: 8). Boas himself, however, never elaborated on the question of cultural integration and the

problem was left up to his students to tackle later on. As Stocking (1974: 5) points out, "On the one hand, culture was simply the accidental accretion of individual elements. On the other, culture—despite Boas' renunciation of organic growth—was at the same time an integrated spiritual totality that somehow conditioned the form of its elements."

For Boas, cultures were conglomerates of traits and ideas accumulated over long periods of time:

> [Cultures] are not organic growths, but have gradually developed and obtained their present form by accretion of foreign materials. Much of this material must have been adopted ready-made, and had been adapted and changed in form according to the genius of the people who borrowed it (Boas 1940: 286).[12]

Boas's extrication of culture from biological factors left him with only one determinant causal force, culture itself. It was culture that shaped and molded human thought and behavior everywhere (Boas 1940: 259; Keesing and Keesing 1971: 382). **Cultural determinism,** which can be expressed in the axiom that culture-comes-from-culture, was Boas's answer to the biological determinism of the evolutionists. If culture is distinct from biology, and if culture is a determinant causal form, then it follows that culture can only be explained in terms of culture (cf. Hatch 1973: 49).

Unfortunately, Boasian cultural determinism is based upon faulty logic (i.e., circular reasoning, begging the question). Cultural determinist explanations say very little and take the form of: Culture X is different from culture Y because they are different. Yet this is the typical kind of explanation forwarded by cultural determinists (Lett 1987). The question of causal forces operating upon culture is ignored and culture is "both the *necessary* and *sufficient* cause of this thing" (D'Andrade 1999: 88).

Boas's culture-comes-from-culture principle taken to extremes bestows ontological autonomy upon culture. **Ontology** refers to premises about the nature of reality; that is, about what ultimately exists or is real (Williams 2001: 6–7). In such a construal, culture becomes a force that is above and beyond nature, something self-generating that imposes determinative influence upon nature but is itself independent of nature.

The problematic nature of this formulation and its implications for the anthropological enterprise are noted by the anthropologist Dan Sperber (1996: 10):

> The thesis of the ontological autonomy of culture is generally expressed as a series of denials: cultural facts are not biological facts; they are not psychological facts; they are not the sum of individual facts. But what, then, are they? How are they related to other kinds of facts? There are no well-argued answers to these questions. The obvious result of assuming that there is a fundamental discontinuity between the biological or the mental on the one side and the cultural on the other is to insulate anthropology from both biology and psychology, and to reject as a priori mistaken any contribution and, even more, any criticisms coming from outside. To achieve this dubious outcome, one need not develop in any detail the idea of the autonomy of culture; postulating it is enough.[13]

The ontological autonomy of culture inherent in the culture-comes-from-culture equation central to Boasian anthropology means that culture is beyond the domain of nature and not amenable to scientific analysis and all such efforts have been doomed to failure from the start (cf. Ross 1980: xv). This view, however, is highly compatible with cultural constructionist positions in anthropology. As such, the concept of culture has been an endless source of epistemological problems in American anthropology.

Boas's cultural determinist position resulted in a host of other difficulties. Geographical, ecological, economic, and demographic factors were virtually excluded as irrelevant for the explanation of cultural phenomena. With respect to environmental and geographical factors, Boas (1940: 266) wrote that

> [e]nvironmental conditions may stimulate existing cultural activities, but they have no creative force. . . . the same environment will influence culture in diverse ways. . . . Thus it is fruitless to explain culture in geographical terms.[14]

This view of the environment as a passive background that sets limits but has no determinative influence later became known as **possibilism** (see Milton 1996: 45–46). While this led a few anthropologists to carefully investigate human-environment interactions (e.g., Richards 1932, 1939), for the most part possibilism justified the near total neglect of ecological questions during most of the first part of the twentieth century (cf. Ellen 1986: 24).

Surprisingly, during his Baffin Island work (1884) Boas had focused upon the important role of geographic/environmental factors. In his book *The Central Eskimo* (1888) he in fact documented the close linkages between the location of sea ice, the movement of inshore seals, and Eskimo settlements. This, as Ellen (1986: 24) has put it, is one of the first convincing ethnographic human-environment correlations.

However, the culture-comes-from-culture perspective that Boas adopted led him to relegate ecological and environmental factors to the background. It was the same with economic explanations:

> Economists believe that economic conditions control cultural form. Economic determinism is proposed as against environmental determinism. Undoubtedly the interrelation between economics and other aspects of culture is much more immediate than that between geographical environment and culture. Still it is not possible to explain every feature of cultural life as determined by economic status. We do not see how art styles, the form of ritual or the special form of religious belief could possibly derive from economic forces. On the contrary, we see that economics and the rest of culture interact as cause and effect, as effect and cause (Boas 1940: 256).[15]

Demographic variables were similarly dismissed: "there is no evidence that density of population, stability of location, or economic status is necessarily connected with a particular system of relationship and behavior connected with it" (Boas 1938: 680).

Thus, the Boasian paradigm, centered on the idea of cultural determinism, led to the exclusion and neglect of some of the most salient process from anthropological analysis. It was only in the work of later generations of anthropologists that the significance of demographic variables and human–environment relations came to light. Such works revealed that sociocultural systems "adjust themselves in patterned and predictable ways to ecological and demographic constraints" and clarified many issues mystified by Boas's approach (Lett 1987: 91; see Boserup 1965; Cohen 1995; Graeber 1991, 1992; Harris 1997; Hawkes 1993; Keely 1988; Pfaffenberger 1992).

CULTURAL RELATIVISM

Treating each culture as a unique and distinct entity raises the problem of how one might go about investigating cultures different from that of our own. Clearly, applying standards applicable in our own culture to another is inappropriate. So what is the anthropologist to do? Boas recommended the following:

> The attempt has been made too often to formulate a genetic problem as defined by a term taken from our own civilization, either based on analogy with forms known to us or contrasted to those with which we are familiar. Thus concepts, like war, the idea of immortality, marriage regulations, have been considered units and general conclusions have been derived from their forms and distributions. It should be recognized that the subordination of all such forms, under a category with which we are familiar on account of our own cultural experience, does not prove the historical or sociological unity of the phenomenon (Boas 1940: 258).[16]

Boas stressed a relativistic point of view and advocated the concept of **cultural relativism,** the idea that each culture must be studied in its own

context and in terms of its own values and ideals rather than those of the observer. A corollary of this view is that since all standards are relative to particular cultures, the idea that one culture is superior to another is erroneous.

Cultural relativism was central to the Boasian paradigm and was treated as the precondition for "scientific objectivity." According to Boas (1938: 666), "We must . . . investigate primitive life purely and objectively." The way to do that was for the anthropologist to "divest himself entirely of opinions and emotions based upon the particular social environment into which he is born. He must adapt his own mind, so far as feasible, to that of the people whom he is studying" (Boas 1901: 1).

The kind of relativism advocated by Boas was wedded to an idiographic approach that magnified cultural differences and understated similarities. For this reason, Boas saw the task of cross-cultural comparisons as eminently problematic because of the difficulties of establishing whether units of culture being compared were in fact equivalent categories or dissimilar ones bearing only surface likenesses to each other. This kind of relativism remains a part of anthropological thought in the United States today and is the rational for the continual rejection of generalizing scientific approaches. Reduction to absurdity leads from this stance to radical epistemological relativism, in which all standards, including scientific standards, become relative and culture specific.

The question that one might raise is this: Are cultures so unique as to preclude comparisons? If so, then why aren't there as many different kinship systems as there are cultures? Why aren't there as many economic, subsistence, or political systems as there are cultures? Why is it that there are no cultures organized upon the pattern of beehives or bat colonies instead of the patterns familiar to anthropologists? Clearly, cultures have many things in common, and there are no reasons why those things cannot be fruitfully compared.

Yes, it is true that in one respect every culture is unique, just as every individual, or every grain of sand, leaf, and snowflake may be said to be unique. Those who want to look for differences between cultures, individuals, grains of sand, snowflakes will have no difficulties in identifying them (cf. Kaplan and Manners 1972: 8). However, there are similarities as well. In fact, in order to establish that something is unique in the first place we must contrast it with some other thing with which it has particular similarities. Stating differences hinges as much upon comparisons as stating similarities. Those who choose the relativistic point of view and retreat into ethnographic particularism do so on the basis of personal choices, not because of any real epistemological obstacles posed by the phenomena under investigation.

Cultural relativists ignore similarities by choice and are not concerned with their explanation. This kind of relativism stands as a needless barrier to attempts to explain cross-cultural similarities. As Kaplan and Manners (1972: 7) pointed out, taken to its logical conclusion

> all such knowledge—including the doctrine of cultural relativism itself—would be relative to the culture in which it originated or developed. And we would thus end up with an Eskimo anthropology, a Trobriand anthropology, a Nuer anthropology, and so on—with a series of cultural configurations, each of which is defined as unique and therefore not comparable.[17]

The thrust of the cultural constructionist perspectives in vogue in anthropology today is precisely in the direction noted by Kaplan and Manners.

BOAS'S FIELD METHODS

Boas is generally credited for establishing fieldwork as an essential component of anthropology. However, he did not invent ethnographic field research, nor did he develop innovative field research strategies. There was already an established tradition of fieldwork in the United States when Boas arrived on the scene (Gruber 1967). As early as the 1890s Henry Schoolcraft (1793–1864) had been engaged in intensive fieldwork among Native Americans. Then there was Lewis Henry Morgan and his field research among the Iroquois and other Native American groups (White 1951). James Mooney (1861–1921) did remarkable fieldwork focusing on the rise and spread of the Ghost Dance religion. Finally, Frank Hamilton Cushing (1857–1900) conducted five years of intensive fieldwork among the Zuñi. Cushing had not only mastered the local language, but he also lived among and participated in the daily lives of the Zuñi. There is some justification, therefore, for some writers to credit Cushing as being the pioneer of the participant-observation method in North America (Hinsley 1983: 56).

The field methods Boas himself employed were not all that different from the procedures of his contemporaries, although he tended to be more inclusive and systematic. Boas was also more diligent and critical than his contemporaries. His adherence to the high standards of empirical research was without parallel. Moreover, Boas demanded that the fieldworker learn the local language and to try and capture the "native's point of view." Boas himself often worked through interpreters (see Rohner and Rohner 1969: xxvii).

Boas also encouraged the recruitment and training of local people to collect ethnographic data in their own language. To ensure the least amount of bias during data collection, he would allow his informants to convey information without any attempts to direct the conversation towards any specific topic (Oswalt 1972: 54). He transcribed what his informants had to say verbatim and published the texts in the original language with interlinear English translations. This was an effort to allow the facts to speak for themselves, which is an analogue of what in the rhetoric of present-day antiscience writers would be referred to as an attempt to make "discursive space" for "the voices" of the Other to be heard.

In addition to the collection of texts, Boas also gathered vocabularies and investigated the grammatical features of local languages. He thus amassed a vast amount of firsthand information and, as one writer has perhaps overenthusiastically pointed out, "his success in the broadscale collection of raw data is unparalleled in the history of ethnography" (Oswalt 1972: 55). Boas also gathered data on bodily measurements through **anthropometry,** collected skeletal materials, and took photographs of human body forms (Rohner and Rohner 1969: xxiv).

A large part of Boas's fieldwork among the Kwakiutl was in the form of survey research. He moved from place to place, stayed for short intervals, and after working out a particular problem, moved on. Seldom did he live among and participate in the lives of the people he was studying. This approach was necessary in part because at the time so little was known about the area and its people (Rohner and Rohner 1969: xxvii). Thus, although Boas insisted that fieldwork was central to the anthropological enterprise, he did not approach anything close to Bronislaw Malinowski's conception of extended fieldwork through participant observation, which is discussed in a later chapter.

BOASIAN SCIENCE AND METHODOLOGY

As noted previously, Boas did not formulate an alternate theoretical scheme to replace the evolutionary paradigm. He simply offered as a substitute an idiographic approach wedded to an extremely relativistic outlook. Details were what mattered most, the idea being that once all the details were described and understood, or once all the facts were in, they would "speak for themselves" (Radin 1939: 301). As his student Ruth Benedict (1943: 33) put it, "The detailed study of particulars seemed to him more rewarding than the building of systems." Boas (1940: 644) himself wrote that "the mere occurrence of an event [a fact] claims the full attention of our mind, because we are affected by it, and it is studied without any regard to its place in the system." Boas's dictum of gather facts now and theorize later was a recipe for inductive research, in which data collection always precedes the formulation of theories (Bell 1994: 143).

Boas adopted a descriptive, inductive historical perspective over the methodology of the physical sciences on the basis of a distinctions made in German thought at the time between the natural sciences and the human sciences. Whereas the former were appropriate for the study of the physical world, they were deemed inappropriate for the study of humans. Human sciences were based upon interpretive understanding of the spiritual and aesthetic dimensions of the human experience (Stocking 1974: 10–11).

The distinction between the human sciences and natural sciences is a mistaken one. The requirements of science remain the same regardless of the subject of study. This distinction, as Spiro (1986: 274) has noted in another context, stems from a misunderstanding of the difference between method and technique. Technique refers to the empirical procedures used for acquiring data, whether it is participant observation, interviewing, or experimentation. The investigation of different phenomena requires different techniques because you obviously cannot study star clusters, genes, or people using the same techniques. Method refers to the standards by which data are evaluated. In science method remain the same.

Boas's approach required that his anthropological investigation be centered upon the individual case (Boas 1940: 268). As he put it,

> The material of anthropology is such that it needs must be a historical science, one of the sciences the interest of which centers in the attempt to understand the individual phenomena rather than in the establishment of general laws (Boas 1940: 258).[18]

"Historical" in this context referred simply to the concern with the geographical spread and distribution of cultural elements, not historiography as undertaken by historians (Adams 1998: 315). To Boas the historical method was not counter to or different from science, rather it was a different mode of scientific analysis (Stocking 1974: 11–12). This as noted above was a mistake on Boas's part.

Boas's strategy was to construct anthropological knowledge by going from fact to theory, and not the other way around. In science, induction or inductive reasoning means going from the specific to the general, in which the facts are the premises for the development of hypotheses that not only account for the facts in question, but also predict the properties of unobserved phenomena (see Chapter 2). Boas, however, never ventured much beyond the observation of facts. Empirical generalizations were few, hypotheses were completely absent, there were no attempts to put generalizations to the test, and there were certainly no efforts at linking the verified propositions into "higher-order" abstracted systems, which inductive research entails (cf. Pelto and Pelto 1979: 254).

For Boas, going beyond the facts would be "forcing phenomena into the straightjacket of a theory," which he found unacceptable because it departed from "the actual relations of definite phenomena" (Boas 1940: 270). His anthropology was about the individual case:

> For each individual case we can arrive at an understanding of its determination by inner and outer forces, but we cannot explain its individuality in the form of laws. . . . Cultural phenomena are of such complexity that it seems to me doubtful whether valid cultural laws can be found. The causal conditions of cultural happenings lie always in the interaction between individuals and society, and no classificatory study of societies will solve this problem. The morphological classification of societies may call to our attention many problems. It will not solve them. In every case it is reducible to the same source, namely, the interaction between individual and society (Boas 1940: 257).[19]

Boas later added that

> on account of the uniqueness of cultural phenomena and their complexity nothing will ever be

found that deserves the name of a law excepting those psychological, biologically determined characteristics which are common to all cultures and appear in a multitude of forms according to the particular culture in which they manifest themselves (Boas 1940: 311).[20]

Boas's inductivism was based upon the assumption that one could collect the facts outside a theoretical framework. This simply cannot be, as discussed in Chapter 2. Boas's approach has been compared to Francis Bacon's (1561–1626) method of building scientific knowledge (Harris 2001b: 287). Bacon's method, which is called **classical induction,** was to start with the facts. These he treated as absolutes, little bits of absolute truth to be collected with minimal imposition. Once all the facts were in, lawlike formulations would emerge by themselves. For Bacon the defining condition of scientific knowledge was for all propositions to be reducible to facts (Bell 1994: 148). Such propositions, being based upon absolute facts, would yield absolute truths. Therefore, any proposition not reducible in this way to the facts was unscientific and science was about the generation of absolute truths.

What Boas failed to grasp is that science does not yield absolute certainty or truths, only probabilistic truths. The anthropologist Leslie White (1987d: 204–205), who emerged as one of Boas's harshest critics, was particularly disparaging on this point:

> Another theoretical weakness of the work under review . . . is the notion that one can achieve universals, or laws, by the inductive method. Boas and his students have virtually made a fetish of induction, with a corresponding repudiation and ridicule of deduction. To Boas, deduction meant "unbridled imagination" and "wild conjecture": deduction was characteristic of "social evolutionists and armchair philosophers." Induction on the other hand meant patient, laborious field work and research, the piling of fact upon fact, until something came of it. Generalizations arrived at deductively were easy, Boas argued, but scientifically worthless. Sound generalizations can be won only through induction. Thus Boas maintained

that "we recognize the fact that before we seek for what is common to all culture, we must analyze each culture by careful and exact methods" (1900: 4). "Unless we know how the culture of each group of man came to be what it is, we cannot expect to reach any conclusions in regard to the conditions controlling the general history of culture" (1932: 609). . . . This is a *reductio ad absurdum*. In the first place it is impossible to analyze the culture of each group of man by any kind of methods, exact or otherwise. . . . Nowhere has science been able to examine each and every member of a class—every fish, every flower, meteorite, ray of light, atom of copper, etc. In the second place it is not necessary to do this in order to come to sound and valid generalizations, as every science will testify. And finally, the basic principles, the great generalizations of science, are not arrived at inductively.[21]

As Bell (1994: 158) has observed, "Induction from facts can generate knowledge that is probable but not certain, and knowledge is legitimate—scientific—if it is reducible to the facts within an acceptable range of probability."

Inductive reasoning begins with specific observations that are true in order to generate a conclusion. Take, for example, a series of observations: Foraging culture 1 is egalitarian; foraging culture 2 is egalitarian; foraging culture 3 is egalitarian (and so on): Therefore, all foraging cultures are egalitarian. In this example, the individual premises are true and supply evidence from which the conclusion is derived. Note, however, that the evidence is incomplete because foraging culture 10 may turn out not to be egalitarian. It is in fact the case that not all foraging cultures were egalitarian (see Chapter 10).

Therefore, while we have greater justification for reaching the conclusion that all foraging cultures are egalitarian after looking at a large number of cases, the conclusion is probabilistic, not absolute. It holds for the cases observed, but not necessarily for all cases (cf. Hospers 1988: 250).

Boas, like Bacon, assumed that scientific laws exist in nature independently of the observer. Such propositions were treated not as probabilistic statements but as "eternal truths" (Stocking

1974: 12). To find these truths Boas believed that the inductive method was better than beginning with hypotheses and the deductive approach. This view meant, in terms of the preceding example, that Boas really did need all the facts to be in, not just for cultures 1 to 10, but for all foraging cultures. This was a mistake. As Kaplan and Manners (1972: 21) observe,

> The notion that we may record all the facts is an obvious absurdity. We observe and filter facts through a screen of interest, predisposition, and prior experience. And all of our descriptions are inevitably interpenetrated by theoretical considerations. *Thus the notion that there is such a thing as pure description is a mistaken notion* (emphasis added).[22]

Facts do not exist outside of theoretical frameworks. All observations, as noted in Chapter 2, are influenced by implicit or explicit interpretive frameworks that tell us where to look and what to ignore. As White (1987c: 91) cogently put it,

> Facts do not speak for themselves; they require imaginative intellects to speak for them. Facts as facts lie inert and meaningless until they are quickened into life and meaning by the creative power of intelligence.[23]

Consider, for example, the question, Why look at foraging cultures to being with? This question is not conjured out of thin air but is generated by a theoretical framework that incorporates assumptions about the relationships among certain forms of technology, adaptive strategies, modes of subsistence, and particular ecological and economic conditions.

Although Boas was fully committed to the empirical accuracy of field data, his perspective was entirely anti-scientific in its relativistic, idiosyncratic, or particularizing emphasis. For this reason the praises lavished upon Boas as a scientist by his students are misplaced. As Margaret Mead (1959: 35) put it, "[Boas was] the man who made anthropology into a science." Leslie White (1963) rejected such portrayals, pointing out that "Boas came fairly close to leaving the 'chaos of beliefs and customs' just about where he found it." White added,

> Students of Boas . . . like to point to his "merciless logic," his "scientific rigor," his "acidly critical faculty," on the one hand, and his "abhorrence" of generalizations and systems, his impatience with theory, in short, with a creative, synthesizing intelligence. . . . Thus, the defects and shortcomings of Boas' ethnology, his anti-scientific traits—for without theory and philosophic systems there can be no science—have been transformed into virtues (White 1987c: 92; 1987a: 146).[24]

ASSESSMENT

The Boasian paradigm, as I noted at the beginning of this chapter, is a useful illustration of the futility of research programs that lack the essential elements of a viable scientific approach, such as a parsimonious, generalizing perspective, material causation, and evolutionary holism. Boas's research program was rigorously empiricist, but it lacked these other essential elements. One of the defects of the paradigm was the ontological autonomy it granted culture. This has created irresolvable problems that have taxed the generations of anthropologists that came after Boas.

Given the inherent flaws of Boas's perspective, it comes as no surprise that his anthropological efforts, for the most part, were a failure. His "sense of definiteness of problem, of exact rigor of method, and of highly critical objectivity," as Kroeber (1935: 540) put it, resulted in masses of data on the Kwakiutl. Boas wrote over five thousand pages on the Kwakiutl, yet he was never able to write a coherent ethnographic monograph on the subject. As George Murdock (1949: xiv) found,

> Despite Boas' "five-foot shelf" of monographs on the Kwakiutl, this tribe falls into the quartile of those whose social structure and related practices are least adequately described among the 250 covered in the present study.[25]

Boas did not generate systematic accounts of the Kwakiutl because he felt that such accounts had

to wait until all the facts were in hand (cf. Rohner and Rohner 1969: xxiii). This was an unobtainable ideal.

Another defective aspect of Boas's enterprise was that he did not assign causality to any cultural element. Everything was treated as being equally important with no end result in mind (Smith 1959: 52–53). This amounted to a kind of sampling exercise. As Smith (1959: 49) pointed out, "This exhaustive collection of data which seemed at the time to have little or no connection with any specific problem is a feature of [Boas's] approach. . . . There is a fascination in following the details of a subject just for its intrinsic interest. . . . Masses of data may therefore be worked over with no clear knowledge of what is to be gained at the end."

Boas's Northwest Coast materials, which were amassed in this way, were a veritable mine of seeming chaos. Boas's idiographic interpretive framework, which highlighted differences and understated similarities, led him to believe that uniformities did not exists, and hence his skepticism regarding "laws of culture." The realm of sociocultural phenomena appeared to him as a vast and chaotic place, a viewpoint nicely captured by Lowie's (1920: 441) construal of culture as a "planless hodgepodge," a "thing of shreds and patches."

The confused and baffling picture that confronted Boas was to a large degree an artifact of his own theoretical framework. On this point Leslie White (1987d: 200) attacked him without mercy:

> Not only did [Boas] fail to see the forest for the trees, he could scarcely see the tree for the branches, or the branches for the twigs. And no two twigs were alike. Diversity is what impressed him. The ultimate was the concrete event which was, of course, unique. . . . The picture of culture that Boas produced, working from this point of view, was precisely what might have been expected. There was no order, no rhyme or reason, to the great mass of cultural phenomena that make up the history and life of mankind.[26]

Finally, although Boas insisted that the facts should be allowed to speak for themselves and that the ethnographer must not impose frameworks, models, or "preconceived philosophical positions" (Smith 1959: 49) upon the data, his own theoretical biases led him to focus almost exclusively upon the mental life of people and the symbolic domain of culture; in other words, he stressed emic over etic descriptions. This was a reflection of his assumption about the nature of cultural phenomena as ontologically autonomous. As Honigmann (1976: 199) pointed out, "The bias against deductive interpretation favored what came to be known in post–World War II anthropology as an emic point of view."

What interested Boas the most were language, religion, mythology, folklore, and art, on which he kept copious notes. He neglected the ecological, sociopolitical, and economic aspects of the cultures he studied (Rohner and Rohner 1969: xxiii). In Boas's research agenda the "native's point of view" was given highest priority. At the same time those aspects of sociocultural systems that are beyond the conscious awareness of members of a culture were slighted or totally ignored (R. Barrett 1991: 135). American anthropology was thus set on an idealist trajectory that many practitioners continue to follow to this day.

ACADEMIC POLITICS AND BOASIAN ANTHROPOLOGY

Boas and the large group of students he trained constituted an academic cohort: They shared the same epistemological assumptions and were committed to the same intellectual agenda (Darnell 1998: 272–272). As Stocking (1974: 17) has put it, "much of twentieth-century American anthropology may be viewed as the working out in time of various implications in Boas' own position." As a group, Boas and his students for the most part controlled the teaching of anthropology in the United States as well as dominating the major professional organizations (Miele

2001: 28). These anthropologists constituted something that had not existed before, a school of anthropological thought, although members denied that such was the case (cf. Service 1985: vii; see Kroeber 1935: 540; Mead 1959: 31).

What was significant about this development is that schools of thought are associated with what Service (1985: vii) has described as "disciple-ism, despotism, and collegial rivalries and alliances [which] become . . . significant to the acceptance or rejection of ideas." This was the milieu of academic politics and breeding ground of the kind of rancorous rivalries that characterizes the culture wars in American anthropology today. The elitist intellectual hegemony imposed by the Boasians in effect determined how anthropology was practiced in the United States for a very long time. The same sort of political tactics have enabled present-day cultural constructionists to achieve control over many of the major departments of anthropology and key organizations and journals and to exercise similar exclusionary and elitist intellectual agendas. It is for this reason that the subject of academic politics and institutional basis of anthropology are both important and require a separate study in their own rights.

THE BOASIANS AND AMERICAN ANTHROPOLOGY

Boas set the agenda for American anthropology. As Stocking (1974: 18–19) has pointed out,

It is out of Boas' critique of evolutionary assumptions that certain of the most fundamental orientations of modern American cultural anthropology derive: on the one hand, the rejection of the traditional nineteenth-century linkage of race and culture in a single hierarchical evolutionary sequence; on the other, the elaboration of the concept of culture as a relativistic, pluralistic, holistic, integrated and historically conditioned framework for the study of the determination of human behavior.[27]

Attempts to develop scientific paradigms during the mid–1930s, and again during the late 1940s and early 1950s, failed to make lasting impact. Scientific anthropology (as opposed to what was called scientific anthropology, i.e., the Boasian program) remained peripheral in American anthropology. By the close of the 1960s the theory phobia and the relativistic and particularistic pursuit of the individual case established so firmly by Boas and his followers once again dominated the intellectual landscape (Stocking 1974: 20).

Postmodern anthropology and its distrust of theory and science found fertile soil in departments of anthropology in the United States (cf. Layton 1997: 29). Anthropologists operating under the auspices of this perspective have surpassed Boas in their hostile attitude toward science and theory construction.

Chapter 7

After Boas: The Development of American Anthropology

Franz Boas created a new anthropological paradigm centered upon the idea of "culture" and the axiom of cultural relativism. The concept of culture was the unifying theme of the Boasian perspective (Darnell 1998: 274). In the next phase of development in American anthropology, the cadre of students trained in the Boasian tradition would tackle in force questions pertaining to the nature of culture, the relationship between culture and biology, and the influence of culture upon human behavior (see Adams 1998: 316–328). This was the age of Boasian anthropology. Honigmann (1976: 199–200) summarizes the developments of this period:

> Along with making frequent field trips, usually to western American Indian tribes, American anthropologists between the first and second world wars accumulated and partially systematized a body of concepts and propositions about the nature and structure of culture, relationships between culture and the geographical milieu, the individual's role in culture, and other matters.

Boas's diverse interests that encompassed a whole spectrum of anthropological topics covering all four fields of the discipline, from whence developed the holistic orientation of American anthropology (Magli 2001: 78), provided his students with leads to follow along a number of avenues of research. American anthropology took shape through the different versions of historical particularism espoused in the work of these researchers (cf. Langness 1993: 73). Although some of Boas's students departed from the views of their teacher on various issues, they were as one in terms of the basic epistemological principles to which they subscribed. We find, therefore, that what is lacking from the works of many of the Boasians were the same elements absent in the works of their teacher (i.e., a parsimonious, generalizing perspective, material causation, and evolutionary holism).

As I noted in the previous chapter, the present-day antiscience, impressionistic interpretive perspectives in American cultural anthropology embody much that was central to the Boasian paradigm. For this reason the works of the Boasians require a detailed review. An overview of Boasian anthropology, from Wissler's culture area studies to Margaret Mead's Samoan research, is highly instructive in two ways. First, such a brief can help us situate the current anti-science movement within the discipline's overall historical trajectory. Second, such an overview illustrates the kinds of theoretical blunders and dead ends that ensue when one pursues anti-science, antigeneralization, idiosyncratic, and impressionistic avenues of research.

THE DIFFUSION OF TRAITS AND CULTURE AREAS

During the first part of the twentieth century diffusionism dominated American anthropology. The type of diffusionism espoused did not endure for more than a few decades and no one has since conceived of culture in quite the same way. A review of the main ideas of the period, however, helps illustrate one of the fruitless lines of research engendered by Boas's relativistic and antitheory cultural determinism.

Diffusionist studies emerged from Boas's concerns with the chronological and spatial distribution of cultural elements. Boas, we might recall, saw culture not as an "organic growth" but rather as the accretions of elements that were integrated into the whole according to the "genius" of the people. By careful examination of the spatial distribution of traits in limited geographical areas, it was thought, one could differentiate and work out the relationships between various Native American cultures and even explain cultural similarities and differences. Moreover, the classification of traits was aimed at the discovery of patterns of cultural organization. The rationale behind these studies was that an understanding of the spread and acquisition of cultural traits would in the end reveal macropatterns that would amount to nothing less than a reconstruction of the prehistory of the Americas (Adams 1998: 316).

Melville Herskovits, one of Boas's distinguished students, described the historical particularist construal of culture and the role of diffusion in the formation of culture as follows:

One of the most significant aspects of culture [is that] disparate elements, whose distribution can be individually traced, are combined and recombined into . . . different expressions of a given basic concept; each complex or aggregate forming an integrated whole whose every part is not only accepted but held as symbolically essential by the people in whose particular culture it is found (Herskovits 1955: 395).

The historical particularists noted that although no two cultures are identical, those people who lived in close proximity to one another tended to have much more in common with each other than with cultures elsewhere (Herskovits 1955: 396). Thus cultural similarities and differences could be explained in terms of geographical contiguousness. This led to the idea that particular cultures may correspond with particular geographical areas. Given that culture is learned, the reasoning went, people are able to borrow elements and learn from cultures with which they come into contact. Thus, frequent contact between people living close to one another allows for a higher frequency of borrowing. As a result, cultures in an area, Herskovits (1955: 296) pointed out, "form clusters . . . sufficiently homogenous that regions in which they occur can be delimited on a map. *The area in which similar cultures are found is called a culture area.*"

The idea of culture areas was implicit in Boas's debate with Otis Mason, noted in Chapter 6. However, it was Boas's student Clark Wissler (1870–1947) who provided a systematic treatment of the concept. As curator of the American Museum of Natural History in New York, Wissler undertook the classification of Native American "tribal cultures" by attempting to correlate dominant cultural traits with geographical locations, or culture areas. What constituted dominant cultural traits could not be determined, however, unless a complete list of traits for a culture was compiled (Wissler 1923: 51). A "tribal culture," according to Wissler (1929: 341) "is the aggregate of standardized beliefs and procedures followed by the tribe."

In his book *The American Indian* (1938 [1917]), Wissler pointed out that

If . . . we take all traits into simultaneous consideration and shift our point of view to the social, or tribal units, we are able to form fairly definite groups. This will give us culture areas, or a classification of social groups according to their culture traits (Wissler 1938: 220).

Wissler (1929: 345) noted that the classification of "tribes" based upon similarities in culture results in "regional distributions that closely conform to the ranges of the animals and plants upon which the tribes base their economic life." In other words, a culture area was seen as a geographical region/physical environment occupied by a number of independent groups with similar cultures and modes of subsistence.

Using the criterion of subsistence as the primary factor, Wissler identified the following culture areas (Figure 7.1):

Area	Subsistence
Eskimo	Caribou
Great Plains	Bison
North Pacific Coast	Salmon
California	Wild Seeds
Southeast Woodland	Eastern Maize
Southwest, Nahua—Mexico, Chibcha, Inca—Peru	Intensive Agriculture
Amazon, Caribbean	Manioc
Guanaco	Guanaco

Wissler posited the presence of a "cultural center," construed as a circle, within each culture area associated with "the most favorable environment for that culture type," and where the identified traits occur in their highest concentration. Traits most compatible with a particular habitat, according to Wissler, are drawn in and worked into the cultural repertoire. Then these traits radiate "outward" in all directions from the cultural center to peripheral areas or "culture margins," where the traits decrease or fade out and mingle with traits from the adjacent culture area (Wissler 1926: 182–183).

For example, the main characteristics of the Great Plains culture area included the skin teepee, use of a circular shield, geometric artistic style, developed leatherwork, band-level social organization, the **Sun Dance** ceremony, sweat-house observances, absence of agriculture, basketry, and pottery, and so forth. Groups in the cultural center possessed all of these traits while cultures on the margins possessed fewer of these traits (Wissler 1926: 221–224).

Wissler was clearly aware of a significant correlation between cultures and particular environmental settings. He noted, for instance, that maps of culture areas correspond quite closely with ecological areas (Harris 2001: 663). As Wissler (1926: 216–217) put it,

> We have . . . made progress in our search for the environmental factors, since it appears that the rule that, whenever in aboriginal America, a well marked ecological area can be delineated, there one will find a culture area and that the centers of distribution for the constituent [cultural] traits will fall in the heart of the ecological area. There must then be some determining condition that produces this uniformity, some ecological relation here, and no doubt a mechanism involved, which when laid bare, will give an adequate scientific explanation of the phenomenon. This discussion has at least set us on the trail of this mechanism, for its place of function is the ecological area, and it is most in evidence at the center.[1]

Wissler, however, was at a loss as to the reasons for such a correspondence. This was symptomatic of Boasian anthropology, with its theoretical focus on the differences and particularities of each culture rather than similarities and uniformities. The anthropologists operating under the auspices of this paradigm could offer no explanations for, and were often mystified or bewildered by, the diversity of cultures they encountered. They were mystified because, while they operated in the idiom of science, they eschewed the notion of material causality (Ellen 1986: 49).

Thus, Wissler was content to treat the development of culture centers in terms of historical accidents and purely cultural determinants, rather than in terms of any environmental or ecological factors. However, as subsequent research has shown, the trend toward convergence in culture areas involves many additional factors other than

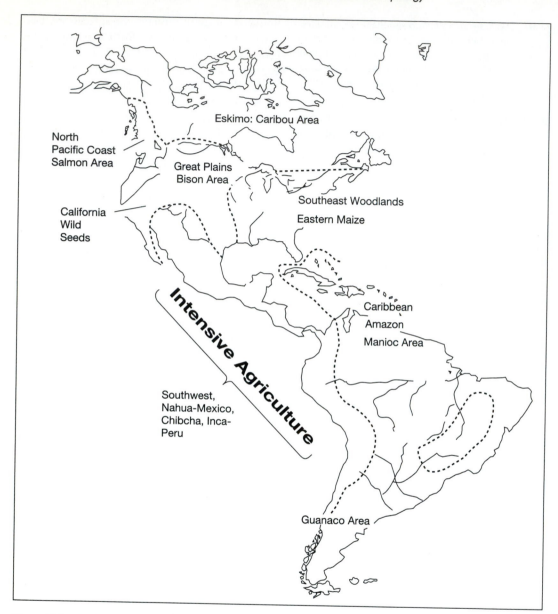

Figure 7.1   Culture areas based on subsistence.   *After Wissler (1938).*

the mechanical or accidental operation of diffusion (Murphy 1989: 228). The similarities among groups in a given culture area arise as a consequence of similar ecological adjustments to a common environment. Common environment also enhances intensive communication and movement of people throughout the culture area, such as occurred, for example, in the Great Plains of North America or in the North Pacific Coast. These are important factors that account for why traits are readily passed on between groups in such areas (Murphy 1989: 228).

Wissler failed to take into account these additional factors. He clearly acknowledged that the ceremonial practices of the Inuit are confined to the limits of the Arctic environment and the Sun Dance to the plains. But he maintained that "no one has been able to demonstrate a causal relation between the environment and such non-material traits of culture" (Wissler 1929: 338). Wissler (1926: 372) also asserted that

> the origin of a culture center seems due to ethnic factors more than to geographical ones. The locations of these centers is largely a matter of historic accident, but once located and the adjustments made, the stability of the environment doubtless tends to hold each particular type of culture to its initial locality, even in the face of many changes in blood and language.[2]

The "culture-comes-from-culture" viewpoint instilled by Boas, which excluded all noncultural variables, is clearly evident here. Wissler's position, moreover, reflected the theory-phobia characteristic of the Boasian perspective. This compelled him to "speak and deal with the cultures of the world with a minimum of commitment" (Wissler 1929: 345).

"The culture area," Wissler (1929: 357) pointed out, "is a diffusion area. Regional phenomena imply free diffusion within a more or less circumscribed area. Likewise a culture center is conceived as a center from which diffusion takes place." Thus, diffusion was thought of as the process that could explain the cultural patterns in given tribal areas as well as accounting for the spread of particular traits from one place to another.

Wissler also used the idea of the distribution of traits to infer a trait's point of origin and its relative age, a formulation referred to as **the age–area hypothesis.** This amounted to the assumption that the wider the distribution of a trait around a culture center the greater its age. Wissler (1929: 336) provided the method of gripping a bow and arrow, in archery, as an example:

There are three main types of arrow release . . . which may be designated as A, B, and C. A stands for the various methods of holding the arrow between the thumb and the first finger; B, for the so-called Mediterranean release, where the arrow is held between the first and second fingers; C, for the special Mongolian pull. As may be surmised, the Mongolian form is peculiar to a zone extending through the middle of Asia; type B occurs in zones on either side of C, whereas A lies outside of B. From the distribution alone, we may infer that A is the primitive form of arrow release and that C is the latest. The question, however, arises as to whether A once prevailed in the zones now given over to B and C. The inference is that it did. Also it would follow that B once prevailed in the region now characterized by C, assuming that the inventions followed the time order A, B and C.[3]

Attempts to make the culture area approach more reliable resulted in exacting efforts to accumulate comprehensive trait lists. Alfred Kroeber suggested the use of statistical correlations in order to identify the representative traits and thus demarcate culture areas with more precision. However, the results of these efforts were theoretically inconclusive.

There were several major culture area studies produced during this period. Wissler published *The American Indian* (1917), a brilliant essay on the spread of the horse (Figure 7.2) and its impact upon the cultures of the Great Plains (Wissler 1914, see 1923), and the book *The Relation of Nature to Man in Aboriginal America* (1926). In addition, there was Leslie Spier's (1893–1961) books, *The Sundance of the Plains Indians* (1921), and *The Prophet Dance of the Northwest and its Derivatives* (1935). Finally, we have Alfred Kroeber's books *Handbook of the Indians of California* (1925) and *Cultural and Natural Areas of Native North America* (1939), to which I shall refer later.

Despite considerable effort invested in the culture area perspective for over two decades, in the end such studies proved sterile because of numerous inherent problems that I shall discuss later. However, culture area studies did lead to the accumulation of systematic data on many

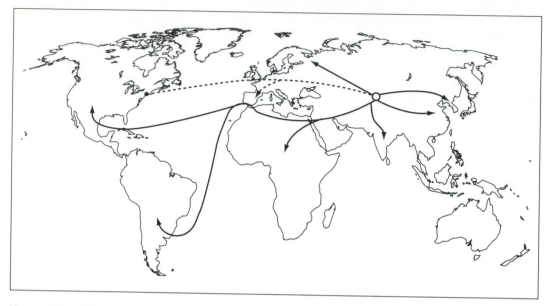

Figure 7.2 Diffusion of the horse complex. *After Wissler (1923).*

disappearing cultures (Moore 1997: 72). Moreover, because such work demanded detailed analysis of traits, it brought to light aspects of culture and the processes of culture change that had hitherto escaped attention. One of the theoretically significant implications of this research was that it revealed an undeniable and complex interrelationship between culture and environment, leading subsequent researchers, such as Julian Steward, who was trained by Kroeber, to explore ecological variables in a more detailed and systematic manner (see Chapter 10).

SHORTCOMINGS OF THE CULTURE AREA STUDIES

Culture area studies suffered from numerous defects. First, there was the problem of scale, which entailed continents and subcontinents and environmental complexity on the ground that could not possibly be taken into account theoretically (Vayda and Rappaport 1968: 481). The limited number of variables used for delineating culture

areas, areas of immense cultural and environmental variability, rendered the validity of the whole exercised questionable from the very start (Ellen 1986: 9).

Second, the variables employed in such research posed problems. For example, there was a lack of consensus as to what constituted a typical cultural trait with which culture areas were to be defined. Was a tent to be counted as a single unit, a living place, or several traits based on the number of poles, the type of skin covering, and the decorations on it? Also problematic was the fact that all traits were treated more or less as being of equal significance. Hence, in one sense the number of tent poles and number of spouses were handled as being of equal diagnostic importance. Also, differences in the function and significance of a trait that was found in two different cultures (for example, pyramid-like structures serving as tombs versus those serving as temples) were not taken into consideration.

Third, culture areas overlapped and it was impossible to establish any objective criteria for delimiting the boundaries of different culture areas. In other words, the question of where one culture area ended and another began could not be resolved. Later studies have shown that cultures and groups on the ground interact in intricate ways and may even exhibit complex **symbiotic relationships** with one another, as Fredrik Barth's (1956) work in Northern Pakistan demonstrated. Here different ecological zones in one geographical region are exploited by three distinct ethnic groups, ranging from sedentary Pathan agriculturalists, to agro-pastoral Kohistanis, to the nomadic pastoral Gujars. Each group pursues a different mode of production and engages in various political and economic relationships with the others. Barth's study clearly pointed out that the same "culture area" often contains people with significant differences, despite the fact that they may share many traits.

Not mindful of such complexities and intricacies in human-environment relations, when the Boasians assigned different groups to particular culture areas, they often overlooked factors related to economy, technology, group interactions, ethnic diversity, social organization, and environmental variability. In other words, the traits used to assign groups to a particular culture area were based upon arbitrary categories established by the anthropologist rather than reflecting the circumstances on the ground.

Wissler (1938: 16) himself was aware of the problem of complexity. He wrote of the agricultural areas, "The reader may be appalled by the complexity and variety of peoples in this area; hence it is fortunate that we are able to see one element of unity in the whole." Wissler, however, did not appreciate the true theoretical implications of this observation, which basically cast doubt upon the methodology itself, a methodology that led to the grouping of culturally diverse groups into single categories.

Fourth, the culture area approach was based on the assumption that "free diffusion" occurs within culture areas, which ignored the fact that frequently there is as much resistance to borrowing traits as there is receptivity to them, as noted in Chapter 5. Resistance and receptivity and the factors they entail needed to be taken into account, but they were not.

Fifth, cultures were treated as being stable and fixed, and because creativity was thought to be restricted to the culture centers, changes in peripheries over time were not taken into consideration. This was because diffusion, when construed as a universal and primary historical process, necessarily entails the assumption that independent inventions are few and far between and that cultures develop and change primarily by borrowing of innovations from a limited number of centers of creativity. This, we might recall, was also an assumption shared by the British and German diffusionists. Archaeological and ethnographic evidence, however, has shown the widespread occurrence of independent inventions and worldwide parallelisms (for example, pottery, metallurgy, calendars, writing, domestication of plants and animals, the rise of the state, just to name a few), thus refuting this central diffusionist assumption.

Sixth, there is no way of proving that traits diffuse evenly and at even rates in all direction. Subsequent research has in fact revealed that diffusion often tends to be unidirectional and moreover that the rates of diffusion vary considerably (Malefijt 1974: 179).

Finally, the extent to which traits are distributed over a geographical area does not necessarily imply antiquity; otherwise one could conclude that personal computers were invented long before electric typewriters.

Despite these defects, in fairness one might add that what culture area studies anthropologists were attempting was not altogether invalid. They simply lacked the computational hardware/software, such as the geographic information systems (GIS) computer technology now available for the collection, integration, storage, and manipulation/modeling of geographically referenced data, to accomplish what they were attempting.

ALFRED KROEBER

One among the Boasians who attempted to push anthropology toward new directions was Alfred Kroeber (1876–1960). Kroeber was born in New Jersey into a German-American family. He received an M.A. in English from Columbia University. His interest in anthropology developed after he enrolled in a seminar on Indian languages offered by Franz Boas. A three-month field trip among the Arapaho in 1899 and a trip among the Arapaho, Ute, Shoshone, and Bannock in 1900 led to his shift to anthropology as a career.

In 1901 Kroeber received the first Ph.D. from Boas's anthropology department at Columbia after completing a 28-page dissertation on Arapaho art entitled "Decorative Symbolism of the Arapaho" (1901). In the same year Kroeber took up a position as instructor of anthropology at the newly formed department of anthropology at the University of California, Berkeley.

Like his teacher at Columbia, Kroeber had to build a department of anthropology from the ground up. Kroeber was one of several of Boas's students to establish a department of anthropology, as noted in the previous chapter. This was part of the process of the institutionalization and entrenchment of Boasian anthropology, or the Boasian school of thought.

Kroeber is considered to be one of the key figures in the development of American anthropology (Steward 1961: 1039) whose work had a tremendous impact upon the field. As the anthropologist Eric Wolf (1923–1998) wrote of Kroeber, "For anthropologists of my generation, Kroeber was the living embodiment of American anthropology. His books and his words accompanied us through graduate school, and he appeared in our professional lives again and again" (Wolf 1981: 36).

Kroeber's specialty was Native American cultures of California and the Great Plains, although his research interests and writings covered a wide range of topics and areas, such as trait distribution studies, archaeological work in

Alfred Kroeber, a major figure in American anthropology during the first half of the twentieth century, who was instrumental in establishing the Boasian program in the United States.

Mexico and Peru, linguistic research, and the analysis of complex societies or "high civilizations." He wrote prodigiously, contributed to all the four fields of the discipline and the bibliography of his works is staggering (see Gibson and Rowe 1961: 1060–1087).

Kroeber fully accepted Boas's focus on empirical data collection through firsthand fieldwork and his repudiation of deductive approaches. Moreover, he adopted Boas's holistic and relativistic perspectives in the study of culture. Like his teacher, Kroeber also treated each culture as comprising a unique pattern or configuration that could only be understood in its own terms and in its own context.

Kroeber outlined his methodology in a paper entitled "Causes in Culture" (1952 [1947]), which he pointed out was modeled after linguistics. The reason for this, he noted, is that linguistics is impersonal, historical in orientation, emphasizes patterns, and offers explanations in terms of historic contexts, relevance, and value significance. Kroeber wrote that

> on transposition of these criteria—impersonality, historic orientation, pattern emphasis, absence of causality, value significance—to studies of culture . . . it is evident that standard ethnography, archaeology, and both kinds of culture history—that of disparate traits and that devoted to culture-wholes—pursue mainly the method of linguistics. In contrast, consciously functional anthropology, social anthropology, and sociology tend to be non-historical, reductionistic, and interested in cause (Kroeber 1952: 107).[4]

The attempt to construct anthropological approaches modeled upon linguistics has a long history and continues to this day (cf. Adams 1998: 178). The version of Historical Particularism expounded by Kroeber retained the idealist (culture as mental rules) antiscience, no-laws-and-causality-in-culture, interpretive, and particularistic thrust of the Boasian program. Here I shall highlight some of the basic aspects of Kroeber's work and their impact on American anthropology.

Kroeber: Anthropology as a Historical Discipline

Kroeber construed anthropology as a historical discipline. For him, anthropology was about understanding events/phenomena in their spatial and temporal contexts and trying to identify patterns within those events/phenomena. Viewing things in their contexts, as opposed to seeking causal connections outside the domain of culture, is the hallmark of interpretive anthropology, an enterprise devoted to the subjective appreciation of aesthetic and symbolic features of culture.

As Kroeber (1952: 3) put it, "My natural and first interest always has been in phenomena and their ordering: akin to an aesthetic proclivity." Kroeber (1952: 5) described the historical perspective as follows:

> The essential quality of the historical approach as a method of science I see as its integration of phenomena into an ever widening phenomenal context, with as much preservation as possible—instead of analytic resolution—of the qualitative organization of the phenomena dealt with. The context includes the placing in space and time and therefore, when knowledge allows, in sequence. . . . Patterns or configurations . . . are what it seems most profitable and productive to distinguish and formulate in culture.[5]

Elsewhere, Kroeber elaborated upon the distinction between his own subjective/interpretive, particularistic nongeneralizing perspective and the scientific approach:

> The essential characteristic of the historic approach appears to be the endeavor to achieve a conceptual integration of phenomena while preserving the quality of the phenomena. This quality the strictly scientific approach does not attempt to preserve. On the contrary, it destroys phenomena as phenomena in utilizing them for its own conceptualizations of a different order. Time and space certainly enter into the considerations and results of science proper; but its findings or end-results are timeless and spaceless formulations, in the sense that they are independent of specific or particular time and place. The findings of the historical approach on the other hand are necessarily always given in terms of specific time and space—phenomenal space and time, we might say, in contrast to the abstract measure of time and space in science. A dateless and placeless finding in human history, natural history, palaeontology, geology, or astronomy would make no sense. If a dateless and placeless block of phenomena is discovered, the first problem of any historical discipline is recognized to be the finding of its date and place. Conversely, where a phenomenal lacuna appears in the date-place frame, the filling of this lacuna with the relevant phenomena is felt to be a need and a problem. The historical approach is therefore always reconstructive in its nature—reconstructive as to the phenomena themselves and to their dates and places (Kroeber 1952: 70).[6]

This is idiographic interpretive research with its emphasis upon context and contextuality. It is a viewpoint very much like the one sported by present-day interpretivists who juxtapose their perspective against science and its claims to universality and timeless uncontextual validity, which is the gist of Kroeber's statement.

Kroeber maintained that the subject matter of anthropology (i.e., culture, which he considered to be distinct from nature) demanded a historical approach. To apply the method of the physical sciences to cultural phenomena, construed as closed, internally consistent, self-generating symbolic (emic) systems, he felt, was a fundamental mistake:

> It is the nature of culture to be heavily conditioned by its own cumulative past, so that the most fruitful approach is a historical one. I recognize the distinction of nomothetic [generalizing] and idiographic [particularizing] method, but not as an absolute dichotomy between science as investigation of nature and history as the study of man or spirit or culture. Both approaches, I hold, contrariwise, can be applied to any level of phenomena—as the simple example of historical sciences shows—and should ultimately be applied. But on the basic inorganic level it is the mathematically formulable, experimentally verifiable, analytic approach that is most immediately rewarding. On the upper levels, especially on the uppermost one of culture, it is the qualitative and the contextual associations of phenomena that are important, and isolation of specific causal factors tend to be both difficult and, so far as we can see, of less significance. After all, the history of a particular civilization has obvious meaning; the history of a particular stone on the beach . . . has very little meaning as history. . . . A "physics" or "physiology" of culture would be desirable enough and may ultimately and gradually be attainable. But to transfer the method of the physicochemical sciences of the inorganic to culture would be a fallacy. By eliminating the history of a cultural situation, we cut off its largest component or dimension (Kroeber 1952: 4–5).[7]

Present-day postmodern/interpretive/literary anthropological writers share most of Kroeber's ontological assumptions, such as culture being apart from nature, rejection of generalizing approaches in the study of culture, and an anti-science bias. The one difference being that unlike many present-day interpretivists, Kroeber admitted the possibility of a science of culture at some future date.

Kroeber's argument against a science of culture is an old one. E. B. Tylor wrote of it in his day (see Chapter 3). It is a viewpoint that at present appears in the discourses of interpretivists such as Clifford Geertz (1983: 3), who tells us that a "social physics" of culture is dead. It is also the point of contention by the cadre of postmodern and cultural constructionist writers, such as Herzfeld (2001: 43), who clamor against anthropology based on "the old Newtonian models," as if such things really ever existed.

Kroeber: The Rejection of Science

Throughout his career, Kroeber maintained that laws of culture do not exist, that cultural phenomena are not amenable to analysis through the scientific method, and that there are no causal explanations in culture (cf. Harris 2001: 336–337). This adamant and unwavering anti-science stance by Kroeber demonstrates how powerfully Boas' epistemological assumptions had shaped the thinking of those under his influence. "[The] findings of history," Kroeber wrote, "can never be substantiated by proofs like the proofs of natural science" (Kroeber 1952: 79).

For Kroeber, recurring phenomena, such as feudalism, clans, cross-cousin marriages, and the like, arose from diverse beginnings (polygenetic origins) and merely gave the illusion that regularities exist (Kroeber 1952: 89). "Allegations of regular recurrences in culture," he argued, "refer to shadowy large resemblances which are not precisely definable" (Kroeber 1952: 131). This was the same argument Boas had used in his efforts to demolish nineteenth-century evolutionism and its generalizing approach. Kroeber insisted that

> The problem remains unresolved of how far general forms, therefore recurrent forms, can be demonstrated in culture. The difficulty has been that the recurrent forms are lax and ill defined. With strict analysis, the stable content of concepts like feudalism, clan, mana, soul and taboo shrinks increasingly. This seems to be because the cultural content of their historical development, which is always complex and always tending toward the unique, as historians have long ago learned to take for granted. The general or recurrent remnant in these seemingly recurrent phenomena is usually not cultural but of lower level, especially psychological (Kroeber 1952: 134).[8]

In other words, Kroeber was invoking the idea of the radical plurality of cultures, stressing individuality and uniqueness of each culture while downplaying and blurring similarities, all of which were part of the Boasian intellectual legacy.

Kroeber's Ethnographic Program

Kroeber's ethnographic research in California led him to tackle questions related to the delineation of cultural boundaries, reconstruction of precontact cultures, and how the process of contact between cultures could be quantitatively gauged.

Struck by the diversity of Native American cultures (and languages) in California, Kroeber attempted to measure the range of diversity by means of cultural trait lists. Kroeber was committed to quantification of the data. He organized a four-year survey project during which 254 tribal and tribal subdivisions west of the Rocky Mountains were surveyed through the use of massive trait lists ranging from 400 to over 6000 elements (Steward 1961: 1057). These studies were also tied to Kroeber's efforts to gather as much information on the disappearing Native American cultures of California. Kroe-

ber's commitment to systematic quantification reflected the general Boasian commitment to systematic empirical data gathering. Like the endeavors of his colleagues, Kroeber's efforts were allied to a profoundly particularistic orientation that was completely antiscientific in nature (cf. Sanderson 1990: 47).

The surveys were methodologically defective because they were based upon data from "one or two members of a series of tribes" believed to be "qualified tribal informants" (Kroeber 1952: 263). Moreover, the resultant studies based on the surveys suffered from the shortcomings of the culture element studies noted previously and failed to yield significant theoretical results. Here again one might note that in part the failure had to do with the lack of the appropriate computational technology, such as the GIS, without which the sort of patterns Kroeber attempted to detect is nearly impossible.

On the positive side, Kroeber's project did yield a significant body of descriptive ethnographic data and resulted in the publication of twenty-five separate monographs (see Aginsky 1943; Driver 1937, 1939; Drucker 1950; Klimek 1935; Steward 1941). Kroeber's research also led to the publication of his massive *Handbook of the Indians of California* (1925), which is nearly a thousand pages in length.

In the *Cultural and Natural Areas of Native North America* (1939), Kroeber left the statistical approach behind and adopted a position similar to Wissler, in which cultures were associated with geographical areas on the basis of criteria such as subsistence and population densities. In this work, Kroeber attempted to refine the culture area concept by introducing the ideas of "cultural intensity" and "cultural climax." These referred to different degrees of and variations in cultural complexity. By *cultural intensity* Kroeber meant

> a precise calendar system, a complex interrelation of rituals or social units, invariably embodies special cultural material as well as intensity of its development and organization. Simple culture

material cannot well be highly systematized; refined and specialized material seems to demand organization. What we call intensity of culture therefore means both special content and special system. A more intensive culture normally contains not only more material—more elements or traits—but also more material peculiar to itself, as well as more precisely and articulately established interrelations between the materials. An accurate time reckoning, a religious hierarchy, a set of social classes, a detailed property law, are illustrations of this. . . . Granted this interdependence of richness of content and richness of systematization, it should be possible to determine approximately objective measures of culture intensity by measuring culture content—by counting distinguishable elements, for instance (Kroeber 1952: 338).[9]

Kroeber described culture climax

as the point from which the greatest radiation of cultural material has taken place in the area. But it is always necessary to remember that as a culture becomes richer, it also tends to become more highly organized, and in proportion as its organization grows, so does its capacity to assimilate and place new material, whether this be produced within or imported from without. In the long run, accordingly, high-intensity cultures are the most absorptive as well as the most productive. It is by the interaction of both processes that culture culminations seem to be built up. Consequently, an unusually successful degree of absorption tends to lead to further "inventive" productiveness and outward influencing . . . until the process fails somewhere and a condition of stability is reached or a decline sets in; or a newer center begins to dominate the old (Kroeber 1952: 339).[10]

As this passage clearly indicates, Kroeber's focus was entirely upon culture as the cause of culture. Thus, he never entertained the possibility that specific environments and technologies might be causally associated with particular types of social organizations, as Julian Steward would later propose (Ellen 1986: 53). Kroeber himself considered this line of inquiry to be his more important contribution to the field rather than the ecological or environmental correlations dis-

cussed in his *Cultural and Natural Areas of Native America* (Harris 2001: 340). It is not surprising therefore that the concept of "adaptation" is altogether absent form Kroeber's work (Wolf 1981: 52).

Kroeber, like Wissler, attributed only a limiting role to the natural habitat, a perspective known as **possibilism:**

While it is true that cultures are rooted in nature, and can therefore never be completely understood except with reference to that piece of nature in which they occur, they are no more produced by that nature than a plant is produced or caused by the soil in which it is rooted. The immediate cause of cultural phenomena are other cultural phenomena (Kroeber 1939: 1).

Later on Kroeber (1939: 205) reiterated the same point: "Culture can be understood primarily only in terms of cultural factors, but . . . no culture is intelligible without reference to the non-cultural or so-called environmental factors with which it is in relation and which condition it." In Kroeber's anthropology, the "so-called environmental factor" remained always in the background, if considered at all, despite such acknowledgements of their importance. Indeed, by treating environmental factors as constraints, possibilists like Kroeber could acknowledge the environment, without attributing to it any sort of causal significance or status (Ellen 1986: 24).

As Ellen has pointed out, while possibilism led to a recognition of the importance of empirical investigation of environmental conditions, it was methodologically and theoretically deficient. It entailed a "crude inductionism" and "a logically vacuous circularity in argument" (Ellen 1986: 49). This is because it was coupled with an antimaterialist ideology, rejected evolutionary holism, and entailed circular thinking based on the culture-comes-from-culture premise.

Although Kroeber paid careful and systematic attention to the relationship between environmental and cultural variables, mapped the distribution of cultigens ("cultivated crops"), and provided estimates of pre-Columbian populations of the Americas, his Boasian particularist perspective prevented him from moving beyond possibilism (Ellen 1986: 24–25). The complexity of culture-environment relationships mystified him, rather than leading to the generation of empirically useful generalizations (Kroeber 1939: 205).

Kroeber: Cultural Patterns and the Superorganic

Kroeber's ethnological interests, however, went well beyond the plotting of culture traits and the study of culture areas. He shifted his focus to broad macrolevel cultural patterns. He wrote that "basic patterns are nexuses of culture traits which have assumed a definite and coherent structure, which function successfully, and which acquire major historic weight and persistence" (Kroeber 1952: 92).

As already noted, Boas viewed culture as the result of the accretion of traits through diffusion. Cultural elements, he believed, were integrated into the whole "according to the genius of the people who borrowed these." This integration was psychological in nature being the result of the *Geist* or spirit of a people. Although Boas was aware of the wholeness of culture, he never elaborated on the question of cultural integration. In general, interest in trait distribution hindered Boas and many of his students from fully exploring the notion of cultural unity (Langness 1993: 72). These anthropologists continued to see culture as a jumble of odds and ends and accidental accretions in which no rhyme or reason could be found. In his *Primitive Society*, Lowie (1920: 441) described culture (civilization) as "a planless hodgepodge, that thing of shreds and patches." The problem of cultural integration was thus left up to Kroeber and Boas's other students to tackle.

Kroeber perceived culture as an emergent phenomenon that was qualitatively different from and irreducible to chemical, biological, or psychological phenomena, possessing its own inner dynamics, principles, and its own "regularities of form." It was on this issue that Kroeber departed significantly from Boas.

> Primary, it seems to me, is the recognition of culture as a "level" or "order" emergent of natural phenomena, a level marked by a certain distinctive organization of its characteristic phenomena (Kroeber 1952: 4).[11]

By this he meant that culture was a **"superorganic"** phenomenon (a term he borrowed from Herbert Spencer) that had to be studied in its own terms as something above or outside nature. Culture, according to this view, is something *sui generis* (unique, in a class by itself) that exists through people, but constitutes an order distinct from biology or psychology. In culture the personal and the individual play no significant role, according to this view.

Kroeber's idea of culture as superorganic is an analogue of the antimaterialist view of the French sociologist Émile Durkheim (Ellen 1986: 27). As Kroeber pointed out,

> Qualities of culture are: (1) It is transmitted and continued not by the genetic mechanism of heredity but by interconditioning of zygotes. (2) Whatever its origins in or through individuals, culture quickly tends to become supra-personal and anonymous. (3) It falls into patterns, or regularities of form and style and significance. (4) It embodies values, which may be formulated (overtly, as mores) or felt (implicitly, as in folkways) by the society carrying the culture (Kroeber 1952: 104).[12]

Behavioral and individual psychological factors had no part in cultural phenomena.

> The level which I have personally chosen . . . is the cultural one. . . . it seems the most consistent with an integrative-contextual or "historical" approach. . . . [I] separate out the purely cultural aspects of phenomena and to interrelate these among themselves, eliminating or "holding constant" the social and individual factors (Kroeber 1952: 7).[13]

It is true that, in the study of culture by deliberate suppression of individuals as individuals, the element of human behavior is eliminated. One investigates, provisionally, the interrelation of collective and patterned products of the behavior of personalities, with these personalities and their behavior no longer taken into account. For myself, I have carried out this methodological suppression without qualms (Kroeber 1952: 8).[14]

Kroeber attempted to demonstrate the transcending or supra-individual nature of culture by pointing to the many examples of independent inventions. These include the theory of natural selection by Charles Darwin and Alfred Wallace, the independent creation of calculus by Leibnitz and Newton, and the simultaneous independent rediscovery of Mendel's principles of genetics, to make the point that "the history of inventions is a chain of parallel instances" (Kroeber 1952: 45). Parallel inventions, what Kroeber called the "principle of simultaneity of invention," demonstrate that a force more powerful than any individual is in operation, the force of the superorganic. As Kroeber observed,

> Knowing the civilization of an age and a land, we can then substantially affirm that its distinctive discoveries, in this or that field of activity, were not directly contingent upon the personality of the actual inventors that graced the period, but would have been made without them (Kroeber 1952: 45).[15]

In other words, when the right cultural conditions arise, the inventors will appear and not just once but many times. Kroeber rejected the "great man theory of history." Indeed, for him, individual geniuses were merely "indicators of coherent pattern growths of cultural value."

> When we cease to look upon invention or discovery as some mysterious faculty of individual minds which are randomly dropped in space and time by fate; when we center our attention on the plainer relations of one such advancing step to the others, when, in short, interest shifts from individually biographic elements . . . and attaches wholeheartedly to the social or civilizational, evidence on this

point will be infinite in quantity, and the presence of majestic forces or sequences pervading civilization will be irresistibly evident (Kroeber 1952: 45).[16]

What contributes to the development of the appropriate cultural matrix conducive to the appearance of geniuses who then distill out the appropriate new ideas? For this Kroeber had no answers. For him, the locus of causality rested in the domain of culture as a self-generating force with its own dynamics and principles operating outside the constraints of the natural or organic world. For this reason, Kroeber was unable to specify the mechanisms to account for the occurrence of the "right" cultural conditions that beckon the genius at the right time. These conditions simply happened.

Kroeber opposed any attempts to explain culture in terms of individual psychological factors or economic or environmental factors. Here again we see Boas's conception that culture comes from culture and culture can only be understood in terms of itself in its fullest manifestation, although cast in a mode that would irritate Boas immensely. Kroeber (1952: 132) wrote that

> what is operative is a powerful system of circular causality. The human beings who influence culture and make new culture are themselves molded; and they are molded through the intervention of other men who are culturalized and thus products of previous culture. So it is clear that, while human beings are always the *immediate* causes of cultural events, these human causes are themselves the result of antecedent culture situations, having been fitted to the existing cultural forms which they encounter.[17]

Kroeber viewed culture as possessing two distinct characteristics, basic features (*reality culture*) and secondary features (*value culture*). Basic cultural features are associated with practical needs such as subsistence and are grounded in nature. Secondary features, however, which comprise the aesthetic domains, are autonomous and subject to their own internal principles operating independently of external factors (Hatch 1973:

99; Kroeber 1963: 62). It was the latter that Kroeber made his focus of study.

As he did not acknowledge any extracultural causality or any causal relationships between technology, economy, ecology and culture, Kroeber was content to focus exclusively on the aesthetic domain, the domain of creativity, play, styles and fashions. This is how he justified his point of view:

> When one finds the culture inventories of even neighboring lowly tribes invariably differing in a whole series of features, although their physical environment and external cultural exposure are essentially identical; when one people or small group of tribes has evolved a really suburb art, an intricate and specialized legal, economic, or ritual system, an amazingly novel recombination of elements of social organization, a successful political fabric, or a system of mythological-symbolic thought, out of much humbler antecedents, one must . . . accord our species with a very strong latent impulse toward play, innovation, and experiment, a true originality and inventiveness (Kroeber 1952: 218).[18]

The simplistic conceptualization of human-environment relationships that was typical of Boasian anthropology led to the impression that the environment had very little or nothing to do with the elaboration of cultural patterns and institutions. These things happened in terms of mysterious cultural forces. Kroeber noted that "secondary culture" tends to develop historically through growth curves in styles. All the anthropologists could do was to focus on customs and traditions, appreciate them for themselves in their particularities, and trace their macropatterns over time. The task Kroeber set for himself, the task of anthropology as he saw it, therefore, was to examine, classify, and search for connections between the patterns discernable in culture, whether that culture was large scale or small scale, transitory or persistent, local or worldwide (Wolf 1981: 50, 54).

To the majority of the Boasians, all of this was heresy and they would not stand for it. We must remember, as noted before, that this was academic anthropology, a time of an anthropological school which went with "disciple-ism," "despotism," and collegial rivalries and alliances that were crucial factors as to whether ideas would be accepted or rejected (cf. Service 1985: vii).

The challenge came from Edward Sapir (1884–1934), who, as well as being a pioneer in anthropological linguistics, also had a great interest in the relationship between culture and personality (White 1987: 12; see Sapir 1964). Sapir (1917: 442) stressed the important role of the individual and rejected Kroeber's notion of the superorganic. As Sapir put it,

> Had [Kroeber] occupied himself with the religious, philosophical, aesthetics, and crudely volitional activities and tendencies of man, I believe that Dr. Kroeber's case for the non-cultural significance of the individual would have been a far more difficult one to make (Sapir 1917: 442).

Sapir had thus issued a challenge to Kroeber to prove his point by tackling the aesthetic domain of culture.

Kroeber's notion of culture as a superorganic phenomenon, a force outside and above human agency, also drew considerable criticism from other highly annoyed Boasians. Ruth Benedict (1934: 231) accused him of expressing himself in "mystical phraseology" for resorting to "a force he calls the superorganic to account for the cultural process." Boas himself objected, calling Kroeber's superorganic "a mystical entity that exists outside the society of its individual carriers, and that moves by its own force."

Kroeber took up Sapir's challenge by undertaking his famous study of fashion changes in women's evening dress, which exemplifies his concern with stylistic patterns in the domain of secondary culture. The data for the study came from Parisian fashion magazines, fashion plates, and engravings dating back to the 1780s. Using measurements of dress length and width, among others, Kroeber was able to show through statistical analysis the occurrence of regular cyclical swings in such variables as length of skirt, for example, from short to long every one hundred years or so. Pointing out such trends, Kroeber demonstrated the presence of patterns unrecognized by individuals in the culture.

When talking about more general cultural patterns, Kroeber (1963: 41) wrote that every stylistic pattern "tends to develop and progress, later to degenerate and die." Kroeber employed the concept of superorganic and the idea of stylistic growth curves in his *Configuration of Culture Growth* (1944). In this study, he examined the developmental trajectories of patterns of form and style in such aesthetic domains as philology, sculpture, painting, drama, literature, and music in the major civilizations of the Old World. He wrote that

> the kind of general problems I treated in *Configuration of Culture Growth* could hardly have been even defined except in terms of assuming races and individuals to be uniform in mass effect. Thereafter, it was possible to explore more clearly the "movement" and "behavior" of the civilizational [cultural] phenomena treated (Kroeber 1952: 7).[19]

Kroeber was able to identify growth curves characterized by abrupt outbursts of great creativity, their culmination, exhaustion, and decline in one or several aesthetic domains. Each culture had many patterns, which altogether created a "whole-culture pattern."

In *Configuration*, Kroeber was also able to demonstrate how superorganic forces were not under the will of individual genius but called forth geniuses when the time was ripe.

> Genius is seen as a product which is a function of cultural growth. This growth, in developing a style-like pattern, evokes or releases the required innate individual talents or creative abilities which presumably are always potentially present in larger quantity than utilized. As the pattern is realized, a culmination is attained; with its exhaustion, decline sets in, until a new pattern is evolved. With this culture-level approach, we have at least made a beginning of understanding how civilizations

come to be and develop, instead of merely taking them for granted as miracles or accidents or deriving them from impossibly remote causes like physical environment (Kroeber 1952: 8).[20]

Having confined his analysis to the ideological and aesthetic domains of culture, which he could treat more or less as a closed system, Kroeber found no predictable trajectories because each trajectory was in effect a historically unique event. This was the application of Boas's doctrine of cultural relativism to whole civilizations (cf. Erickson and Murphy 1998: 78). Kroeber wrote that

> in reviewing the ground covered, I wish to say at the outset that I see no evidence of any true law in the phenomena dealt with; nothing cyclical, regularly repetitive, or necessary. There is nothing to show either that every culture must develop patterns with which a florescence of quality is possible, or that, having once so flowered, it must wither without chance for survival (Kroeber 1944: 761).[21]

This only confirmed what Kroeber had maintained previously; namely that cultural phenomena were irreducible to anything but culture itself (Moore 1997: 76).

Unfortunately, attempting to explain culture in terms of culture led Kroeber down a path to nowhere. After peering through the pages of Kroeber's tome, we are not one bit more informed about the operation of sociocultural systems than when we start out.

Although Kroeber vigorously advocated the idea of the superorganic nature of culture for several years, in 1948 he recanted his views, thus returning to the Boasian fold. The first anthropological school was whole again. Thus Kroeber wrote that

> I take this opportunity for formally and publicly recanting any extravagances and overstatements of which I may have been guilty through overardor of conviction in my "Superorganic. . . . As of 1948, it seems to me both unnecessary and productive of new difficulties, if, in order to account for the phenomena of culture, one assumes any entity,

substance, kind of being, or set of separate, autonomous, and wholly self-sufficient forces (Kroeber 1952: 112).[22]

If we are to accept Harris's (2001: 332) view that a scientific study of culture is contingent upon the assumption that individual behavior is the result rather than cause of cultural forces, then Kroeber made a quick foray into science, only to retreat in an 180-degree turnabout.

Given the preceding discussion, it is surprising that anthropologists George Murdock, Leslie White, and Julian Steward endeavored to highlight the scientific nature of Kroeber's work. They neglected to note that Kroeber's methodology and epistemological assumptions were wholly incompatible with a scientific approach. As Harris (2001: 342) summed it up,

> Kroeber's anthropological style, which in every respect remained well within the Boasian program, inheriting all of its initial limitations of theory and method, adding to them only in ways appropriate to a frank denial of scientific pretense.[23]

Edward Sapir, cultural anthropologist and comparative linguist trained by Boas who was the expositor of configurationalism and the idea of linguistic relativity.

EDWARD SAPIR: LANGUAGE, CULTURE, AND PERSONALITY

While Kroeber sought an integrating principle underlying the "shreds and patches" view of culture in the realm of the superorganic, other of Boas's students turned to the investigation of the relationship among language, culture, and personality. In part, the shift in this direction was a reaction to Kroeber's conception of culture and his view regarding the insignificance of the individual in culture.

Edward Sapir set the groundwork for this line of research. Sapir used ideas he developed in his book *Language* (1921) to investigate cultural processes (cf. Keesing and Keesing 1971: 392). He fully subscribed to the Boasian relativistic perspective, noting that the languages spoken by members of different cultures were fully developed and equally capable of conveying complex thoughts. According to his famous statement,

Both simple and complex types of language of an indefinite number of varieties may be found spoken at any desired level of cultural advance. When it comes to linguistic form, Plato walks with the Macedonian swineherd, Confucius with the head-hunting savage of Assam (Sapir 1921: 234).

Sapir pointed out that culture, like language, is symbolic and is based upon shared and communicated meanings. Just like language, which is part of culture, he reasoned, other components of culture are internalized as well. He believed that there is an underlying unconscious pattern or "configuration" of cultural behavior comparable to the grammar of language (cf. Keesing and Keesing 1971: 392). This view has been referred to as **configurationalism** and was elaborated further by Sapir's friend and colleague Ruth Benedict (Salzman 2001: 69–70). Behavioral patterns observable by the anthropologist are an expression of this underlying configuration in the minds of individuals.

In an article entitled "Cultural Anthropology and Psychiatry," Sapir (1932: 432–433) wrote that

> the true locus of culture is in the interactions of specific individuals and, on the subjective side, in the world of meanings which each one of these individuals may unconsciously abstract for himself from his participation in these interactions.

Sapir thus defined culture as, to use present-day jargon, a dialogical multisubjective and negotiated reality remarkably similar to the construal of culture by postmodern anthropological writers (see Clifford 1986a: 7, 14–15; Marcus and Fischer 1986: 8). To reiterate a point made earlier, this convergence between postmodernist formulations and the work of Sapir is not surprising, as the former incorporates many elements of the Boasian perspective. What is surprising is that present-day anthropologists treat postmodern thought as new, cutting edge, and innovative, whereas in fact much of its formulations either comes directly from, or was anticipated in, Boasian anthropology.

Another area of convergence between present-day postmodern interpretivists and Sapir is in his views on the relationship between language and perception. Sapir noted, for example, that as individuals learn language they internalize it and thereafter can only perceive the world through their particular linguistic categories and classifications. Sapir (1929: 209, 214) wrote that

> [language] powerfully conditions all our thinking about social problems and processes. Human beings do not live in the objective world alone, nor alone in the world of social activity as ordinarily understood but are very much at the mercy of the particular language which has become the medium of expression for their society. It is quite an illusion to imagine that one adjusts to reality essentially without the use of language and that language is merely an incidental means of solving specific problems of communication or reflection.

> The fact of the matter is that the "real world" is to a large extent unconsciously built up on the language habits of the group. No two languages are ever sufficiently similar to be considered as representing the same social reality. The worlds in which different societies live are distinct worlds, not merely the same world with different labels attached. . . . We see and hear and otherwise experience very largely as we do because the language habits of our community predisposes certain choices of interpretation.[24]

These ideas along with contributions from Benjamin Whorf (1941), a student of Sapir, form the basis of what became known as **the Sapir-Whorf hypothesis,** or more recently **linguistic relativity** (see Lucy 1997). The Sapir-Whorf hypothesis holds that language and culture are interrelated and that people's thoughts and perceptions of reality are powerfully influenced by the language they speak (for an overview see McNeill 1987: 173–198). Similar views regarding language inform the discourse of postmodern philosophers and have contributed to cultural constructionist views in American anthropology. For example, Jacques Derrida (1976: 145) espouses an extreme version of this idea (cf. Layton 1997: 194). A careful assessment of linguistic relativism/determinism is highly useful at this point.

The Sapir-Whorf hypothesis posits that people are born into linguistic communities that already have languages with lexicons, labels, categories, concepts, and grammatical rules that guide and direct the way people think and perceive reality. In a paper called "The Relation of Habitual Thought and Behavior to Language" (written in 1939 and published in 1941), Whorf compared the manner in which speakers of English and speakers of Hopi made reference to time. Whorf pointed out that English speakers use spatial metaphors to refer to time (for instance, a long time, short time) and refer to time in terms of units much like the way they refer to things and objects (e.g., two seconds, two minutes, two cars, two people) (Peoples and Bailey 1994: 56).

Another point Whorf noted was that speakers of English construe time in terms of past, present, and future tenses. Hopi, on the other hand, does not have equivalent linguistic categories as these. From this, Whorf concluded that Hopi speakers and speakers of English perceive the passage of time very differently.

These ideas, which are referred to as the Sapir-Whorf hypothesis, imply that language has a powerful effect upon our perceptions of the world and universe. In other words, that language in effect determines peoples' perceptions of reality, worldviews, and cultures (cf. Bohannan and Glazer 1988: 151). How powerfully this determinism is treated depends on whether a particular researcher is using the "weak version" or the "strong version" of the Sapir-Whorf formulation (Bonvillain 2000: 51–52).

This kind of linguistic relativism, which holds that symbols/language act like a curtain interposed between our consciousness and the external world, opens the road toward cultural constructionist views and the epistemological relativism they entail (cf. D'Andrade 1995: 149). Present-day cultural constructionists espouse an extreme version of the Sapir-Whorf viewpoint, asserting that language does not simply influence perceptions of reality, but rather that it creates reality.

Whorf's analysis of the Hopi language has been severely criticized (see Malotki 1983; Pinker 1994), and the notion that language determines culture, which the Sapir-Whorf hypothesis implies, is not widely accepted. There is a lot of evidence that the type of linguistic determinism implied by the Whorfian and postmodern views is unwarranted. As Peoples and Bailey (1994: 56–57) have put it,

> First, if a language greatly shapes the way its speakers perceive the world, then we would expect a people's world view to change only at a rate roughly comparable to the rate at which their language changes. Yet there is no doubt that world views are capable of changing much more rapidly than language. How else can we explain the fact

that the English language has changed little in the past 150 years compared to the dramatic alteration in the world views of speakers of English? How else can we explain the spread of religious traditions such as Islam and Christianity out of their original homes among people with enormously diverse languages? . . . Second, if language strongly conditions perceptions, thought patterns, and entire world views, we should find that speakers of languages that have a common ancestor show marked cultural similarities. More precisely, we would expect to find the cultural similarities between speakers of related languages to be consistently greater than the cultural similarities between speakers of languages that are less closely related. Sometimes we do find this; unfortunately, we often do not.[25]

I shall say more about linguistic determinism/relativity in later chapters.

RUTH BENEDICT: CONFIGURATIONALISM AND THE PATTERNS OF CULTURE

Sapir's idea of configurations of culture was picked up and developed by his friend Ruth Benedict (1887–1948), also a student of Boas (for an overview, see Barnouw 1985: 59–75). Configurationalism was "a latter-day Boasian paradigm," the leading expositors of which were Sapir, Benedict and Margaret Mead (Adams 1998: 318). However, this perspective was soon adopted by a number of anthropologists, such as Morris Opler, Cora DuBois, and Clyde Kluckhohn, who were not trained by Boas but who shared his idealist epistemological point of view (Adams 1998: 318).

Benedict came to anthropology from a background in English literature at Vassar College. She was also a published poet who wrote under the pen name Anne Singleton (S. Barrett 1996: 57). Benedict received her doctorate at Columbia under Franz Boas in 1923 and thereafter remained closely associated with her teacher until his retirement in 1936. Benedict's early works, including her Ph.D. dissertation, were based on

Ruth Benedict, Boasian cultural anthropologist known for her interest in the relationship between culture and personality.

library research. She conducted a brief field study of the Serrano in southern California, in 1922, and subsequently conducted several summer field studies in the Southwest. Benedict's work among the Zuñi became an important aspect of her most famous work, *Patterns of Culture* (1934).

Like many of her colleagues, Benedict shared her teacher's beliefs in cultural determinism and the idea of cultural relativism. "To the anthropologist," Benedict (1934: 1) wrote,

> our customs and those of a New Guinea tribe are two possible social schemes for dealing with a common problem, and in so far as he remains an anthropologist he is bound to avoid any weighting of one in favor of another.[26]

Moreover, like Sapir and other Boasians, Benedict was fully committed to a humanistic

anthropology. In words reminiscent of present-day interpretive anthropologists, such as Clifford Geertz (1983: 19; see Chapter 13), Benedict (1948: 585) observed that

> to my mind the very nature of the problems posed and discussed in the humanities are closer, chapter by chapter, to those in anthropology than are the investigations carried on in most of the social sciences.

Benedict was well aware that the diffusionist studies of culture had failed to yield any integrating principle. Instead, such studies demonstrated that when cultural traits are passed from one group to another they were combined in different ways with other traits in a random fashion and the degree of importance that a particular trait acquired as part of a new trait constellation varied from culture to culture. Benedict's 1923 library based Ph.D. research on the role of the "guardian spirit" among Native North Americans, which followed the Boasian diffusionist approach, confirmed this. Benedict found, for example, that among one group the concept of guardian spirit was associated with male puberty rites, among another it was a hereditary lineage marker, and among still another it appeared in association with vision quests (Benedict 1934: 39–43). Benedict (1923: 84–85) concluded that

> it is, so far as we can see, an ultimate fact of human nature that man builds up his culture out of disparate elements, combining and recombining them; and until we have abandoned the superstition that the result is an organism functionally interrelated, we shall be unable to see our cultural life objectively, or to control its manifestations.

As Benedict's anthropological thought matured, however, she became uncomfortable with the diffusionist view espoused by Boasians such as Lowie, that cultural integration is nothing more than the totality of the linkages between its traits (cf. Leaf 1979: 222). Boas (1938: 680) himself had in his later years begun to entertain the "superstition," namely the idea that cultures are integrated: "It seems more desirable and worth while to understand each culture as a whole and to define its character."

Benedict undertook the search for an underlying explanatory principle, or as Margaret Mead (1959: 204) put it, "some integrating principle that would explain both the disparate origins of elements of which a culture was built and the wholeness which she felt was there in each culture." Benedict came upon an answer sometime in the late 1920s and early 1930s. For her it was a people's shared basic attitudes and values that gave uniformity to behavior. Benedict presented an elaboration of her ideas in her highly influential book *Patterns of Culture* (1934), which gained her an international reputation (Mintz 1981: 144). Like the work of Kroeber, Benedict's work represents another permutation of the culture-comes-from-culture perspective, but along a different line, which led her to consider human psychological factors.

Benedict argued that cultural integration occurs not at the level of traits, trait complexes, technologies, economies, or ecological settings, but rather in the pattern of ideas and emotions characteristic of any given culture. In other words, order, what ties a culture together, exists in the minds of the members of the culture (cf. Leaf 1979: 223). These patterns make cultures into "articulated wholes" consistent with the temperament of their members. For Benedict "pattern" referred to a distinct underlying set of values and emotions people have that pervades and integrates their cultures. How traits are integrated in a particular culture is to a large degree determined by the emotional theme characterizing that culture. Benedict (1934: 49) wrote that

> If we are interested in cultural processes, the only way in which we can know the significance of the selected detail of behaviour is against the background of the motives and emotions and values that are institutionalized in that culture.[27]

Like Boas, Benedict stressed the plasticity of human behavior and the powerful impact of

culture in shaping that behavior. Moreover, the starkly contrasting patterns of culture Benedict described among such groups as the Zuñi, the Kwakiutl, and the people of Dobu served as examples of the primacy of culture over biology, which, as we have seen, was an essential feature of Boasian anthropology.

Benedict viewed each culture as occupying a segment of a vast continuum of variability, or "great arc" of culture. In other words, each cultures was seen as having its own particular primary focus point to which considerable energy is devoted.

> In culture . . . we must imagine a great arc on which are ranged the possible interests provided either by the human age-cycle or by the environment or by man's various activities. A culture that capitalized even a considerable proportion of these would be as unintelligible as a language that used all the clicks, all the glottal stops, all the labials, dentals sibilants, and gutturals from voiceless to voiced and from oral to nasal. Its identity as a culture depends upon the selection of some segments of this arc. Every human society everywhere had made such selection in its cultural institutions. Each from the point of view of another ignores fundamentals and exploits irrelevancies. One culture hardly recognizes monetary values; another had made them fundamental in every field of behaviour. In one society technology is unbelievably slighted even in those aspects of life which seem necessary to ensure survival; in another, equally simple, technological achievements are complex and fitted with admirable nicety to the situation. One builds an enormous cultural superstructure upon adolescence, one upon death, one upon after-life (Benedict 1934: 24).[28]

Benedict elaborated on the idea that different cultures may come to emphasize particular features that then become central and around which other aspects of that society are organized:

> The diversity of cultures can be endlessly documented. A field of human behaviour may be ignored in some societies until it barely exists; it may even be in some cases unimagined. Or it may

almost monopolize the whole organized behaviour of the society, and the most alien situations be manipulated only in its terms. Traits having no intrinsic relation one with the other, and historically independent, merge and become inextricable, providing the occasion for behaviour that has no counterpart in regions that do not make these identifications. It is a corollary of this that standards, no matter in what aspect of behaviour, range in different cultures from the positive to the negative pole (Benedict 1934: 45).[29]

She reiterated this point of view in her 1938 paper on religion:

> Religion is a spotlight that swings quite indiscriminately, in one region bringing it about that property and all the concepts that center around it are religiously guaranteed, and in another leaving property entirely secular; in one region centering upon weather control, in another upon curing (Benedict 1938: 648).[30]

Benedict was expressing the Boasian assumption that institutions are purposeless (i.e., spotlights that swing indiscriminately) and operate virtually independently from the material requirements of human life.

The selection of any segments of the arc of human possibilities by any culture, as Benedict saw it, was not dictated by external factors such as economy, environment, demography, or technology. The reason one domain of culture takes on great significance in one place and another domain elsewhere is to be accounted for entirely in terms of internal cultural dynamics. This approach was perfectly consistent with Boas's teachings that cultural integration was psychological in nature, according to the *Geist* or spirit of a people, and was based upon unconscious categories and dominant ideas (cf. Stocking 1974: 8).

For Benedict (1934: 37) cultural variations and permutations were infinite: "[t]he possibilities are endless and the adjustments are often bizarre." She added, "The diversity of the possible combinations is endless, and adequate social

orders can be built indiscriminately upon a great variety of these foundations" (1934: 44).

In Benedict's view, any culture could develop along any trajectory because of its internal dynamics. However, Benedict maintained that it was impossible to specify why individual cultures developed along any given pattern (R. Barrett 1991: 84). Benedict (1934: 254) added that "any society selects some segment of the arc of possible human behavior, and in so far as it achieves integration its institutions tend to further the expression of its selected segments and inhibit its opposite expressions." Cultures, in other words, come in infinite varieties and why any particular culture develops along a particular trajectory cannot be explained.

Benedict attributed total determining force to culture by arguing that once a set of values came into existence they acquired a determining influence of their own completely detached from external factors. Placing the locus of cultural organization and integration in the level of subjective thought was again consistent with Boas's ideas (Hatch 1973: 80).

It was the influence of Benedict's work that, in accordance with Boas's teachings, further emphasized the idea of "cultures" in the plural in American anthropological thought. Her work led, once and for all, to the abandonment of the conception of culture in the singular, which was most often equated with "civilization" (Langness 1993: 108).

For Benedict (1934: 48), all aspects of culture were subject to the determining force of the underlying emotional pattern or configuration. For this reason, some refer to Benedict's formulation as **configurationalism** (Salzman 2001: 70). This is because "all miscellaneous behavior directed toward getting a living, mating, warring, and worshipping the gods, is made over into consistent patterns in accordance with unconscious canons of choice that develop within the culture." The circularity of reasoning here is fairly easy to see.

Each culture, according to Benedict, not only has a distinct and unique configuration of traits, but each one also has its own unique emotional configuration (feelings and motivations). "Cultures from this point of view," wrote Benedict (1932: 24), "are individual psychology thrown large upon the screen, given gigantic proportions and a long time span." Culture, in turn, determines people's personality by favoring "temperament types" best suited to it (Benedict 1934: 258). For psychological anthropologists **personality** refers to

> a more or less enduring organization of forces within the individual associated with a complex of fairly consistent attitudes, values, and modes of perception which account, in part, for the individual's consistency of behavior (Barnouw 1985: 8).

Benedict postulated a one-to-one relationship between culture and personality. The primary mechanism through which a culture's core values are instilled in its members, a process called **enculturation,** is through child-rearing practices. Parents using positive and negative sanctions teach their offspring the traits from their culture's segment of the arc, thereby molding the child into a particular personality type (Benedict 1949: 342–343). Thus human nature is shaped by the primary values of the culture to the degree that nearly all members come to believe that "their particular institutions reflect an ultimate and universal sanity" (Benedict 1934: 254). This does not mean, however, that Benedict (1934: 220) thought every member of a particular culture had the same temperament:

> No anthropologist with a background of experience in other cultures has ever believed that individuals were automatons, mechanically carrying out the decrees of their civilization. No culture yet observed has been able to eradicate the differences in the temperament of the persons who compose it. It is always a give-and-take.[31]

Benedict observed that every culture contains individuals that deviate from the "personality type selected by their culture." However, because cultural values are relative, deviance itself is relative as well. Thus one culture's madman can easily be another culture's saint or prophet. Among the Dobu, the man who is friendly is a deviant, while the man held in the highest esteem among the Plains cultures would be the deviant among the Pueblos. Similarly, the prestigious Potlatch chief of the Kwakiutle would be a megalomaniac paranoid in Euro-American culture (Benedict 1934: 195).

For Benedict, the personality types of entire cultures could be described in terms of a single trait. Thus the Dobuans of Melanesia were "paranoid," the Kwakiutl of the Northwest Coast of North America were "megalomaniacs," and the Pueblos of New Mexico, passive and unemotional. These characterizations were more than simply stereotypes, Benedict maintained, but were generalizations made on the basis of a careful comparison of the entire institutional and ideological aspects of each culture.

Because culture determines personality, people from different cultures therefore act, feel, and think differently. The implication here is that cultures are not only entities unique unto themselves but also that they are incommensurable with one another. Benedict was espousing the idea of the "radical plurality" of culture, arguing that each culture produces a set of unique and culturally particular human characteristics. The uniqueness of cultures, in turn, implies that the range of cultural diversity, the great arc of potentialities, is all but limitless. Human thought and behavior are therefore the product of each distinct culture, rather than "pan-human culture." Because cultures are radically different, they are incommensurable with one another.

Benedict's ideas reflect the Boasian particularistic and relativistic perspective that each culture can only be studied in its own terms. Stiffened variants of these ideas, as we shall see, reappear in the writings of present-day epistemophobic, antitheory interpretive anthropologi-

cal writers, who go on to argue that culture produces an essential "otherness" or difference between humans. Related to this is their fixation
on the "politics of identity," which as one anthropologist put it "makes for little dramas, but
doesn't do anything meaningful politically."

For postmodern anthropological writers this
"otherness" precludes the possibility of anyone
ever achieving true cross-cultural understanding.
Benedict, however, never entertained the idea
that it was impossible to understand another culture. As she pointed out in her book *The
Chrysanthemum and the Sword* (1946),

> A conviction of difference is dangerous only if a
> student rests content with saying simply that these
> differences are so fantastic that it is impossible to
> understand such people. The anthropologist has
> good proof in his experience that even bizarre be-
> havior does not prevent one's understanding it
> (Benedict 1946: 10).[32]

The present-day notion of the difference of the
"cultural Other" has in fact led cultural constructionist anthropologists to rest content by
saying that these differences are indeed so fantastic that it is impossible to understand other
cultures.

Benedict's idea that culture was the primary
determinant of the personality of its members
became the central thesis of the **culture and
personality** approach in American anthropology (Barnouw 1985; Langness 1993: 108).
Among the first noteworthy works to investigate the relationship between culture and personality was Cora Du Bois's study of the inhabitants of the Indonesian island of Alor. In her
study *The People of Alor* (1944), Du Bois relied
upon a statistical concept called **modal personality.** Modal personality refers to a central
tendency that appears in a society with a higher
frequency distribution and entails the use of
projective techniques, such as the administration
of the **Rorschach test** and the **thematic apperception test** to sample populations. Today,
many psychological anthropologists speak of a

basic modal, or typical personality, when referring to personality configurations in a given
culture.

Inspired by Benedict's ideas, other anthropologists conducted studies focusing upon the relationships between personality and child-rearing
practices such as swaddling (Gorer and Rickman 1949), contact between mother and child
(Caudill and Weinstein 1969), and economic
factors and modes of production (Barry et al.
1959; Edgerton 1965; Goldschmidt 1965).

Benedict: The Configuration of Cultures in New Mexico and the Great Plains

Benedict's psychological portraits of the Pueblo
Indians of New Mexico and the Indians of the
Great Plains enables us to gain insight into her approach to the study of culture and personality. To
describe the cultural configurations among different groups, Benedict adopted terms from the
German philosopher **Friedrich Nietzsche**'s
study of Greek drama. Benedict thus characterized Pueblo culture as "Apollonian" and the
Great Plains Indians as the diametrically opposite
"Dionysian." She explicated the contrast as
follows:

> The basic contrast between the Pueblos and the
> other cultures of North America is the contrast
> that is named and described by Nietzsche in his
> studies of Greek tragedy. He discusses two diamet-
> rically opposed ways of arriving at the values of
> existence. The Dionysian pursues them through
> "the annihilation of the ordinary bounds and lim-
> its of existence"; he seeks to attain in his most val-
> ued moments escape from the boundaries imposed
> upon him by his five senses, to break through into
> another order of experience. The desire of the
> Dionysian, in personal experience or in ritual, is to
> press through it toward a certain psychological
> state, to achieve excess. The closest analogy to the
> emotions he seeks is drunkenness, and he values
> the illuminations of frenzy. With Blake, he believes
> "the path of excess leads to the palace of wisdom."
> The Apollonian distrusts all this, and has often lit-

tle idea of the nature of such experiences. He finds means to outlaw them from his conscious life. He "knows but one law, measured in the Hellenic sense." He keeps the middle of the road, stays within the known map, does not meddle with disruptive psychological states. In Nietzsche's fine phrase, even in the exaltation of the dance he "remains what he is, and retains his civic name" (Benedict 1934: 78–79).[33]

Benedict construed the cultures she studied in these terms. She described the Pueblos as having a suspicion of individualism and valuing the submergence of the will of the individual into the will of the group. Restraint, conformity to tradition and precedence, and moderation were exalted over individual initiative and innovation, according to Benedict. Furthermore, according to her description, the Pueblos were placid, unemotional and avoided excesses. Ecstatic religious experiences, the use of hallucinogenic drugs, and self-mutilation, so prominent among the Great Plains cultures, were absent among the Pueblos.

In stark contrast, Benedict depicted the Dionysian Plains Indians as warlike, individualistic, self-reliant, ambitious, and competitive. They valued "all violent experiences" and sought individual supernatural powers to help them in the vagaries of warfare and aggressive competition. Benedict (1934: 81) described the vision quest of the Plains warriors as follows:

On the western plains men sought these visions with hideous tortures. They cut strips from the skins of their arms, they struck off fingers, they swung themselves from tall poles by straps inserted under the muscles of their shoulders. They went without food and water for extreme periods. They sought in every way to achieve an order of experience set apart from daily living. It was grown men, on the plains, who went out after visions. Sometimes they stood motionless, their hands tied behind them, or they staked out a tiny spot from which they could not move till they had received their blessing. Sometimes . . . they wandered over distant regions, far out into dangerous country. Some tribes chose precipices and places especially

associated with danger. At all events a man went alone, or, if he was seeking his vision by torture and someone had to go out with him to tie him to the pole from which he was to swing till he had his supernatural experience, his helper did his part and left him alone for his ordeal.[34]

Benedict was drawing a contrast between cultures that accentuated conformity and moderation with those that stressed extravagance and individual display (R. Barrett 1991: 84). As far as Benedict was concerned, her typology of the Pueblo and Plains Indians in terms of cultural configurations she called Apollonian and Dionysian was sufficient to explain the differences between the two groups. In other words, the two groups were different because their cultures differed.

The differences in question between the Pueblo and Plains Indians, of course, are explicable in terms of different subsistence systems and different ecological adaptations. The Pueblos were farmers who lived in villages and followed a routine of planting, harvesting, and storage of crops in an annual cycle. Conformity to precedence and tradition was desired, as in all agrarian communities, while individual initiative and inventiveness that would disrupt the agricultural cycle were viewed with suspicion and discouraged.

The Great Plains Indians, on the other hand, were nomadic horseback buffalo hunters who engaged in intense marauding warfare. They possessed institutions that engendered self-reliance through demonstrations of bravery and tolerance of pain and hardship and extolled the virtues of the warrior, all characteristics necessary for survival in the highly competitive and warlike environment of the Great Plains. These traits were also necessary for success as nomadic horseback buffalo hunters, which required reliance upon individual initiative, resourcefulness, and quick thinking.

The marauding warfare complex in the Great Plains, which evolved following European contact and the introduction of horses and firearms, has been described as a system of free enterprise (R. Barrett 1991: 84). There were opportunities for any man to attain great status through displays of individual acts of bravery in warfare, seizing enemy horses or weapons, being victorious in hand-to-hand combat, and competing with one another for prestige.

What Benedict provided in her *Patterns of Culture* was description, not explanation. She did not address the question of why the Plains Indian cultures were so different from those of the Pueblos. Benedict did not believe that there were any causal connections between ecology, subsistence, and culture. As we have seen, she thought that it was impossible to specify why cultures developed along any particular pattern. Just as in the works of Kroeber, the idea of adaptation was absent from Benedict's work as well. True to the Boasian program, she seemed content to artfully describe the diversity of human cultural patterns without seeing the need to explain them.

In this, Benedict's work has much in common with that of present-day writers who have retreated to ethnographic particularism. Her answer to why the Plains Indians were so different from the Pueblos was simply to say that cultures are different because they are different and quoting a saying from among the Digger Indians:

> God gave to every people a cup, a cup of clay, and from their cup they drank their life. . . . They all dipped in the water . . . but their cups were different (Benedict 1934: 21–22).[35]

The statement that cultures are different because they are different is a proposition in which the conclusion is already present in the premise. The logically vacuous circularity in argument is all too evident and entails the logical fallacy of begging the question. As such, Benedict's formulations do not advance our understanding of sociocultural phenomena.

Benedict has been criticized for selective omission and de-emphasis of contradictory and incompatible ethnographic data in constructing the psychological configurations described in *Patterns of Culture*. Moreover, Benedict has been criticized for a lack of methodological rigor and highly impressionistic and scientifically unreliable procedures (Harris 2001: 404, 407). Her attempt to describe the personality types of whole cultures under a single label is also seen to be a gross oversimplification.

Benedict and the Samurai: Anthropology from a Distance

During World War II, Benedict worked for the Bureau of Overseas Intelligence, in the Office of War Information in Washington, D.C. During this time a number of anthropologist were recruited to conduct research to promote the war effort. Benedict was asked to provide anthropological information on Japanese cultural values and how these might influence Japanese behavior during the war.

Benedict's attempt to discern the "national character" of the enemy, which had to be done without fieldwork, since the United States was at war with Japan, came to be known as "cultures at a distance" or **national character studies** (see the volume edited by Mead and Métraux 1953). Benedict had to relying on written accounts by Westerners, interviews with Japanese-Americans, and a variety of other materials, such as Japanese films, mythology, and propaganda pamphlets.

She applied the idea of cultural configurations to the study of the dominant theme or core values of Japanese culture. Her findings were presented in the book *The Chrysanthemum and the Sword* (1946), from which I earlier cited a passage. In this work, Benedict described the Japanese in terms of dual traits, preoccupation with aesthetics (hence the chrysanthemum) and militarism (hence the sword). *Chrysanthemum and the Sword* became the model for many other national character studies that were motivated by the endeavor during World War II to understand the character of enemies and allies. Geoffrey Gorer (1943) produced a similar study on the Japanese. Erik Erikson (1963: 326–358) provided an analysis of German national character and the cultural reasons for Hitler's appeal to German youth.

The adequate description and interpretation of the personality patterns of other cultures requires a depth of understanding and familiarity with those other cultures that was lacking in the studies cited here. Stereotyping was therefore the end result in most cases.

In general, the one lesson of national character studies was not that they shed light on the personality structure of other peoples but rather what they reveal regarding the follies of research based on over simplifications and insubstantial data (see Haring 1949).

Benedict's work, regardless of its serious shortcomings, was influential in pointing out to anthropologists the importance of considering personality as an aspect of the cultures they studied. This led to a number of attempts to develop more sophisticated methods for measuring and describing personality traits and personality structures cross-culturally in a trend generally known as "culture and personality" studies, as noted previously (see Barnouw 1985; Suárez-Orozoco et al., 1994; Wallace 1970; Whiting and Child 1953).

Although the theoretical contributions of Benedict's work (and the work of her student Margaret Mead, which I shall discuss next) were far from being earth shattering, this was not the case with respect to the intellectual impact of her work. As Harris (2001: 409) put it,

> The artful presentation of cultural differences to a wide professional and lay public by Mead and Benedict must be reckoned among the important events in the history of American intellectual thought. The significance of their contributions as far as cultural theory is concerned cannot be regarded as of a similar magnitude.[36]

MARGARET MEAD: COMING OF AGE IN AMERICA

The last Boasian anthropologist to be discussed in this chapter is Margaret Mead (1901–1978). She was among the shining stars of American anthropology until her work came under massive criticism in the early 1980s. Mead was the first American female anthropologist to conduct fieldwork in a faraway place. She was a prolific

Margaret Mead and a Samoan friend. Mead is best known for her Samoan ethnography and study of child rearing practices and personality.

writer who made anthropology a household word. Mead's total scholarly output during the period between 1925 and her death in 1978 numbers some 1400 items, including books, articles, reports, audio recordings, and films (Gordan 1976). Mead's major monographs include *Coming of Age in Samoa* (1928), *Growing up in New Guinea* (1930), and *Sex and Temperament in Three Primitive Societies* (1935).

Mead came to anthropology in her senior year as an English and psychology major. Fascinated by a course she took from Franz Boas, Mead decided to pursue graduate work in anthropology. Her decision was in part also due to the influence of Ruth Benedict, then Boas's teaching assistant (Moore 1997: 103). As a student of Boas and Benedict, Mead became versed in the configurationist approach and was involved in the intellectual discussions that led Benedict to formulate the ideas presented in *Patterns of Culture* (Mead 1959: 207). Like her mentor, Benedict, Mead's Ph.D. work, a study of the material culture of Polynesia, was based on library research.

Mead's entrance into anthropology coincided with a period when Boas was trying to establish the validity of his cultural determinist paradigm over hereditarian theories (the nature/nurture debate). The prevailing viewpoint in the United States was espoused by G. Stanley Hall (1904), a noted psychologist who affirmed that the stress of adolescence had a biological basis. The Boasians realized that if they could find a cultural setting in which adolescence was stress free they could demolish such hereditarian views once and for all.

The challenge for Boas was to how translate his cultural determinist paradigm into a set of propositions that would lend themselves to empirical analysis. What Boas settled upon was to instruct Mead to compare a particular stage in individual psychological development in two cultures. This approach would be enough to demonstrate the biopsychological plasticity of human behavior (Harris 2001: 408). Thus, to find evidence for this point of view, Boas sent the young Margaret Mead to American Samoa.

Mead arrived in American Samoa in 1925, not knowing that the work she would engage in over the next few months would propel her to the status of anthropological superstar. She stated the questions that brought her there as follows: "Are the disturbances which vex our adolescents due to the nature of adolescence itself or to the [culture]? Under different conditions does adolescence present a different picture?" (Mead 2001 [1928]: 17).

What did Mead find in Samoa? She found life in Samoa to be serene, the people free of sexual inhibitions and guilt, permissive sexual attitudes, and stress-free adolescent sexuality. The conclusion was that the stress of adolescence in the United States could not be biological in nature, but was caused by culture. Thus Mead wrote that

one by one, aspects of behavior which we had been accustomed to consider invariable complements of our humanity were found to be merely as result of [culture], present in the inhabitants of one country, absent in another country, and this without a change in race. . . . neither race nor common humanity can be held responsible for many of the forms which even such basic human emotions as love and fear and anger take under different social conditions (Mead 2001 [1928]: 12–13).[37]

The Boasian cultural determinist paradigm had been proven. It was nurture over nature. Boas was delighted.

The Boasian paradigm remained uncontested until the American anthropological community learned of an Australian anthropologist by the name of Derek Freeman (1916–2001), a specialist in Samoan culture with close to four decades of field experience. In a book called *Margaret Mead and Samoa: The Making and Unmaking of an Anthropological Myth* (1983), Freeman stated that Mead was wrong, completely wrong. Samoa was

Derek Freeman, Australian anthropologist best known as the debunker of Mead's Samoan ethnography.

lies and playful hoaxes by her friends and informants (Freeman 1983: 282–302; 1998).

Freeman went on to charge Mead of committing the scientific sin of going into the field with answers already in hand, answers derived from Franz Boas's "absolute" cultural determinist perspective. Mead was "a stooge for Franz Boas" (Freeman 1983: 282–283). Mead's defenders took issue with this charge, stating that Boas was not "a doctrinaire cultural determinist" (Barnouw 1985: 100). This argument, however, is impossible to sustain, as the discussion in the previous chapter suggests.

The questions Freeman raised had serious implications for American anthropology. How could one of the most famous and well-respected anthropologists of her generation, one of the founding figures of the discipline, so to speak, be so mistaken? *Margaret Mead and Samoa* struck many in the American anthropological community like a bolt of lightning and set off a "media feeding frenzy." The debunker rose to prominence.

Not until the publication of Patrick Tierney's *Darkness in El Dorado* (2000), in which that writer raises a host of spurious and fallacious charges against the anthropologist Napoleon Chagnon (Shankman 2001: 48; Shermer 2001), would the anthropological community encounter similar circumstances. The parallels between the two cases are interesting. They both center upon the Other and the "representation" of the Other. Also, the media hype in both cases overshadowed the weaknesses of the debunkers' cases, which included great liberties with the evidence, specious allegations, and misrepresentation of the works being attacked (see Shankman 2001; Shermer 2001).

Freeman's own account has some of the same kinds of shortcomings for which he criticized Mead's ethnographic endeavors (Holmes 1987: 151, 173; Orans 1996: 12; Schneider 1983: 6; Shankman 1996, 2001; Womack 1998: 128–129). Nevertheless, he must still be highly commended

nothing like the picture depicted in *Coming of Age in Samoa.*

In Freeman's (1983: 238–239, 289) account the Samoans are sexually inhibited, puritanical, prudish, aggressive, competitive, and jealous. More than that, according to Freeman, the Samoans have a propensity for suicide, murder, assault, and rape. Freeman (1983: xii, 289) mercilessly attacked Mead's conclusions as being "fundamentally in error" and some "preposterously false." Mead had failed, Freeman argued, because of her inexperience, inability to speak the language fluently, the short duration of her stay (months instead of years), and her tendency for oversimplifying cultural phenomena. Finally, Freeman maintained that Mead had fallen victim to the mischievous for revealing a major defect in an academic enterprise that has naively accepted a work that is so wrong for such a long time (see Freeman 1983: 95–96).

The fallout of what became known as the Mead–Freeman controversy was, among other things, a lot of soul searching and plenty of recriminations. At issue was the question that if anthropology is a science, then how is it possible for Mead's work, which was so flawed, to stand unchallenged?

The anthropologist Martin Orans (1996: 1) attributes the uncritical reception of Mead's *Coming of Age in Samoa* by anthropologists and the American public to the fact that the book had a message that everyone wanted to hear (see MacClancy 1996: 18). Americans, Orans writes, had a great desire for confirmation of the "ideological" claim that culture not biology is a key determinant of human behavior, and Mead gave them that confirmation. In part the uncritical reception of Mead's work was also due to the Boasians' near total hegemony over the field, which created an intellectual atmosphere in which the savants could express their views without much risk of being challenged.

For Orans, Mead's Samoan research is thus an indictment of American cultural anthropology as a discipline (Orans 1996:10). He observes that Mead's work stood unchallenged even by reviewers who had a grasp of the most fundamental principle of science, which is that propositions must be verifiable and they must be accepted or rejected based upon how well they accord with empirical observations. Orans is absolutely correct, although there were several anthropologists who had pointed out the essentially unscientific nature of Mead's anthropology (e.g., Gold 1983; Harris 2001: 409–413, 1983a, 1983b).

What happened in Samoa all those years ago? Why was Mead so off the mark? There are no surprises here. As with other members of the Boasian school, Mead (1962: 134–135) did not believe that the scientific model was applicable

to anthropological investigations. The fact that members of Boas's school peppered their writings with the honorifics "science" and "scientific" does not change the fundamentally unscientific nature of their undertaking. Mead opted for the intuitive approach to the individual case. Take, for example, Mead's (2001 [1928]: 169) description of her methodology:

> As the physician and the psychiatrist have found it necessary to describe each case separately and to use their cases as illumination of a thesis rather than as irrefutable proof such as is possible to adduce in the physical sciences, so the student of the more intangible and psychological aspects of human behaviour is forced to illuminate rather than demonstrate a thesis.[38]

Mead justified her approach on the grounds that her own judgment as an authority "who had been there" was sufficient and whatever other measures, such as systematic sampling would only be useful in convincing others (Orans 1996: 127):

> Would it be more acceptable if I could devise some method of testing the similarity of attitudes among the girls, in a quantitative way. . . . I wouldn't feel any wiser after collecting information in that style but maybe the results would be strengthened (Mead's letter to Boas, in Orans 1996: 127).[39]

This was a huge mistake because Mead rejected the very thing she needed in order to assess the validity of her findings. Aside from the absence of rigorous testing, Mead also failed to investigate whether adolescence is more stressful than other phases of Samoan life. This is crucial because without taking other phases of life into consideration there is no way for one to gauge the relative stress of adolescence. Nor is there evidence of any standard measure that would enable one to compare "stress" in Samoa and "stress" in 1920s United States (Orans 1996: 154). Instead of attending to these important requirements, Mead relied upon her own subjective impressions and anecdotal accounts found in the popular literature (Orans 1996: 154).

Given Mead's immense departure from the standards of scientific research, it is remarkable that cultural constructionists writers parade her anthropology as an example of scientific anthropology and then commence upon profound discussions of the follies of a science of culture (e.g., Clifford 1986b: 102–103). Marcus and Fischer (1986: 3), two other notable cultural constructionists, dubbed the Mead-Freeman controversy as a "scientific scandal" and an example of "the enduring anthropological problem of what constitutes an adequate account of another culture in the face of contrasting interpretations." They add that

> if one prominent lesson of this controversy is that the knowledge which anthropology offers of cultural alternatives cannot be conceived according to the conventional notion of scientific precision and certainty, then on what authority can it offer itself as a critic of its own society? (Marcus and Fischer 1986: 3)[40]

Thus in the furious debate over the Mead-Freeman issue the majority of the protagonists failed to realize that the debate was not about the merits or lack thereof of a scientific approach in anthropology, but about a work that does not even approach the bare minimum standards of scientific research. This is an illustration of how grossly uninformed many anthropologists are regarding even the elementary requirements of science and scientific research.

Orans's assessment of American anthropology, with reference to the Mead-Freeman issue supports a point that I have made in the previous chapters:

> From its inception [American anthropology] has often been profoundly unscientific and positively cavalier in its willingness to accept generalizations without empirical substantiation. It tends to make little use of logic and mathematics in expressing relationships and seldom employs reasonably well-defined concepts. It therefore produces propositions that are untestable. Relationships and concepts tend to be so ill-defined that they provide too much "wiggle room"— opportunity to claim

that whatever test has been offered to falsify a claim has missed the intended meaning (Orans 1996: 125).[41]

Not everyone was blind to the circumstance of the practice of American anthropology. In fact, years before member of the American anthropological community had heard Freeman's name, Harris (2001: 411) had specifically pointed out the unscientific nature of Mead's methodology, described previously, and the problematic nature of her "intuitive prerogatives of a clinical diagnostician."

Nonetheless, there is no point in arguing with Orans's (1996: 10) astute observation that: "From the outset most cultural anthropologists have practiced the discipline as though unaware of the requirement of verifiability." They simply could not tell that Mead had it all wrong. Nor have circumstances changed for the better. Indeed, Orans's observations are well worth noting:

> If the pioneers in cultural anthropology were in practice unscientific, many of the leading lights among contemporary anthropologists practice an anthropology that is avowedly nonempirical on the grounds that verifiability is inappropriate to the investigation of human behavior. . . . The requirement of verifiability is considered by these anthropologists to be a manifestation of "positivism," which they regard as outmoded. The most extreme position within this camp is that all understanding is a "construction" devised to serve the interests quite independent of knowing the truth; indeed, these extremists would scoff at the notion of "truth" as anything other than a perspective related to one's position in society or in space. This they think is consistent with the relativistic findings of modern physics [Heisenberg's uncertainty principle]. Freed from the constraints of empirical verification, many of these anthropologists speak a language almost totally unintelligible to those of us who are looking for empirical referents and relational terms whose meanings we clearly grasp. It is a kind of speaking in tongues perhaps emulative of certain French savants of great erudition but no understanding of science. It

is from this perspective that many of the reviews of the Mead-Freeman debate were written (Orans 1996: 11).[42]

Instead of a more rigorous approach and attention to methodological and theoretical considerations, the new anthropologists are calling for an epistemological free-for-all as an answer to the problem of bias in anthropological research. Orans (1996: 137) adds that

> the ambiguous notion of multiple truths has become a charter for the idea that "anything goes," that you have your truth and I have mine, and ultimately for a rejection of empirical verification. In its most egregious form this approach holds truth to be merely a label employed by competing interest groups to sanctify beliefs useful for furthering their ends. From this perspective, evidence for propositions is of little interest; competing claims are seen simply as furthering competing ends, and the demand that propositions be stated in a manner capable of verification is vilified as ethnocentric positivism and doubtless the tool of some ruling class.[43]

The main point that has been overlooked in the Mead-Freeman case is that whatever flaws there are in Mead's research they are there because she discarded scientific criteria and standards of validation, not because she adhered to these principles. She failed terribly because she did not even heed the minimum standards of scientific research.

The Mead-Freeman controversy has important implications for anthropology, but not the ones that the cultural constructionists have focused upon. The controversy tells us that all sorts of blunders and follies await those who spurn the scientific requirement for validation and the testing of propositions against empirical evidence. As Orans (1996: 155) points out,

> Mead should have attended to that most scientific of all questions—what evidence she would consider inconsistent with her hypothesis. Without such an understanding her work may properly be damned with the harshest scientific criticism of all,

that it is "*not even wrong,*" for without such consideration the meaning of her claim has not been adequately specified (emphasis added).[44]

The most important question to be raised about Mead and her research pertains to the epistemological basis of anthropological knowledge. Is the debate beyond resolution? Should we purge our scientific pretensions and embrace the dubious idea that in the final analysis, knowledge is hopelessly problematic, that everyone has *a* truth, but not *the* truth? In other words, should we acquiesce to the view that that when it comes to sociocultural phenomena, the question of the veracity of propositions can never be established? Cultural constructionists will no doubt answer in the affirmative; others do not.

There are those anthropologists who do not view the problem of knowledge to be insurmountable and feel that the world is knowable and that not all claims about the world can be correct. The solution to the problem, these anthropologists would say, is to go back to the evidence. There is a huge corpus of ethnographic and historical information not yet tapped fully that can shed light on the central issues in the debate, specifically regarding the accuracy of Freeman's historical reconstruction (Shankman 1996: 564). This data set can also allow us to generate better reconstructions (Shankman 1996: 564). As I have stated before, "the problem of knowledge" is not insoluble. The critical conceptual tools are there for anyone who wishes to use them. Obtaining reliable understandings of the world is not easy, but it can be done.

ASSESSMENT

The Boasians are generally credited with setting American anthropology on a solid scientific footing. Moreover, works generated under the auspices of the Boasian paradigm are treated as exemplars of scientific anthropology. As the preceding discussion indicates, however, such a construal is highly misleading. Boasian anthropologists, from Wissler to Mead, who set the intellectual agenda for anthropological research in the United States during the first half of the twentieth century, were committed to nonscientific or antiscientific historical, relativistic, and particularistic perspectives. The culture wars in American anthropology today are rooted in the antiscience epistemological foundations set forth by the founding figures under the banner of a fierce commitment to empirical data gathering.

Discussions of the unscientific nature of Boasian anthropology often evoke surprise and even indignation, especially from members of the older generation of American anthropologists. Unfortunately, they are defending a science that is not science. As I have already noted in reference to Boas's program, empirical data collection alone does not a science make. The other components include material causation, evolutionary holism, the development and testing of hypotheses, and the endeavor to establish cross-culturally valid generalizations about sociocultural phenomena. These latter elements are noticeably absent from the Boasians' research agenda.

Chapter 8

Bronislaw Malinowski, Functionalism, and Modern Anthropology

Modern anthropology as we know it began with Bronislaw Malinowski (1884–1942). Malinowski was born into an aristocratic family in Cracow (Poland) in 1884. His father was a distinguished professor of Slavic philology at Cracow's Jagellonian University, where Malinowski himself received a Ph.D. in mathematics and physics in 1908. Malinowski, like Franz Boas, turned from physics to anthropology. For Malinowski, however, the reason for the switch was illness, which prevented him from pursuing a career in physics. While recuperating, Malinowski took up reading Sir James Frazer's *The Golden Bough,* which he said was a turning point in his life (Richards 1943: 1). Under the spell of Frazer's colorful prose, Malinowski decided that he would make anthropology his new career.

In 1910, Malinowski began postgraduate work at the London School of Economics under Charles G. Seligman (1873–1940), one of the great fieldworkers of the day, and the noted sociologist/anthropologist Edward Westermarck (1862–1939). Seligman had been a member of

the Torres Straits Expedition (see Haddon 1901), an important project that literally set the standards for systematic field research techniques in British anthropology. Malinowski received his doctorate in anthropology in 1913 after writing a dissertation entitled *The Family Among the Australian Aborigines,* based on documentary sources (Kuper 1999: 11). In 1914, with funding secured for him by Seligman, Malinowski went to Australia to undertake firsthand field research.

Malinowski was in Australia when World War I broke out. This changed his circumstances because as an Austrian subject he was technically an enemy alien and stood a real chance of being sent to an internment camp. The Australian authorities, however, not only allowed Malinowski to proceed with his plans to conduct ethnographic research in their territory, but they also provided funding for his project. Less fortunate was the hapless German historical ethnologist Fritz Graebner, who was also in Australia at the time and was detained for five years as an enemy alien.

Members of the Torres Straits Expedition: Alfred Haddon (seated), standing left to right, William H. Rivers, Charles Seligman, Sidney Ray, and Anthony Wilkins, who set the standards for ethnographic fieldwork in Malinowski's time.

MALINOWSKI'S FIELDWORK

At the start of his field studies Malinowski realized that the ethnographic enterprise posed problems that existing approaches to fieldwork could not accommodate. He described these problems in his diary:

My ethnological explorations absorb me a great deal. But they suffer from two basic defects: (1) I have rather little to do with the savages on the spot, and do not observe them enough, and (2) I do not speak their language. This second defect will be hard enough to overcome although I am trying to learn Motu [the language most widely spoken in the region] (Malinowski 1989: 13).[1]

When Malinowski undertook research among the Mailu of Toulon Island, off the south coast of New Guinea (September 1914 to March 1915) he had already dealt with the language problem by mastering Motu. Malinowski stressed the importance of the ethnographer's proficiency with the local language or dialect.

The ethnographer, he wrote, must achieve the degree of fluency in the local language that enables him/her to record thoughts and expressions without having to first translate them.

Malinowski's stay among the Mailu led to another breakthrough that was to be of great importance in his later efforts. This occurred when he found an opportunity to spend three nights in a men's house among the local people in order to observe a feast (Stocking 1992: 43). Such close or intimate contact with indigenous people would have been out of the question for most ethnographers of the time, who were content to interview natives on the decks of steamships, and so forth.

Malinowski's experiences among the Mailu led him to develop an approach to understanding another culture that had not hitherto been attempted. He noted that "it was not until I was alone in the district that I began to make some headway; and at any rate, I found out where lay the secret to effective field-work" (Malinowski 1922a: 6).

Malinowski developed his field research strategy around the idea that the ethnographer must immerse himself/herself in another culture and conduct research by means of direct engagement and firsthand observations. This approach, which would become known as **participant observation,** would forever change the nature of ethnographic research. As he put it,

> My experience is that direct questioning of the native about a custom or belief never discloses their attitude of mind as thoroughly as the discussion of facts connected with the direct observation of a custom, or with a concrete occurrence, in which both parties are materially concerned (Malinowski 1915: 275).[2]

Malinowski had thus hit upon a new and novel way of conducting ethnography. His work in the Trobriand Islands, where he applied his new approach, transformed him into a giant in the field. It is for this reason that he is identified as the master of ethnographic research and the person who invented modern fieldwork (Kardiner and Preble 1962: 185; Kuper 1999: 9, 12).

EPISTEMOLOGY AND FIELDWORK METHODOLOGY

Malinowski addressed the epistemological and theoretical issues related to fieldwork in his first Trobriand ethnography, which was entitled *Baloma: The Spirit of the Dead in the Trobriands* (1916) (Stocking 1992: 45). He noted that fieldwork was a process of interpretation, not simply the collection of raw facts floating around awaiting the ethnographer. As he put it, it is impossible "to wrap up in a blanket a certain number of facts 'as you find them' and bring them all back for the home student to generalize upon" (Malinowski 1916: 238).

The point Malinowski was trying to make was that ethnography is theory driven; one cannot gather facts without a theory that defines those facts. Cultural constructionists often accuse modern anthropologists of simpleminded assumptions that they can render "other realities 'exactly as they are,' not filtered through [their] own values and interpretive scheme" (Pratt 1986: 27). This is a straw man argument that cannot be supported, as Malinowski's statements indicate. Malinowski's understanding that ethnography is theory based constituted a radical departure from the ethnological perspective of the day (Firth 1957: 2; Kuper 1999: 32).

Malinowski laid out the central principles of his new approach, now standards in the field, in his major monograph *Argonauts of the Western Pacific* (1922). He did this in the context of describing his first encounter with the Other in the Trobriands:

> Soon after I had established myself in Omarakana [a village on Kiriwina in the Trobriands], I began to take part, in a way, in the village life, to look forward to the important festive events, to take personal interest in the gossip and the developments of the small village occurrences; to wake up every morning to a day, presenting itself to me

Bronislaw Malinowski conducting field research among the Trobriand Islanders.

more or less as it does to the native. I would get out from under my mosquito net, to find around me the village life beginning to stir, or the people well advanced in their working day according to the hour and also to the season, for they get up and begin their labours early or late, as work presses. As I went on my morning walks through the village, I could see intimate details of family life, of toilet, cooking, taking meals; I could see arrangements for the day's work, people starting on their errands, or groups of men and women busy at some manufacturing task. . . . Quarrels, jokes, family scenes, events usually trivial, sometime dramatic but always significant, formed the atmosphere of my daily life, as well as of theirs. It must be remembered that as the natives saw me constantly every day, they ceased to be interested or alarmed, or made self-conscious by my presence, and I ceased to be a disturbing element in the tribal life which I was studying, altering it by my very approach, as always happens with a newcomer to every savage community. In fact, as they knew that I would thrust my nose into everything, even where a well-mannered native would not

dream of intruding, they finished by regarding me as part and parcel of their life, a necessary evil or nuisance, mitigated by donations of tobacco (Malinowski 1922a: 7–8).[3]

What Malinowski's approach entailed was to situate the ethnographer at the very center of community life. From this position the ethnographer is able not only to observe human activities all around, but also to take part in those activities. As Malinowski put it,

It is good for the Ethnographer sometimes to put aside camera, note book and pencil, and to join in himself in what is going on. He can take part in the natives' games, he can follow them on their visits and walks, sit down and listen and share in their conversations. . . . Out of such plunges into the life of the natives—and I made them frequently not only for study's sake but because everyone needs human company—I have carried away a distinct feeling that their behaviour, their manner of being, in all sorts of tribal transactions, became more apparent and easily understandable than it had been before (Malinowski 1922a: 21–22).[4]

Participant observation would thereafter become a standard in the field that all subsequent generations of anthropologists would try to emulate.

Only through immersion in and engagement with another culture, Malinowski argued, is the ethnographer able to gain an understanding that would evade the gaze of the casual visitor. Moreover, there are dimensions of sociocultural phenomena, what he called the "imponderabilia of actual life," that elude simple observation and description and can only be rendered through experience and intimacy of contact.

> Living in the village with no other business but to follow native life, one sees the customs, ceremonies and transactions over and over again, one has examples of their beliefs as they are actually lived through, and the full body of abstract constructions. . . . [Thus] the Ethnographer is enabled to add something essential to the bare outline of tribal constitution, and to supplement it by all the details of behaviour, setting and small incident. He is able in each case to state whether an act is public or private; how a public assembly behaves, and what it looks like; he can judge whether an event is ordinary or an exciting and singular one; whether natives bring to it a great deal of sincere and earnest spirit, or perform it in fun; whether they do it in a perfunctory manner, or with deliberation. . . . In other words, there is a series of phenomena of great importance which cannot possibly be recorded by questioning or computing documents, but have to be observed in their full actuality. Let us call them *the imponderabilia of actual life*. Here belongs the routine of a man's working day, the details of his care of the body, the manner of taking food and preparing it; the tone of the conversation and social life around the village fires, the existence of strong friendships or hostilities, and of passing sympathies and dislikes between people; the subtle yet unmistakable manner in which personal vanities and ambitions are reflected in the behaviour of the individual and in the emotional reactions of those who surround him (Malinowski 1922a: 18–19).[5]

The distinction made here is between the "real" and the "ideal," between what people say and what they do. Thus Malinowski noted that, "it would be well to check rules [what people say things are like] as against the actual performances of the people" (Malinowski 1944: 45). It was necessary, therefore, to set apart information based upon the "native's point of view" and the ethnographer's own formulations, a distinction between the emic and the etic.

For Malinowski, the way to access another culture was to "penetrating the mental attitudes expressed in social action":

> If we remember that these imponderable yet all important facts of actual life are part of the real substance of the social fabric, that in them are spun the innumerable threads which keep together the family, the clan, the village community, the tribe—their significance becomes clear. Taking full account of the imponderabilia of life is necessary if one wants to bring the reality of native life to ones readers back home. This can only be done through insight and empathy, rather than following any precise rules of data gathering, although it is important to allow the facts to speak for themselves, to note the variations and deviations and well as the ordinary and the conventional (Malinowski 1922a: 19).[6]

Highly sensitive to the complexities confronting the ethnographer, Malinowski pointed out that

> in every act of tribal life, there is, first, the routine prescribed by custom and tradition, then there is the manner in which it is carried out, and lastly there is the commentary to it, contained in the native mind. A man who submits to various customary obligations, who follows a traditional course of action, does it impelled by certain motives, to the accompaniment of certain feelings, guided by certain ideas. These . . . are molded and conditioned by the culture in which we find them, and are therefore an ethnic peculiarity of the given society. An attempt must be made, therefore, to study and record them (Malinowski 1922a: 22).[7]

By stressing the importance of accessing "the native's views and opinions and utterances,"

Malinowski was advocating what later became known as gaining the "insider's point of view." As he put it, the ultimate objective of ethnographic fieldwork which "the Ethnographer must never lose sight . . . is to grasp the native's point of view, his relation to life, to realise *his* vision of *his* world." Such an understanding was a significant and indispensable part of the ethnographic experience and central to cross-cultural translation.

But for Malinowski, ethnographic research was more than the investigation of the insider's view of another culture. Such research also had to focus upon the organizational features of culture and the relationships between its constituent elements. Malinowski approached ethnographic research with the understanding that cultures are regulated, well ordered, and governed by laws and complex bonds of kinship, rather than being things of shreds and patches. He treated culture as being integrated, with its parts connected in various subtle and not so subtle ways to the whole. It fell upon the ethnographer to pinpoint and describe the connections between institutions and situate them in the context of the culture as a whole.

In his own work, Malinowski pursued such connections in detail. It is for this reason that the ethnographic monographs Malinowski produced possessed a completeness that was absent in the works of his contemporaries. As he put it,

The first and basic ideal of ethnographic fieldwork is to give a clear and firm outline of the social constitution, and disentangle the laws and regularities of all cultural phenomena from irrelevancies. The firm skeleton of the tribal life has to be first ascertained. The ideal imposes in the first place the fundamental obligation of giving a complete survey of the phenomena, and not picking out the sensational, singular, still less the funny and quaint. The time when we could tolerate accounts presenting us the native as a distorted, childish caricature of a human being are gone. This picture is false, and like many other falsehoods, it has been killed by Science. The field Ethnographer has seriously and soberly to cover the full extent of the phenomena in each aspect of tribal culture stud-

ied, making no difference between what is commonplace, or drab, or ordinary, and what strikes him as astonishing and out-of-the-way. At the same time the whole area of tribal culture *in all its aspects* has to be gone over in research. The consistency, the law and order which obtain within each aspect make also for joining them into one coherent whole. . . . An Ethnographer who sets out to study only religion, or only technology, or only social organisation cuts out an artificial field of inquiry, and he will be seriously handicapped in his work (Malinowski 1922a: 10–11).[8]

Moreover, Malinowski (1922a: 17) added that

each phenomenon ought to be studied through the broadest range possible of its concrete manifestations; each studied by an exhaustive survey of detailed examples. If possible, the results ought to be tabulated into some sort of synoptic chart, both to be used as an instrument of study, and to be presented as an ethnological document. With the help of such documents and such study of actualities the clear outline of the framework of the natives' cultures in the widest sense of the word, and the constitution of their society, can be presented.[9]

Malinowski was offering this systematic, rigorous, and detailed ethnographic approach as a corrective to the ethnocentric, racist, and prejudicial representations of native life by contemporary ethnologists. This is what he was referring to when he said that the false picture presented in the works of his contemporaries has been "killed by science." In fact, Malinowski made such analytical and methodological rigor and the specification of the conditions under which data were collected a condition of the ethnographic enterprise:

I consider that only such ethnographic sources are of unquestionable scientific value, in which we can clearly draw the line between, on the one hand, the results of direct observation and of native statements and interpretations, and on the other, the inferences of the author, based on his common sense and psychological insight (Malinowski 1922a: 3).[10]

He added further that the ethnographer must not only present his/her findings "in a manner absolutely candid and above board," but also with "the full searchlight of methodic sincerity," specifying "by what actual experiences the writers have reached their conclusions" (Malinowski 1922a: 2–3). In other words, Malinowski was advocating what interpretive/postmodern anthropologists were touting during the 1980s, namely that the ethnographer must specify who speaks, who writes, and so on, an idea postmodernists claim to be distinctive of their own approach (e.g., Clifford 1986: 13).

Malinowski's emphasis upon accountability on the part of the ethnographer and upon getting the facts right was a radical departure from the wild conjectures rampant in anthropology at that time. That is the crucial point. Critics maintain that Malinowski's emphasis upon systematic, empirically rigorous analyses of other cultures was really an attempt to "usurp authority" from the other genre of writing" and to perpetuate the fantasy that cultural realities can be described exactly "exactly as they are" (Pratt 1986: 27) (i.e., that science is about absolute truths).

Criticisms of this sort directed at the *Argonauts* imply that there is more being said than simply an attempt to provide a clear set of instructions on how to gather, organize, and analyze ethnographic information. Malinowksi, critics note, was telling the story of his research to persuade his readers that this kind of anthropology can be done, and that he succeeded in doing it (Clifford 1988: 28; Stocking 1992: 52–53). Such views entail the logical fallacy of the red herring and the straw man argument. Malinowski's critics seem to have conflated "the setting of standards" with myth (Firth 1988: 32) and "story of research."

There are several facts that cannot be overlooked with respect to Malinowski's work, despite such attacks upon his anthropological efforts. First, *Argonauts* offered a highly useful and clear set of guidelines on gathering ethnographic data. These guidelines not only transformed the manner in which ethnographic research would be conducted thereafter in Britain and the United States (cf. Leach 1982: 27) but also led to the generation of numerous solid and factually accurate ethnographic monographs that make up the ethnographic record.

Second, these guidelines enabled Malinowski himself to produce a rich, lucid, empirically grounded, and powerful account that, as Annette Weiner has put it,

> continues to enthrall each generation of anthropologists through its intensity, rich detail, and penetrating revelations. The distinctive quality of Malinowski's ethnographic writing remain potent, emphatically and personally instructing the reader how to enter into the lives of Trobrianders, cautioning them to beware of ethnocentric conclusions, and explaining how seemingly strange behaviors have pragmatic functions and must be understood in their own terms (Weiner 1987: xiv–xv).

Third, whatever one might say about Malinowski's motives and his literary strategies, this does not in any way render his ethnographies obsolete (Rabinow 1986: 244).

Malinowski's emphasis on rigorous data gathering involving the detailed analysis of the systematic linkages between cultural elements in a documented manner was not an end in itself. He sought to go beyond description in order to produce useful generalization about sociocultural phenomena (cf. Kaberry 1957: 72). To do this, it would be necessary to gather a large and comprehensive empirical database: "The collecting of concrete data over a wide range of facts is . . . one of the mains points of field method" (Malinowski 1922a: 13).

Although Malinowski was interested in developing abstract conceptual systems, he did not hold the naïve view that the ethnographer could render other realities "exactly as they are." Highly sensitive to the complexities of the ethnographic experience, Malinowski paid careful attention to the issues surrounding translation and interpretation (contra Asad 1986: 142) and the gap or slippage between the reality of native life, the ethnographer's experience of that reality, and the written account emerging from that experience:

> In Ethnography, the distance is often enormous between the brute material of information—as it is presented to the student in his own observations, in native statement, in the kaleidoscope of tribal life—and the final authoritative presentation of the results (Malinowski 1922a: 3–4).[11]

Malinowski was thus completely cognizant of the fact that the ethnographer's renderings of cultures are of a different order than what exists in the empirical world. Anticipating points made by postmodern and literary anthropologists in the 1980s, Malinowski wrote that "in obtaining a precise formula for them from the collection of data and native statements, we find that this very precision is foreign to real life, which never adheres rigidly to any rules" (Malinowski 1922a: 17).

CULTURAL RELATIVISM

Malinowski used his Trobriand material to stress that each culture has its own workable and internally consistent sets of values, ideals, and traditions. Moreover, he stressed that behaviors related to these beliefs make logical sense once seen in their own cultural contexts. He wrote that

> when you enter a new cultural setting, the behaviour, individual or collective, of the new type of human beings seems strange, unmotivated, irrational, in short incomprehensible. You learn the language, you gradually adopt the strange habits and the new points of view—and imperceptibly what was alien becomes familiar and you feel at home in what recently had been an exotic milieu. The universally human running through all the cultures is the common measure of comprehension and adaptation. . . . Even in such cases as eating of human flesh, underdone beef, or plum pudding, playing golf, running amok, and the practice of *couvade,* the anthropologist may attempt to survey the psychological raw material of the pursuit, can assume a certain diversity of taste in human

beings, and define the pursuit in terms of the universally human (in Leach 1966: 565).[12]

Each culture, according to Malinowski, has its own set of values and traditions and the traditions of one culture are no better or worse than those of another. Each represents a workable solution to common human problems people face everywhere. Malinowski therefore accepted the principle of "cultural relativism" (Leach 1966: 565).

On the basis of this principle, Malinowski entered into a debate with the proponents of Freudian psychoanalysis, which was highly popular at the time. Malinowski used his Trobriand data to challenge the Freudian **Odepius complex,** which he considered to be culture-bound and not easily applicable to other cultures. He observed, for example, that among the Trobrianders, who are matrilineal and have **avunculocal** families, a boy's mother's brother and his biological father share between them the social role fulfilled by the European father. In the Trobriands it is the boy's mother's brother who exercises authority over him. The Trobriand boy thus resents his mother's brother for his authority, not his biological father, with whom he has a warm and close relationship. As Malinowski put it in his *Sex and Repression in Savage Society* (1957 [1927]: 80),

> In the Trobriands there is no friction between father and son. . . . The ambivalent attitude of veneration and dislike is felt between a man and his mother's brother, while the repressed sexual attitude of incestuous temptations can be formed only towards his sister.[13]

]Therefore, Malinowski concluded, there are limitations to the application of the Oedipus complex to other cultures (see Spiro 1982 for an opposing view; for a discussion of Freud's views on totemism, taboo, and incest, see Chapter 11).

Malinowski's cultural relativism, however, did not lead him to the conclusions it led Boas and his followers (i.e., that each culture is unique unto itself and therefore efforts to build a science of culture are frivolous and meaningless). Nor did his relativism lead him down the path towards epistemological relativism and solipsism as it has taken many present-day cultural constructionists.

Indeed, Malinowski rejected particularizing approaches of all kinds. Perspectives that stress the unique and individual in each culture by isolating and focusing on such elements as cannibalism, head-hunting, **couvade, Potlatch,** Kula, cremation, mummification, and other peripheral "freaks" and "eccentricities" are unscientific, he wrote. They are unscientific, Malinowski observed, because they do not specify on the basis of relevancy what that culture's significant elements are and how the "isolated" trait fits in with those significant elements. Approaches based on the examination of "isolates" fail to take into account that what seem strange and bizarre are basically related to "universal and fundamentally human cultural elements" (Malinowski 1944: 41). These universal elements, such as the need for food, shelter, reproduction, and psychological well-being, for Malinowski were reflected in the psychobiological rational beneath all cultural institutions and provided the starting point for cross-cultural comparisons.

CULTURE AND
THE INDIVIDUAL

Malinowski insisted that the subject of anthropological research is the individual and human nature, rather than human society (Leach 1982: 29; 1957). This too was a radical departure from the reigning paradigms of the day, which were more concerned with trait distributions based on the belief that traits or customs were "free-floating entities" that went here and there independently of people (Leach 1966: 566). Malinowski insisted that anthropology is the study of humans, not the analysis of "customs" as phenomena existing independently of people. Thus he concentrated upon human beings and their

biopsychological characteristics as they related to culture.

> The most important thing for the student, in my opinion, is never to forget the living, palpitating flesh and blood organism of man which remains somewhere at the heart of every institutions (Malinowski 1934: xxxi).

For Malinowski, culture did not grip the individual, as in the deterministic schemes of Boas and Benedict. The latter sought answers to human behavior in cultural configurations that they saw as overriding all inborn biological tendencies. Malinowski believed that human behavior and motivation in the final analysis were rooted in the natural human biopsychological dispositions. In this respect, Malinowski's work foreshadowed the development of sociobiological theories, or **sociobiology.**

People, for Malinowski, act according to their inborn natural impulses, fear, anxiety, affection, the desire for prestige, and so on. Different cultures provide different means of responding to these natural impulses. Ambition for renown among the Plains Indians expresses itself in ostentatious feats of bravery in warfare. For an up-and-coming Euro-American corporate executive the same emotions and desires are dealt with by feats of cunning in the boardroom, while among the Zuñi a man attains this objective by avoiding strife and flamboyant exhibitionism (cf. Hatch 1973: 308–309).

The question Malinowski did not address, however, was why different cultures vary so greatly in the rules they provide for responding to human biopsychological needs that presumably are constant among all groups. The reason he did not ask this question is due to the perennial problem of the functionalist model in which there is no room for environment or ecology as elements of causal processes (cf. Ellen 1986: 26).

Malinowski was also concerned with the relationship between individuals and their culture. Individuals are not gripped in the iron clutches of traditional rules, he pointed out, but rather manipulate these rules according to their own feelings and motives in order to achieve their own goals in ways most advantageous to them. The ethnographer must therefore examine the manner in which people manipulate rules rather than assume that the ideals reflect actual behavior (Malinowski 1934: xxv):

> The hasty field-worker, who relies completely upon the question and answer method, obtains at best that lifeless body of laws, regulations, morals, and conventionalities which *ought* to be obeyed, but in reality are often only evaded. For in actual life rules are never entirely conformed to, and it remains, as the most difficult but indispensable part of the ethnographer's work, to ascertain the extent and mechanism of the deviations (Malinowski 1932: 509).

This does not mean that human cultural experience is a free-for-all. To some extent the process of enculturation functions to instill a sense of reverence and commitment to traditions on the part of the individual. However, Malinowski pointed out that these traditions are often at odds with the innate tendencies that all humans have in common, such as ambitions, desire for status, fears, and anxieties. Therefore, individuals will do their best to manipulate cultural rules toward their own ends, through evasion or deception. Cultural behavior entails the continual process of negotiation. When a person conforms, he or she conforms out of self-interest, in the sense that lack of conformity would be more costly socially than conforming. In other words, the individual adheres to rules and regulations, duties, and obligations only to the extent that he or she can avoid humiliation and loss of prestige.

FUNCTIONALISM: MALINOWSKI'S THEORY OF CULTURE

The theoretical perspective associated with Malinowski is known as functionalism or the "functional school of anthropology." In humor,

Malinowski (1932: xxix) wrote that "the magnificent title of the Functional School of Anthropology has been bestowed by myself, in a way on myself, and to a large extent out of my own sense of irresponsibility." The functional paradigm was born entirely from Malinowski's ethnographic studies in the Trobriand Islands when during the process of his research he came to construe cultures as integrated, functional wholes. As he put it,

A. Culture is essentially an instrumental apparatus by which man is put in a position the better to cope with the concrete specific problems that face him in his environment in the course of the satisfaction of his needs.

B. It is a system of objects, activities, and attitudes in which every part exists as a means to an end.

C. It is an integral part in which the various elements are interdependent.

D. Such activities, attitudes and objects are organized around important and vital tasks into institutions such as family, the clan, the local community, the tribe, and the organized teams of economic coöperation, political, legal, and educational activity.

E. From the dynamic point of view, that is, as regards the type of activity, culture can be analyzed into a number of aspects such as education, social control, economics, systems of knowledge, belief and morality, and also modes of creative and artistic expression (Malinowski 1944: 150).[14]

Malinowski's paradigm was centered upon the biological and psychological needs, or "basic imperatives," that people everywhere have in common. These include the need for food, shelter, reproduction, psychological well-being, health care, and defense. To attend to these, Malinowski noted, humans rely upon "organized systems of behavior" such as kin groups and social and political institutions. These institutions serve to ensure that the basic imperatives are met in orderly, repetitive, and predictable ways.

These organized systems of behavior, or, we could say, cultural arrangements, in turn produce what Malinowski referred to as "derived needs" or "secondary environments" necessitating still other cultural arrangements to ensure and perpetuate those arrangements over time. As Malinowski (1944: 37) pointed out,

> It is clear that the satisfaction of the organic or basic needs of man and of the race is a minimum set of conditions imposed on each culture. The problems set by man's nutritive, reproductive, and hygienic needs must be solved. They are solved by the construction of a new, secondary, or artificial environment. This environment, which is neither more nor less than culture itself, has to be permanently reproduced, maintained and managed. This creates in what might be described in the most general sense of the term as a new standard of living, which depends on the environment, and on the efficiency of the group. A cultural standard of living, however, means that new needs appear and new imperatives or determinants are imposed upon human behavior. Clearly, cultural tradition had to be transmitted from each generation to the next. Methods and mechanisms of an educational character must exist in every culture. Order and law have to be maintained, since coöperation is the essence of every cultural achievement. In every community there must exist arrangements for the sanctioning of custom, ethics, and law. The material substratum of culture has to be renewed, and maintained in working order. Hence some forms of economic organization are indispensable, even in the most primitive cultures.[15]

In the process of how cultural arrangements function to meet individual biopsychological needs, Malinowski saw an explanatory model, his functional theory:

> The analysis . . . in which we attempt to define the relation between a cultural performance and a human need, basic or derived, may be termed functional. For function can not be defined in any other way than the satisfaction of a need by an activity in which human beings cooperate, use artifacts, and consume goods (Malinowski 1944: 39).[16]

This perspective is really "a theory of needs," which Malinowski described as follows:

> Here I would like to suggest that we must take our stand on two axioms: first and foremost, that every

culture must satisfy the biological system of needs, such as those dictated by metabolism, reproduction, the physiological conditions of temperature, protection from moisture, wind, and the direct impact of damaging forces of climate and weather, safety from dangerous animals or human beings, occasional relaxation, the exercise of the muscular and nervous systems in movement, and the regulation of growth. The second axiom in the science of culture is that every cultural achievements that implies the use of artifacts and symbolism is an instrumental enhancement of human anatomy, and refers directly or indirectly to the satisfaction of a bodily need. If we were to start with an evolutionary consideration, we could show that as soon as the human anatomy is supplemented by a stick or a stone, a flame or a covering wrap, the use of such artifacts, tools, and commodities not only satisfies a bodily need, but also establish derived needs (Malinowski 1944: 171).[17]

Malinowski stressed that in order to achieve their purposes through cultural behavior humans must organize their activities. Malinowski (1944: 39) labeled such units of organization "institutions":

> This concept implies an agreement on a set of traditional values for which human beings come together. It also implies that these human beings stand in a definite relation to one another and to a specific physical part of their environment, natural and artificial. Under the charter of their purpose or traditional mandate, obeying the specific norms of their association, working through the material apparatus which they manipulate, human beings act together and thus satisfy some of their desires, while also producing an impression on their environment.[18]

The institution as the unit of analysis is different from a trait complex as understood by the Boasians. As Malinowski put it,

> The functional isolate that I have labeled Institution differs from the cultural complex or trait-complex, when defined as "composed of elements which stand in no necessary relation to each other," in that it does postulate such a necessary relationship. In fact, the functional isolate is con-

crete, that is, can be observed as a definite social grouping. It has a structure universally valid for all types of isolates; and it is a real isolate in so far as we can not only enumerate its abstract factors, but also concretely draw a line around it. Functionalism would have no true claim to deal with culture in its fundamental aspects, such as educational, legal, economic, or pertaining to knowledge, primitive or developed, and religion, unless it were able to analyze and thus define each, and relate them to the biological needs of the human organism (Malinowski 1944: 158).[19]

Malinowski (1944:40) adds that

our two types of analysis, functional and institutional, will allow us to define culture more concretely, precisely and exhaustively. Culture is an integral composed of partly autonomous, partly coordinated institutions. It is integrated on a series of principles such as the community of blood through procreation; the contiguity of space related to cooperation; the specialization in activities; and last but not least, the use of power in political organization. Each culture owes its completeness and self-sufficiency to the fact that it satisfies the whole range of basic, instrumental and integrative needs. To suggest therefore, as has been recently done, that each culture only covers a small segment of its potential compass [i.e., Benedict's arc of culture], is at least in one sense radically wrong.[20]

Malinowski noted that a scientific study of culture was possible, not by focusing on the particular and the unique in each culture, but upon cross-culturally recurring "universal and fundamentally human cultural elements."

Taking an individual culture as a coherent whole, we can state a number of general determinants to which it has to conform, we shall be able to produce a number of predictive statements as guides for field-research, as yardsticks for comparative treatment, and as common measures in the process of cultural adaptation and change. From this point of view culture will not appear to us a "patchwork of shreds and tatters," as has been quite recently described by one or two competent anthropologists [i.e., Lowie]. We shall be able to reject the

view that no common measure of cultural processes are vague, insipid, and useless (Malinowski 1944: 38).[21]

Finally, Malinowski stressed the usefulness of the functional approach in terms of fieldwork and collection of ethnographic data:

The functional theory, as here presented, claims to be the prerequisite for field-work and for the comparative analysis of culture into institutions and their aspects. If you imagine a field-worker supplied with such guiding charts, you will see that they might be helpful to him in isolating, as well as relating, the phenomena observed. It is meant primarily to equip the field-worker with a clear perspective and full instructions regarding what to observe and how to record (Malinowski 1944: 41).[22]

We can summarize Malinowski's functional theory as follows:

1. He saw cultures as being integrated and coherent wholes, in which parts are related to each other and to the totality, where a change in one element would cause changes in other elements as well. When describing the Trobriand trade enterprise called Kula, for example, Malinowski traced the ways this central institution articulates with other aspects of Trobriand life, such as the institution of chiefdomship, magic, canoe building, gardening, kinship, and myth. By tracing these interconnections, Malinowski was able to shed light on customs that otherwise remained incomprehensible or seemed "absurd" from the outsider's point of view. As he put it, "A belief, which appears crude and senseless in isolation, a practice which seems queer and 'immoral,' becomes often clear and even clean if understood as part of a system of thought and practice" (Malinowski 1922b: 218).

2. Malinowski saw utility in all cultural elements. Culture is a coherent whole "of objects, activities, and attitudes in which every part exists as a means to an end" (Malinowski 1944: 150).

3. The third feature of Malinowski's functionalism is that all of the needs that culture functions to fulfill are traced to the individual and his/her biopsychological requirements and desires.

INTELLECTUAL CONTEXT

Like Boas, Malinowski's paradigm developed in relation to prevailing theoretical perspectives. Malinowski's notion of functional integration was a simultaneous refutation the Boasians' diffusionist idea that culture was a thing of shreds and patches and of nineteenth-century evolutionism, based upon the cross-cultural comparisons of isolated customs (cf. Cheater 1989: 24). It might be noted, however, that functionalism itself is not a negation of evolutionism (Hallpike 1988: 7) but of the models associated with nineteenth-century evolutionism (see Chapters 3 and 4).

Rejecting the speculative reconstructions of the nineteenth-century evolutionists, Malinowski pointed out that in nonliterate societies the past was impenetrable. Thus, oral narratives about the former ages and how things came to be as they are were to be treated as mythical, not as historical accounts. Malinowski thus rejected the "myth-as-history" perspective. Instead he paid particular attention to the narrative performances of myths and audience-narrator interactions.

For Malinowski, the meaning of myths was easily discernable and he saw the function of myths as charters for social institutions and a means of legitimizing existing social and political relationships. It was in this respect that the study of myths fell within the scope of anthropological inquiry (cf. Cheater 1989: 24). Malinowski's "myth-as-charter" and "myth-as-performance" approach stands in contrast to the "myth-as-text" approach with an emphasis on encrypted meanings associated with the perspective of the French anthropologist Claude Lévi-Strauss (Hicks 1999: 29), whose work we shall examine in Chapter 11.

In contrast to the diachronic evolutionary perspectives of the day that sought origins of institutions and the like, Malinowski's approach had a present-time, or **synchronic,** orientation that emphasized the analysis of what was present rather than conjectures about origins. Because of this synchronic focus Malinowski's functionalism has been criticized for being ahistorical, or ignoring history.

THE KULA AND THE ARGONAUTS OF THE WESTERN PACIFIC

The highlight of Malinowski's work on the Trobriand Islands was the analysis of the Kula. This was a vast indigenous enterprise that linked many different islands by means of a special ceremonial relationship called trade partnerships (Figure 8.1). According to Malinowski,

> The tribes who live within the sphere of the Kula system of trading . . . inhabit the eastern-most end of the mainland of New Guinea and those islands, scattered in the form of the long-drawn archipelago, which continue in the same south-easternly trend as the mainland, as if to bridge over the gap between New Guinea and the Solomons (Malinowski 1922a: 27).[23]

The item exchanged between trade partners on different islands, includes ornamental shell armbands and necklaces:

> The Kula is a form of exchange, of extensive, inter-tribal character; it is carried on by communities inhabiting a wide ring of islands, which form a closed circuit. . . . Along this route, articles of two kinds, and these two kinds only, are constantly travelling in opposite directions. In the direction of the hands of a clock, moves constantly one of these kinds—long necklaces of red shell, called *soulava.* In the opposite direction moves the other kind—bracelets of white shell called *mwali.* Each of these articles, as it travels in its own direction on the closed circuit, meets on its way articles of the other class, and is constantly being exchanged for them. Every movement of the Kula articles, every

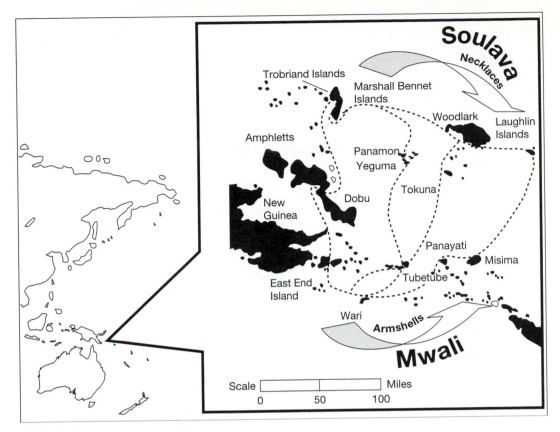

Figure 8.1 The Kula Ring, a vast indigenous enterprise that links many different islands through a special ceremonial relationship called trade partnerships (after Malinowski 1922).

detail of the transactions is fixed and regulated by a set of traditional rules and conventions, and some acts of the Kula are accompanied by an elaborate magical ritual and public ceremonies (Malinowki 1922a: 81).[24]

Kula ornaments comprise armband and necklaces made of shell. These objects have no practical utility but are prized for their beauty and fame much in the same way that a Euro-American values an antique artifact or a painting. The exchange is restricted only to the two items, armband for necklaces. Armbands travel in one direction, and necklaces in the other. A particular Kula object, after circulating for years, and going from owner to owner and island to island, will eventually return to its point of origin,

but from the opposite direction. Then it circulates once more.

What makes the Kula object valuable is not the workmanship needed in its production or the material from which the item is crafted. Rather, its value is based upon the how long it has been in circulation and how many famous individuals have at one time possessed it. A trade object therefore has its own particular history that indicates where it has traveled, for how long, and by whom it was owned.

The flow of armbands and necklaces in opposite directions along the circular trade route prevents partners from trading objects of the same kind, necklaces for necklaces or armbands for armbands, thereby ensuring that the circuit incorporates as many islands as possible (Harris 1991: 112).

> On every island and in every village, a more or less limited number of men take part in the Kula— that is to say, receive the goods, hold them for a short time, and then pass them on. Therefore every man who is in the Kula, periodically though not regularly, receives one or several *mwali* (arm-shells), or a *soulava* (necklace or red shell discs), and then has to hand it on to one of his partners, from whom he receives the opposite commodity in exchange. Thus no man ever keeps any of the articles for any length of time in his possession. One transaction does not finish the Kula relationship, the rule being "once in the Kula, always in the Kula," and a partnership between two men is a permanent and lifelong affair. Again any given *mwali* or *soulava* may always be found travelling and changing hands, and there is no question of its ever settling down, so that the principle "once in the Kula, always in the Kula" applies also to the valuables themselves (Malinowski 1922a: 81–82).[25]

Kula expeditions are planned well in advance. Canoes are built, provisions are gathered, magical spells are pronounced, and the dates set to coincide with the most auspicious times are specified. Following these preparations, on the appointed date, the expedition sets sail over open seas on risky journeys to reach trade partners on other islands.

Every man involved in the system has trade partners on different islands. Upon landfall, trade partners greet each other as kinsmen and exchange minor gifts. The partners then go to their host's village, where Kula ornaments change hands. The transaction takes place on the basis of the principle of **balanced reciprocity.** Those who receive a gift are obligated to reciprocate with an object of equal or greater value, either at the time of the exchange, or at some future date.

It is usually the more important men who take part in the Kula and only the most important of these is able to acquire Kula objects of

Specially constructed Kula Canoe from the Trobriand Islands.

great renown. Strategy, negotiation skills, and planning are all ingredients for success enabling a person to obtain more desired objects and postpone the repayments of debts. The institution of Kula therefore enables the high-ranking men on different islands to develop and maintain a network of personal relationships. Kula is thus connected to the prestige hierarchy and success in the enterprise is a means of obtaining and enhancing prestige. This depends upon the number of renowned Kula ornaments a person is able to possess and strategically exchange with high-ranking trade partners.

Malinowski (1922a: 98–99) described the strategies and rules of the Kula exchange:

Let us suppose that I, a Sinaketa [a major coastal Trobriand village] man, am in possession of a pair of big armshells. An overseas expedition from Dobu, in the d'Entrecasteaux Archipelago, arrives at my village. Blowing a conch shell, I take my armshell pair and I offer it to my overseas partner, with some such words, "This is a *vaga* (initial gift)—in due time, thou returnest to me a big *soulave* (necklace) for it!" Next year, when I visit my partner's village, he either is in possession of an equivalent necklace, and this he gives to me as *yotile* (restoration gift), or he has not a necklace good enough to repay my last gift. In this case he will give me a smaller necklace—avowedly not equivalent to my gift—and will give it to me as a *basi* (intermediary gift). This means that the main gift has to be repaid on a future occasion and the *basi* is given in token of good faith—but it, in turn, must be repaid by me in the meantime by a gift of armshells. The final gift, which will be given to me to clinch the whole transactions, would be then called *kudu* (equivalent gift) in contrast to the *basi*. . . .

Although haggling and bargaining are completely ruled out of the Kula, there are customary and regulated ways of bidding for a piece of *vaygu'a* known to be in the possession of one's partner. This is done by the offer of what we shall call solicitary gifts, of which there are several types. If an inhabitant of Sinaketa happens to be in possession of a pair of armshells more than usually good, the fame of its spreads. It must be noted that

each one of the first-class armshells and necklaces has a personal name and history of its own, and as they all circulate around the big ring of the Kula, they are all well-known, and their appearance in a given district always creates a sensation. Now all my partners—whether from overseas or from within the district—compete for the favour of receiving this particular article of mine, and those who are specially keen try to obtain it by giving me *pokala* (offerings) and *kaributu* (solicitory gifts).[26]

Malinowski's analysis revealed that groups over a vast geographical area are linked by means of the Kula exchange. The enterprise itself, he noted, was founded upon specific rules and obligations, rather than being haphazard and erratic, as Westerners tended to describe indigenous economic enterprises.

The Kula is . . . an extremely big and complex institution, both in its geographical extent, and in the manifoldness of its component pursuits. It welds together a considerable number of tribes, and it embraces a vast complex of activities, interconnected, and playing into one another, so as to form one organic whole (1922a: 82–83).[27]

Malinowski added that

the Kula is not a surreptitious and precarious form of exchange. It is, quite on the contrary, rooted in myth, backed by traditional law, and surrounded with magical rites. All its main transactions are public and ceremonial, and carried out according to definite rules. It is not done on the spur of the moment, but happens periodically, at dates settled in advance, and it is carried on along definite trade routes, which must lead to fixed trysting places. Sociologically, though transacted between tribes differing in language, culture, and probably even in race, it is based on a fixed and permanent status, on a partnership which binds into couples some thousands of individuals. This partnership is a lifelong relationship, it implies various mutual duties and privileges, and constitutes a type of intertribal relationship on an enormous scale. As to the economic mechanism of the transactions, this is based on a specific form of credit, which implies a high degree of mutual trust and commercial honour—

and this refers also to the subsidiary, minor trade, which accompanies the Kula proper (Malinowksi 1922a: 85–86).[28]

The Kula therefore functioned to promote peaceful relations between potentially hostile neighbors by means of the personal and lifelong relations between trade partners, who are honor bound to act toward one anther as they would toward kinsmen. The honorable intentions of the trade partners were symbolically depicted by means of the armbands and necklaces. Also, Kula transactions involved many individuals in a kind of game of strategy in which success was accompanied by greater prestige for individual participants.

But Malinowski also noted that the Kula had another function—the exchange of practical goods. This takes place in the beaches following the ceremonial gift exchanges among trade partners. The Kula canoes bring not only the ornamental objects but are also full of many economically useful consumer goods. These items are traded under that banner of safe conduct facilitated by the ritual trade partnerships (see Irwin 1983; Scoditti 1983).

> The ceremonial exchange of the two articles is the main, the fundamental aspect of the Kula. But associated with it, and done under its cover, we find a great number of secondary activities and features. Thus, side by side with the ritual exchange of arm-shells and necklaces, the natives carry on ordinary trade, bartering from one island to another a great number of utilities, often unprocurable in the district to which they are imported, and indispensable there (Malinowski 1922a: 83).[29]

Another function of the Kula, Malinowski added, was that it enabled the circulation of locally unobtainable trade goods and facilitated trade in useful commodities between islands:

> Voyaging to far-off countries, endowed with natural resources unknown in their own homes, the Kula sailors return each time richly laden with these, the spoils of their enterprise. Again, in order to be able to offer presents to his partner, every outward bound canoe carries a cargo of such

things as are known to be most desirable in the overseas district. Some of this is given away in presents to partners, but a good deal is carried in order to pay for the objects desired at home (Malinowski 1922a: 100).[30]

If the goods desired on the island of one's trade partner are not available in one's own district, then the Kula participants have to procure them from other districts before setting off.

Malinowski's analysis reveals that the Kula had a number of functions. Some of these were intended and known to the participant; others were unintended and outside the awareness of the participants. These two different types of function would later be called **manifest functions** and **latent functions** (Merton 1957: 51).

MALINOWSKI ON THE FUNCTION OF MAGIC

Among the areas of Trobriand life that greatly interested Malinowski was magic. He wrote that

> magic—the very word seems to reveal a world of mysterious and unexpected possibilities! . . . Partly perhaps we hope to find in it the quintessence of primitive man's longings and of his wisdom—and that, whatever it might be, is worth knowing. Partly because "magic" seems to stir up in everyone some hidden mental forces, some lingering hopes in the miraculous, some dormant beliefs in man's mysterious possibilities (Malinowski 1948: 70–71).[31]

Malinowski's functional approach to magic centered upon the way in which magical beliefs fulfilled the psychological/emotional needs of the individual. He took the "emotionalist approach" to magic/religion/ritual, which stands in contrast to Tylor's "intellectualist approach" (cf. Morris 1988: 145–147). By approaching the ethnographic analysis of magic in this way, Malinowski was able to reveal how beliefs and practices that might appear irrational to the outsider make perfect sense.

Malinowski maintained that magic should not be treated merely as "primitive science," a view taken by Frazer, nor as a manifestation of prelogical mentality and superstition, as advocated by Lévy-Bruhl. Magic, he added, is rooted in tangible human emotions that emerge in times of frustration or uncertainty (Morris 1988: 147–149).

Malinowski noted that the Trobrianders deemed magic a necessary procedure associated with certain enterprises, such as open-ocean voyages or gardening. For example, Trobrianders believe that their gardens would not produce yams unless they use magic (Malinowski 1935: 62). Magic and gardening, while they appear to be different activities, are interrelated:

> To the natives, magic is as indispensable to the success of gardens as competent and effective husbandry. It is essential to the fertility of the soil: The garden magician utters magic by mouth; the magical virtue enters the soil. . . . Magic is to them an almost natural element in the growth of the gardens (Malinowski 1935: 62).[32]

The question Malinowski asked was, Why do people who are proficient in gardening feel that they need to resort to magic? He discovered that despite the Trobrianders' expertise in horticulture, there are aspects of gardening that are beyond their control. These include variations in such things as temperature, rainfall, and amount of sunshine hours that can influence the yields obtained from the same garden from one year to the next. When confronted with forces beyond their comprehension and control, the Trobrianders resort to magic.

The anthropologist George Gmelch (1982) reached a comparable conclusion in his study of "baseball magic," noting that players resort to the use of magic in situations of uncertainty. Thus just as magic alleviates anxieties over the vicissitudes of gardening for the Trobriand farmer (Malinowski 1948: 29), it alleviates the anxieties over the vicissitudes of hitting the next home-run for the American baseball player.

Another area of uncertainty in which the Trobrianders rely upon magic is during open-ocean fishing, an enterprise that is both unpredictable and dangerous. In contrast, they rely upon their skills rather than magic when fishing in the calm lagoons, which is not hazardous and fairly easy (Malinowski 1935: 17, 433). Malinowski concluded therefore that

> magic, as the belief that by spell and rite results can be obtained . . . always appears in those phases of human action where knowledge fails man. Primitive man cannot manipulate the weather. Experience teaches him that rain and sunshine, wind, heat and cold, cannot be produced by his own hands, however much he might think about or observe such phenomena. He therefore deals with them magically (Malinowski 1944: 198).[33]

As Malinowski saw it, magic was basically an institutional expression of human emotional states (Hatch 1973: 301). Magic therefore really works. Not in the way that those performing magical rites might think—yams don't grow larger, and fish don't bite with greater frequency, and so forth—but rather because magic creates effects upon the individuals and their psychological needs.

ASSESSMENT

Malinowski basically transformed his ethnographic method of looking for linkages between customs and institutions, developed in order to gather systematic field data, into a general theory of culture (Jarvie 1964: 182–183, 1973; Nadel 1970: 190). His work in the Trobriand Islands, a small-scale and insular society, led him to view culture as an integrated functional whole (referred to as **functional unity**). As such, Malinowski assumed that every part of culture has a function (referred to as **universal function**). Therefore there can be no **dysfunctional** or functionless elements. Everything has a place and cultural systems tend to be in a state of balance or equilibrium.

Critics have attempted to infer nefarious motives for what amounts to serious shortcomings in Malinowski's theoretical perspective. Barrett maintains, for example, that functionalism was an ideology in the service of colonial powers. How? Barrett (1996: 66) notes that "after all, if society is harmonious, in a state of equilibrium and every pattern of action has its purpose, why attempt to change things?" This is a remarkable statement on two counts. First, colonialism has never been about equilibrium and the status quo but about changing things. Second, there is no evidence that Malinowski was in collusion with the forces of imperialism or colonialism. Malinowski was in fact highly critical of colonial policies (Cheater 1989: 28). His book *The Dynamics of Culture Change* (1945) provides a critical analysis of societies under colonial rule.

Many of the shortcomings of Malinowski's functionalism are related to his construal of culture. If cultures are integrated functional wholes, then the task of the ethnographer is to chart the linkages and document the functions of the components of the culture as they relate to the whole. In turn, the culture as a whole can be explained in terms of these functions (Jarvie 1964: 182). In other words, explanation depends upon comprehension of how various aspects of a culture are integrated, a description of how every institution functions to meet the practical biopsychological needs of individuals, and explanation of the existence of those institutions in terms of the biopsychological needs.

Malinowski's perspective suffers from two defects. First, such reasoning entails the logical fallacy of affirming the consequent: If X then Y: Y therefore X, discussed in Chapter 2. Logically fallacious propositions, as discussed before, do not contribute to knowledge.

Second, Malinowski substituted description for explanation. As he put it, "to identify is the same as to understand" (Malinowski 1944: 71). To describe the effects of a cultural element, however, is not the same as explaining it. The reason for this is that the cultural elements in question do not bear upon survival to the extent that their effects can account for their persistence (Sperber 1996: 48). Also, the effects of a

phenomenon cannot explain why the phenomena developed in the first place. Valid functional explanations require some form of feedback mechanism (Sperber 1996: 47). Malinowski merely described the useful effects of some institutions but rarely sought to isolate feedback mechanisms themselves.

Later in his career Malinowski himself realized the logical problems of his functional approach:

> This type of functional analysis is easily exposed to the accusation of tautology and platitude, as well as to the criticism that it implies a logical circle, for obviously, if we define function as the satisfaction of a need, it is easy to suspect that the need to be satisfied has been introduced in order to satisfy the need of satisfying a function. Thus, for instance, clans are obviously an additional, one might say, supererogatory type of internal differentiation. Can we speak of a legitimate need for such differentiation, especially when the need is not ever present; for not all communities have clans, and yet they go on very well without them (Malinowski 1944: 169–170).[34]

Malinowski went on to acknowledge that the main value of the functional approach was after all as a "heuristic device" to guide to the collection and presentation of ethnographic field data (Evans-Pritchard 1981: 199).

The other problem associated with Malinowski's functional approach was that although it was oriented toward the development of parsimonious generalizations, it excluded material causation and evolutionary holism by leaving out ecological and demographic factors from analytical consideration altogether. As such, it could not lead to a truly scientific perspective.

But perhaps the greatest defect of Malinowski's anthropology is that he took his theoretical model based upon the idea of culture as an integrated functional whole as an article of faith, rather than considering it as a group of propositions that needed to be tested against empirical data (Jarvie 1964: 184, 187).

Chapter 9

From Functionalism to Structural Functionalism: The Anthropology of Radcliffe-Brown

Bronislaw Malinowski played a key role in shaping British social anthropology and holds a special position as the virtuoso of ethnographic fieldwork. His success as a theoretician, however, was limited and fairly brief. It was Alfred Reginald Radcliffe-Brown (1881–1955) who emerged during this period as a major theoretician in British social anthropology. He too espoused a functionalist approach, but one that was considered more sophisticated than that of Malinowski. This perspective became known as structural functionalism. In this chapter I shall examine some of the works and theoretical contributions of Radcliffe-Brown.

Born in Birmingham, England, in 1881, Radcliffe-Brown (A. R. Brown then) studied anthropology at Trinity College, Cambridge. There he was influenced by two of the leading anthropologists of the day, William H. R. Rivers, creator of the genealogical method and later diffusionist (see Chapter 5), and Alfred C. Haddon, leader of the anthropological expedition to the Torres Straits that had set the standards of anthropological field research.

Radcilffe-Brown conducted fieldwork from 1906 to 1908 in the Andaman Islands, off the southern coast of Burma, in the Bay of Bengal. He finished his dissertation in 1909, but the work was not published until 1922, the watershed year for British anthropology, which also saw the publication of Malinowski's *Argonauts of the Western Pacific* (Leach 1982: 25).

From 1910 to 1912, Radcliffe-Brown undertook fieldwork among the Karera and other aboriginal peoples in western Australia (Radcliffe-Brown 1913, 1918). During this period, his anthropological orientation underwent a significant transformation due to the influence of the works of the French sociologist Émile Durkheim (1858–1917). As a result, Radcliffe-Brown abandoned the diffusionist perspective he had acquired from Rivers and took up what seemed to him to be a sociologically more sophisticated and fruitful approach (Stocking 1984a).

As a fieldworker Radcliffe-Brown was undistinguished in comparison to Malinowski, who, as we have seen, redefined the enterprise during

Alfred Reginald Radcliffe-Brown, expositor of the structural functional approach in British social anthropology.

his work in the Trobriand Islands between 1914 and 1918. Radcliffe-Brown's impact upon the field was entirely in the area of theory. His theoretical ideas were expressed in his monograph on the Andaman Islanders (Radcliffe-Brown 1933 [1922]), in his articles, and through his many lectures in diverse international academic settings (Evans-Pritchard 1981: 200).

Radcliffe-Brown's influence upon American anthropology came as a result of his years of teaching at the University of Chicago (1931–1936). As the anthropologist Robert Redfield, who studied under him at Chicago, put it,

> Professor Radcliffe-Brown brought to this country a method for the study of society, well defined and different enough from what prevailed here to require American anthropologists to reconsider the whole matter of method, to scrutinize their objec-

tives, and attend to new problems and new ways of looking at problems (in Eggan and Warner 1956: 545).

Radcliffe-Brown's structural functionalism thus offered American anthropologists a theoretical alternative to the prevailing Boasian perspective. Soon a cadre of students and associates, the likes of Redfield, Morris Opler, Sol Tax, Fred Eggan, and Edward Spicer assembled around Radcliffe-Brown, and Chicago emerged as a major center of anthropological theory in the United States (Adams 1998: 326).

The Chicago anthropologists represented the first non-Boasian anthropological school whose members were committed to a nomothetic approach (Adams 1998: 352). They posed a serious but somewhat short-lived challenge to the Boasian idealist perspectives that had held sway up to that point in American anthropology (Adams 1998: 325).

Radcliffe-Brown held a number of academic positions during his long and distinguished career, including posts at the University of Cape Town (1921–1926), the University of Sydney (1926–1931), the University of Chicago (1931–1936), and the University of Oxford (1937–1946). After his retirement from Oxford, he taught at Farouk I University in Cairo and later at Grahamstown in South Africa. Radcliffe-Brown could be called the first "international" anthropologist, and he is credited specifically for helping to create a bridge between British and American anthropology (Eggan and Warner 1956: 547).

THE NOMOTHETIC APPROACH

Radcliffe-Brown was responsible for developing a rigorous set of concepts for ordering anthropological data (Kuper 1999: 35; see Radcliffe-Brown 1952, 1957, 1958, 1977). Radcliffe-Brown (1952: 3) considered social anthropology to be a branch of comparative sociology, which he defined as the "theoretical or nomothetic study of which the aim is to provide acceptable generalisations." He distinguished his own theoretical perspective from idiographic approaches to the study of social institutions:

> In an idiographic enquiry the purpose is to establish as acceptable certain particular or factual propositions or statements. A nomothetic enquiry, on the contrary, has for its purpose to arrive at acceptable general propositions (Radcliffe-Brown 1952: 1).[1]

For this reason, Radcliffe-Brown's vision of social anthropology as a nomothetic science was opposed to the idiographic, or particularizing, "shreds and patches" historical ethnology of the Boasians.

Radcliffe-Brown was particularly intolerant of the anti-science view of Boas's students that no generalizations were possible in the study of culture.

> I have found it impossible to know what they mean, or on what sort of evidence (rational or empirical) they would base their contention. Generalisations about any sort of subject matter are of two kinds: generalisations of common opinion, and generalisations that have been verified or demonstrated by a systematic examination of the evidence afforded by precise observations systematically made. Generalisations of the latter kind are called scientific laws. Those who hold that there are no laws of human society cannot hold that there are no generalisations about human society because they themselves hold such generalisations and even make new ones of their own. They must therefore hold that in the field of social phenomena, in contradistinction to physical or biological phenomena, any attempt at the systematic testing of existing generalisations or towards the discovery and verification of new ones, is, for some unexplained reason, futile, or, as Dr. Radin puts it, "crying for the moon". Arguments against such a contention is unprofitable or indeed impossible (Radcliffe-Brown 1952: 187).[2]

Radcliffe-Brown took on the task of building a generalizing, or nomothetic science of society. His efforts were not particularly original per se because he drew upon the sociological works of Durkheim and Comte, among others, who had already dealt with many of the issues Radcliffe-Brown chose to tackle. Moreover, attempting to develop a nomothetic science operating from a Durkheimian perspective constituted one of the weaknesses of Radcliff-Brown's anthropology. This is because Durkheim's work led him to reject two crucial elements of a scientific paradigm: material causation and evolutionary holism.

In his books *The Elementary Forms of Religious Life* (1915) and *Rules of Sociological Method* (1938), Durkheim elaborated the sociological functionalist perspective that Radcliffe-Brown incorporated into his own anthropological perspective. Durkheim's approach was idealist and was based upon the dictum that the social realm represents an emergent phenomenon, something *sui generis* (unique, in a class by itself), constituting an order distinct from biology or psychology. Related to this was Durkheim's idea of the **collective consciousness,** or group thought, an ideological force that exists outside the individual members of society, but exercises a determinative influence upon their thoughts and behavior.

For Durkheim (1938: 110), "the determining cause of a social fact should be sought among social facts preceding it and not among the states of the individual consciousness." In other words, "social facts" (social phenomena) can only be understood in terms of other "social facts" and in terms of the functions they fulfill in maintaining the social system as a whole. (Durkheim's sociological theory of religion, which illustrates these points, is discussed in Chapter 11.) An analogue of Durkheim's axiom that sociological phenomena can only be understood in terms of other sociological phenomena (i.e., that sociological phenomena are superindividual) is Kroeber's idea of culture as the **superorganic** (Ellen 1986: 27) and Boas's culture-comes-from-culture principle. These ideas involve similar circularity of reasoning and have identical theoretical and methodological implications.

The significance of this idealist twist in British social anthropology via the work of

Radcliffe-Brown cannot be underestimated. The epistemological alignment with Durkheimian sociology meant that British anthropologists could virtually ignore ecological or environmental questions, which again parallels developments in Boasian anthropology. As the anthropologist Robert Netting (1977: 57) put it, anthropologists operating under the auspices of the Radcliffe-Brownian paradigm were more interested in "rain dances than in rain." And as Gray (1964: 6) observed,

> The tendency in social anthropology has been to study societies as if they were isolated, self-sufficient systems, subsisting on thin air, with no visible roots in the soil. The guiding principle, derived in part from Durkheim and more explicitly from Radcliffe-Brown, has been that social facts require sociological explanations.[3]

Although operating in the idiom of science, Radcliffe-Brown's Durkheimian sociological perspective and its version of the culture-comes-from-culture axiom compelled him to eschew questions of material causality (cf. Ellen 1986: 27). To construct an anthropological paradigm that rejected material causation and at the same time aspired to be scientific would lead Radcliffe-Brown into a number of conceptual difficulties.

SYNCHRONIC APPROACH

Radcliffe-Brown opposed historical perspectives in anthropology. He reasoned that the acceptability of historical approaches depends upon the completeness of the historical records. Such records did not exist for the "primitive" societies that make up the subject matter of social anthropology. Anthropologists who insisted that their discipline is historical in nature therefore have to fall back upon conjecture, pseudohistorical explanations, and speculative reconstructions. These speculations, as Radcliffe-Brown saw it, were not just useless, they were "worse than useless." He objected to all conjectural histories, not on the grounds that they were historical, but

rather that they were conjectural (Radcliffe-Brown 1952: 50).

Radcliffe-Brown's did not view history as an unimportant part of anthropological inquiry, but he thought that it had little bearing upon what he was interested in, namely the analysis of causal relations in the present (Stocking 1984b: 151). He therefore rejected the **diachronic approach** in favor of a **synchronic approach** (Radcliffe-Brown 1957: 88–89). In this he was inspired by Durkheim's *The Rules of Sociological Method* (1938), which calls for a synchronic approach to the analysis of social facts (Stocking 1984b: 150).

In Radcliffe-Brown's view, therefore, in order for social anthropology to be a scientific and generalizing discipline it had to concern itself with social facts, with the concrete, observable, phenomenal reality in a synchronic framework. As he put it, social anthropology is concerned with

> the observation, description, comparison and classification of . . . the process of social life. The unit of investigation is the social life of some particular region of the earth during a certain period of time. The process itself consists of an immense multitude of actions and interactions of human beings, acting as individuals or in combinations or groups. Amidst the diversity of the particular events there are discoverable regularities, so that it is possible to give statements or descriptions of certain *general features* of the social life of a selected region. A statement of such significant general features of the process of social life constitutes a description of what may be called *a form of social life*. My conception of social anthropology is as the comparative theoretical study of forms of social life amongst primitive peoples (Radcliffe-Brown 1952: 4).[4]

RADCLIFFE-BROWN'S USE OF THE COMPARATIVE METHOD

The comparative approach was a fundamental aspect of the nomothetic science that Radcliffe-Brown attempted to construct. He wrote, "if there is to be a natural science of human societies, its methods will be the method of comparing, one with another, social systems of different kinds" (Radcilffe-Brown 1957: 38). The approach advocated was controlled comparisons, which I discussed in Chapter 3.

In his classic paper "The Comparative Method in Social Anthropology" (1951), Radcliffe-Brown attempted to demonstrate the utility of the comparative approach for the generation of nomothetic principles (in Radcliffe-Brown 1977: 53–69). This paper is also significant because it reveals the development of another theoretical direction in Radcliffe-Brown's work, namely, structural analysis. This is an important aspect of Radcliffe-Brown's work that is frequently overlooked in introductory texts, which tend to lump him together with Malinowski under the common heading of functional anthropology. The paper in question is thought to have provided the inspiration for the French structural anthropologist Claude Lévi-Strauss's influential study *Totemism,* published in 1962 (Leach 1970: 42). Lévi-Strauss went on to transform structural analysis into an anthropological paradigm know as structural anthropology, which acquired extraordinary popularity during the 1960s and 1970s (see Chapter 11).

The objective of the comparative method, according to Radcliffe-Brown, is "to explore the varieties of forms of social life as a basis for the theoretical study of social phenomena." Without a comparative perspective, he added, "anthropology will become only historiography and ethnography. Sociological theory must be based on, and continually tested by, systematic comparison" (Radcliffe-Brown 1977: 53, 54).

Radcliffe-Brown demonstrated the analytical usefulness of the comparative method in his examination of totemic representations of the divisions of exogamous moieties of the Australian aborigines in the interior of New South Wales. Societies based on **moieties,** from the French word *moitié* for "half," are divided into two descent-based halves. **Totemism** involves the use of aspects of nature (plant/animal/elements)

to refer to the human social world (for a detailed discussion see Chapter 11). Among the groups in question, Radcliffe-Brown noted that members of the moieties belonged to two separate social categories. One category was named the Eaglehawk and the other the Crow (Radcliffe-Brown 1977: 55). A man may take a wife from the group to which he does not belong, and his children will be members of the division of their mother.

Radcliffe-Brown was curious as to why these social divisions were identified with reference to two natural species of birds. To answer this question he took note of the existence of other moieties in which the dual divisions are associated with other pairs of animals, such as two species of kangaroo or bees. He observed further that the Australian moieties are merely one case of a much wider cross-cultural phenomenon of totemism involving the use of natural species to identify and distinguish social groups or divisions (Radcliffe-Brown 1977: 57). Thus, Radcliffe-Brown (1977: 57) pointed out that

> from a particular phenomenon we are led, by the comparative method, to a much more general problem—How can we understand the customs by which social groups and divisions which are distinguished by associating a particular group or division with a particular natural species?[5]

Radcliffe-Brown was interested in elucidating the principle by which pairs such as the Eaglehawk and the Crow are chosen to represent moieties of duel division? In the case he was working on, he wanted to know why Eaglehawk and Crow were used. Radcliffe-Brown observed that tales from different parts of Australia indicated that Eaglehawks and Crows are always depicted as opponents in some form of conflict (Radcliffe-Brown 1977: 57). For example, he recorded the following account from Western Australia:

> Eaglehawk was the mother's brother of Crow. In these tribes a man marries the daughter of a mother's brother so that Eaglehawk was the

possible father-in-law of Crow, to whom therefore he owed obligations such as that of providing him with food. Eaglehawk told his nephew to go and hunt wallaby. Crow, having killed a wallaby, ate it himself, an extremely reprehensible action in terms of native morality. On his return to camp his uncle asked him what he had brought, and Crow, being a liar, said he had succeeded in getting nothing. Eaglehawk then said, "but what is in your belly, since your hunger-belt is no longer tight?" Crow replied that to stay the pangs of hunger he had filled his belly with the gum from the acacia. The uncle replied that he did not believe him and would tickle him until he vomited. . . . The crow vomited the wallaby that he had eaten. Thereupon Eaglehawk seized him and rolled him in the fire; his eyes became red with the fire, he was blackened by the charcoal, and he called out in pain, "Wa! Wa! Wa!" Eaglehawk pronounced what was to be the law, "You will never be a hunter, but you will for ever be a thief." And that is how things are now (Radcliffe-Brown 1977: 58).[6]

Radcliffe-Brown noted many parallels among the Australian tales in which resemblances and differences of animal species are cast in the form of friendship and conflict, solidarity and opposition. From this, he made the following observations: (1) In these tales the resemblances and differences of animal species are represented in terms of social relationships of friendship and animosity, comparable to human social relationships; and (2) animal species are placed in pairs of opposites. Eaglehawk and Crow, for instance, can be positioned in this manner because they resemble each other and yet are different. Both Eaglehawk and Crow are birds that eat meat, but one is a hunter, the other a carrion eater.

From these observations Radcliffe-Brown concluded that the reason the Eaglehawk and the Crow are chosen to represent the duel divisions is because they have a type of relationship that may be called one of opposition. He observed further that the two categories of classification, a natural one and a cultural one have the same structure; one is a **transformation** of the other. He explained this in the following terms:

The Australian idea of what is here called "opposition" is a particular application of that association by contrariety that is a universal feature of human thinking, so that we think by pairs of contraries, upwards and downwards, strong and weak, black and white. But the Australian conceptions of "opposition" combines the ideas of a pair of contraries with that of a pair of opponents in the sense of being antagonists. They are also contraries by reason of their differences of character, Eaglehawk the hunter, Crow the thief (Radcliffe-Brown 1977: 60).[7]

Here Radcliffe-Brown refers to the tendency of humans to cast things in terms of "binary oppositions," an idea that Lévi-Strauss would later use to characterize the structure of the human thought process (see Chapter 11).

Radcliffe-Brown noted that the use of contrariety is a phenomenon widespread not just in Australia, but also in Melanesia, and America. The general law that results from these observations is that wherever the social structure of exogamous moieties exist, the moieties are thought of as being in a relation that is characterized by opposition (Radcliffe-Brown 1977: 61). The opposition of moieties is expressed in the institution of moiety exogamy, where marriages are between members of opposite divisions. The marriage relationship established between the two divisions is often expressed by the custom of avoidance and the **joking relationship.** A man must avoid contact with his wife's mother and other members of the generation to which she belongs. Associated with this is the joking relationship, which requires a man to insult members of his wife's kin that belong to his own generation. These practices are conventional means through which compound relationships of friendship or solidarity and opposition are established and maintained. In this way the opposition functions as a mode of social integration.

Thus, Radcliffe-Brown was able analytically to reduce a complicated social phenomenon to its underlying structural principle, that of social solidarity.

Our comparative study enables us to see the eagle-hawk-crow division of the Darling River tribes as one particular example of a widespread type of the structural principle. The relation between the two divisions, which has here been spoken of by the term "opposition" is one which separates and also unites, and which therefore gives us a rather special kind of social integration which deserves special study. But the term "opposition" which I have been obliged to use because I cannot find a better one, is not wholly appropriate, for it stresses too much what is only one side of the relationship, that of separation and difference. The more correct description would be to say that the kind of structure with which we are concerned is one of the union of opposites (Radcliffe-Brown 1977: 64).[8]

Lévi-Strauss (1963 [1962]), for whom totemism became a topic of great interest, as noted previously, made similar observations, pointing out that the lexical categories pertaining to the classification of the natural world have logical analogues in the classification of the social world (see Chapter 11). Thus, the functions, rights, and obligations of the various clans and their positions in the social hierarchy are symbolically coded by principles derived from the classification of totemic things in the natural environment (Kaplan and Manners 1972: 174). According to this view, totems function as metaphors to depict the relationships between clans and to underscore the idea that the unity and division that characterize human social relations obtain in nature as well (Kaplan and Manners 1972: 175). Such social appropriation of nature, nature as a metaphor for the social, formed the basis of both British and French structuralist perspectives (Sahlins 1976: 113).

Through the use of the comparative method, Radcliffe-Brown moved from a particular institution in a specific area (i.e., exogamous moieties identified as Eaglehawk and Crow in Australia) to the wider ethnographic context and a more general problem. The specific case is thus shown to be part of a more widespread anthropological phenomenon. Radcliffe-Brown went on to yet another level of generalization, to investigate the nature of social relationships of oppositions and how they are used as a mode of social integration. Thus, he pointed out that the comparative method enables us to understand a particular feature of a specific society by relating it to a general class of social phenomena and then associating it with certain general propositions relating to universal tendencies of human societies. This, in Radcliffe-Brown's view, was science.

CULTURE VERSUS SOCIAL STRUCTURE

Radcliffe-Brown was concerned with the study of forms of social life, or social structure, and not culture, the concept that was central to the works of Malinowski and the Boasians. Radcliffe-Brown considered culture as one aspect of social life and not as something that encompassed the whole of social life. As he put it,

> If we treat social reality that we are investigating as being not an entity but a process, then culture and cultural tradition are names of certain recognisable aspects of that process, but not, of course, the whole process (Radcliffe-Brown 1952: 5).[9]

To illustrate his point that social system takes analytical precedence over culture, Radcliffe-Brown used the example of language:

> Culture cannot exist of itself even for a moment; certainly it cannot continue. What, for example, is the basis of the continuity of a language? . . . A language you recognized as a body of speech usages, and you can describe it in terms of a set of rules. It is quite clear that a set of speech usages does not remain unchanged, even for a comparatively short period. But English today is still English, though not that spoken in the eighteenth century. We recognize a certain fundamental continuity. What is the basis of it? It is that at any moment of time between the eighteenth century and the present day we could put our finger on a certain body of human beings who constituted the English speaking community of the time *and had a structural continuity as a group*. The continuity of the language

depends on the continuity of the social structure. Just so does the continuity of the whole of culture as characteristics of the group. . . . The social structure consists of the social behavior of actual individual human beings, who are *a priori* to the existence of culture. Therefore if you study culture, you are always studying the acts of behavior of a specific set of persons who are linked together in a social structure (Radcliffe-Brown 1957: 107).[10]

By focusing upon social structure rather than culture, Radcliffe-Brown attempted to avoid the kind of reification and essentialism that seems to occur in the works of anthropologists that have made culture their principle concept (see Chapters 6 and 7). Radcliffe-Brown employed an analytical model based on the idea that any form of "social life" comprises a system. In any given system, "there are relations of interconnection and interdependence, or . . . relations of solidarity, amongst the various features" (Radcliffe-Brown 1952: 5). The notion of social systems, Radcliffe-Brown added, is theoretically significant because "our first step in an attempt to understand a regular feature of a form of social life . . . is to discover its place in the system of which it is a part" (Radcliffe-Brown 1952: 6). Social systems were thus conceive as coherent wholes in which features of social life are seen to be interconnected, and the system as a whole is considered to possess internal consistency and functional unity. Radcliffe-Brown posited further that the systematic investigation of the interconnections of the features of social life holds the key to understanding human societies (Radcliffe-Brown 1952: 6).

FROM SOCIAL STRUCTURE TO STRUCTURAL FUNCTIONALISM

Radcliffe-Brown recognized two sets of problems for anthropological investigation: the conditions of persistence of social systems, or social statics, and the conditions of change, or social dynamics, concepts first elaborated by August Comte (Radcliffe-Brown 1952: 7). Radcliffe-Brown himself was more concerned with the conditions of persistence of systems, or social statics, the understanding of which he believed would also shed light on dynamics. This does not mean that Radcliffe-Brown dismissed system change or suggested that sociocultural systems do not entail conflict and contradictions, but rather he thought that the analysis of persistence would shed light on change as well.

In order to analyze relationships internal to the system it was heuristically necessary to assume that social systems tend toward homeostasis. Critics attribute a more nefarious motive to Radcliffe-Brown's anthropology. Because structural functionalsim "downplayed conflict" and ignored social change (Barrett 1996: 66), they argue, it supported European colonial domination and imperialism and was therefore morally wicked, as if colonial governments needed the dreary articles of functionalist anthropologists published in arcane journals to ratify their policies. Writers such as Radcliffe-Brown and other "functionalists," such as Malinowski, Schapera, Evans-Pritchard, and Gluckman, did in fact address change, conflict, and did engage the colonial situation in many of their writings (Salzman 2001: 40).

Criticisms of the sort noted here entail the politicization of the theoretical weakness of an analytical model in an attempt to score points in favor of the critics' own moralistic agendas and are based on the red herring and straw man fallacies. Functionalist equilibrium models were indeed problematic and they did emphasize system stability for heuristic reasons. Perhaps this was a bad choice theoretically, but it does not automatically place proponents of structural functionalist models into the camp of the handmaidens of imperialism.

Radcliffe-Brown's (1952: 7) basic assumption regarding conditions of existence and persistence of social systems was that "for any form of social life to persist or continue the various features must exhibit some kind and measure of coherence or consistence." In order to investigate the coherence of social systems, it is necessary to delimit its structure, the components of this structure, and the process through which the different components operate to ensure the continuity of the system. By structure, Radcliffe-Brown (1952: 9) meant

[the] ordered arrangement of parts or components. A musical composition has a structure, and so does a sentence. A building has a structure, so does a molecule or an animal. The components or units of social structure are *persons,* and a person is a human being considered not as an organism but as occupying position in a social structure.[11]

For Radcliffe-Brown, the network of observable social relations that exists between people acting as members of groups comprised the social structure. This concept thus gave the field-worker an organizing theme for data collection:

Let us consider what are the concrete, observable facts with which the social anthropologist is concerned. If we set out to study, for example, the aboriginal inhabitants of a part of Australia, we find a certain number of individual human beings in a certain natural environment. We can observe the acts of behaviour of these individuals, including, of course, their acts of speech, and the material products of past actions. We do not observe a "culture", since that word denotes, not any concrete reality, but an abstraction, and as it is commonly used a vague abstraction. But direct observation does reveal to us that these human beings are connected by a complex network of social relations. I use the terms "social structure" to denote this network of actually existing relations. It is this that I regard as my business to study if I am working, not as an ethnologist or psychologist, but as a social anthropologist. I do not mean that the study of social structure is the whole of social anthropology, but I do regard it as being in a very important sense the most fundamental part of the science (Radcliffe-Brown 1977: 26–27).[12]

The issue for Radcliffe-Brown was anthropological abstractions and their place in the scientific perspective he was attempting to construct.

He noted that although social structure was something that was concrete and observable, the task of the social anthropologist was to abstract the structural form of the society being studied.

In the study of social structure the concrete reality with which we are concerned is the set of actually existing social relations, at a given moment of time, which link together certain human beings. It is on this that we can make direct observations. But it is not this that we attempt to describe in its particularity. Science (as distinguished from history or biography) is not concerned with the particular, the unique, but only with the general, with kinds, with events which recur. The actual relations of Tom, Dick, and Harry or the behaviour of Jack and Jill may go down in our field notebooks and may provide illustrations for a general description. But what we need for scientific purposes is an account of the form of the structure. For example, in an Australian tribe I observe in a number of instances the behaviour towards one another of persons who stand in the relation of mother's brother and sister's son, it is in order that I may be able to record as precisely as possible the general or normal form of this relationship, abstracted from the variations of particular instances, though taking account of those variations (Radcliffe-Brown 1977: 28–29).[13]

For Radcliffe-Brown, the study of specific cases was important to provide evidence for cross-cultural comparisons and not as an end in itself (Radcliffe-Brown 1952: 184).

Radcliffe-Brown elucidated the nature of anthropological abstractions in his discussion of the distinction between structure and structural form:

This important distinction, between structure as an actually existing concrete reality, to be directly observed, and structural form, as what the field-worker describes [abstracts], may be made clearer perhaps by a consideration of the continuity of social structure through time, a continuity which is not static like that of a building, but a dynamic continuity, like that of the organic structure of a living body. Throughout the life of an organism its structure is being constantly renewed; and similarly the social life constantly renews the social structure. Thus the actual relations of persons and groups of persons change from year to year, or even from day to day. New members come into a community by birth or immigration; others go out of it by death or emigration. There are marriages and divorces. Friends may become enemies, or enemies may make peace and become friends. But while the actual structure changes in this way, the general structural form may remain relatively constant over a longer or shorter period of time. Thus if I visit a relatively stable community and revisit it after an interval of ten years, I shall find that many of its members have died and others have been born, the members who still survive are now ten years older and their relations to one another may have changed in many ways. Yet I find that the kinds of relations that I can observe are very little different from those observed ten years before. The structural form has changed little (Radcliffe-Brown 1977: 29).[14]

What Radcliffe-Brown was suggesting is that structure consists of the social morphology, or that which can be observed in social roles. But structure entails not just visible behavioral manifestations but also structural principles on the basis of which the relationship between people are organized that cannot be seen but which can be inferred from the behavioral dimension and can be expressed as general principles. In other words, he was talking about logico-empirical abstractions based upon observational data of actual human behavior.

Leach (1954: 4) criticized Radcliffe-Brown's assertion that social structure was something real and observable, noting that social structure is a model that merely exists inside the researcher's head. Jarvie (1964: 192) suggested that Radcliffe-Brown's assertion that social structures are observable things was his rationalization for committing the "positivist's" sin of dealing with nonempirical or metaphysical things. These comments imply that abstractions are unreal, which is a misunderstanding of a fundamental postulate of empirical science. This postulate holds that there is a reality outside of the observer the nature of which can be known through interacting with it by means of observations, logical operations, and experimentation (Harris 1997: 413). Therefore, all known things, from galaxies and atomic particles to moieties and social structures, are in part created by means of observations and logical operations (Harris 1997: 413). This, however, does not make these things unreal, contra to what Leach and Jarvie seem to be implying. The problems of Radcliffe-Brown's approach were not so much that he was dealing with unreal things, but rather that he eschewed material causality and virtually ignored ecological and demographic factors.

Thus, it was perfectly reasonable for Radcliffe-Brown to maintain that social structure was something real and observable because, unlike the concept of culture, which is construed as sets of values, ideals, and norms, it refers to concrete entities. When the anthropologist is ready to undertake the scientific tasks of classification and comparison, social forms must be abstracted (Kuper 1999: 51). This is necessary because the ultimate objective of scientific anthropology is the formulation of generalizations applicable to all societies.

For Radcliffe-Brown the analysis of social structure took priority over everything else. Social structures are not random assemblages, he noted, but are based upon definite structural principals.

> The social relationships of which the continuing network constitute [the] social structure, are not haphazard conjunctions of individuals, but are determined by the social process, and any relationship is one in which the conduct of persons in their interactions with each other is controlled by norms, rules or patterns. So that in any relationship within a social structure a person knows that he is expected to behave according to these norms and is justified in expecting that other persons should do the same. The established norms of conduct of a particular form of social life it is usual to refer to as *institutions*. An institution is an established norm of conduct recognised as such by a distinguishable

social group or class of which therefore it is an institution (Radcliffe-Brown 1952: 10).[15]

The elements of the social system thus fit together. Radcliffe-Brown used the term *coaptation* (fitting together) to refer to the process by which the conduct of persons in their interactions with each other is controlled. "The most characteristic thing about any society . . . is that the individual members of the society have their behavior fitted together in some way so as to maintain a social life as a result of that fitting together" (Radcliffe-Brown 1957: 90). This fitting together was referred to as **functional unity:**

> Such a view implies that a social system (the total social structure of a society together with the totality of social usages in which that structure appears and on which it depends for its continued existence) has a certain kind of unity, which we may speak of as functional unity. We may define it as a condition in which all part of the social system work together with a sufficient degree of harmony or internal consistencies, i.e., without producing persistent conflicts which can neither be resolved nor regulated [opposition, i.e., organized and regulated antagonism, is, of course, and essential feature of every social system] (Radcliffe-Brown 1952: 181).[16]

Central to Radcliffe-Brown's thinking were the relationships among structure, functions, and the conceptualization of social systems as analogues of living organisms (organic analogy). Maintenance of social life, or continuity of the system, was one of Radcliffe-Brown's main concerns, as noted previously: "Continuity in forms of social life depends on structural continuity, that is, some sort of continuity in the arrangements of persons in relation to one another" (Radcliffe-Brown 1952: 10). An important concept in understanding the continuation of structure was the idea of "function."

> For the . . . elucidation of the concept it is convenient to use the analogy between social life and organic life. . . . An animal organism is an agglomeration of cells and interstitial fluids arranged in relation to one another not as an aggregate but as

an integrated living whole. . . . The system of relations by which these units are related is the organic structure. As the terms here used the organism is *not* itself the structure; it is a collection of relations; the organism *has* a structure. Two mature animals of the same species and sex consist of similar units combined in a similar structure. The structure is thus to be defined as a set of relations between entities. . . . As long as it lives the organism preserves a certain continuity of structure although it does not preserve the complete identity of its constituent parts. It loses some of its constituent molecules by respiration or excretion; it takes in other by respiration and alimentary absorption. Over a period its constituent cells do not remain the same. But the structural arrangement of the constituent units remain similar. The process by which this structural continuity of the organism is maintained is called life. The life-process consists of the organism, the cells, and the organs into which the cells are united. . . . As the word function is here being used the life of an organism is conceived as the *functioning* of its structure. It is through and by the continuity of the functioning that the continuity of the structure is preserved. If we consider any recurrent part of the life-process, such as respiration, digestion, etc., its *function* is the part it plays in, the contribution to makes to, the life of the organism as a whole. As the terms are here being used a cell or an organ has an *activity* and the activity has a *function* (Radcliffe-Brown 1952: 178–179).[17]

Thus, turning to social life, Radcliffe-Brown wrote that

> if we examine such a community as an African or Australian tribe we can recognize the existence of a social structure. Individual human beings, the essential units in this instance, are connected by a definite set of social relations into an integrated whole. The continuity of the social structure, like that of an organic structure, is not destroyed by changes in the units. Individuals may leave the society, by death or otherwise; others may enter it. The continuity of structure is maintained by the process of social life, which consists of the activities and interactions of the individual human beings and of the organised groups into which they

are united. The social life of the community is here defined as the *functioning* of the social structure. The *function* of recurrent activity, such as the punishment of a crime, or a funeral ceremony, is the part it plays in the social life as a whole and therefore the contribution it makes to the maintenance of the structural continuity. . . . The concept of function as here defined thus involves the notion of a *structure* consisting of a set of relations amongst *unit entities,* the *continuity* of the structure being maintained by a *life process* made up of the *activities* of the constituent units (Radcliffe-Brown 1952: 180).[18]

Radcliffe-Brown employed the organic analogy and functional approach in his monograph on the Andaman islanders:

> Every custom and belief of a primitive society plays some determinate part in the social life of the community, just as every organ of a living body plays some part in the general life of the organism. The mass of institutions, customs and beliefs forms a single whole or system that determines the life of the society, and the life of a society is not less real, or less subject to natural laws, than the life of an organism. To continue the analogy, the study of the meaning of savage customs is a sort of social physiology, and it is to be distinguished from the study of origins, or changes of custom in just the same way that animal physiology is distinguished from the biology that deals with the origins of species, the causes of variation, and the general laws of evolution (Radcliffe-Brown 1933: 229–230).[19]

Thus, because Radcliffe-Brown's notion of function referred to the contribution of a particular institution made toward the maintenance and perpetuation of the social structure, then it followed that the explanation of institutions lay in their functions.

ANDAMAN CHILDBIRTH TABOO AND STRUCTURAL FUNCTIONAL ANALYSIS

Radcliffe-Brown's structural functionalist approach is nicely exemplified in his analysis of Andaman taboos relating to childbirth, which I

shall briefly examine here. He noted that cross-culturally taboos involve ritually prohibited actions or behaviors. For example, the people of the Andaman Islands observe certain taboos relating to childbirth. Andaman islanders give a name to the child while it is still in the womb. From that time until the birth of the child, no one is allowed to use the personal names of the mother and father, but must instead resort to **teknonymy,** that is, refer to them in terms of their relation to the child (i.e., X's mother, X's father). During this time the prospective parents ritually abstain from certain foods. The infraction of the taboo is believed to lead to a negative change in the ritual status of the individual who has broken the rule. Such a person, as a consequence of his or her infraction, is in danger of some misfortune, such as illness (Radcliffe-Brown 1952: 135).

Radcliffe-Brown (1952: 139) approached the taboo from the perspective of its effects upon the network of social relationships rather than how it affected particular individuals and their psychological states. He noted that anything that is the object of a taboo has ritual value, as evidenced by the behavior adopted toward it. Values, he added, are what binds members of society together. Indeed, social relations require common interests and social values among members of society.

> A social system can be conceived and studied as a system of values. A society consists of a number of individuals bound together in a network of social relations. A social relation exists between two or more persons when there is some harmonisation of their individual interests. . . . a society cannot exist except on the basis of a certain measure of similarity in the interests of its members. Putting this in terms of values, the first necessary condition of the existence of a society is that the individual members shall agree in some measure in the values [moral, aesthetics, economic, etc.] that they recognise (1952: 140).[20]

Radcliffe-Brown observed that one could study rituals in terms of their purposes as related by individuals or members of the community who observe those rites. However, he added, these can be vague and it is problematic to suppose that the reason given is a valid anthropological explanation (Radcliffe-Brown 1952: 142). There is a sense in which people always know the meaning of their own symbols, but they do so "intuitively and can rarely express their understanding in words" (Radcliffe-Brown 1952: 143). Thus Radcliffe-Brown, like Malinowski, was cognizant of the differences between the native's perspective and the perspective of the observer.

To seek explanations for ritual actions in their attested purposes, Radcliffe-Brown noted, is to erroneously treat rituals as if they are technical acts. In a technical act, such as building a canoe, the purpose constitutes an explanation. But ritual acts, such as the observation of a taboo, are different from technical ones because they have a symbolic dimension. Ritual acts must thus be studied in terms of the social values and the socially shared symbolic meanings they embody and must be analyzed in sociological terms. Meanings, however, do not lie on the surface. Thus, the real question was how to discover the sociologically significant meanings of rituals.

Radcliffe-Brown rejected guesswork and intuition as a way of determining the symbolic meanings of rites. Thus, his approach stands in contrast with the avenue taken by interpretive anthropologists such as Clifford Geertz, whose methodology for arriving at the meaning of symbols is through intuition and guesswork (see Chapter 13). Rites, according to Radcliffe-Brown, not only have psychological effects, but they also have effects on the social structure, or the network of social relations that bind individuals together in an ordered life.

Radcliffe-Brown contrasted his own position with Malinowski's functional anthropology, which focused upon the psychological functions of rites, as illustrated by his studies of Trobriand magic and religion. Thus, Malinowski would interpret the taboos associated with childbirth

among the Andaman Islanders as a cultural mechanism that functions to alleviate anxiety over the dangers of childbirth. Radcliffe-Brown dismissed such an explanation, pointing out that

> for certain rites it would be easy to maintain with equal plausibility an exactly contrary theory, namely, that if it were not for the existence of the rite and the beliefs associated with it the individual would feel no anxiety, and that the psychological effect of the rite is to create in him a sense of insecurity or danger (Radcliffe-Brown 1952: 148–149).[21]

Radcliffe-Brown rejected psychological explanations of any kind, including the formulations of Malinowski and the Boasians in the United States.

In the case of the Adamanese childbirth taboo, Radcliffe-Brown noted that a psychological explanation was problematic because among the Andaman islanders the taboo is observed for a period even after the child is born, and the stress and anxiety over childbirth are no longer an issue. This is how he described his approach:

> I did not obtain from the Andamanese any statement of the purpose or reason for this avoidance of names. Assuming that the act is symbolic, what method, other than that of guessing, is there of arriving at the meaning? I suggest that we may start with a general working hypothesis that when, in a single society, the same symbol is used in different contexts or on different kinds of occasions there is some common element of meaning, and that by comparing together the various uses of the symbol we may be able to discover what the common element is. This is precisely the method we adopt in studying an unrecorded spoken language in order to discover the meaning of words and morphemes (Radcliffe-Brown 1952: 146).[22]

Radcliffe-Brown went on to examine other social contexts in which the Andamand islanders observed the name-avoidance taboo. For example, he noted that among the islanders the name of a dead person is avoided until the end of the mourning period. Also, the names of those mourning a dead relative are avoided. The names of adolescent girls going through puberty rites are likewise not mentioned until after the ceremonies are complete. The same is true of the names of a bride and bridegroom, which are not mentioned until after the marriage ceremony. Radcliffe-Brown argued that the personal name is "a symbol of social personality, i.e., of the position that an individual occupies in the social structure and the social life." A person whose name is temporarily avoided is therefore in an abnormal social status. From this he reached the following conclusion:

> In a given community it is appropriate that an expectant father should feel concern or at least should make an appearance of doing so. Some suitable symbolic expression of his concern is found in terms of the general ritual or symbolic idiom of the society, and it is felt generally that a man in that situation ought to carry out the symbolic or ritual actions or abstentions. For every rule that *ought* to be observed there must be some sort of sanction or reason. For acts that patently affect other persons the moral and legal sanctions provide a generally sufficient controlling force upon the individual. For ritual obligations conformity and rationalisation are provided by the ritual sanctions. The simplest form of ritual sanction is an accepted belief that if rules of ritual are not observed some undefined danger is likely to occur. In many societies the expected danger of sickness, or, in extreme cases, death (Radcliffe-Brown 1952: 150).[23]

This explanation is not concerned with the question of historical origins of the ritual, nor does it attempt to explain ritual in terms of human psychology. Instead, it focuses on the social functions of the ritual and ritual values in terms of their effects upon the community as a whole, as it exists as a living, and functioning entity. Thus

> By this theory the Andamanese taboos relating to childbirth are the obligatory recognition in a standardised symbolic form of the significance and importance of the event to the parents and to the community at large. They thus serve to fix the social value of occasions of this kind. . . . The primary

basis of ritual . . . is the attribution of ritual value to objects and occasions which are either themselves objects of important common interests linking together the persons of a community or are symbolically representative of such objects (Radcliffe-Brown 1952: 151–152).[24]

In Radcliffe-Brown's work, the analysis of symbolic meaning is directly tied to actual social relationships, rather than simply being the analysis of symbols themselves:

> My own view is that the negative and positive rites of savages exist and persist because they are part of the mechanism by which an orderly society maintains itself in existence, serving as they do to establish certain fundamental social values. The beliefs by which the rites themselves are justified and given some sort of consistency are the rationalisations of symbolic actions and of the sentiments associated with them (Radcliffe-Brown 1952: 151).[25]

As the discussion above suggests, Radcliffe-Brown's conception of function was fundamentally different from the manner in which Malinowski employed the term. As he put it, "This theory of society in terms of structure and process, interconnected by function, has nothing in common with the theory of culture as derived from individual biological needs" (Radcliffe-Brown 1977: 52).

As Radcliffe-Brown saw it, the concept of the "functional unity of a social system" opened up a range of questions for anthropological inquiry:

> The concept of function . . . constitutes a "working hypothesis" by which a number of problems are formulated for investigation. No scientific enquiry is possible without some such formulation of working hypotheses. Two remarks are necessary here. One is that the hypothesis does not require the dogmatic assertion that everything in the life of every community has a function. It only requires the assumption that it *may* have one, and that we are justified in seeking to discover it. The second is that what appears to be the same social usage in two societies may have different functions

in the two. Thus the practice of celibacy in the Roman Catholic Church of today has very different functions from those of celibacy in the early Christian Church. In other words, in order to define a social usage, and therefore in order to make valid comparisons between the usages of different peoples or periods, it is necessary to consider not merely the form of the usage but also its function. . . .

The acceptance of the functional hypothesis . . . results in the recognition of a vast number of problems for the solution of which there are required wide comparative studies of societies of diverse types and also intensive studies of as many single societies as possible. In field studies of simpler peoples it leads, first of all, to a direct study of the social life of the community as the functioning of a social structure. . . .

. . . [the] subject-matter of social anthropology is the whole social life of a people in all its aspects. For convenience of handling it is often necessary to devote special attention to some particular part or aspect of the social life, but if functionalism means anything at all it does mean the attempt to see social life of a people as a whole, as a functional unity (Radcliffe-Brown 1952: 184–185).[26]

ASSESSMENT

Radcliffe-Brown had as much of a role in the shaping of British social anthropology as Bronislaw Malinowski. His influence upon the discipline began to grow particularly strong from the mid-1930s onward, when functionalism was replaced by structural functionalism as the dominant perspective in British social anthropology (Jarvie 1964: 189). Thereafter, Malinowski remained the unmatched virtuoso of fieldwork, while Radcliffe-Brown became the personification of theoretical anthropology in Britain.

Both functionalism and structural functionalism employed an organic analogy. However, Malinowski's approach construed society as an organism, the parts (institutions) of which functioned to contribute to the survival of individuals by meeting their biopsychological needs. For Radcliffe-Brown, institutions were explicable in terms of their function in ameliorating conflict and contributing to the survival and perpetuation of the social system. Moreover, all aspects of the social system and all functional relationships were, in the final analysis, linked to social structure, to which Radcliffe-Brown gave analytical priority.

Radcliffe-Brown treated social structure as the foundation upon which every other aspect of social life was constructed. By placing primacy upon social structure, he felt that he could build a scientific understanding of sociocultural systems and generate explanatory laws to account for cultural similarities and differences. Radcliffe-Brown stressed the comparative method and the importance of comparing a sufficient number of different cultures for the formulation of universal laws. He himself, however, compared only certain aspects of cultures, such as taboos, totemism, and kinship reckoning.

The sociological laws Radcliffe-Brown was able to discover were in the nature of general statements such as, In order for social systems to continue to exist its constituent parts must have a degree of functional consistency. Or, The principal function of rituals is to express and maintain sentiments necessary for social cohesion. Thus, for any particular social system, he could demonstrate the functional cohesion of its constituent parts. He could show how a ceremonial observance, a totemic rite, ancestor worship, lineal descent, or a body of cosmological ideas reflected structural principles and functioned to maintain social structural cohesion and continuity. As such, Radcliffe-Brown's work shed light on the interconnections among different elements within social systems.

Under his influence, anthropological analysis shifted toward the analysis of social institutions and their role in the maintenance and perpetuation of the social system. For this reason, American anthropologists such as Robert Redfield, Morris Opler, Sol Tax, Fred Eggan, and Edward Spicer found in Radcliffe-Brown's work a refreshing alternative to the Boasian anthropology at home. This is by no means an indication of the triumph of nomothetic perspective over the entrenched Boasian idealist approach. The effects of Radcliffe-Brown's nomothetic structural functionalist approach was transitory and it failed to squelch the mentalist and idiographic orientation that Boas had instilled. Subsequently, Spicer, Redfield, Opler, and Tax returned to the Boasian historical/idealist point of view (Adams 1998: 353). Thus, I think that Robin Fox's (1997: 327) construal of the Functionalist period as the Golden Age of scientific anthropology, which lasted up to the 1950s, when humanistic interpretive approaches gained currency, is not quite accurate in the context of American anthropology.

One of the main problems with Radcliffe-Brown's approach was that, while structural functional analysis could demonstrate how parts related to wholes, it could not account for the similarities and differences between wholes. The wholes (i.e., social structures) were treated as a given. For this reason, Radcliffe-Brown could show that the form taken by a particular institution is determined by social structure, but he could not tell us what determined the social structure.

Another problem was Radcliffe-Brown's treatment of causal relationships. For him, to demonstrate that unilineal descent reckoning had a functional value of preventing conflict because such systems clearly specify rights and obligations was to explain this type of descent reckoning. In other words, the "cause" of this form of descent lay in its functional value (Hatch 1973: 237). Thus, as in the case of Malinowski's functional analysis, Radcliffe-Brown's approach was also prone to conflating the antecedent and the consequent.

The epistemological status of Radcliffe-Brown's sociological laws was problematic. As we have seen, he sought to provide scientific explanations for sociocultural phenomena by isolating underlying principles from behavioral patterns. As concise descriptive statements referring to particular features of the social structure, these principles have a utility (Kaplan and Manners 1972: 102). However, using these principles as explanations entails the error of treating description as explanation, a problem also evident in Malinowski's functionalism. As Kaplan and Manners (1972: 102) noted,

> Since the principles are themselves derived from the very pattern of behavior they are intended to explain, to see them as having explanatory value is to engage in tautological thinking.[27]

The perennial quandary of a paradigm that is based upon the axiom that the sociological can only be explained by the sociological, which provides no room for any sort of material causation, and which excludes ecological, demographic, and environmental factors, is to fall back upon logically problematic circular explanations. Fox (1997: 341) is correct in characterizing Radcliffe-Brown's generalizations or general laws as "teleological truisms."

In his later writings Radcliffe-Brown acknowledged the role of ecological factors, but he still placed analytical priority upon social structure as the locus of causal relationships. Radcliffe-Brown wrote, for example, that social systems have three analytically distinguishable components: ecological, institutional, and cultural.

> There is the way in which the social system is adjusted to the physical environment, and we can . . . speak of this as the æcological adaptation. Secondly, there are the institutional arrangements by which an orderly social life is maintained, so that . . . co-operation is provided for and conflict is restrained or regulated. This we might call . . . the institutional aspect of social adaptation. Thirdly, there is the social process by which an individual acquires habits and mental characteristics that fit him for a place in the social life and enable him to participate in its activities. This . . . could be called

cultural adaptation, in accordance with the earlier definition of cultural tradition as process (Radcliffe-Brown 1952: 9).[28]

But for Radcliffe-Brown all aspects of the social system and all functional relationships were, in the final analysis, linked to social structure, which he construed as a closed and fixed system in which all its components were thought to have more or less equal causal effects.

Finally, critics have pointed out a related problem, which is that many of Radcliffe-Brown's laws were merely truisms. For example, the proposition that where moieties exist these units are in a state of balanced opposition, a combination of agreement and disagreement, or solidarity and difference, is a truism which exists in the definition of moieties (fallacy of begging the question) and can in fact be extended to any social group (Evans-Pritchard 1981: 201). Other of Radcliffe-Brown's laws were criticized for being supported by a few selected illustrations, which were either too general to be of any analytical use or were based on slender evidence and exclusion of contradictory data.

Radcliffe-Brown must be lauded for introducing a new theoretical approach that challenged (unsuccessfully) the reigning Boasian paradigm in American anthropology. His attempt to build a scientific paradigm and the emphasis upon cross-cultural comparisons as part of that effort must also be treated as a highly praiseworthy effort. He must be faulted, however, for adopting theoretical principles that rejected material causality and evolutionary holism that were inimical to the development of a viable scientific approach.

The defects of Radcliffe-Brown's approach are not related to its scientific aspirations but are related to the problematic features of structural functionalism itself and its epistemological assumptions regarding sociocultural phenomena. Thus, to argue that Radcliffe-Brown's formulations represent science and then to conclude that since structural functionalism was defective therefore science is defective entails a *non sequitur.*

Chapter 10

Cultural Evolution Returns: Leslie White and Julian Steward

While the functionalist perspectives were being forged in Britain, other developments were taking place in the United States that would bring evolutionary thinking back into cultural anthropology. The revival of evolutionism in American anthropology is the topic of this chapter.

By the end of 1900, Boas had completed his critique of evolutionism (Stocking 1974: 6). Robert Lowie's books *Culture and Ethnology* (1917) and *Primitive Society* (1920) (with its famous "shreds and patches" statement) are considered to be the culmination of the Boasian critique of evolutionary theory in cultural anthropology (Herskovits 1933: 82; Parsons 1920; Sapir 1920a, 1920b; Stocking 1974: 6).

As noted before, the Boasians were the practitioners of academic anthropology—they formed a school of thought that went along with "disciple-ism, "despotism," and alliances that played an important part in the acceptance or rejection of ideas (cf. Service 1985: vii). They had established complete intellectual hegemony over the anthropological landscape. Their favorite theories and epistemological orientation defined the discipline during this time. It is unequivocal that

Boas and his students stood together in their negative opinion of evolutionary theory in cultural anthropology and the possibility of a science of culture. To bring evolutionary thinking back into anthropological thought would require challenging this powerful academic clique.

Leslie White (1987a [1947]), who emerged as a staunch critic of Boasian anthropology and who singlehandedly took on this puissant coterie of anthropologists, seemed to have delighted in putting together strings of antievolutionary statements by Boas's students that he had complied over the years. White noted that Sapir (1920a: 377; 1920b: 46) called evolutionists "closet philosophers" and referred to their theory "not as science but a pseudo-science like medieval alchemy." Goldenweiser (1921: 55; 1924: 433) referred to the field of cultural evolution as "a happy hunting ground for the exercise of the creative imagination" and dubbed the theory itself "a substitute for critical thought." Herskovits (1941: 273) wrote, "I am glad . . . to reaffirm my belief that the use . . . of such a concept as 'stages of development' implies a belief in a type of social evolution that cannot

. . . be established as valid." Mead and Benedict concurred with the antievolutionism of their teacher and colleagues.

Although the formidable Boasians demolished nineteenth-century evolutionary schemes, none of them denied that cultures change (e.g., Goldenweiser 1921: 65; Kroeber 1917: 164). At issue was the mechanism of change, not whether change takes place, and on this point no one seemed to have an acceptable response.

For some Boasians the answer lay in the random diffusion and combination of traits. Others were not convinced that diffusion was the mechanism and sought answers in psychological factors and cultural configurations. What the Boasians were unanimous in was their suspicion of the talk about laws of cultural evolution and theoretical generalizations. Such ideas were simply not acceptable to Boasian sensibilities for reasons discussed in Chapters 6 and 7.

INTELLECTUAL CLIMATE: THE BOASIAN THEORY PHOBIA

The Boasian construal of science as an enterprise deeply committed to systematic empirical data gathering but allied to a profoundly idiographic orientation was totally inimical to science (Sanderson 1990: 47). As Radin (1987 [1933]: 253) put it, Boas and his students not only rejected evolutionary theory but they managed to make "the distrust of theories of whatever description" an epistemological feature of American cultural anthropology. This was entirely the accomplishment of Boas himself, who cleverly used the refutation of individual hypotheses to delegitimize the nomothetic scientific enterprise as a whole (cf. Wax 1956: 63). The net effect of the Boasian hostility toward evolutionary theory, in other words, was not only the repudiation of the theories of Tylor and Morgan, but also the eschewal of all efforts at theory construction.

The Boasian theory phobia of American anthropologists was so trenchant that Clyde Kluckhohn (1939: 333) wrote "to suggest that something is 'theoretical' is to suggest that it is slightly indecent." The intellectual climate of the Boasian period during the first half of the twentieth century was in many respects very much like the antiscience atmosphere in which American anthropologists find themselves today.

The Boasians dominated the American anthropological scene until the 1950s. Prior to that, with the exception of the challenge posed by Radcliffe-Brown's group at Chicago, their views held sway, with proponents well beyond the circle of Boas's immediate students. One of these was Berthold Laufer, whose laudatory review of Lowie's *Culture and Ethnology* illustrates the impact of Boas's antitheory view on writers of period:

> The theory of cultural evolution, to my mind one of the most inane, sterile, and pernicious theory ever conceived in the history of science (a cheap toy for the amusement of big children) is duly disparaged. . . . Culture cannot be forced into the straitjacket of any theory whatever it may be, nor can it be reduced to chemical or mathematical formulae. Nature has no laws, so culture has none. It is as vast and free as the ocean, throwing its waves and currents in all directions. . . . All that the practical investigator can hope for, at least to study each cultural phenomenon as exactly as possible in its geographical distribution, its historical development and its relation or association with other kindred ideas. The more theories will be smashed, the more new facts will be established, the better for the progress of our science (Laufer 1918: 90).

Laufer's passage reveals the powerful impact of Boas's antitheory perspective. Fifty years of antiscience had a profound influence upon American cultural anthropology. Boas's Historical Particularism faded, but not the antiscience/antitheory perspective that he and his students had inculcated. Today, this attitude is powerfully expressed in the cultural constructionist perspectives glossed as interpretive/postmodern/literary anthropology.

LESLIE WHITE AND THE EVOLUTION OF CULTURE

It was largely due to the efforts of Leslie White (1900–1975) that American cultural anthropology once again became receptive to evolutionary theory and a scientific approach to the study of culture (Trigger 1998: 126–129). His drive set the stage for other anthropologists, such as Julian Steward and the British archaeologist V. Gordon Childe, to broach the subject of sociocutural evolution in different ways.

White took up the study of anthropology after having earned B.A. and M.A. degrees in psychology. He was not a student of Boas himself (contra W. Adams 1998: 326) but was trained in the Boasian antievolutionary tradition by Alexander Goldenweiser, Edward Sapir, and Fay-Cooper Cole, who were all Boas's students.

White pursed his Ph.D. work at the University of Chicago, where he enrolled in 1924. For his dissertation, he proposed to write a theoretical library thesis that dealt with culture as a superorganic phenomenon and a number of related ideas he would develop during his professional career (Carneiro 1981: 213). Benjamin Faris, the Chair of the Department of Sociology at Chicago, rejected White's proposal as too the-

Leslie White, who singlehandedly battled Boasian anti-evolutionism and brought evolutionary thinking back into anthropology.

oretical and overambitious. This ignited a serious dispute between Faris and Cole, the senior anthropologist in the department.

The outcome of this academic feud was a split and the establishment of a separate department of anthropology under Cole (Carneiro 1981: 213; Service 1976: 612). Caught up in the violence of departmental politics, which were apparently as fierce then as they are now, White was forced to give up his proposal and was compelled to select another topic for his dissertation. He undertook a year of fieldwork in the Acoma Pueblo in New Mexico and completed a Ph.D. dissertation entitled "Medicine Societies of the Southwest." He received his degree in 1927.

After graduation, White continued his ethnographic field research in the American Southwest. This work resulted in the publication of major monographs on the Acoma (1932a), the Pueblo of San Felipe (1932b), the Pueblo of Santo Domingo (1934), the Pueblo of Santa Ana (1942), and the Pueblo of Sia (1962). These ethnographies, which earned White recognition as an authority on the Southwest, were descriptive in nature and he seldom cited them in his theoretical writings. For this reason, the British social anthropologist Evans-Pritchard (1981: 204) criticized White for not appealing to his own ethnographic data to support his theoretical formulations. A similar lack of articulation exists in White's ideas about the science of culture, or **culturology** as he referred to it, and his evolutionary theory. It is best, therefore, to evaluate each aspect of White's work independently.

White's major theoretical works include *The Science of Culture* (1949), which deals with the concept of culture, the scientific study of culture, and cultural evolution; and *The Evolution of Culture* (1959), which traces the development of culture over a vast expanse of time from an evolutionary point of view. In addition, White published the edited volumes *Extracts from the European Journal of Lewis Henry Morgan* (1937) and *Pioneers in American Anthropology: The Bandelier-*

Morgan Letters, 1873–1883 (1940), which document the works and life of Lewis Henry Morgan.

CONVERSION TO EVOLUTIONISM

In 1927 White accepted a position at the Buffalo Museum of Science, a job that also entailed teaching classes at the University of Buffalo. The most important event in White's intellectual development, which transformed him into "the dragon slayer of Boasianism," as his student, the archeologists Lewis Binford (1972: 6) referred to him, took place when he was at the University of Buffalo. White recalled that while teaching Boasian antievolutionism, his students asked him why the theory of evolution, which was so crucial in the biological sciences, was excluded from ethnology. White (1987b: 13) wrote that

> they challenged me on this issue. I repeated all the reasons the Boasians offered for rejecting the theory of cultural evolution. . . . They pushed me into a corner. Before long I had realized that I could not defend the doctrines of anti-evolutionism; then I realized that I could no longer hold them; they were untenable.[1]

The questions that occupied White (1987b: 13) thereafter were as follows: "if the theory of evolution was so pervasive in science, if it was fundamental and fruitful in all other fields, why was it rejected in ethnology? Why did anti-evolutionism flourish both in orthodox theology and American ethnology?"

White's two years at Buffalo had a major impact on his departure from Boasian anthropology. Buffalo was close to the Tonawanda Indian Reservation, where Lewis Henry Morgan had worked with the Seneca Iroquois. White became involved with the Seneca and, as Robert Carniero (1981: 214) his student tells us, this led him to read Morgan's books *The League of the Iroquois* (1851) and *Ancient Society* (1877). What

White found in those works was unexpected. Rather than finding "the comprehensive weak mind," or a work that "was hopelessly antiquated," as the Boasians described Morgan and his research, he found many effective ideas and "a remarkable scholar, savant, and personality" (Barnes 1960: xxvi).

White then turned to the works of the other classical evolutionists, such as Tylor and Spencer. Therein he found much that was valid and useful. Thereafter White set himself the task of restoring Morgan to his rightful intellectual place and resuscitating evolutionary theory.

WHITE, THE SOVIET UNION, AND MARX

Another crucial event that had a lasting impact on White's intellectual growth was a visit in 1929 to the Soviet Union (Barnes 1960: xxvi). During this trip, White came into contact with Soviet anthropologists and was familiarized with the works of Karl Marx and Fredrick Engels. These social theorists, as noted earlier, had incorporated Morgan's anthropological ideas into their own works (see Chapters 4 and 14).

White found Marx's historical materialist approach attractive and full of possibilities for anthropology (Carneiro 1981: 216). Marx's theoretical perspective, stated in the preface of his *Contribution to the Critique of Political Economy* (1904 [1859]), has become one of the cornerstones of cultural materialist perspectives in American anthropology (see Chapter 14). Marx wrote that

> in the social production which men carry on they enter into definite relations that are indispensable and independent of their will; these relations of production correspond to a definite state of development of their material powers of production. The sum total of these relations of production constitutes the economic structure of society—the real foundation, on which rise legal and political superstructures and to which correspond definite

forms of social consciousness. The mode of production in material life determines the general character of the social, political, and spiritual processes of life. It is not the consciousness of men that determines their existences, but, on the contrary, their social existence determines their consciousness (Marx 1904: 10–11).

The ideas expressed in this passage appear in many of White's writings, although he never cited Marx directly (Carneiro 1981: 216). This reluctance to refer to Marx is understandable. In the political climate in which White was working, anyone writing favorably about Marx put his or her career in jeopardy.

The years after World War II were a time when the United States was in the grips of the "red scare," a hysterical fear of communism. American politicians such as Congressman Richard Nixon, Senator Joseph McCarthy, and several others played a significant role in inculcating a climate of fear and suspicion that pervaded American society. White's materialist perspective, his link with Soviet ideas, and his defense of Morgan, who had become associated with Marxism, were sufficient for him to be branded as a dangerous subversive (Bloch 1983: 129; Sanderson 1990: 90; Trigger 1998: 131).

White's enemies, Catholic priests and other religious types along with some anthropologists, tried to use his so-called Marxist connections to have him dismissed from his job. The anthropologist Morris Opler (1961), who had pretensions of being an expert in Marxist theory, unscrupulously denounced White's scientific-materialist perspective by pointing out that his theoretical position was based on Communist dogma, knowing full well that his denouncements could jeopardize the career of his colleague.

The paper in which Opler launched his attack was a response to an article by the anthropologist Betty Meggers (1960), entitled "The Law of Cultural Evolution as a Practical Research Tool," which was based upon White's formulations. Opler (1961: 8–9) methodically linked White's evolutionary theory with "communism," insinuating that it was a "strange coincidence" that White's ideas were parallel to those of N. I. Bukharin "one of the inner group of Old Bolsheviks and a Marxist whom Lenin called 'the most valuable and greatest theoretician of the party.'" Opler's paper is full of ominous snide remarks and innuendoes, such as the practical tool kit Dr. Meggers urges upon anthropology containing "a somewhat shopworn hammer and sickle" (Opler 1961: 9, 13).

Opler's interpretation of White's work as being Marxist was in error. What separated White from the kind of Marxism espoused by Soviet thinkers was that he did not employ the **dialectical method** (see Chapter 14). For this reason, none of Opler's Old Bolsheviks, or new ones for that matter, would have classified White as a Marxist. Had Opler really been versed in Marxism, as it was claimed, he would have noticed this difference (on Soviet anthropology see Gellner 1980).

The period in question was a sad and tragic time for beleaguered American intellectuals, who were assailed by opportunistic politicians capitalizing on the idea of "un-American activities" as a popular platform to advance their own careers. The anti-red rhetoric and the climate of fear greatly resembled the witch hunt years in early modern Europe. Indeed, the anthropologist Rebecca Cardozo (1970) referred to the events as "an American witch-craze."

Langness (1993: 126) describes the red-scare mentality of the time as an "unpleasant and shortsighted chapter in the history of American anthropology." Harris (2001b: 638) compares the political climate under which materialist theorists were operating at the time with the circumstances facing Mendelian geneticists under the regime of Stalin and his watchdog Trofim Lysenko (see Medvedev 1969). It is a pity that an anthropologist such as Opler would find the political climate opportune to besmirch two of his colleagues and in fact endanger their careers and reputations.

White's marginalization because of his Marxist connection may have been the consequence of national and international politics, but academic politics had a role in this as well. Taking on the Boasian's theoretical hegemony had its costs: marginalization, ridicule, and abuse. However, White remained steadfast. During the 1940s and 1950s, he wrote a number of articles in which he challenged Boasian antievolutionism and laid bare their misinterpretations of the evolutionary theory.

For years, however, White was alone in his challenge. Eventually, Julian Steward and the British archeologists V. Gordon Childe (1892–1957) joined in the struggle to bring evolutionary thinking back into anthropology (see Childe 1950, 1951). But at this stage their contributions were limited in comparison to those of White (Carneiro 1981: 229). As Steward (1960b: 144) himself acknowledged, "For many years Leslie White stood virtually alone in his uncompromising support of the 19th century cultural evolutionists and in opposition to the followers of Franz Boas."

It was after long years of battle with his foes, and some fifteen years after the publication of his important article "Energy and the Evolution of Culture" (1943), that the tide turned in White's favor (Carneiro 1981: 231). White succeeded not so much because he was able to convince the staunch antievolutionists, but because he found a receptive ear among the younger generation of anthropologists. His success was also due to the "notable obituaries" of Boas's students, "following their master in death as they had in life," as White (1987b: 15) sarcastically put it.

As evolutionary theory gained renewed credence in American cultural anthropology, the new perspective came to be known as **neoevolutionism** (see Orlove 1980). White was adamant, however, that the evolutionary theory he was espousing was not new, but a continuation of the theories of Morgan and Tylor. In the preface of his major work, *The Evolution of Culture* (1959), White wrote,

Let it be said, and with emphasis, that the theory set forth here cannot properly be called

V. Gordon Childe, the British archaeologist who contributed to the renewed interest in the evolution of human culture and evolutionary theory.

WHITE'S EVOLUTIONARY PERSPECTIVE

The Boasians, we might recall, objected to evolutionary schemes on the basis of several arguments. First they maintained that evolutionary stages, which were based on the comparison of other cultures with European civilization, were ethnocentric and invalid. Second, they contended that the notion of "progress" was subjective and based upon ethnocentric criteria and did not have a place in scientific analysis of cultural development. Third, they noted that there are no "objective" criteria by means of which cultures can be evaluated. Fourth, the Boasians asserted that diffusion negates evolution.

White had to develop his own theory and at the same time engage the antievolutionary polemic of the Boas group. This illustrates well how new paradigms do not emerge in an intellectual vacuum, but are forged through a dialectical relationship with existing paradigms. White attempted to address all of the key points that the Boasians used to reject evolutionary theory.

On the question of evolutionary stages, White elaborated upon the basic principle stated by Tylor:

> On the whole, it appears that wherever there are found elaborate arts, abstruse knowledge, complex institutions, these are results of gradual development from an earlier, simpler, ruder state of life. No stage of civilization comes into existence spontaneously, but grows or is developed out of the stage before it. This is the great principle which every scholar must lay firm hold of, if he intends to understand either the world he lives in or the history of the past (Tylor 1881: 20).

White (1987c: 70) observed that evolution is the process whereby "one form grows out of another in chronological sequence: evolution is a temporal sequence of forms." By form, White meant that cultural elements are functionally integrated patterns that undergo transformation over time. White derived the concept of functional integration of culture (and the idea of culture a *sui generis* phenomenon) from the works

"neoevolutionism," a term proposed by Lowie, Goldenweiser, Bennett, Nunomura (in Japan), and others. Neoevolutionism is a misleading term: it has been used to imply that the theory of evolution today is somehow different from the theory of eighty years ago. We reject such a notion. The *theory* of evolution set forth in this work does not differ one whit in principle from that expressed in Tylor's *Anthropology* in 1881, although of course the development, expression, and demonstration of the theory may—and it does—differ at some points (White 1959: ix).[2]

However, as I shall point out later, although there are some points of convergence between White's model and those of the classical evolutionists from the nineteenth century, there are also fundamental epistemological differences, which White did not appreciate, or chose not to discuss.

of Émile Durkheim and the writings of Malinowski and Radcliffe-Brown (Carneiro 1981:
217).

Starting with the idea that one form grows
out of another, and that therefore there is continuity in culture, White (1987c: 67) saw the
means by which the cultural anthropologists
could reconstruct developmental stages of
culture.

> We assume that one form grows out of another
> instead of being created independently, then we
> may be in many situations to reconstruct a series.
> We would begin, naturally, with the present, with
> what we have before us. Then we would arrange
> other forms in a series in accordance with their
> likeness or dissimilarity to the present, with what
> we have before us. Then we would arrange other
> forms in a series in accordance with their likeness
> or dissimilarity to the present form. Thus of the
> various forms of the horse we would put those
> most like the present nearest the end of the series
> and those most different at the beginning. . . .
> Lacking an established chronology would anyone
> question the use of this method in reconstructing
> a developmental series of automobiles? Would we
> not be justified in placing those types which most
> closely resemble the present forms nearest to them
> and those with the fewest similarities farther down
> the scale? Could not one arrange a series of looms,
> locomotives, knives, guns, etc., in a developmental
> series?[3]

The method is sound, White argued, as long
as it is used critically and with care. Just because
early evolutionists made mistakes, White argued,
does not mean that the method is false. It is the
same thing with, for example, statistics. Indeed,
"One could commit stupid blunders with statistics; but this does not invalidate statistics as a
method" (White 1987e: 108). Rejecting statistics
on the basis of errors in a particular statistical
analysis involves a *non sequitur*. One of Boas's
fortes was to use this type of reasoning to deal
with the views of his rivals, which involved
using the refutation of a particular hypothesis in
order to justify the rejection a generalizing science of culture as a whole (see Chapter 6).

White went on to caution, however, that simply because a group of phenomena, such as automobiles, or looms, or axes, can be arranged in
a sequence does not mean that all groups of
phenomena are to be arranged in this manner.
The phenomena arranged in a developmental
sequence must belong to the same formal class.
Thus arranging the Navajo, Bantu, Chinese, and
Eskimo languages into a sequence in terms of
their similarities or differences with English
would be as incorrect as arranging squirrels,
bears, pigs, and manatees in a sequence on the
basis of their resemblances to the human form
(White 1987c: 68–69).

On the question of progress and the evaluation of cultures, White observed that the
Boasians conceded that progress could be identified in the development of mechanical inventions. In other words, one could show logical
progression in the development of better axes, in
which the development of later forms depends
upon earlier developments. However, the
Boasians were adamant that questions of evaluation are meaningless and misleading when it
comes to the nontechnical aspects of culture,
such as ethical ideas, aesthetic expression, art
forms, and social organization. They considered
these to have "unknown ends." Moreover, they
viewed institutions as being purposeless and operating virtually independently of any utilitarian
requirement of human life (Hatch 1973: 135).
For the relativistic Boasians, things such as ethical codes, aesthetics, artistic expression, and religious beliefs could only be evaluated aestheti-
cally and only from the natives' point of view.

White did not subscribe to the "shreds and
patches" view of culture, but instead saw culture
as a functionally integrated whole. He soundly
criticized Boas and his followers of mystification
for using their anthropology to produce an endless array of cases in order to show that culture
has no-rhyme-or-reason and that there are no
laws of culture.

For White nontechnical aspects of culture did
not appear mysterious and incomprehensible.
As he saw it, culture was a mechanism that

functioned as the adaptive means that made life secure, perpetual, and worthwhile (White 1959: 8). Culture had a utility and its emic dimensions were fully articulated with its etic components.

> Culture is man's own way of carrying on the struggle for existence. It is a means of obtaining need-serving materials from nature, a means of combating disease, of finding protection from the elements, etc. We may distinguish technological, sociological, and philosophic aspects of culture, but all have a common purpose and a common goal: the security and continuity of life. Social systems are social means of operating technological systems; one type being geared to a hunting technology, another to a fishing, agricultural, pastoral, medical, military, etc., technology. Philosophies (using the term in a broad sense to embrace the sum total of thought and belief of a people) also are means of carrying on the struggle for existence on all fronts: subsistence, military, medical, morale, etc. Social solidarity is important too in the struggle for existence, and we find institutions—clubs, societies, kinship systems, clans, ceremonial groups, etc.—myths, lore, legends, art forms, rituals, fetishes, etc., working to build morale, to strengthen group solidarity. Recreation and diversion in games and in the arts build moral; they give zest to life and make it seem worthwhile; they comfort, soothe, inspire, and encourage. Human beings have to be related to each other in an effective manner in order to carry the business of life successfully. Social, political, ethical, artistic, ecclesiastical, and educational systems operate to accomplish this purpose. They are the means of coordinating, integrating, regulating, and directing human endeavor toward the goal of all life: a secure and agreeable existence (White 1987c: 73–74).[4]

Cultures could therefore be compared as functional totalities or integrated wholes and assessed in terms of how well they operated as means of organizing the relationship of members of society with respect to one another and with the relationship of the society to its natural habitat. Cultures vary widely in these respects, White maintained, and they could therefore be evaluated in terms of their effectiveness. Thus, he pointed out that

a culture is . . . a means of adjustment, regulation, and control. Means vary; some are better than others, "Superior" and "inferior" are measured in terms of security and survival. We can measure cultures by a number of objective and vitally significant indexes: amount of food and other human-need-serving goods produced per unit of human labor; infant mortality; death rates for various diseases; life expectancy, etc. The best single index, however, by which all cultures can be measured, is amount of energy harnessed per capita per year. This is the common denominator of all cultures (White 1987c: 76).[5]

White suggested the criterion of quality of life as a measure for assessing cultural systems.

Evaluating other cultures without slipping into ethnocentrism is a problem that has taxed anthropologists since the days of Boas. The anthropologists Walter Goldschmidt (1952: 135) tackled the problem years ago and provided a set of criteria that still have utility and which corresponds to many of the indices noted by White. The anthropologist John Bodley has stated in his book *Victims of Progress* (1975) that Goldschmidt's indices are less ethnocentric and more universally applicable than such measures as standard of living, gross national product, and annual per capita income. According to Bodley, Goldschmidt's measures include

> the nutritional status and general physical health and mental health of its population, the incidence of crime and delinquency, the demographic structure, family stability, and the society's relationship to its natural resource base (Bodley 1975: 151).[6]

White used such measures to evaluate evolutionary development, while Goldschmidt and Bodley were more concerned with issues of economic development in contemporary non-western societies (Bodley 1975: 150–151; see also Fox 1968: 290).

In White's formulations evolution is associated with progress and betterment in terms of material benefits, in which he equates more energy with higher standards of living, more leisure time, better health, longer life spans, and greater civil security (Sanderson 1990: 97).

White's position is problematic, however, because there is no empirical basis for the conflation of evolution with betterment. It is now pretty clear that the shift from low-energy systems based on hunting and gathering to high-energy systems based upon the cultivation of crops and animal husbandry led to longer working hours, lower standards of living, and poorer quality of life in terms of health and nutrition (Figure 10.1). In addition, unlike hunter-gatherers, farming people had to contend with political subordination, socioeconomic inequalities, differential access to strategic resources, intensification of violence and large-scale warfare (Sanderson 1990: 132, 151, 196). Hunting-gathering peoples, in other words, were much better off than farmers. Also, whatever betterment in terms of material benefits that high-energy systems have yielded has been confined to only a small minority of the world's elite because of the massive socioeconomic and political inequalities that characterize such systems (Sanderson 1990: 132, 151, 196). Many present-day evolutionists have rejected White's views on this issue.

Returning to White's diatribe with the Boasians, he disagreed with their position that the non-technical aspects of culture had to be evaluated from the natives' point of view. White wrote,

> Who is to judge in scientific matters, the scientist or the folk? People may disagree on the proper way to treat trachoma, but if some are trained physicians while others are pre-literate savages, is equal weight to be given to all views? Which is to be the judge of foods, the science of nutrition or folk custom and prejudice? Suppose that ten persons claim that a charm will prevent malaria for every one who advocates the use of screens and mosquito-killers; suppose that ten million "prefer" democracy, only one thousand vote for anarchy; four hundred million pledge allegiance to Buddhism, only ten million to Judaism—what does all this prove or mean? The values of medicines, machines, organizations, philosophies, etc., in the conduct of the life of man as an animal species, are not to be ascertained by appeal to the opinions of laymen or even by taking a poll among experts.

They are to be gauged by *objective measurement*. It is curious that Boas, Lowie, Goldenweiser, *et al.,* should be willing to place the opinions, tastes, and preferences of tribesmen and laymen—which after all are cultural traits themselves, data of anthropological inquiry—on the same plane as the investigations and conclusions of the scientific anthropologist (White 1987c: 76).[7]

Present-day cultural constructionists have gone well beyond the Boasian stance by ridiculing science as the conceited, ethnocentric, and context-dependent metaphysics of Euro-American culture. In its place they advocate the idea that folk knowledge (opinions, preferences, assumptions of local people) are the only valid forms of anthropological knowledge (see Chapters 2 and 15).

White also refuted the Boasians' assertion that diffusion negates evolution as a mechanism of culture change. Lowie expressed this position in his *Primitive Society* (1920: 434):

> One fact . . . encountered at every stage and in every phase of society, by itself lays the axe to the root of any theory of historical laws [i.e., evolutionary theory]—the extensive occurrence of diffusion. Creating nothing, this factor nevertheless makes all other agencies taper almost into nothingness beside it in its effect on the total growth of human civilization.

The Boasians argued, for example, that because of diffusion some African cultures went directly from the level of stone technology directly into the iron age, skipping the intermediary bronze age. Therefore, evolutionary process as a whole could not be operative. The stone age–iron age case was in fact part of one of the Boasians' standard antievolutionist arguments.

White countered this view by pointing out that the Boasians had erroneously conflated the evolution of culture with the culture history of a people (White 1987e: 105). The evolutionary principle, according to White, posits that the art of metallurgy passes through the sequences, not that every culture must go through all the stages sequentially. He stressed the fundamental difference between history and evolution. Historical

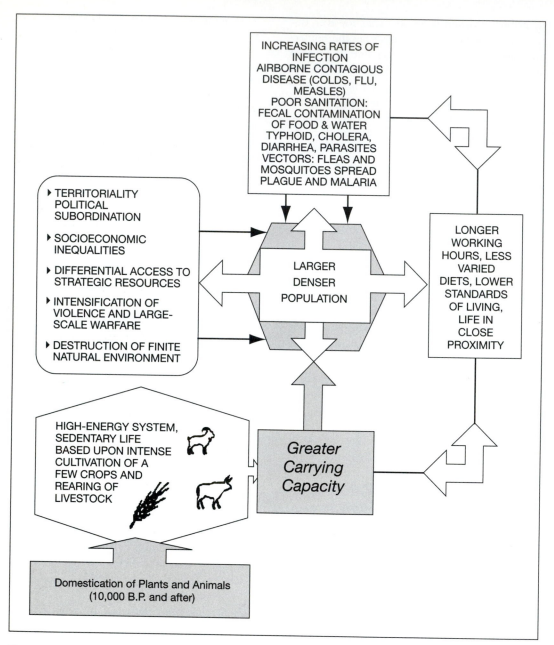

Figure 10.1   Negative consequences of agriculture.   *After Lenkeit (2001).*

descriptions deal with sequences of events that are unique in time and space. Evolutionary descriptions deal with sequence of forms that apply to culture as a whole, with one form growing out of another with no necessary relation to a particular time or place. Moreover, evolutionary processes are orderly and predictable and subject to scientific generalizations. Thus there are scientific laws that apply to the evolution of culture as a whole. In contrast, historical processes are random, with no predictions possible, except in a limited sense (White 1987e: 111; the problems with this view are discussed later).

Finally, White pointed out that the Boasians were using a straw man argument because Tylor and Morgan did not discount diffusion, as discussed in Chapters 3 and 4. Not only did Morgan and Tylor take diffusion into consideration, but they also saw diffusion as working harmoniously with evolution. White observed further that the development of a trait and its diffusion are separate processes, but that they may work together. Once a trait evolves in one place it spreads to other areas. This in no way alters the fact that evolution is at work.

WHITE'S MODEL OF CULTURAL EVOLUTION

White saw the development of culture through human history, from foraging bands to complex agrarian state-level societies and complex industrial states in terms of technological changes and consequent increases in the amount of energy available for use per capita per year.

> In the beginning, the cultural system had only the energy of the human organism to draw upon. Until the domestication of animals or the cultivation of plants, energy from this original source was supplemented to an insignificant extent by utilization of fire, wind, and flowing water. The domestication of animals to a limited extent, and the cultivation of plants to a much greater extent, were means of adding materially to the energy resources of cultural systems. They were able to develop ex-

tensively as a consequence. After hundreds of thousands of years of meager development, so long as the human organism was the chief source of energy for culture building, culture leaped forward prodigiously after the development of agricultural arts. The great civilizations of Egypt, Mesopotamia, India, China, Peru, Mexico, and Middle America followed quickly upon the heels of the Neolithic Ages. At a later day, energy in fuel form, harnessed by engines, again sent culture forward. And today we are on the threshold of a new era of energy available for use in cultural systems. If it does not wreck civilization, it may advance it as far beyond the Age of Coal as this age was in advance of the Age of Cereals, or as it in turn was beyond the Age of Hunting and Gathering (White 1987e: 118–119).[8]

Culture evolves as the amount of energy increases or more efficient means of using energy are perfected. More efficient use of energy, however, has an upper threshold. Further cultural transformations are dependent upon additional amounts of energy incorporated and put to work:

> Technological evolution is a matter of tools as well as of energy. There must be means of harnessing energy and means of putting it to work. These means may vary; some are better than others. If the energy factor is constant, culture can advance as the means of harnessing energy and putting it to work are improved. But improvement of tools and machines is not unlimited; sooner or later they are brought to a condition of maximum efficiency and then cultural advance stops—unless the amount of energy is increased. Improvement of tools can advance culture only within limits. When these boundaries are reached cultural advance can come only from further additions of energy. Tools and energy both play a part in technological evolution, but it is the energy factor that is of prime importance. Improvement of tools and machines will keep pace with the harnessing of energy; it is the energy factor that moves the whole process forward (White 1987e: 119).[9]

Energy itself, according to White, was an index for evaluating cultures, by distinguishing high-energy systems from low-energy ones.

We can, therefore, use energy as the basic index of cultural evolution. Culture grows as the amount of energy harnessed and put to work per capita per year increases. Cultures may be graded in terms of energy: the more energy harnessed the higher the culture (White 1987e: 119).[10]

White viewed culture as an energy-capturing system. In his book, *The Science of Culture* (1949), he described culture as "an elaborate thermodynamic, mechanical system" (White 1949: 367–368). All cultural activities, according to White, require the expenditure of energy, whether this be cooking, weaving, or saying a prayer. "Every event that takes place in the universe," White wrote (1987f: 215), "whether it be physical, biological, or cultural, is an expression of energy, an instance of energy transformation." Thus all cultural systems could be reduced to the "common denominator" of energy.

White's measure, the amount of energy harnessed per capita per year, has been labeled **the basic law of cultural evolution.** This was White's unique contribution to evolutionary thought in cultural anthropology. White continuously stated that his ideas were a continuation of the nineteenth-century evolutionism; however, his basic law of evolution has no counterpart in the works of his acknowledged predecessors (Harris 2001b: 636). Thus, White's evolutionism has a dimension that is absent in the works of Tylor, Morgan, and the other evolutionists of that time.

The greater the amount of energy flowing through a system the greater its complexity. Low-energy systems, therefore, are less complex than high energy ones. Culture evolves, in White's view, "as the amount of energy harnessed per capita per year is increased, other factors remaining constant" (White 1987e: 119). White presented the following formula: $E \times T = C$, in which E stands for energy, T for the efficiency of technology, and C is culture.

According to the **second law of thermodynamics,** White pointed out, the universe is winding down towards greater disorder or positive entropy. Living systems, however, are able to capture free energy from their surroundings and develop more internal differentiation and structural complexity, become "more differentiated structurally and more specialized functionally," and attain "higher energy potentials" (White 1959: 39–40). Higher forms are achieved through negative entropy.

The implication of this is that in the evolutionary process, systems whose populations convert and control greater quantities of energy are favored by natural selection. In other words, societies that have been able to increase the amount of energy under their control have an adaptive advantage over low-energy societies (Richard Adams 1975: 126; the basic formulation of the relationship among energy, evolution, and natural selection was by the biologist Alfred Lotka 1922a, 1922b, 1945; see Rambo 1991b for a positive assessment of White's law).

White saw the technological, sociological, and philosophical aspects of culture as being integrated and interacting with and influencing one another, but he placed primary causal emphasis on the technological sector. "The technological aspect is the most important by far; the sociological and ideological aspects are depended upon the technological and are to a large extent given form and content by it" (White 1987e: 117).

Because White saw the ideological dimension of culture as being causally and functionally related to the technological aspects, he observed that technological changes are accompanied by corresponding ideological change. "As technology changes the philosophy changes" (White 1987e: 117). By this White was not saying that knowing the technology of a culture meant that one could predict the specifics of a people's ideological system, such as beliefs in the number of souls. Instead, White suggested that particular types of technologies are associated with particular types of belief systems.

The nontechnological dimensions of culture could thus be seen as being integrated with and functioning to ensure the efficient operation of the technological components of culture. This, however, was a fairly simplistic view that overlooks the subtle manner in which ideological systems articulate with other aspects of culture. However, we must bear in mind that White was engaged in a polemic with the idealist Boasians and this may account for his exaggerations and overstatements of many of his points.

One of the more significant errors in White's evolutionary ideas is the great emphasis that he placed upon the role of technology. White construed cultural evolution primarily in terms of technology and technological change because it is through technology that humans obtain their basic life support requirements, food, shelter, and defense. As he put it, these processes "are technological in a broad, but valid sense, i.e., they are carried on by material, mechanical, biophysical and biomechanical means" (White 1959: 19).

> [The process of cultural evolution] rests upon the material mechanical, physical, chemical means by which man is articulated with the earth beneath him and the cosmos around him. Social systems and philosophies are sociological and ideological functions of the technological culture; as it changes they are altered accordingly. Cultural evolution as a whole, therefore, is a function of technological evolution in particular (White 1987e: 118–119).[11]

The primacy of technology lay in its role in harnessing and using greater amounts of energy.

> The evolution of technology is a matter of harnessing energy and of putting it to work. . . . Just as biological systems evolve by capturing free energy and utilizing it to build more highly organized systems, organisms with greater degrees of control over their environments, so do cultural systems evolve by capturing more and more free energy from the outside world and utilizing it to develop more highly organized systems of greater degrees of control over their respective environments. Cultural evolution is a continuation of the process of biological evolution on a higher plane (White 1987e: 119).[12]

White summarized his position on the evolution of culture as follows:

> (1) Culture evolves; one form grows out of another. There is form and continuity in the cultural process. A clan, an alphabet, a telescope, a language, a king, or a table of logarithms does not "just happen"; each grows out of previous organizations of cultural elements. (2) An evolutionary stage is simply one of a succession of forms in the developmental process. . . . the keystone arch, the plow, a symbol for zero, representative government, antiseptics, relativity, etc., represent stages of cultural development. (3) We may properly speak of progress in cultural development not only in the sense of more recent forms in the successive series but also in terms of higher and better. . . . Culture advances as the amount of energy harnessed per capita increases. The criterion for the evaluation of cultures is thus an objective one. The measurements can be expressed in mathematical terms. The goal—security and survival—is likewise objective; it is one that all species, man included, must live by. . . . (4) We can evaluate cultures and arrange them in a series from lower to higher. This follows, of course, from the establishment of a scientifically valid criterion of value and means of measurement (White 1987c: 76–77).[13]

White's ideas regarding energy in the evolution of culture has inspired a number of studies. For example, the anthropologist Richard Adams (1975) elaborated upon the role of energy and energy flows and their relationship to social power and systems of valuation. Adams also reformulated White's idea of the evolutionary significance of energy in terms of a society's control over its environment as a measure of evolutionary development (see also Odum 1971; Pimentel and Pimentel 1979).

THE EPISTEMOLOGICAL BASIS OF WHITE'S EVOLUTIONISM

As far as the epistemological basis of White's evolutionary formulation and his idea of causation are concerned, the answer is pretty clear, as Sanderson (1990: 87) has pointed out. White viewed culture as an adaptive mechanism geared towards harnessing and putting energy to work. He saw evolution and the direction of evolutionary development as the outcome of the interaction and causal relationships between a set of variables. According to Sanderson's (1990: 88) assessment, White construed the directional tendency of sociocultural evolution not in terms of the "unfolding of latent potentialities" or "immanences" but rather in terms of specific "causal relationships between specific variables at specific times."

Tim Ingold, however, has argued that White's conception of evolution was essentially similar to the nineteenth-century models based on immanences and directional laws (Ingold 1986: 82). Ingold's views apply most directly to White's

culturological formulations, which I shall discuss shortly.

ERRORS AND PROBLEMS: WHITE'S TECHNOLOGICAL DETERMINISM

As noted previously, White's treated technology as a prime mover and this represents a major weakness in his model. White's **technological determinism** is at variance with more recent materialist evolutionary perspectives. For example, in the case of the **Neolithic Revolution** (Figure 10.2), many researchers treat technology as dependent on other transformations. Among the new evolutionary perspectives are theories focusing upon population pressure, climatic

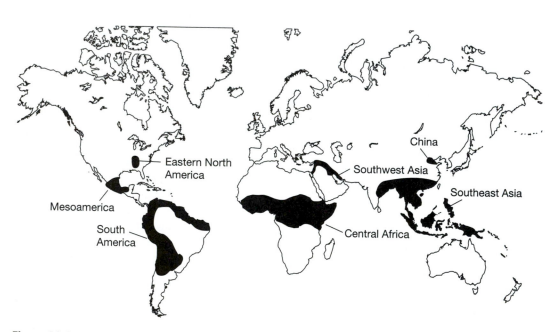

Figure 10.2   Centers where the domestication of plants and animals took place independently as instances of parallel development. Unlike Leslie White's evolutionary schema, present-day evolutionary models treat technology as dependent variable in the development of agro-pastoral production systems indicated here.

shifts, resource stress, and Darwinian cultural selectionist models (Sanderson 1999: 36–51; Trigger 1998: 124–151).

Demographic theories focus upon population growth and population pressure on resources as the causal forces that necessitated an increased reliance upon undesirable food resources, leading to a technological shift toward modes of production based upon domesticated plants and animals (Cohen 1977).

Climatic theories focus on changes, such as global warming circa 13,000 B.P. (before present), which led to a proliferation of wild grasses, the ancestors of wheat and barley, in the Near East. The appearance of this abundant source of food enabled foragers to settle down. The new mode of subsistence could not be maintained, however, as human populations increased and subsequent drier climatic conditions around 11,000 years ago led to resource depletions. These conditions led to the adoption of farming as a mode of production (Henry 1989; McCorriston and Hole 1991).

Resource stress models focus upon ecological transformations following the retreat of glaciers circa 13,000 B.P., causing disruptions in the existing human population/resource base balance, as grasslands were transformed into forests and the number of large game animals dwindled and were eventually hunted out. The solution to the problem was to shift to economies based upon domesticated plants and animals (Harris 1991; Hyden 1981). Finally, evolutionary Darwinian models place the interaction of humans/plants/animals within an ecosystem framework, in which the domestication of plants and animals is treated as the outcome of evolutionary selection operating at a systemic level, rather than being the result of purposeful human activities (Rindos 1984; Toumlin 1981).

As this brief review suggests, few present-day sociocultural evolutionary perspectives give technology the place it has in White's formulations. Although technology correlates closely with evolutionary transformations, technology and technological change are not seen as the prime movers in the evolution of culture (Sanderson 1990: 98).

CULTUROLOGY: THE SCIENTIFIC STUDY OF CULTURE

An important feature of White's anthropology was his conception of and the scientific study of culture, which he called **culturology**. Here White shares Boasian idealism, which is evident in the convergence of his work with that of Kroeber, whom William Adams (1998: 327) calls "the quintessential American idealist." White's view of culture as an extrasomatic suprabiological phenomenon is identical to Kroeber's concept of the **superorganic.**

For these reasons, White's materialist evolutionary formulations do not articulate with his culturological work. Moreover, it is in this domain of White's theoretical work that the problem of "unfolding latent potentialities and immanences" is most evident.

White saw culture as a uniquely human attribute: "Man is unique: he is the only living species that has a culture. By culture we mean an extrasomatic, temporal continuum of things and events dependent upon symboling" (White 1959: 3). For White the ability to symbol refers to the human capacity to create and attribute meaning to objects and events.

Culture and man as a human being began simultaneously; both originated in symboling. Symboling produced culture: an organization of beliefs, customs, tools, and techniques. In a relatively short time, every society of men acquired a complete, even though simple and crude, culture, and in so doing these men became completely humanized. This culture was transmitted from one generation to another; it flowed down through time indefinitely. It acquired a life of its own, so to speak. It became a process *sui generis,* self-contained, self-determined, and autonomous. To be sure culture could not exist without human beings; it is culture that determines the behavior of peoples. The behavior of the culture process, or of cultural systems, is not a function of the human mind; on the contrary, the behavior of peoples is a function of the extrasomatic tradition that is culture (we say peoples, not individuals, because the behavior of an individual is a function of his biological make-up as well as of his culture). The culture process, or cultural systems, behave in accordance with the principles and laws of their own. Culture is to be explained culturologically rather than biologically or psychologically. There is, of course, a necessary and intimate relationship between culture as a whole and the human species. If man were not the kind of animal he is, his culture in general would not be what it is. But we cannot explain variations of culture in terms of the biological factor of man. The culturologist approaches the problems of culture change as if the human race did not exist (White 1987g: 301).[14]

White saw culture as the determinant of human behavior, rather than human behavior exercising control over cultural phenomena, which exist as a force outside the human being:

It is . . . culture that determines the behavior of man, not man who controls culture. And culture changes and develops in accordance with laws of its own, not in obedience to man's desire or will. A science of culture would disclose the nature and direction of the culture process, but would not put into man's hands the power to control or direct its course (White 1948b: 213).[15]

Indeed, White (1949: 141) added that

to introduce the human organism into consideration of cultural variations is therefore not only irrelevant but wrong; it involves a premise that is false. Culture must be explained in terms of culture. Thus, paradoxical though it may seem "the proper study of mankind" turns out not to be Man, after all, but Culture. The most realistic and scientifically adequate interpretation of culture is one that proceeds as if human beings did not exist.[16]

White's construal of culture left no room for individual thought and action. This drew considerable opposition from those whose professional careers were invested in the study of individual psychological phenomena (cf. Carneiro 1981: 234–235).

In White's view the individual is the carrier or utensil, "it is culture that supplies the content." For example, new discoveries and inventions are not due to the individual genius, but are cultural in nature, and are conceived and realized in the medium of culture itself. The "individual is merely the neural locus in which the advance occurs" (White 1987g: 299). Thus the "development of mathematics, like the development of technology or medicine, is an evolutionary process: new forms grow out of preceding forms" (White 1949: 14). Like Kroeber (before he recanted his superorganic sins), White rejected the "great man theory of history."

In a paper dealing with the introduction of monotheism by the Pharaoh Ikhnaton, entitled "Ikhnaton: The Great Man vs. the Culture Process" (1948a), White argued that "Ikhnaton originated nothing": Monotheism was inevitable and developed out of a synthesis of previous cultural knowledge. Ikhnaton was simply the medium through which cultural evolution expressed itself.

In the process of cultural development, a Great Man is but the neural medium through which an important synthesis of culture takes place. Darwin, Newton, Beethoven, and Edison were men of this type. They were the neurological loci of important cultural events. . . . had they been reared as swineherds, Greatness would not have found them (White 1949: 280).[17]

White therefore did not believe in the idea of the "fortuitous clustering of genius." Rather, he saw new cultural developments and inventions as the terminal points of converging lines of cultural growth, when fusion and synthesis occur. The inventors are merely the "loci or vehicles of expression of this process." For White (1959: 283), explaining events in terms of a hypothetical person who "got the idea" does not explain the occurrence or nonoccurrence of that idea. When the cultural conditions are right, when fusion and synthesis take place, then the right idea will occur as well.

But what leads to the fusion and synthesis at a particular point in time? What is the mechanism that impels cultural change? White seemed to believe that the accumulations of changes of degree could culminate in changes in kind as a certain cultural threshold is reached (White 1959: 282). The force impelling culture toward more complexity lay in the symbolic nature of culture that enables the preservation and continuity and therefore accumulation of knowledge and inventions; "preservation means accumulation and progress" (White 1949: 30). White explained the evolution of agriculture in these terms.

This idea that agriculture developed as a result of the growth and accumulation of knowledge and was hence an automatic and self-evident process is basically the notion of "unfolding" of latent potentialities." This idea goes back to the works of the nineteenth-century evolutionists and was also held by the British Archeologist Gordon Childe (Harlan et al., 1976). This position is linked to White's culturology.

However, White did not argue that agriculture appeared because new facts became available. In other words, White rejected the "eureka" hypothesis and observed that ancient peoples had a complete understanding of the manner in which plants and animals propagate, as contemporary foraging people do. He was suggesting that

> Agriculture began when the old equilibrium of hunting and gathering was upset, and a new type of adjustment, a new kind of relationship to local flora, became requisite to survival (White 1959: 284).[18]

This makes sense in terms of White's materialist/evolutionary construal of culture as an adaptive mechanism that enables humans to adjust to their environment. Thus "an equilibrium can be established culturally between man and habitat [that] may continue indefinitely" (White 1959: 283). This equilibrium, however, can be disrupted or upset, White observed, "by the intrusion of a new factor, the disappearance of an old one, or a radical change in the cultural configuration" (White 1959: 284). Clearly, he is taking about causality in terms of specific variables during particular times. White (1959: 284–285) suggested demographic pressures as the stimulus for the evolution of farming, the factor that disrupted the equilibrium. This supports the idea that White's materialist/evolutionary perspective is epistemologically closer to modern views on sociocultural evolution rather than the formulations of the nineteenth-century ethnologists.

THE DISARTICULATION BETWEEN WHITE'S MATERIALIST STRATEGY AND CULTUROLOGY

In the case of the "agricultural revolution," White (1959: 284–285) suggested demographic pressures as the factor upsetting the foraging equilibrium. However, in general, White seems to have placed the locus of change in the realm of culture itself, which he construed as being governed by its own laws and principles, rather than in extracultural variables. White (1959: 51) observed, for example, that

> although natural habitat exerts an influence upon culture, we can learn more about this influence from a consideration of the culture and its degree of development than by a mere inventory of environmental features. . . . if one wishes to discover how cultural systems are structured and how they function as cultural systems, then one does not need to consider the natural habitat at all.[19]

White added that

> a cultural tradition is a stream of interacting cultural elements—of instruments, beliefs, customs, etc. In this interactive process, each element impinges upon others and is in turn acted upon by

them. The process is a competitive one: instruments, customs, and beliefs may become obsolete and eliminated from the stream. New elements are incorporated from time to time. New combinations and syntheses—inventions and discoveries—of cultural elements are continually being formed in this interactive process. A cultural system is therefore a dynamic system, powered by natural forces which it harnesses, that behaves and grows in terms of its own principles and laws. It may be regarded as a system *sui generis* (White 1959: 286–287).[20]

White therefore subscribed to the axiom that "culture comes from culture." This is not exactly the same thing as the nineteenth-century notion of directional law and unfolding of latent potentialities. White's definition of culture in terms of symbols rather than behavior implies something else: that symbols cause other symbols (Murphy 1981: 185). This being the case, White clearly moved from a categorically materialist position to an entirely idealist stance.

For these reasons, White's view of culture as a superorganic phenomenon was incongruous with his materialist theory of cultural evolution. This is because on the one hand, he placed primacy on material factors, such as energy and technology but, on the other hand, he suggested the symbolic domain as the locus of change. He wrote, for example, that culture develops and changes "by capturing more and more free energy from the outside world and utilizing it to develop more highly organized systems of greater degrees of control over their respective environments" (White 1987e: 118–119). In this view, extracultural factors, such as energy from the environment, have a determining influence on the characteristics of culture.

On the other hand, White maintained that culture is *sui generis,* a phenomenon unique and in a class by itself, an autonomous realm subject to its own internal laws and principles. White insisted that "culture is to be explained in terms of culture." For this reason, the anthropologist Elman Service (1976: 613) noted that White's

Culturology, the science of culture as he presented it, is not the same thing as, nor does it even imply a connection to, his ideas about the *evolution of culture.* A comparison of his two major theoretical works, *The Science of Culture* and *The Evolution of Culture,* should make this clear.[21]

White himself noticed the inconsistency between these aspects of his work but was not able to resolve it (Carneiro 1981: 236).

CULTURE AND CULTURES IN WHITE'S WORK

White's culturology has been criticized on the grounds that this approach excluded external environmental or ecological factors. White might argue that in part, this criticism stems from a misunderstanding of the two ways he used the term culture, the differences in the level of analysis and abstraction each entailed, and the kinds of evolutionary forces involved in each. As White (1959: 30–31) saw it,

> Culture may be regarded as a one or as many, as an all-inclusive system—the culture of mankind as a whole—or as an indefinite number of subsystems of two different kinds: (1) the cultures of peoples or regions, and (2) subdivisions such as writing, mathematics, currency, metallurgy, social organization, etc. Mathematics, language, writing, architecture, social organization, etc. may each be considered as one or as many, also; one may work out the evolution of mathematics as a whole, or a number of lines of development may be distinguished. Evolutionist interpretations of culture will therefore be both unilinear and multilinear. One type of interpretation is as valid as the other; each implies the other.[22]

When discussing the evolution of culture, therefore, White was expressing culturological laws pertaining to the development of **C**ulture as a whole, throughout the entire course of human existence on earth. In this case, at issue are abstractions dealing with the temporal sequence of forms "taken as classes rather than unique occurrences." White felt that the effects of the environment could be averaged out to form a constant factor and removed from the conceptualization of broad evolutionary developments.

When talking about culture**s,** White was referring to the cultural systems of specific societies. In the analysis of particular cultural systems, more attention had to be given to the role of the environment because environmental factors have a significant impact in the development of individual societies by creating diversity through adaptive modifications.

This distinction between the general and the specific posed some confusion because, as Sanderson (1990: 85–86) has pointed out, White appears to be suggesting that evolution pertains to culture as a whole and not to particular societies. The problem here is what does "culture as whole" mean? Does such a thing exist apart from societies and populations of people? And if there are evolutionary laws that pertain to culture as a whole, do they tell us anything about the particular case?

Harris (2001b: 649) challenged White on this point, observing that a generalization that says nothing about the particular cannot be treated as an empirical proposition. He thus inquired:

> Does the law of gravitation tell us nothing about particulars? When one predicts a particular eclipse on a particular sun by a particular moon, has this no relation to the general law? White undoubtedly means to say something else to wit: no general law tells us everything about particulars.[23]

Harris is probably correct in suggesting that what White really meant to say was that a general law does not tell us everything about specific cases. As Sanderson (1990: 86) has pointed out, in the substantive analysis presented in *The Evolution of Culture,* White avoids this analytical confusion and incorporates the particular in order to illustrate his general analysis. In other words, in practice White abandons the idea that evolution and culture history are distinct, and he interrelates overall evolutionary development

and adaptive modification in particular cultures (Sanderson 1990: 96).

The differences between the two levels of analysis were conceptualized as representing different but interrelated evolutionary processes. This was clarified and expressed succinctly by Marshall Sahlins (1960: 12–13) during the materialist phase of his career (Figure 10.3):

> In both its biological and cultural spheres evolution moves simultaneously in two directions. On one side, it creates diversity through adaptive modification: new forms differentiate from old. On the other side, evolution generates progress: higher forms arise from, and surpass, lower. The first of these directions is Specific evolution, and the

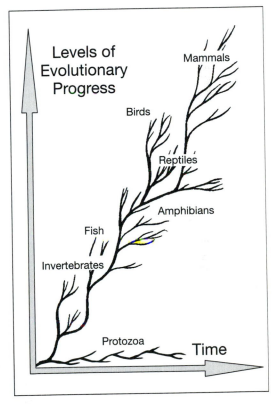

Figure 10.3 General and Specific evolution as two levels of analysis conceptualized as representing different but interrelated evolutionary processes. *After Sahlins and Service (1960).*

second, General Evolution. But note that specific and general evolution are not different concrete realities; they are rather aspects of the same total process.[24]

ASSESSMENT

White evolutionary formulations have been criticized on a number of points. First, critics assert that he overemphasized of the role of technology in the evolution of culture. Second, that he proposed laws too general to be applicable to specific cases. There are also the problems stemming from the lack of articulation between White's views on cultural evolution and his science of culture.

However, it is important to note that despite shortcomings, White's work as a whole had considerable influence by generating interest in the relationship between culture and environment, both in ethnology and archeology (Carneiro 1981: 239). This is one of his substantial contributions to the field.

White is also credited, although very begrudgingly, with the formulation of the cultural materialist strategy in anthropology. As Harris (2001b: 650–651) writes,

> White's energy "law" . . . possess utility as a kind of meta-generalization. . . . It is this reformulation which actually deserves our greatest attention, because it amounts to nothing less than a statement of the research strategy through which one proposes to arrive at the formulation of the most productive statements of diachronic and synchronic regularities. This is the strategy which often reluctantly acknowledges its debt to Marx: The most powerful generalizations about history are to be found by studying the relationship between qualitative and quantitative aspects of culture energy systems as the independent variables and the quantitative and qualitative aspects of the other domains of sociocultural phenomena as the dependent ones. It must be emphasized that the meta-generalization embodied in the cultural-materialist strategy is fully analogous to and at least as well vindicated by specific cases as the vaunted "principle of natural selection" in biology.[25]

But Harris (2001b: 651) adds that

> the implication in White's proposals concerning the nomothetic explanations to which we must take vigorous exception is that cultural materialism as a general strategy leads only to highly abstract evolutionary sequences. It must be affirmed that this strategy need not limit itself to the vapid generalizations with which White has sometimes tried the patience of his colleagues. It leads as well to the understanding of particular cases in all their detail in so far as such an understanding can be achieved with reference to nomothetic, as distinct from strictly historical, relations. We may credit White therefore with the formulation of this strategy (under the pseudonym of evolutionism), but must also note his failure to apply it to specific cases.[26]

White must also be lauded for his great intellectual courage. He began his efforts to reestablish a scientific and evolutionary anthropology at a time when Boas's students were at the height of their powers and firmly entrenched in the major departments of anthropology throughout the country. White was confronted by an influential cohort of anthropologists who had close personal associations with their teacher and with each other and who shared a "disciplinary culture" (cf. Darnell 1998: 272–273). White fought a lonely war. It is perhaps for this reason that he strongly objected to academic schools of thought based on personal associations, which he felt were detrimental to the intellectual advancement of the discipline (Service 1976: 615).

White's (1987d: 123) criticism of the Boasian "chaotic, no-rhyme-or-reason-in-the-realm-of-culture" anthropological paradigm made him the subject of considerable hostility. As Eric Wolf (1964: 27–28) noted, "For many years, Leslie A. White was an evolutionist prophet crying in an antievolutionary wilderness that yielded no sympathetic echo." White's views not only made him a target of anthropologists the likes of Opler, but also antievolutionist religious organizations. He was also branded a communist sympathizer. But White persisted in his task despite these considerable adversities. As the anthropologist Robert Murphy (1977: 28) put it, "the efforts of Leslie White . . . to revive the works of Morgan must rate as one of the most courageous intellectual stands ever taken by an anthropologist."

Whatever the faults of his evolutionary perspective and culturology, White's major accomplishment was to once again bring respectability to theoretical generalizations in cultural anthropology, after close to fifty years of the fruitless relativistic, particularistic experiment of the Boasians. As a result of White's labors, for a time theory would no longer be deemed as something "indecent." White reminded his colleagues of a basic epistemological point: "facts do not and cannot speak for themselves; they must have a creative intelligence to make them intelligible and meaningful" (White 1987a: 146). He added that "facts as facts lie inert and meaningless until they are quickened into life and meaning by creative intelligence" (White 1987a: 91).

The importance of this accomplishment cannot be overestimated. White provided an alternative to the chaotic, purposeless vision of culture promulgated by the dogmatically relativistic Boasians. He saw culture as an organic whole, a system operating according to its own laws and principles that were amenable to rational inquiry. He attempted to demonstrate that cultures evolved in patterned and predictable ways (Lett 1987: 91), rather than "through borrowings due to chance contact," as Lowie (1920: 411) and the diffusionists would have it.

Moreover, White attempted to show that there were objective ways of conceptualizing and comparing cultures and that one did not need to elevate the native's point of view above those of the scientist. White therefore brought a new optimistic outlook into a discipline made dismal by Boasian dogmatism by stressing that the task of anthropology as a science was to advance our understanding of cultural phenomena, not to demonstrate the hopelessness of our ever understanding it.

White's optimistic view, however, did not survive the twentieth century. Today, cultural constructionists have adopted the position that the understanding of culture is an insurmountable problem and have resigned themselves to the fate that we can never really know much of anything. These writers console themselves by reciting poems and writing fiction. This view, however, curiously diverges from Boas' pessimism in one significant way. Although Boas maintained that there were innumerable obstacles to understanding other cultures, he foresaw a day when those obstacles would be overcome, when more data was available, when new theoretical frameworks were constructed, and so on. The science-bashing interpretivists, on the contrary, not only consider the obstacles to cross-cultural understanding to be insurmountable, but they consider it a necessary condition for the validity of their theoretical perspective. That perspective, we might recall is based on a rejection of rationality and science and a definition of knowledge, based upon subjective moralistic criteria, which embraces local understandings and the native's point of view.

JULIAN STEWARD: CULTURAL ECOLOGY AND EVOLUTION

Another anthropologist who made a significant contribution to the re-establishment of evolutionary theory and a scientific approach in American anthropology was Julian Steward (1902–1972). Steward attempted to develop a perspective that treated sociocultural evolution in terms of **positive feedback** relationships between sets of variables situated within particular ecological circumstances (Sanderson 1990: 95; Trigger 1998: 128–129). The epistemological assumptions underlying Steward's evolutionary formulations pertain to material causality and his position therefore excludes the notion of unfolding of latent immanence of the nineteenth-century ethnologists.

Steward attempted to address significant questions concerning the interface between culture and its ecological context and the issue of "**adaptation**" in a way that would avoid the problems of crude environmental determinism and the theoretically vacuous concept of possibilism.

STEWARD: BACKGROUND AS A BOASIAN

Steward was trained by two of Franz Boas's star pupils, Alfred Kroeber, who established the department of anthropology at Berkeley, and Robert Lowie, who joined Kroeber at Berkeley in 1921. Steward received his Ph.D. in 1929. His dissertation, which was based on library research, was entitled "The Ceremonial Buffoon of the American Indian." It dealt with the psychology of humor and ritualized clowning and role reversals (Murphy 1977: 4).

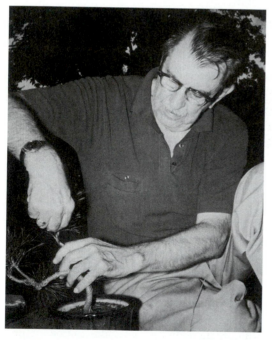

Julian Steward, expositor of cultural ecology who introduced the concept of multilinear evolution.

Although he specialized in cultural anthropology, Steward was also trained as an archeologist and functioned in that capacity as much as in that of a cultural anthropologist for most of his early career. Steward is credited with pioneering **settlement pattern archeology** with a focus on ecological and functional features of culture. This approach transformed the focus of the field of archaeology from a concern with the study of stylistic variations toward a sociological orientation and the application of the idea of culture as an adaptive system. This orientation became popular in the 1960s (Murphy 1977: 27; see Binford 1962, 1968; Flannery 1968). Steward also stressed the importance of ethnographic data for archeological investigations and urged archeologists to draw upon ethnological data to interpret the archaeological record.

In 1930, Steward accepted a teaching job at the University of Utah, where he taught anthropology and initiated an archaeological field project excavating Pueblo sites (Manners 1973: 889). In 1933–1934, Steward returned to Berkeley as a lecturer. During this time he began two years of intensive fieldwork among the Great Basin cultures studying Shoshone and Northern Paiute groups in the eastern part of California, as well as in Nevada, Utah, and Idaho. As we shall see, Steward's Great Basin ethnographic work had a decisive impact on the development of his theoretical ideas.

From 1935 to 1946, Steward joined the Smithsonian Institute's Bureau of American Ethnology as Associate Anthropologist. Here he initiated several research projects. Among these was the compilation of the encyclopedic treatise, *Handbook of South American Indians* (1946–1950), which Steward organized on the basis of **culture types.** As well as editing the volume, he also contributed important theoretical sections (Murphy 1977: 7). Aside from assembling a vast body of data on South America, with submissions by some one hundred leading scholars in the field from a dozen countries, the *Handbook* delimited major theoretical issues. These concerns would guide field research in the area for the next thirty years (Manners 1973: 892; Murphy 1977: 7).

In 1946 Steward accepted a teaching position at Boas's department of anthropology at Columbia University, where he trained a number of students. Steward also began a major collaborative ethnographic research project in Puerto Rico. This was the first anthropological endeavor to examine the cultures and subcultures of a complex society from an historical and ecological framework within a larger political and economic setting (Murphy 1977: 11). The findings were presented in *The People of Puerto Rico* (1956). The Puerto Rico project also inspired Steward to write *Area Research: Theory and Practice* (1950), in which he provided insights into the study of complex societies in terms of different levels of integration characterizing family, community, and state institutions.

Steward left Columbia in 1952 for a research professorship at the University of Illinois, where he would remain for the rest of his career. At Illinois he initiated a collaborative project to study cultural regularities based upon cross-cultural ethnographic research in Africa, Asia, Mexico, and Peru. The results were published in a volume entitled *Contemporary Change in Traditional Societies* (1967) edited by Steward. In 1955 Steward published *The Theory of Culture Change* and *Native Peoples of South America* in 1959. The latter volume was written in collaboration with the anthropologist Louis Faron. Toward the end of his life, Steward (1960a) also wrote a biography of his teacher Alfred Kroeber.

SCIENCE AND CAUSALITY

From the start of his career as an anthropologist, Steward viewed anthropology as a science and considered the "search for causality" his long-life endeavor (Manners 1973: 887). Thus, like Leslie White, Steward departed from the Boasian program of his teachers.

Steward had to simultaneously engage in epistemological and theoretical debates with the Boasians as well as with White while formulating his own perspective, which departed from the views of both in various ways. Steward's epistemological position was that there is an objective reality and that this reality can be apprehended. Moreover, he believed that cultural phenomena are orderly, that significant regularities exist in cultures, that certain cultural elements are causally connected to one another, and that the regularities in culture are amenable to rational inquiry. His approach was based upon categories and concepts meaningful to the scientist, rather than meaningful from the native's point of view, which again was a radical departure from the Boasian idiographic and hyperrelativist program.

Although Steward was mindful of inductive research and the gathering of empirical data, he brought deductive reasoning back into anthropology. This Boas had more or less exorcised from the discipline. As Murphy (1977: 20–21) remarked,

> Steward did not eschew the world of evidence and the senses . . . but he was among the first anthropologists to introduce a strong element of deductive process in his scientific reasoning. He formulated hypotheses on the basis of scattered evidence combined with logic and then went to the field, or to the library, for fuller corroboration. He was one of the first anthropologists to undertake fieldwork with a firm sense of problem, formulated in advance, rather than to simply obtain a general description of culture. This affinity for educated conjecture was paralleled by an equally strong propensity toward generalization.[27]

Thus Steward's work in many ways hailed the end of the age of induction and of the German science which Boas taught to his numerous students (Murphy 1977: 21). It was, as Harris (2001b: 657) put it, "the triumph of the nomothetic mode over the idiographic." However, we must not forget the contributions of White in this direction as well.

Steward was interested in discovering causal connections and this meant the search for laws of culture (Murphy 1977: 17). However, his objectives were more modest in this regard than White's quest for universally applicable propositions. In his classic paper "Cultural Causality and Law" (1949), Steward outlined his scientific perspective as follows:

> The present need is not to achieve a world scheme of culture development or a set of universally valid laws, though no doubt many such laws can even now be postulated, but to establish a genuine interest in the scientific objective and a clear conceptualization of what is meant by regularities. It does not matter whether the formulations are sequential (diachronic) or functional (synchronic), on a large scale or small scale. It is more important that comparative cultural studies should interest themselves in recurrent phenomena as well as in unique phenomena, and that anthropology explicitly recognize that a legitimate and ultimate objective is to see through the differences of cultures to similarities, to ascertain processes that are duplicated independently in cultural sequences, and to recognize cause and effect in both temporal and functional relationships. Such scientific endeavor need not be ridden by the requirement that cultural laws or regularities be formulated in terms comparable to those of the biological or physical sciences, that they be absolutes and universals, or that they provide ultimate explanations. Any formulations of cultural data are valid provided the procedure is empirical, hypothesis arising from interpretation of fact and being revised as new facts become available (Steward 1955: 180).[28]

This paper, despite its cautious and modest orientation, was among Steward's most substantive contributions in the effort to reintroduce evolutionism in American anthropology (Sanderson 1990: 92).

The period in which this paper appeared was a brief but happy time in American cultural anthropology when, as Murray Wax put it, researchers sought both to generalize about cultures as well as to describe particular human groups. It was a time when "the differently di-

rected activities within the discipline [might] fruitfully assist each other, and a joint store of particular facts, generalizations about process, and insightful interpretations and understandings came to be accepted as valid" (Wax 1956: 66).

As Steward's passage above indicates, he was looking for cause-effect relationships operating in a narrowly defined and limited area, rather than seeking universal laws of culture. He was concerned with particular ethnographic instances and attempted to ground his explanations in empirical evidence. In this respect, Steward's approach was considerably different from White's disarticulated culturology and evolutionism, which involved the search for general laws of evolution that applied to all culture in all times and places and operated at a more abstract level of analysis. As Steward observed,

> The cultural-ecological method of analyzing culture change or evolution differs from that based on the superorganic or culturological concept. The latter assumes that only phenomena of a cultural level are relevant and admissible, and it repudiates "reductionism," that is, consideration of processes induced by factors of a psychological, biological, or environmental level. The evolutionary hypothesis based upon this method deals with culture in the generic or global sense rather than with individual cultures in a substantive sense, and they postulate universal processes. Cultural ecology, on the other hand, recognizes the substantive dissimilarities of cultures that are caused by the particular adaptive processes by which any society interacts with its environment (Steward 1977a: 44).[29]

Since Steward gave priority to the analysis of particular environmental adaptations, which he saw as a prerequisite to the formulation of more general laws, he was critical of White's evolutionary formulations. In his review of White's book, *Evolution of Culture,* Steward (1960b: 146) pointed out that

> regarding the causal chain that begins with technology and control of energy and runs through society to religion, there can be little disagreement with the self-evident proposition that "as the

amount of energy harnessed by sociocultural systems increase per capita per year, the systems not only increase in size, but become more highly evolved, i.e., . . . more differentiated structurally and more specialized functionally" (pp. 39–40). But this does not at all explain what kinds of social structures arise from the utilization of technologies in particular environments. White concedes (p. 41) that "technological and environmental factors both operate to produce cultural differences quite apart from the source and magnitude of energy harnessed," but he is not interested in these differences and states (p. 51) that "if one . . . wishes to discover how cultural systems are structured and how they function . . . then *one does not need to consider the natural habitat at all*," for he is really concerned with "*how and why the culture of mankind as a whole has grown.*" He makes no use of the heuristic concept of cultural ecology and attaches no importance to social variations which relate in part to differences between such subsistence activities as food collecting (dispersed Shoshoni and Alacaluf families), fishing (e.g., large Northwest Coast villages), hunting and collecting in areas rich in food resources (small California villages), pastoral nomadism (multi-family Mongol bands), irrigation farming (early and New and Old World civilized societies), and many others.

For Steward the ethnographic investigation of causality entailed the following type of reasoning: "Given conditions A, B . . . then C will probably result" (Murphy 1977: 18). Steward sought cause-and-effect relationships in historical and ethnographic situations that could be validated by cross-cultural comparisons and tests of **covariance.** Steward not only fully subscribed to the comparative method, but he also made it respectable once again. Murphy outlines Steward's methodology as follows:

> The relatedness of two elements in society or culture depends upon a test of co-variance. This can be effected in the hard sciences by experimentation, the setting up of an artificially bounded and isolated situation in which one or more of the variables under study may be manipulated. In human societies it is impossible to isolate the variables, just as it is often politically or ethically unde-

sirable or impossible to change them. The only way that we can study co-variation in natural setting situations is to find a variety of such situations in our inventory of cultures. Thus, if we are interested in demonstrating a relationship between A and B on the one hand and C on the other, then we can review all the societies that have A and B to see whether C is always present; or we may look at all the societies where C is found in order to determine whether A and B are present. The actual situation in comparison is always more complex than this, of course, but this is the essential method in anthropology, and the one followed by Steward (Murphy 1977: 18).[30]

The problems that would arise related to the poor quality of the available ethnographic data at Steward's disposal. In addition to this, some critics also objected to Steward's methodological approach, which entails finding certain cultural features that covary, or are functionally related, locating their occurrence in a particular environment, and then concluding on the basis of this that a causal connection exists between the variables. However, correlation does not necessarily mean that a causal relationship has been verified (see Ellen 1986: 63; Vayda and Rappaport 1968: 483–487).

Critics also raised issues regarding Steward's sampling procedures, his reliance on nonstatistical generalizations, as well as faulting him for not searching for cases in which the postulated causal relationships between environmental and cultural variables might not hold true.

While some of the criticisms have merit, we must not let them overshadow Steward's most important contribution to anthropology, that is, to shift the direction of anthropological research away from the Boasian idiographic mode of analysis toward a nomothetic one (Harris 2001b: 657). Moreover, it must also be noted that some of the most important cases Steward presented, such as parallelism in the evolutionary trajectories of sociocultural systems located in different parts of the world, are now widely accepted by archeologists and cultural anthropologists (cf. Sanderson 1999: 69).

STEWARD AGAINST BOASIAN DIFFUSIONISM

Unlike his teachers, Kroeber and Lowie, Steward's concern with causal connections led him to construe similarities between cultures as the result of the same causes leading to parallel developments. The Boasians, as we have seen, dismissed cultural parallels and offered their own principle that "unlike causes produce like effects" (Boas 1887: 485). The Boasians suggested the mechanism of diffusion as the explanation for the phenomenon of parallel developments. Diffusion was also one of the primary factors they felt negated any sort of recurrent evolutionary cultural developments, as I have already pointed out. This was, of course, an expression of the Boasian no-rhyme-or-reason-in-the-realm-of-culture point of view that White found so annoying and unacceptable.

Steward (1955: 182) saw diffusion as an inadequate causal mechanism and a nonexplanation:

> The use of diffusion to avoid coming to grips with problems of cause and effect not only fails to provide a consistent approach to culture history, but it gives an explanation of cultural origins that really explains nothing. Diffusion becomes a mechanical and unintelligible, though universal, cause, and it is employed, as if in contrast to other kinds of causes, to account for about 90 percent of the world's culture.[31]

Steward saw cultures as functionally integrated systems comprising of central institutional complexes. For this reason, he doubted whether entire institutional complexes, as opposed to individual cultural elements, could spread by borrowing/imitation. In Steward's view, diffusion could account for the dispersion of particular traits, such as myths, rituals, the practice of smoking tobacco, or the manufacture of paper (see Ember and Ember 1990: 472; 2002: 272–273) and thus influenced the outward features of particular cultures. However, he did not think that diffusion could account for the development of whole institutional complexes such as, for example, state-level organization.

State-level societies first appeared as instances of parallel development, as noted in Chapter 5. Subsequent spread of state-level organization by diffusion leading to the emergence of secondary states could take place only under particular circumstances. Secondary states evolved under the impetus of primary states only if the suitable or necessary conditions were already present, such as intensive agriculture, long-distance trade, occupational specialization, and population densities of a certain magnitude (Murphy 1977: 19). Whether a diffused trait would be incorporated or not is "always contingent upon local potentialities." This is why there are many tribal societies that may be called "**chiefdoms,**" in Asia, Oceania, and South America, that have been in contact with state-level societies for long periods of time, without themselves adopting state organization (Gross 1992: 435; see Kirch 1984; Sahlins 1958).

Believing that causal relationships would be much easier to discover in simple rather than complex societies, Steward undertook fieldwork among the Shoshoni of the Great Basin. During his research he also collected information as part of the Culture-Element Surveys project directed by his teacher Alfred Kroeber, which was discussed in Chapter 7 (Steward 1941). Steward, however, was never fully convinced of the usefulness of the trait-list approach. His ethnographic research in the Great Basin area suggested an alternative that he would then develop into a theoretical and methodological perspective. This alternative was that ecology was central to understanding cultural patterns, integration, and change.

THE HUNTING AND GATHERING BAND: ECOLOGICAL FOCUS

Steward's study of the ecology, economy, and social organization of the Shoshoni, which led to the publication of his classic monograph, *Basin-Plateau Aboriginal Sociopolitical Groups* (1938), clearly demonstrated the analytical strengths of the cultural ecological approach and was the stimulus for Steward's theory of culture change (Murphy 1977: 5–6). Steward noted a close correlation between Shoshoni sociopolitical and economic organization, their mode of production, and the ecological context in which they operated.

Unlike the Boasians, who saw the environment as imposing a backdrop upon which different traits could be reshaped and recombined in a random and endless fashion, Steward noted that adaptive cultural arrangements were more likely to persist over other patterns. This meant that cultures can only vary within certain limits, "otherwise the people will obviously not survive." The implication of this was that, as Steward observed, "the types of culture forms being limited in number, the same type is frequently evolved" (Steward 1938: 261).

Once again, the striking parallelisms in the development of state-level societies illustrate this point. Even in instances of political evolution that did not lead to true statehood, complex polities called chiefdoms did appear, for example in Asia, Polynesia, North America, and South America outside Peru. These polities exhibit remarkable parallels with zones where state formation took place (Sanderson 1999: 69; for Polynesia see Kirch 1984; for South Asia see Sidky 1996; for the Americas see Fiedel 1987).

In his study of the Shoshoni, Steward detected a causal connection between the major social features and adjustments associated with adaptation to the resource-scarce arid Basin-Plateau region. He later wrote that "empirical studies disclose that among the simpler and earlier societies of mankind, to whom physical survival was the major concern, different social systems were fairly direct responses to the exploitation of particular environments by special techniques" (Steward 1977a: 44). The crucial relationships Steward observed were those between available resources, technology, labor patterns necessary for the exploitation of resources, and the effects of labor patterns upon other social institutions. Steward thus developed a method that focused upon the articulation of human subsistence strategies and the natural habitat in order to arrive at causal principles to account for cultural differences and similarities.

Inspired by his Shoshoni research, Steward wrote a paper in 1934 entitled "The Economic and Social Basis of Primitive Bands" (1936) in which he noted many parallels between historically and geographically unrelated peoples, such as the Australian Aborigines, the Bushmen of South Africa, the Semang of Malaysia, and other hunter-gatherers. An expanded version of this study appeared under the title of "The Patrilineal Band" in Steward's important book, *Theory of Culture Change* (1955: 122–142; for a recent assessment of Steward's Shoshoni work see Clemmer et al. 1999). He posited that similar ecological conditions lead to the emergence of groups with band-level social organization. Steward (1977a: 181) summed it up as follows: "Certain features of the relationship of man to his environment are very similar and have produced almost identical social patterns."

Steward's 1936 paper was rejected at first by several anthropological journals because of the novelty of the ideas expressed in it (Manners 1973: 890). He was, we must remember, operating in a stultifying antiscience intellectual environment, not unlike that of today, in which the idea of the radical plurality of cultures and an antipathy towards cross-cultural generalizations were the dominant themes. Moreover, it was a time of Boasian idiographic approaches, hyperrelativism, and trait lists, when the number of poles in a teepee could well be deemed a major differentiating cultural feature (Manners 1973: 890).

Steward developed his model of the hunting-gathering band on the basis of a number of assumptions, formulated upon poor ethnographic data and misleading analysis by other anthropologists, which have been disproved by later ethnographic research. These assumptions included the idea that hunter-gathering populations are at the mercy of their environments, that all their efforts are directed towards subsistence, that hunting comprises the most important subsistence activity, that band composition is fairly inflexible, and that bands are patrilocal land-owning units. The last idea, hunting-gathering bands as land-owning patrilineal/patrilocal groups, is specifically attributable to erroneous interpretations of data on "Australian tribes" by Radcliffe-Brown (1913, 1918), whose ideas influenced Steward (Bodley 1994: 29).

The classic modern ethnographic monographs on hunter-gather societies include Colin Turnbull's (1961) study of the Mbuti of central Zaire, James Woodburn's (1968) work on the Hadza in Tanzania, and Richard Lee's (1979) research among the !Kung San of southern Africa (Figure 10.4). These and other studies have shown that members of hunting-gathering or **foraging bands,** with a few exceptions (e.g., the Inuit), have a satisfactory food supply and obtain a high return for relatively little effort in subsistence activities. Moreover, their diets are adequate both in terms of calories and protein consumed daily (Cashdan 1989; Ellen 1986: 56; Lee 1969). Based on such data, Sahlins (1972, 1982, 1997) suggested that the foraging band represents "the original affluent society" (cf. Sanderson 1999: 21).

Subsequent ethnographic work also suggests that aside from the arctic region, vegetable foods comprise the greater part of the calories consumed by foraging populations (Lee 1969; see Lee and DeVore 1968, 1978). Thus, it is the female gatherers rather than the male hunters who provide the bulk of the calories consumed. Furthermore, field studies have shown that foraging bands possess considerable flexibility, with members having extensive social links with other groups through kinship, **fictive kinship,** marriage, trade, and so on. Also, foraging bands are characterized by **flux** or a **fission-fusion** pattern as an essential part of their adaptation, with group size and composition changing with seasonal fluctuations in the availability of water and other resources (Lee 1972, 1993: 65; Marshall 1960; Oliver 1962; Stiles 1992; Turnbull 1961, 1968).

Finally, modern ethnographic data indicate that foraging bands are not kinship units, are not corporate in nature, and do not own territory. We also know that foraging populations exhibit a pattern of **egalitarian** social relations (Lee 1990; Lee and DeVore 1968; also see Lee and Daly 1999; Lee and Guenter 1991, 1995; Schrire 1984; Stiles 1992; Wilmsen and Denbow 1990 for more recent debates in this area).

Parenthetically it must be noted also that some prehistoric hunter-gatherer societies did not fit the pattern based upon the ethnographic record. Unlike the foraging groups today, prehistoric hunter-gatherers did not occupy marginal environments. Moreover, archaeological evidence suggests that some prehistoric hunter-gatherer societies had characteristics such as social ranking and hierarchy, large sedentary populations, developed political leadership, and occupational specialization, not found among hunter-gatherers described by ethnographers (Price and Brown 1985). This may have been especially the case in the period just prior to the "Neolithic Revolution," which marked a transition to farming modes of production. Also, foraging communities in the Northwest Coast of North America, such as the Kwakiutl described by Boas (see Boas 1966; Drucker 1965), were stratified chiefdoms, which depart from the ethnographic cases described above (Sanderson 1999: 23). Many of these findings are at variance with Steward's formulation.

The importance of Steward's pioneering article stemmed not so much from the ethnographic and empirical accuracy of his model of hunting gathering bands, although attempts were made to modify it in various ways (e.g., Service 1979), but rather from its methodological approach. As Ellen (1986: 53) has observed, Steward's 1936 article was of enormous theoretical significance because it represented the first systematic treatment of how human/culture-environment could be analyzed in causal terms, without slipping into particularism.

In other words, Steward pointed out how technological and environmental interactions

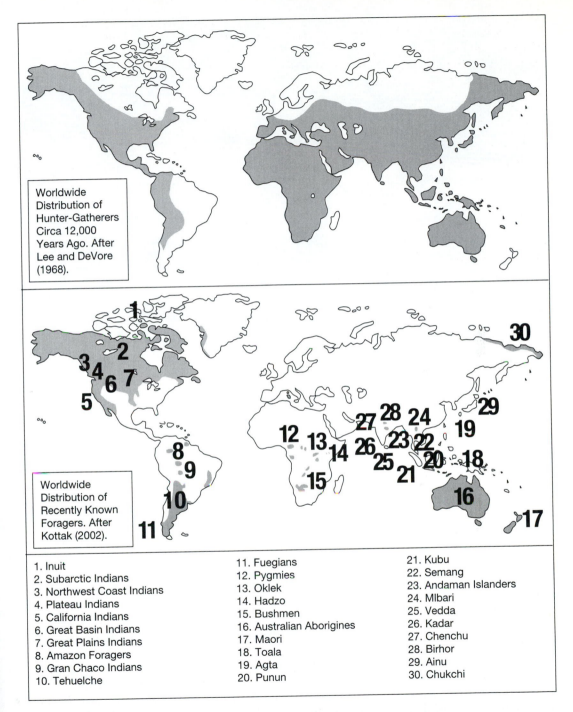

Worldwide
Distribution of
Hunter-Gatherers
Circa 12,000
Years Ago. After
Lee and DeVore
(1968).

Worldwide
Distribution of
Recently Known
Foragers. After
Kottak (2002).

1. Inuit
2. Subarctic Indians
3. Northwest Coast Indians
4. Plateau Indians
5. California Indians
6. Great Basin Indians
7. Great Plains Indians
8. Amazon Foragers
9. Gran Chaco Indians
10. Tehuelche

11. Fuegians
12. Pygmies
13. Oklek
14. Hadzo
15. Bushmen
16. Australian Aborigines
17. Maori
18. Toala
19. Agta
20. Punun

21. Kubu
22. Semang
23. Andaman Islanders
24. Mlbari
25. Vedda
26. Kadar
27. Chenchu
28. Birhor
29. Ainu
30. Chukchi

Figure 10.4 Distribution of Hunter–Gatherers.

Scientific ethnography conducted by anthropologists such as Richard Lee (shown here with the San of the Kalahari Desert) has greatly contributed to our understanding of the foraging adaptive pattern.

could account for the structural and ideological characteristics of hunting-gathering bands without the need to rely upon the specific contents of these cultures, or idiographic explanations (Harris 2001b: 669). Steward's work was also instrumental in illustrating how comparable adaptive ecological adjustments among different cultures are often concealed by the specific contents of these cultures (Harris 2001b: 666). This marked what would be the beginning of the cultural ecological approach to ethnographic research, a perspective that seemed to avoid the tautological trap in which British functionalism and Boasian cultural anthropology had been caught (Baker 1962).

In recent years the pendulum has swung back toward the idiographic relativistic perspectives in the study of hunter-gatherer societies (Joachim 1996; Kelly 1995; Kent 1996). These studies are concerned with ethnographic particularism

based upon something similar to what Boas used to shift attention toward the particular (i.e., that "unlike causes produce like effects").

We must bear in mind, however, as I have noted in Chapter 6, that in one respect or another every culture is unique, just as every person, or leaf, or grain of sand, or snowflake is unique. Finding differences between things is easy. But these things that are classified as different, be they cultures, snowflakes, or grains of sand, also have similarities with other cultures, snowflakes, or grains of sand.

To find out that something is different we have to contrast it with something else, with which it has certain similarities. In other words, statements about differences depend as much upon comparisons as statements about similarities. The retreat to ethnographic particularism is therefore a matter of personal preference not something dictated by the ontological attributes of the phenomena anthropologists study. There are simply too many parallelisms in sociocultural phenomena (e.g., the transition to farming, the development of chiefdoms, the rise of the state, the invention of writing, ceramics, metallurgy, calendars, to name just a few) to be accounted for in terms of dissimilar causes producing superficial similarities.

CULTURAL ECOLOGY

Steward's cultural ecology is considered to be one of his major contributions to anthropological theory. In the concept of ecology Steward (1955: 30) saw a means "to determine the creative process involved in the adaptation of culture to the environment." Cultural evolution, for Steward, basically entailed the continuing process of adaptation to the environment. Environment was construed in ecological terms as "the total web of life wherein all plants and animal species interact with one another and with physical features in a particular unit of territory" (Steward 1955: 30).

Steward, however, espoused an ecological approach for the investigation of cultural adjustments, rather than treating humans as one of many elements in an ecosystem framework. This distinguished his work from those of the later ecological anthropologists, such as for example Roy Rappaport's groundbreaking study of a highland population in New Guinea. Rappaport construed the idea of ecosystem in a manner commensurable with general ecology as

> a demarcated portion of the biosphere that includes living organisms [including humans] and non-living substances interacting to produce a systemic exchange of material among the living components and with the non-living substances (Rappaport 1984: 225).[32]

In his later works, however, Rappaport (1993) attempted to address some of the limitations of the ecosystem approach by entertaining the idea of "anthropocentric" ecosystems, in which emphasis is placed upon the role of humans "putting nature to their own purposes," making the cultural dimension more apparent.

Steward (1955: 31) was interested in "how culture is affected by its adaptation to environment." The superorganic had to be accommodated in his ecological framework as a phenomenon distinct from environmental factors. Steward wrote that

> man enters the ecological scene . . . not merely as another organism which is related to other organisms in terms of his physical characteristics. He introduces the super-organic factor of culture, which also affects and is affected by the total web of life (Steward 1955: 31).[33]

According to this view, humans differ from other biotic assemblages in the way they interact with the total web of life in two major respects. First, humans adapt to their environments through culture (i.e., the superorganic) rather than genes. Second, the web of life in which humans participate often extends well beyond their particular unit of territory. Thus attempts to elucidate the causes of similarities and differences in culture from a cultural ecological framework must contend with a different set of problems than those confronting general ecologists:

> Cultural ecology differs from human and social ecology in seeking to explain the origin of particular cultural features and patterns which characterize different areas rather than derive general principles applicable to any cultural-environmental situation. It differs from the relativistic and neo-evolutionist conceptions of culture history in that it introduces the local environment as the extra-cultural factor in the fruitless assumption that culture comes from culture. Thus cultural ecology presents both a problem and a method. The problem is to ascertain whether the adjustments of human societies to their environment require particular modes of behavior or whether they permit latitude for a certain range of possible behavior patterns. . . . the problem of cultural ecology must be further qualified, however, through use of a supplementary conception of culture. According to the holistic view, all aspects of culture are functionally interdependent upon one another. The

degree and kind of interdependency, however, are not the same with all features (Steward 1955: 36).[34]

For Steward, therefore, all sectors of culture did not have the same status in terms of causal relationships. In order to identify the causally crucial sectors, Steward (1955: 40–41) offered the methodology of cultural ecology, which involves the following basic procedures:

1. Analysis focusing upon the interrelationship between the exploitative or productive technology and the environment
2. The analysis of the human behavioral patterns involved in the exploitation of a particular resource through the use of a particular technology
3. The determination of the degree to which the behavior patterns involved in exploiting the environment affect other sectors of culture

There are four interrelated concepts that together make up Steward's research perspective. These are (1) **culture core;** (2) **secondary institutions;** (3) **culture types;** (4) **levels of cultural integration** (Figure 10.5). As noted previously, Steward construed culture in terms of functional integration:

> Culture is not an entirely fortuitous assemblage of unrelated elements but consists of parts which in some degree predetermine, condition, or delimit one another. The problem, then, is to ascertain the nature and degree of this interrelationship (Steward 1940: 480).

Steward saw a difference between the diverse sectors of a culture in terms of their part in the adaptive process; for this reason he attempted to isolate the most important sectors for analysis. He called these sectors the culture core, which was his key concept. Steward defined the culture core as

> the constellation of features which are most closely related to subsistence activities and economic arrangements. The core includes such social, political, and religious patterns as are empirically determined to be closely connected with these arrangements (Steward 1955: 36–37).[35]

In other words, the culture core refers to those sectors of a sociocultural system in which environmental resources, tools, cultural knowledge used to appropriate those resources, and human behavior in the form of patterns of labor and labor allocation necessary to effectively employ technology, and appropriate ideologies are brought together. Elsewhere Steward defined the culture core as follows: "basic features ... which have similar functional interrelationships resulting from local ecological adaptations and similar levels of sociocultural integration" (Steward 1955: 6).

Steward distinguished the culture core from other aspects of culture, which he referred to as secondary cultural features:

> Innumerable other features may have great potential variability because they are less strongly tied to the core. These latter, or secondary features, are determined to a greater extent by purely cultural-historical factors—by random innovations or by diffusion—and they give the appearance of outward distinctiveness to cultures with similar cores. Cultural ecology pays primary attention to those features which empirical analysis shows to be most closely involved in the utilization of environment in culturally prescribed ways (Steward 1955: 36–37).[36]

For Steward the organization of production, which was determined by the environment/resources and available technology, had a determinant causal effect upon other social institutions. Human behavior in the pursuit of subsistence, such as work patterns, division of labor, the organization, management, and timing of work, was the key to understanding cultural similarities and differences (Murphy 1977: 22).

Cultural ecology was therefore the study not just of culture nor just of the environment or ecosystem, but rather of the interaction between culture (technology, knowledge) and environmental resources and the effects of the interaction between these upon culture as a whole. Steward's focus upon the interface between behavioral and cultural variables and environmental variables enabled him to avoid the pitfalls of simplistic one-to-one culture/environment

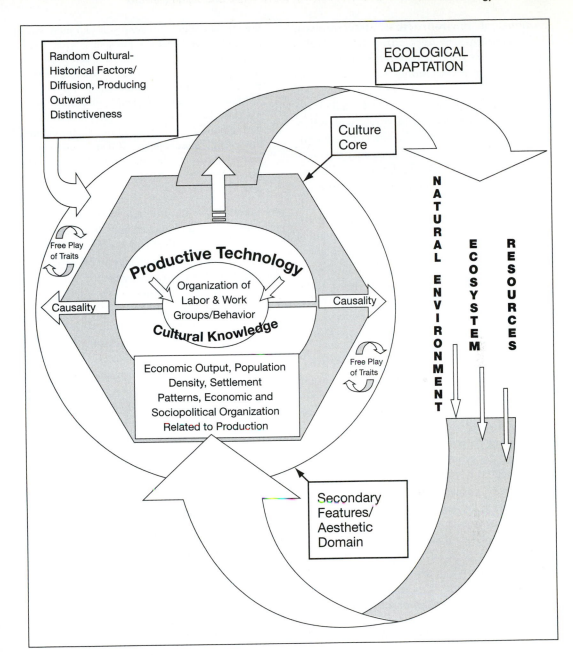

Figure 10.5   Steward's cultural ecological model.

relations, or **environmental determinism.** This is because he recognized that different human groups respond to similar environments in different ways, according to existing social structural patterns and types of technologies. He thus solved a problem that had baffled the Boasians, i.e., the presence of groups with different cultural configurations in the same environment, leading them into thinking that the environment was merely the backdrop that limited, but did not otherwise impinge upon culture.

For Steward, institutions comprising the culture core are those directly associated with the exploitation of resources from the environment and are central to a society's cultural adaptation. Secondary or peripheral institutions are less directly associated with the adaptive process and are subject to forces of change emanating either from within the culture or from outside factors. Steward saw wide latitude of free play in these sectors as opposed to the core.

Steward's core and secondary institutions are similar to Kroeber's view of culture as possessing two distinct elements, basic features (reality culture), and secondary features (value culture). Kroeber defined reality culture as those sectors associated with practical needs, such as subsistence, that are grounded in nature. He saw value culture, which he defined as being comprised of the aesthetic domains and which he made his focus of study, as autonomous and subject to its own internal principles operating independently of external factors (Hatch 1973: 99, 117; Kroeber 1963: 62). Steward attempted to work out the linkages between reality culture and value culture within a broader ecological framework.

Steward's conceptualization of culture, which attributed causal priority to some cultural elements over others, was at considerable variance with the views of most of his contemporaries. As he put it,

> This conception of culture is in conflict with an extreme organic view, which regards culture as a closed system in which all parts are of equal importance and are equally fixed. It holds that some features of culture are more basic and more fixed than others and that the problem is to ascertain those which are primary and basic and to explain their origin and development. It assumes that although the secondary features must be consistent and functionally integrated with the primary ones, it is these latter that are more susceptible to fortuitous influences from inside or outside the culture, that change most readily, and that acquire such a variety of aspects that they give the impression that history never repeats itself (Steward 1955: 185).[37]

As Steward saw it, although secondary features of culture can undergo change in a fortuitous fashion, the cultural system as a whole will not change unless there is a change in its core institutions. The chain of causality went from culture core to secondary features with greater force than the other way around.

Steward's formulations regarding the culture core pose certain difficulties because elsewhere, he includes aesthetic features alongside economic, social, political, religious, and military patterns as also belonging to the culture core (Steward 1955: 93). In White's conception of culture as an adaptive mechanism, emic dimensions, such as aesthetic features are fully articulated with their etic components. However, because Steward included elements from nearly every sector of culture, both emic and etic, under the category of core institutions we encounter a logical problem in determining causality. The more inclusive Steward became in his definition of the culture core, the closer he came to equating the entire cultural pattern with the core. Thus it becomes impossible to determine whether it is subsistence, or the economic, political, religious, military, medical, or aesthetic sectors that determine any particular culture type (cf. Harris 2001b: 661).

A related problem was Steward's suggestion that the elements that comprise the culture core vary from one society to another. In other words, Steward attempted to address the problem of investigating human-environment interactions by suggesting the concept of culture core (i.e., activities closely connected to subsistence and economic arrangements). However, he then went on to point out that the constituents of the culture core vary from case to case. This lack of precision regarding what comprises the core posed difficulties when investigators attempted to apply the concept to the ethnographic case (Ellen 1986: 61). For these reasons, Harris (2001b: 660) referred to Steward's key concept as "the core of confusion."

Another problem arising from the concept of culture core was that Steward made no allowance for feedback between social relations and the environment (Ellen 1986: 64). The chain of causality went one direction. Also, Steward's emphasis was upon the culture core and he made no allowance for any feedback from the secondary features to the core.

Steward's focus upon human-environment interactions in terms of technology, labor patterns and allocation, and associated behavioral patterns/social relations, has also led to the criticism that he ruled out the possibility that system-transforming forces could emanate from other sectors, a point raised by Marxist theorists (e.g., Friedman 1974: 462). Most other critics reiterate the same issue and really contribute nothing new to the discussion (e.g., Herzfeld 2001: 178–179; Milton 1996: 43–45). Marxist perspectives ultimately place the locus of causality in the context of systemic contradictions at the level of social relationships (see Chapter 14) and are therefore epistemologically incompatible with approaches that attempt to link causality to ecological variables. Thus writers espousing Marxist viewpoints would treat the exclusion of social relations/ideologies, i.e., elements beyond the technical relations of production, as sources of system transformations as problematic (Friedman 1974: 462).

LEVELS OF SOCIOCULTURAL INTEGRATION

Steward classified cultures with similar cores as belonging to the same **culture type.** For Steward (1955: 180) the development of a typology of "cultures, patterns, and institutions" was one of the requirements for the understanding of cultural regularities and developing cross-cultural generalizations. Culture types can be arranged according to sociocultural complexity, or in terms of what Steward called **levels of sociocultural integration** (Figure 10.6). This refers to the largest social grouping in a culture that can undertake collective action (Kaplan and Manners 1972: 48). Steward recognized three general levels of integration: **family, tribe,** and **state.** These were analytical concepts useful for arranging data for the purposes of cross-cultural comparison:

> The concept of levels of sociocultural integration . . . is simply a methodological tool for dealing with cultures of different degrees of complexity. It is not a conclusion about evolution. . . . The . . . concept provides a new frame of reference and a new meaning to pattern; and it facilitates cross-cultural comparison (Steward 1950: 52).[38]

Others later reformulated Steward's levels in terms of sociopolitical integration as bands, tribes, chiefdoms, and states (Service 1962; Sahlins 1968), or in terms of the emergence of inequality as egalitarian, ranked, stratified, and state-level societies (Fried 1967). Typologies based upon both sets of categories appear in the writings of present-day anthropologists (cf. Sanderson 1999: 53–58).

The levels of sociocultural integration was central to Steward's cultural ecology, which he summed up as follows:

> Cultural ecology had been described as a methodological tool for ascertaining how the adaptation of a culture to its environment may entail certain changes. In a larger sense the problem is to determine whether similar adjustments occur in similar environments. Since in any given environment, culture may develop through a succession of very unlike periods, it is sometimes pointed out that environment, the constant, obviously has no relationship to cultural type. This difficulty disappears, however, if the level of sociocultural integration represented by each period is taken into account.

	Bands	Tribes	Chiefdoms	States
Primary Mode of Subsistence	Foraging	Agriculture/Pastoralism		Intensive Agriculture
Primary Mode of Distribution	Reciprocity	Redistribution		Market
Population Size	Small/Low Density			Large/High Density
Level of Social Differentiation	Egalitarian			Caste/Class

(a)

SERVICE'S TYPOLOGY	FRIED'S TYPOLOGY
States	States
Chiefdoms	Stratified Societies
Tribes	Ranked Societies
Bands	Egalitarian Societies

(b)

Figure 10.6 (a) Steward's levels of sociocultural and economic integration as bands, tribes, chiefdoms, and states. *After Ferraro (1992).* (b) Typologies based upon Steward's level of sociocultural integration. *After Bogucki (1999).*

Cultural types, therefore, must be conceived as constellations of core features which arise out of environmental adaptations and which represent similar levels of integration. . . . Cultural diffusion, of course, always operates, but in view of the seeming importance of ecological adaptations its role in explaining culture has been greatly overestimated. The extent to which the large variety of world cultures can be sytematized in categories of types and explained through cross-cultural regularities of developmental process is purely an empirical matter. Hunches arising out of comparative studies suggest that there are many regularities which can be formulated in terms of similar levels and similar adaptations (Steward 1955: 42).[39]

CULTURAL ECOLOGY AND ECOLOGICAL ANTHROPOLOGY

Steward's cultural ecology inspired a number of studies. Among the more notable are Louise Sweet's (1965, 1970) study of Bedouin camel pastoralism, Sahlins's (1958) analysis of the relationship between island topography, resource patterns, and social and political evolution in Polynesia, and Netting's (1968) study of Kofyar farming in central Nigeria.

However, when attempting to **operationalize** the strategy for ethnographic fieldwork, researchers adopting Steward's ecological approach encountered problems such as how to identify the precise constituents of the culture core. Field application was only possible after considerable modifications to Steward's original formulation (Moran 1993: 10).

There were other problems as well. Critics objected to the idea of culture core because it could not address all the complexities of human-environment relationships and they criticized Steward for placing too much emphasis upon culture (Geertz 1963; Moran 1993: 10; Vayda and Rappaport 1968). The superorganic element prevented Steward from treating humans in terms of the same relationships and energy/material flows that link all other organisms within an ecological matrix in an ecosystem (Ellen 1986: 65).

Drawing inspiration from the Eugene Odum's influential book *Fundamentals of Ecology* (1953) and Marston Bates's article "Human Ecology" (1953), some anthropologists moved toward a biological paradigm in which the unit of analysis was the ecosystem (Moran 1993: 8; for an historical overview see Turner et al. 1997). The ecosystem approach seemed more promising because it advocated evolutionary holism in studies of humans in their environment. More-

over, **systems theory** (or General Systems Theory, GST), which became part of this approach, offered a scientific framework for the description and analysis both of the internal dynamics of systems and their development and transformation, as well as a way of assimilating humans into nature (Ellen 1986: 67; Moran 1993: 11).

The most influential (and later most criticized) study which employed the ecosystem approach in anthropology was Roy Rappaport's *Pigs for the Ancestors* (1984 [1968]). This was a groundbreaking analysis of the culture of the Tsembaga Maring highlanders in New Guinea (Moran 1993: 15; for criticisms of the ecosystems approach in anthropology, see Vayda and MacKay 1975 and Winterhalder 1984; for an assessment of Rappaport's work, see Lambeck 2001: 244–276; Messer 2001: 1–38; Stewart and Strathern 2001: 277–290).

MULTILINEAR EVOLUTION

Steward's cultural ecology was the methodology behind his theory of cultural evolution, which he termed **multilinear evolution.** As Steward (1977a: 72) pointed out, "processes may operate cross-culturally only a few times to produce similar structures and . . . many lines of development could be described as 'multilinear evolution.'"

An illustration of this perspective is to be found in Steward's discussion of the rise of the **hydraulic states** in Mesopotamia, Egypt, northern China, northern Peru, and Mesoamerica. Steward drew upon the **irrigation hypothesis** (Figure 10.7) proposed by the political theorist and sinologist Karl Wittfogel (1957) for his theory of state formation (see Sidky 1996: 20–25). As Steward observed,

> Irrigation farming is the major organizing factor of another line of evolution, which covered a considerable span of the early prehistory and history of China, Mesopotamia, Egypt, the north coast of Peru, probably the Indus Valley, and possibly the Valley of Mexico. This line had three stages. In the

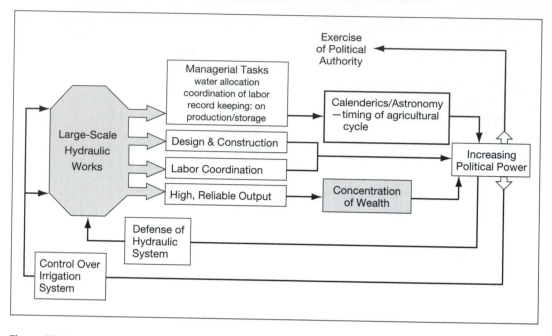

Figure 10.7   Karl Wittfogel's Hydraulic model of state formation.   *After Gross (1992).*

first period primitive groups apparently began to cultivate food plants along moist banks of rivers or in the higher terrain where rainfall was sufficient for crops. They occupied small but permanent villages. The second stage started when people learned to divert the river waters by means of canals to irrigate large tracts of land. Irrigation farming made possible a larger population and freed farmers from the need to spend all their time on basic food production. Part of the new-found time was put into enlarging the system of canals and ditches and part into developing crafts. This period brought the invention of loom weaving, metallurgy, the wheel, mathematics, the calendar, writing, monumental and religious architecture, and extremely fine art products. . . . When irrigation works expanded so that the canals served many communities, a coordinating and managerial control became necessary. This need was met by a ruling class or a bureaucracy whose authority had mainly religious sanctions, for men looked to the gods for the rainfall on which their agriculture depended. Centralization of authority over a large territory marked the emergence of the states. . . . That state developed in these irrigation centers by

no means signifies that all states originated in this way. Many different lines of cultural evolution could have led from kinship groups to multi-community states. For example, feudal Europe and Japan developed small states very different from the theocratic irrigation states. . . . The irrigation state reached its florescence in Mesopotamia between 3000 to 400 B.C., in Egypt a little later, in China about 1500 or 2000 B.C., in northern Peru between 500 B.C. and 500 A.D., in the Valley of Mexico a little later than in Peru. Then, in each case, a third stage of expansion followed. When the theocratic states had reached the limits of available water and production leveled off, they began to raid and conquer their neighbors to exact tribute. The states grew into empires. The empire was not only larger than the state but differed qualitatively in the ways it regimented and controlled its large and diversified population. Laws were codified; a bureaucracy was developed; a powerful military establishment, rather than a priesthood, was made the basis of authority. The militaristic empires began with the Sumerian Dynasty in Mesopotamia, the pyramid-building Early Dynasty in Egypt, the Chou periods in China, the Toltec and

Aztec periods in Mexico, and the Tiahuanacan period in the Andes. . . . Since the wealth of these empires was based on forced tribute rather than on increased production, they contained the seeds of their own undoing. Excessive taxation, regimentation of civil life, and imposition of the imperial religious cult over the local ones led the subject peoples eventually to rebel. The great empires were destroyed; the irrigation works were neglected; production declined; the population decreased. A "dark age" ensued. But in each center the process of empire building later began anew, and the cycle repeated. Cyclical conquests succeeded one another in Mesopotamia, Egypt, and China for nearly 2000 years. Peru had gone through at least two cycles and was at the peak of the Inca Empire when the Spaniards came. Mexico also probably had experienced two cycles prior to the Spanish conquest (Steward 1977a: 64–65).[40]

For Steward these cases were prime examples of parallel developments illustrating that "like causes produce like effects" (Figure 10.8). He was careful to point out, however, that not all states evolved as a result of the establishment of large-scale irrigation works.

The hydraulic thesis was a hypothesis to be tested against empirical data. Such testing has shown that in the case of Mesopotamia irrigation systems began as small-scale enterprises and were expanded after state-level polities evolved (see Robert McC Adams 1966; Carneiro 1970, 1987; Haas 1982). Similarly, irrigation works seem not to have been an important causal factor in the emergence of the state in Egypt (Butzer 1976), China (Chang 1986), and Mesoamerica (Robert McC Adams 1966). Steward (1977c: 91–95) himself later called for an empirical revision of the hydraulic hypothesis.

The irrigation hypothesis is no longer favorably endorsed. However, irrigation agriculture as a general factor may have played a significant part in the development of complexity (Sanderson 1999: 79; see Sidky 1996 for an ethnographic case). Moreover, while the evidence does not show large-scale irrigation systems temporally preceding the evolution of state-level

Karl Wittfogel, political theorist and sinologist who first proposed the Hydraulic theory of the rise of the state.

political complexity, Harris (1991: 233–247) has attempted to defend the irrigation hypothesis by suggesting a step-by-step parallel correspondence between scale of irrigation works and scale of political complexity is probably a reasonable one. My own ethnographic study supports this point of view (Sidky 1996).

As for the cases of evolutionary parallelism noted by Steward, the theoretical and epistemological importance of these cannot be overstated. This is because they suggest that sociocultural systems tend to evolve along certain trajectories with greater frequency than others, which implies that regularities exist in sociocultural processes, and therefore a science of culture is feasible (Harris 2001a; Lett 1987). As Sanderson (1999: 69) has pointed out with respect to

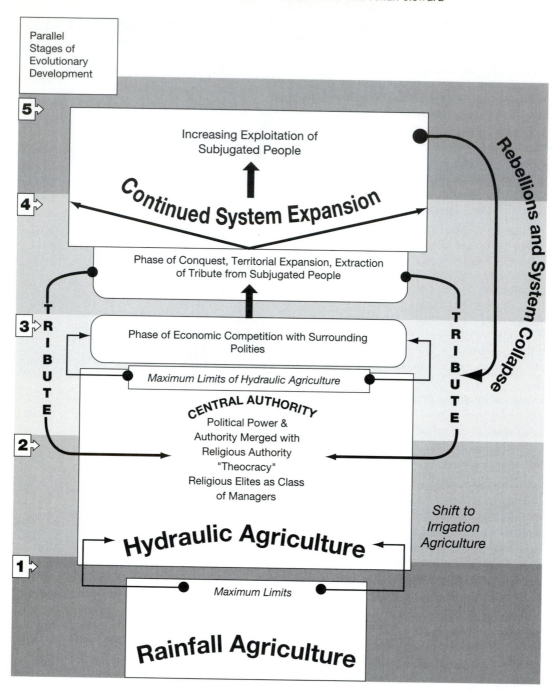

Figure 10.8   Steward's parallel sequence (1–5) of evolutionary development in Southwest Asia, Egypt, China, Peru, and Mesoamerica.

Large-scale irrigation project in China (Beijing, 1972). According to the Hydraulic hypothesis in ancient times the coordination and employment of such a massive labor force towards the construction of large-scale hydraulic works contributed to the evolution of state-level societies (Photo by H. Sidky).

the rise of the state, parallel developments represent "the single most important thing that must be explained by any theory of the rise of the state."

AMBIGUITIES IN STEWARD'S WORK

Steward's writings on evolution contain a number of ambiguities based upon the conflation of methodology and the phenomena being investigated. Steward (1955: 14) wrote, for example, that cultural evolution "may be defined broadly as a quest for cultural regularities or laws." Leslie White (1987d: 124) took issue with this by pointing out that evolution is not a quest for laws, but rather a process that takes place in the external world of "real things and events in terrestrial time and space." The enterprise of searching for cultural laws is not evolution. The searching refers to a methodology by means of which evolutionary processes may be sought. Steward, however, identified multilinear evolution as a methodology:

> Multilinear evolution is essentially a methodology based on the assumption that significant regularities in cultural change occur, and it is concerned with the determination of cultural laws (1955: 18–19).[41]

This is confusing because the analytical procedures based upon the assumption that significant regularities in culture change occur represent the methodology for discovering instances of multilinear evolution, the latter itself is not a methodology (cf. Harris 2001b).

ASSESSMENT

In order to distinguish his own perspective from that of White's and the position of the nineteenth-century evolutionists, Steward (1955: 14–15) maintained that

> first, *unilinear evolution,* the classical nineteenth-century formulation, dealt with particular cultures, placing them on stages of a universal sequence. Second, *universal evolution*—a rather arbitrary label to designate the modern revamping of unilinear evolution—is concerned with culture rather than with cultures. Third, *multilinear evolution,* a somewhat less ambitious approach than the other two, is like unilinear evolution in dealing with developmental sequences, but it is distinctive in searching for parallels of limited occurrence instead of universals.[42]

Steward (1955: 29) went on to extol the virtues of his own perspective:

> For those who are interested in cultural laws, regularities, or formulations, the greatest promise lies in analysis and comparison of limited similarities and parallels, that is multilinear evolution rather than unilinear evolution or universal evolution. Unilinear evolution is discredited, except as it provides limited insights concerning the particular cultures analyzed in detail by the nineteenth-century students of culture. Universal evolution has yet to provide any very new formulations that will explain any and all cultures. The most fruitful course of investigation would seem to be the search for laws which formulate the interrelationships of particular phenomena which may recur cross-culturally but not necessarily universal.[43]

Steward's characterization of his theoretical perspective echoes elements of historical particularism:

> [The] method [of multilinear evolution] is empirical rather than deductive. It is inevitably concerned with historical reconstruction, but it does not expect that historical data can be classified in universal stages. It is interested in particular cultures, but instead of finding local variations and diversity troublesome facts which force the frame of

reference from the particular to the general, it deals only with those limited parallels of form, function, and sequence which have empirical validity. What is lost in universality will be gained in concreteness and specificity. (Steward 1955: 18–19).[44]

White (1987d: 126–127) criticized Steward for vacillating between idiographic interpretations and nomothetic explanations and for being suspended between the particular and the general. White observed that many of the cases that Steward called evolution were actually cases of "like causes producing like effects," which are not necessarily the same thing.

Thus, while White was willing to accept that Steward's parallel hydraulic civilizations as instances of "genuine evolution," he was not so agreeable in other cases. For example, White denied that the parallels between the Mundurucú Indians of the Amazon and the Algonquians of eastern Canada could be called an instance of evolutionary development. The cases were discussed in a classic paper entitled "Tappers and Trappers: Parallel Processes in Acculturation" (1956), which Steward wrote jointly with Robert Murphy (see Steward 1977b: 151–179). This study, which is clearly limited in empirical scope, is illustrative of Steward's cautious approach (Sanderson 1990: 94).

Steward and Murphy attempted to demonstrate how the Mundurucú and the Algonquians, who originally had different forms of social organization, developed similar social patterns as a result of contact with white traders. The Mundurucú became rubber-tappers and the Algonquians fur-trappers. Dependence upon trade with Europeans led to the abandonment of previous modes of life among both groups, with villages and bands breaking down to individual families as the units of production, dependent on the outside economy for clothing and food. Steward considered this as a case of parallel evolutionary development. White disagreed.

White also took issue over Steward's objection to universal laws because they cannot explain the specific features of particular cultures. White (1987d: 127) wrote,

> Of course they cannot! This is precisely the characteristic of a generalization or a law: particulars are subsumed under the universal. The law of gravitation cannot tell us whether the falling body is a rock or a feather, much less whether the one is sandstone or the other a heron plume. And this is precisely why the law of gravitation—like any other scientific law—has value: because it is universal, i.e., it tells us nothing about particulars as particulars.[45]

White noted further that because Steward conflated idiographic and nomothetic perspectives he confused history and evolution:

> Two quite different kinds of processes are involved here. One is a chronological sequence of particular events: the alphabet originated at a certain time and a particular place and subsequently diffused to other regions at specified times. This is an idiographic temporal process which may properly be called history, or historical. The other process is characterized by a temporal sequence of forms: writing developed through three stages—pictographic, rebus, and phonetic. . . . This is a nomothetic temporal process which may properly be called evolution. The historical process is particularizing; the evolutionary process, generalizing (White 1987d: 127).[46]

For Steward (1955: 18–19), however, the answer lay in the particular cases. As he put it,

> Multilinear evolution . . . has no a priori scheme or laws. It recognizes that the cultural traditions of different areas may be wholly or partly distinctive, and it simply poses the question of whether any genuine or meaningful similarities between certain cultures exist and whether these lend themselves to formulation.[47]

Steward also left open the idea that in the final analysis, we may yet find an infinite diversity of cultural forms:

> A taxonomic scheme designed to facilitate the determination of parallels and regularities in terms of concrete characteristics and developmental processes will have to distinguish innumerable culture types, many of which have not as yet been recognized (Steward 1955: 24).[48]

For Harris (2001b: 656) this smacks of the Boasian anthropological program. Harris finds Stewards concept of multilinear evolution fraught with problems. What is most valuable in Steward's method of cultural ecology is not what it can tell us about evolutionary processes, Harris (2001b: 66) points out, but because it shows that the interaction between culture and environment can be studied without lapses into geographical determinism or Boasian particularism. Steward is therefore credited with devising a method of applying White's cultural materialist formulations to concrete ethnographic cases concerning cultural similarities and differences. This contributed to the development of ecological anthropology as well as the scientific paradigm of **cultural materialism** (Murphy 1976: 10–11), which I shall discuss in Chapter 14.

Despite problems and criticisms, the works of Julian Steward and Leslie White are important and have made a significant contribution to the development of American anthropology. Sanderson (1990: 100) has summed it up well:

> In essence, they established a new version of materialist evolutionary analysis that, while unacceptable in many ways, was moving in the right direction. They set social scientists along a path that allowed many of their own errors to be corrected and many new theoretical leads to emerge. Through their influence, it has been possible for social scientists to produce a materialist evolutionary model that is far more empirically defensible and less conceptually vulnerable to criticisms of today's antievolutionists.[49]

What Sanderson is describing is a perspective that has built upon past mistakes, corrected errors, opened up many new directions of research, and has led to the cumulative growth of knowledge. Old ideas and debates reoccur but they are seldom restated in the exactly the same manner. Such an augmentation of our knowledge is a hallmark of science (cf. Ellen 1986: 274).

SOCIOCULTURAL EVOLUTION TODAY

Present-day interpretive and cultural constructionist anthropologists dismiss sociocultural evolutionary theory, suggesting that it is merely the outdated and prejudicial views of nineteenth-century ethnologists passed off as new paradigm. Barrett (1996: 83) describes modern evolutionary theory as follows:

> the theoretical approach which had been attacked so vigorously by the historical particularists and the structural functionalists as inappropriate, misleading, and almost unethical in its assumptions was dusted off and marched back on stage.[50]

Postmodern interpretivists treat the concept of "adaptation" as an expression of "transhistorical human drive for mastery" and an analogue of the nineteenth-century notion of progress, which entails the assumption of betterment/improvement (Sanderson 1990: 5). However, the idea of adaptation and evolution as betterment does not have a place in modern evolutionary thought. Such criticisms are merely the expression of the longstanding hostilities and entrenched antiscience stance by those subscribing to symbolic/interpretive perspectives that dominate the field (cf. Rambo 1991a: 25).

Critics overlook the central epistemological divergences between modern evolutionary theory and the perspectives of Tylor or Morgan. Nineteenth-century evolutionary models were developmental, directional, and teleological in which evolutionary change was construed as immanent, the "unfolding" of latent potentialities inherent is all social systems (Sanderson 1990: 17–18). Moreover, there was no place in nineteenth-century evolutionism for functional, ecological, demographic factors, and specific historical conditions. In contrast, modern sociocultural evolutionary models construe evolutionary processes in terms of the interaction of historical conditions and ecological and demographic factors at work at a particular time within the context of particular constraints, the overall effects of which result in successive sequences of evolutionary development (Sanderson 1990: 17–18). Moreover, directionality is not treated as inherent in evolutionary development, and orderly patterns, rather than being assumed a priori, are identified after they emerge (Sanderson 1990: 17–18).

Sociocultural evolutionary theories have continued to command considerable attention and interest since the days of White and Steward, as evident by the publication of significant evolutionary studies spanning the last four decades or so (Claessen and Skalník 1982; Fried 1967; Hallpike 1988; Haas 1982; Ingold 1986; Johnson and Earle 1987; Sahlins and Service 1960; Sanderson 1990; Service 1962, 1971, 1975). Sociocultural evolution remains a dominant paradigm in archaeology today (Fagan 1999; Trigger 1998).

Why is there so much interest in what is supposedly a defunct point of view that is "inappropriate, misleading, and almost unethical in its assumptions"? The reason is simple. There is an overwhelming body of scientific ethnographic, historical, and archaeological evidence for sociocultural evolution. No valid anthropological perspective can legitimately dismiss this body of evidence and still claim to be anthropology. As Hallpike (1986: 13) has put it, "social evolution is much too important a subject just to disappear because it is unfashionable."

Chapter 11

French Structuralism: The Anthropology of Claude Lévi-Strauss

At the time when White and Steward were assembling elements of a materialist, evolutionary paradigm in the United States, a new nonmaterialist paradigm was in the making through the efforts of the French/Belgian anthropologist Claude Lévi-Strauss (b. 1908). Structural anthropology is a European import. As Kaplan and Manners (1972: 171) have put it, "To talk structuralism . . . is to talk of French structuralism, and to talk of French structuralism is to talk of Lévi-Strauss's theoretical schema." Ortner (1984) calls structuralism the only original social science paradigm to be developed in the twentieth century, although Lévi-Strauss acknowledges his intellectual debt to the ideas of structural linguists such as Ferdianand de Saussure and Roman Jakobsen. Lévi-Strauss himself has been called the greatest French anthropologist (Langness 1993: 140), or he at least enjoyed that status for a period of time.

Structural anthropology is a research strategy that seeks to discover the universal structure of human thought. Although completely idealist, detached from the material world, ahistorical, and epistemologically opaque, the paradigm rapidly acquired a degree of popularity that is hard to fathom. In the 1960s and 1970s, Lévi-Strauss himself attained the stature of a great genius of incomparable erudition, a French savant par excellence (for an overview, see Hénaff 1998; Penner 1998; Werner 1973). The British anthropologist Edmund Leach (1910–1989) wrote of Lévi-Strauss's work, "The outstanding characteristic of his writing is that it is difficult to understand; his sociological theories combine baffling complexity with overwhelming erudition" (Leach 1970: 2). Lévi-Strauss is lauded not only for the originality of his ideas, but also for the novel ways in which he applied them. Finally, he is credited for having introduced something new in anthropology, a new way of looking at old established facts (Murphy 1980: 177).

Lévi-Strauss displays the vexatious tendency of many French intellectuals to dabble in word games, double entendres, "calculated ambiguity" and other obscurantisms (Adams 1998: 359). Weighty and seemingly perspicacious prose can be generated in this way. But we must not forget that "overwhelming erudition" is sometimes merely "clever talk" and clever talk can be

Claude Lévi-Strauss, the originator of structural anthropology.

Today, structuralism has fallen out of favor. Its fall from grace was as rapid as its rise to prominence. The realization that structural anthropology consisted of more clever talk than substance probably accounts for the paradigm's swift decline (for a stout defense of Lévi-Strauss, see Hénaff 1998).

LÉVI-STRAUSS: BECOMING AN ANTHROPOLOGIST

Lévi-Strauss was born in Brussels, Belgium in 1908 (for a chronology, see Hénaff 1998: 245–259). He attended the University of Paris from 1927 to 1932, receiving a degree in law and philosophy. In 1934 he accepted the position of Professor of Sociology at the University of São Paulo, in Brazil, where he remained until 1937. It was at this time that Lévi-Strauss became interested in anthropology after reading Robert Lowie's book *Primitive Society* (1920). However, the most significant events in his shift to anthropology were several trips into the interior. These encounters with "the primitives" had a profound and lasting effect upon his intellectual outlook.

In 1938 Lévi-Strauss obtained financial support from the French government to conduct research in central Brazil, where he worked among the Nambikwara and Tupi-Kawahib. This is the closest he came to actual fieldwork (Leaf 1979: 254). However, he had not mastered the local languages and his fieldwork involved short-duration stays in various places and involved interviews of special informants and the use of interpreters. (Leach 1970: 12). Lévi-Strauss's fieldwork therefore was more like that of Franz Boas, rather than the intensive approach based on Malinowski's model.

Lévi-Strauss first anthropological piece was an article on the social organization of the Bororo, which was published in 1936. This paper brought him to the attention of two eminent anthropologists, Robert Lowie and Alfred Métraux, who would later play a key role in his

mistaken for wisdom, a point clearly demonstrated by the reception of French postmodern obscurantism that reached American anthropological circles in the 1980s.

Structuralism made greater headway in Britain and much earlier, in the 1950s, than it did in the United States. Adams (1998: 360) attributes this to the Fracophile tendencies of British intellectuals, who have always shown receptivity to French influences, and to their ability to read French, in contrast to "functionally monolingual" American anthropologists. It was not until the translation of Lévi-Strauss's major works into English in the mid- to late-1960s that American anthropologists adopted the new perspective. Not surprisingly, structuralism turned out to be highly compatible with mainstream American cultural anthropology where Boasian mentalism was deeply entrenched (cf. Adams 1998: 361).

career as an anthropologist. In 1939 Lévi-Strauss was back in France, where he hoped to write up his ethnographic materials. The outbreak of World War II and the Nazi occupation forced him to leave France. He traveled to New York by way of Martinique and Puerto Rico. Lowie and Métraux, having become aware of Lévi-Strauss's circumstances, managed to secure a teaching post for him at the New School of Social Research in New York, where he taught from 1942 to 1945. From 1946 to 1947 he held the post of French Cultural Attaché in the United States.

In New York, Lévi-Strauss had a chance to interact with some of the leading anthropologists of the day, including Boas, Linton, Benedict, Mead, Kroeber, and Lowie (Moore 1997: 218). He was thus exposed to the Boasian anthropological program. At the New School of Social Research Lévi-Strauss also met the linguist Roman Jakobson, one of the principle thinkers of the Prague School of structural linguistics, whose work had a profound effect in shaping his anthropological thinking. He also met the philosopher Jean-Paul Sartre, founder of existentialism, with whom he would engage in lengthy debates in the years to follow (Bohannan and Glazer 1988: 423; Kuper 1999: 160).

While Lévi-Strauss was in New York, he began writing his major work on kinship, which he presented as his thesis to the Sorbonne in 1948, earning the degree of *Doctoret et Letters*. The work was published in 1949 under the title of *Elementary Structures of Kinship* (1969a). In 1950 Lévi-Strauss was appointed Director of Studies at the *Ecole pratique des hautes études* (Laboratory of Social Anthropology), at the University of Paris, the post once occupied by the famous Marcel Mauss.

Lévi-Strauss's ethnographic travel book, *Tristes Tropiques* (1974), appeared in 1955 and the first volume of *Structural Anthropology* (1967) was published in 1958. By this time Lévi-Strauss had been propelled to the level of intellectual superstar in France. In 1959 he was appointed to the prestigious post of Chair of Social Anthropology at the Collège de France, where he taught until 1982.

In addition to over a hundred important articles, some of the major works Lévi-Strauss produced during his tenure at the Collège de France include *Totemism* (1963), *The Savage Mind* (1966), *The Raw and the Cooked* (1969b), *From Honey to Ashes* (1973), *The Origins of Table Manners* (1978), *The Naked Man* (1981), and *Anthropology and Myth, Lectures 1951–1982* (1987). He continued to publish after his retirement, producing *View from Afar* (1985), *The Jealous Potter* (1988), and a book of photos taken during his fieldwork, *Saudades do Brasil: A Photographic Memoir* (1995). As of this writing, Lévi-Strauss remains active in anthropological research.

In American anthropology, Lévi-Strauss's structuralism made its greatest impact upon symbolic and interpretive approaches (McGee and Warms 2000: 332). Structuralism, however, had a greater influence upon British social anthropology, already influenced by the social theories of French thinkers such as Durkheim and Mauss. The leading British structuralists, or those heavily influenced by this approach, included Edmund Leach, Rodney Needham, and Mary Douglas (Kuper 1999: 161).

STRUCTURAL ANTHROPOLOGY

Structural anthropology is concerned with the search for subconscious grammar of culture, or "deep structures" embedded in the human mind. These are said to be invariant pan-human thought processes underlying all cultural forms. Although Lévi-Strauss owes an intellectual debt to predecessors such as Émile Durkheim and Marcel Mauss, his approach to the analysis of cultural forms, which focuses upon the elemental structure of human thought, is an innovative idea of his own.

This departure enabled Lévi-Strauss to resolve the long-standing enigma posed by Durkheimian sociology, namely the idea of collective conscience as something external and coercive upon members of society. Lévi-Strauss addressed this by implanting "collective conscience" firmly in the human unconscious. As Barrett (1984: 117) has put it,

> For well over half a century Durkheim tortured anthropologists and sociologists with an enigmatic half-truth: the external, coercive collective conscience. Lévi-Strauss pulled it down from the clouds and placed it firmly in the unconscious, an entity about which Durkheim was ignorant.[1]

For Lévi-Strauss culture is the symbolic expression of the subconscious properties of the human mind. Edmund Leach, who has been called Lévi-Strauss's public relations agent in the English-speaking world (Barrett 1996: 147), outlines the basic premises of structural anthropology his book, *Claude Lévi-Strauss* (1970):

> The general argument runs something like this. What we know about the external world we apprehend through our senses. The phenomena we perceive have the characteristics we attribute to them because of the way our senses operate and the way the human brain is designed to order and interpret the stimuli which are fed into it. One very important feature of this ordering process is that we cut up the continua of space and time with which we are surrounded into segments, so that we are predisposed to think of the environment as consisting of vast numbers of separate things belonging to named classes, and to think of the passage of time as consisting of sequences of separate events. Correspondingly, when, as men, we construct artificial things (artifacts of all kinds), or devise ceremonials, or write histories of the past, we imitate our apprehension of nature: the products of our culture are segmented and ordered in the same way as we suppose the products of nature to be segmented and ordered (Leach 1970: 15–16).[2]

As Lévi-Strauss himself put it,

> If, as we believe to be the case, the unconscious activity of the mind consists in imposing forms upon content, and if these forms are fundamentally the same for all minds—ancient and modern, primitive and civilized (as the study of symbolic function, expressed in language, so strikingly indicates)—it is necessary and sufficient to grasp the unconscious structure underlying each institution and each custom, in order to obtain a principle of interpretation valid for other institutions and other customs, provided of course that that analysis is carried far enough (Lévi-Strauss 1967: 21–22).[3]

The idea that the human mind provides the categories of thought is central to the rationalist perspective first espoused by René Descartes, as opposed to the empiricist view that knowledge derives from experience, a position associated with David Hume. Lévi-Strauss's structuralism has been described as a form of ultra-rationalism (Kaplan and Manners 1972: 180).

In some respects, Lévi-Strauss's structural principles of thought bear a resemblance to the Cartesian transformational-generative grammar model of linguistics developed by Noam Chomsky in the United States (for an overview, see Haley and Lunsford 1994; Maher and Groves 1997). Chomsky (1966, 1972) posits that underneath the surface structure of language there exists a "deep structure," a finite set of organizing principles based on a linguistic blueprint, or **universal grammar,** genetically programmed into the human brain. One can uncover these "deep structures" through the analysis of individual languages. Chomsky believes that the surface structure of language, what linguists have traditionally focused upon, gives the impression of greater diversity between languages than really exists. At the deeper level, all languages share a finite set of principles.

Chomsky's ideas imply that culture as well must be based on innate structural principles. However, the relationship between the work of Chomsky and that of Lévi-Strauss is general in nature. In other words, Chomsky leads us somewhere close to the general view espoused by Lévi-Strauss but not exactly to it (cf. Malefijt 1974: 335). Chomsky's perspective has been instrumental in legitimizing cognitive and mentalist approaches, including structuralism, and the view that culture is based upon codes and rules for generating behavior, rather than engendering anthropological structuralism (Harris 2001a: 282).

THE NATURE OF STRUCTURAL EXPLANATIONS

The task of structural anthropology is to search for the unconscious structural principle at the basis of cultural institutions and customs. Lévi-Strauss was thus searching for unity underneath the apparent surface diversity of cultures, or attempted to solve the longstanding anthropological problem of reconciling cultural diversity and the underlying sameness of culture (Barrett 1984: 123). As such, Lévi-Strauss was aiming to construct a new epistemological foundation for anthropology, one which bypassed the chaotic surface variation of the empirical world in order to discover underlying universal logical struc-

tures for all cultures (Barrett 1984: 124). For Lévi-Strauss developing parsimonious understanding of sociocultural phenomena lies in these underlying structures of thought.

Lévi-Strauss ejected the conventional, positivistic science from his paradigm (Barrett 1996: 149). The goal of structural anthropology, as he put it, is "to grasp, beyond the conscious and always shifting images which men hold, the complete range of unconscious possibilities" (Lévi-Strauss 1967: 23). The argument is that surface diversity can be reduced to the underlying unity of the human mind that operates in the same way everywhere. The rules are logical.

The human mind itself, which in Lévi-Strauss's view is like a computer, is structured and operates on the principle of binary oppositions (up/down, right/left, good/evil, light/dark, etc., Figure 11.1). The binary nature of human thought is expressed in all cultural forms, but through a sequence of **transformations** and **inversions** that hide and mask it (Barrett 1984: 120). All sociocultural phenomena everywhere

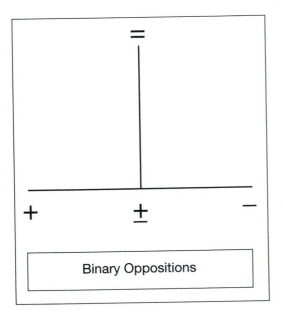

Figure 11.1 The binary operation of human cognition. *After Lévi-Strauss (1967).*

are constrained and shaped by the structural operations of the human mind. Cultural phenomena such as myths, totemism, kinship systems, incest taboos, and cuisine are all examples of **objectified thought** (i.e., the tangible expression of underlying principles). What structural anthropologists want to find, therefore, is how humans think, not what they think. "The final aim of anthropology," Lévi-Strauss writes (1969b: 13), "is to contribute to a better knowledge of objectified thought and its mechanisms."

Lévi-Strauss (1969b: 13) uses the metaphor of code and maintains that myths, kinship systems, totemic systems, and even cuisine, which are all expressions of the underlying structure of human thought, can be decoded to reveal the deeper hidden message underneath the surface manifestations. These coded messages are made up of pieces of sensory data that are familiar, such as sun, moon, animals, plants, which are derived from the realm of experience. These bits of data are then assembled according to logical rules underlying the operation of human thought (Murphy 1980: 190). Once put together these sensory data assume new meaning in the same way that words acquire meaning on the basis of their place in a sentence, or how the colors red, yellow, and green acquire a particular meaning by their arrangement in the traffic light (Honigmann 1976: 324).

Lévi-Strauss seeks relationships of contrast and opposition, such as between fire and water, sun and moon, eaglehawk and crow, the raw and the cooked (both foods, but different in how they are prepared), and other similar double pairs of mutually exclusive, but complementary, symbols (Honigmann 1976: 324). These are then linked by Lévi-Strauss to the universal process of human thought.

Leach uses the example of the traffic lights to demonstrate the binary principle behind human thought:

> With traffic lights on both railways and roads, green means go and red means stop. For many situations this is sufficient. However, if we want to devise a further signal with an intermediate mean-
>
> ing—*about to stop/about to go*—we choose the color yellow. We do this because, in the spectrum, it lies midway between green and red. . . . In this example the ordering of the colors green-yellow-red is the same as the ordering instructions go-caution-stop; the color system and the signal system have the same "structure," one is a transformation of the other (Leach 1970: 17).[4]

Leach explains how this transformation occurs:

> The color spectrum exists in nature as a continuum. The brain interprets this continuum as if it consisted of discontinuous segments. The brain searches for an appropriate representation of a binary opposition plus/minus and selects green and red as a binary pair. Having set up this polar opposition, the human brain is dissatisfied with the resulting discontinuity and searches for an intermediate position: not plus/not minus. It then goes back to the original natural continuum and chooses yellow as the intermediate signal because the brain is able to perceive yellow as a discontinuous intermediate segment lying between green and red. Thus the final cultural product—the three-color traffic light—is a simplified imitation of a phenomenon of nature—the color spectrum—as apprehended by the human brain (Leach 1970: 17–18).[5]

This is a wonderfully neat example from Euro-American culture with which to illustrate the binary properties of the human mind and the rational behind Lévi-Strauss's paradigm. Because it pertains to Euro-American culture, and not to the culture of some remote and unfamiliar tribe, such as the Bororo, it offers a useful case with which to test the reliability of the structuralist position. If Leach is correct, if the color of traffic lights is a true example of the human mind breaking a continuum into binary opposites, then red and green must always mean stop or go and no color other than yellow can mean caution (Harris 2001a: 198).

Unfortunately, the well-documented history of the development of traffic signals, which goes back to early nineteenth-century England, does not support the structuralist claim. The choice of colors was dictated not by an unconscious binary principle of human thought but evolved in the context of a number of technological developments. Initially blue was ubiquitously used to denote danger/stop. By 1839 Liverpool and Manchester railways used red and blue flags to signal stop. Black was also used to indicate stop. At night a green light was used to indicate caution.

In his study of the development of railway and highway traffic signals, Fredrick Gamst (1980: 383) has demonstrated that red has several meanings and, moreover,

> other colors [aside from red] also mean "stop." And, most important of all, even if red were (for whatever reason) exclusively the stop color, the interrelations found between red ("stop") and other colors and indications in railway signals are not those cognitively patterned after nature![6]

Gamst's study also shows that "color signal categories are not a closed cognitive domain. They relate functionally to other domains of culture as they change through time." Violet lights were also used to indicate caution. It was not until after the turn of the century that yellow was adopted for this purpose. Blue still means caution under all cases in the British railway system. A similar use of different colors is the case with automobile traffic signals. Flashing blue lights, not red, are used on emergency vehicles in the United States to indicate danger and emergencies.

Leach's traffic light example, which pertains to a phenomenon known to most Euro-Americans, clearly reveals the problems with some of Lévi-Strauss's main assumptions. In Lévi-Strauss's own work many of these difficulties remain hidden because the reader is seldom familiar with the cultures from which examples are taken. It therefore becomes difficult to determine whether the binary oppositions discussed are really present in the ethnographic materials or whether they are the inventions of the anthropologist himself.

WHAT IS THE STRUCTURALIST'S STRUCTURE?

The structures that interest Lévi-Strauss lies deep within the human psyche, hidden by "inaccurate conscious models lying across the path which leads to it" (Lévi-Strauss 1967: 274). Leach (1970: 21–22) explains:

> It is important to understand just what is being proposed. In a superficial sense the products of culture are enormously varied, and when an anthropologist sets out to compare, let us say, the culture of Australian Aborigines with that of the Eskimo or the English he is first of all impressed by the difference. Yet since all cultures are the product of human brains, there must be, somewhere beneath the surface, features common to all.[7]

These underlying commonalties are the structure of the structuralists. Structure refers to this unconscious reality, the structure of the human mind or the logical ordering that takes place in the mind. Barrett (1984: 123) calls it neurological reductionism—another version of the psychic unity of humankind. However, it is not neurological structure of the brain that Lévi-Strauss seeks, but the structure of human cognition (Lett 1987: 100).

Lévi-Strauss models his perspective on structural linguistics of the **Prague School of Linguistics** associated with Nikolai Troubetzkoy (1890–1938) and Roman Jakobson (1896–1982). This model is based on the observation that most native speakers of a language are not aware of the phonological and grammatical rules of speech they use. However, they are able to communicate effectively. The rules in question exist at an unconscious level. When a linguist studies an unknown language his/her job is to identify the hidden grammatical and phonological rules that exist at the unconscious level, far removed from the surface manifestation of linguistic expressions (Kaplan and Manners 1972: 171). Identification of the rules enables the explanation of language.

Most linguists acknowledge that languages vary in their basic structural principles and do not make it their task to seek commonalties. Some, however, are concerned with the discovery of the universal structural principles that underlie all languages. These linguists have provided Lévi-Strauss with the model for his anthropological approach (Kaplan and Manners 1972: 171).

Another idea adopted from the Prague School by Lévi-Strauss is that words are constructed on the basis of binary oppositions between units of sound, or phonemes, rather than being aggregates of sounds. On the basis of this, Lévi-Strauss argued that the human mind operates according to the principles of binary oppositions, an idea anticipated by Radcliffe-Brown, as noted in Chapter 9.

Lévi-Strauss describes the basic operations he has adopted from structural linguistics.

> First, structural linguistics shifts from the study of *conscious* linguistic phenomena to the study of their *unconscious* infrastructures; second, it does not treat terms as independent entities, taking instead as its basis of analysis the relations between terms; third, it introduces the concept of *system* . . . finally, structural linguistics aims at discovering *general laws* (Lévi-Strauss 1967: 31).[8]

LÉVI-STRAUSS AND THE INCEST TABOO

The **incest taboo** is among the cross-cultural universals and has long attracted the attention of anthropologists and psychologists. This taboo refers to rules that culturally prohibit sexual activity with particular categories of relatives. Rules against incest pertain to sexual relations with certain categories of kin, while marriage rules specify the kind of kin considered to be eligible/ineligible as marriage partners. The two rules often do coincide in that individuals with whom one cannot have sexual relations are also ineligible as spouses, but they may not necessarily do so (Fox 1967a: 54–55).

What has fascinated anthropologists is that people everywhere have a fear of incest. The following myth from among the Mehinaku of Central Brazil, which tells of a boy named Araukuni who had sexual intercourse with and impregnated his own sister, captures the human abhorrence of incest:

> Oh, the mother was angry. She struck Araukuni and beat him with a club. She cut down his hammock and burned it. She burned his bow, his arm bands and his belt. All of these she burned. She would not make bread for him. She would not give him manioc porridge or fish stew. All she would do was beat him, beat him, beat him. All the time she beat him. . . . Araukuni grew sad. Araukuni went off into the forest. In his village, Araukuni's family and friends said it was so much better that he had gone. "Good riddance," said his father. "He had sex with his sister" (Gregor 1985: 180, in Gross 1992: 340).[9]

Severe punishments are often meted out for those who violate the incest taboo. The penalty among the Ashanti of Africa was death, in Feudal Japan violators were banished, in the United States it is often imprisonment along with psychiatric treatment (Gross 1992: 340).

The anthropologist Mary Douglas, whose work has been highly influenced by the ideas of Lévi-Strauss, has made an observation about the structure of human thought that may help clarify the revulsion evoked by the violation of the incest taboo. As she points out, in the way human thought is structured there are things that should be joined and things that should be separate. "Separating that which should be joined or joining that which should be separate" evokes a sense of defilement of danger and pollution (Douglas 1966: 113).

There appears to be no known culture today that permits sexual relations within the "nuclear family," or **nuclear incest,** that is, matings between mother-son, father-daughter, and brother-sister. Exceptions to this in the form of brother-sister marriages occurred among members of the royal lineages in Inca Peru and Ptole-

Cleopatra, Queen of Egypt, was the offspring of 11 generations of sister-brother marriages.

maic Egypt (Bixler 1982) and in the royal lineage in ancient Hawaii. In the case of the Incas and Pharaohs, who were considered to be divine beings, and Hawaiian rulers, who were imbued with **mana,** brother-sister marriages may have served as a means of safeguarding the divinity of the royal lineage as well as keeping political and economic power concentrated. However, brother-sister marriages also occurred and seemed to be preferred among commoners in Roman Egypt (Hopkins 1980: 304; Middleton 1962); many of these marriages involved half-siblings, but some involved full siblings as well.

Aside from the cases noted previously, the incest taboo seems to be a cross-cultural universal, although following different genealogical trajec-tories, and that universality has challenged anthropologists to provide explanations. Lévi-Strauss has offered a structural explanation for the origins of the incest taboo.

In his book *The Elementary Structures of Kinship* (1969a), Lévi-Strauss applies his method to the analysis of kinship. Here he draws upon Marcel Mauss's (1872–1950) *The Gift: The Form and Reason for Exchange in Archaic Societies* (2000 [1924]). Mauss was interested in the nature of reciprocal social exchange in primitive societies, its rules and its significance. Exchange occurs in the context of obligations between groups to give, receive, and reciprocate. Mauss noted that reciprocal exchange functioned to establish and ratify alliances between groups. The gift symbolizes the alliance made possible through its exchange and its economic value, but as a symbol of the alliance the gift is more important for society than its particular economic value.

Mauss attempted to reduce all such exchanges to their "elementary structure," which he argued was an underlying principle of reciprocity ingrained in the human mind. People engage in reciprocal gift giving, not because of economic motives, but in order to satisfy a powerfully ingrained human need for giving, receiving, and repaying (Harris 2001b: 487). There is, in other words, a universal psychological need for gift giving/receiving. All forms of gift giving found cross-culturally, Mauss observed, involve a "circulation of objects side by side with the circulation of persons and rights" (in Harris 2001b: 486–487). The ingrained logic of reciprocity therefore extends not just to economic transactions, according to Mauss, but applies as well to other aspects of human life, such as kinship and social organization.

Lévi-Strauss employs Mauss's principle of reciprocity and the cycle of reciprocal exchange of valuables to the phenomenon of the incest taboo in an attempt to uncover its underlying mental structure. The question Lévi-Strauss is really attempting to answer, as Fox (1967b: 161) reminds us, is, What distinguishes humans from proto-humans and animals? What separates humans from Nature and yet leaves them a part of Nature? In *The Elementary Structures of Kinship,* Lévi-Strauss shows how the incest taboo and marriage rules represent the transition from nature to culture, from promiscuous matings to cultural order of **exogamy.** For Lévi-Strauss, the incest taboo marks the changeover of humans from protohumanity. According to this view, only when the distinction between Self and Other is made, a distinction upon which the incest taboo is predicated, does symbolic communication, and hence culture itself, begin (Hénaff 1998: 50; Malefijt 1974: 327).

As Lévi-Strauss sees it, the incest taboo transforms promiscuous sexual intercourse presumably found in nature into an ordered system of marriage found in culture. Marriage ties, established and perpetuated through the exchange of gifts, mediate between people who are a part of the realm of nature but who have been changed into kinsmen through marriage, an aspect of culture. The incest taboo thus introduces an alteration in human relations by adding to social relationships based entirely on **consanguinity,** or "blood ties," those relationships based upon marriage or **affinity.**

The importance of the incest taboo hinges upon the distinction it entails between the contrasting categories of Us/Them and Self/Other. As Lévi-Strauss puts it, "starting from the moment that I prohibited the use of a woman to myself, who thus becomes available for another man, there is somewhere, a man who renounces a woman who then becomes disposable for me" (Lévi-Strauss 1969a: 65). Thus, for Lévi-Strauss, the taboo functions to ensure the perpetual reciprocal exchange of women. The principle of reciprocity bridges or mediates the gap between the Us/Them, or Self/Other contrasts.

The incest taboo, according to Lévi-Strauss, obligates men to give their sisters and daughters to other men in marriage. There are diverse ways in which such exchange takes place, all of them based upon the same principles. One form occurs directly in societies organized into moieties (duel divisions based on descent), which Lévi-Strauss calls **restricted exchange.** Here a man from group A takes a wife from group B, and a man from B marries a woman from group A. The exchange can take place among men of the same generation, or it can be completed in the next generation. In another form, an indirect exchange, called **generalized exchange,** a man from group A marries a woman from group B, but men of B do not take a wife from A, but from group C. Men of group C always marry women from group A.

Why do people take part in such an exchange? Reciprocity, according to Lévi-Strauss, functions to enhance social solidarity, it confers an advantage to the group exercising control over the distribution of females, and it offers the benefits of making available a larger pool of women from which mates may be selected (Lévi-Strauss 1969a: 55–56). All systems of kinship and marriage are founded upon the Mine/Yours distinction and are treated as variant systems of women exchange (Harris 2001b: 490).

We may summarize Lévi-Strauss's view on the incest taboo as follows. The most fundamental symbolic exchange, which is the prototype for all other exchanges, is the exchange of women (Leach 1970: 45). The incest taboo, which implies the capacity to distinguish between categories of women (wife, sister, daughter), enforces an ordered or structured exchange of women between groups and also serves as the foundation of marriage rules and kinship systems. Thus mating among humans is ordered/regulated, in contrast to random and promiscuous mating presumed to exist in the animal world. The incest taboo also highlights the dichotomy between culture and nature (Malefijt 1974: 327).

As Lévi-Strauss sees it, the incest taboo is a product of the structure of the human thought process that operates upon the principle of binary oppositions and the basal dialectic between Self and Other, Us and Them, Culture and Nature. In the final analysis, for Lévi-Strauss, the incest taboo did not arise because it confers any economic or survival benefits per se, although it may achieve these effects, but rather because it is rooted in "certain fundamental structures of the human mind" (Lévi-Strauss 1969a: 108).

Other anthropologists have attempted to provide different explanations for the incest taboo that encompass causal mechanisms other than the structure of human thought. Two varieties of explanations have been forwarded: those focusing upon genetic reasons and psychological aversions, and those based on the socioeconomic, demographic, political, and ecological advantages conferred by marriages outside the nuclear family. A brief review of some of these explanations will help highlight the differences

between Lévi-Strauss's structural paradigm and other perspectives in cultural anthropology.

The anthropologist Edward Westermarck (one of Malinowski's mentors) suggested that individuals raised together have a natural aversion toward sexual interactions and the incest taboo was therefore a manifestation of this aversion (Westermarck 1894). This phenomenon has been referred to as the **Westermarck effect.** Studies of children brought up together in Israeli *kibbutzim* (a *kibbutz* is a village commune) appear to support this view; that is, children raised in these communities tend not to marry one another (Shepher 1983; Talmon 1964; but see Hartung 1985).

However, such correlations may be deceptive because what has been overlooked is that Kibbutz youth sign up for compulsory service with the Israeli army in their late teens, around the time they reach the age of marriage, and go elsewhere and come into contact with many other potential mates. Thus the fact that their marriage partners are not from among those with whom they grew up is hardly surprising (Leavitt 1990). Also, cases of adolescent heterosexual relations have been reported in these communes, which run counter to Westermarck's idea (Kaffman 1977; Leavitt 1990). Finally, the evidence from Roman Egypt, which suggests that the commoners preferred brother-sister marriages, further disconfirms the **natural aversion theory** (Leavitt 1990; Wolf 1993).

Other evidence cited in support of the natural aversion theory comes from Taiwan, where very young girls from poor families are adopted by other families as future wives and are raised with the boys to whom they will be married. This has been referred to as the "adopt-a-daughter-in-law-marry-a-sister" custom. Marriages resulting from this arrangement, which involves couples raised together as children, are said to be very unfulfilling, hence confirming Westermarck's position (Wolf 1966, 1970, 1995). However, an alternate explanation may be that such marriages are unsatisfactory because the customary exchange of wealth between the families of the bride and groom to help the new couple are minimal or absent altogether. Given this economic factor, it is difficult to attribute unsatisfactory marriages to the Westermarck effect (Harris 1997: 255).

Finally, there is the evidence that the incest taboo is violated with considerable frequency. In North American it is estimated that 10 to 14% of children under 18 years of age have been involved in some form of incestuous relationship, which cannot be accounted for by Westermarck's hypothesis (Whelehan 1985: 678).

Another problematic element of Westermarck's hypothesis, as Staski and Marks (1992: 646) have observed, is that if natural aversion exists, then why are there specific cultural rules that prohibit something that humans do not want to do in the first place? A rule banning something no one wants to do is meaningless and superfluous. There are cultural rules that forbid homicide because there are some people who want to commit murder, and so there are regulations to prevent them from doing so. Thus it is no less reasonable to assume that rules against incest are meant to prevent people from committing incest because they might want to commit incest, not because they have an innate biological/psychological tendency not to do so (Staski and Marks 1992: 646; White 1949: 309).

Sigmund Freud (1856–1939) proposed a psychological explanation, pointing out that the fear expressed over the idea of incest is an unconscious defense against the powerful erotic desires experienced by sons towards their mothers. This was the basis of what Freud called the **Oedipus complex,** after *Oedipus Rex,* the Greek drama about King Oedipus who unwittingly slew his own father and married his own mother (Freud 1920). So great was the shame of this deed that upon realizing what he had done, Oedipus blinded himself.

Freud suggested that the incest taboo is a reaction to powerful incestuous desires. As such, this explanation is incompatible with Lévi-Strauss's position, which attempts to account for the taboo in terms of an inherent psychological need for giving and receiving gifts and the importance of the social ties created in the process of men exchanging women. However, like Lévi-Strauss, Freud also considers the adoption of the incest taboo and exogamous marriage rules as the key process in the emergence of humankind, although for different reasons (Morris 1988: 267).

Freud's explanation, which hinges upon the Oedipus complex, fails to account for why there is a taboo against brother-sister matings. Also, in documented cases, it is father-daughter incest that occurs with greatest frequency, with sibling incest ranging from one third to less than half that of father-daughter cases, while mother-son incest is the most infrequent (Barnouw 1985: 215; Willner 1983: 139–140). Finally, there is the fact that the Oedipus complex is a culture-bound phenomenon, as Malinowski pointed out with respect to the Trobrianders.

Inbreeding theories posit that marriages among closely related individuals result in deleterious effects because of the presence of harmful recessive genes, which have a greater frequency of being expressed as a result of matings between individuals that carry them. It may be assumed that ancient peoples who adopted cultural practices forbidding incestuous marriages recognized the harmful nature of such close marriages. The problem here is that if ancient peoples suffered high mortality rates from a variety of causes it would have been difficult for them to discern between individuals who died from genetically related and genetically unrelated causes (Gross 1992: 343).

However, it is possible that the taboo persisted because it conferred an adaptive advantage. Matings that would be construed as incestuous by humans are rare among non-human primates closely related to us, which suggests that the roots of incest avoidance go back into our biological history and may have an evolutionary basis (Bischof 1975; Parker 1976; Pusey 1980). This is because incestuous marriages decreased a population's genetic variability, making it susceptible to disease and higher mortality rates. Groups that practiced the incest taboo would have been favored by natural selection, versus those that did not, by having more children that survived to a reproductive age. Such groups would have higher genetic diversity, fewer harmful recessive alleles, better health, and lower mortality rates (Campbell 1979: 74). Reproductive success may account for the taboo, or at least for its persistence (Ferraro 1992: 199). If correct, this explanation, although not necessarily incompatible with Lévi-Strauss's position, renders it superfluous.

Inbreeding explanations are based upon the assumption that incest results in a high incidence of deformities or congenital diseases. However, in small foraging bands infants with deformities are eliminated and consequently close marriages will actually reduce the group's harmful genetic load after a few generations (Livingston 1982). Also, the widespread practice of preferential cousin marriages around the world, which also entails high genetic risks, runs counter to the inbreeding theory that the incest taboo arose as a response to the harmful effects of close matings (Bittles et al. 1991; Harris 1997: 256).

Malinowski (1927) provided a functional, sociological explanation for the incest taboo, noting that marriages between parents and children and between siblings would create intense jealousies and sexual rivalries and disrupt parental authority that would hinder domestic groups from functioning. Such matings would also produce **role ambiguity.** For example, in the case of a mother-son mating, the offspring's father is also his half-brother and its mother is also its grandmother. Given that the parental and sibling roles entail distinct rights, duties, and expectations the results would be confusion within the domestic group. Malinowski's explanation focuses on group dynamics and functional requisites necessary for the smooth operation of domestic units, an approach that is also at variance with to Lévi-Strauss's structural explanation.

The weakness of Malinowski's hypothesis is that brother-sister marriages do not necessarily have to be disruptive, as evidence from Roman Egypt suggests. Moreover, because human role relationships are very flexible, rules could have been devised to avoid the disruptions that such marriage arrangements could create (Ember and Ember 1990: 336: Gross 1992: 344).

Another explanation focuses on the positive economic, demographic, and ecological advantages of incest avoidance and marriages outside the domestic group (Leavitt 1989). This perspective is called the **expanding alliance/cooperation hypothesis.** Tylor noted the importance of rules that led to marriages outside of the group:

> Exogamy, enabling a growing tribe to keep itself compact by constant unions between its spreading clans, enables it to overmatch any number of small, intermarrying groups, isolated and helpless. Again and again in the world's history, savage tribes must have had plainly before their minds the simple practical alternative between marrying out and being killed out (Tylor 1889: 267).

The incest taboo promotes exogamy by making it necessary for members of the domestic group to find marriage partners from among other groups. This leads to the establishment of a network of marriage alliances between separate domestic groups, which would contribute to better group cooperation and enhance survival. Leslie White (1949: 303–329) developed Tylor's view, noting that incest rules facilitated group cooperation, provided security against enemies, and a buffer against scarcity. In this respect, the expanding alliance/cooperation hypothesis is compatible with Lévi-Strauss's perspective, but there are some points of variance.

For a foraging band of 25 to 35 individuals exogamy means the establishment of a wide network of kin providing flexibility for the movement of personnel between bands, access to other territories, reciprocal exchange of goods and access to a large pool of potential marriage partners. Because the sort of flexibility achieved through the establishment of networks of alliances is an essential part of their adaptive strategy, it is difficult for foraging bands to exist as closed, self-sufficient units. Bands practicing **endogamy** would lack social and geographical flexibility, they would not have economic relations with other groups, and they would be denied access to marriage partners beyond their own membership. For such isolated endogamous bands, localized resource failures, a string of male births, or the deaths of several females of reproductive age could mean disaster. Thus given the small size of such groups the advantages of exogamy as a means of expanding social alliances and fostering reciprocal relationships are considerable (Harris 1997: 256).

For village level societies, exogamy offers similar advantages, by enhancing the overall productive and reproductive powers of the intermarrying groups, promoting trade, integrating different groups, and increasing the size of the labor force that can be called up for various tasks and communal projects (Harris 1997: 257). Also, where warfare is a threat, the ability to muster up allies contributes to group survival (Harris 1997: 257). Oscar Lewis's (1955) study of the village of Rani Khera in the Delhi District, Northern India indicated that 226 women living in the village had come from 200 different villages, and almost as many women from that village had married out (Lewis 1955: 163). Through marriage exchanges, Rani Khera was connected to hundreds of other communities in that part of India. Thus, the practice of marrying out based on the motive to avoid incest operates to integrate Indian society (Ferraro 1992: 200).

Where the expanding alliances explanation runs counter to Lévi-Strauss's formulation is that he posits that early humans lived in isolated endogamous, sexually promiscuous self-sufficient bands and that the incest taboo and the rules of exogamy evolved jointly marking the transition from protohumanity to humanity. However, such groups could have adopted the marriage rule of exogamy while still practicing incestuous sexual relationships. The incest taboo and exogamy do not necessarily have to coincide, as noted previously.

There is also the evidence from among nonhuman primates that indicates that incest avoidance is common in the animal world (Bischof 1975; Parker 1976; Pusey 1980). Hence any protohuman group, such as Lévi-Strauss has in mind, would not have been sexually promiscuous. Finally, the incentives for the establishment of marriage alliances can be adequately explained in terms of the economic, demographic, social, and political advantages of such arrangements, without reference to structures in the mind.

LÉVI-STRAUSS AND THE AVUNCULATE

To demonstrate the applications of structural analysis in elucidating cultural phenomena, Lévi-Strauss has also tackled the "mother's brother and sister's son" problem in kinship studies, which Radcliffe-Brown tackled years earlier in his article "The Mother's Brother in South Africa" (1924; see 1952a). Lévi-Strauss begins with Radcliffe-Brown's paper on the maternal uncle which he describes as "the first attempt to grasp and analyze the modalities of what we may call the 'general principle of attitude qualification'" (Lévi-Strauss 1967: 39). In the ethnographic literature this problem is referred to as the **avunculate.** It involves the relationship between ego and his maternal uncle, referred to as a **joking relationship.** At issue are the great liberties ego enjoys in his interaction with his maternal uncle and the latter's wives and property.

The avunculate, as Radcliffe-Brown demonstrated, involves not simply a set of kinship terms but it also entails a system of attitudes. His explanation was that in these societies the kind of relationship that ego has with his mother is extended to all members of her patrilineage, and the kind of relationship ego has with his father is extended to all members of his patrilineage. Respect and formality characterize ego's relationship with his father, while his relationship with his mother is warm and affectionate. Thus mother and mother's brothers and sisters display warm and tolerant attitudes and great familiarity toward ego. Father's relationship with ego is stern and formal. Thus father's sisters and brothers have a formal and stern relationship with ego.

Radcliffe-Brown also called attention to the principle that in "primitive societies" there is a great deal of difference in the behavior of a man toward other men and toward women. Any considerable degree of familiarity is only permitted between individuals of the same sex (Radcliffe-Brown 1952a: 20). Thus, ego's has the greatest degree of familiarity with mother's brother, who is treated as male mother. Conversely, ego's relation with his father's sister is even more distant and formal because she is a woman and because she is construed as a "female" father.

Lévi-Strauss picks up the problem at this point and criticizes Radcliffe-Brown for being too narrowly focused:

> First, the avunculate does not occur in all matrilineal or all patrilineal systems, and we find it present in some systems which are neither matrilineal nor patrilineal. Further, the avuncular relationship is not limited to two terms, but presupposes four, namely, brother, sister, brother-in-law, and nephew. An interpretation such as Radcliffe-Brown's arbitrarily isolates particular elements of a global structure which must be treated as a whole (Lévi-Strauss 1967: 39–40).[10]

Lévi-Strauss cites a number of examples. Among the matrilineal Trobriand Islanders the relationship between father and son is "free and familiar," but there is "a marked antagonism" between uncle and nephew. Lévi-Strauss then goes on to describe sets of relationships not considered by Radcliffe-Brown. Among the Trobrianders, husband and wife live in "tender intimacy," but the relations between brother and sister is dominated by a rigid taboo. Among the patrilineal Cherkess of the Caucasus, there is hostility between father and son, while the maternal uncle is on friendly terms with his nephew, assists him, and gives him a horse upon his marriage. Here the relations between brother and sister are tender. However, relation between spouses is rigid. According to Lévi-Strauss, these examples indicate that the correlation of attitudes should include not only those between father/son and maternal uncle/sister's son, but also brother/sister, husband/wife. From this Lévi-Strauss derives the following principle:

> In both groups, the relation between maternal uncle and nephew is to the relation between brother and sister as the relation between father and son is to that between husband and wife. Thus if we know one pair of relations, it is always possible to infer the other (Lévi-Strauss 1967: 40).[11]

Lévi-Strauss extends his analysis to other examples. Among the patrilineal Tonga, in Polynesia, husband-wife relations are "harmonious." Nephew and maternal uncle have a relationship of freedom and familiarity. In contrast, the father-son relationship is formal. Also, there is a formal and rigid relation between sister and brother. Among the matrilineal Siuai of Bougainville, brother-sister relations are "friendly." Father-son relations involve no hostility or stern authority. But the nephew-maternal uncle is stern and the boy stands in awe of his mother's brother. Moreover, husband-wife relations are not harmonious. Lévi-Strauss writes,

> What can we conclude from these examples? The correlation between the types of descent and forms of avunculate does not exhaust the problem. Different forms of avunculate can coexist with the same type of descent, whether patrilineal or matrilineal. But we constantly find the same fundamental relationships between the four pairs of oppositions required to construct the system (1967: 42).[12]

The four pairs of oppositions (Figure 11.2) are given as follows:

	Trobriand	Siuai	Cherkess	Tonga
uncle/nephew	−	−	+	+
bro/sis	−	+	+	−
fa/son	+	+	−	−
hus/wi	+	−	−	+

Lévi-Strauss characterizes relations marked + as "free and familiar relations" and those depicted

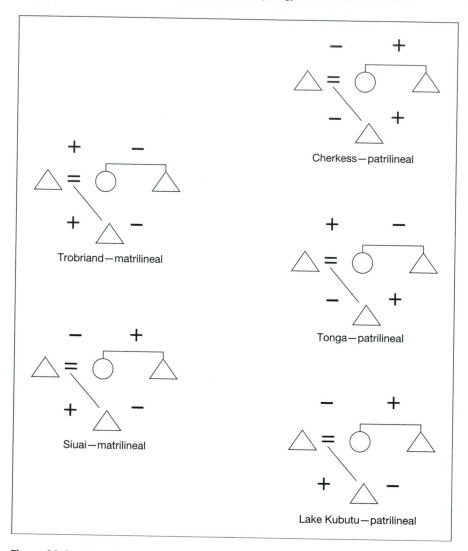

Figure 11.2 Lévi-Strauss's structural analysis of the avunculate. *After Lévi-Strauss (1967).*

as − as characterized by "hostility, antagonisms, and reserve." Lévi-Strauss adds,

> Thus we see that in order to understand the avunculate we must treat it as one relationship within a system, while the system itself must be considered as a whole in order to grasp its structure. This structure rests upon four terms (brother, sister, father, and son), which are linked by two pairs of correlative oppositions in such a way that in each

of the two generations there is always a positive relationship and a negative one. Now, what is the nature of this structure, and what is its function? The answer is as follows: This structure is the most elementary form of kinship that can exist. It is, properly speaking, *the unit of kinship*. . . . One may give a logical argument to support this statement. In order for a kinship structure to exist, three types of familial relations must always be present: a relation of consanguinity, a relation of affinity, and a relation of descent—in other words, a relation between siblings, a relation between spouses, and a relation between parent and child (Lévi-Strauss 1967: 43).[13]

This fundamental unit of kinship, according to Lévi-Strauss, is the result of the incest taboo:

> The primitive and irreducible character of the basic unit of kinship, as we have defined it, is actually a direct result of the universal presence of the incest taboo. This is really saying that in human society a man must obtain a woman from another man who gives him a daughter or a sister. Thus we do not need to explain how the maternal uncle emerged in the kinship structure: He does not emerge—he is present initially. Indeed, the presence of the maternal uncle is a necessary precondition for the structure to exist. The error of traditional anthropology, like traditional linguistics, was to consider the terms, and not the relations between the terms (Lévi-Strauss 1967: 44–45).[14]

Thus Lévi-Strauss ties the incest taboo and all of the kinship relations encompassed in his analysis of the avunculate to marriage exchange systems, the foundation of kinship, that are based upon the contrast between Us/Them, or consanguinity and affinity mediated by means of reciprocal woman exchange. The avunculate becomes understandable, therefore, only when seen within the structural relations of binary attitudinal oppositions within the basic unit of kinship. Lévi-Strauss's basic unit of kinship illustrates the fundamental propensity of the human mind to construct logical categories through binary oppositions.

Critics have raised a number of the questions regarding Lévi-Strauss's analysis (see Harris 2001b: 496). For example, are the emotional attitudes and relationships in question really reducible to positive and negative oppositions? Also, Lévi-Strauss's treatment of these relationships leaves out important questions regarding the descent systems, such as, Why is it that among the Trobrianders the relationships are minus, minus, plus, plus?

Also, the important question left out is, Why are the Trobrianders matrilineal, while the Tonga are patrilineal? Moreover, since Lévi-Strauss includes the mother's brother in the elementary unit of kinship, why is the avunculate not universal? The answer he provides is particularly unsatisfactory:

> Let us point out first, that the kinship system does not have the same importance in all cultures. For some cultures it provides the active principle regulating all or most of the social relationships. In other groups, as in our own, this function is either absent altogether or greatly reduced. In still others, as in the societies of the Plains Indians, it is only partially fulfilled. The kinship system is a language; but it is not a universal language, and a society may prefer other modes of expression and action. From the point of view of the anthropologist this means that in dealing with a specific culture we must always ask a preliminary question: Is the system systematic? Such a question, which seems absurd at first, is absurd only in relation to language; for language is the semantic system par excellence; it cannot but signify, and exists only through signification. On the contrary, this question must be rigorously examined as we move from the study of language to the consideration of other systems which also claim to have semantic functions, but whose fulfillment remains partial, fragmentary, or subjective, like, for example, social organization, art, and so forth. (Lévi-Strauss 1967: 46).[15]

But if these contrasting characteristics are expressed in some societies and not others how can they stem from universal binary contrasts? Lévi-Strauss dismisses cases that do not support the validity of his laws of negative and positive contrasts as unimportant. However, one might argue that through such procedures any structural hypothesis could be validated (cf. Harris 2001b: 497).

THE STRUCTURAL ANALYSIS OF MYTHS

Lévi-Strauss's search for underlying structures of human thought extends to his analysis of myth. Myths are narrative accounts that embody symbolically encoded messages. Every culture has its own myths often set in the context of a broader cultural narrative system. The originators of the myths are often unknown. Many European people are familiar with myths from ancient Greek literature. The myth of the hapless Oedipus, who unknowingly kills his father and marries his own mother, has various strata of symbolic meaning and has been the subject of study by philosophers, psychoanalysts, and anthropologists, among others.

Often myths relate events dealing with culture heroes and supernatural entities and occurrences and are set in mythic time rather than in any specified historical period. Some myths deal with how humans or some aspect of the human condition originated. These are referred to as **origin myths.** Thus the myth of Prometheus, who gave humankind fire after stealing it from the gods, for which he was condemned to suffer eternally, is an origin myth. Other myths involve accounts dealing with the creation of people, the world, the universe and everything in it. These are known as **creation myths.**

Usually a myth has been told and retold countless times as it has been transmitted through the centuries across space and time. It is often possible to identify variants of a particular myth, sometime from around the world. For example, folklorists have collected more than 500 versions of the Cinderella tale from Europe, Asia, and America (see Aarne 1961; Cox 1893; Dundes 1983). Some of these were due to the process of diffusion, but others, such as the Native American story of Ash boy, which Lévi-Strauss maintains is structurally similar to the Cinderella tale, appear to have emerged independently (Gross 1992: 78).

During the nineteenth century, anthropologists treated mythology as pseudohistory or tall tales told in order to explain misunderstood astronomical, meteorological, and other such natural phenomena. This was the position of the nineteenth-century anthropologist James Frazer (1854–1941), the author of the *Golden Bough* (1919–1927). Later anthropologists treated myths as cultural products embodying symbolically en-

coded messages often in the form of sacred tales. Franz Boas and his followers treated myths as the repositories of significant cultural information from which one could glean anthropologically useful information. Malinowski and his students stressed the important sociopsychological functions of myths as "charters" that sanctioned various cultural institutions of the social order. Myths therefore had to be understood in their social and political contexts, rather than as timeless texts (for an overview of anthropological treatment of myths during the nineteenth and early twentieth centuries, see Bidney 1967: 286–326; see also Segal 1996, 1998).

Modern anthropological studies of myth fall into two broad categories, those associated with Lévi-Strauss's structural perspective, and those associated with the symbolic and interpretive approaches associated mainly with the works of Clifford Geertz and Victor Turner, whose works are treated in Chapter 13 (Pandian 1991: 21).

Lévi-Strauss's focus on myths departs from most approaches. His mode of analysis is based upon the premise that human thought is least encumbered and more inventive in the realm of myth, art, and poetic language, whereas other aspects of human culture are constrained by the practical considerations of everyday life (Honigmann 1976: 324). Therefore, myths are a system of communication in which the human mind, free of the encumbrance of empirical reality, communes with itself (Lévi-Strauss 1969a: 10). Myths are determined by the nature of thought itself, the mind imitating itself as an object (Murphy 1980: 191). Because myths are unencumbered by the exigencies of everyday life, mental structures are said to be easiest to detect here.

For Lévi-Strauss myths are systems with elements that relate to each other and to the whole. Moreover, he treats any corpus of myths that pertains to the same theme, regardless of their culture of origin, as belonging to the same system. Myths from different parts of the world that deal with the same themes are merely the expression of the same thought patterns in different ways. Similarities between myths are not a matter of diffusion or historical accident, but rather due to the fact that all myths emanate from the same source, namely the human mind, and are merely transformations, reversions, or redefinitions of the same themes (Honigmann 1976: 325). This also applies to the "myths" found in complex industrial societies. For example, the anthropologist Peter Claus (1982), who applied Lévi-Strauss's structural analysis to American television serials, has found that they share the same structure as the myths found in nonindustrial traditions.

Although myths may appear to have no practical utility, to Lévi-Strauss they represent "objectified thought" that is concerned with significant human dilemmas (oppositions) that produce tensions that the mind attempts to resolve or ameliorate. These include the quandaries posed by life and death, the autochthonous origins of humankind versus the idea that humans come from the sexual union between men and women, and most fundamentally, the relationship between culture/order and nature/randomness (Honigmann 1976: 325). The culture/nature contrast is as central to Lévi-Strauss's ideas, as the Oedipus myth is to the Freudians (Honigmann 1976: 325).

One of the quandaries humans must contend with is the idea of descent from a first man, which presents the dilemma of the origins of the first nonincestuous mate. In other words, where did the first woman come from? In the biblical origin myth Eve is created from Adam's flesh; thus the first union was incestuous. There is also the contradiction of humankind's dual character, being part of nature and yet set apart from it by culture.

It is in the universe of myth that the mind dabbles freely with these contradictions and transposes and mediates them symbolically. This is because for Lévi-Strauss the mind strives to find the midpoint between such oppositions (McGee and Warms 2000: 331). The dichotomy between life and death is thus rephrased in terms of the opposition between an antelope, which is an herbivore, and a lion, a carnivore, and inter-

jecting a hyena, which eats animals it does not kill, to negate the contradiction represented by the juxtaposition of antelope and lion (Keesing and Keesing 1971: 311). As Leach (1970: 62–63) put it,

> Another contradiction . . . is that the concept of life entails the concept of death. A living thing is that which is not dead; a dead thing is that which is not alive. But religion endeavors to separate these two intrinsically interdependent concepts so that we have myths which account for the *origin* of death or which represent death as "the gateway to eternal life." Lévi-Strauss has argued that when we are considering the universalist aspects of primitive mythology we shall repeatedly discover that the hidden message is concerned with the resolution of unwelcome contradictions of this sort. The repetitions and prevarications of mythology so fog the issues that irresolvable logical inconsistencies are lost sight of even when they are openly expressed.[16]

Lévi-Strauss's application of structural analysis to the trickster in Native American mythology illustrates how the dichotomy between life and death is transformed in mythical thought (see Lett 1987). He writes that

> The trickster of American mythology has remained so far a problematic figure. Why is it that throughout North America his role is assigned practically everywhere to either coyote or raven?[17]

The solution is as follows:

> If we keep in mind that mythical thought always progresses from the awareness of oppositions toward their resolution, the reason for these choices becomes clearer. We need only assume that two opposite terms with no intermediary always tend to be replaced by two equivalent terms which admit of a third one as mediator; then one of the polar terms and the mediator become replaced by a new triad, and so on (Lévi-Strauss 1967: 220–221).[18]

Lévi-Strauss arrives at the structural explanation for the role of the coyote as the supernatural trickster by establishing an opposition between Life/Death, the initial pair. Life/Death pose a dichotomy, they are oppositions with no intermediaries and must be replaced by two equivalent terms that admit a third term as mediator to negate them (Figure 11.3). The analogous opposition to Life/Death is Agriculture/Warfare. Agriculture sustains life and so means life—warfare leads to killing and therefore signifies death. The mediator between agriculture and warfare is hunting which sustains life by war against animals. This is the first triad. Agriculture is associated with plant-eating animals and hunting with beasts of prey. The mediator between these two terms are carrion-eating animals, which are anomalous, being like beasts of prey because they eat animal flesh but also like plant eaters because they do not kill what they eat.

Thus because the anomalous coyote mediates between Life/Death, it becomes the trickster: "the trickster is a mediator. Since his mediating function occupies a position halfway between two polar terms, he must retain something of that duality—namely an ambiguous and equivocal character" (Lévi-Strauss 1967: 223).

This example illustrates how in mythical thought the dichotomy between life and death can be rephrased in terms of different sets of op-

positions and is as intriguing as it is elegant. However, a few words need to be said about this exposition as an explanation for the recurrence of a cultural element. Lévi-Strauss's analysis suggests that the binary operations of the human mind determine the recurrence of the coyote as a trickster. There are difficulties with this analysis, not the least of which is the fact that coyotes are not exclusively carrion eaters (Harris 2001a: 200). These intelligent animals do in fact hunt small creatures like rabbits, rats, mice, and birds, as well as being opportunistic. Moreover, coyotes are extremely intelligent creatures. Thus a more plausible and parsimonious explanation for their role as the tricksters could be that Native Americans recognized coyotes as tricky animals. Thus Lévi-Strauss structural explanation, some critics have argued, misdirects us from the obvious to the obscure and improbable (Harris 2001a: 201).

THE MESSAGE IN THE MYTH

Lévi-Strauss is intrigued by the similarities between myths from different cultures around the world. As he points out,

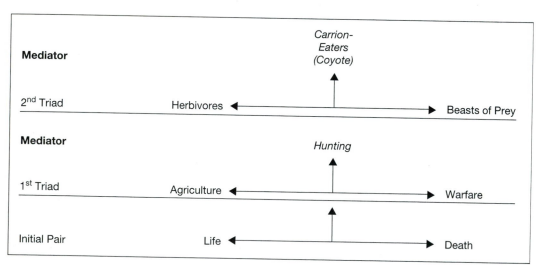

Figure 11.3   Lévi-Strauss's structural explanation for the role of the coyote as "the Trickster." *After Lett (1987).*

Mythology confronts the student with a situation which at first sight appears contradictory. On the one hand it would seem that in the course of a myth anything is likely to happen. There is no logic. Any characteristic can be attributed to any subject; every conceivable relation can be found. With myth, everything becomes possible. But on the other hand, this apparent arbitrariness is belied by the astounding similarity between myths collected in widely different regions. Therefore the problem: If the content of a myth is contingent, how are we going to explain the fact that myths throughout the world are so similar? (Lévi-Strauss 1967: 204)[19]

Lévi-Strauss maintains that looking at a corpus of myths superficially, we note considerable variety of details, a great deal of repetition, and reoccurring themes, such as incest, parricide, fratricide, and cannibalism (Leach 1970: 60). However, beneath these surface features, there exists another level of meaning, an encoded message that can be deciphered. Myths, in other words, embody hidden messages. When seen in this way, myths become the medium of communication between generations, between the past and the present. The task of the anthropologists is therefore to detect and decipher the messages in myths.

As Lévi-Strauss sees it, the message is not necessarily contained in a single myth but rather in the corpus of mythology of a people. Messages are transmitted or handed down from long-dead ancestors (the senders) to the present generation (the receivers). Parts of the message contained in any single myth may be distorted in the process of transmission from generation to generation, however, when the myths are analyzed together as a set, the complete message is detected. Leach gives the following analogy:

Let us imagine the situation of an individual A who is trying to get a message to a friend B who is almost out of earshot, and let us suppose that communication is further hampered by various kinds of interference—noise from wind, passing cars, and so on. What will A do? If he is sensible he will not be satisfied with shouting his message just once; he will shout it several times, and gives a different wording to the message each time, supplementing his words with visual signals. At the receiving end B may very likely get the meaning of each of the individual messages slightly wrong, but when he puts them together the redundancies and the mutual consistencies and inconsistencies will make it quite clear what is "really being said" (Leach 1970: 63–64).[20]

Thus, let us say that the message consists of eight constituent units, or mythemes, 1 to 8, and the message was shouted five times (a to e) from A to B. Let us also say that each time the message is transmitted a different segment is lost in a particular message through distortion. Thus B would receive five versions (a) to (e), each one containing a different segment of the total message. B would receive the following information: (a), 1, 2, 4, 7, 8; (b) 2, 3, 4, 6, 8; (c) 1, 4, 5, 7, 8; (d) 1, 2, 5, 7; (e) 3, 4, 5, 6, 8.

Looking at the five messages in which different segments of the sequence are present, we end up with a string of elements: 1, 2, 4, 7, 8, 2, 3, 4, 6, 8, 1, 4, 5, 7, 8, 1, 2, 5, 7, 3, 4, 5, 6, 8. Reading the elements of the message as a unilinear series will not reveal the message. The elements must be reorganized in the correct order:

(a)	1	2		4			7	8
(b)		2	3	4		6		8
(c)	1			4	5		7	8
(d)	1	2			5		7	
(e)			3	4	5	6		8

This resembles a group of chords in an orchestral score (Leach 1970: 63–64). Lévi-Strauss maintains that a corpus of myth makes up just such an orchestral score and that the message of the ancestors is contained in the whole set, rather in any individual myth. The message can now be identified if we read it vertically, from left to right.

Lévi-Strauss maintains that the ancient people, the ancestors, were sensible and they sent many versions of their messages, knowing that only portions of each version would actually reach the intended recipients and that the whole message would only be apparent from the totality of versions. This is intriguing and even ingenious. But there are problems. We could go along with this as long as Lévi-Strauss is working with a corpus of myth precisely located in a specific cultural area. The operation becomes highly problematic, however, because Lévi-Strauss roams across the world, oblivious to cultural or temporal boundaries, in order to constructing the myth orchestral scores. Thus, in the case of the preceding example, myths (a) could come from one continent and cultural group in one time period, (b) and (c) from another area, and (d) and (e) from an unrelated cultural group from yet another time period. Thus an orchestral score could be composed of elements from different cultures and time periods of Europe, China, and the Americas (see Leach 1970: 65).

In some instances, Lévi-Strauss has been known to combine elements of myths from different cultures, such as from Kwakiutl and Bella Bella, in order to synthesize a version of a myth that contains the needed dichotomies necessary to demonstrate the power of structural analysis (Harris 2001a: 215). This operation, as Harris (2001a: 215) put it,

> is clearly not a case of the analysis of myths worthy of anthropological science, but a pure and unadulterated case of myth-making in order to con us into believing that we need structuralism in order to understand how people think.[21]

Lévi-Strauss, however, feels justified in engaging in such myth-making because he is not interested in the narrative content of myths, but rather what he believes to be their more significant aspect, the basic structural core that appears in all myths. The reason for the similarity in the underlying structure of myths is because all myths stem from the structure of the human mind or human thought process. The structural core therefore contains the key to unlocking the universal structure of the human thought process. To uncover this underlying structure,

one must focus not on a myth's narrative but on the formal arrangements and logical relationship of its elements.

STRUCTURAL ANALYSIS OF TOTEMISM

From the nineteenth century to the present, anthropologists, philosophers, psychologists, sociologists, and scholars of religion have been interested in the phenomenon of **totemism** (e.g., Bleakley 2000; Smith 1889). The term **totem** comes from the Ojibwa of Canada, whose expression *ototeman* means, "he is a relative of mine" (Morris 1988: 270). It was first recorded by John Long, a fur trader who wrote a book called *Voyages and Travels of an Indian Interpreter and Trader* (1791). Among the Ojibwa, clans were named after particular animal species, and members of those clans were not permitted to eat or harm their totems. The word was transformed into a general concept when it was applied to other cases where social groups appeared to stand in a certain relationship, usually a ritual one, to animal or plant species (Morris 1988: 270).

The nineteenth-century Scottish evolutionary anthropologist John F. McLennan (1827–1888), the person who first coined the terms *endogamy* and *exogamy,* considered totemism as a type of religion based upon the worship of plants and animals (McLennan 1869). Subsequent writers simply followed along (Morris 1988: 270).

Among the important sources of information regarding totemistic beliefs were the ethnographic descriptions of the Australian aborigines. Writers such as James Frazer and Émile Durkheim, among others, who wrote on the subject, were either inspired by the ethnographic data on the Australian aborigines or else they used these data as evidence in support of their theoretical formulations. Nineteenth-century writers were under the false impression that Australian aborigines represented the most primitive stage of human evolutionary development and therefore used ethnographic data on the aborigines in order to answer questions pertaining to the origins of religion.

It is necessary, therefore, to first say a few words about Australian aboriginal cultures, which have provided much, but not all, of the information on totemism (see Bodley 1994: 18–44; Bourke et al. 1998; Isaacs 1980; Tonkinson 1991). I shall also look briefly at how different writers have attempted to explain the meaning and significance of totemism, and the extent to which these depart from Lévi-Strauss's formulations.

The Australian aborigines pursued a hunting and gathering or foraging mode of subsistence, lived in multi-family nomadic bands, called **hordes** by nineteenth- and early twentieth-century anthropologists, and were associated with "ritual" or "religious estates." These comprised territories over which bands had use-rights but which were associated with clans, or exogamous descent groups composed of related lineages. Clans as descent groups should not to be con-flated with bands, which were land-using social units with diverse membership (Bodley 1994: 28–29). The religious estates although associated with clans were accessible to others who simply had to ask permission to enter the area. Modern anthropologists see the clan-band-estate relationship as a resource conservation mechanism.

In the universe of the Australian aborigines, humans and their environment are brought together through a pervasive and complex **cosmology** (conceptions about the world/universe and the place of people in them) called the **Dreamtime,** or **Dreaming.** Dreamtime is a spiritual worldview that all at once encompasses different human groups, human ancestors, plant and animal species, and the physical landscape, in the past, present, and future, whose relationships and interactions are symbolically defined (cf. Tonkinson 1991: 20–25). Particular geographical locations and features are **sacred sites,** which, according to aboriginal **cosmogony** (beliefs regarding the origins of the world/universe and

Aboriginal dance ceremony. Aboriginal culture has been the source of speculation and interest among anthropologists, sociologists, and psychologists since the nineteenth century.

Uluru (Ayers Rock) in central Australia has numerous sacred sites associated with the dreamtime (Photo by H. Sidky).

everything in them), were created by **totemic beings,** or Dreamtime ancestors, and represent a tangible physical connection among them, humans, and the natural landscape. These sites are the centers of ritual activities.

Sacred sites are linked by **Dreamtime paths,** sometimes called **song lines,** which represent the routes taken by the totemic beings as they dotted the landscape with sacred sites. These paths are hundreds of miles long and traverse the territories of many clans and tribes (Bodley 1994: 33–36). The spiritual potency of the totemic beings who created particular sites manifest themselves at these places, which are also locations where rituals can harness those spiritual powers. Some sites exude spiritual essence associated with animal species and through ritual means humans are thought to be able to increase the numbers of those animals. Pregnancy and conception among humans are associated with spiritual essences emanating from some Dreaming sites and thus

totemic beings and human beings are spiritually linked (Bodley 1994: 33–36).

Anthropologists have referred to the incorporation of the human and natural worlds in the Dreamtime as totemism (Bodley 1994: 33–36). Each clan is named after a particular **totem** animal or plant species (sometimes objects and natural phenomenon are used as well). Australian aborigines symbolically depict totems on stones called **churinga** or on wood used as **bullroars.**

Members of a totemic group often maintain a ritual attitude toward their totem. Totem species are treated as sacred and must not be eaten or injured by members of the group. However, during certain religious ceremonies the totem species may be ritually sacrificed and consumed.

Among societies with exogamous clans, such as the Australian aborigines, totem animal species are treated as mythical ancestors and as identifying emblems (cf. Tonkinson 1991: 79–82). Totems also serve to symbolically represent the relationship

Aboriginal elder discussing a dreamtime story associated with a sacred site in Cave Hill, central Australia (Photo courtesy of Dr. Deborah Akers, Miami University).

between human groups and their ecosystem with which the totem animals stand in a specific relationship. Finally, totems serve to define aspects of the social world, such as relationships between human groups and their rights and obligations toward one another, including which groups are permitted or forbidden from intermarriage.

The anthropologist James Frazer devoted a four-volume work to the topic of totemism, entitled *Totemism and Exogamy* (1968 [1910]). For Frazer totemism was both a primeval religion associated with the worship of animals, plants, objects, as well as a system of kinship classification, which served to sort out individuals and groups with common lineal ancestors. Frazer saw totemism as the consequence of primitive igno-

rance regarding the biology of conception that required the development of a means of labeling people in order that incestuous relationships may be avoided.

The French sociologist Émile Durkheim took up the analysis of totemism in his book, *The Elementary Forms of the Religions Life* (1915). Durkheim thought that he had found the answer to question of the origins of religion in the phenomenon of totemism. His views departed from those of the evolutionists, who treated religion in terms of primitive man's cognitive processes.

For Durkheim religion is a sociological phenomenon, a manifestation of the power of the collective/society, which cannot be reduced to the level of individual psychological/cognitive

The French sociologist Émile Durkheim, whose ideas on the origins and nature of religion, expressed in The Elementary Forms of the Religious Life (1915), were formulated on the basis of ethnographic materials on the Australian aborigines.

states or characteristics. Religion, according to this view, represents a group phenomenon, which comprises sets of shared beliefs and attitudes toward the sacred. These shared beliefs bring individuals together into a single "moral community." This, for Durkheim, held the key to understanding religion. Durkheim's sociological conception of religion is based on the distinction between the ordinary realm of human existence, or the **profane,** and the realm of the extraordinary, the **sacred.** The sacred is distinguished and differentiated from the profane by means of rituals, ritual behavior, recitations, sacred objects and emblems, and taboos.

In order to investigate how the "sacred" first appeared Durkheim sought out data on what was construed to be the most primitive of all religions, the totemistic beliefs of the Australian aborigines. The information came from Spencer

and Gillen's ethnography, *The Northern Tribes of Central Australia* (1904), five chapters of which deals with totems, totemic ceremonies and associated objects, and the eating of totemic plants and animals.

Durkheim noted that it is during the time of the gathering of clans that the sacred is manifested. For it is when the groups come together that the power of the collective consciousness, the collective thought of the aggregate as a whole, presents itself to the individual as an awesome and external force. From the collectivity of the clans emanates collective power, which appears impersonal and transcends the individual and which, because it is a manifestation of the collective, endures beyond the earthly existence of individuals and impinges upon them as an outside force. It is this that becomes the focus of worship and ritual. Thus the object of reverence and worship is the collective, or society, itself (Evans-Pritchard 1965: 58–61). For Durkheim this was the basis of all religions.

According to the Durkheimian view, the manner in which totemic species are identified and defined stems from the imposition of the social or sociological domain upon the natural world. Evans-Pritchard (1965: 58) expressed this as follows:

> The social structure thus provides the model for the classification of natural phenomena. Since the things so classified with the clans are associated with their totems, they also have a sacred character; and since the cults mutually imply each other, all are co-ordinated parts of a single religion, a tribal religion.[22]

By contrast, as we shall see, for Lévi-Strauss totemism represents parallels between natural and social categories, in which the human mind creates categories, groups, and units based upon nature.

Needless to say, Durkheim's view on the origins of religion has met with criticisms. Robert Lowie (1952: 114) put the "ax to the root of the theory," as he put it, by pointing out that totemism is "a widespread but far from universal phenomenon" and hence cannot be the universal source for the origins of religion.

Sigmund Freud (1938) attempted to explain totemism in terms of human psychological factors. Again, the Australian aboriginal cultures were the inspiration. In his book *Totem and Taboo* (1952), a sort of intuitive allegorical evolutionary reconstruction first published in 1913, Freud began with "the primal horde" headed by the senior male who had exclusive sexual rights over all females in the band (Freud 1952: 141–143). This "violent primal father" was feared and envied by his sons. As Freud (1952: 141–143) put it, "the tumultuous mob of brothers were filled with the same contradictory feelings which we can see at work in the ambivalent-father complexes of our children and our neurotic patients."

Freud was operating on the assumption that the emotional states of primitive people were

Sigmund Freud, noted psychologist, whose influential work Totem and Taboo (1952) was based on ethnographic materials on the Australian aborigines.

childlike and abnormal, which is expressed in the book's subtitle, which is "Resemblances Between the Psychic Life of Savages and Neurotics." It comes as no surprise, therefore, that Boasian anthropologists, whose sensibilities would not allow them to stand for such ethnocentrism, poorly received Freud's work (see Kroeber 1920).

In Freud's reconstruction, the psychosexually frustrated sons of the violent primal father, who was hated because he was the obstacle to the sons' sexual desires but who also loved and admired by them, slew their father and being "cannibal savages" ate their victim. This act marked the end of the "patriarchal horde" and the transition to humanity. Well fed, but overwhelmed by guilt and remorse over what they had done, the victim's sons agreed that they would never again disobey their father's rules and renounced the fruits of their deed by resigning their claims to the women they had desired, their mothers and sisters. They adopted the incest taboo and the rule of exogamy. The guilt-ridden sons then chose a totem species to symbolically depict their father and vowed not to kill the totem animal, except during particular times of ritual. The totem as the representation of the father was thus the object both of jealous hatred and love.

For Freud (1952: 141–143), the ritual slaying and eating of the totem animal represented a commemoration or reenactment of the original horrifying primal act of parricide and cannibalism. It was also an expression and resolution of deep psychosexual guilt and tensions, which served to bolster the incest prohibition and reinforce exogamy (Malefijt 1974: 295). This was how Freud reconstructed the origins of totemistic beliefs, the practice of exogamy, and the human revulsion of incest.

Freud placed great significance upon this development because in the process he saw the transition of mankind from animal-like protohumans to *Homo sapiens*, which was an event that occurred when people became exogamous (Fox 1967b). For Freud, the evidence of how this transition transpired was to be found in the totemistic beliefs of groups such as the Australian aborigines (Fox 1967b). On the question of the transition to humanity, or humankind's transition from nature to culture, Freud's views are similar to those of Lévi-Strauss regarding the incest prohibition, discussed previously, but on other points there is a marked divergence.

Lévi-Strauss in general has been highly influenced by the theoretical ideas both of Durkheim and Freud. From Durkheim he has taken the idea of symbolic classifications, and from Freud, the notion that primitive cultures offer a gateway into the unconscious structures of the human mind (Pandian 1991: 23). However, on the subject of totemism Lévi-Strauss has rejected the views of both these writers.

I have already noted the divergence between the Durkhemian view of totemism representing society superimposed upon nature and Lévi-Strauss's position that totemism represents parallels between natural and social categories, in which the human mind creates categories based upon nature. There is as well another related and fundamental point on which Lévi-Strauss departs from other writers in his analysis of totemism. Here Lévi-Strauss (1963: 4–5) follows the lead provided by the Boasian anthropologist Alexander Goldenweiser (1880–1940) in an article entitled "Totemism: An Analytical Study" (1910).

Operating in the standard idiographic, diffusionist Boasian mode, Goldenweiser pointed out that in the works of such writers as McLennan, Frazer, and Durkheim, three separate traits had been conflated under the one conceptual category of totemism. These traits included clan organization, the association of clans and natural species, and the idea of a ritual relationship between clans and particular animal species (Morris 1988: 270). Goldenweiser reported the independent occurrence of these elements and questioned the usefulness of the then current usage of the concept and urged particularistic studies.

Following Goldenweiser's lead, Lévi-Strauss drops the idea of totemism as a religion and chooses to focus on one aspect of the problem, what totemistic categories say about the operation of the human mind. Here he also follows a lead provided by Radcliffe-Brown in his 1951 paper, "The Comparative Method in Social Anthropology" (Radcliffe-Brown 1977). In his book *Totemism* (1963), Lévi-Strauss develops Radcliffe-Brown's idea that totemism involves the symbolic use of plants, animal species, and other elements from the natural world that are similar and yet different, such as for example the Eaglehawk and the Crow, to refer to the social world (see Chapter 9). Lévi-Strauss goes on to elaborate upon the point stressed by Radcliffe-Brown, that totemic systems involve human groups who are similar by belonging to the same tribe but are at the same time different because of their membership in different descent groups. Thus, totemism employs the differences in similar animal species to signify symbolically or metaphorically the social differences between human groups. As a consequence, there appear categories of totems that are associated with specific categories of human groups. In other words, contrasting features of the natural world are used to convey symbolically coded messages about people (Honigmann 1976: 328).

The two classification systems (the natural and the symbolic) have the same structure because one is a **transformation** of the other. This enables people to classify and order elements of their culture and metaphorically relate them to one another and to a similar ordering in the natural world (Kaplan and Manners 1972: 174). Characteristics of particular animal species are employed to convey the message that humans, although different, are also alike. For Lévi-Strauss certain animals are selected as totems not because they are "good to eat," as earlier anthropologists thought (e.g., Radcliffe-Brown 1952b) but because they are "good to think" (Lévi-Strauss 1963: 89).

We could say, therefore, that totemism is based upon a symbolic code modeled after the classification of totemic objects in the natural environment that logically correspond to aspects of the social world (Kaplan and Manners 1972: 175). This code, which consists of categories derived from nature, is a logical classificatory system that is used to render the social world by specifying the roles, relationships, obligations, and differences among clans. Structural analysis reveals the basic rationality underlying cultural phenomena. This rationality is based upon logical categories and relationships or the logical organization that stems from the binary operation of the human mind (Kaplan and Manners 1972: 176).

Totemism thus mediates the Culture/Nature opposition, by revealing the similarities between the two contrasting realms. In the same way, exogamy between totemic groups mediates the opposition between them by showing that although different, they are also alike, being members of a single society in which women are shared. Thus, exogamy, which is made possible by means of the exchange of women, functions to solidify the relations of totemic groups with each other and to society as a whole (Honigmann 1976: 328).

ASSESSMENT

Structural anthropology addresses fascinating and intriguing questions about humans and human thought. As a research strategy it has numerous shortcomings. The anthropologist Dan Sperber has cogently specified the nature of these defects. Sperber (1996: 45) points out that structural analysis entails interpretations of representations in order that structural relationships between them might be established. However, Sperber adds, Lévi-Strauss provides no guidelines for the interpretation of representations other than subjective procedures, such as intuition. Given this fact, structural analysis proceeds on the basis of interpretations made outside any explicit methodologies, steered by intuition, and motivated by the paradigmatic objectives to find similarities, oppositions, and inversions or transformations (Sperber 1996: 46). The outcome of this procedure is that systematic similarities and differences, inversions, and the like, often become apparent only in the interpretations and are not evident in the data themselves. In other words, the oppositions simply exist in the mind of the anthropologist performing the analysis.

Moreover, Sperber adds further, structural analysis does not constitute explanation, it merely leads to classification of the data. Once the data are classified Levi-Strauss links his analyses to a postulated underlying structure of thought. Here some major theoretical difficulties of the paradigm arise because cultural phenomena are extremely complex and exhibit innumerable properties, most of which are epiphenomenal in nature, rather than being fundamental properties of those cultural phenomena. Epiphenomenal aspects of cultural phenomena are generated by the fundamental properties of those cultural phenomena, but they are not themselves part of those fundamental properties and have no causal role in the appearance of those phenomena and therefore cannot explain the phenomena themselves (Sperber 1996: 46–47).

Structural analysis may tell us that some phenomena have certain systematic properties, but it does not provide the means to set apart fundamental properties from epiphenomenal properties (Sperber 1996: 47). Without the means of distinguishing fundamental and epiphenomenal aspects of the cultural phenomena being analyzed, structural analysis amounts to nothing more than a lot of guess work, intuitive insights, and creative imagination. Validation and the replication of results are impossible to achieve. The most problematic aspect of structural analysis is that its methodological procedures are impossible to replicate. Moreover, there are no clearly established criteria by which to determine the soundness or validity of a structural analysis (Werner 1973: 295).

Although validation no longer seems to be part of the intellectual vocabulary of many of today's interpretive/literary anthropological writers, for those who believe that knowledge of the world must be checked against experience, and that getting the facts right is crucial, it is a significant criterion. Structural anthropology does not provide any guidelines with which different analysts can adduce the same structural principals in the same cases. The only criterion offered is that the more correct analysis is the one that has the most forceful intuitive or intellectual appeal (Lett 1987: 103).

A good structural analysis, one could say, is one that is "good to think." For Lévi-Strauss soundness is equated with logical validity, not empirical validity (Honigmann 1976: 322). Logical validity, as we have discussed in Chapter 2, tells us only whether conclusions are justified by their premises, not whether the premises themselves are correct. In order to determine the validity of our premises, we have to rely on something other than logic. To achieve this, science turns to empirical evidence or the crucible of human experience.

Lévi-Strauss has stated that the structures he is interested in have nothing to do with empirical reality. The implication here is that structuralism has no real relevance to the empirical world (Malefijt 1974: 331). By shifting analytical focus to the structure of human thought, structuralism diverts the anthropological enterprise away from the examination of socially significant human problems, such as war, crime, inequality, poverty, and environmental degradation (Barrett 1984: 129).

The subject matter of structural anthropology is "deep structure," something not directly accessible in empirical terms. The "deep structures" and "transformations" with which Lévi-Strauss is concerned are hypothetical. In order to arrive at these hypothetical constructs, he undertakes numerous convoluted and sometimes fanciful mental operations based upon rules he himself seems to set. One might recall the structuralist interpretation of the coyote as trickster. Additional examples come from Lévi-Strauss's book *From Honey to Ashes* (1973), in which he equates

eating raw honey with eroticism. Cooking honey is equated with incest. Honey, which is eaten raw, becomes the opposite of tobacco, which is burned before being consumed.

Do these oppositions and equivalences exist in the myths and in the minds of its tellers and hearers, or are they a product of Lévi-Strauss's own creative imagination? The problem is that we have no way of determining what is the case. The method for finding oppositions and mediations that appear as transformations at the level of surface phenomena is to apply progressively more removed and arcane analogies based on contrasts (Harris 2001a: 169). Lévi-Strauss is thus able to discover binary oppositions everywhere he looks.

An observation Lévi-Strauss (1967: 203) makes when criticizing functionalists and psychoanalytical interpretations of myths applies equally to his own work: "Whatever the situation, a clever dialectic will always find a way to pretend that a meaning has been found." As Kaplan and Manners (1972: 179) note in this regard,

> To be certain, all sciences employ such inferred entities as explanatory devices. And provided these constructs are utilized to link two sets of observable phenomena, and are therefore open to possible refutation, they present no logical difficulties. Lévi-Straussian structural principles, however, can be utilized, if one is ingenious enough and employs the appropriate transformations, to account for virtually *all* possible variations in cultural performance. To many adherents of structuralism, it is precisely this all-encompassing nature of Lévi-Straussian theory that is most appealing and is taken as a measure of its explanatory power. But a theory that is capable of explaining everything should be suspect.[23]

Structural explanations are immune from falsification and cannot be replicated. They are presented as self-validating (Lett 1987: 117). Thus, like French postmodernism, French structuralism affords one the luxury of presenting nearly any explanation without the risk of ever being proven wrong.

D'Andrade (1995: 249) suggests that the reason for the abandonment of the structuralist agenda was not due simply to a shift in intellectual fads, but to the shortcomings associated with perspectives that are inherently unverifiable.

> No one could build on what was done before, because building requires criticism, modifications, and selection of what is sound from what is unsound, and this is not possible in a world where there is no way of knowing what is better and what is worse (D'Andrade 1995: 249).[24]

I suspect that a similar fate awaits the formulations of the current epistemophobic cultural constructionists.

Rather than tackling the complexity of the empirical world, Lévi-Strauss's program dismisses empirical reality as irrelevant. He totally glosses over intercultural and intracultural variations (Leaf 1979: 259). What structuralists fail to consider is that complexity neither rules out the existence of relevant causal relationships, nor does it justify dismissing empirical phenomena as a hindrance to the understanding of culture (see Lévi-Strauss 1967: 274). Yet Lévi-Strauss suggests that empirical evidence is not relevant since his own thoughts are sufficient to illustrate the binary operations of the human mind:

> Let me say again that all the solutions put forward are not presented as being of equal value, since I myself have made a point of emphasizing the uncertainty of some of them; however, it would be hypocritical not to carry my thought to its logical conclusion. I therefore say in advance to possible critics: *what does it matter?* For if the final aim of anthropology is to contribute to a better understanding of objectified thought and its mechanisms, it is in the last resort immaterial whether in this book the thought process of the South American Indians take shape through the medium of my thoughts, or whether mine take place through the medium of theirs. What matters is that the human mind, regardless of the identity of those who happen to be giving expression, should display an increasingly intelligible structure as a result of doubly reflexive thought movement of two thought processes acting as one upon the other, either of which can in turn provide the spark or tinder whose conjunction will shed light on both (Lévi-Strauss 1969b: 13).[25]

The problem, of course, is that if Lévi-Strauss's thoughts are conflated with the thoughts of the "Indians," we have no way of determining if the oppositions and equivalences he writes about are figments of his own imagination or characteristics of the thought of the people he writes about.

Moreover, Lévi-Strauss asserts that it is the unconscious mind that imposes structure on cultural phenomena and therefore what the natives consciously think about their myths, masks, totems, and taboos is beside the point. Yet Lévi-Strauss claims to be able to fathom the unconscious operations of his own mind. How can this be? A stronger case could be made if structuralists could demonstrate that the makers of the traffic lights or South American Indians recognize the binary contrasts identified and derive some sort of mental gratification from them; that is, that they are "good to think" (cf. Lett 1987: 107). However, whether the actors themselves recognize or are conscious of the dialectics of their thought is not relevant for Lévi-Strauss and his followers.

Another problem relates to the claim structuralists make that they are able to decode the cryptic messages in the myths of "exotic cultures." They claim to be able to do this because of the assumption that all myths embody the universal cognitive structures of the human mind. In other words, that beyond the unfamiliar signifiers there exists a familiar message (Layton 1997: 93). Hence one could undertake the task of decoding myths of other cultures from the confines of a study in Paris, as easily as in a village along the Orinoco River. This may account for, what Gamst (1980: 386) called "a cavalier armchair detachment for the empirical world," which characterizes French structuralism.

Structuralists acknowledge that the empirical world or observable cultural phenomena undergo constant change, yet they restrict their analysis to the invariant principles underlying the ever-changing surface manifestations, or objectified thoughts, which they use to deduce those invariant principles. The problem here is that if objectified thought is generated from invariant dialectical structural principles of the mind, why are these surface manifestations so ephemeral? If objectified thought is "good to think" why does it change all the time? (Lett 1987: 103). Also problematic is Lévi-Strauss's attempt to account for the variable surface manifestation of cultures by means of a limited set of invariable principles of thought. The difficulty here is that a variable cannot be explained in terms of a constant (see White 1949: 139). Lévi-Strauss is able to bypass the problem through sheer sophistry, suggesting that the underlying universal structures of thought work within various cultural settings but do not determine cultural patterns (cf. McGee and Warms 2000: 330), yet the main thrust of his own work suggests otherwise.

Another deficiency of structural anthropology is the exclusive focus on "primitive" peoples based on the unsubstantiated assumption that among the "savages" one is dealing with a timeless and changeless universe operating on the basis of changeless logical principles. Lévi-Strauss and his followers therefore ignore the dimension of history. However, cognitive domains are functionally related to other domains of culture and change as other domains undergo historical transformations. A simple example of this is the color signal categories for which Leach attempted to provide a structural explanation. Gamst (1980) work on traffic signals clearly shows such a historical transformation. However, Lévi-Strauss treats the categories he deals with as closed and static cognitive domains.

Moreover, the manner in which Lévi-Strauss uses ethnographic data is problematic. First, Lévi-Strauss makes statements that are said to be valid for all cultures on the basis of one or a few exam-

ples. Thus, the few cases that seem to support Lévi-Strauss's laws of negative and positive contrasts in his analysis of the avunculate are considered sufficient to validate the claim that these laws apply to all cultures in all times and places.

Second, Lévi-Strauss has a tendency to selectively cull myths from around the world without paying heed to any cultural, temporal, or spatial boundaries in order to find corroborating cases to construct unitary messages inherent in the architecture of the human mind (Leach 1970: 65). In this respect, his use of ethnographic materials is analogous in some ways to the practices of nineteenth-century evolutionists, such as the James Frazer. As the formidable Edmund Leach, himself later a structuralist convert (before accepting the Writing Culture creed of the postmodernists in the late 1980s), wrote that

> [Lévi-Strauss] always seems to be able to find just what he is looking for. Any evidence, however dubious, is acceptable so long as it fits with logically calculated expectations; but wherever the data run counter to the theory Lévi-Strauss will either bypass the evidence or marshal the full resources of his powerful invective to have the heresy thrown out of court. So we need to remember that Lévi-Strauss' prime training was in philosophy and law; he consistently behaves like an advocate defending a cause rather than a scientist searching for ultimate truth (Leach 1970: 13).[26]

For reasons such as these, critics have charged that the structures that Lévi-Strauss talks about are fictional and unreal and exist only in his own mind (Harris 2001a: 167, 202–215; Jenkins 1979; Leaf 1979: 261). The anthropologist Stanley Diamond (1974: 325) described Lévi-Strauss's structural anthropology as a "triumph of inauthenticity."

Finally, perhaps the most serious shortcoming of structural anthropology is its failure to meet its own goals. Lévi-Strauss's anthropology has not yielded any profound insights about human thought other than that it is structured and operates in a binary pattern (Malefijt 1974: 331). So, we could indeed ask, what does it matter?

Chapter 12

Ethnoscience and Cognitive Anthropology: The Problem of Local Knowledge

At a time when Lévi-Strauss was developing his structural paradigm, a small cadre of anthropologists in the United States set out to revamp the way ethnographic research was to be conducted. The approach was called "the new ethnography," ethnosemantics, or ethnoscience (Sturtevant 1972), later subsumed by what became known as cognitive anthropology. The label "cognitive anthropology" was not in use during the formative period of the paradigm but was popularized by the volume *Cognitive Anthropology* (1969), edited by Stephen Tyler.

For anthropologists operating under the auspices of ethnoscience, putting ethnography on solid grounds was crucial because of the importance of ethnographic research in comparative and theoretical work in cultural anthropology (Wallace 1972: 111). The recognition of the significant place of ethnography in anthropological research and the need to solidify the slippage that exists between experience and the ethnographic texts led these anthropologists to devise more rigorous methods for the acquisition of ethnographic information. Ethnoscience was based upon the assumption that cultural phenomena are amenable to rational inquiry and its practitioners were committed to building a body of anthropological knowledge and advancing our understanding, all highly commendable endeavors.

The new ethnographers in the 1960s and 1970s were primarily anthropologists trained in the Boasian tradition or else they were powerfully influenced by the Boasian cultural determinist perspective that has had wide and lasting influence on anthropological thought in the United States. They were heavily influenced by Boasian linguistics as well as by developments in the field of structural linguistics (e.g., Bloch and Trager 1942; Gleason 1955; Z. Harris 1951; Pike 1947). Unlike many of the other paradigms we have examined so far, ethnoscience/cognitive anthropology has no single architect. The individuals most closely associated with this perspective include, among others, Harold Conklin, Charles Frake, Ward Goodenough, and William Sturtevant.

Ethnoscientists derived their inspiration in part from the longstanding interest by the Boasians in native knowledge of botany, zoology,

Anthropologist Ward Goodenough, one of the principal exponents of ethnoscience.

Anthropologist William Sturtevant, one of the principal exponents of ethnoscience.

geography, astronomy, and other similar domains of culture. Ethnoscience made all of these as well as other areas of native knowledge its subject matter. "Native knowledge" was presented by these writers with the prefix "ethno-" attached (for example, ethnobotany, ethnozoology) to indicate reference to "the system of knowledge and cognition typical of a given culture" (Sturtevant 1972: 130; see Berlin 1992).

Highly critical of traditional ethnographic accounts that described other cultures in terms of categories and concepts meaningful to the outside observer, the new ethnographers proposed to understand other cultures according to how they are perceived and categorized from the "insider's point of view." Thus, they chose to tackle head on a problem that has engaged anthropologists since at least the days of Bronislaw Malinowski.

The ethnoscientific agenda to attain the insider's perspective was not something new in itself. Indeed, this was a central feature of Boas's particularistic program. As Boas pointed out,

In natural science we are accustomed to demand a classification of phenomena expressed in a concise and unambiguous terminology. The same term should have the same meaning everywhere. We should like to see the same in anthropology. As long as we do not overstep the limits of one culture we are able to classify its features in a clear and definite terminology. We know what we mean by the terms family, state, government, etc. As soon as we overstep the limits of one culture we do not know in how far these may correspond to equivalent concepts. If we choose to apply our classification to alien cultures we may combine forms that do not belong together. The very rigidity of definition may lead to a misunderstanding of the essential problems involved. . . . If it is our serious purpose to understand the thoughts of a people the whole analysis of experience must be based on their concepts, not ours (Boas 1943: 314).[1]

Attaining the insider's view was also part of Malinowski's (1922: 22) ethnographic research agenda, captured in his statement that the final objective of ethnographic fieldwork "is to grasp the native's point of view, his relation to life, to realise *his* vision of *his* world" (Sturtevant 1972: 131).

Ethnoscientists/cognitive anthropologists assumed that somehow the insider's perspective will yield a better understanding of human behavior and the operation of sociocultural systems in comparison with perspectives based upon the analytical concepts and categories of the outside observer. For the ethnoscientists, the anthropologist had to get inside peoples' heads and semantics offered a way to do this (cf. D'Andrade 1995: 246). Thus by recording only the insider's point of view, these anthropologists assumed, they could reach the really "real" about his or her culture. This approach was also thought to eliminate the observer's perspective from the equation and hence produce bias-free ethnographic accounts.

Malinowski (1944: 7), it might be pointed out, did not share these additional assumptions, noting that "there is no such thing as description completely devoid of theory [i.e., the observer's analytical framework]." Moreover, Malinowski did not maintain that the "native" had the really real picture of his or her culture. For example, while describing the Kula he wrote that

> [the Trobrianders] have no knowledge of the total outline of any of their social structure. They know only their own motives, know the purpose of individual actions and the rules which apply to them, but how, out of these, the whole collective institution shapes, this is beyond their mental range. Not even the most intelligent native has any clear idea of the Kula as a big, organised social construction, still less of its sociological function and implications. If you ask him what the Kula is, he would answer by giving a few details, most likely by giving his personal experiences and subjective views on the Kula, but nothing approaching the definition just given here. Not even a partial coherent account could be obtained. For the integral picture does not exist in his mind; he is in it and cannot see the whole from the outside (Malinowski 1922: 83).[2]

Radcliffe-Brown would have also rejected the idea that the really real of another culture resides within the insiders' point of view, despite the fact that he often took native report as objectively true. Leslie White, during his diatribe with the Boasians, categorically dismissed the elevation of the "native's point of view" over that of the trained observer. White (1987a: 76) did so on the grounds that this approach entails placing the "the opinions, tastes, and preferences of tribesmen and laymen—which after all are cultural traits themselves, data of anthropological inquiry—on the same plane as the investigations and conclusions of the scientific anthropologist."

Why did White, Radcliffe-Brown, and Malinowski reject making the native's point of view their primary objective? This question is more significant than being merely of passing interest in the history of anthropological thought. Present-day cultural constructionists emphatically reject the observer/observed distinction in ethnographic research. Scientific anthropologists disagree with this point of view. The reason, as Richard Barrett (1991: 133–135) has observed, is that to make the native's point of view the ultimate and sole objective of anthropological inquiry is to overlook a considerable range of sociocultural phenomena that members of a culture participate in simply because of tradition. They neither understand nor are aware of the reasons for their behavior. This dimension of culture is taken for granted. In other words, people adhered to many customs without giving them any thought. When asked to account for what they do, they often supply "folk explanations" for their actions, which may sound reasonable but which are post hoc rationalizations. Thus, Barrett (1991: 135) adds, there is a large segment of culture that remains outside the "objective awareness" of members of society. The treatment of this aspect of culture requires that the anthropologist seek explanations "that surpass the native's understanding."

Given their exclusive emphasis on the insiders' point of view of another culture, the new ethnographers were firmly grounded in the extreme cultural relativism of the Boasians. As Stephen Tyler (1969: 14), another expositor of the new anthropology and later converted cultural constructionist postmodern guru, pointed out, the theories of cognitive anthropology "constitute complete accurate descriptions of particular cognitive systems" and no general theory of culture is possible until the particular descriptions are complete and their logical properties revealed." For this reason, the new ethnographers, like Boas himself decades earlier, called for a halt on all cross-cultural comparisons between systems and advocated a shift to a focus on comparison of facts within the same system, at least "until the facts themselves are adequately described" (Tyler 1969: 15). If all of this sounds familiar it is because these assertions are merely a restatement of Boas' dictum, which was that all theorization should stop until the "facts are in" (see Chapter 6).

As is to be expected, the ethnoscientists, like their Boasian predecessors, were deeply committed to rigorous and systematic empirical data gathering wedded to a particularistic orientation. For the new ethnographers, each culture is described as embodying a distinct and unique category of "native" thought, containing, so to speak, a particular theory of culture.

Those interested in developing a generalizing science of culture objected to this position because the focus upon the individual case, in all its particularities, requires that at some point one is able to move to more general theories (cf. Kaplan and Manners 1972: 183; Spiro 1986: 273). Ethnoscientists were never able to adequately address the question of how to proceed from the theory of particular cultures to the general theory of culture, although this was one of their ultimate goals.

ETHNOSCIENCE AND THE INFLUENCE OF KINSHIP STUDIES

The central issue for the new ethnographers was the fact that people from different cultures do not see and categorize things or classify experi-

ence as Euro-Americans do (Frake 1972: 193; Sturtevant 1972: 135). Without an understanding of the insider's categories, these anthropologists reasoned, it would be difficult to understand how a particular cognitive system is organized.

To illustrate this point, take for example the category of relatives that Euro-Americans would label as *cousins*. Cousins are the male and female offspring of **ego**'s mother's brother and sister and ego's father's brother and sister. No distinctions are made in the English language between cousins. The same is true of ego's parent's siblings, who are referred to as aunts and uncles. The Euro-American classification reflects how these relatives are perceived (for a treatment of American kinship and English kin terms, see Bria 1998; Farber 1981; Kronenfeld 1996: 55–72; Oswalt 1970; Schneider 1968; Schneider and Cottrell 1975).

People in another culture, however, may have completely different linguistic categories for ego's mother's brother's offspring and mother's sister's offspring. Moreover, they may call their father's sister and mother's sister by different terms, rather than collapsing them into a single category of "aunt" as Euro-Americans do. This means that in cultures that make such distinctions, these categories of relatives are perceived differently from the way Euro-Americans perceive them. Moreover, the non-Euro-American kinship categories into which relatives we refer to as cousins or aunts are placed would occupy a different structural position than they would in the Euro-American kinship system. Clearly, then, imposing our own conceptions upon another culture would distort its salient and culturally significant cognitive distinctions.

Those engaged in kinship studies recognized this long ago and hence the study of kinship terminological systems had developed well beyond the mere translation of labels, or of finding a "tribe's" word for cousin, uncle, or nephew. As Frake put it,

> The recognition that the denotative range of kinship categories must be determined empirically in

each case, that the categories form a system, and that the semantic contrasts underlying the system are amenable to formal analysis, have imparted to kinship studies a methodological rigor and theoretical productivity rare among ethnographic endeavors (Frake 1972: 193).[3]

Frake went on to point out that kinship or genealogical relations are not the only kinds of phenomena for which people have elaborate classificatory systems. Therefore, "there is no reason why the study of a people's concepts of these other phenomena should not offer a theoretical interest comparable to that of kinship studies" (Frake 1972: 193). In other words, the general principles employed in the study of kinship terms could be extended to other terminological systems or classifications as well. Frake's (1961) own classic ethnoscientific study involved the analysis of disease categories and diagnosis among the Subanun of Mindanao, in the Philippines.

Cognitive anthropologists maintained that by carefully describing a culture in terms of the codes, rules, and conceptual categories a native needs to know in order to be able to behave appropriately in different social settings in that culture one could achieve new standards of accuracy and replicability in ethnographic research. As already noted, ethnoscience was meticulously empiricist and scientific in its methodology for gathering emic data and its criteria for verification (Harris 2001a: 268).

Ethnoscience concerns itself principally with the analysis of terminological systems or folk classifications. This is based on the premise that the way a culture divides up the world of people, animals, plants, and things is mirrored in the categories of the language of the bearers of that culture. From this it follows that to learn linguistic categories of another culture is to learn native cognitive categories and to perceive the world as the native does. Thus, as Frake put it, the investigation of native classification systems of plants, animals, soils, weather, social relations, supernatural beings, navigation techniques, and

the like will provide "a sketch map of the world in the image of the tribe" (Frake 1972: 194).

Stated differently, the task of the new ethnography was to discover a culture's "cognitive world." Here, language becomes of central interest. As Frake (1972: 194) put it,

> Culturally significant cognitive features must be communicable between persons in one of the standard symbolic systems of the culture. A major share of these features will undoubtedly be codable in a society's most flexible and productive communication device, its language.[4]

Tyler (1969: 6) pointed out,

> What do we describe and how do we describe it? Obviously, we are interested in the mental codes of other people, but how do we infer these mental processes? Thus far, it has been assumed that the easiest entry to such processes is through language, and most of the recent studies have sought to discover codes that are mapped in language. Nearly all of this work has been concerned with how these names are organized into larger groupings. These names are thus both an index to what is significant in the environment of some other people, and a means of discovering how these people organize their perceptions of the environment. Naming is seen as one of the chief methods for imposing order on perception.[5]

These were the reasons why the methodology of ethnoscience was modeled after studies that employed semantic analysis for the investigation of kinship terms. Two papers, one written by Lounsbury (1956) and the other by Goodenough (1956a), are considered as the landmark works in the development of ethnoscience (D'Andrade 1995: 17). The methodology employed for the identification and analysis of "units of ideas" in these papers seemed applicable to other domains of culture. Thus, as the anthropologist D'Andrade (1995: 17) points out, "It was this body of methods and goals which was to become the agenda of cognitive anthropology."

The thrust of ethnoscientific research was not simply to focus upon indigenous knowledge and explore ways of incorporating it into frameworks for economic development (e.g., Grenier 1998) or in relation to intellectual property rights and environmental issues (see Ellen et al., 2000). The objective was much loftier. It was to discern the nature of cognitive processes and to find cognitive ordering principles or, to put it another way, to describe "the grammar of culture." This was an objective that was no less ambitious than Lévi-Strauss' efforts to elucidate the structure of human thought.

ETHNOSCIENCE AND THE CONCEPTION OF CULTURE

Cognitive anthropologists considered culture as the focus of their study and they define it as "the sum of a given society's folk classifications, all of that society's ethnoscience, its particular ways of classifying the material and social universe" (Sturtevant 1972: 130–131). Along the same lines, Goodenough (1957: 167) noted that

> a society's culture consists of whatever it is one has to know or believe in order to operate in a manner acceptable to its members, and do so in any role that they accept for any one of themselves. Culture, being what people have to learn as distinct from their biological heritage, must consist of the end product of learning: knowledge, in a most general, if relative, sense of the term. By this definition, we should note that culture is not a material phenomenon; *it does not consist of things, people, behavior, or emotions. It is rather an organization of these things.* It is the form of things that people have in mind, their models for perceiving, relating and otherwise interpreting them. As such, the things people say and do, their social arrangements and events, are products or by-products of their culture as they apply it to the task of perceiving and dealing with their circumstances (emphasis added).[6]

It followed that if cultures are studied by the appropriate methods it would be possible to discover the underlying conceptual principles of those cultures (Frake 1972: 192). The implications of this for the conduct of ethnographic research were, as Wallace (1972: 112) put it, that

the research operations of the ethnographer produce primarily not naturalistic or statistical descriptions of regularities in overt behavior but descriptions of the rules which the actors are presumably employing, or attempting to employ, in the execution and mutual organization of this behavior.[7]

Goodenough added that

> ethnographic description, then, requires methods of processing observed phenomena such that we can inductively construct a theory of how our informants have organized the same phenomena. It is the theory, not the phenomena alone, which ethnographic description aims to present (Goodenough 1957: 167–168).[8]

The new ethnography was therefore associated with a conception of culture that was entirely ideational/mentalist in nature and it excluded human behavior and the material dimensions of life altogether. As Spradley (1972: 6) observed,

> The *cognitive definition* [of culture] excludes behavior and restricts the culture concept to ideas, beliefs, and knowledge. While most early definitions *included* the cognitive dimensions, they were not restricted to them.[9]

The complicated and messy behavioral patterns that ethnographers encounter on the ground and find so difficult to fathom have been completely exorcised from this definition of culture.

No one would deny that culture consists of "forms of things that people have in mind, their models for perceiving, relating, and otherwise interpreting them," as Goodenough suggests. But it is not just models for perceiving. While there is nothing objectionable about the efforts to comprehend what these models are, how they are constructed, and what their logical structures may be, it is when anthropologists being treating culture as if they are nothing but models and rules that problems arise. Treating culture as though it consisted of rules and mental models and nothing else is the direction that cognitive anthropology took.

This idealist twist in American cultural anthropology was not a new development but was solidly rooted in the cognitivism inherent in Boasian anthropology. This idealism apparently received new impetus as a result of the influence of the sociologist Talcott Parsons, founder of the Harvard's Department of Social Relations, who touted his own idealist form of structural functionalism in American sociology (see Parsons 1964, 1968). It is thought that Parsons's influence on the anthropologist Clyde Kluckhohn, cofounder of the department, in turn influenced the latter's friend Alfred Kroeber, the reigning Boasian anthropologist of the day (Harris 2001a: 280).

Kroeber and Kluckhohn went on to write the influential book *Culture: A Critical Review of Concepts and Definitions,* in 1952, in which they espoused a mentalist view of culture (Kroeber and Kluckhohn 1963: 357). Leslie White (1987b: 168), who was naturally annoyed by the turn of events, acridly described this construal of culture as a shift from "concrete mindedness to traffic in abstractions."

Kroeber formally ratified the Boasian idealist conception of culture, reenergized by Parsons's mentalism, in a paper he wrote jointly with Parsons in 1958:

> We suggest that it is more useful to define culture for most usages more narrowly than has generally been the case in the American anthropological tradition, restricting reference to transmitted and created content and patterns of values, ideas, and other symbolic-meaningful systems as factors in shaping human behavior (Kroeber and Parsons 1958: 583).

It is such a conception of culture that informs the thinking of most present-day symbolic and interpretive anthropologists.

COGNITION AND BEHAVIOR

The new conception of culture, construed entirely in terms of symbolic-meaningful systems, excluded not only human behavior and action from the definition but also treated behavior as something shaped by values and symbols (Honigmann 1976: 251). Kroeber and Parsons's definition, as Harris (2001a: 281) noted, "is an encapsulated statement of the research strategy of cultural idealism, since it explicitly gives research priority to the principle that ideas determine behavior."

Cognitive anthropologist wholeheartedly adopted this idealist definition of culture (cf. Spradley 1972: 7). Moreover, Parsonian idealism would become the basis of another emic anthropological research strategy that came to be known as **symbolic anthropology** (see Chapter 13). From Harvard, the new conception of culture was transmitted to Princeton by the Harvard-trained anthropologist Clifford Geertz, and to Chicago by his fellow Harvard-trained anthropologist David Schneider (see Harris 1980; Harris 2001a: 281; Salzman 2001: 71; Schneider 1968: 1).

As I have pointed out, cognitive anthropology was constructed upon the epistemological foundation that culture comprises a set of logically structured cognitive models. Thus, understanding the chaotic surface or empirically accessible aspects of culture depended on the comprehension of subsurface rules and categories of cognition. Cognitive anthropologists were not concerned with the sorts of deep structures that interested Lévi-Strauss and others operating under the auspices of French structuralism. American cognitivists were more concerned with the learned rules and codes through which actors conceptualized the world (Honigmann 1976: 242).

Ultimately, however, American cognitivism and French structuralism both sought answers to cultural phenomena in the human mind and this led to a number of points of convergence between them. For example, both perspectives treated culture like a language and both relied upon formal analysis of categories of thought. Also, both perspectives were based upon models derived specifically from structural linguistics and approached cognition from a logical perspective. Ethnoscience departed from structuralism in its attempt to analyze culture from the point of view of the native actors rather than striving to infer the innate structures of human thought. However, the idea of innate structures was not far from the minds of ethnoscientists, especially in light of the influence of Chomsky's (1970) transformational-generative grammar model in linguistics.

Given their orientation, it is understandable that ethnoscience made an epistemological distinction between cultural behavior and cultural knowledge (Spradley 1972: 8). Goodenough described this distinction as follows:

> In considering any society's culture, anthropologists have been talking about *two different orders of reality* as if they were part of the same order. Many of the disagreements among anthropological schools of thought in the past have reflected differential emphasis on one or the other of these distinct orders. One is the phenomenal order of observed events and the regularities they exhibit. A human community, like any other natural universe in a state of near equilibrium, exhibits the statistical patterns characteristic of internally stable systems, as with homeostasis in the living organism. Similar, but never identical events occur over and over again and are therefore isolable as types of events and patterned arrangements. Certain types of arrangements tend to persist and others to appear and reappear in fixed sequences. An observer can perceive this kind of statistical patterning in a community without any knowledge whatever of the ideas, beliefs, values, and principles of action of the community's members, the ideational order. The phenomenal order is a property of the community as a material system of people, their surroundings, and their behavior. The ideational order is a property not of the community but of its members. It is their organization of their experience within the phenomenal order, a product of cognitive and instrumental (habit forming) learning. The ideational order, unlike the statistical order, is nonmaterial, being composed of ideal forms as they exist in people's minds, a proposition about their interrelationships, preference ratings regarding them, and recipes for their mutual or-

dering as means to desired ends. And as an organization of past experience, the ideational order is a means for organizing and interpreting new experience (Goodenough 1964: 11, emphasis added).[10]

Although acknowledging the existence of recurrent patterns of behavior in the "material system of people," cognitive anthropologists considered the primary objective of ethnographic research to be the description of the ideational order.

In a passage that echoes Sapir (1949: 546–547), Anthony Wallace, another major figure associated with this theoretical perspective, explained why ethnoscientists give priority to the cognitive rather than the behavioral dimension of culture:

> The work of the ethnographer, in describing the cognitive processes which have been culturally standardized in society, may perhaps best be made clear by an analogy. Let us suppose that a nonmathematician is given the task of describing a new mathematical calculus which is in active use by a group of people who have not bothered to formulate their system of calculation in a text or monograph. It has, in other words, been developing informally over the years, is currently being used in developed form, and is being taught to new users by example and by oral instruction. The investigator is allowed to interview and observe— that is, he may ask questions during coffee breaks, watch people computing, save scraps of paper from the wastebasket, take photographs of the machines employed, talk a few times with a project director, listen to people teaching one another the right way of doing things, and make other such minimally interfering kinds of observations and inquiry. He may even be permitted—and he will certainly be well advised—to join the group as a novice and learn to use the calculus himself. . . . Now, as he analyzes the data collected in these various ways, he does not merely tabulate the frequencies and intercorrelations of various classes of observed behavior in order to arrive at the calculus; if he did this, he would be giving equal weight to misunderstood jokes, learners' mistakes, slips of the pen, plain sloppy work, gibberish produced by broken computers, legpulling, and competent pro-

fessional operations. What he does, instead, is to infer the system of rules which these people are attempting to apply. The assurance that he is on the way to an adequate understanding of these rules will give him by the logical completeness of the system he infers and by his ability, when using it, to produce behavior which an expert will reward by saying, in effect, "That's right; that's good; now you've got it." Sometimes, of course, a sociologist or a psychologist will say to him, "But it is the behavior that is real, not this abstract system which no one actually applies perfectly and completely and which is merely the asymptote of the real curve of behaviors." To this the investigator simply replies that culture—conceived in this sense is a collection of formal calculi—is just as real as algebra, Euclidean geometry, and set theory, which are also "merely" asymptotes of the "real" behavior of fallible students, professional mathematicians, and machines. Indeed, he will point out, these other calculi *are* aspects of a culture, and their apparently greater tangibility is attributable to the incidental circumstances that they have been the object of more intensive study, in order to make their elements and operations explicit, than the undescribed calculus which he has just been investigating (Wallace 1972; 112–113).[11]

The analogy of fieldwork Wallace uses here is not a representative one, although it accurately depicts the orientation of an ethnographer who is unconcerned with ecological, demographic, and technological factors and whose theoretical framework excludes material causation and evolutionary holism.

While rules of calculus, written or not, are explicit in the minds of people, just like traffic rules, or the rules for football, and can be solicited with the appropriate questions, a great many rules exist at different levels of consciousness and cannot be accessed through such questioning. Moreover, many people are fuzzy and unclear even about explicit rules, such as traffic regulations, and one often finds drivers hesitating or not heeding such simple operations as giving the right of way to other drivers at four-way stops. Wallace's suggestion that ethnographic

research is about the search for rules is too narrow and limited a perspective.

In Wallace's scenario the ethnographer would also want to know why, for example, is the project in progress to begin with? Who is funding it and why? Why are the people in question there and using their informal calculus? Why the leg pulling? Why the jokes? Why the project supervisors? and sundry other questions that make up the social context of the group in question.

THE EMIC AND ETIC DISTINCTION

Linguists studying the sound systems of a language look at phonemes (the basic units of sound) in terms of how sounds are vocalized or formed mechanically (phonetics) and how they work within a specific language (phonemics). Phonetics entails observation, whereas phonemics requires looking at sound from within the language (Perry 2003: 65; see Headland, Pike, and Harris 1990). What we have are two modes of analysis, an emic (from phon*emic*) and an etic (from phon*etic*) one. According to the linguist Kenneth Pike, who first coined the two terms,

> [The emic approach] is an attempt to *discover* and to describe the pattern of the particular language or culture in reference to the way in which the various elements of that culture are related to each other in the functioning of the particular pattern, rather than attempt to describe them in reference to a generalized classification derived in advance of the study of that culture (Pike 1954: 8).[12]

Pike adds that

> An etic analytical standpoint . . . might be called "external" or "alien," since for etic purposes the analyst stands "far enough away" from or "outside" of a particular culture to see its separate events, primarily in relation to their similarities and differences, as compared to events in other cultures, rather than in reference to the sequence of classes of events within that one particular culture (Pike 1954: 10).[13]

Etic criteria have the appearance of absolutes, within the range of sensitivity of the measuring instrument (or the expertness of the analyst); emic criteria savor more of relativity, with the sameness of activity determined in reference to a particular system of activity (Pike 1954: 11).[14]

We can get a better idea of the difference between emic and etic modes of inquiry if we recall the example of the Euro-American kinship category "cousin" given earlier. Etically, ego has eight biological relatives that Euro-Americans gloss as cousins, the male and female offspring of his mother's brother and sister and the male and female offspring of his father's brother and sister. However, emic rules can result in different classifications of these individuals that Euro-Americans categorize under the single label of "cousin."

By way of illustration, we might think of a community made up of two exogamous patrilineal descent groups. Communities with such a dual division are based upon the moiety principle, mentioned in Chapter 9, and its divisions are called **patrimoieties,** such as the dual divisions among of the Mardu (Mardudjara) Aborigines in Australia (Tonkinson 1991: 75). Members of each moiety claim descent from a common ancestor and belong to separate named exogamous social categories (for example, A and B). Being patrilineal, members of each of the two social groups trace their descent along the father's line (Figure 12.1).

The result of such descent reckoning and dual division, looking at it from the point of view of a particular individual, or ego in group A, is that some of ego's cousins belong to his descent group, while others do not. Those cousins who belong to ego's descent group (A) are considered equivalent to and are referred to by the kin terms "brother" and "sister," and as such marriage between ego and these individuals is prohibited and sexual relations between these individuals would be considered incestuous. However, other of ego's cousins fall in descent group B, they are not considered siblings, and

ego is permitted to have sexual relations with and marry women from this group. In other words, ego takes a wife from the group to which he does not belong, and his children, because descent is reckoned along the father's side, will be members of his division.

The basis of this classification of cousins is patrilineal descent reckoning, dual divisions, and a distinction between two kinds of **parallel cousins** and **cross cousins.** The children of parents of the same sex on either side (i.e., mother's sister and father's brother) are ego's parallel cousins, while the children of parents of the opposite sex (i.e., father's sister and mother's brother) are ego's cross cousins. Ego's mother belongs to group B as do her sister and brother. Because the community is based upon moiety organization, ego's mother's sister is married to a man from group A, and her children, ego's parallel cousins on his mother's side, belong to their father's descent group. Ego's father's brother is married to a woman from B, but again because descent is traced patrilineally, his children, ego's parallel cousins on his father's side, belong to descent group A.

Ego's father's sister belongs to group A, but she is married to a man from group B and her children, ego's cross cousins on his father's side, belong to their father's descent group. Ego's mother's brother is married to a woman from group A, but his children, ego's cross cousins on his mother's side, belong to group B. In societies that trace descent unilineally, the differences between parallel and cross cousins are crucial.

What this example demonstrates is that the kinship terms ego uses are emic, culturally defined categories and may not correspond with etic, biological relationships. This also reveals the epistemological significance of the emic-etic distinction and why many science-oriented anthropologists acknowledge the importance of such distinctions.

The anthropologist Ward Goodenough elaborated upon the emic-etic contrasts, arguing that emic and etic modes of inquiry refer to "two or-

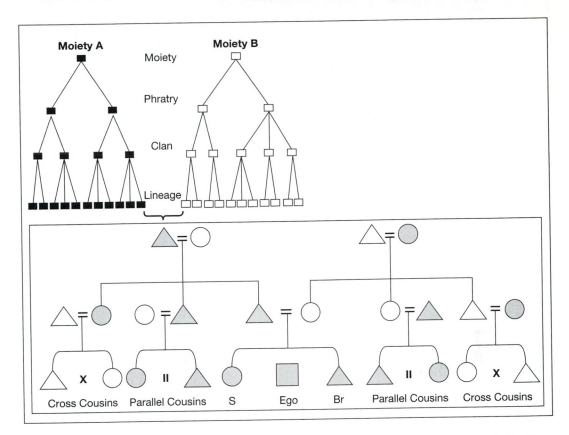

Figure 12.1 Shaded individuals belong to Patrimoiety A, unshaded ones to Patrimoiety B. Patrilineal descent reckoning and dual division means that parallel cousins belong to ego's descent group (A) by virtue of the membership of their father into that division and are considered equivalent to and are referred to by the kin terms "brother" and "sister." Marriage and sexual relations between ego and these individuals is prohibited. Cross cousins fall in descent group B, by virtue of the membership of their father into that division, and are not considered siblings, and ego is permitted to have sexual relations with and marry women from this group.

ders of reality" (Figure 12.2) and that the development of culture theory hinges upon anthropologists keeping these orders of reality distinct rather than treating them as if they refer to the same order (Goodenough 1964: 11; 1970). The anthropologist Marvin Harris, whose work I shall examine in Chapter 14, appropriated the emic/etic concepts from linguistics, reformulating them as a distinction between insider/outsider or science/folklore perspectives, and

stressed their theoretical significance in the scientific analysis of sociocultural phenomena (cf. Johnson and Johnson 2001: viii).

ETHNOSCIENCE IN ACTION: "DOING DOPE" ON CAMPUS

The objective of ethnoscience is "to find out what people know" and how people perceive and organize their reality through "their cus-

Phenomenal Order Events, Artifacts, Behavior	Ideational Order Values, Rules, Norms, i.e. Culture
1. Material system of people, their surroundings, and their behavior.	1. A nonmaterial system of ideas, beliefs, and values.
2. It is characteristic of a human community.	2. It is characteristic of a community's members.
3. It is observable without communication with members of a community.	3. It is not observable and can only be discovered by communicating with members of a community.
4. It involves patterns of action.	4. It involves principles of action.
5. It can be described as statistical patterns in a community.	5. It can be described as ideal forms in people's minds.
6. It forms part of the basis for a community's ideational order.	6. It is the organization of the member's experience of the phenomenal order.

Figure 12.2   Goodenough's distinction between phenomenal and ideational orders (etic–emic).   *After Goodenough (1964) and Spradley and McCurdy (1975: 8–9).*

tomary ways of categorizing the world around them" (Spradley and McCurdy 1975: 59). The focus of this kind of research is upon the "folk concepts" of another culture, or meaning, which is based upon how folk concepts are organized (Spradley and McCurdy 1975: 86). One must identify these concepts and then strive to discover how they are organized. To illustrate, I will refer to the example of an ethnographer investigating student drug culture on a university campus in the 1960s, based upon research conducted by Spradley and Janice Allen (Spradley and Mc-Curdy 1975). Ethnoscientific research may be broken down into the following eight steps (the discussion is drawn directly from Spradley and McCurdy 1975: 74–107).

(1) Collect Native Terms

To obtain the conceptual system of another culture one must look for the "things that go with words" (Spradley and McCurdy 1975: 74). It is important for the ethnographer to avoid interjecting his or her own analytical concepts and instead concentrate upon folk concepts. In our example, these concepts include words such as *freak, head, acid head* (as three different types of drug users), terms such as *smoking a roach, smoking a water pipe, hyperventilating* (as methods of doing dope), and words like *red death, peyote,* and *Acapulco Gold* (as types of dope).

(2) Formulate Culturally Appropriate Questions

The ethnographer formulates culturally appropriate questions on the basis of the statements obtained from informants in the context of their daily activities. For example, implicit in an informant's statement: "I smoke Acapulco Gold" are several questions:

> Who did dope? (I did.)
> What way did you do dope? (I smoked it.)
> What kind of dope did you do? (It was Acapulco Gold.)

Imbedded in these are more general questions that provide information on the larger conceptual domain:

> What kinds of people do dope?
> What are all the different ways to do dope?
> What are the different kinds of dope?

Determining culturally appropriate questions enables one to elicit answers that give more in-depth access to the culture.

(3) Identify Cultural/ Semantic Domains

A domain is a cultural category or class of objects that share at least one common feature of meaning that distinguishes these objects from things in other domains. Identifying cultural domains is important to the ethnoscientist because "like a rough map of the world that identifies the continents and oceans, the domains of a culture reveal the broad contours of a culture" (Spradley and McCurdy 1975: 78–79).

Domains have labels, called *cover terms.* One can discover cover terms by asking the appropriate cultural questions that generate an extensive list of terms. For example, an informant's statement, "I was smoking dope because I was bored," can be taken as one reason for doing dope, which can lead to the question, "are there other reasons students have for doing dope?" If this question generates a long list of answers (i.e., "reasons for doing dope"), this would comprise a cultural domain.

Semantic domains are sets or classes of related things/ideas/perceptions for which there are words in a language. Domains are often labeled with a word that encompasses all the items they contain. Thus, in English the word *color* is the label of the domain that contains all the words denoting coloration, such as *red, white, blue, green.* The labeled items in the domain are referred to as **lexemes.** For example, in English the color green is broken down into different kinds of green, such as kelly, mint, lime, olive, and avocado. Blue is broken down into teal, navy, royal, aqua, and so on. The meanings encoded in lexemes are garnered from their relationship to the other lexemes in the same domain, such as kelly green and lime green, or navy blue and royal blue.

Recording the main cultural domains serves as a general guide or map of the cultural terrain (Spradley and McCurdy 1975: 79). The ethnographer can then begin a detailed analysis of the cultural landscape.

(4) Identify Domain Members

In the case of the college drug culture in our example, one domain is the how drug users classify their social world into different types of people: "straights," "acid heads," "pot heads," "mescaline heads," "dealers," "smokers," "needle freaks." These terms bear significant information and provide rules about how to behave in reference to different people (i.e., straights, dealers, etc.). By learning the meaning and usage of the terms in this domain, the ethnographer can ostensibly operate in the cultural setting "as a native" (Spradley and McCurdy 1975: 80).

Aside from terms relating to people, there is also the domain for "kinds of drugs" or chemical substances. These number close to one hundred words and include marijuana, LSD, heroin, opium, "Red Hash," peyote, "red death," "downer," "Acapulco Gold," "ganga," "old basement," DMT, "kief," "Mary Jane," and "Kentucky Blue."

Meaning depends upon context, and the ethnographer must describe the variations in meaning with enough detail to enable one to use and interpret the terms in the same way as the member of the culture. For example, among many students marijuana is the primary drug. In situational contexts, the ethnographer will hear it referred to as *dope,* although in other contexts this term refers to other drugs as well. Other references to marijuana include "stuff," "Mary Jo Juana," "joint," "shit," "boo," "tea," "pot," "weed," "Alice B.," all of which are part of the domain of *names for dope.*

The ethnographer would also focus upon the social dimensions of drug use, which includes the contexts of use and the influence of culture upon the effects of chemical substances. There are concepts pertaining to the domain of *experiences when stoned* (Spradley and McCurdy 1975: 84). These are terms used for organizing subjective states, such as being "high" or "stoned," "coming on," "peaking," "coming down," "crashing," and "munchies." Other terms pertaining to subjective experiences include "silly," "mellow," "intense," "discorporated," "paranoid," "bummed out," "not together," and "introverted." The objective of this line of inquiry is to provide a complete ethnographic account that can serve as

> a recipe that an outsider could use to know which feelings and experiences were appropriate. One would know when to feel hungry or drowsy and be able to act in a manner judged acceptable by students (Spradley and McCurdy 1975: 85).[15]

The analysis of a cultural domain requires detailed look at cultural meanings. For example, the domain of "ways to do dope" contains many subcategories, as indicated in Figure 12.3.

The ability of the ethnographic description to reflect what one's informants know depends upon identifying all the domains that make up the cultural knowledge of the student drug

1. Smoking dope	16. Snorting a stem
2. Blowing grass	17. Drinking tea
3. Turkeying	18. Smoking a joint
4. Eating brownies	19. Eating a pizza
5. Smoking a sneaky peak carburetor	20. Drinking water
6. Eating gingerbread	21. Hyperventilating
7. Snorting a roach	22. Snorting a pipe
8. Eating dope	23. Snorting from a pipe
9. Smoking from a scuba tank	24. Snorting dope
10. Eating cookies	25. Eating in peanut butter
11. Smoking a pipe	26. Eating a roach
12. Eating grass	27. Eating kief
13. Eating it plain	28. Taking a nose hit
14. Drinking dope	29. Eating an Alice B. Toklas
15. Smoking a water pipe	30. Smoking a hookah

Figure 12.3   Ways of "doing dope."   *After James Spradley and David McCurdy* Anthropology: The Cultural Perspective *(1975). New York: John Wiley & Sons, p. 86.*

users. To grasp the student users' point of view, or "cultural meaning," the ethnographer must determine "how they organize their knowledge" (Spradley and McCurdy 1975: 81). As Spradley and McCurdy (1975: 86) have pointed out,

A culture is like a map for finding your way in the vast complexity of human experience. Our culture provides each of us with a blueprint for identifying the significant features of our environment, for selecting goals and achieving them, and for locating ourselves in time and space. But cultural meaning involves more than using folk concepts to identify persons, places and objects. Meaning is based on the way folk concepts are organized. As we acquire our culture, we learn to arrange the elements of experience into larger categories that are linked together and interrelated in a complex network, a pattern of cultural meaning. It is the various parts that are arranged into relationships that constitute the structure of a particular culture.[16]

Finding out how domains are internally structured/organized is important because it is thought to supply tacit knowledge that remains outside the conscious awareness of the members of the culture (Spradley and McCurdy 1975: 87). Thus the identification of cultural domains is followed by the investigation of how folk concepts are organized.

(5) Discover Taxonomic Structure

To discover the principles used by the students to organize their cultural concepts entails looking at *folk taxonomies*. Taxonomies are based upon "the principle of inclusion" based upon the use of a general category to refer to more specific categories. In the example here, the investigation of taxonomic structure begins with the study of the domain of "doing dope." The names of all the different ways of doing dope (e.g., "hyperventilating" or "taking a nose hit") are written on slips of paper that the informants are asked to sort into groups. Such a procedure reveals that the students have four primary

methods of doing dope: drinking dope, eating dope, snorting dope, and smoking dope. The taxonomic structure is provided in Figure 12.4.

(6) Select Contrast Set for Analysis

The next step entails looking for things that are treated as being different. This involves an investigation of how members of the culture organize the world by looking at which things they group together and what things they set apart. This indicates that what something means is connected to what something does not mean. A contrast set basically refers to an assemblage of terms within a taxonomy that are included under a single term in a higher level. Figure 12.5 shows the contrast sets in the taxonomy of doing dope. Thus, to grasp what smoking a joint means, one must understand how that process is different from "hyperventilating," smoking a scuba tank, smoking a pipe (Spradley and McCurdy 1975: 94).

The meaning of concepts is differentiated by the attributes that are linked to them. Figure 12.6 indicates the attributes linked to the concept of *smoking a roach*. This shows the numerous significant aspects, formal and emotional, of the activity in the culture of the students. In this case, smoking a roach is contrasted to other kinds of highs. Attributes together make up the overall cultural meaning of a cultural category.

(7) Look for Attributes

Members of a contrast set are differentiated by their attributes. The investigation of the attributes associated with the categories in a set is called **componential analysis.**

Looking at the contrast sets of "ways to do dope," the anthropologists will pay attention to how informants interpret their behavior. For example, one method is called "sneaky peak carburetor," which involves taking a toilet paper roll and making a hole on one side close to the end and then placing joint in it. Covering one end of

W A Y S T O D O D O P E	Drinking Dope	Drinking tea
		Drinking in water
		Drinking in wine
	Eating Dope	Eating in peanut butter
		Eating grass
		Eating brownies
		Eating gingerbread
		Eating a roach
		Eating cookies
		Eating on pizza
		Eating kief
	Snorting Dope	Snorting a roach
		Snorting a stem
		Snorting from a pipe
		Taking a nose hit
	Smoking Dope	Smoking a water pipe
		Turkeying
		Smoking a pipe
		Smoking a joint
		Smoking a sneaky peak carburetor
		Smoking from a scuba tank
		Hyperventilating

Figure 12.4   Taxonomic structure of ways to do dope.   *After James Spradley and David McCurdy* An-thropology: The Cultural Perspective *(1975). New York: John Wiley & Sons, p. 90.*

the roll by hand, the user inhales. This causes the roll to fill with smoke, and once the hand is re-moved concentrated smoke blasts into the user's lungs, producing a powerful "rush." This method has the attribute of using equipment, which is shared with smoking a pipe, a scuba tank, or a roach. It is set apart from smoking a joint by the attribute of resulting in a more intense high.

To discover attributes the anthropologist will ask informants to name the distinguishing at-

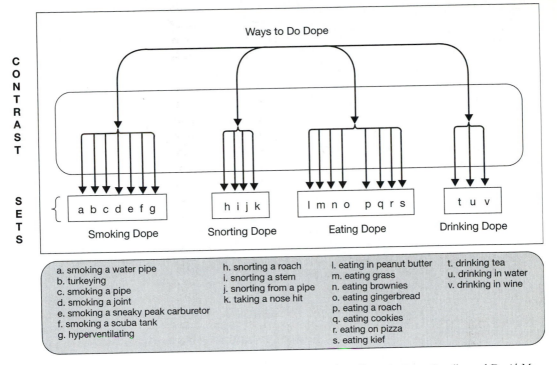

Figure 12.5 Contrast sets in the taxonomy of "ways to do dope." *After James Spradley and David McCurdy Anthropology: The Cultural Perspective (1975). New York: John Wiley & Sons, p. 94.*

tributes of contrasting terms, such as How is "smoking a joint" different from "smoking a water pipe"? Informants will then provide a number of attributes: Smoking a water pipe is a preferred method because it is less harsh on the throat. It is smoother than smoking a joint because grass smoke is harsh and hard to inhale. A water pipe is especially smooth if one uses wine instead of water.

One way to get such information is to ask informants to sort several of their concepts into sets according to similarities and differences. Asking a student to sort the several ways of smoking into two or more groups would get the following result: (1) smoking a water pipe, from a scuba tank; (2) smoking a joint, a pipe, a sneaky peak carburetor, a roach, and hyperventilating. Inquiring why the informant has created cate-

gories, you would find that method (1) requires a larger quantity of marijuana in comparison with method (2).

(8) Construct a Paradigm

Representing that major attributes for a set of terms graphically enables one to determine which categories have the greatest differences. Recording the attributes of a set of terms reveals multiple relationships. To depict this, the anthropologist will use a "paradigm" as in Figure 12.7. A paradigm "organizes a set of terms that share at least one feature of meaning and can all be distinguished by at least one . . . attribute" (Spradley and McCurdy 1975: 100). Here the category of ways to smoking dope has six dimensions. Each dimension has several possible

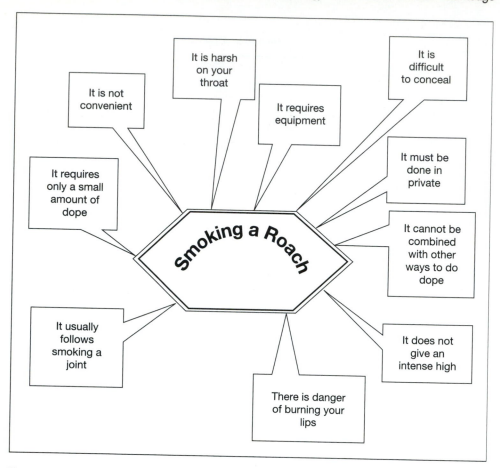

Figure 12.6 Attributes of smoking a roach. *After James Spradley and David McCurdy Anthropology: The Cultural Perspective (1975). New York: John Wiley & Sons, p. 96.*

attributes indicated below the paradigm in numerical and alphabetical form. This diagram depicts the more significant information that members of the culture use to organize their behavior. The choice of one method over another is in response to the questions: "Is it convenient?", "Will it be harsh on my throat?", "Will it give me a more intense high?"

Through these procedures the anthropologist attempts to decode the information contained in cultures as systems of meaning. As Spradley and McCurdy (1975: 101) observe,

> Culture . . . is a set of rules for interpreting experience and generating appropriate behavior. College

students who use drugs employ their culture in much the same way that corporate executives or tribal hunters employ theirs.[17]

THEORETICAL ISSUES

Ethnoscientists start with the identification of native terms and the investigation of semantic domains, the categories that people in different cultures use to sort and classify information. Repeated intensive structured interviews are used to elicit information on native categories. Examples of semantic domains, apart from the preceding example, are kinship systems, categories of

Dimensions of Contrast						
	A Harsh on Throat?	**B** Combined with Others?	**C** Convenient?	**D** More Intense High?	**E** Large Amount Required?	**F** Easily Concealed?
Smoking a water pipe	No	1	No	No	Yes	No
Smoking a joint	Yes	2	2	No	No	1
Smoking a pipe	Yes	No	1	No	No	Yes
Smoking a sneaky peak carburetor	Yes	No	3	Yes	No	No
Smoking from a scuba tank	No	No	4	No	Yes	2
Hyperventilating	XX	3	3	Yes	No	XX
Smoking a roach	Yes	No	3	No	No	No
Turkeying	Yes	No	2	Yes	No	No

Dimensions of Contrast: Ways to Smoke

(A) Harsh on Throat
No: Smoke is cooled by water or other process.
Yes: Although temperature may vary, depending on nearness to heat, all are harsh.

(B) Combines with Other Ways to Do Dope
1: May drink water or liquid in water pipe.
2: Eat grass dropped while preparing joint.
3: Combines with any type of inhalation.
No: Generally not combined with other ways to do dope.

(C) Convenience
1: Most convenient.
2: It is convenient, but still requires additional equipment or action.
3: Not as convenient as 2 because it requires additional equipment or action.
4: Temporary inconvenience but results in a convenient supply of smoke to inhale.

(D) More Intense High
Yes: A higher concentration of smoke is inhaled, resulting in heightened sensations.
No: Normal result that can vary with amount over time.

(E) Large Amount Required
Yes: Amount varies depending on size of water pipe and scuba tank.
No: Can ingest dope with relatively small amount.

(F) Easily Concealed
No: Must be done in private.
Yes: May be done in private.
1: May be done in public and easily concealed depending on type of joint.
2: Substance is very well concealed but would not be used in public.
XX: Not applicable to this term.

Figure 12.7 Paradigm of ways to smoke dope. *After James Spradley and David McCurdy* Anthropology: The Cultural Perspective *(1975). New York: John Wiley & Sons, p. 99.*

disease, experience of disease, colors, methods of open sea navigation, rock music, and art.

Success in this line of research depends on the exhaustive elicitation of lexemes in each domain. Among the problems posed by this kind of research is determining whether or not the data obtained exhaust a particular domain. In other words, the researcher must somehow establish that all the lexemes in a domain have been recorded and that their informants have a reasonable familiarity with the domain in question, something that is not as simple as it may sound (Eastman 1990: 114).

Analysis of semantic domains has revealed that people from different cultures do organize and think about things differently. Harold Conklin's (1955) paper on the color categories of the Hanunóo, in the Philippines, is a classic ethnoscientific study of a semantic domain in one language. However, the cross-cultural study of color terminology by Brent Berlin and Paul Kay (1969) is far more ambitious and requires comment.

Berlin and Kay analyzed the color terms in close to one hundred languages and identified 11 basic color terms: white, black, red, green, yellow, blue, brown, purple, pink, gray, and orange. They found a wide range of diversity in color terms cross-culturally. Not all languages have all of the eleven terms; however, no language has less than two colors. Some cultures have as few as two color terms (white/black or light/dark) (for example, the Jalé of Papua New Guinea), whereas some have terms for all the basic colors (for example Zuñi of New Mexico, the Dinka of the Sudan, and the Tagalog of the Philippines).

Berlin and Kay proposed that when a new color is incorporated into the lexicon, it everywhere follows the same sequence (Figure 12.8). Thus, in a language with two colors, the terms will be white/black. In a language with three colors, they will be white/black/red. In a language with four colors, they will be either white/black/red/yellow or white/black/red/green. A language that has five color terms will either add yellow or green, depending on which term is already present. In languages with six colors, the sixth will be blue. In a language with seven color terms, the seventh will be brown. Languages with more than seven colors include the words for purple, pink, orange, and gray (Berlin and Kay 1969: 152–156). Some languages—for example, Japanese, Inuktitut (Arctic Canada), and Aguaruna (Peru)—have terms for the blue-green wavelength of the color spectrum for which English does not have an equivalent term. Kay (1975) designated this blue-green color category as **grue.**

What are the implications of this range of variation in the color terminologies of various languages? Does this show that people such as the Jalé, whose language according to Berlin and Kay contains only two color words, are unable

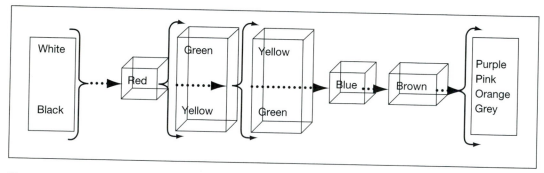

Figure 12.8   Sequence of color term acquisition.   *After Berlin and Kay (1969).*

to distinguish red from green? No. They are able to do so in the same way that speakers of English can distinguish between green and grue, even though their language does not have a specific word for grue. There may be some biological variation in color perception between people with lighter eyes and darker eyes in how easily they can distinguish the blue-green range of the color spectrum (Bornstein 1973; Ember 1978). However, this does not mean the people do not see colors in the same way.

In fact, Berlin and Kay asked subjects to identify from a set of color chips the one that was the purest example of that color and to indicate when the chips on the color chart became another color. They found that speakers of all languages were able to pick out the purest example. This means that people perceive color in the same way despite the fact that they may have different labels or lack labels for them (Eastman 1990: 107). The number of words for color in a particular language seems to become greater with increasing technological and economic complexity (Kay and Mc-Daniel 1978; see Thompson 1995).

These findings contradict the strong version of the Sapir-Whorf hypothesis of linguistic determinism, as well as its ancillary, the contention that reality is culturally constituted or culturally constructed without any reference to the objective world. What the preceding examples show is that cultures breakup experience differently and create dissimilar categories working with the objective characteristics of things by attributing or not attributing importance to those differences of experience. This means, in other words, that cultural models "are strongly shaped by the ordinary world of normal perception" and that "cultural reality is more often reality-shaped than culturally constituted" (D'Andrade 1999: 88). This is an important observation to bear in mind when we turn to the cultural constructionist assertions that reality is determined wholly and exclusively by culture.

The primary method used in ethnoscience is componential analysis. Componential analysis is applied to semantic domains in order to search for attributes and investigate the relationship between the components of meaning within a domain. Semantic domains possess a hierarchical structure of inclusive levels and can be taxonomically displayed as a branching diagram. The hierarchy divides the domain by means of contrasts and exclusions. Thus, in the English domain of fruits, categories on the same level are placed in terms of their contrasts (for example, oranges, grapefruits, lemons, limes), while all of these categories are included as being similar at the level above, as citrus fruits, and so on.

The assumption behind this procedure is that the comparison of lexical items within a domain would contribute to an understanding of the meaning of the domain as a whole (Eastman 1990: 113). By determining the criteria used in classifying things within a domain, one could discover the principles of organization, or "logical calculus" in a domain and hence the principles of cognition.

Ethnoscientists operate on the assumption that each culture's semantic domains encodes different segments of a universal set of cognitive ordering principles, or the "grammar" underlying culture (cf. Bernard 1995: 239). The investigation of the cognitive domains of various cultures altogether would thus reveal the set of universal cognitive principles. Frake (1972: 203) lauded the new ethnography by pointing out its explanatory potential:

> The principles by which people in a culture construe their world reveal how they segregate the pertinent from the insignificant, how they code and retrieve information, how they anticipate events . . . how they define alternative courses of action and make decisions among them. Consequently a strategy of ethnographic description that gives a central place to the cognitive processes of the actors involved will contribute reliable cultural data to problems of the relations between language, cognition, and behavior; it will point up critical dimensions for meaningful cross-cultural comparisons; and, finally, *it will give us productive*

descriptions of cultural behavior, descriptions which, like the linguists' grammar, succinctly state what one must know in order to generate culturally acceptable acts and utterances appropriate to a given socio-ecological context (emphasis added).[18]

The test of ethnoscience is whether it can generate the kind of data that would let the researcher think like and see the world as "the natives" do, as Frake (1972: 203) suggested it could. If it cannot do this then the question must be raised about what the data of cognitive anthropology really do.

Other ethnoscientists also claimed that the plans and rules they were after could elucidate behavior. For example, Spradley (1972: 4) wrote that people "use plans to organize their behavior in the pursuit of goals," and Tyler (1969: 3) pointed out that people use these rules to "organize and use their cultures." However, at the same time cognitivists maintained that the cultural rules with which they were concerned had little to do with actual behavior. Tyler (1969: 13), for example, pointed out that behavior is irrelevant to the cognitivists' theory of culture by falling back upon an analogy with linguistics.

> There is no necessity to assume that the cognitive order is either systematically derivative of or a predictor of substantive actions. Just as the grammar of a language provides no information on what an individual speaker will say on any given occasion, so too a cognitive description of a culture does not pretend to predict the actual behavior of any individual. The formal analysis of culture, like a grammar, is concerned only with what is expected and appropriate. And just as an adequate grammar is neither contingent upon prior assumptions concerning the developmental processes nor necessarily explains them, a grammar of culture need make no assumptions about nor attempt to explain these processes (Tyler 1969: 13).[19]

One might question the relevance of an anthropology that, by Tyler's own admission, has no bearing upon how people behave. Harris (2001b: 590) highlights the problem relating to the correspondence between the grammar of culture and actual behavior:

> If permitted to develop unchecked, the tendency to write ethnographies in accord with the emic rules of behavior will result in an unintentional parody of the human condition. Applied to our own culture it would conjure up a way of life in which men tip their hats to ladies; youths defer to old people in public conveyances; unwed mothers are a rarity; citizens go to the aid of law enforcement officers; chewing gum is never stuck under tables and never dropped on sidewalks; television repairmen fix television sets; children respect their aged parents; rich and poor get the same medical treatment; taxes are paid in full; all men are created equal; and our defense budget is used only for maintaining peace.[20]

Another question is this: Is it really a grammar of culture that cognitive anthropologists uncover? Critics have questioned whether componential analysis really provides the investigator with information about what people think, or with the necessary knowledge, something like "the linguists' grammar," that would enable one to think or behave like a native. While such an analysis may reveal the patterns of thought about the lexemes within the domains analyzed, it is unlikely that it tells us anything significant about cognition, which entails more than classification (Gross 1992: 82).

A still greater problem pertains to the relationship between the semantic domains. As more data were gathered in semantic domains relating to such things as firewood, curers, ethnobotanical systems, agriculture, betel chewing, pottery, verbal play, color categories, kinship, water, and navigation, it became evident that these were more or less separate entities independent of one another. As D'Andrade (1995: 249) put it, "Each cultural model is 'thing-like,' but all the models together do not form any kind of thing." Thus, the end result of the Boasian influenced cognitive anthropological research perspective was a shreds and patches conception much like the one in which the Boasians themselves were entangled.

PROBLEMS OF FORMAL ANALYSIS

The cognitivists were particularly enthralled by the formal and quasi-mathematical manipulations that could be performed on culture when it is treated as a language. As Tyler (1969: 14) put it,

> At issue here are two contrasting views of cultural anthropology. The central issue is, Is cultural anthropology a *natural* or a *formal* science? Traditional cultural anthropology is based on the assumption that its data are discrete material phenomena which can be analyzed like the material phenomena of any other natural science. Cognitive anthropology is based on the assumption that its data are mental phenomena which can be analyzed by formal methods similar to those of mathematics and logic. Each particular culture consists of a set of logical principles which order relevant material phenomena. To the cognitive anthropologist these logical principles rather than the material phenomena are the object of investigation. For the cognitive anthropologist cultural anthropology is a formal science. It seems likely that the logical operations underlying principles of ordering are finite and universal, but capable of generating an infinite number of possible specific orderings. . . . In this limited sense, cognitive anthropology constitutes a return to Bastian's search for the "psychic unity of mankind."[21]

The commitment to formal analysis amounted to a disregard for behavior and a rejection of material causation and evolutionary holism. Having ejected these ingredients, cognitive anthropologists were left with the problem of figuring out cognitive rules entirely on the basis of semantic relationships. This they did by constructing formal models to capture "ideal forms as they exist in people's minds." Such models involve sets of carefully defined elements that are combined by means of logical rules (Kaplan and Manners 1972: 165, 167).

The appealing aspect of this approach was that there were explicit instructions derived from structural linguistics that specified how an analytical model should be developed. For this reason the methods of cognitive anthropology were embraced by many because they seemed to offer objective and replicable procedures in comparison to the conventional "impressionistic" approaches of the time.

However, the logical rigor that formal analysis requires comes at the cost of forfeiture of a significant amount of empirical ethnographic data through the shedding of variables (cf. Honigmann 1976: 256). While the models work in that they do reveal that certain formal relationships exist between variables, and are reproducible, they do not say anything about whether these relationships hold true empirically. This is the major weakness of all perspectives based upon formal analysis, including cognitive anthropology and French structuralism. As Honigmann (1976: 256) put it,

> Less was said about the comparative validity of the new methods; a moment's reflection reveals that there need be no necessary connection between a reproducible procedure and the truth of what it reveals. The attractiveness of formalism stemmed partly from the explicitness of the rules put forward for studying particular systems of culture, and the ease with which the rules could be learned. When critics examined the value of what the rules were revealing, formal semantic analysis could marshal few arguments in its defense.

Ethnoscientists assumed that there is only one "right" and logical way to organize a semantic domain (Pelto and Pelto 1979: 59). In other words, the assumption was that the relationships revealed through logical manipulation corresponded to the one shared by members of the culture in question. This, sadly, is not the case. In an article entitled "Cognition and Componential Analysis: God's Truth or Hocus-Pocus?" (1964), Robbins Burling demonstrated that using only four items it is hypothetically possible to create 124 models for the domain. With more items, the possibilities become almost infinite. The paradigm offered few guidelines for choosing between alternate models generated in this manner. Thus, Burling expressed strong doubts that componential analysis would ever lead to the discovery of the grammar of culture or how people construe the world.

> Students who claim that componential analysis or comparable methods of semantic analysis can provide a means for "discovering how people construe the world" must explain how to eliminate the great majority of logical possibilities and narrow the choice to the one or few that are "psychologically real." I will not be convinced that there are not dozens or hundreds of possible analyses of Subanun disease terms until Frake presents us with the entire system fully analyzed and faces squarely the problem of how he chooses his particular analysis. In the meantime, I will doubt whether any single analysis tells us much about people's cognitive structure, even if it enables us to use terms as a native does (Burling 1964: 26).[22]

Burling added that

> linguists, in referring to attitudes toward grammatical analyses, have sometimes made the distinction between the "God's truth" view and the "hocus pocus" view. . . . When a linguist makes his investigation and writes his grammar, is he discovering something about the language which is "out there" waiting to be described and recorded or is he simply formulating a set of rules which somehow work? Similarly, when an anthropologist undertakes a semantic analysis, is he discovering some "psychological reality" which somehow speakers are presumed to have or is he simply working out a set of rules which somehow take account of the observed phenomena? The attitude taken in this paper is far over on the "hocus-pocus" side. It is always tempting to attribute something of more importance to one's work than a tinkering with a rough set of operational devices. It certainly sounds more exciting to say we are fiddling with a set of rules which allow us to use terms the way others do. Nevertheless, I think the latter is a realistic goal, while the former is not. I believe we should be content with the less exciting objective of showing how terms in language are applied to objects in the world, and stop pursuing the illusory goal of cognitive structures (Burling 1964: 27).[23]

PROBLEMS OF THE EMIC APPROACH AND CROSS-CULTURAL GENERALIZATIONS

Some anthropologists have criticized the cognitivists' theoretical objective to describe cultures from the emic mode of inquiry. All descriptions entail discrimination and selection, including the descriptions based on "the native's point of view." While the native's categories may be necessary to address some questions, these certainly do not encompass all the aims of cultural anthropology (Kaplan and Manners 1972: 181). There are innumerable questions of interest to anthropologists that cannot be treated by using native categories. It goes without saying that the same observations apply in the case of present-day interpretive perspectives that advocate a retreat into ethnographic particularism, referred to in the current jargon as "narrative ethnographies of the particular" (e.g., Abu-Lughod 1991: 150–151).

A related problem is that exclusive focus upon the insider's point of vies hinders any hopes of cross-cultural comparisons, because each culture, described in its own terms, becomes unique unto itself. While in the antiscience and relativistic intellectual climate of today this might not present itself as a problem, it was perceived as such for those who at the time were attempting to build a generalizing science of culture. As Spiro pointed out in his book *Burmese Supernaturalism* (1967),

> As between the "emic" and "etic" approaches, then, my approach is unabashedly etic. The former approach leads to a descriptive and relativistic inquiry whose interest begins and ends with the parochial. The latter approach leads to a theoretical and comparative inquiry in which the parochial is of interest as an instance of the universal. If the former issues in ethnography, the latter (although based on ethnography) issues in science. Since I am interested in science, the explanations offered in this study use concepts which are analytic rather than substantive; there reference is usually to a theoretical construct rather than to an ethnographic

category; and their domain is usually the class "supernaturalism" and not merely Burmese supernaturalism (Spiro 1967: 6).[24]

The problem that Spiro is referring to is one alluded to earlier in this chapter, namely that of going from specific and particularistic accounts to general theoretical constructs.

Goodenough attempted to address this issue with respect to a problem he encountered during his fieldwork in Micronesia. Goodenough (1956b) and John Fischer (1958) both conducted research on residence forms in a community on the island of Romonum in Truk Lagoon, in Micronesia. These two anthropologists were there within three years of one another. The problem that surfaced was a discrepancy in their findings regarding Trukese **postmarital residence patterns.** Both anthropologists relied upon censuses for their data on residence patterns, although Fischer's survey was more extensive in geographical scope and less detailed for individual communities (Fischer 1958: 509).

Goodenough's data indicated that three-quarters of the Trukese lived in **matrilocal** residence and hence he concluded that the society was matrilocal. Fischer's figure indicated that half the married couples lived in matrilocal residence and a third **patrilocally.** On the basis of these data, Trukese society could be classified as **bilocal.** As Goodenough noted,

> In short, two censuses of the same community within three years result in differences of a magnitude sufficient to suggest a different classification of its residence customs. Fischer's and my conclusions were both based on accepted census procedures. Either there were radical changes in residence practices and physical shifts of household accordingly in three years' time or we were honestly interpreting similar census data in very different ways (Goodenough 1956b: 23).[25]

Goodenough (1956b: 24) rejected radical change as an explanation and believed that the discrepancies were due to different interpretations of the data.

Fischer (1958: 510) saw the solution to the problem in terms of modifications of the typology in use. Goodenough's solution, however, was to urge that the ethnographers search for rules significant from the point of view of the indigenous people, in this case the Trukese, rather than applying an a priori anthropological typology of residence. The assumption was that this prescription would make "cultural descriptions replicable and accurate" and hence "advance the whole of cultural anthropology" (Sturtevant 1972: 132). In other words, the anthropologist should use terms and categories meaningful to the native, rather than those meaningful to the observer.

Goodenough's conclusion was therefore that the source of the problem was disciplinary bias. He noted, for example, that when the ethnographer says that a society is patrilocal, he or she is really stating that there are residence customs of a nature unascertained but such that he feels they should be classified as patrilocal for comparative purposes. Then this assertion is treated as if it is a descriptive ethnographic statement. To address this uncertainty, Goodenough suggested that descriptive ethnography should be separated from any sort of comparative work and treated as "a legitimate scientific end in itself."

> What we do as ethnographers is, and must be kept, independent of what we do as comparative ethnologists. An ethnographer is constructing a theory that will make intelligible what goes on in a particular social universe. A comparativist is trying to find principles common to many different universes. His data are not the direct observations of an ethnographer, but the laws governing the particular universe as the ethnographer formulates them. It is by noting how these laws vary from one universe to another and under what conditions, that the comparativist arrives at a statement of laws governing the separate sets of laws which in turn govern the events in their respective social universes. Although they operate at different levels of abstraction, both ethnographer and comparativist are engaged in theory construction. Each must, therefore, develop concepts appropriate to his own level of abstraction, and in the case of the

ethnographer to his particular universe. When we move from one level to the other we must shift our conceptual frameworks in accordance with systemic transformation procedures (Goodenough 1956b: 37).[26]

One must grant that Goodenough was concerned with making ethnographic descriptions more reliable by pointing out the problems of using Euro-American conceptual categories so that such accounts can be more reliable and replicable, which are admirable scientific goals. Ethnoscientists had ultimate scientific goals that did not preclude cross-cultural comparisons at some stage. However, this was in actuality also an advocacy for a retreat to the particularistic studies of the kind associated with Franz Boas (i.e., we must understand how each particular culture works before we can undertake comparisons). Moreover, this view entails the assumption that the ethnographer can somehow operate unencumbered by any theoretical predispositions or biases and can operate entirely using native categories, which is questionable. Goodenough is to be criticized for ignoring the interplay between theory and empirical data collection. Moreover, Goodenough's use of the term theory to refer to particular cultures, which suggests that the ethnography of a given culture holds a theory of that culture, is in error. This view is clearly reiterated by Tyler (1969: 5), who states that ethnographic "description itself constitutes the 'theory' for that culture, for it represents the conceptual model of organization used by its members."

This view is unacceptable and is based upon a misunderstanding of the relationship between theory and empirical data because it ignores the constant interplay between them (Kaplan and Manners 1972: 183). This viewpoint is comparable to the assertion made by present-day interpretive anthropologists that the only valid and meaningful generalizations, if there are any to be found at all, are those that are culturally specific, context dependent, and relative (cf. Spiro 1986: 262). The idea of generalizing within cultures is

also programmatic for Geertz (1973: 26), one of the gurus of interpretive anthropology. Although Geertz is highly critical of cognitive anthropology (see Chapter 13), his own emic perspective converges with those of the cognitivists on several points.

As critics see it, the problem with cognitivist formulations is, of course, that a generalization that applies only to a single case is a contradiction in terms (Harris 2001b: 285). If each culture or cultural institution is described in "native" categories and concepts, and hence is treated as an entity unique unto itself, cross-cultural comparisons would be impossible. The transformation procedures necessary in order to move from Goodenough's ethnographic case to a general theory of culture would require that the descriptive materials to be decontextualized (Kaplan and Manners 1972: 183). In other words, ethnographic descriptions using native concepts and categories are not amenable to comparative analysis until those concepts and categories have been translated into nonnative terms and categories.

Theory requires comparison, something that Goodenough's approach does not permit. As Kaplan and Manners (1972: 183) noted,

> When Goodenough argues, therefore, that there is a broad conceptual gap between an ethnographic description framed wholly in native terms and categories and the formulation or testing of comparative propositions, he is, in effect, emphasizing the limitations of such descriptions for the development of a theoretical anthropology.[27]

For some anthropologists working in the 1960s and 1970s the issue of cross-cultural comparisons and the development of a generalizing science of culture was important, and it is for this reason that they raised objections to the ethnoscience research agenda. Today, there are a number of writers who categorically dismiss the idea of cross-cultural comparisons and generalizations on the grounds that such efforts are irrelevant to the understanding of the "Other." Therefore the epistemological implications of what Goodenough and other cognitivists were advocating would pose no problems for these writers.

ASSESSMENT

If Goodenough's solution to the problem of more accurate fieldwork leads to theoretical difficulties, does it at least solve the problem of producing more reliable descriptions? No. This is because cognitivists assume unambiguity and semantic homogeneity when eliciting data from their informants. Yet ill-informed or uninformed informants abound, and ambiguity in the meanings of lexical terms is a manifest feature of many semantic domains. A good example comes from Euro-American kinship terminology. Few Americans can agree on the distinctions between first and second cousins and first and second cousins twice removed. Nor is there agreement on the appropriate term for father's second wife or wife's brother's wife's brother (Harris 2001a: 272). This problem is not confined to American culture, or just to kinship categories, but is also true of people from other cultures and in other domains (e.g., Hamill et al. 2002).

Ambiguities of the kind that resulted in the discrepancies in the ethnographic works of Goodenough and Fischer on Truk are not always necessarily the attributes of data gathering procedures but may be due to semantic heterogeneity in the community and the representativeness of the informants. Such variations can be significant. As Dolgin, Kemnitzer, and Schnieder (1977: 3) noted,

> Some beliefs are *shared* by all the members of a group; others are specific to one or another subgroup or category of persons within a larger group; and others still are held by individuals only. Each of these constitutes systems at different levels; the system of beliefs shared (more or less) by all members of a group is called a "culture" or "ideology"; an individual's system of beliefs—the totality of what a person shares with others and what is unique to that person—is an aspect of personality;

the beliefs of a subgroup are often called a "subculture."

These issues pose an especially insurmountable problem for perspectives that focus on the native's point of view and emic rules, while at the same time excluding from the explanatory frame of reference all forms of nonverbal behavior, such as material conditions, actual social relationships, and technology (Pelto and Pelto 1979: 60).

Clifford Geertz (1973: 11–12) referred to the methods of cognitive anthropology as "extreme subjectivism . . . married to extreme formalism" and criticized the "cognitivist fallacy" of treating culture as mental phenomena that can me analyzed by formal methods resembling mathematics and logic. He also raised the issue noted above, of whether the folk taxonomies, paradigms, tables, "and other ingenuities" really reflect what the natives think, or are merely clever simulations, "logically equivalent but substantively different, of what they think."

A problem of a different sort is that componential analysis takes a very long time, a shortcoming recognized early on. For example, Sturtevant (1972: 158) wrote that

> ethnoscience raises the standards of reliability, validity, and exhaustiveness in ethnography. One result is that the ideal goal of a complete ethnography is farther removed from practical attainment. The full ethnoscientific description of a single culture would require many thousands of pages published after many years of intensive fieldwork based on ethnographic methods more complete and more advanced than are now available. The interest in ethnography will therefore continue to be guided by ethnological, comparative, interests. Some domains will receive more attention that others.[28]

It is telling that a perspective that started out with the goal of elevating the standards of field research should settle for partial and incomplete accounts of limited domains of culture. So, what happened to the better and more precise ethnographies that were anticipated? Berreman

(1966: 410) referred to Sturtevant's admission as "exhaustion, if not exhaustive" and doubted that an ethnoscientific ethnography would ever be produced. He was not wrong.

Thus, in addition to the problems and shortcoming of cognitive anthropology already mentioned, there was the problem of what the perspective could actually achieve on the ground. Frake (1969: 135) summarized these as follows:

> No one working with [ethnoscientific] procedures has yet described a complete culture, but some have succeeded in producing descriptions of remarkable variety of cultural manifestations. Metzger and Williams, for example, emerged from one field session with descriptions of firewood . . . terms of personal reference . . . curers . . . and weddings. Conklin has described ethnobotanical systems, agriculture, betel chewing, pottery, verbal play, color, kinship, and water. . . . None of these descriptions, whatever its faults, can be called superficial and each says a great deal about the topics at hand but also about the cultures being investigated and about the culture in general.[29]

Commenting on these, Berreman (1966: 351) made the following observations:

> None of these descriptions, whatever their virtues, can in themselves be called very significant. They sound like ethnoscientific trait lists. They remind me of Mill's warning that many sociologists have gotten to the point where they overlook what is important in their research for what is verifiable, and some of them break down the units of analysis so minutely that truth and falsity are no longer distinguishable. Many have worked so hard on what is trivial that it comes to appear important—at least triviality and importance have become indistinguishable when fitted into the molds of formal analysis.[30]

The problems therefore were numerous. By the mid-1970s, these difficulties led to a shift in research focus. There was a move away from attempts to discover people's whole cognitive systems and structures, or grammars of culture. The shift was toward a less ambitious goal, that of providing accurate descriptions of cultural representations, or "how terms in a language are applied to objects in the world" (Burling 1964: 27; D'Andrade 1995: 251).

Any perspective with unattainable goals is not worth much, no matter how grand those goals might be. What is remarkable to me is that a parallel trajectory taken by cognitivists in the 1960s and 1970s is being followed by today's cultural constructionist/postmodern/interpretive anthropology. The latter also began with the admirable goal of elevating the standards of ethnographic fieldwork. They too have had to settle for far more humble results in the form of ethnographies that are "inherently *partial*—committed and incomplete" (Clifford 1986: 7).

There is, however, a significant difference between the two theoretical perspectives. Ethnoscience, or cognitive anthropology, unlike present-day postmodern interpretivism, was based upon the assumption that cultural phenomena are amenable to rational inquiry and its practitioners were committed to advancing knowledge and they attempted to push the frontiers of anthropological knowledge toward a new direction with that objective in mind. For this they cannot be commended enough. In contrast, today's new anthropologists offer us despair over the thought that we can never know anything, and solipsism and poetry in the place of reliable, well-researched ethnographies. What is different between the two perspectives also is that whereas the ethnoscientists recognized the shortcomings of their approach and sought to enhance their methods, the postmodernists revel in it and accept it as a necessary condition of their intellectual enterprise.

Chapter 13

Symbols, Symbolic Anthropology, and the Interpretation of Culture

A theoretical perspective known as symbolic or interpretive anthropology emerged during the 1960s in the United States (McGee and Warms 2000: 467). Proponents of this approach were interested in exploring systems of meaning and signification. Their efforts were directed toward establishing a humanistic and interpretive, or **hermeneutic** (from Greek for interpretive), framework for the analysis of cultural phenomena.

Interest in the symbolic domain of culture goes back to the works of Franz Boas and his students and their concerns with the symbolic and psychological basis of culture. Symbolic anthropologists are highly influenced by the Boasians' construal of culture as a system of symbols, meanings, and values and their axioms that culture comes from culture and the culture must be explained in terms of culture.

Leslie White also devoted considerable attention to the role of symbols in culture and wrote a number of important papers on the subject (White 1949, 1962, 1977 [1959]). In his article "The Symbol: The Origin and Basis of Human Behavior," White wrote that

all culture . . . depends upon the symbol. It was the exercise of the symbolic faculty that brought culture into existence and it is the use of symbols that makes the perpetuation of culture possible. Without the symbol there would be no culture, and man would be merely an animal, not a human being (White 1949: 33).[1]

In another paper, White elaborated upon the importance of symbols in shaping human perceptions of the universe and everything in it:

[With symbols] man built a new world in which to live. To be sure, he still trod the earth, felt the wind against his cheek, or heard it sigh among the pines; he drank from streams, slept beneath the stars, and awoke to greet the sun. But it was not the same sun! Nothing was the same anymore. Everything was "bathed in celestial light"; and there were "imitations of immortality" on every hand. Water was not merely something to quench thirst; it could bestow the life everlasting. Between man and nature hung the veil of culture, and he could see nothing save through this medium. He still used his senses. He chipped stone, chased deer, mated and begat offspring. But permeating everything was the essence of words: the meaning and values that lay beyond the senses. And these

305

meanings and values guided him—in addition to his sense—and often took precedence over them (White 1977: 247).[2]

One of the significant differences between White's position and that of the symbolic anthropologists is that the latter make the symbolic domain of culture their only and exclusive concern.

As a humanistic and interpretive enterprise, with greater affinities with the humanities rather than the sciences, symbolic anthropology is idealist and ethnographically particularist in orientation. It is about context and understanding ideas and meanings in the context of the broader conceptual systems in which they are embedded. It excludes material causation and evolutionary holism from the intellectual agenda.

The symbolic perspective held the promise of elucidating an important but limited domain of human experience. However, problems emerged when its proponents began to treat the domain of symbols as the only legitimate subject of anthropological inquiry.

THE EPISTEMOLOGICAL FOUNDATIONS OF SYMBOLIC ANTHROPOLOGY

Symbolic anthropology is based upon the assumption that human life is about the meaning of experiences rather than causality. Meaning being what it is varies from one culture, place, and time to another. This being the case, human experience is thought to be random and capricious. The understanding of human life and experiences therefore hinges not upon the concern with why people do what they do, but rather upon the interpretation of what the things people do mean to them in the context of the symbolic systems specific to their culture (O'Meara 1989: 355).

The centrality of meaning for symbolic anthropologists is sustained through the dismissal of the vast body of ethnographic and archaeological evidence that suggests that sociocultural

systems adjust themselves "in patterned and predictable ways to ecological and demographic constraints" (Lett 1987: 91) and that a lot of human behavior is nonrandom and predictable (Bernard 1995: 17). If this were not the case, we would be confronted with hundreds of different culture types, kinship systems, modes of subsistence, religious configurations, sociopolitical patterns, and so on, rather than the limited number known to anthropologists.

Symbolic anthropologist are unconcerned with these issues. For them the task of anthropology is to investigate the shared, culturally constituted systems of meanings particular to each society or group. Meaning entails symbols (Dolgin et al., 1977: 18). A symbol, according to Schneider's (1968: 1) definition, is "something which stands for something else, or some things else, where there is no necessary or intrinsic relationship between the symbol and that which it symbolizes." Thus the word *cat* in the phrase "go round the world to count the cats in Zanzibar" does not bear any resemblance to, nor does it sound like, the animal it signifies. In the same vein, White noted that "a symbol may be defined as a thing the value or meaning of which is bestowed upon it by those who use it" (White 1949: 25).

Put another way, a symbol is a shared, agreed-upon meaning ascribed to phenomena. As such, symbols are arbitrary. Richard Barrett (1991: 55) provides a good example to illustrate the nature of symbols:

> Take, for example, a day of the week such as a Tuesday. What is a Tuesday and how is it recognized? It should be obvious that it cannot be found in nature. We cannot look at the sky and differentiate a Tuesday from a Sunday. It is simply the name given to an otherwise indistinguishable twenty-four hour period. If a sailor, shipwrecked on an uninhabited island, should fail to keep track of the days from the beginning of his ordeal, he could never again be certain of the day or date. It is difficult to define a Tuesday, since to do so we must resort to similar symbolic divisions: we say that it is the third day of the week (another man-

made category), or it is the day following Monday or that it precedes Wednesday. . . . no other animal has [Tuesdays]; they are the sole possession of humanity. Nonhuman animals live in the real world of wind, trees, water, rocks, and earth. Their lives are regulated by the weather, by the seasons, and by their own physiology but definitely not by meanings that they themselves impose on nature. Ducks and beavers cannot even recognize Tuesdays, let alone organize their lives around them.[3]

It is through symbols that humans infuse the world, universe, and everything in them with meanings and significance. They then act out their lives, order nature, structure experience, create philosophies and construct ideologies according to these meanings. Being human is inexorably tied to symbols and symbolic systems.

Symbolic anthropologists begin by observing that human life "must have meaning . . . [which] entails a system of signs or symbols in which this meaning is embedded and expressed" (Dolgin et al., 1977: 33–34). These anthropologists address the following questions:

> What are the conditions of existence? How is life defined? What kinds of units are specified and differentiated according to what assumptions or premises about the nature of the universe? How are these formulated, and how are they expressed? (Dolgin et al., 1977: 20).

For symbolic anthropologists "symbols and meanings represent the reality of the world in which [people] live their lives" (Dolgin et al., 1977: 33). Taking the domain of symbols and meanings as a given, these writers endeavor to somehow penetrate the conceptual realities in which humans "live their lives" (Geertz 1973: 24). The manner in which these anthropologists define culture, as a reality apart from patterns of behavior or "actual occurrences" (Schneider 1968: 5–6), represents an intellectual return to the Boasian cultural determinist perspective, a place where American anthropologists have always been most secure. Like the Boasians, American symbolic anthropologists also treat culture as if it possesses ontological autonomy.

The volume *Symbolic Anthropology* (1977), edited by Dolgin, Kemnitzer, and Schneider, outlined the central epistemological premises of symbolic anthropology. Symbolic anthropologists, Dolgin et al. (1977: 34) point out, are concerned with "how people formulate their reality." The symbolic anthropologist begins

with the premise that social action tends to be orderly, to be, in some degree, predictable or understandable by both participants and observers. Social life—made up of people, of gods and ghosts and ghouls, of beliefs about the possible and about the actual and about that which is right and that which is wrong as well as actions, things, relationships, and institutions—is constituted logically, attaining coherence for those who live it out in its particularity. One person, may, for instance, argue that ghosts exist, as another may argue that they do not, but among those who do believe in ghosts, they are treated as real. Our concern is not with whether or not the views a people hold are accurate in any "scientific" sense of the term—whether they hold up against the scrutiny of the rather particular domain of Western belief and knowledge called Science; in social actions, that which is thought to be real is treated as real: and that treatment, by self and others, both contributes confirmation of "reality" and constitutes a decisive aspect of the meaning of the situation of action (Dolgin et al., 1977: 4–5).

The treatment of what "is thought to be real . . . as real" sets symbolic anthropology along the road to epistemological relativism (cf. D'Andrade 1995: 148). This is because what follows is the notion "that there exist a multiplicity of 'truths' and 'goods'; and that these are *made* by various peoples" (Dolgin et al., 1977: 8). This entails the relativist fallacy discussed in Chapter 2, that posits not simply that beliefs are relative to culture, but rather that truth is relative to each culture. The epistemological premises of symbolic anthropology in the 1960s and 1970s served as the foundation upon which was built the full-fledged relativistic cultural constructionist approaches glossed as postmodern/interpretive anthropology prevalent today.

Two kinds of symbolic anthropology were being espoused during the 1960s and 1970s, one operating within the parameters of American cultural anthropology and the other in the context of the British structural functionalist tradition. David Schneider and Clifford Geertz (whose work is rooted in Weberian/German sociology) were the main proponents of symbolic anthropology in the United States. In Great Britain, the symbolic approach was associated with the works of Victor Turner and Mary Douglas, both of whom were influenced by the sociology of Émile Durkheim and the writings of Radcliffe-Brown. Douglas has also been influenced by Lévi-Strauss's structuralism, which made a significant impact upon British anthropology as early as the 1950s, as discussed in Chapter 11.

VICTOR TURNER: SYMBOLS AND RITUALS

Victor Turner (1920–1983) completed his graduate work at Manchester University, where Max Gluckman (1911–1975) had established his prestigious department of anthropology. Gluckman had developed a structural functionalist approach incorporating elements of Marxist theory, which departed from mainstream structural functional approaches by focusing not upon how social solidarity and integration are maintained and perpetuated but on how integration is sustained despite the presence of structural contradictions (cf. Ortner 1984: 130). Gluckman (1954, 1956, 1965) was interested, for example, in how cathartic effects of the ritual expression of conflict, what he called "rituals of rebellion" contributed to social integration. Influenced by this perspective, Turner undertook fieldwork from 1950 to 1954 among the Ndembu of northwestern Zambia (then Northern Rhodesia), situated on the border between Angola and Zaire, in Central Africa.

Turner obtained his doctorate in 1955 and then joined the anthropology department at

Anthropologist Victor Turner, one of the leading British symbolic anthropologists, best known for his study of ritual symbols.

Manchester. In 1961–1962 he was a fellow at the Institute for Advanced Study in Behavioral Sciences in Stanford. In 1964, he returned to United States as Professor at Cornell. He then went to the University of Chicago, and in 1977 moved to the University of Virginia in Charlottesville, where he remained until his death in 1983. Turner was among the important theoreticians in British social anthropology whose work also had a significant impact upon American anthropology.

Gluckman's influence is most evident in Turner's book *Schism and Continuity in an African Society* (1957), a study of conflict among the Ndembu. Turner developed his theoretically innovative approach to the study of symbols, social dramas, and ritual out of his rich and extensive field experience among the Ndembu. This perspective is elaborated in his books *The Forest of*

Symbols (1967), *The Drums of Affliction* (1968), *The Ritual Process* (1969), and *Drama, Fields, and Metaphors* (1974), as well as in numerous articles. Turner's approach to ritual and symbolism was an alternative to Lévi-Strauss's structural approach.

In his *Schism and Continuity in an African Society* (1957), Turner examined how Ndembu society achieved and maintained solidarity in the presence of inherent embedded social structural contradictions. The principal sources of the strife were conflicts of interest over inheritance rights and succession to office generated as a consequence of the opposing principles of matrilineal social organization and **virilocality** (women having to live in their husband's village separated from their mothers and matrilineal kin). Turner demonstrated how inherent structural contradictions are concealed and made to appear consistent through multiple layers of rituals and symbols.

Turner developed his theoretical perspective upon realizing that the prevailing structural–functionalist model, based upon a biological metaphor or analogy, could not be applied to the field circumstances that he encountered in Africa. He describes his transformation as follows:

> With my conviction as to the dynamic nature of social relations I saw movement as much as structure, persistence as much as change, indeed persistence as a striking aspect of change. I saw people interacting, and, as day succeeded day, the consequences of their interactions. I then began to perceive a form in the process of social time. This form was essentially *dramatic* (Turner 1974: 32).[4]

One of the features of Ndembu social life Turner noted was the propensity toward conflict. This manifested itself in what he called **social dramas.** One aspect of Turner's (1974: 33) anthropology was to take social dramas, "aharmonic phases in the ongoing social process," as units of analysis. As he observed,

> Conflict seems to bring fundamental aspects of society, normally overlaid by the customs and habits of daily intercourse, into frightening prominence.

People have to take sides in terms of deeply entrenched moral imperatives and constraints, often against their own personal preferences. Choice is overborne by duty (Turner 1974: 35).[5]

Conflict brought hidden, inherent structural strains and contradictions to the surface. By using the concept of social drama Turner could present his analysis of how conflicts developed, worked themselves out, and were resolved. The analysis is formulated after Gluckman's model of conflict (Kuper 1999: 145). Social dramas, Turner (1974: 36) noted, are structured and their structure is based upon models or metaphors carried in the actors' heads. Elsewhere Turner (1974: 13) wrote that social actions acquire form through the "metaphors and paradigms in their actors' heads" that are "put there through explicit teaching and implicit generalization from social experience."

These dramas arising from conflict situations begin with a breach of norm-governed social relations. The breach, unless rapidly sealed, escalates to involve the widest divisions of the community to which the antagonists belong. This is followed by redressive action, which, depending on the nature of the crisis may range from informal mediation to elaborate rituals to seal the breach. In the final phase either there is reintegration or a social recognition of the irreparable schism between the antagonists, which leads to village fissioning. While not all social processes are of this nature, such as for example socioeconomic enterprises, social dramas are recurrent aspects of life. It was by studying such events that Turner was led to develop what he called a processual approach to the analysis of human behavior.

In his subsequent works, Turner took up the analysis of symbols as the catalysts for social action. In Turner's scheme, symbols play a principle role in the sociocultural process (Lett 1987: 114). For Turner (1974: 33) the "humanistic coefficient" was crucial in any attempt to make sense of human social processes. The human element is crucial because the meaning and existence of cultural systems depend upon the participation of conscious, volitional human agents and their ongoing and altering relations with one another (Turner 1974: 33). Indeed, Turner observed that the very development of an authentic anthropology depended upon the humanistic coefficient:

> I plead with my colleagues to acquire the humanistic skills that would enable them to live more comfortably in those territories where the masters of human thought and art have long been dwelling. This must be done if a unified science of man, an authentic anthropology, is ever to become possible. I am an advocate not of abandoning the methods of behavioral science but of applying them to the behavior of an innovative, liminal creature, to a species whose individual members have included Homer, Dante, Shakespeare, as well as Galileo, Newton, and Einstein (Turner 1974: 18).[6]

RITUAL SYMBOLS, COMMUNITAS, AND LIMINALITY

Ritual symbols are semantic structures that operate as the means whereby people and the norms and categories of their society are synchronized and through which contradictions are ameliorated and the social order reproduced. Turner's ideas are developed in his ethnographic work on the Ndembu. In his book *The Forest of Symbols* (1967), Turner presents an approach to the study of rituals and symbols. For Turner (1967: 19), "Symbols are observable, empirical objects, relationships, gestures, and spatial units in a ritual situation." Symbols have a semantic structure. Each symbol in a ritual presents and conveys particular messages about aspects of the social order. Meaning is bestowed upon objects that stand as symbols in rituals by mutual consent. People bestow symbolic meaning upon objects or artifacts, such as trees, water, food, colors, wood, holes, hens, utensils and the like, because of analogous properties and associations they have in everyday life. These resemblances are im-

ported into ritual because of their symbolic significance and they are sometimes exported back to the nonritual sphere (Murphy 1979: 321). A symbol, Turner observed, "is a thing regarded by general consent as naturally typifying or representing or recalling something by possession of analogous qualities or by association in fact or thought" (1967: 19).

For example, among the Ndembu, the sapling of a tree that exudes a white milky latex substance when its bark is scratched signifies aspects of female body imagery, such as milk, suckling, breasts, girlish slenderness (Turner 1977: 185). Thus, the Ndembu use these properties when they employ the sapling of the milk tree in the girl's puberty ritual. The symbol, according to Turner, "is the smallest unit of ritual which still retains the specific properties of ritual behavior; it is the ultimate unit of specific structure in a ritual context" (Turner 1977: 19).

Rituals represent configurations of symbols akin to a musical score in which the individual symbols are comparable to musical notes. Turner described ritual in the following terms:

> A ritual is a stereotyped sequence of activities involving gestures, words, and objects, performed in a sequestered place, and designed to influence preternatural entities or forces on behalf of the actors' goals and interests (Turner 1977: 183).

Symbols, when arranged in a particular sequence during ritual, like the notes in a musical score, convey meaning in various ways and possess the power to produce social transformations, such as in the case of rites of passage.

Turner elaborated on the property of symbols to simultaneously convey and express multiple meanings as follows:

> This property of individual symbols is true of ritual as a whole. For a few symbols have to represent a whole culture and its material environment. Ritual may be described, in one aspect, as a quintessential custom in that it represents a distillate or condensation of many secular customs and natural regularities. Certain dominant or focal symbols conspicuously possess this property of multivocal-

ity which allows for the economic representation of key aspects of culture and belief. Each dominant symbol has a "fan" or "spectrum" of referents, which are interlinked by what is usually a simple mode of association, its very simplicity enabling it to interconnect a wide variety of significata [meanings]. For example, the association provided by "whiteness" enables white clay . . . to stand for a multiplicity of ideas and phenomena, ranging from biological referents as "semen," to abstract ideas such as "ritual purity" (1977: 50).

"Condensation" results in certain symbols being loaded with multiple and disparate meanings and can concurrently represent "many ideas, relations between things, actions, interactions, and transactions" (Turner 1977: 184). The dissimilar meanings are linked to one another through analogy or by association. Turner referred to meaning-packed elements of signification as dominant symbols. Extreme **multivocality** and a wide range of semantic meanings characterize dominant symbols.

> Such symbols come in the process of time to absorb into their meaning-content most of the major aspects of human social life, so that, in a sense, they come to represent "human society" itself. In each ritual they assert the situational primacy of a single aspect or of a few aspects only, but by their mere presence they suffuse those aspects with the awe that can only be inspired by the human total. All the contradictions of human social life, between norms, and drives, between different drives and between different norms, between society and the individual, and between groups, are condensed and unified in a single representation, the dominant symbols. It is the task of the analyst to break down this amalgam into its primary constituents (Turner 1977: 44).

Turner (1977: 50) also noted that different meanings of the same symbol often come into play at different stages in the same ritual. Thus

> the same symbol may be reckoned to have different senses at different phases in a ritual performance, or rather, different senses become paramount at different times. Which sense shall become paramount is determined by the ostensi-

ble purpose of the phase of the ritual in which it appears. For a ritual, like a space rocket, is phased, and each phase is directed towards a limited end which itself becomes a means to the ultimate end of the total performance. . . . There is a consistent relationship between the end or aim of each phase in a ritual, the kind of symbolic configuration employed in that phase, and the senses that become paramount in multivocal symbols in that configuration (Turner 1977: 52).

Furthermore, Turner pointed out that in any given ritual only a limited number of the total range of meanings embodied in a symbol is ever expressed. For this reason the anthropologist must have familiarity with the entire range of meanings of the symbols in question in order to understand ritual symbols. The meaning of rituals must be inferred from the symbolic pattern and behaviors associated with it. This is possible

> only if he has previously examined the symbolic configurations and the meanings attributed to their component symbols by skilled informants, of many kinds of ritual in the same total system. In other words, he must examine symbols not only in the context of each specific kind of ritual, but in the context of the total system (Turner 1967: 43).[7]

This approach allows the investigator to examine the ritual as a system of meaning that is part of the larger ritual system. Turner explained the theoretical significance of this approach:

> It is in comparison with other sectors of the total system, and by reference to the dominant articulating principles of the total system, that we often become aware that the overt and ostensible aims and purposes of a given ritual conceal unavowed, and even "unconscious" wishes and goals. We also become aware that a complex relationship exists between the overt and the submerged, and the manifest and the latent patterns of meaning (Turner 1967: 46).[8]

Finally, symbols refer to two poles of meanings, ideological and sensory. Ideological meanings refer to aspects of the moral and social order. Sensory meanings refer to phenomena that stimulate desires and feelings. Symbols in ritual can convey lengthy messages or arguments in abridged form because they are condensations of semantic wealth. For Turner, a symbol has a dynamic nature; it is alive:

> It is alive only in so far as it is "pregnant with meaning" for men and women, who interact by observing, transgressing, and manipulating for private ends the norms and values that the symbol expresses. If the ritual symbol is conceptualized as a force in a field of social action, its critical properties become intelligible and explicable. On the other hand, conceptualizing the symbol as if it were an object and neglecting its role in action often lead to a stress on only those aspects of symbolism which can be logically and consistently related to one another to form an abstract unitary system (Turner 1967: 44).[9]

Symbols are thus construed as "a force in a field of social action" through which multiple and possibly conflicting meanings are created in various contexts by different groups and individuals and maintained alongside each other. This enables us to see cultural phenomena as a dynamic process and performance, as opposed to a manifestation of static structures. Performances of ritual are seen as elements in the social process and ritual is understood as a factor in social action. Symbols themselves are seen in terms of human interests and objectives (Turner 1967: 20).

Putting it differently, Turner viewed symbols as catalysts for social action:

> It must not be forgotten that ritual symbols are not merely signs representing known things; they are felt to possess ritual efficacy, to be charged with power from unknown sources, and to be capable of acting on persons and groups coming in contact with them in such a way as to change them for the better or in a desired direction. Symbols, in short, have an orectic [relating to desire or appetite, willing and feeling] as well as a cognitive function. They elicit emotion and express and mobilize desire (Turner 1967: 54).[10]

Ritual symbols operate to combine meanings, convey messages, and resolve contradictions as follows:

> In my view [ritual symbols] condense many references, uniting them in a single cognitive and affective field. . . . In this sense ritual symbols are "multivocal," susceptible of many meanings, but their referents tend to polarize between physiological phenomena (blood, sexual organs, coitus, birth, death, catabolism, and so on) and normative values of moral facts (kindness to children, reciprocity, generosity to kinsmen, respect for elders, obedience to political authorities, and the like). At this "normative" or "ideological" pole of meaning, one also finds reference to principles of organization: matriliny, patriliny, kingship, gerontocracy, agegrade organization, sex-affiliations, and others (Turner 1967: 54).[11]

The meanings of symbols are exchanged and juxtaposed in the context of the ritual process:

> The drama of ritual action—the singing, dancing, feasting, wearing of bizarre dress, body painting, use of alcohol or hallucinogens, and so on, causes an exchange between these poles in which the biological referents are ennobled and the normative referents are charged with emotional significance. I call the biological referents, insofar as they constitute an organized system set off from the normative referents, the "orectic pole," "relating to desire or appetite, willing and feeling," for symbols, under optimal conditions, may reinforce the will of those exposed to them to obey moral commandments, maintain covenants, repay debts, keep up obligations, avoid illicit behavior. In these ways *anomie* is prevented or avoided and a milieu is created in which a society's members cannot see any fundamental conflicts between themselves as individuals and society. There is set up, in their minds, a symbiotic interpenetration of individual and society (Turner 1974: 55–56).[12]

But Turner (1974: 56) noted that ritual works only if there is a high level of **communitas,** a "generic bond" that is recognized to exist beneath all of society's hierarchical and **segmentary oppositions** and contradictions.

Turner (1967: 93–111; 1969; 1974: 231–299; 1984) developed the concept of communitas during his study of the forms and attributes of **rites of passage,** following a theme first developed by Arnold van Gennep (1873–1957), a folklorist/anthropologist. Rites of passages are associated with changes in status, social position, and age. Such rites are found in all societies, Turner (1967: 93) points out, but find their maximal expression in small-scale societies that are structured through kinship bonds.

Van Gennep (1960) noted that all rites of passage are tripartite, involving the stages of separation, marginality or **liminality,** and reincorporation (Figure 13.1). The cross-cultural tripartite structure of rites of passage becomes intelligible in terms of Lévi-Strauss's dialectical structural principles of binary oppositions and mediator. During liminality, limbo or statusless-

ness, the individuals are "betwixt and between all recognized fixed points in space-time of structural classification," when normal social relations and time itself are suspended (Turner 1967: 97). Such individuals are "no longer classified and not yet classified" (Turner 1967: 97).

The liminal *persona* is defined by a complex and sometimes "bizarre" set of animal or natural symbols, such as bird feathers, grass skirts, animal masks, and the like. Liminality is symbolically likened to death and invisibility. It is "a moment in and out of time" and "in and out of secular social structure" (Turner 1969: 96). The initiates as liminal beings are ground down to be created anew. They are stripped of all distinctions of rank, status, and gender and reduced to passivity and humility. In this state the initiates develop an intense comradeship and egalitarianism among themselves and lowliness and sacredness,

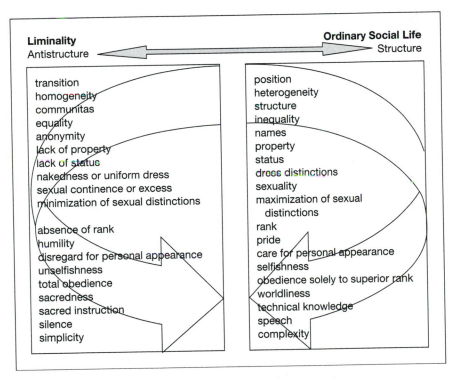

Figure 13.1   Turner's contrast between liminality and normal social life.   *After Kottak (2002).*

homogeneity and comradeship are merged. The initiates are thus able to grasp a glimpse of a social bond between them that in secular life is broken up either into caste, class, rank hierarchies, or segmentary oppositions.

Emerging from this is the realization that there are two modalities of human relationships:

> The first is of a society as a structured, differentiated, and often hierarchical system of politico-legal-economic positions with many types of evaluation, separating men in terms of "more" or "less". The second, which emerges recognizable in the liminal period, is of society as an unstructured or rudimentarily structured and relatively undifferentiated *communitas,* or community, or even communion of equal individuals who submit together to the general authority of the ritual elders (Turner 1969: 96).[13]

Communitas is "antistructure," it is a process in which the ordinary ties of social structure are undone, and it impresses upon the individuals a realization of the common human bond among members of society. This seems to be one of the important features of communitas:

> It is . . . a matter of giving recognition to an essential and generic human bond, without which there would be *no* society. Liminality implies that the high could not be high unless the low existed, and he who is high must experience what it is like to be low (Turner 1969: 97).[14]

Communitas is a dimension of all societies, ancient and modern. Structure imposes differences between males and females, elders and juniors, commoners and chiefs, masters and servants. Membership in society, be it simple or complex, modern or archaic, commits the individual to structure and the antagonisms that come with structural differentiation. As Turner (1969: 130) adds,

> Even in the simplest societies, the distinction between structure and communitas exists and obtains symbolic expression in the cultural attributes of liminality, marginality, and inferiority. In different societies and at different periods in each society,

one or the other of these "immortal antagonists" comes uppermost. But together they constitute the "human condition," as regards man's relations with his fellow man.[15]

Turner saw social life itself as a dialectical process involving successive experiences of communitas and structure, homogeneity and differentiation, equality and inequality and the transition from one to the other by means of the limbo of statuslessness. The "opposites . . . constitute one another and are mutually indispensable" (Turner 1969: 97). The dialectic between communitas and structure demonstrates the power of symbols upon human behavior. In subsequent works, Turner (1974) went on to demonstrate that liminality and anti-structure also occurs in other kinds of social process as well, such as during carnival, certain stages of millenarian movements, and religious pilgrimages.

TURNER AND THE STUDY OF SYMBOLS

In Turner's approach, symbols are analyzed both by direct observations and in terms of the data obtained from informants. In other words, Turner took into account both emic and etic aspects of ritual symbols, combining observations of behavior with information gained through interviews from members of the culture. Turner's work exemplifies one of the more sophisticated symbolic perspectives. It is for this reason that I provide a detailed description of his approach to the study of symbols in this section.

The significance of ritual symbols, according to Turner, is framed in terms of what they mean to, and what feelings and emotions they evoke in, the participants. This is coupled with what the investigator is able to discern from the social context of the ritual in relation to others in the total ritual system of a people and in relation to the wider context of their society as a whole. Thus Turner writes,

I found that I could not analyze ritual symbols without studying them in a time series in relation to other "events," for symbols are essentially involved in social process. I came to see performances of ritual as distinct phases in the social processes whereby groups became adjusted to internal changes and adapted to their external environment. From this standpoint the ritual symbol becomes a factor in social action, a positive force in an activity field. The symbol becomes associated with human interests, purposes, ends, and means, whether these are explicitly formulated or have to be inferred from the observed behavior. The structure and properties of a symbol become those of a dynamic entity, at least within its appropriate context of action (Turner 1967: 20).[16]

Turner approached the study of ritual symbols in terms of several distinct levels of meaning.

When we talk about the "meaning" of a symbol, we must be careful to distinguish between at least three levels or fields of meaning. These I shall call: (1) the level of indigenous interpretation (or, briefly, the exegetical meaning); (2) the operational meaning; and (3) the positional meanings (Turner 1967: 50).[17]

Turner explained the differences between these levels of meaning as follows:

The exegetical meaning is obtained from questioning indigenous informants about observed ritual behavior. Here again one must distinguish between information given by ritual specialists and information given by laymen, that is, between esoteric and exoteric interpretations. One must also be careful to ascertain whether a given explanation is truly representative of either of these categories or whether it is a uniquely personal view. . . . On the other hand, much light may be shed on the role of the ritual symbol by equating its meaning with its use, by observing what the Ndembu do with it, and not only what they say about it. This is what I call the operational meaning, and this level has the most bearing on problems of social dynamics. For the observer must consider not only the symbol but the structure and composition of the group that handles it or performs mimetic acts with direct reference to it. He must further note the affective qualities of these acts, whether they

are aggressive, sad, penitent, joyful, derisive, and so on. He must also inquire why certain persons and groups are absent on given occasions, and if absent, whether and why they have been ritually excluded from the presence of the symbol. . . . The positional meaning of a symbol derives from its relationship to other symbols in a totality, a *Gestalt*, whose elements acquire their significance from the system as a whole. This level of meaning is directly related to the important property of ritual symbols mentioned earlier, their polysemy. Such symbols possess many senses, but contextually it may be necessary to stress only one or a few of them only (Turner 1967: 50–51).[18]

Turner's description of the Ndembu girl's puberty ritual illustrates the nature of ritual symbols and his mode of analysis:

At *Nkang'a,* the girl's puberty ritual, a novice is wrapped in a blanket and laid at the foot of a *mudyi* sapling. The *mudyi* tree . . . is conspicuous for its white latex, which exudes in milky beads if the thin bark is scratched. For Ndembu this is its most important observable characteristics, and therefore I propose to call it "the milk tree" henceforth. Most Ndembu women can attribute several meanings to this tree. In the first place, they say that the milk tree is the "senior" . . . tree of the ritual. Each kind of ritual has this "senior" or, as I will call it, "dominant" symbol. . . . dominant symbols are regarded not merely as means to fulfillment of the avowed purposes of a given ritual, but also and more importantly refer to values that are regarded as ends in themselves, that is to axiomatic values. Secondly, the women say with reference to its observable characteristics that the milk tree stands for human breast milk and also for the breasts that supply it. They relate this meaning to the fact that *Nkang'a* is performed when a girl's breasts begin to ripen, not after her first menstruation, which is the subject of another less elaborate ritual. The main theme of *Nkang'a* is indeed the tie of nurturing between mother and child, not the bond of birth. This theme of nurturing is expressed at the *Nkang'a* in a number of supplementary symbols indicative of the act of feeding and of foodstuff. In the third place, the women describe the milk tree as "the tree of a mother and her child." Here the reference has shifted from description of a biological act, breast feeding, to a social tie of profound significance both in domestic relations and in the structure of the widest Ndembu community (Turner 1967: 21).[19]

The Ndembu, according to Turner, attribute broader symbolic significance to the milk tree, which is considered as the place of all mothers of the lineage; the tree represents the ancestress of women and men; and it is thought to be where the ancestress slept when she was initiated. Thus, Turner adds,

> At one level of abstraction the milk tree stands for matriliny, the principle on which the continuity of Ndembu society depends. Matriliny governs succession to office and inheritance of property, and it vests dominant rights of residence in local units. More than any other principle of social organization it confers order and structure on Ndembu social life. Beyond this, however, "*mudyi*" means more than matriliny. . . . It stands for tribal custom . . . itself. The principle of matriliny, the backbone of Ndembu social organization, as an element in the semantic structure of the milk tree, itself symbolized the total system of interrelations between groups and persons that make up Ndembu society. Some of the meanings of important symbols may themselves be symbols, each with its own system of meanings. At the highest level of abstraction, therefore, the milk tree stands for the unity and continuity of Ndembu society. Both men and women are components of that spatiotemporal continuum (Turner 1967: 21).[20]

Turner points out that informants discuss the symbolism of the milk tree in the context of the girl's puberty ritual by noting its harmonizing aspects. They emphasize the dependence of child upon mother in the symbolism, for the child depends upon its mother for milk and for instruction in cultural customs, for mother's role is the archetypal protector, provider of nourishment, and teacher. However, Turner also notes that while the informants stress the harmonizing aspects of the ritual, their actual behavior suggests that the milk tree represents social differentiation and opposition between the elements of society, which it is said to depict as a harmonious whole.

For Turner, this raised the problem of the **uncomprehended symbol,** symbolic meanings of which the participant in the culture are unaware. For example, in the *Nkang'a,* the milk tree symbolizes the exclusiveness of women and mobilizes them in opposition to men. When the women are dancing around the initiate in a circle they taunt men in song and will not allow them to dance at one stage of the proceedings. At the operational level, the milk tree distinguishes women as a social category and symbolizes their solidarity. The milk tree also sets the novice herself apart from other women at the time by symbolizing her new social identity and celebrating her coming of age. It also symbolizes the conflict between the girl and the moral community of women she is about to enter.

In yet another context, the milk tree expresses the opposition of the girl's mother and the adult women. She is excluded from the circle of dancing. The ritual symbolizes the mother's loss of her child, although she gains her later as co-member of her lineage. Here the conflict between the matricentric family and wider society is evident. In another phase of the ritual the mother and daughter exchange pieces of their clothing, which Turner relates to the mortuary custom in which mourners wear pieces of the deceased's clothing. Turner interprets this as depicting the termination of a significant aspect of the relationship between mother and daughter.

Another representation of the conflict between the initiate's mother and mature female society occurs at the end of the first day of the ritual. The mother cooks a meal of cassava and beans. Before the meal is served, the women go and dance around the milk tree. Then the women scramble to be the first to seize and eat from a large spoon carried by the mother of the initiate. The spoon is said to represent the novice in her role of a married woman and the food symbolizes her productive and reproductive capacities. If the person who succeeds in seizing the spoon comes from the girl's own village then it is said that the girl upon her marriage will remain close to her natal village. If not, it is said that the girl will go far away to a distant village, where she will reside until the end of her life. This, for Turner, symbolizes the deep conflict between the matricentric family and mature female society. It alludes to the major principle of Ndembu society, virilocal postmarital residence, according to which the woman must move to and live in her husband's village, sometimes located at great distances from her mother's community.

In the milk tree ritual, the women represent the matrilneal core of the village, and each village seeks to gain control over the novice's labor. Women also wish that their children will be raised in their own village, adding to its numbers and enhancing its prestige.

Finally, the attempts of the members of the novice's matrilineal kin to seize the spoon, signifies the solidarity and exclusiveness of each matrilineage in the village in relation to other such corporate groups. These are aspects of behavior associated with the milk tree symbolism that the members of the culture are unaware of and are unable to interpret, but which Turner believes he has been able to penetrate.

UNCOMPREHENDED SYMBOLS AND THE NATIVE'S POINT OF VIEW

Much of the analysis above entails symbolic meanings of which the participant in the culture are unaware. The idea of the "uncomprehended symbols" raises problems for the anthropologist as the interpreter of such symbols. Turner (1967: 26) queried that, "if the Ndembu do not recognize the discrepancy between their interpretation of the milk tree symbolism and their behavior in connection with it, does this mean that the discrepancy has no relevance for the social anthropologist?"

Some anthropologist have chosen to focus entirely on what the actors recognize and ex-

clude all other symbolic elements as irrelevant and even non-symbols. For example, Siegfried Nadel (1903–1956), a distinguished anthropologist known for his study of witchcraft as well as the place of "status" and "role" in human behavior, pointed out that "uncomprehended symbols have no part in social inquiry" (Nadel 1954: 108; see Nadel 1952, 1947, 1964).

Postmodernist anthropologists react vehemently to the idea that the anthropologist might understand what members of the culture do not. This implies that the native's point of view does not encompass the whole picture, that epistemology belongs to the anthropologist alone and clashes with the postmodern egalitarian view of knowledge. Moreover, this position entails the imposition of analytical categories, analytical judgments, a distinction between the observer and observed, a distinction between "our knowledge" and "their knowledge" which simply cannot be tolerated (Herzfeld 2001: 10, 22, 174). For writers like Herzfeld all of this is intellectual imperialism and "intellectual apartheid" and entails the amoral and ethnocentric assumption of a rationality transcending cultural boundaries that cannot be admitted. By contrast, scientific anthropologist maintain that if the objective of anthropological inquiry is to enhance our understanding of the empirical world and human experience in it, then the axiomatic separation of the observer and observed is essential.

Turner took a Durkheimian sociological point of view in addressing the problem of "uncomprehended symbols." For Durkheim rituals convey messages about society emanating from the collective consciousness of society. The messages are projections of society about itself and are best understood in those terms. Turner adopted such a view by treating ritual symbols, both in terms of what the participants believe and in terms of meanings that they convey above the level of individual comprehension.

One of the strengths of Turner's approach, and that of modern anthropology in general, is that the native's point of view is not the ultimate and sole objective, as it seems to be for symbolic anthropologists such as Clifford Geertz and the postmodern interpretivists. This is an important aspect of modern ethnographic research. As Richard Barrett (1991: 133–135) has pointed out,

> The interpretation of a society that an anthropologist obtains never derives entirely from the statements and beliefs of informants. There are many things about a society, and about their own behavior in it, that most individuals simply do not understand. This is because many actions are of a traditionalist, rote kind; they are engaged in because the individuals have been taught to perform them and not because they know the specific reasons behind their actions. . . . customs are adhered to with very little thought given to them. This unanalyzed nature of culture is not as obvious as it might be because of the propensity of individuals to offer folk explanations . . . for various aspects of their behavior. When they do not know the origin or purpose of a custom they invent, or repeat, reasonably sounding explanations. . . . there is a portion of any culture that remains covert, or at least that lies outside of the objective awareness of members of society. When anthropologists deal with these aspects of culture they must preforce seek explanations for cultural practices that surpass the native's understanding. This disparity between the native's comprehension and that of the scientific observer becomes particularly apparent when anthropologists deal with, and try to interpret, the expressive symbolism of culture.[21]

Turner not only considered this level of meaning to be significant, but maintained that the anthropologist stood in the unique position "to interpret a society's ritual symbols more deeply and comprehensively than the actors themselves" (Turner 1967: 26). Turner was certain of this because, as he put it,

> each participant in the ritual views it from his own particular corner of observation. He has . . . his own "structural perspective." His vision is circumscribed by his occupancy of a particular position, or even of a set of situationally conflicting positions, both in the persisting structure of his society,

and also in the role structure of the given ritual. Moreover, the participant is likely to be governed in his actions by a number of interests, purposes, and sentiments, dependent upon his specific position, which impair his understanding of the total situation (Turner 1967: 27).[22]

The anthropologist is in a position to render the deeper meanings of ritual symbols for several reasons.

> In the first place, the anthropologist, by the use of his special techniques and concepts, is able to view the performance of a given kind of ritual as occurring in, and being interpreted by, a totality of coexisting social entities each as various kinds of groups, sub-groups, categories, or personalities, and also barriers between them, and modes of inter connexion. . . . In other words, he can place the ritual in its significant field setting and describe the structure and properties of that field. . . . [Moreover] the anthropologist who has previously made a structural analysis of Ndembu society, isolating its organizational principles, and distinguishing its groups and relationships, has no particular bias and can observe the real interconnections and conflicts between groups and persons, in so far as these receive ritual representation. What is meaningless for an actor playing a specific role may well be highly significant for an observer and analyst of the total system (Turner 1967: 26–27).[23]

According to Turner (1967: 20), the anthropologist must take into account three dimensions of symbols, the exegetic, the operational, and the positional, which were discussed previously.

> The exegetic dimension consists of the explanations given the investigator by actors in the ritual system. Actors of different age, sex, ritual role, status, grade of esoteric knowledge, and so forth provide data of varying richness, explicitness, and internal coherence. The investigator should infer from this information how members of a given society think about ritual (Turner 1977: 190).

> In the operational dimension, the investigator equates a symbol's meaning with its use—he observes what actors do with it and how they relate to one another in the process. He also records

their gestures, expressions, and other nonverbal aspects of behavior and discovers what values they represent—grief, joy, anger, triumph, modesty, and so on. . . . formalized prayers or invocations . . . fall into this category. Here verbal symbols approximate nonverbal symbols. The investigator is interested not only in the social organization and structure of those individuals who operate with symbols on this level, but also in what persons, categories, and groups are absent from the situation, for formal exclusion would reveal social values and attitudes (Turner 1977: 190).

In the positional dimension, the observer finds in the relation between one symbol and other symbols an important source of meaning. I have shown how binary opposition may, in context, highlight one (or more) of a symbol's referents by contrasting it with one (or more) of another symbol's referents. When used in a ritual context with three or more other symbols, a particular symbol reveals further facets of its total "meaning." Groups of symbols may also be arrayed as to state a message, in which some symbols function analogously to parts of speech and in which there may be conventional rules of connection. The message is not about specific actions and circumstances, but the given culture's basic structures of thought, ethics, esthetics, law, and modes of speculation about new experience (Turner 1977: 190–191).

ASSESSMENT

The weaknesses of Turner's approach are the same as those perpetually besetting all other perspectives that offer interpretative accounts of cultures in terms of "beliefs and meanings," to the exclusion of material causation and evolutionary holism. There is also the problem of validation. Interpretative accounts are immune to any systematic mode of validation or replication. How is Turner (1974: 36) sure that he has accessed the "models" or "metaphors" carried in the actors' heads that figure in the "social dramas" he used as units of analysis? Turner (1967: 20) says that part of his analysis involves inferences drawn from human behavior. The problem here is that ideological features such as norms,

cultural themes, ethos, and values, which are inferred from behavior, are in turn applied to explicate the same behavior. This entails an error in logic because it conflates consequent with antecedent, as discussed in Chapter 2.

Finally, there is the difficulty posed by the multivocality of symbols. As Dolgin et al. (1977: 22–23) note,

Symbols have many meanings, that is, they are polysemic, multivocal, or mulivalent. . . . The polysemous character of symbols is significant for understanding the relations of symbolic structures to process; if a symbol has several meanings, then the *relationship between* its various meanings becomes important and often problematic.

Symbols are open to different interpretations and only a specific range of their meanings is expressed in any given ritual or sociological context. Interpretative ethnographies lend themselves to the production of wonderfully imaginative and clever stories, especially if the ethnographer is inclined toward the idea of ethnography as fiction, as in the case of present-day postmodern interpretivists. But many questions remain. How is the investigator to be certain that the particular meanings that make up his or her interpretation are the right or appropriate ones? How do we know whether the interpretation offered is clever talk or sheer deftness on the part of the anthropologist, rather than being an aspect of the system of meaning of the culture in question? Or does this no longer matter in anthropology? This problem is compounded in light of the fact that informants are often unable to clarify various meanings of their symbols, and that there are strata of meaning that they do not consciously comprehend, as noted previously.

Turner's solution, that meanings can be inferred only if the investigator has studied many kinds of rituals in the total ritual system of the people in question, seems a monumental task indeed. However, Turner's approach is to be commended because it requires immersion in and an empirical understanding of another culture that takes into account observational sociological factors. This approach has not substituted glib labels and slick catchphrases for hard work on the ground. Also, Turner is to be highly commended because he does not resort to clever rhetorical ploys, such as labeling all ethnographies fictions, each as good as the other, in order to bypass the required hard work in the field. Nor does he appeal to his own authority and special intuitive powers or privileged access to justify referring to exercises in creative writing as "authentic" ethnographies.

MARY DOUGLAS: PURITY, POLLUTION, TABOO, AND SYMBOLS

Mary Douglas (1921–) is best known for her studies of the symbolic domain of culture and her works have inspired many interested in the study of meaning (Wuthnow et al., 1984: 13). Douglas conducted ethnographic fieldwork among the Lele of Zaire, in Africa, from 1949 to 1950, with additional work in 1953. She received her doctorate from Oxford University in 1951 under the supervision of Edward Evans-Pritchard. After a brief period of teaching at Oxford, Douglas went to University College in London, where she taught from 1951 to 1977. In 1977 Douglas accepted the position of Director of Research at the Russell Sage Foundation (1977–1981) and moved to the United States. She was one among a number of prominent anthropologists, including Victor Turner, F. G. Bailey, John Middleton, Robin Fox, and Talal Asad, to leave Britain as a result of the crisis precipitated in the 1970s by cutbacks in the British university system (Kuper 1999: 180).

Douglas's anthropology was shaped in part by the humanistic approach of Evans-Pritchard and Durkheimian sociology, which historically had a strong influence upon British social anthropology. She was also influenced by French structuralism, although she criticized Lévi-Strauss for discounting the importance of the cultural content of symbols and the emotional power they are capable of evoking. Lévi-Strauss (1967:

Anthropologist Mary Douglas, one of the leading British symbolic anthropologists, best known for her study of purity, pollution, taboos, and cultural classification systems.

21–22), we might recall, maintained that the unconscious activity of the mind imposes form upon content, that the form is the same for all minds, and it is therefore necessary to focus on the form, rather than content. Douglas, following Turner, focused on the sociological significance of meaning, the psychic content of symbols in human experience (Kuper 1999: 174).

Douglas's ethnographic research is presented in her books *Peoples of the Lake Nyasa Region* (1950) and *The Lele of Kasai* (1963), as well in a number of articles. Her theoretical works, for which she is better known, include *Purity and Danger* (1966) and *Natural Symbols* (1973). It is Douglas's work on the universal patterns of symbolism and their interpretation that will concern us here.

Douglas is interested in accounting for the concepts of purity, pollution, and taboo, with which cultures everywhere are preoccupied. Douglas employs a conception of culture as a symbolic system that people superimpose upon nature to create order. Order is established by classification, which entails labeling and putting things into logical mental categories. Cultural classifications are constructs.

> In perceiving we are building, taking some cues and rejecting others. The most acceptable cues are those which fit most easily into the pattern that is being built up. Ambiguous ones tend to be treated as if they harmonised with the rest of the pattern. Discordant ones tend to be rejected. If they are accepted the structure of assumptions has to be modified. As learning proceeds objects are named. Their names then affect the way they are perceived the next time: once labeled they are more speedily slotted into the pigeon-holes in future (Douglas 1966: 36).[24]

For Douglas (1966: 2), therefore, culture enables humans to symbolically organize or re-order the environment "making it conform to an idea." The way this is done is by contrasting certain qualities with other qualities, according to Douglas (1966: 4), "by exaggerating the difference between within and without, above and below, male and female, with and against." Following Lévi-Strauss's idea of binary oppositions, Douglas suggests that nature is ordered through the use of polar categories or polar terms.

There is a rationale or logic operating in this cultural ordering of nature. The rationale is that things that are classified as being apart must be kept apart, and things that are classified as being together must be kept together. These distinctions are expressions of the basic categories of thought and any breach of their boundaries conflicts with the logical operation of the human thought process. As such, these boundary-breaching things must somehow be mediated lest they undermine the cultural classification system as a whole.

The dilemma people face everywhere, Douglas points out, is that not everything falls neatly into their culturally constructed classification systems. When something does not fit, or is out of place, it creates ambiguities. People are uncomfortable when dealing with ambiguous or anomalous things because these things are slippery and they make us feel uneasy. Along these lines, as discussed in Chapter 11, Lévi-Strauss has suggested that the coyote assumes the role of the trickster in Native American myths because it is out of place. Being a carrion eater it occupies a position midway between life and death. For this reason, to reiterate, the coyote is deemed a trickster, because "the trickster is a mediator. Since his mediating function occupies a position halfway between two polar terms, he must retain something of that duality—namely an ambiguous and equivocal character" (Lévi-Strauss 1967: 223).

Following Lévi-Strauss's lead, Douglas attempts to explain the ideas of pollution, purity, and taboo in similar terms. She suggests that when something defies classification, and is hence out of place, it arouses a sense of defilement. One way people deal with such out of place things is to classify them as being impure, polluting and dangerous. Ideas about contagion are reactions to anomaly, according to Douglas.

Thus to say that something is polluting or dirty is really to say that it out of place. There are two elements here: first a conception of order, of where things belong; second, the notion that the order has been violated, of something being out of place. Thus, Douglas adds,

> Dirt then, is never a unique, isolated event. Where there is dirt there is system. Dirt is the by-product of a systematic ordering and classification of matter, in so far as ordering involves rejecting inappropriate elements. This idea of dirt takes us straight into the field of symbolic systems of purity (Douglas 1966: 38).[25]

Like Turner, Douglas argues that symbols cannot be understood in isolation, but in terms of the larger structures of meaning of which they are a part. "No particular set of classifying symbols can be understood in isolation, but there can be hope of making sense of them in relation to the total structure of classifications in the culture in question" (Douglas 1966: vii). Moreover, she adds, "A symbol only has meaning from its relation to other symbols in a pattern. The pattern gives the meaning. Therefore no one item in the pattern can carry meaning by itself isolated from the rest" (Douglas 1973: 11). Thus dirt and uncleanness are to be understood in relation to other symbols in their broader contexts.

> Defilement is never an isolated event. It cannot occur except in view of a systematic ordering of ideas. Hence any piecemeal interpretation of the pollution rules of another culture is bound to fail. For the only way in which pollution ideas make sense is in reference to the total structure of thought whose key-stone, boundaries, margins and internal lines are held in relation by rituals of separation (Douglas 1966: 41).[26]

Douglas points out that European ideas about dirt, transformed by the "germ" theory of disease transmission developed during the nineteenth century, make it difficult to see dirt outside the context of pathogenic transmission. Yet if we look beyond this, we find that Europeans also employ the same logic as that used in "primitive cultures" (i.e., that dirt is matter out of place) (Douglas 1966: 35). We can take this to mean that the same structure of thought underlies both the modern Euro-American conceptions of "dirt" and "primitive" notions of pollution.

> We can recognise in our own notions of dirt that we are using a kind of omnibus compendium which includes all the rejected elements of ordered systems. It is a relative idea. Shoes are not dirty in themselves, but it is dirty to place them on the dinning table; food is not dirty in itself, but it is dirty to leave cooking utensils in the bedroom, or food bespattered on clothing; similarly, bathroom equipment in the drawing room; clothing lying on chairs; out-door things in-doors; upstairs things

downstairs; under-clothing appearing where over-clothing should be, and so on. In short, our pollution behaviour is the reaction which condemns any object or idea likely to confuse or contradict cherished classifications (Douglas 1966: 36).[27]

Douglas goes on to apply her idea of dirt as things that are out of place to elucidate the nature of cultural ideas of pure/holy, impure/unholy, ritual pollution, and taboos.

ANOMALIES, TABOOS, AND PIGS

The same logic underlying the association of dirt as things out of place is involved when that which is anomalous is defined as being unholy or ritually polluting. That which is out of place is treated as such because things that do not fit into the pattern or classification scheme, things that overlap boundaries of cultural categories, become unnerving and problematic, and jeopardize the entire classificatory system. Transgression of boundaries summons forth dangers, according to Douglas. Pollution possesses power and this power is not vested in humans or animals, although human action can release them. That power resides in the symbolic order, which appears as an external force, mystically potent and dangerous. Here Douglas's views are very similar to the way that Durkheim construed the power of collective consciousness, the collective thought of the aggregate as a whole, which presents itself to the individual as an awesome and external force.

The power of pollution resides in the structure of human thought, in the structure of ideas that punish "a symbolic breaking of that which should be joined or joining that which should be separate." "The power which presents a danger for careless humans," Douglas (1966: 113) writes, "is very evidently a power inhering in the structure of ideas, a power by which the structure is expected to protect itself." Douglas is basically suggesting that the symbol, a thing potent and infused with life and a power of its own, is mightier than the proverbial sword.

Douglas (1966: 36–37) points out further that "uncomfortable facts which refuse to be fitted in, we find ourselves ignoring or distorting so that they do not disturb these established assumptions." Anomalies can be dealt with by ignoring them or by not perceiving them. Alternatively, the anomalies could be dealt with by creating new categories for them. But this is easier said than done because, while it may be easy for an individual to revise his or her personal classification schemes, it is not so when it involves a whole community of people for whom their culture appears as an external and coercive supraindividual power:

> Culture, in the sense of public, standardised values of a community, mediates the experience of individuals. It provides in advance some basic categories, a positive pattern in which ideas and values are tidily ordered. And above all, it has authority, since each is induced to assent because of the assent of others. But its public character makes its categories more rigid. A private person may revise his pattern of assumptions or not. It is a private matter. But cultural categories are public matters. They cannot so easily be subject to revision. Yet they cannot neglect the challenge of aberrant forms. Any given system of classification must give rise to anomalies, and any given culture must confront events which seem to defy its assumptions. It cannot ignore the anomalies which its scheme produces, except at risk of forfeiting confidence (Douglas 1966: 38–39).[28]

For this reason, Douglas observes, cultures have various means of contending with ambiguous or anomalous events and experiences. One is to provide an alternate interpretation. Thus, when a deformed child is born among the Nuer, the defining line distinguishing people from animals is imperiled, and the anomaly is dealt with by treating the newborn as a baby hippopotamus, accidentally born to a human. Labeled as such, it is laid by the river where it is thought to properly belong. Alternatively, anomaly may be physically restrained. If it were believed that the same womb could not possible bear two humans at the same time, the solution would be to kill all twins at birth.

Another way of dealing with anomalies is to subject them to condemnation. It is under these circumstances that taboos and the idea of ritual impurity spring into action. Rules of avoidance are instituted to make the anomalous a tabooed object, a thing that is unholy or ritually polluting and dangerous. The idea of pollution and the associated behaviors of avoidance and purification thus serve to affirm and bolster the belief system by bringing symbolic meanings of purity and uncleanness into sharper definition (Douglas 1966: 39–40). Conformity with the taboo reinforces the belief system that gave rise to the interdiction. "Reflection on dirt involves reflection on the relation of order to disorder, being to non-being, form to formlessness, life to death" (Douglas 1966: 5). Thus Douglas suggests that the ideas of purity and pollution operate to ensure that people do not transgress the boundaries of cultural order and hence order is preserved.

Douglas employs this approach in her analysis of the dietary prohibitions among the ancient Israelites. Leviticus (xi) and Deuteronomy (xiv) list the creatures whose consumption was permitted by humans and those that were forbidden:

> These are the living things which you may eat among all the beasts that are on the earth. Whatever parts the hoof and is cloven-footed and chews the cud, among the animals you may eat. Nevertheless among those that chew the cud or part the hoof, you shall not eat these: The camel, because it chews the cud but does not part the hoof, is unclean to you. And the rock badger, because it chews the cud but does not part the hoof, is unclean to you. And the hare, because it chews the cud but does not part the hoof, is unclean to you. And the swine, because it parts the hoof and is cloven-footed but does not chew the cud, is unclean to you. Of their flesh you shall not eat, and their carcasses you shall not touch; they are unclean to you (Leviticus xi).

True to the dictum of interpretive analysis, which entails placing cultural features in their specific contexts, Douglas begins by pointing out that "since each of the injunctions is prefaced by the command to be holy, so they must be explained by that command. There must be contrariness between holiness and abomination which will make over-all sense of all the particular restrictions" (Douglas 1966: 49). Douglas proceeds by examining notions of holiness in the passages of Leviticus and Deuteronomy. Holiness is equated with wholeness:

> We can conclude that holiness is exemplified by completeness. Holiness requires that individuals shall conform to the class to which they belong. And holiness requires that different classes of things shall not be confused. . . . Holiness means keeping distinct the categories of creation (Douglas 1966: 53).[29]

Douglas also equates ideas of holiness to order; being holy is being orderly. Thus she adds, "To be holy is to be whole, to be one; holiness is unity, integrity, perfection of the individual and of the kind. The dietary rules merely develop the metaphor of holiness on the same lines" (Douglas 1966: 54)

Douglas suggests that living an orderly life among the ancient Israelites was to abide by the symbolic categories and not to transgress their boundaries. These symbolic categories included the zoological taxonomy in the Bible. Certain animals, such as the herds of cattle, camels, sheep and goats upon which the Israelites depended for their livelihood were symbolically incorporated within the social order. Thus, these beasts, like people, received the blessing of God. The continued fertility of the land and livestock depended upon the blessing and both were drawn into the divine order, the order of creation. It was the obligation of people to preserve this order.

For the Israelites, what distinguished domesticated livestock from the wild beasts, was that the wild beasts had no covenant to protect them. Cloven hoofed, cud chewing ungulates were the model of the appropriate kind of food. Animals that are not cloven-hoofed were specifically excluded. Similarly cloven-hoofed animals that are not ruminants, such as the pig were excluded. Douglas points out,

> Note that this failure to conform to the two necessary criteria for defining cattle is the only reason given in the Old Testament for avoiding the pig; nothing whatsoever is said about its dirty scavenging habits. As the pig does not yield milk, hide nor wool, there is no other reason for keeping it except for its flesh. And if the Israelites did not keep pig they would not be familiar with its habits. I suggest that originally the sole reason for its being counted as unclean is its failure as a wild boar to get into the antelope class, and that in this it is on the same footing as the camel and the hyrax, exactly as stated in the book (Douglas 1966: 54–55).[30]

Douglas (1966: 55) concludes that, "in general the underlying principle of cleanness in animals is that they shall conform fully to their class. Those species are unclean which are imperfect members of their class, or whose class itself confounds the general scheme of the world." In other words, pigs are considered unclean because they are anomalous, they have cloven hoofs, but do not chew the cud. Pigs fail to conform to the divine order. Therefore, they are polluting and unfit for humans to eat or even touch.

Here we can see the influence of French structuralism on Douglas's thinking because her argument is similar to the one Lévi-Strauss proposes in his book *The Raw and the Cooked* (1969) (i.e., that people select foods not because they are "good to eat" but because they are "good to think"). The taboo, in other words, is a manifestation of the structure of human thought. The explanation for the taboo on pork can be expressed in the structuralist formula (Harris 2001: 190):

pig : livestock :: disorder : order :: dirty : clean :: nature : culture

Douglas's ideas are an analogue of the culture-comes-from-culture argument because it is cultural categories imposed upon nature that define the status of animals such as pigs, rather than any intrinsic characteristics of these creatures themselves. For Douglas it does not matter that there is no pan-human reason to rule out pigs from being good to eat and good to think (Harris 2001: 92). It is also of no consequence whether the tabooed animal was the rock badger, the hare, the pig, or the swarming creatures in the water. What matters is that pigs were anomalous in the mental binary code of the Israelites. What matters also is the taboo itself and the avoidance behaviors with which it was associated. The observance of the taboo on pork conveys an encoded symbolic message, according to Douglas, and that message reaffirms the cultural order. Thus food is really a code and the message it encodes relates to cultural categories that must be maintained.

Douglas goes on to emphasize that the idea of pollution and the associated behaviors of avoidance and purification serve to affirm and bolster the belief system by bringing symbolic meanings of purity and uncleanness into sharper definition (Douglas 1966: 39–40). In other words, observances of the taboos reinforce the symbolically ordered relationships that gave rise to them. Thus Douglas writes,

> If the proposed interpretation of the forbidden animals is correct, the dietary laws would have been like signs which at every turn inspired meditation on the oneness, purity and completeness of God. By rules of avoidance holiness was given a physical expression in every encounter with the animal kingdom and at every meal. Observance of the dietary rules would thus have been a meaningful part of the great liturgical act of recognition and worship which culminated in the sacrifice in the Temple (Douglas 1966: 57).[31]

In a subsequent paper, Douglas elaborates on the message encoded in the rules governing the Jewish meal. "It would seem that whenever a people are aware of encroachment and danger, dietary rules controlling what goes into the body would serve as a vivid analogy of the corpus of their cultural categories at risk" (Douglas 1972: 79).

Exploring the implications of her findings, Douglas points out that one of the cultural categories for which dietary rules served as an analogue included approved and disapproved sexual relations.

> [The pig] carries the odium of multiple pollution. First it pollutes because it defies the classification of ungulates. Second, it pollutes because it eats carrion. Third it pollutes because it is reared as food (and presumable as prime pork) by non-Israelites. An Israelite who betrothed a foreigner might have been liable to be offered a feast of pork and hence propelled into pollution, according to Douglas. By these stages it comes plausibly to represent the utterly disapproved form of sexual mating and carries all the odium that this implies (Douglas 1972: 79).[32]

Thus, according to Douglas, the taboo on pork served as a symbolic measure to prevent the Israelites from marrying foreigners. What Douglas overlooks, however, is that the pig taboo was found not just among the Israelites, but also among the inhabitants of a zone of pastoral nomadism extending from North Africa through the Middle East into Central Asia as well as in a number of adjacent river valleys (see Simoons 1961: 36–43). Thus attempting to explain the taboo in terms of symbolic meanings, values, and the like, specific to the Israelite cultural categories runs into difficulties (Harris 1991: 203).

ASSESSMENT

Douglas's work is highly intriguing and seems insightful. However, it suffers from many of the same shortcomings associated with other interpretive/symbolic perspectives, including contemporary varieties, such as the position espoused by Clifford Geertz. As Spiro (1968: 391) points out,

[Douglas's] symbolic analysis . . . proceeds neither from a general theory of symbolism, from which the meaning attributed to a symbol can be logically deduced, nor from a set of psychological data on social actors, from which the putative meaning of a symbol is empirically induced. In the absence of both bases for the derivation of meaning, symbolic analyses become arbitrary, and conviction of their validity must stem from the persuasiveness of the argument.[33]

Rather than providing evidence for purported symbolic meanings, the presumed meanings are provided as self-evident, self-validating truths much in the same manner that Lévi-Strauss presents his structural explanations.

Douglas herself appears to ascribe a referential meaning to things and behaviors, for example, dirt being construed "matter out of place," or "reflection on dirt" evoking a reflection on ideas of order and disorder, form and formlessness, and so on without offering any data or strong argument for equating these things with one another (Spiro 1968). How does Douglas determine that dirt evokes such reflections universally? Does everyone see upstairs thing being downstairs as "dirty"? Do people object to shoes on dinning tables because they contradict cherished classifications or because frequently shoes have on them clumps of mud, chewing gum, and other noxious substances found on the streets of modern towns and cities?

Douglas reaches these conclusions not on the basis of cross-cultural evidence but because these things are a contradiction of her own notions of order (Douglas 1966: 2). These personal and ethnocentric impressions are then transmuted through rhetorical alchemy into a human cultural universal (cf. Harris 2001: 196–197). It appears that Douglas is in agreement with Lévi-Strauss, who finds no difficulties in using his own thoughts as sufficient evidence to illustrate the universal properties of the structure of human thought. Lévi-Strauss, we might recall, observes that "in the last resort it is immaterial whether . . . thought process of the South Amer-

ican Indians take shape through the medium of my thoughts, or whether mine take place through the medium of theirs" (Lévi-Strauss 1969: 13).

Finally, Douglas's work suffers from the same kind of vagueness characteristic of other interpretive approaches. Her use of the terms *meaning* and *symbolic* are so broad as to allow anything including feelings, intentions, motives, significance, or anything related to these to be defined as having symbolic meaning (O'Meara 1989: 363–364). Thus, as Spiro (1968: 391) has noted, Douglas's idea of "ritual pollution" appears to mean "dirt, disorder, defilement, danger, power, taboo, the beliefs pertaining to them, the rituals concerning them, the (magical) punitive consequences attendant upon contact with, or violation of, them."

THE SYMBOLIC/ INTERPRETIVE ANTHROPOLOGY OF CLIFFORD GEERTZ

The third symbolic perspective that I shall examine in this chapter is associated with the American cultural anthropologist Clifford Geertz (b. 1926). Geertz obtained his Ph.D. from Harvard University in 1956. He conducted fieldwork in Java and Bali and later in Morocco. He taught at the University of Chicago from 1960 to 1970 and thereafter took a position at the Institute for Advanced Study in Princeton, where he founded the Department of Social Sciences. Geertz is considered to be one of the principle architects of symbolic perspective in American cultural anthropology (see Ortner 1999).

Geertz's theoretical perspective is outlined in his articles "Thick Description: Toward an Interpretive Theory of Culture" (in Geertz 1973) and "Blurred Genres: The Reconfiguration of Social Thought" (1980, in Geertz 1983) and in his book, *The Interpretation of Culture* (1973).

Clifford Geertz, the main expositor of interpretive anthropology.

Geertz's work is a continuation of the Boasian idiographic approach that was in turn grounded in nineteenth-century German idealism (cf. Darnell 1984: 271). For this reason Geertzian anthropology is remarkably similar in various respects to its Boasian predecessor.

The concept of culture is central to this approach. Like other symbolists, Geertz takes the domain of symbols and meanings as a given. Culture is construed as a set of symbols infused with meaning and these, as Geertz (1973: 127) puts it,

> are felt somehow to sum up, for those for whom they are resonant, what is known about the way the world is, the quality of emotional life it supports, and the way one ought to behave while in it.[34]

The emphasis on meaning is associated with a commitment to an emic mode of inquiry. For example, as Geertz (1973: 5) puts it,

The concept of culture I espouse . . . is essentially a semiotic one. Believing, with Max Weber, that man [sic] is an animal suspended in webs of significance he himself has spun, I take culture to be those webs, and the analysis of it to be therefore not an experimental science in search of law but an interpretive one in search of meaning.[35]

Elsewhere Geertz (1973: 89) writes that

> the culture concept to which I adhere has neither multiple referents nor, so far as I can see, any unusual ambiguity; it denotes an historically transmitted pattern of meanings embodied in symbols, a system of inherited conceptions expressed in symbolic forms by means of which men communicate, perpetuate, and develop their knowledge about and attitudes toward life.[36]

Culture is defined in a way that excludes behavior. The mode of inquiry is emic and the insider's viewpoint becomes the sole concern of the anthropologists who strives to comprehend the specific and the particular by putting these in their unique and particular symbolic contexts.

Geertz treats symbolic systems (i.e., cultures) as a self-contained, self-referential system that must be understood exclusively in reference to understandings that derive from insider's point of view (Geertz 1983: 55–70). The treatment of culture as closed, self-referential systems of meaning, subject to their own internal dynamics, removes culture from the realm of nature. Culture has ontological autonomy. Objective measures therefore become inapplicable to the realm of culture defined in this way (Ross 1980: xx). Culture comes from culture in this formulation. Culture is therefore no longer amenable to rational, scientific inquiry. If cultures are closed symbolic systems, then cultures are arbitrary because symbols are arbitrary.

Geertz describes his approach as "an attempt to come to terms with the diversity of the ways human beings construct their lives in the act of leading them" (Geertz 1983: 16). The objective is to enter into the inner world of meanings, the conceptual symbolic realities rather than a search for nomothetic explanations. Anthropology, for

Geertz, is not about hypothesis testing and objectively valid knowledge but about attaining the insiders point of view, or "local frames of awareness" through interpretation (Geertz 1983: 6, 16).

In the analysis of human affairs, it follows that the anthropologist must rely upon sympathetic identification rather than objective methodologies. The analytical tools brought to bear on the subject are intuition, empathy, and other subjective procedures (cf. Kaplan and Manners 1972: 27). There are no established explicit methodologies or criteria for validating interpretive accounts other than the subjective means through which the accounts are generated. It is the "inherent persuasiveness" of an account that leads to acceptance or rejection (Lett 1997: 3).

The idea behind Geertz's anthropology is to probe deeper and deeper into the domain of meaning and the layers of significations that constitute the symbolic worlds humans construct (Bohannan and Glazer 1988: 530). Geertz calls this approach **thick description.**

> What the ethnographer is in fact faced with . . . is a multiplicity of complex conceptual structures, many of them superimposed upon or knotted into one another, which are at once strange, irregular, and inexplicit, and which he must contrive to somehow grasp and then to render (Geertz 1988: 536).

Interpretive anthropologists seek to provide ever "thicker" descriptions. Greater validity depends upon greater thickness (i.e., more specificity and detail). The call for thick description is really a call for a retreat into ethnographic particularism. Geertz is interested in what is unique and particular in each culture (Geertz 1984: 275). The focus is upon the local frames of references and cultural alternatives. Diversity of views and plurality of voices are pursued for their own sake without any theoretical goals in mind. This is a direction Boas and his students took long ago with disappointing results.

How does one go about thickly describing alien conceptual systems? Geertz does not provide an answer. There is nothing in his books and papers that resembles "a theory or methodology for interpreting" or for attributing meaning to symbolic systems (cf. Reyna 1994: 572–573). What Geertz does instead is to suggests that interpretation is "one of those things like riding a bicycle that is easier done than said;" it is like "grasping a proverb, catching an allusion, seeing a joke" (Geertz 1983: 10, 70). What this means is that the ethnographer's subjective impressions and sensitivities become the basis of the ethnographic enterprise.

Given its humanistic orientation and a construal of culture as a closed system of meaning—which enables symbolic anthropologists to disregard the idea that their accounts must be validated against empirical data—this approach transforms ethnographic research into a kind of literary exercise, an activity that is to be appreciated in the same way that one appreciated a good novel or book. As Geertz has put it,

> A number of things, I think are true. One is that there has been an enormous amount of genre mixing in intellectual life in recent years, and it is, such blurring of kinds, continuing apace. Another is that many social scientists have turned away from a laws and instances ideal of explanation toward a cases and interpretation one, looking less for the sort of things that connects planets and pendulums and more for the sort that connects chrysanthemums and swords. Yet another is that analogies drawn from the humanities are coming to play the kind of role in sociological understanding that analogies draw from the crafts and technology have long played in physical understanding. Further, I not only think these things are true, I think they are true together; and it is the culture shift that makes them so that is my subject: the reconfiguration of social thought (Geertz 1983: 19).[37]

The reconfiguration of social thought or paradigm shift away from scientific laws and instances toward "chrysanthemums and swords" is how Geertz characterized the perspective he advocates. His construal of the development in the field, however, is based upon a misrepresentation because laws and causes have never dominated American cultural anthropology. Geertz's own perspective is firmly embedded in and is a continuation of the broad anti-science, interpretive tradition of Boas and his students that continues to dominate and shape anthropological thought.

Shankman (1984: 261) has summarized Geertz's intellectual agenda for anthropology:

> The programmatic side of Geertz's work is an attempt to refocus anthropology—indeed all of social science—away from the emulation of the natural sciences and toward a reintegration with the humanities. Geertz has proposed that social scientists study meaning rather than behavior, seek understanding rather than causal laws, and reject mechanistic explanations of the natural-science variety in favor of interpretive explanations. He has invited his colleagues to take seriously the possibilities of analogy and metaphor, to consider human activity as text and symbolic action as drama. In other words, he has asked social scientists to rework, if not abandon, their traditional assumptions about the nature of their intellectual enterprise.[38]

Geertz's interpretive, humanistic anthropology, which excludes material causality, evolutionary holism, and the objective of providing scientific explanations for sociocultural phenomena, transforms anthropological into an entirely ethnographic enterprise (Salzman 2001: 74). As Geertz (1973: 5) put it,

> In anthropology . . . what the practitioners do is ethnography. And it is in understanding what ethnography is, or more exactly what doing ethnography is, that a start can be made toward grasping what anthropological analysis amounts to as a form of knowledge.[39]

Geertz describes ethnography as follows:

> Doing ethnography is like trying to read (in the sense of "construct a reading of") a manuscript—foreign, faded, full of ellipses, incoherencies, suspicious emendations, and tendentious commentaries, but written not in conventionalized graphs of sound but in transient examples of shaped behavior (Geertz 1973: 10).[40]

Culture is "an ensemble of texts, themselves ensembles, which the anthropologist strains to read over the shoulder of those to whom they properly belong" (Geertz 1973: 452). The job of the ethnographer is to read and interpret this text that is written in "shaped behavior." If cultures are like texts, then it follows that embedded in each culture is its own unique interpretation.

Geertz strives hard to assure his readers that his anthropology is grounded in the concrete. Cultures are texts written in behavior, they are public, acted out texts, he points out. Cultures are public because meanings are shared and therefore public (Geertz 1973: 12). He adds, "Whatever, or wherever, symbolic systems . . . may be, we gain empirical access to them by inspecting events, not by arranging abstracted entities into unified patterns" (Geertz 1973: 17).

One could argue from this that if meaning is public therefore it is amenable to empirical analysis. While this is what Geertz seems to be suggesting, he has something else in mind. When Geertz begins the process of interpreting the empirically accessed symbolic system, the empirical or public dimension is lost. This is because an interpretative account is treated as a construct, a thing made up by the ethnographer (Geertz 1988: 540).

Related to Geertz's metaphor of culture-as-text is the metaphor of ethnography as fiction. Ethnographic accounts "are fictions; fictions in the sense that they are 'something made up,' 'something fashioned'—the original meaning of *ficto*—not that they are false, unfactual, or merely 'as if' thought experiments" (Geertz 1988: 540). Given that symbolic anthropology does not accommodate procedures by means of which interpretations may be tested against additional empirical data to see how well they accord with what is on the ground, what we are left with are simply the interpretations or "fictions" that must be accepted at face value.

Ethnographies are fictions because they are *interpretations* of cultural texts that make no references outside the text. Each one is a sort of "reading," and there can be a many readings as there are readers. In this sense, the task of the ethnographer is no different from that of the literary critic analyzing a poem. Each reading is treated as being as valid in its own way, just as each interpretation of a poem is valid.

The emphasis on the fashioned or made-up aspect of ethnographic accounts is important. This is because a great deal hinges upon how an ethnographic account is made-up or written and upon the ethnographer's authorial skills. "Substantive content" and "mode of representation" become blurred, according to this view. In other words, anthropological knowledge is not grounded upon empirical reality, data, or the way the world is but rather upon what Geertz (1973: 16) calls "scholarly artifice."

Geertz adds that ethnography is not about "its author's ability to capture primitive facts in faraway places and carry them home like a mask or a carving but on the degree to which he is able to clarify what goes on in such places" (Geertz 1973: 16). But there are no standards on the basis of which one can say whether the clarifications are not imaginary ones or not utter nonsense. Adroitness of the prose rather than "the way the world is," is offered as the only basis of whether an account is worthwhile or not. This entails the logical fallacy of style over substance, discussed in Chapter 2.

Take, for example, Geertz's famous article, "Deep Play: Notes on the Balinese Cockfight." In this article Geertz (1973: 412–453) provides an account of the place of cockfighting in Balinese society. He says that the cockfight is a symbolic reenactment of Balinese society and worldview which people savor and contemplate, and in which they discover facets of their temperament and "their society's temper." The conclusion is offered as self-evident and we have no means of assessing whether or not such is the case. We must go by Geertz' authority and his skills as a writer. This is not sufficient, not if we want to be sure that were are not being bamboozled.

The issue becomes more problematic once we learn that the paper in question is not an account of a particular cockfight that is analyzed in depth through public means, but rather a composite of Geertz's own literary contrivance based upon numerous cockfight matches (Crapanzano 1986: 75).

This raises an important question: If anthropological knowledge is all about mode of representation or scholarly artifice, then what ever happened to the description and the native's point of view or the local frames? Furthermore, if it is indeed the case that anthropological knowledge is all about modes of representation, then why engage in fieldwork in the first place? Clever stories can be written more effectively in the comfortable confines of one's office in Chicago as opposed to, let's say, a mud hut in a remote village in Afghanistan.

Geertizian anthropology offers no mean for the reader to evaluate the ethnographic account or a way of determining whether the clever story presented is an interpretation, a misinterpretation, or something wholly fantastic. Given the absence of any methodological framework or independent standards for assessment, it is not surprising that scholarly artifice and mode of representation come to assume such a central place in Geertz's ethnographic enterprise. But this is true only of the narratives produced by interpretive anthropologists, for whom it is not what they describe that is important, but how they describe it.

The problem of validation is connected with the nature and kinds of information generated through interpretation. Interpretation, as Geertz (1973: 20) has put it, involves guessing at meanings, assessing the guesses, and drawing explanatory conclusions from the better guesses, not discovering the Continent of Meaning and mapping out its bodiless landscape.[41]

Explanatory conclusions amount to reveling in the particular of the particular in all its details as perceived by the ethnographer in entirely subjective terms. For symbolic anthropologists "a good interpretation of anything—a poem, a person, a history, a ritual, an institution, a society—takes us into the heart of that which it is the interpretation" (Geertz 1973: 18). But how does one decide which interpretation does or does not take use into the heart of the matter? No such guidelines exist in Geertz's enterprise (Shankman 1984: 263). There is no oversight here, no guidelines exist because they are unnecessary for an intellectual enterprise that is akin to "grasping a proverb, catching and illusion, seeing a joke" or "riding a bicycle" (Geertz 1983: 10, 70).

Symbolic anthropologists object vigorously when called to account for how they know what they know or when asked to address the scientific criteria of validation or falsification (e.g., Farrer 1984). These writers also demand that their works not be evaluated in terms of coherence or completeness because the real world is a confusing jumble and all interpretations are "as inherently inconclusive as any others" (Geertz 1973: 23).

A perspective that rebukes accountability is intellectually irresponsible. Geertz is not interested in attending to methodological concerns so that the reliability of ethnographic accounts is enhanced. Instead, he passes of the greatest failing of his perspective as its greatest asset.

> The besetting sin of interpretive approaches to anything—literature, dreams, symptoms, culture—is that they tend to resist, or to be permitted to resist, conceptual articulation and thus escape systematic modes of assessment. You either grasp an interpretation or you do not, see the point of it or you do not, accept it or you do not. Imprisoned in

the immediacy of its own detail, it is presented as self-validating, or, worse, as validated by the supposedly developed sensitivities of the person who presents it; any attempt to cast what it says in terms other than its own is regarded as a travesty—as, the anthropologist's severest term of moral abuse, ethnocentric (Geertz 1973: 24).[42]

Geertz's answer to the problem of knowledge is to treat the whole issue of validation as obsolete and superfluous for the ethnographic enterprise and label those who demand validation as ethnocentric. Yet the position he advocates as better alternative to scientific approaches leaves one open to all sorts of ethnocentric subjective biases. Spiro's (1986: 275) remarks in this regard are relevant:

> For if ethnographic interpretations are processed through all those subjective filters, an objective—a public and replicable—method is required for deciding whether an interpretation should be accepted or rejected. The scientific method, which assesses the validity of interpretations by the logical procedure of testing their predictive or retrodictive [predicting the past] consequences, constitutes such a method. . . . [If we reject this method], and if consequently competing interpretations are merely variant "readings" then anything goes. And if anything—well, almost anything—goes, a scholarly discipline is not intellectually responsible.[43]

ASSESSMENT

Geertz's efforts to steer anthropology down the path of ethnographic particularism has produced innumerable problems. This is the same trajectory to nowhere that Boas took years ago. Boas at least may be excused for taking this sterile direction because he was a pioneer venturing into undiscovered country. One cannot make any such excuse for present-day interpretivists intent upon repeating the mistakes of the past.

Interpretive anthropology, which is incapable of going much beyond the individual case, constitutes a barrier to the growth of anthropological knowledge. Geertz acknowledges this problem and attempts to address it by stressing comprehension over analysis:

> It must be admitted that there are a number of characteristics of cultural interpretation which make the theoretical development of it more than usually difficult. . . . The tension between the pull of [the] need to penetrate an unfamiliar universe of symbolic action and the requirements of technical advance in theory of culture, between the need to grasp and need to analyze, is, as a result, both necessarily great and essentially irremovable. Indeed, the further theoretical development goes, the deeper the tension gets. This is the first condition for cultural theory: it is not its own master. As it is unseverable from the immediacies thick description presents, its freedom to shape itself in terms of its internal logic is rather limited. What generality it contrives to achieve grows out of the delicacy of its distinctions, not the sweep of its abstractions (Geertz 1973: 24).[44]

What is being said here is that the "immediacies of thick description" are theoretically useless. Each thick ethnography represents a new beginning and does not permit one to build upon previous findings. Geertz (1973: 25) attempts to justify his stance in this matter:

> Rather than following a rising curve of cumulative findings, cultural analysis breaks up into a disconnected yet coherent sequence of bolder and bolder sorties. Studies do build on other studies, not in the sense that they take up where the others leave off, but in the sense that, better informed and better conceptualized, they plunge more deeply into the same things. Every serious cultural analysis starts from a sheer beginning and ends where it manages to get before exhausting its intellectual impulse. Previously discovered facts are mobilized, previously developed concepts used, previously formulated hypotheses tried out: but the movement is not from already proven theorems to newly proven ones, it is from an awkward fumbling for the most elementary understanding to a supported claim that one has achieved that surpasses it. A study is an advance if it is more incisive—whatever that may mean—than those that

preceded it; but it less stands on their shoulders than, challenged and challenging, runs by their side (Geertz 1973: 25).[45]

Geertz ends up saying that all his enterprise can be is "the awkward fumbling for the most elementary understanding" with no prospects for advancing our knowledge. We are given hints of failure and asked to embrace tentative, inconclusive and incomplete accounts. Geertz (1973: 29) writes that

> cultural analysis is intrinsically incomplete. And, worse than that, the more deeply it goes the less complete it is. It is a strange science whose most telling assertions are its most tremulously based, in which to get somewhere with the matter at hand is to intensify the suspicion, both your own and that of others, that you are not quite getting it right. But that, along with plaguing subtle people with obtuse questions, is what being an ethnographer is like. . . . The fact is that to commit oneself to a semiotic concept of culture and an interpretive approach to the study of it is to commit oneself to a view of ethnographic assertion as . . . "essentially contestable."[46]

I find here cryptic excuses for a vacuous paradigm and reparation for an ethnographer's failure to do a thorough job. Geertz concludes his classic article with a number of caveats that are intended to demonstrate his grasp of the problematic nature of knowledge generated through "the interpretation of culture":

> My own position . . . has been to try to resist subjectivism on the one hand and cabbalism on the other, to try to keep the analysis of symbolic forms as closely tied as I could to concrete social events and occasions, the public world of common life, and to organized it in such a way that the connections between theoretical formulations and descriptive interpretations were unobscured by appeals to dark sciences. I have never been impressed by the argument that, as complete objectivity is impossible in these matters (as, of course, it is), one might as well let one's sentiments run loose. (Geertz 1973: 29–30).[47]

Nothing will discredit a semiotic approach to culture more quickly than allowing it to drift into a combination of intuitionism and alchemy, no matter how elegantly the intuitions are expressed or how modern the alchemy is made to look (Geertz 1973: 30).[48]

The danger that cultural analysis, in search of all-too-deep-lying turtles, will lose touch with the hard surfaces of life—with the political, economic, stratificatory realities within which men are everywhere contained—and with the biological and physical necessities on which those surfaces rest, is an ever-present one. The only defense against it, and against, thus, turning cultural analysis into a kind of sociological aestheticism, is to train such analysis on such realities and such necessities in the first place (Geertz 1973: 30).[49]

Nothing in Geertz's work gives any indication that he has heeded his own caveats. Geertz is an extremely clever writer and a master of rhetoric and intentional ambiguity. Like the French savants with whom he is so enamored, Geertz too has the vexatious proclivity to dabble in word games, double entendres, intentional ambiguities and other ingenuities. Verbal dexterity and the ability to phrase arguments with great rhetorical skill have allowed Geertz to make incongruous assertions and contradictory claims. This is how he reformulated ethnography into an enterprise devoted entirely to the pursuit of the particulars in all their particularities. Moreover, he has been able to convince others to abandon methodological rigor and elevate guesswork and personal opinion to the level of anthropological theory.

As I see it, Geertz is the individual responsible for setting the intellectual course of American anthropology toward the postmodern incarnation of interpretive anthropology, under the negative effects of which the discipline has languished so terribly for so long. In the hands of postmodernists, who today occupy sundry departments of anthropology, many of Geertz's theoretical formulations have been taken to their logical extremes, producing a full-fledged anti-science epistemology (Salzman 2001: 9–10). I shall treat the works of Geertz's postmodern progeny in a later chapter.

Chapter 14

Scientific, Materialist, and Marxist Anthropology

While the symbolic/interpretive approach in American cultural anthropology has capitalized upon the longstanding antiscience, particularistic, and relativistic perspective established by Boas and his disciples, there remains an equally entrenched materialist and scientific anthropological research perspective emanating from an entirely different intellectual tradition. This is the paradigm of cultural materialism.

The leading expositor of cultural materialism is the anthropologist Marvin Harris (1927–2001), although the paradigm has many other proponents (see Johnson and Johnson 2001; Murphy and Margolis 1995b). It was Harris who coined the label "cultural materialism" in his influential book *The Rise of Anthropological Theory* (2001b [1968]), although the strategy itself is said to be based upon a macrotheoretical approach to the evolution of sociocultural systems that was already known (Harris 2001b: 3).

The development of the cultural materialist paradigm and the explicit statement of its epistemological and theoretical principles are to be found in Harris's books *The Rise of Anthropological Theory* (1968), *Cultural Materialism: The Strug-*

gle for a Science of Culture (2001a [1979]), and *Theories of Culture in Postmodern Times* (1999). The application of the theoretical principles of cultural materialism to a wide range of anthropological problems, what Harris called "the riddles of culture," are to be found in his books *Cow, Pigs, Wars and Witches* (1974), *Cannibals and Kings* (1977), *America Now* (1981), *Good to Eat* (1985), and *Our Kind* (1989).

Harris's (2001a: xii) objective is "to create a pan-human science of society whose findings can be accepted on logical and evidentiary grounds by the pan-human community." Johnson and Johnson (2001: vi) describe cultural materialism as "a research orientation that develops strong theories that are frankly exposed to challenge on logical and empirical grounds and that equally develops specific and direct critiques of competing theories." Toward these objectives cultural materialism is based upon the epistemological principles of science.

Cultural materialism, as the anthropologist Brian Ferguson (1995: 21) has pointed out,

> is an explicitly scientific and deliberately practical research strategy for discovering the causes of sim-

Marvin Harris, the leading expositor of cultural materialism.

ilarities and differences in sociocultural form. While in no way denying the validity and importance of efforts to understand or interpret the symbolic, meaningful world of "others," cultural materialism follows another anthropological tradition in seeking to explain culture. The goal is to develop a consistent set of propositions that can be tested cross-culturally in order to establish regularities of social existence. With better explanations [of] how the world really works, we may be in a better position to ameliorate some of the most pressing human problems.[1]

All scientific perspectives refer to events and entities that are subject to sense experience and observations (aided by instrumentality). Science is based on the belief in

the existence of a reality apart from consciousness that can only be known by interacting with it: it may not be known purely by imagination and contemplation. In fact, imagination has the dangerous property that it is not only capable of but

also prone to creating images that distort or even deny external realty (Johnson 1995: 8).[2]

In anthropology, science entails "the objective, comparative analysis of cultural similarities and differences which ... place the study of human behavior and thought within the province of a general evolutionary paradigm" (Ross 1980c: xv).

Cultural materialism generates a wide range of interrelated theories that are applicable to numerous sociocultural problems (Lett 1987: 91). As Harris recently stated,

Cultural materialism . . . is a processually holistic and globally comparative scientific research strategy. It is concerned with diachronic and synchronic, long term and short term, emic and etic, behavioral and semiotic phenomena. In addition, it prioritizes material, behavioral, and etic conditions and processes in the explanation of the divergent, convergent, and parallel evolution of human sociocultural systems (Harris 1999: 141).[3]

Thus, cultural materialism is relevant to nearly all the fields and subfields of anthropology. It is for this reason that cultural materialists include not only cultural anthropologists, but also archaeologists, linguists, and biological anthropologists. Unlike the interpretive/postmodern anthropologists, for whom anthropology is an exclusively and narrowly defined ethnographic or rather literary enterprise, cultural materialists see the focus of the discipline differently. For them, anthropology is about "the exchange of data and theories among different fields and subfields concerned with the global, comparative, diachronic, and synchronic study of humankind" (Harris 1994: 62).

One striking feature that sets cultural materialism apart from other paradigms or research strategies is the explicitness of its epistemological and theoretical principles (Lett 1987: 91).

The aim of cultural materialism in particular is to account for the origin, maintenance, and change of the global inventory of sociocultural differences and similarities. Thus cultural materialism shares with other scientific strategies an epistemology which seeks to restrict fields of inquiry to events, entities, and relationships that are knowable by means of explicit, logico-empirical, inductive-deductive, quantifiable public procedures or "operations" subject to replication by independent observers (Harris 2001a: 27).[4]

In accordance with the epistemological principles of science, cultural materialists seek to obtain knowledge through public, replicable operations:

> The aim of scientific research is to formulate explanatory theories that are (1) predictive (or retrodictive), (2) testable (or falsifiable), (3) parsimonious, (4) of broad scope, and (5) integratable or cumulative within a coherent and expanding corpus of theories (Harris 1994: 64).[5]

A scientific research strategy, Harris (1994: 65) observes, is advantageous, not because it guarantees absolute truths, free of all subjective biases, errors, or frauds, but rather "because science is the best system yet devised for reducing subjective bias, error, untruths, lies and frauds."

The strategy in question, which is based upon the principle of the primacy of infrastructure, appears in different forms in three compatible traditions of materialist theories: Karl Marx's (1818–1883) political economy; Leslie White's evolutionism; Julian Steward's cultural ecology (cf. Ferguson 1995: 34; Margolis 2001: x; Sanderson 1990: 164). Having already treated the works of White and Steward in Chapter 10, here we shall examine the following topics: (1) the Marxist roots of cultural materialism; (2) the theoretical and epistemological differences between cultural materialism and Marxist anthropology; (3) the epistemological and theoretical principles of the paradigm of cultural materialism.

MARXIST AND MATERIALIST ANTHROPOLOGY

Marx's research principles, which have the most immediate significance to cultural materialists, are outlined in the Preface to his work *The Cri-*

Karl Marx, whose materialist conception of history and society has influenced cultural materialism.

tique of Political Economy (1859), which I have already cited in Chapter 10:

> The general conclusion at which I arrived and which, once reached, continue to serve as the leading thread in my studies may be briefly summed up as follows: In the social production which men carry on they enter into definite relations that are indispensable and independent of their will; these relations of production correspond to a definite stage of development of their material powers of production. The sum total of these relations of production constitutes the economic structure of society—the real foundation, on which rise legal and political superstructures and to which correspond definite forms of social consciousness. The mode of production in material life determines the general character of the social, political, and spiritual processes of life. It is not the consciousness of men that determine their existence, but on the contrary, their social existence determines their consciousness (Marx 1959a: 43).[6]

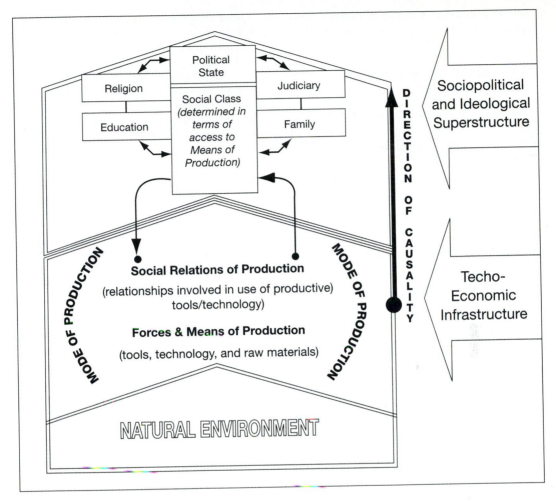

Figure 14.1   Key subsystems in Marx's model of sociocultural systems.

The key subsystems of Marx's model of sociocultural systems include techno-economic infrastructure and the sociopolitical and ideological superstructure (Figure 14.1). The processes associated with production are central to Marx's conceptualization of sociocultural systems. These comprise the relations of production and forces of production and the material powers of society. Together these processes determine who controls strategic resources, who controls production, what is produced, how and

by whom, and who controls the products of human labor.

What is significant here is that Marx provides a causal diachronic evolutionary model that has potential applicability to the anthropological analysis of the nature and evolution of sociocultural systems. This aspect of Marx's work has been the source of considerable interest to anthropologists from a variety of theoretical backgrounds (for an overview of Marx's ideas and Marxist anthropology, see Diamond

1979; Gailey 1992; Kahn and Llobera 1981; Layton 1997: 8–18, 127–156; Seddon 1978; Wessman 1981).

DIALECTICAL ANALYSIS AND MARXISM

Marx goes on to describe the mechanism by which sociocultural systems are transformed. Here he depends upon the dialectical logic espoused by the idealist German philosopher Georg Wilhelm Friedrich Hegel (1770–1831). Hegel construed the driving force of history as a metaphysical process of thought he called "the Idea," or "Spirit" and suggested that history is impelled toward a particular direction by this force. Hegel considered the Idea as the "demi-urgos" or the creative Spirit of the world (Marx 1959a: 146). Thought or abstract reason is the actual reality, according to this view, while the empirical world is merely a reflection of "the Idea." What appears to the senses as tangible is merely appearance, only shadowy images of reality that the limited human senses are capable of perceiving. Reality itself is in constant flux and therefore cannot be known. What humans can know are the constant dialectical processes driving reality.

In other words, beneath surface phenomena there are hidden internal and invariant dialectical laws that can only be apprehended by analytical procedures. These metaphysical laws have their own dynamics and purpose, continuously changing through the outgrowth of internal contradictions, leading to the negation of opposites and their eventual resolutions into a higher unity. This is expressed in repeated triads of **thesis-antithesis-synthesis** (Adams 1998: 275). This is the law of dialectics, or dialectic of mind, which in the context of Hegel's work and in the hands of Friedrich Engels (1820–1895), the world's number two Marxist, became the explanatory principle for the evolution of human history (see Engels 1964).

The anthropologist Robert Murphy (1980: 95) provides a concise explanation of Hegelian dialectics:

Things are not to be understood as fixed entities but are in a continual state of transition into other forms of themselves. The structure of reality is a structure of oppositions, of elements that contradict each other and limit each other's possibilities. Out of this clash of antagonistic tendencies, new forms arise that incorporate the opposing elements, albeit in altered form and with their contradictions now resolved. States of being contain their contradictions as a condition of their existence, and they realize their possibilities by transcending these limitations and passing on to another phase. But the latter is also found to breed its own opposition, and the resultant world view is one of continual movement and transformation. Underlying the oppositions of the sensate, phenomenal world, then, there lies another, deeper reality, which is the process through which the contradictions are contained within a unity—a transcending of their mutual negation through synthesis, which is a "negation of the negation."

The dialectical process is conceived to be in operation everywhere. Everything is constantly colliding with its opposite, the opposites become contradictions, and move beyond what they are to a new state of being (Murphy 1980: 96). All social forms contain their own negation, or the seeds of their own destruction, which will result in a progressive transformation to a different order. Thus historical change and sociocultural evolution are the outcomes of this dialectical process of the recurring triads of thesis-antithesis-synthesis (Figure 14.2). Hegelian dialectics is based upon change as immanent, necessary and teleological, which is subject to directional laws and the manifestation of the "unfolding" of latent potentialities present in social systems from their onset (cf. Sanderson 1990).

DIALECTICAL MATERIALISM

For Hegel "contradictions" in the metaphysical realm of thought are the mechanism of historical change. What is different with Marx's use of dialectics in his theory of sociocultural evolution is that he takes Hegel's dialectic of Mind and

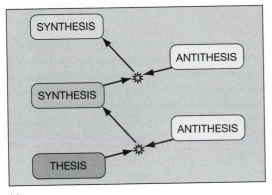

(a)

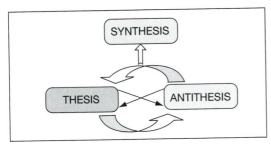

(b)

Figure 14.2 (a) Hegel's dialectical model of historical development. (b) Hegel's dialectic thesis-antithesis-synthesis triad.

brings it down to earth, or turns it on its head, making it the dialectic of the material forces of production and the relations of production. Unlike dialectics in the hands of Lévi-Strauss, which is confined to mental phenomena, Marx's dialectics is linked to the interactions between social organization and technological and economic factors (cf. Barrett 1984: 81).

This position is clearly stated by Marx and Engels in the exposition of their materialist strategy in *The German Ideology:*

In direct contrast to German philosophy, which descends from heaven to earth, here we ascend from earth to heaven. That is to say, we do not set out from what men say, imagine, conceive, nor from men as narrated, thought of, imagined, conceived, in order to arrive at men in the flesh. We set out from real, active men, and on the basis of their real life process we demonstrate the development of the phantoms formed in the human brain are also, necessarily, sublimates of their material life process, which is empirically verifiable and bound to material premises. Morality, religion, metaphysics, all the rest of ideology and their corresponding forms of consciousness, thus no longer retain the semblance of independence. They have no history, no development; but men, developing their material production and their material intercourse, alter, along with this, their real existence, their thinking, and the products of their thinking. *Life is not determined by consciousness, but consciousness by life.* In the first method of approach the starting point is consciousness taken as the living individual; in the second it is the real, living individuals themselves, as they are in actual life, and consciousness is considered *solely* their consciousness (Marx and Engels 1959b: 247–249; emphasis added).[7]

For Marx, the material forces receive priority over ideas and he maintains that ideas are merely "the material world reflected by the human mind and translated into forms of thought" (Marx 1959a: 145). For this reason Engels referred to Marx's materialist perspective as **dialectical materialism.**

Marx's insistence that "life is not determined by consciousness, but consciousness by life" expresses the foundation of his materialist perspective, which stands in opposition to idealist formulations of writers such as Max Weber, founder of interpretive sociology (Layton 1997: 94). Weber, whose works have inspired a variety of nonmaterialist/antimaterialist cognitive and symbolic perspectives in American anthropology stressed that ideas have a causal role in history. In his book *The Protestant Ethic and the Spirit of Capitalism* (1930), Weber argues that beliefs inside people's head, such as the Protestant ethics of hard work and deferred gratification, were the major force that gave rise of **capitalism** (Ringer 1997: 163–167).

Marx saw history as a succession of **social formations,** one growing out of the other (from "the womb of the old society") through the process of dialectical change (Marx 1959b: 44). He envisioned this change in terms of the playing out of inherent contradictions in the material base of life in the form of class struggle (in state-level societies), which he saw as the result of the exploitation of the subordinate working classes by the ruling classes. The outcome of this class struggle is the negation of one existing order and the emergence of another.

Marx posited that revolutionary changes occur in terms of the dynamics internal to systems, the result of the systemic contradictions that ensue when the **material forces of production** and the existing **relations of production** in the context of the given **mode of production** come into conflict (Figure 14.3). Forces of production refers to techno-economic factors, such as raw materials, tools, machinery, while relations of production signifies the social relations established between those who control the **means of production** and producers in the process of work (cf. Terray 1972: 98). Mode of production refers to the complex structure resulting from the articulation of forces of production and relations of production (Althusser and Balibar 1997: 104, 317).

Marx's resultant schema is a diachronic functionalist evolutionary model based upon the interplay between components of the system in which growing conflicts and system stress lead to system transformation over time (for an overview of classical Marxist evolutionism, see Trigger 1998: 89–93). Moreover, Marx's model specifies those aspects of the system that have causal priority over other components. This model stands in stark contrast to the synchronic functionalist models associated with twentieth-century British and American anthropologists. The latter models are detached from materials conditions and construe all components of the system as contributing more or less equally towards the maintenance and equilibrium of the whole, with dysfunctional

traits either downplayed or ignored (Harris 2001b: 235; Layton 1997: 132; O'Laughlin 1975: 344).

However, we might remind ourselves that the charge that functionalists ignored change and were therefore in collusion with imperialism and the forces of evil and oppression is greatly exaggerated, as I noted in Chapter 8. The underemphasis of system change was due to a heuristic choice, not part of a political agenda or imperialistic conspiracy, as such. The main weakness of functionalist models was in how they treated causality and material conditions. In contrast, Marx's work provides the causal mechanisms by means of which anthropologists could conceptualize contradictions and system transformations within a materialist framework.

Dialectics serve as the principal causal mechanism in Marx's analysis of capitalist society. As Marx observed,

> At a certain stage of their development the material forces of production in society come into conflict with the existing relations of production or—what is but a legal expression of the same thing—with the property relations within which they had been at work before. From forms of development of the forces of production these relations turn into their fetters. Then comes a period of social revolution. With the change of the economic foundation the entire immense superstructure is more or less rapidly transformed. In considering such transformations the distinction should always be made between the material transformation of the economic conditions of production, which can be determined with the precision of natural science, and the legal, political, religious, aesthetic, or philosophic—in short, ideological—forms in which men become conscious of this conflict and fight it out (Marx 1959b: 43–44).[8]

The ultimate direction of change set into motion by the dialectical processes, as viewed by Marx, would be the emergence of a new stage in cultural evolution, with a utopian, classless society arising out of the debris of the capitalist system. While some writers have attempted to defend Marx's evolutionary model as one based on

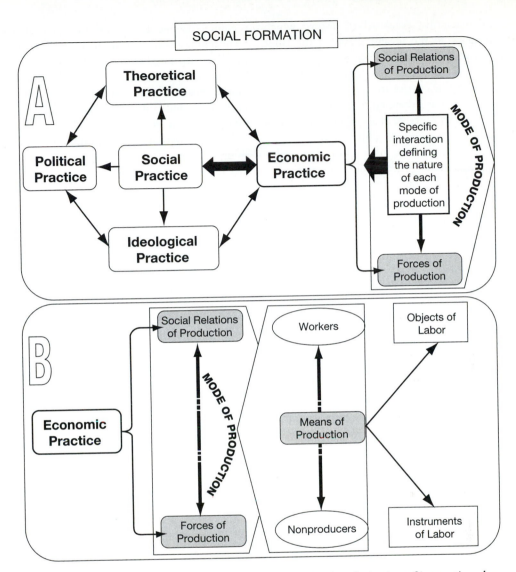

Figure 14.3 Marx's social formation. Economic practice is a derivative of interactions between forces of production (specific labor processes that transform raw materials into use value) and relations of production (how surplus labor is expropriated). Economic practice determines the nature of all other practices.   *After Taylor (1979) and M. H. Sidky (1987).*

ordinary causality (Sanderson 1990: 51–61), it is often difficult to sustain this argument. The fact that Marx's schema was wedded to a utopian ideology implies that ultimately change is immanent, necessary and teleological, a manifestation of "unfolding" of latent potentialities present in social systems from inception. In this respect, Marx's model is akin to the evolutionary models of the nineteenth-century anthropologists discussed in Chapters 3 and 4; the main difference was his materialist construal of history, which was contrary to the idealist views of the latter group of writers (Trigger 1998: 89).

We must not forget that Marx did not propose a theory strictly for the analysis of sociocultural systems, but presented a political doctrine based upon the unity of theory and practice. Dialectical materialism not only foretold of the great social transformations to come, but it also set forth a strategy for how best to hasten the arrival of the new order. As Marx and Engels wrote in their "Manifesto of the Communist Party,"

The communists disdain to conceal their views and aims. They openly declare that their ends can be attained only by the forcible overthrow of all existing social conditions. Let the ruling classes tremble at the communistic revolution. The proletarians have nothing to lose but their chains. They have a world to win. Workingmen of all countries, unite! (Marx and Engels 1959a: 41).[9]

MARXISM, MATERIALISM, AND AMERICAN ANTHROPOLOGY

Leslie White had incorporated many elements of Marxist theory into his formulations during the 1940s. However, in White's work the driving force of sociocultural evolution is the control of energy and not the dialectical dynamics associated with class exploitation based upon the control of labor, technology, and access to strategic resources, which is the central causal mechanism in Marx's evolutionary model (Layton 1997: 127; Salzman 2001: 99–103).

Marxism made its greatest and direct impact upon American anthropology during the 1960s among radicals vexed over the Vietnam War and critical of U.S. "imperialism" and imperialism and colonialism in general (Adams 1998: 345). Marxist theory, with its concepts of exploitation, dominance, and inequality and a mechanism of sociocultural evolution, offered a new way of viewing cultural systems. It made it possible to

reconnect the economic and the political as interrelated processes, which in classical economics had been separated since the start of the twentieth century (Adams 1998: 345–347). One result of this separation was that economics had been virtually excluded from the anthropologist's cultural categories (Adams 1998: 345).

The separation of economy and politics, along with the disconnection of other aspects of the human condition, had been further augmented as a result of the emergence of academic disciplines of economics, political science, psychology, sociology, and anthropology. Each of these disciplines treated its own circumscribed domain of inquiry as independent and subject to its own internal dynamics (Wolf 1982: 1–27). But these things are connected and Marxist theory and Marx's conception of **political economy** pointed out the connections between these aspects of life in terms of material relationships of power, class exploitation, modes of production, and the circulation of goods, services, and people (Salzman 2001: 57–58).

Moreover, Marx's conception of political economy enabled anthropologists to conceptualize sociocultural systems in terms of broader political, economic, and demographic relationships operating at the local, regional, national, and international levels and which are embedded in the **capitalist world-economic system** (Wolf 1982: 1–27). This line of inquiry led to the development of a fruitful theoretical perspective referred to as **world systems theory** (see Sanderson 1999; Shannon 1989; Wallerstein 1979).

All of the perspectives mentioned thus far are considered to be materialist in orientation. We must remember that there are different kinds of materialism and the differences between them stem from conflicting epistemological and ontological assumptions regarding the material world (Sperber 1996: 10–12). Thus, in addition to cultural materialism, there is world systems theory, dialectical or historical materialism, and structural Marxism. Proponents of these different perspectives all claim to be materialists but hold different ontological premises. The disregard of ontological and epistemological differences among these different approaches has led some writers to erroneously lump them together and then refer to the disagreements between their proponents as an indicator of the weakness of the materialist approach (e.g., Salzman 2001: 131).

A MARXIST ANTHROPOLOGY

In addition to the impact upon cultural materialism and world systems theory, the works of Marx has led some writers to follow another "materialist" line of inquiry, referred to as French structural Marxism. The proponents of this perspective touted it as the only legitimate and authentic Marxist perspective in anthropology. As such, a review of the main features of this approach can help us better understand the differences that set apart the materialist paradigms in anthropology.

A number of problems confront those attempting to develop a Marxist anthropology. First there are the ambiguities in Marx's writings, which lend themselves to alternate interpretations or "readings." There is, therefore, considerable room for idiosyncratic interpretations of the relevant works. Second, particular ideological orientations and theoretical interests on the part of various Marxist writers have resulted in some texts being emphasized and highlighted, while others have been ignored or discounted (cf. Bailey 1981: 90). For example, in an attempted to disassociate Marx from any hints that he might have attributed causal priority to productive forces over relations of production (e.g., G. A. Cohen 2001)—something pejoratively referred to as **techno-environmental determinism**—several writers have asked for particular readings of Marx (cf. Godelier 1975: 15).

Bloch (1983: 136) urges that interpretations of the Preface to *The Critique of Political Economy* should take into account the fact that Marx overstated his case in that text in order to stress the difference between his stance and Hegel's idealist position that ideas come from mysterious sources. Toward the same objective of saving Marx from charges of techno–economic determinism, Friedman (1974: 30) asks that *The German Ideology* and *The Contributions to the Critique of Political Economy* be discarded altogether.

Still others have given priority to the works of the "mature" Marx, who was keen on structures and systems and who wrote *Capital,* over those of the early or "immature" Marx, who was concerned with individual consciousness (Althusser 1969; Althusser and Balibar 1997). The shift in Marx's epistemological and theoretical position from an approach based on the essence of "man" to a perspective focusing on systems, modes of production, relations of production and so forth is thought to have occurred in 1845–1846 and is first evident in *The German Ideology.* Those in the quest of a theory of **precapitalist social formations** in the works of Marx must contend with these inconsistencies. For example, is it the young Marx or the mature Marx who is to be the source of a Marxist theory of precapitalist social formations?

SOURCES FOR A MARXIST ANTHROPOLOGY

Efforts to develop a Marxist anthropology have been hampered by additional obstacles. The problems stem from the fact that Marx's primary focus was the explication of the **capitalist mode of production.** Thus, the theoretical formulations of his major work *Capital,* which deals with the evolution of capitalism in Europe, are not directly applicable to the nonindustrial, small-scale sociocultural systems that have traditionally interested anthropologists. However, there are aspects to Marx's formulations that have potential anthropological application, which I shall mention briefly.

Marx's papers and notes in which he outlined his ideas regarding non-Western cultures, mentioned in certain places in *Capital,* appear in a volume entitled *Pre-Capitalist Economic*

Formations (1964). Marx's notes are based upon his reading of nineteenth-century evolutionists such as Morgan, Lubbock, and Maine, among others. The notes were written late in Marx's life, when precapitalist social formations began to assume greater theoretical significance in his thinking and provide an evolutionary model.

Marx's model is far more sophisticated than many of those proposed by the nineteenth-century evolutionary anthropologists because it entails a multilinear evolutionary development, rather than a unilineal one (Figure 14.4). Marx envisions three evolutionary trajectories respectively leading from a presumed stage of primitive

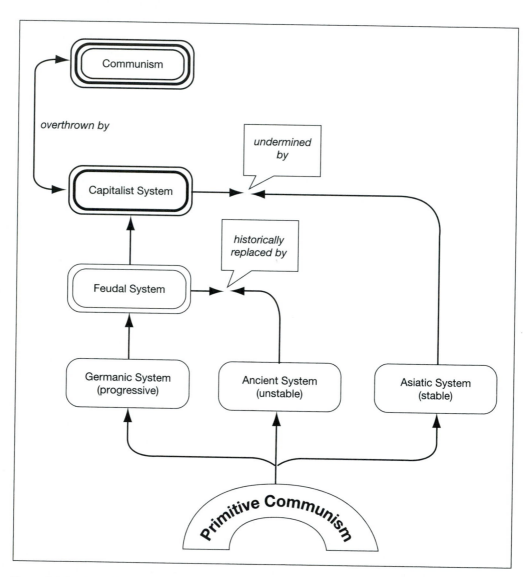

Figure 14.4 Marx's multilinear evolutionary model. *After Layton (1997).*

communism far back in time, to the emergence of what he called the Ancient, the Germanic, and the Asiatic modes of production (Layton 1997: 16–18). The first two, exemplified by classical Greece and ancient Rome, evolve into and are replaced by the feudal mode of production and characterize historical developments in Europe (also Japan). The Asiatic mode leads to a different evolutionary pathway.

Marx's concept of the **Asiatic mode of production,** which he developed on the basis of the analysis of Asian and African societies, was intended for use in the analysis of non-Western cultures (Sidky 1996: 27). As such, the Asiatic mode of production has attracted the interest of anthropologists.

The Asiatic mode of production, exemplified by precolonial social formations of India, Peru, and Mexico, follows a trajectory different than those in Europe in which this mode of production is not replaced by a feudal mode but is instead undermined by capitalist modes of production (Layton 1997: 16). In the Asiatic mode, the landing-holding village commune partially organized on the basis of kinship is the independent, self-sufficient unit of food and crafts production. The village commune is integrated into a wider political system governed by a king, to whom the village turns over its surplus production in the form of tribute (Layton 1997: 16). Urban centers are absent and occur only in places where trade is conducted with other societies. Because of its structural organization the Asiatic mode of production is highly stable and often outlasts ruling dynasties (Layton 1997: 16; on the Asiatic mode of production see Dunn 1982; Friedman 1979; Sawer 1977; Wittfogel 1957).

One of the problems encountered by those attempting to make anthropological use of these formulations is that Marx's interest in precapitalist societies was intended to shed light on aspects of capitalism rather than to provide a general theory of precapitalist social formations for its own sake (Kahn and Llobera 1981: 301). More-over, Marx did not use the concept of Asiatic mode of production in a sustained and systematic way and his works do not contain a readily discernable theory of precapitalist societies (Kahn and Llobera 1981: 302). Any theory based on these sources must necessarily depend upon specific readings and extrapolations that encompass sources external to the corpus of Marx's own writings (Kahn and Llobera 1981: 303). Nevertheless, some writers have attempted to apply Marx's Asiatic mode of production to the analysis of non-European societies, with various results.

An alternative for the derivation of a "genuine" Marxist theory of precapitalist societies is to turn to Marx's principal text, *Capital* itself. In other words, one could try and deduce a general theory from Marx's work pertaining specifically to the capitalist mode of production, which would be applicable to all modes of production (Kahn and Llobera 1981: 303). This approach, which was taken by the French philosopher Louis Althusser (1918–1990), also entails specific readings and interpretation that again takes us outside the boundaries of Marx's own formulations.

Finally, one could turn to another source for a Marxist anthropology, this being the works of the number two Marxist, Friedrich Engels, who was interested in such anthropological questions as the evolution of the family, development of property rights, and the rise of the state (see Woolfson 1982). Using Engels to complete Marx's anthropological theory is to assume that both men were in total theoretical agreement, which, as some have argued, they were not (see Sanderson 1990: 64).

However one looks at it, the development of a Marxist anthropology requires a wide latitude in how the works of Marx and Engels are interpreted. French Marxism, which appeared in the 1960s and 1970s, was one such effort (Bloch 1983; Kahn and Llobera 1981). This perspective was the creation of French intellectuals based largely upon their own particular interpretations and specific readings of Marx's works. Moreover, the direction which French Marxists would take anthropological thought would lead them in a circuitous way to postmodern thought and its antimaterialist, antiscience, nihilistic formulations. This was a surprising and unfortunate twist for Marxist anthropology.

FRENCH STRUCTURAL MARXIST ANTHROPOLOGY

For French Marxist writers such as Maurice Godelier and Claude Meillassoux, who were dissatisfied with party-bound Soviet dogmatism but interested in applying Marxist theory to non-Western, tribal peoples, the obvious starting place was Marx's writings on precapitalist societies. The disillusionment with Soviet Marxism was in part due to the realization that it did not apply to "tribal" peoples, whose diverse cultures were then under the close scrutiny of French anthropologists led by Lévi-Strauss. The framework through which Soviet theoreticians dealt with prestate societies was Morgan's discredited evolutionary scheme, which had been imported into Marxism by Engels and formed an essential component of party-bound Soviet Marxism (cf. Trigger 1998: 93–95).

The interest in precapitalist societies, engendered by Lévi-Strauss's highly popular writings, was in part fueled by the furious **formalist-substantivist controversy** in economic anthropology (see Cook 1966; Polanyi 1968) taking place at the time in which French Marxists such as Godelier, Meillassoux, P. P. Rey, and others were involved. At issue in the debate was the nature of the difference between capitalist and noncapitalist economic systems and associated patterns of economic decision making and economic behavior.

The **formalists** maintained that all economic systems possess the same basic characteristics (see Cook 1966). They posited that all economic decisions are based upon the principle of economizing, meaning the rational allocation of resources toward utilitarian goals based upon the objective of maximizing profits. In other words, people everywhere make economic decisions based on rational choices and maximization of individual interests.

Formalists maintained that although the idea of maximization of profit in the monetary sense as understood in capitalist societies may not be present in small-scale societies lacking money markets, maximization is still present. However, depending upon the particular case, maximization may be geared not towards accumulating capital, but on the basis of a different index of utility, which could entail a number of other considerations, such as enhancing physical security, social prestige, and expanding alliances. Therefore, the tools and concepts developed by economists studying Western economics systems/institutions, such as "supply and demand," "production and

Maurice Godelier, one of the principal architects of French Structural Marxist Anthropology.

consumption," "investments," "scarcity," and individual profit motives, can be extended for use in the analysis of all economic systems.

The **substantivists,** headed by the British economist Karl Polanyi (1886–1964), charged the formalists of ethnocentrism and *bourgeois* bias. They asserted, much along the lines of present day postmodern interpretivists, that capitalism is a cultural system and its "economic theory" is merely Western people's way of thinking about economic matters; that is, their folk knowledge, erroneously assumed to be universal in nature, transcending cultural boundaries (Gudeman 1986; Herzfeld 2001: 94–97).

Substantivists stressed that there are fundamental differences—differences in kind—between non-Western, small-scale economic systems based upon **reciprocity** and **redistribution** and embedded in institutions outside the market, and capitalist economies based upon **market exchange** geared toward individual motives for profit and accumulation of wealth. For example, in the capitalist market exchange system, production is dominated by the manufacture of goods with **exchange value.** In other words, the objective of production is not simply to produce useful things, but to make a profit and accumulate capital through exchange (Sahlins 1972). In contrast, precapitalist economic systems are dominated by production of items with **use value.**

Marx referred to these two forms of production as (1) "capitalist production," based upon the commodification of labor, wages, and **surplus value,** and uniquely associated with the modern world, and (2) "simple commodity production," characteristic of most of human history (Sanderson 1999: 138). It follows therefore that concepts based upon classical economic theory are inapplicable to small-scale economic systems, in which production, exchange, and consumption are based upon fundamentally different principles, in stark contrast to the maximization principle (Polanyi 1944).

The debate and arguments presented by both sides had an impact upon the development of

economic anthropology. This is because economic exchange does lend itself to analysis by means of concepts and methods of the economists and it is possible to establish standards of value and equivalence in many instances, even in systems without all-purpose money and market exchange. It is also true that precapitalist economic systems are embedded in institutions outside the market and this significant dimension cannot be overlooked. Therefore, economic anthropologists subsequently went on to adopt insights based both upon formalist and substantivist views and grounded their analysis of varying patterns of production, ownership, exchange, and consumption in terms of ecological, demographic and cultural frameworks (Scupin 1992: 117).

The French Marxists came down on the side of the substantivists. They pointed out that "primitive" economies are imbedded in kinship relations, while capitalist economies are embedded in relations involving ownership of property and political economy (Kahn and Llobera 1981: 278). Consequently, the analysis of precapitalist economic systems requires the development of a different set of analytical concepts and methods. However, the French Marxists would go on to present a new set of problems, which I shall discuss shortly, that would altogether bypass the issues central to the formalist-substantive debate.

The interest in Marx's works on precapitalist societies led some French anthropologists to revive the concept of the Asiatic mode of production, which seemed applicable to the types of societies studied by anthropologists. According to Godelier, one of the leading expositors of structural Marxism,

> The very essence of the Asiatic mode of production is the combined existence of primitive, land-holding communities, still partially organised on the basis of kinship, and of a state power which expresses the real or imaginary unity of these communities, controls the use of essential economic resources and directly appropriates part of the

labour and product of the communities which it dominates (in Bailey 1981: 96–97).

Marx's writings on precapitalist societies and the Asiatic mode of production presented French writers with two possibilities. First, these works offered a way of breaking free of the stifling grip that dogmatic party-based Soviet Marxism had established over the field of Marxist theory. In Marx's work on precapitalist social formations could be found a theory of multilineal evolution, discussed previously, that charted different routes to the evolution of the state and class societies and, as such, contradicted the Soviet scheme that had all societies struggling toward socialism along fixed stages. For this reason Marx's texts on precapitalist societies had assumed an apocryphal status in the eyes of Soviet theoreticians and were suppressed and excluded from the official ideology (cf. Bailey 1981: 90).

The second possibility offered by these works was their potential for the development of a truly Marxist anthropological paradigm that combined "analyses inherited from Marx as often as possible" with the corpus of modern anthropological information (cf. Godelier 1977: 121). This was the thrust of the efforts toward establishing a Marxist anthropological paradigm.

Godelier led the merger of Marxism and anthropology. He argued that the emphasis Marx placed upon the Asiatic mode of production suggested that he never fully accepted Morgan's evolutionary scheme (for a contrary view, see Sanderson 1990: 69). Godelier argued that the only reason Morgan's work was incorporated into the corpus of Marxist theory was because at the time it represented the latest anthropological knowledge. Much of this knowledge, however, proved problematic in light of subsequent ethnographic field research. Thus Marx should not be held responsible for the errors of nineteenth-century evolutionism (Godelier 1977: 105).

Given the important advances in anthropology since Morgan's day, Godelier argued, there is really no need to retain antiquated anthropological concepts. Extricating the formulations of nineteenth-

century evolutionary cultural anthropology, he maintained, would not affect Marx's general paradigm. Godelier (1977: 119) proposed therefore to revive the concept of Asiatic mode of production, but only after discarding the "dead parts" and changing it by employing up-to-date anthropological information.

MARX AND LÉVI-STRAUSS UNITED

A second development to take place was the merger of the new Marxist perspective and structuralism. This followed from Godelier's (1977: 46–47) observation that the modes of analyses used by Marx and Lévi-Strauss were basically alike because both eschewed surface appearances and focused instead upon the internal logic of systems and opposed attempts to reduce one structure to another. This observation made Marxism respectable in the eyes of French anthropologists and cleared the way for the incorporation of Marxist theory into anthropology (Bloch 1983: 152).

Partly because of his association with Lévi-Strauss, Godelier has been more concerned with the logical structure of systems of thought than his contemporaries. Meillassoux, Terray, and Rey, however, rejected Lévi-Strauss's work as ideological mystification. Godelier saw the structure of systems of thought as important, even though in the final analysis he attributed causality to the economic infrastructure. Nevertheless, although Godelier saw system transformation emanating from changes in the existing mode of production, he viewed change as being actualized in terms of the cognitive structures or the logic of the mode of production. Thus if kinship is to be changed in relation to alterations in the economic infrastructure, it is changed according to the existing logical structure of the cognitive system associated with the kinship system.

However, Godelier (1975: 14) pointed out that while Lévi-Strauss's approach explained the logic of forms, it could not explain the logic of functions. What separated Godelier from other French Marxists was his insistence that one should not confuse the function of an institution for its form or appearance. Thus he wrote,

> When Marx distinguished between infra- and superstructure and proposed that the deep logic of evolution and history depends in the last analysis on the properties of their infrastructure he did no more than to point out, for the first time, that there is a hierarchy of functions and structural causalities, without in any way prejudging the type of social relations which take on these functions, nor the number of functions that any structure can assume (Godelier 1975: 15).[10]

Thus, just because religion or kinship does not play an important role in the relations of production in capitalist societies it does not mean that this is the case in other types of social formations. For example, Godelier (1977) showed how in the Inca Empire, it was religion that functioned as the relations of production, through which the State extracted surplus from local communities. Similarly, in tribal societies kinship could function both as infrastructure and superstructure at the same time and it is not possible to separate the two.

ALTHUSSER'S READING OF MARX

Another significant event in the shaping of French Marxism was the development of a new analytical approach by the French philosopher Louis Althusser (see Althusser 1969; Althusser and Balibar 1997). Based upon a particular reading of Marx's *Capital,* Althusser extracted the **theory of modes of production** from the specific case to which Marx had applied it in that work (Bloch 1983: 152). This was of great significance for French anthropology because, once detached from the specific case of capitalism, the concept of mode of production could be applied to any society, not just ones characterized by the capitalist political economy (Bloch 1975: xi).

Althusser's reading focused upon Marx's strategy to discover the inner laws of cultural causality for the capitalist mode of production. Surface phenomena (i.e., what actors perceive) obscure the true characteristics or inner logic of the system, of which they are an expression. Thus, an analysis of capitalism, using concepts such as capital, value, labor, and the like, is itself enmeshed in the beliefs associated with the system and fails to penetrate to the internal logic (Bloch 1983: 153). Similarly, according to this view, attempts to explain phenomena associated with the system in terms of other phenomena, such as technology or demography, as is the case with empiricist approaches, are **reductionistic** and also fail to grasp the system's internal logic.

Marx's analysis in *Capital,* according to Althusser, is based on the notion of structural causality centered upon the concept of "mode of production," which he uses to achieve an understanding of **social formations** (see Figure 14.3), the totality of the hierarchical arrangements of subsystems that comprise a sociocultural system. The mode of production is a theoretical construct based upon a group of logically connected relations that comprise the inner link between surface phenomena (Bloch 1983: 154). A mode of production consists of economic, political, and ideological levels/practices, with the economic level determining which of the levels will be dominant in the mode of production. In Althusser's view, which level in a mode of production is dominant varies from one society to the next. In the capitalist social formation, the mode of production comprises the relations that exist between classes, as well as how resources are exploited, the technology used, and the nature of the symbolic-ideological system. In this mode of production, the social relations of production dominate.

Thus, the engines of history, according to Althusser's understanding of Marx, reside in this inner system of interconnections and relationships. According to this view, sociocultural transformation occurs not because of changes in any single subsystem, but due to the contradictions that develop out of the articulation of different subsystems, each of which possesses its own inner logic and characteristics, or structures.

These subsystems, although linked, retain their own distinctive nature and develop differentially according to their own internal contradictions. Because they are articulated they also affect one another in various degrees. Each subsystem also influences the totality, which, in turn, exerts a powerful influence upon the subsystems themselves. According to Althusser, this is what Marx means when he says that

> at a certain stage of their development the material forces of production in society come into conflict with the existing relations of production or—what is but a legal expression of the same thing—with the property relations within which they had been at work before. From forms of development of the forces of production these relations turn into their fetters. Then comes a period of social revolution (Marx 1959b: 43–44).[11]

The system altering force in history emerges out of the tensions, contradictions, and interplay engendered by these interrelationships. Cultural causality is therefore structural and its dynamics reside in the configuration of structural relationships between subsystems. The configuration of subsystems as a whole, according to Althusser, is **overdetermined,** meaning that contradictions arise from the effects of the subsystems on each other, their effects on the whole system, and the effects of the whole on the parts. In other words, there are complex intrasystemic feeback loops. The system as a whole operates under the causal priority to the structure of the social relations of production, which "dominate the entire functioning of the larger system" (Friedman 1975: 164).

Althusser elaborated upon these ideas by pointing out that in each historical case, "the social formation" in a particular location is to be construed as comprising not just one mode of production, but as the articulation of several modes of productions (Bloch 1983: 155–156).

Thus, as a result of colonial penetration it is often the case that a communal or "lineage" mode of production exists in conjunction with a capitalist mode of production that dominates the structural relationships between the two.

Dominant modes of production tend to affect and distort the internal consistency of subordinate modes of production without themselves being affected in a significant way. Thus the focus of analysis must encompass structures internal to each mode of production as well as the structural articulation between those modes of production. The job of the anthropologist is to analytically define the modes of production, at least two in each case, determine their internal contradictions, and specify their structural linkages or "articulation" with one another.

In a sense, because Althusser proposed a new problematic, French anthropologists were able to bypass the formalist-substantivist debate by focusing on the analysis of social formations that were mixtures of capitalist and precapitalist modes of production in Third World nations (Barrett 1984: 90).

A social formation differs from the bounded system of structural functional anthropology because it is an articulation of different structures located in one area, but whose boundaries cannot be confined to a given geographical area (Bloch 1983: 157). Thus, Althusser's conception of social formation entailing the articulation of distinct structures at odds with one another was seen by its proponents as an alternative to the conventional structural-functionalist views of social systems as integrated unities, the different parts of which came together in a perfect fit.

However, critics of Althusser's reading of Marx have asserted that although his vocabulary is new, the structural model he proposes is highly reminiscent of the structural-functionalist models based upon the works of Durkheim and Talcott Parsons, which also entail intrasystemic feedbacks (Applebaum 1979: 19; Giddens 1979: 52).

What is evident from all this is that Marxist anthropologists under the influence of Althusser and Godelier subscribed to the view that being Marxist was not contingent upon accepting Marx's own ideas on precapitalist social formations. Rather, their claim to being Marxist rested upon what they described as the use of the same type of analysis Marx had employed in his study of capitalism (Bloch 1983: 158). The theoretical perspective they espoused was therefore largely of their own creation.

RESULTS: CLASS IN CLASSLESS SOCIETIES

One of the first statements of the new Marxist anthropology was the publication of Emmanuel Terray's *Marxism and Primitive Society* (1972). Terray called for the abandonment of classificatory schemes of stages and corresponding modes of production (Morgan-like stages, still the standard concepts in party-based Marxism at that time) and stressed the need for the development of new Marxist studies of precapitalist societies according to the new analytical approach (Bloch 1983: 150). Adding to this, P. Rey (1977) stressed the need to focus upon the dynamic nature of sociocultural processes. Rey reintroduced the idea of contradictions emerging out of the inconsistencies between the internal logic of different modes of production and contradictions between classes and between the forces of production and relations of production.

Contradictions between classes and between forces and relations of production were the key mechanism of sociocultural transformation in Marx's analysis of capitalism, and it could not be set aside in any Marxist analysis of precapitalist social formations. The problem was that precapitalist social formations have traditionally been construed as being organized on principles of kinship, rather than in terms of classes. Engels, for example, treated precapitalist societies as classless. For this reason he found himself looking for a substitute theory when it came to the analysis of such societies, for which he turned to Morgan and the nineteenth-century evolutionists.

French Marxists viewed this as an enormous blunder on the part of Engels, which was a detriment to the development of a Marxist science of history. In Marx's formulation, dialectical forces operated through the antagonism that exists between classes. Ethnographic research from a Marxist perspective would go nowhere without the concept of class because without it there could be no dialectical forces, the principle mechanism of cultural evolution in their view. As Bloch (1983: 162) notes,

> Engels had to look for an alternative social theory for primitive society and he vacillated between biological and terminological determinism [Morgan's kinship approach]. The introduction of this type of theory continuously hindered Marxist explanations of primitive societies. Later, this "anthropological" theory even spread its influence to Marxist explanations of other social systems, always with disastrous results, even to the extent that in the hands of such writers as Marvin Harris, who . . . considers himself some sort of Marxist, it became a general social theory.[12]

Rey's solution to the problem was to advocate the use of "class" as an analytical concept for all societies and illustrated how this could be done. This was an important development. The solution to the problem overturned Engels's treatment of precapitalist societies as classless, which had in effect rendered Marxist theory, so powerful in treating capitalist society, irrelevant for the analysis of "primitive" societies (Bloch 1983: 162). Bloch's is mistaken to equate Harris's materialist paradigm with Morgan's idealist perspective. Nevertheless, he is correct about the theoretical significance of Rey's extension of the concept of class to precapitalist societies, at least for Marxist anthropology.

What was Rey's solution? He basically argued that the concept of class could be applied to small-scale societies by, for example, treating lineage elders and juniors in an African society as classes, or women as a class in relation to men, and so forth. Rey was thus applying the blanket statement by Marx and Engels that "the history of all hitherto existing societies is the history of class struggles" (Marx and Engels 1959a: 7). With the concept of class thus extended to societies previously treated as classless, dialectical analysis could now be applied to ethnographic cases.

French Marxist anthropologists therefore constructed an analytical framework, the concept of articulation of different modes of production, that allowed the investigation of the linkages and contradictions between local, colonial, capitalist, and imperial systems (Bloch 1983: 161). They also maintained that complexity and subtleties of sociocultural phenomena could only be captured through dialectical analysis and the application of the concept of class that Marx rightly employed over an empirical approach. So dialectical analysis was retained and Marx and Engels were absolved of the abominable sin of techno-economic determinism to which the **vulgar materialists,** or **mechanical materialists,** such as cultural materialists, and others had supposedly succumbed.

TOWARD POSTMODERNISM: THE DEMATERIALIZATION OF MARX'S MATERIALIST PARADIGM

Although French Marxist anthropologists disagreed with one another on many points, they all concurred that causal primacy rests on the structural relationships internal to the modes of production and the structures linking different modes of production. One implication of the structural Marxist perspective is that in the ethnographic setting one no longer needed to abide by Marx's general materialist strategy but could instead focus upon the identification of structures and the determination of the contradictions emerging from the articulation of these structures in particular social formations.

French Marxist anthropologists also agreed that one subsystem or structure should not be reduced to any other. Moreover, no subsystem could be given causal priority, just as is the case of British structural-functionalist models. By

shifting the level of analysis to intrasystemic dynamics, the causal effects of demographic and techno-environmental factors could be pushed to the status of background effect or altogether obscured.

The shift in the level of analysis to intrasystemic dynamics was tantamount to the abandonment of material causation. It was a significant twist with unfortunate theoretical implications. This is because it led French Marxists to the dematerialization of Marx and a move toward Hegelian idealism. Marxist thought followed a similar trajectory in the hands of the theoreticians associated with the **Frankfurt School** (D'Andrade 1999: 96). This idealist twist was a curious development because Marxism always presented itself as a materialist perspective, an approach that gave primacy to the material forces of production (Gellner 1992: 31). Marx himself treated the realm of thought as the objective world "reflected by the human mind and translated into forms of thought" (Marx 1959a: 145).

Marxism also claimed to be "scientific" with access to "objective" truths. Moreover, as Gellner (1992: 33–34) pointed out, the more sophisticated Marxists, the critical theorists of the Frankfurt School, did not declare that objective scientific understanding was impossible but rather that surface phenomena were not enough to produce an understanding of the objective world. This is because class and political interests and ideology mask the true nature of social relationships. The same philosophical orientation was basically true of the French Marxists. These Marxists accused their adversaries of superficial objectivity and for failing to attain true objectivity, but they did not maintain that objectivity was impossible, just that the positivists had it wrong.

However, the shift of analytical focus toward the inner structures and processes was, as I have said, the road toward Hegelian idealism. The reasons for this are simple. Immense obstacles confront anyone probing into the inner structures lying deep beneath the superficial facts of the shallow empiricists. There are innumerable possibilities and negations, binary oppositions, and contrasts in the deep structures that could "account" for the surface phenomena (Gellner 1992: 33–34). The possibilities increase infinitely when the surface facts are summarily and contemptuously dismissed as illusionary. The shortcomings of the Lévi-Strauss's structural analysis, discussed in Chapter 11, were recapitulated in the efforts of the structural Marxists.

In the absence of any explicit methods or guidelines for selecting the correct combination of inner structures and oppositions, Marxist theorists fell back upon what amounts to is "hocus-pocus, sleight of hand and verbiage" in a remarkable parallel to the present-day postmodern interpretive/literary anthropological writers (Gellner 1992: 34).

The new Marxists gave themselves the widest latitude for intuitive and subjective formulations through which they could pour forth their own private revelations and intuitions about what was wrong with the world and how to correct it (Gellner 1992: 34). Still, lip service was paid to the ideal of objectivity. Nevertheless, the push toward Hegelian idealism continued unabated, with increasing emphasis paid upon ideological forces and discourse. The French antiscience poststructuralists, or postmodernists (D'Andrade 1999: 96), took this trend to its logical nihilistic conclusions.

This is very ironic because Marxism, in principle at least, identified itself with science, rational thought, and objectivity, which were considered to be the best means of fighting the mystifications of the oppressive ruling classes. In actuality, however, there was nothing scientific about the Marxism of Althusser, Godelier, or the Frankfurt School. For this reason radical thinkers of these leanings had no conceptual or epistemological difficulties in casting off their failed Marxist theories and embracing the antiscientific formulations, epistemological relativism, and subjectivism of postmodernism.

The erroneous assumption that Marxism, structural or the Soviet brand, was a scientific enterprise has led to the astonishingly obtuse conclusion that the collapse of the Soviet Union is proof that science and its epistemological foundations are a failed enterprise (cf. Sokal and Bricmont 1998: 192). In other words, the use of the honorific "science" by Marxist theorists and Marxist regimes as a label for their ideological formulations—which fell short of the ideals of science as much as the absurd supernaturalisms of our day—was taken as science.

Take, for example, the comments by the Czech president Václav Havel in 1992, following the collapse of the Soviet Union:

> The fall of Communism can be regarded as a sign that modern thought—based on the premise that the world is objectively knowable, and that the knowledge so obtained can be absolutely generalized—has come to a final crisis (in Sokal and Bricmont 1998: 192).[13]

Havel's statement about absolute generalizations and objectivity is attributable to postmodernist mystifications and its straw man construals or stereotypes of science. The collapse of the Soviet Empire is definitive proof not that science is a failed enterprise, but rather that Marxist theoretical formulations based on subjectivism and intuition were failures. It is a demonstration of the dangers of dismissing the idea that theories must be assessed on the basis of systematic testing and observation against empirical evidence rather than authority, sacred texts, party votes, or clever writing (cf. Sokal and Bricmont 1998: 190).

The fall of Communism has implications for all Marxist theoretical perspectives. This includes cultural materialism, which, as noted previously, is a research strategy based upon the works of Marx. For this reason, I shall revisit this issue later.

THE PARADIGM OF CULTURAL MATERIALISM

Cultural materialism incorporates certain features of Marx's strategy described previously but excludes many others that form the basis of other types of Marxist perspectives. In his book

Cultural Materialism: The Struggle for a Science of Culture (2001a [1979]), which offers a programmatic statement for the paradigm of cultural materialism, Harris acknowledges the contributions of Marx, whom he calls "the Darwin of the social sciences" (Harris 2001a: x–xi).

> Like Darwin, Marx showed that phenomena previously regarded as inscrutable or as a direct emanation of deity could be brought down to earth and understood in terms of lawful scientific principles. Marx did this by proposing that the production of the material means of subsistence forms "the foundation upon which state institutions, the legal conceptions, the art and even the religious ideas of the people concerned have evolved, and in the light of which these things must therefore be explained instead of vice versa as has hitherto been the case." . . . The "materialism" in "cultural materialism" is therefore intended as an acknowledgment of the debt owned to Marx's formulation of the determining influence of production and other material processes (Harris 2001a: x).[14]

While accepting the "objective and empirical aspects of Marx's scientific materialism," cultural materialism departs from Marx in several notable ways. This departure entails taking into account the theories of modern anthropology as well as the jettisoning of one of the basic ingredients of Marxist doctrine—the dialectical mode of analysis. Instead of Hegelian dialectics, cultural materialism is linked to the philosophical tradition of David Hume and the British empiricists (Harris 2001a: xi).

Harris considers Marx's general scientific materialist research strategy, which is based on the recognition of the determinative effects of the material means of production upon the other components of the social system, to be "the closest equivalent in the social sciences to Darwin's principle of natural selection" (Harris 2001b: 229). Marx and Engels expressed this in *The German Ideology:*

> The fact is, therefore, that definite individuals who are productively active in a definite way enter into these definite social and political relations. Empiri-

cal observation must in each separate instance bring out empirically, and without any mystification and speculation, the connection of the social and political structure of production. The social structure and the State are continually evolving out of the life process of definite individuals, but of individuals not as they appear in their own or other people's imagination, but as they really are, i.e., as they are effective, produce materially, and are active under definite material limits, presuppositions, and conditions independent of their will. . . . The production of ideas, of conception, of consciousness is at first directly interwoven with the material activity and material intercourse of men, the language of real life. Conceiving, thinking, the mental intercourse of men appear at this stage as the direct efflux of their material behavior. The same applies to mental production as expressed in the language of politics, laws, morality, religion, metaphysics of people. Men are the producers of their conceptions, ideas, etc.—real, active men, as they are conditioned by definite development of their productive forces and of the intercourse corresponding to these, up to its furthest forms. Consciousness can never be anything else than conscious existence, and the existence of men in their actual life process. If in all ideology men and their circumstances appear upside down, as in *camera obscura,* this phenomena arises just as much from their historical life process as the inversion of objects on the retina does from their physical life process (Marx and Engels 1959b: 247).[15]

Harris dismisses Marx's ideas concerning the manner in which class societies undergo change as part of the Hegelian and revolutionary activist components of Marx's work that "overwhelm" his more general materialist research strategy. Considering "dialectical materialism" to be restricted in scope to a particular historical period in which it was conceived, and hence being a special case of a more general materialist strategy, Harris favors Marx's general materialist program as being applicable to anthropological analysis.

Cultural materialism rejects the Hegelian dialectical metaphysics in Marx's strategy for a number of reasons. First, dialectics does not specify how one is to identify significant aspects of the dialectical process, such as which negations and which contradictions are the causally important ones. Nearly anything can be selected as the negation of anything else. As such, dialectical relationships cannot be falsified and are hence unscientific (Harris 2001a: 145).

Moreover, there is the tragic fact that in countries where Marxist dialectics became part of the official ideology great horrors and follies ensued. In the hands of the power crazed politicians, from Joseph Stalin to Babrak Karmal, Hegelian dialectics often became the justification of all sorts of atrocities, political repression, and the extermination of peoples, classes, and ethnic groups. Dialectics became a convenient tool to explain away all opposition groups by labeling them reactionary forces, deluded class enemies, the dialectical opponents of the people's democracy, and so forth. Dissidents, meaning those who did not accept the current ideology espoused in Marx's name, had to be explained sociologically, their heresies unmasked, the social evils they defended revealed, their presence physically expunged, and the lessons of this exercise taught to all (cf. Gellner 1992: 31). Dialectics therefore become "a breeding ground for fanatical revelations, grand finalities, and impenetrable metaphors" (Harris 2001a: 145).

Another reason cultural materialists reject dialectics is because in the hands of later Marxists, such as V. I. Lenin (1870–1924), leader of the Bolshevik Revolution in Russia, dialectical materialism was harnessed to a political ideology. This political ideology was to serve as an antithesis of bourgeois philosophy and was offered as an alternative to scientific epistemologies and an objective science of society. For this reason, cultural materialists maintain that the objective empirical aspects of Marx's work were overcome by Hegelian dialectics.

The sociocultural processes Marx attempted to account for in terms of dialectics, cultural materialists explain by employing the concept of evolution. Cultural materialism, Harris (2001a: xi) insists,

is concerned with systemic interactions between thought and behavior, with conflicts as well as harmonics, continuities and discontinuities, gradual and revolutionary change, adaptation and maladaptation, function and dysfunction, positive and negative feedback. To drop the word "dialectical" is not to drop any of these interests—it is simply to insist that they must be pursued under empirical and operational auspices rather than as adjuncts to a political program or as an attempt to express one's persona.[16]

Marxist anthropologists object to the discarding of dialectics because they see it as the only way to describe sociocultural complexity (Bloch 1983: 132) in a manner that does not omit the complexities involved in the interactions between economic forces and ideas and values as determined by internal systems contradictions. Because Marx employed the dialectical method, it is argued, he did not construe a direct relationship between economic base and superstructure, which is a characteristic of "mechanical" or "vulgar materialism," a category to which cultural materialism is assigned.

Marxist anthropologists thus view dialectics as an indispensable element of "any form of Marxism." Bloch (1983: 133) claims that techno-economic determinism is not a feature of the works of Marx but derives from Darwinian scientism, as expressed in the works of Morgan and imported into Marxism by Engels, who needed a theory to deal with "primitive societies." Bloch is in error to suggest that Morgan's work was a form of Darwinian scientism. Morgan's work, if anything, is Lamarckian, and his notion of causality is idealist, not techno-economic, as noted in Chapter 4.

In contrast, cultural materialists see Marx's materialist strategy and his elucidation of the relationship between thought and behavior as his major contributions to a science of culture and have made it central to their research program. As Harris (2001b: 231) points out,

There were many predecessor and contemporaries who were convinced that natural law governed the realm of sociocultural phenomena. But Marx and Engels were the first to show how the problem of consciousness and the subjective experience of the importance of ideas for behavior could be reconciled with causation on the physicalist model. If there had been an orderliness in human history, it cannot, as the Enlightenment philosophers supposed, have originated from the orderliness of men's thoughts. Men do not think their way into matrilineality, the couvade, or Iroquois cousin terminology. In the abstract, can a good reason be found why anyone should bother to think up such apparently improbable thoughts? And if one man had thought them, whence arose the compulsion and the power to convince others of their propriety? For surely it could not be that these improbable ideas construed as mere spontaneous products of fancy occur simultaneously to dozens of people at a time. Obviously, therefore, thoughts must be subject to constraints; that is, they have causes and are made more or less probable in individuals and groups of individuals by prior conditions.[17]

The prior conditions could be other ideas, as the Enlightenment philosophers would have it, and this may be argued to be the case in the development of mathematics, where logical links are evident. However, Harris (2001b: 231) argues that there are no logical linkages to prior or subsequent practices in the case of such phenomena as matrilineality and patrilineality, exogamy and endogamy, or other aspects of cultural evolution. Marx's answer to this problem was that the prior conditions that shape ideas about institutions must therefore be the institutions under which they were thought of. Marx went on to explain the origins of the institutions that shape thoughts by distinguishing between different components of the sociocultural systems: the economic structure of society; the legal/political/social organization; and ideology.

According to the cultural materialist interpretation, Marx gave causal priority to the material economic structure. The aspects of Marx's formulation relevant to the cultural materialist model pertain specifically to the linkages between the social relations of production and technology and the sociopolitical and ideological aspects of society. In Marx's model, the level of technology, the "stage" of a society's "material powers of production" exerts a determining force upon relations of production independently of human will, and the totality of the social relations of production shapes other aspects of the system.

Marx's statement is taken by cultural materialists to mean that the stage of a society's material powers of production cannot be changed by mere human will. Society's material powers are the determining force in history and the evolution of sociocultural systems, because they are subject "to a definite order of progression" (Harris 2001b: 232). This is an order of progression, which as archaeologist and ethnographers have shown, is an unbroken chain of cumulative technological innovations, tying the oldest stone tools to the newest computers in a sequence in which there are no shortcuts or diversions. This aspect of Marx's formulations is indisputable. As Harris (2001b: 232) pointed out,

> Stone tools had to come before metal tools; spears *had* to come before bows and arrows; hunting and gathering *had* to precede pastoralism and agriculture; the digging stick *had* to precede the plow; the flint strike-a-light *had* to be invented before the safety match; oars and sails *had* to precede the steamboat; and handicrafts *had* to precede industrial manufacture. Indeed, none of the major opponents of cultural materialism has ever seriously questioned these facts.[18]

Another issue that separates cultural materialism from the various twentieth-century Marxist perspectives pertains to disagreements as to what Marx meant by "relations of production," "the total of the relations of production which constitute the economic structure of society," and "the mode of production" (Marx 1959b: 43). This, despite the fact that Marxists of all kinds have peered over the pages of *Capital* and other of Marx's writings with the same religious diligence and zeal that hermeneutic scholars and sectarians have demonstrated in their scrutiny of the pages of the Bible.

A further point of disagreement is over the fact that Marx combined forces of production (i.e., technology), and relations of production into the economic base or infrastructure. Cultural materialists assign these to different components of the sociocultural system. Cultural materialists attribute causal priority to the forces of production.

Finally, cultural materialists and Marxists disagree over the importance of productive technology in the process of social transformations. The disagreement stems from the fact that in their analysis of the transition from feudalism to capitalism Marx and Engels stressed social organizational factors, such as the development of craft guilds and merchant guilds, rather than technological innovations (Harris 1999: 187). In Marx's historical reconstruction, technological innovations become important in the development of the capitalist mode of production two hundred years after capitalism first appears (Harris 2001b: 233). Marx and Engels focused on the dialectical interplay among sociopolitical aspects of production, or dynamics internal to the sociocultural systems, rather than among sociopolitical patterns and the technological, demographic, or ecological factors cultural materialists stress.

Cultural materialists approach these ambiguities and confusions as merely an aspect of the conceptual haziness that is characteristic of the social sciences when dealing with the question of what constitute the boundaries between economics and technology and culture and environment. But cultural materialists note that "there never has been any confusions concerning the general nature of the factors to which Marx pointed as the key to understanding sociocultural causality" (Harris 2001b: 233). This then is the area which cultural materialists acknowledge their debt to Marx.

Cultural materialists also acknowledge their debt to Marx for his observation that what

people, say, think, imagine, and conceive is different from what people do in their "real life process." Marx and Engels noted that "the phantoms formed in the human brain are . . . sublimates of their material life process" and that "life is not determined by consciousness, but consciousness by life." In other words, the participants in the social process are unable to provide an objective account of their behavior because of rationalizations, the distortions of ideology, or culturally specific ideas about the way things are. For cultural materialists, the distinction between what people say they do and what they actually do is essential for the scientific analysis of sociocultural phenomena. Cultural materialism seeks to ground its theoretical formulation in the "material life process" of human existence rather than on how humans "imagine and conceive" their existence (Harris 2001b: 234–235).

Cultural materialism therefore builds upon those aspects of the works of Marx and Engels deemed most relevant to a scientific perspective of human society and history. It does so by incorporating only a part of Marx's overall theoretical program. As Harris (2001b: 241) observes,

> The admissible sense in which one may propose Marx as the discoverer of the "law of cultural evolution" is that which separates the specific application of the cultural-materialist program on behalf of explaining capitalism from the general strategy set forth in the "Preface" of *The Critique of Political Economy*. This strategy states that the techno-economic processes responsible for the production of the material requirements of biosocial survival. It states that the pressures in favor of certain types of organizational structures and upon the survival and spread of definite types of ideological complexes. It states that in principle, all the major problems of sociocultural differences and similarities can be solved by identifying the precise nature of these selective parameters; yet as a general principle, it does not commit itself to the explanation of any specific sociocultural type or any specific set of institutions. It is possible, in other words, to accept Marx's research strategy without accepting any of his analysis of the specific phenomena of

capitalist and feudal societies. This is not to suggest that Marx's analysis of nineteenth-century capitalism, the French Revolution, or of feudalism can be demeaned or ignored, but simply that in anthropological perspective, a strategy purportedly applicable to the study of three thousand sociocultural systems is an event of far greater significance than the application of that strategy to one or two of them.[19]

Thus, just as the French Marxists extracted elements from Marx's analyses, cultural materialists have adopted other elements, while discarding the rest.

EPISTEMOLOGICAL PRINCIPLES OF CULTURAL MATERIALISM

Having outlined the elements of cultural materialism derived from the works of Marx and the points of divergence between cultural materialists and Marxist anthropologists, we can now proceed to a discussion of the specific epistemological and theoretical principles of the cultural materialist perspective. Cultural materialists recognize that anthropologists are confronted with particular problems when studying humans because humans not only do things, but also have definite thoughts about the things that they do. The problem is how to deal with behavior as well as the ideas, thoughts, and beliefs that people have about their behavior. Often, the thoughts and beliefs that people have about their behavior are rationalizations, uncritical representations of the way things are, or culturally specific ideas that enculturated people hold. Thus, the scientific investigation of the human condition requires the distinction between what people say and think they do from what they actually do (Lett 1987: 67).

Interpretive perspectives, which presently dominate American cultural anthropology, exclude the study of human activity and behavior from their research agendas and consider the study of thoughts, ideas, and discourse as the only legitimate topics for anthropological research. Moreover, interpretivists deem human behavior as largely irrelevant for the understanding of cultural phenomena, which is considered to be arbitrary and operating in complete autonomy from factors extrinsic to the mind. The roots of this idealism are Boasian, which were reincarnated in the ultrarelativistic, idiographic symbolic approaches of the 1960s and 1970s and reenergized as a consequence of the fusion with French postmodern thought in the 1980s.

Culture, according to interpretivists, is subject to its own internal dynamics, the "thermodynamics of the poetic," as Sahlins (1976) put it years ago, and is not objectively knowable or amenable to scientific analysis (cf. Ross 1980a: xix). The most ardent and vocal champions of this idealist antiscience orientation today are the postmodern interpretive/literary anthropological writers.

Cultural materialists, in contrast, emphasize that in order to understand sociocultural phenomena, thought and behavior and their relationships in their historical and materials settings must be taken into account. Thus, as Ross (1980a: xvi) has put it, cultural materialism is

> a manner of anthropological research that locates the forces that shape human institutions, behaviors, and thoughts, not in enigmatic cells of the human mind or the transcendent character of culture, but in the real world; and which contends, and demonstrates, that these forces are real, recurrent, and knowable through systematic, empirical, and historical research.[20]

THE EMIC AND ETIC DISTINCTION

Central to cultural materialist epistemological principles is the distinction between material entities and ideas, between thoughts about things and events and the things and events themselves (Harris 2001a: 30). As noted in Chapter 12, it was the linguist Kenneth Pike (1954) who first made the distinction between emic and etic categories. However, Ward Goodenough developed the emic-etic contrasts and pointed out the theoretical and epistemological importance of keeping these "two orders of reality" distinct (Goodenough 1964: 11; 1970). Harris went on to recast the emic/etic contrasts in terms of insider/outsider (folk knowledge/science) mental/behavioral perspectives. He also stressed the theoretical/epistemological differences between the emic/etic modes of inquiry as two ways of analyzing and interpreting sociocultural phenomena (see Headland, Pike, and Harris 1990). This is considered by some to be one of Harris' major theoretical contributions to anthropology (Johnson and Johnson 2001: viii).

Thus, for cultural materialists the distinction between emic and etic perspectives is central. Harris points out that

> emic operations have as their hallmark the elevation of the native informant to the status of ultimate judge of the adequacy of the observer's descriptions and analyses. The test of adequacy of the analyses is their ability to generate statements the native accepts as real, meaningful, or appropriate. In carrying out research in the emic mode, the observer attempts to acquire a knowledge of the categories and rules one must know in order to think and act as a native (Harris 2001a: 32).[21]

Emics represent "the stereotypical, normative, uncritical representations of reality shared by members of a given culture" (Lett 1987: 62). Emics pertain to participant-oriented studies and are based upon ideas, concepts and distinctions meaningful and significant to the participants themselves (Harris 1999: 31). In contrast,

> etic operations have as their hallmark the elevation of observers to the status of ultimate judge of the categories and concepts used in descriptions and analyses. The test of the adequacy of etic accounts is simply their ability to generate scientifically productive theories about the causes of sociocultural differences and similarities. Rather than employ concepts that are necessarily real, meaningful, and appropriate from the native point of view, the observer is free to use alien categories and rules derived from the data language of science. Frequently, etic operations involve the measurement

and juxtaposition of activities and events that native informants may find inappropriate or meaningless (Harris 2001a: 32).[22]

Put another way, etic accounts entail representations of reality that are meaningful to the scientific community (Lett 1987: 62). Or we could say, etic perspectives are observer-oriented studies and are based upon ideas, concepts, and distinctions meaningful and significant to the observer and the community of scientific observers (Harris 1999: 31). As such, etic accounts are not invalidated if participants of the culture being studied fail to recognize or confirm them.

As I have already pointed in previous chapters, for present-day antiscience critics, such analytical distinctions are inadmissible. This is because it implies that the native's point of view does not encompass the whole picture, that epistemology belongs to the anthropologist alone and clashes with the condescending postmodern egalitarian view of knowledge. Moreover, it entails the imposition of analytical categories, analytical judgments, a distinction between the observer and observed, a distinction between "our knowledge" and "their knowledge" which simply cannot be tolerated (Herzfeld 2001: 10, 22, 174). For writers like Herzfeld all of this is intellectual imperialism and "intellectual apartheid" and encompasses the amoral and ethnocentric assumption of a rationality transcending cultural boundaries that cannot be admitted.

Writers such as Herzfeld stress that the only legitimate ethnographic accounts are those written from the perspective of the participants of the culture themselves. The problem is, however, that not a shred of evidence has been presented, epistemological, empirical, and so on, other than mere opinion offered as self evident truths, to justify this idea, which goes against all the established conventions of science, historiography, and even common sense (cf. Adams 1998: 406). For this reason, materialists reject postmodernists' views on this issue.

For cultural materialists, the development of a science of culture depends upon the distinction between the emics and etics. Emics and etics are analytical concepts and are not related to the ontological status of things, events, and thoughts about them. Things, events, and thoughts are part of empirical reality. It is how these things, events, and thoughts are described that determine whether they are emic or etic. We can talk about emic and etic models, modes of analyses, and descriptions of things, events, and thoughts, but we cannot talk about emic and etic things (Lett 1987: 62–63). In other words, what makes a description emic or etic has to do with the analytical operations used in order to arrive at and validate those descriptions. So there can be emic or etic accounts of thoughts, emotions, intentions, and values, just as there can be emic and etic accounts of behavior, the motion of bodies, and their effects on the surrounding environment (Harris 1999: 37).

Thus psychoanalytic studies of mental categories could be considered as etic descriptions because they are obtained through etic operations (Harris 1999: 37). It is also possible to obtain etic accounts based upon informant understandings of behavioral events, such as the number of people gathered for a ceremony or the number of animals slaughtered by a farmer (Harris 1999: 39). However, discrepancies may and do arise depending upon the reliability of the informant and the manner in which information is solicited. At the same time, it is possible that in some areas there may be a high degree of correspondence between emic accounts based upon the participant's sense of appropriateness and truth and etic descriptions based on the observation of behavior and the observer's categories. The degree of discrepancy between emic and etic descriptions of mental and behavioral events is a measure of the degree to which people may be mystified about their own thoughts and behavior (Harris 2001a: 39).

For the reasons given previously, cultural materialists stress the epistemological significance of the emic and etic distinctions.

> Human behavior not only *can* be described without attempting to infer or elicit intentions, choices, dispositions, and motivations, but such de-

scriptions are *indispensable* in order to allow for the human capacity to lie, obfuscate, forget, and disguise our inner lives; to say one thing and do another; and to produce in the aggregate effects that were not intended by any participant (Harris 1999: 42).[23]

For the cultural materialist, determining the distinctions between emic and etic accounts and the differences between them is indispensable for the comprehension of sociocultural phenomena because

> people tend to have alternative emic prescriptions—often contradictory—that can be brought to saliency by comparison with the etic behavioral record. . . . participants always have recourse to rules for breaking rules. The road to a better understanding of both emic and etics, therefore, lies through the persistent juxtaposition of emic and etic versions of social life (Harris 1999: 45).[24]

An example of such a juxtaposition of emic and etic versions of social life from contemporary American culture comes from the findings of archeologist William Rathje (1992), who conducted research on consumption patterns. Rathje collected two types of information: accounts from household members obtained through interviews and informant reports (emic description); and information obtained through the analysis of the garbage from these households (etic description). Rathje found major discrepancies between what people said about their consumption patterns and what the physical evidence revealed. For example, there were differences between the amount of beer reported to have been consumed and the actual number of beer cans retrieved by the archeologists sifting through the garbage. This example reveals why cultural materialists insist that the understanding of sociocultural phenomena requires both emic and etic data (Murphy and Margolis 1995a: 4).

Lett has specified the criteria that must be met before an account is accepted as etic:

1. The account must be considered meaningful and appropriate by the worldwide community of scientific observers. This is not simply a criterion of consensus. It means that the terms

and concepts employed must satisfy the scientific ideals of precision, reliability, and accuracy. (Emic accounts, of course, are validated by consensus—the consensus of native informants.)

2. The accounts must be validated (or validatable) by independent observers. This means that the procedures employed in the formulation of etic descriptions must be replicable by independent observers and that independent observers must be able to obtain the same test results when attempting to validate etic accounts.

3. The account must satisfy the canons of scientific knowledge and evidence. This means that etic accounts, analyses, and explanations must be falsifiable and that they must not be contradicted by other available evidence. All available evidence must be considered in the formulation of etic accounts.

4. The account must be applicable cross-culturally. This is a necessary but not sufficient condition for etic constructs. It means that etic accounts must not be dependent upon particular, local frames of reference; these accounts must be generalizable. This criterion is intended to ensure that scientists will consider whether their supposedly etic constructs and the tests used to validate those constructs might be dependent upon emic assumptions (Lett 1987: 64–65).[25]

Thus, cultural materialists are epistemologically committed to "restrict fields of inquiry to events, entities, and relationships that are knowable by means of explicit, logico-empirical, inductive-deductive, quantifiable public procedures or operations subject to replication by independent observers" (Harris 2001a: 27). For this reason, cultural materialist explanations must give priority to the objective attributes of the human condition, rather than what people think and feel about their condition (Lett 1987: 66).

THE CULTURAL MATERIALIST ANALYTICAL MODEL

Cultural materialism differs in fundamental ways from research perspectives that focus exclusively upon "culture" defined entirely from an emic standpoint, as shared ideas, values, and sentiments. It also differs from the perspective of the postmodern interpretivists who construe the ethnographic enterprise in terms of texts and specific instances of discourse with the "Other." The difference stems from the epistemological principles of cultural materialism based upon the recognition of the etic/emic distinctions and a focus upon sociocultural systems, rather than "culture." For cultural materialists, the analysis of the relationship between the components of sociocultural systems and the evolution of these components, relationships, and systems are the areas of primary interest (Harris 2001a: 47).

Cultural materialists posit that particular categories of mental and behavioral responses impinge more heavily upon human survival and that it is possible to assess the efficiency with which these responses contribute to the survival and well-being of individuals. As Harris (1994: 68) points out,

> The categories of responses whose costs and benefits underwrite cultural selection and cultural evolution are empirically derived from the biological and psychological sciences that deal with the genetically given needs, drives, aversions, and behavioral drives of *Homo sapiens:* sex, hunger, thirst, sleep, language acquisition, need for affective nurturance, nutritional and metabolic processes, vulnerability to mental and physical disease and to stress by darkness, cold, heat, altitude, moisture, lack of air, and other environmental hazards.[26]

The focal point of causality of sociocultural systems are those components that satisfy these human "biogram needs," or minimal set of pan-human biopsychological needs and drives that must be mediated and satisfied. Thus, cultural materialists contend that an understanding of sociocultural phenomena must start with the biogram needs, which are most significant in human affairs.

Sociocultural systems (Figure 14.5) are posited to possess a universal pattern that includes several components, or subsystems (Harris 1994: 68). The first subsystem of the universal pattern is the etic behavioral infrastructure,

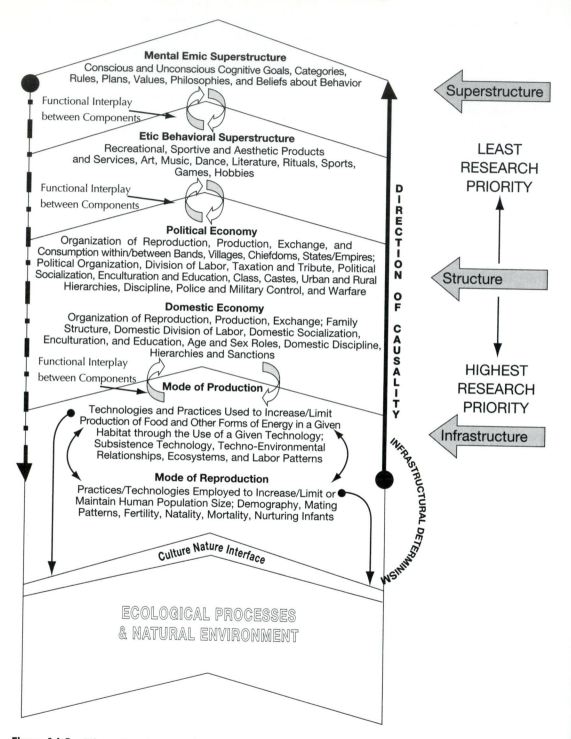

Figure 14.5   The cultural materialist analytical model.   *After Harris (2001b).*

which includes modes of production and **modes of reproduction.** Optimization of costs/benefits to satisfy biogram needs gives determinative priority to the modes of production and reproduction, which comprise the conjunction of demographic, technological, economic, and ecological processes (Harris 1994: 68).

Mode of production entails the technologies and practices used to increase or limit the production of food and other forms of energy in a given habitat through the use of a given technology (Harris 2001a: 52). Subsistence technology, techno-environmental relationships, ecosystems, and labor patterns are all aspects of the mode of production. Mode of reproduction entails those practices and technologies that humans employ to increase, limit, or maintain human population sized. Demography, mating patterns, fertility, natality, mortality, and the nurturing of infants are all aspects of the mode of reproduction (Harris 2001a: 52).

The next subsystem of the universal pattern is the etic behavioral structure. It consists of domestic and political economies. Domestic economies entail the organization of reproduction, production, exchange, and consumption as they occur within camps, houses, and other domestic settings (Harris 2001a: 52–53). Family structure, domestic division of labor, domestic socialization, enculturation, education, age and sex roles, domestic discipline, hierarchies, and sanctions are all aspects of domestic economies.

Political economies entail the organization of reproduction, production, exchange, and consumption as they occur within and between bands, villages, chiefdoms, states, and empires (Harris 2001a: 52–53). Political organization, division of labor, taxation and tribute, political socialization, enculturation and education, class, castes, urban and rural hierarchies, discipline, police and military control, and war are all aspects of political economies (Harris 2001a: 53).

It is important to note that in this model aspects of economy are part of both the infrastructural and structural subsystems. Mode of subsis-

tence, foraging, agriculture, or industrial factory manufacturing are aspects of economics in the infrastructure. In the structure, economy pertains to the organization of economic effort, or what Marx referred to as the "relations of production," which are shaped by patterns of property ownership, wages, and exchange (Harris 1999: 142). Marx, however, assigned relations of production to the infrastructure, treating them as material conditions that exerted an influence upon as well as being influenced by the infrastructure. In the cultural materialist model the relations of production are assigned to the structure.

The third component of the universal pattern is the etic behavioral superstructure, which encompasses the recurrent "productive behavior that leads to etic, recreational, sportive and aesthetic products and services" (Harris 2001a: 52). Art, music, dance, literature, rituals, sports, games, and hobbies are all aspects of this universal component.

The fourth component of the universal pattern is the mental emic superstructure, or the symbolic-ideational subsystem. It includes "the conscious and unconscious cognitive goals, categories, rules, plans, values, philosophies, and beliefs about behavior elicited from the participants or inferred by the observer" (Harris 2001a: 54).

MARX AGAIN

In order to transform Marx's general strategy into a scientific, empirical anthropological perspective, cultural materialists have made a number of modifications and additions. Marx did not have concepts equivalent to emics and etics, and as a result there is a mixing of mental and behavioral phenomena in his schema. First, elements which Marx assigned to the infrastructure, such as the relations of production, which refers to patterns of social organizational (i.e., who owns and has access to productive technology), are shifted in the cultural materialist model to the level of structure. As such, ownership of means of production becomes a dependent variable in terms of the evolution of demographic patterns, technology, ecology, and subsistence economy (Harris 2001a: 64).

Similarly, modes of economic exchange, such as reciprocity, redistribution, commerce, employment, and transactions involving money, are taken from Marx's infrastructure and assigned to the etic structural components, in part, as elements of domestic and political economy and, in part, as aspects of the emic mental superstructure. The theoretical aim here is to allow the prediction of patterns of exchange in terms of more basic variables (Harris 2001a: 65). However, the allowance is made that structure and superstructure could achieve a degree of autonomy in the development of sociocultural systems (Harris 2001a: 65).

Another significant difference between Marx's scheme and the cultural materialist model is that the latter includes demographic factors, or the "mode of reproduction," in the infrastructure as a causal force in the transformation of productive forces. As indicated earlier, Marx saw system-transforming changes as resulting from dialectical processes that holds that all sociocultural patterns are in the process of negating themselves. Thus the build-up of internal contradiction at some stage brings the material forces of production into conflict with the relations of production. For example, in capitalist social formations, private ownership and the quest for greater profits leads to increasing exploitation of labor and comes into conflict with the need for satisfying material requirements. As a result, a period of social revolution ensues, and a new order emerges from the debris of the old. Change in the economic foundation, in turn, results in changes in the superstructure, which is functionally related to the economic base. Cultural materialists view demographic factors as an important determinative force upon the evolution of sociocultural systems, which are given the same weight as the mode of production (Harris 2001a: 66).

DEMOGRAPHY AND MODES OF REPRODUCTION

The reason cultural materialists deem the mode of reproduction to be so important is related to the overall pattern of cultural evolution and the importance of demographic factors in shaping its nature and direction. Population pressure on resources, for example, is a crucial variable in cultural materialist explanations for the transition from foraging to agricultural modes of production, the characteristics of prestate village societies, preindustrial warfare, and the rise of chiefdoms and state-level societies (Binford 1983; Carneiro 1970, 1987, 1988; M. Cohen 1977; Johnson and Earle 1987; Redding 1988; Sidky 1996; see also Boserup 1981; Harris and Ross 1987a, 1987b; Spooner 1972).

A good example to illustrate this point is Harris's evolutionary materialist explanation for the transition from foraging to farming modes of production. As discussed in Chapter 10, ethnographic and archaeological data suggest that the shift from hunting gathering to farming modes of production was not associated with greater material benefits but the reverse. The transition to farming was accompanied by longer working hours, lower standards of living, and poorer quality of life in terms of health and nutrition (Sanderson 1990: 132, 151, 196). Hunting-gathering peoples, in other words, were much better off than farmers.

Also, the "eureka" hypothesis for the Neolithic Revolution is untenable because ancient hunting gathering peoples had a full understanding of the manner in which plants and animals propagate—as do contemporary foragers—long before such knowledge was applied toward the creation of farming economies (Sanderson 1999: 34). The question therefore is: What compelled hunting gathering peoples to switch to farming modes of production?

Harris explains the transition from foraging to farming in terms of shifts in the basic cost-benefits of foraging over those of farming (Harris 2001a: 85–88). Sanderson (1990: 162) calls Harris's schema the **intensification-depletion-renewed intensification model** (Figure 14.6).

Harris begins with global climatic changes at the end of the last ice age roughly 13,000 years ago, which transformed grasslands into forests and resulted in the decreased availability of **Pleistocene megafauna,** which was eventually hunted to extinction. With the loss of large game animals, which had played an important role in hunting economies for thousands of years, the cost-benefits of hunting were altered and the net effect was a shift in the relationship between human populations and their resource base. The same effect seems to have been produced in Southeast Asia due to the inundation of large areas of land as the result of rising sea levels following glacial recessions. Rising sea lev-

els reduced available land areas up to half of what had been accessible earlier, thereby changing the human population/resource base ratios.

Harris's evolutionary schema focuses upon human efforts to cope with such resource depletions and lowered standards of living by intensifying economic production. **Intensification** is achieved first by expansion, by putting more people to work, doing the same thing, harder and for much longer periods relying on existing technologies and making more intensive use of existing resources. This works for a time. However, it is merely a temporary solution that inevitably leads to additional depletions and lowering of standards of living, requiring renewed efforts at intensification.

Intensification based upon doing more of the same thing with existing technologies eventually reaches a ceiling and a **point of diminishing**

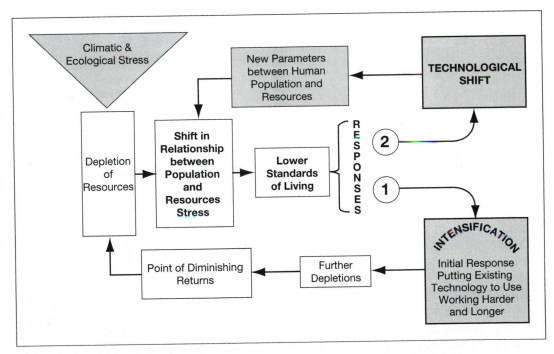

Figure 14.6   Harris's depletion–intensification–depletion model.   *After Harris (2001b).*

returns, in which people find themselves working harder and longer for much less (for a discussion of diminishing returns, see Joseph Tainter's *The Collapse of Complex Societies* [1988]). At this stage, to avoid disaster, technological shift is necessary and the adoption of a new mode of production.

That hard times had befallen foraging peoples at the end of the Pleistocene is indicated by general expansions of the subsistence base, referred to as the **broad spectrum revolution,** to include increasing numbers of small mammals, reptiles, birds, mollusks, and insects (for a discussion of diet and cultural evolution, see Harris and Ross 1987a). Labor cost of foraging increased while benefits decreased, making alternative strategies more appealing.

Drops in available protein in the diet reduced the effectiveness of the **prolonged lactation** method of spacing births (i.e., not weaning a breastfed infant until the ages of 3 or 4), which had acted as a damper on population growth. Prolonged lactation cannot occur without adequately nourished mothers (Harris 1997b: 202; for a discussion of cultural mechanism of population control, see Cowgill 1975; Hassan 1981; Handwerker 1983; Hayden 1981; Jelliffe and Jelliffe 1972; Nag 1983; White 1982). More children per female meant either higher energy costs for women who had to carry children while foraging, or higher rates of abortion or female infanticide. More children also meant higher rates of disease and more hunger (see M. Cohen 1995). All of these factors working in conjunction led to shifts to modes of production and reproduction whose "start-up costs" had been considered to be too great during the previous times of plenty.

Thus under the techno-environmental conditions at the end of the last ice age the foraging way of life became too costly over modes of production based upon farming and herding. Sedentary lifestyle and a farming economy, which provided a wide margin for intensification, in turn, could accommodate and in fact served as an incentive for having more children, since more children meant more labor, and more labor meant more agricultural output.

Harris applies his intensification-depletion-renewed intensification model, in which demographic pressures, declining standards of living, and overintensifications drive the engines of evolutionary change to subsequent developments, such as the rise of state-level societies, the development of hydraulic states, and the evolution of capitalism and industrial modes of production.

Thus, a cultural materialist perspective enables an understanding of the human behavior and thought within the framework of a general evolutionary paradigm (Ross 1980c: xv). It deals with "interactions between thought and behavior, with conflicts as well as harmonics, continuities and discontinuities, gradual and revolutionary change, adaptation and maladaptation, function and dysfunction, positive and negative feedback" (Harris 2001a: xi). It does not posit that all traits are adaptive, that maladaptive traits do not exist, or that cultural systems hold populations in balance with their environments. Such a construal of the paradigm is based upon a faulty understanding of the basic features of this perspective (e.g., Milton 1996: 45–46).

As this outline suggests, the cultural materialist explanation for the origins of Neolithic modes of production encompasses both environmental and technological variables as well as the relationship between population and resources. Cultural materialists insist, therefore, that Marx's contradictions between forces of production and relations of production alone do not shed any light in the transition from foraging to farming modes of production and other evolutionary shifts (Harris 2001a: 88). Also, the mode of reproduction, which is vitally important in this explanation, is absent from Marx's work because he dismissed Malthus's views on population. In doing so, cultural materialists assert, Marx hindered the development of a demographic/ecological theory that could account for the evolution of divergent and convergent modes of production and their associated super-structures (Harris 2001b: 70).

CAUSALITY AND SOCIOCULTURAL SYSTEMS

The cultural materialist schema holds that there is predictable ongoing and dynamic functional interplay between the components of the socio-cultural system (cf. Murphy and Margolis 1995a: 2). Changes in the infrastructure are attributed to alterations in the relationships between human population and its environment (modes of production and reproduction). Changes in the infrastructure, in turn, lead to functionally com-patible transformations in its social and political institutions, or structure, and in its secular and religious ideologies, or the symbolic–ideational subsystem (Murphy and Margolis 1995a: 2). However, the causal linkages are probabilistic, rather than absolute:

> The etic behavioral modes of production and re-production probabilistically determine the etic be-havioral domestic and political economy, which in turn probabilistically determine the behavioral and symbolic–ideational subsystems (Harris 2001a: 55–56).[27]

The explicitness with which the basic episte-mological principles of cultural materialism have been specified has led critics to the unjustified assumption that the paradigm posits a simplistic and mechanical determinism that relegates hu-man thought to the status of epiphenomena (e.g., Bloch 1983: 134; Murphy 1994: 57). Conceptual explicitness, in other words, is incor-rectly equated with simplistic causality. As Mur-phy and Margolis (1995a: 3) have pointed out,

> Regardless of the apparent neatness of this model, cultural materialism does not posit a simplistic, mechanistic correspondence between material conditions (infrastructure) and structural and ideo-logical phenomena. It never suggests that *all* changes in the system under all circumstances

spring from alterations in the infrastructure. Nor does cultural materialism claim that the structure and superstructure are passive entities that do not influence the material base. Rather it proposes a probabilistic relationship between these three lev-els, while at the same time insisting that the *principle* forces of change reside in the material conditions of human existence. Thus, when we note changes in the structure or superstructure, we must first look to its infrastructure for our expla-nations because, according to cultural materialism, that is the most probable sources of change.[28]

The chain of causality from infrastructure to superstructure is referred to as the principle of **infrastructural determinism,** or **primacy of infrastructure** (Harris 1999: 142). According to this principle, innovations arising in the infra-structure that are adaptive (i.e., those that in-crease the efficiency of production and repro-duction, contribute to health and well-being, and fulfill basic human biopsychological needs and drives) will be retained, and those that do not will be eliminated. Moreover, adaptive inno-vations will be selected for even when they are incompatible with the existing structural and su-perstructural subsystems. In these circumstances, the incompatibility will be resolved by changes in the structural and superstructural compo-nents. However, innovations arising in the struc-tural and symbolic-ideational subsystems will be selected against if they are incompatible with the infrastructure (i.e., if they decrease the efficiency of productive and reproductive processes that contribute to health and well-being and fulfill basic human biopsychological needs and drives) (Harris 1999: 143). As Harris (2001a: 71–72) has put it,

> The conceptualization of the interrelationships in question can be improved by introducing a dis-tinction between system-maintaining and system-destroying interdependencies. The most likely out-come of any innovation—whether it arises in the infrastructure, structure, or superstructure—is sys-tem-maintaining negative feedback, the dampen-ing of deviation resulting in either the extinction of the innovation or in slight compensatory

changes in the other sectors, changes which preserve the fundamental characteristics of the whole
system. . . . However, certain kinds of infrastructural changes (for example, those which increase
the energy flow per capita and/or reduce reproductive wastage) are likely to be propagated and
amplified, resulting in positive feedback throughout the structural and superstructural sectors, with
a consequent alteration of the system's fundamental characteristics. . . . Cultural materialism,
unlike classical structural-functionalism, holds that
changes initiated in the etic and behavioral modes
of production and reproduction are more likely to
produce deviation amplifications throughout the
domestic, political, and ideological sectors than
vice versa. Innovations in the etic and behavioral
structural sectors are less likely to produce system-
destroying changes; and innovation arising in the
emic superstructure are still less likely to change
the entire system (due to their progressively remote functional relationships with the crucial infrastructural components).[29]

Cultural materialism differs from other theoretical perspectives because of the causal priority
it places upon the infrastructure in comparison to
the other components of the sociocultural system.
The difference is over the following question:

To what extent can fundamental changes be propagated and amplified by ideologies and political
movements when modes of production and reproduction stand opposed to them? Culture materialism holds that innovations are unlikely to be propagated and amplified if they are functionally
incompatible with the existing modes of production and reproduction—more unlikely than in the
reverse situation (that is, when there is an initial
political and ideological resistance but none in the
modes of production and reproduction). This is
what cultural materialists mean when they say that
in the long run and in the largest number of cases,
etic behavioral infrastructure determines the nature of structure and superstructure (Harris 2001a:
72–73).[30]

Put another way, changes arising in the infrastructure are likely to produce long-term transformations regardless of oppositions that may

exist at the level of superstructure. But this is not
to say that structure and superstructure are mere
reflections or epiphenomena of the infrastructure, as critics mistakenly assume. The nature of
the causal linkages between infrastructure and
the other components of the sociocultural system is frequently misunderstood. Harris (1994:
70) explains:

To say that structure and superstructure are
causally dependent on infrastructure is not to say
that in the process of continuity and change, selection pressure is exerted only from infrastructure to
superstructure. Without structural and superstructural instrumentalities the infrastructural subsystem
would evolve in a radically different direction from
those which we now observe. Structure and superstructure are not mere passive, epiphenomenal
products; rather they actively contribute both to
the continuity and change of infrastructures. But
they do so within the limitations of demo-techno-
econo-environmental conditions. They almost always initiate and select for change in conformity
with but almost never in opposition to those
conditions.[31]

A good example to clarify this point is the
radical alteration of the sexual composition of
the labor force in the United States following
World War II, which was accompanied by major
transformations in American sexual ideology
in spite of vehement superstructural resistance
(Murphy and Margolis 1995a: 2–3). Harris
(1994: 70–71) points out,

Consider the changes in U.S. family life since
World War II with reference to the disappearance
of the male breadwinner role, the demise of multi-
parous stay-at-home housewife, and the rise of
feminist ideologies emphasizing the value of sexual, economic, and intellectual independence for
women. . . . these structural and superstructural
transformations are the determined outcome
of a shift from goods-producing industrialism to
service-and-information-producing industrialism,
mediated by the call-up of a reserve army of
housewives into low-paying service-and-information nonunion jobs. The infrastructural transfor-

mations themselves were related to the use of electronic technologies and to declining productivity in the unionized smokestack industries which created and sustained the male-breadwinner-stay-at-home-housewife families. The rise of a feminist ideology which glamorized the wage labor market and the intellectual, sexual, and emotional independence of women was the determined outcome of the same infrastructural force. However, it is clear that both structural and superstructural changes have exerted and continue to exert an amplifying positive-feedback effect on the infrastructural transformations. As the consequences of the call-up of the female labor force manifest themselves in higher divorce rates, lower first marriage rates, and historically low fertility rates, service-and-information industrialism is in turn amplified into an ever-more dominant mode of production and reproduction. Similarly, as feminist ideologies continue to raise consciousness against the vestiges of male breadwinner sexism, men and women find themselves locked into the labor force as competitors, wages for both are driven down, unions are driven out, and the profitability of the service-and-information industries rises, encouraging more diversion of capital from goods-producing enterprises into service-and-information production (see Harris 1981).[32]

Postwar America also illustrates the existence of a time lag between infrastructural changes and the development of compatible institutional and ideological patterns. As Murphy and Margolis (1995a: 3) note,

Time lag was undoubtedly involved in the case of the "feminine mystique"—the ideology celebrating the joys of domesticity that flourished in this country in the 1950s. According to this ideology, women—most especially married women—should content themselves with home and family and should shun outside employment. . . . But the 1950s was also a decade when married women, in reality, were leaving home to take jobs in record numbers. The ideology seemed inappropriate for the times, however, and belated recognition of women's large-scale employment came with the feminist resurgence more than a decade later. . . .

Still, from the perspective of the cultural materialism, the rebirth of feminism and the blossoming of the women's movement was ultimately a result rather than a cause of women's massive entry into the labor force. Women did not take jobs because a feminist ideology "liberated" them to do so. The reason why so many married women sought employment in the postwar era lies in such material factors as high rates of inflation and an increased demand for female labor (see Margolis 1984).[33]

Innovations in the cultural repertoire appear constantly, and their persistence or demise depends upon how well they contribute to health and well being. They are selected for by consequences. Selected traits are disseminated and passed on, while dysfunctional traits are selected against and eliminated. Sociocultural selection is therefore, opportunistic, rather than **teleological,** because the direction of evolution is unknown to the actors (Harris 1999: 144).

Not all traits are adaptively significant. Some are neutral. Others may be adaptively significant but could represent one among a set of functionally similar choices. Still others may be dysfunctional. However, whether a trait is or is not dysfunctional is an empirical question to be determined in terms of its costs and benefits to various groups or segments of society. In other words, selected innovations contribute to health and well being, but whose health and well being will benefit is another matter. This varies in terms of the presence of different superordinate and subordinate groups, classes, genders, and ethnicities and the power and influence they are able to exercise for their own benefit (Harris 1999: 143). Here symbolic-ideational factors can operate to mobilize groups in favor of certain types of innovations. The success of this mobilization depends upon the extent to which the innovations are compatible with the infrastructural circumstances (Harris 1999: 148). Cultural materialists note that innovations that lead to major alterations in some sectors are usually of the kind that benefits everyone to some degree.

PRIMACY OF INFRASTRUCTURE AND RESEARCH PRIORITIES

The principle of the primacy of infrastructure provides a set of research priorities in which infrastructural variables are treated as "the primary causal factors" (Harris 2001a: 56). Highest priority is given to theories and hypotheses aimed at explaining sociocultural puzzles by testing causal factors in the infrastructure. If factors fail to be identified in the infrastructure, then theories and hypotheses giving structural variables causal priority are to be formulated. Less priority is given to variables in the behavioral superstructure, and even less priority is given to theories that place causal primacy upon the mental superstructure, or symbolic–ideational subsystem.

It is only when testable theories at the level of behavioral superstructure have been rejected that theories that involve variables in the symbolic-ideational subsystem are formulated and tested. Thus, as Harris (2001a: 56) notes,

> Cultural materialism asserts the strategic priority of etic and behavioral conditions and processes over emic and mental conditions and processes, and of infrastructural over structural and superstructural conditions and processes; but it does not deny the possibility that emic, mental, superstructural and structural components may achieve a degree of autonomy from etic behavioral infrastructure. Rather, it merely postpones and delays the possibility in order to guarantee the fullest exploration of the determining influences exerted by the etic behavioral infrastructure.[34]

Thus, components of the etic infrastructure are treated as independent variables, while those of structure and superstructure are dealt with as dependent variables. Infrastructure is given strategic research priority over other components of culture because it is the primary interface between culture and nature. Infrastructure represents "the boundary across which the ecological, chemical, and physical restraints to which human action is subject interact with the principal sociocultural

practices aimed at overcoming or modifying those restraints" (Harris 2001a: 57).

INFRASTRUCTURE, BEHAVIOR, AND THOUGHT

The cultural materialist premise regarding the primacy of the infrastructure outlined above is based on the fact that humans, like all other life forms, must expend energy to get energy and other items necessary for life. In doing so humans run up against immutable physical, chemical, biological, and ecological factors that place limitations upon the amount of control possible over production and reproduction in a given environment using a given technology.

> Infrastructure constitutes the interface between nature, in the form of unalterable physical, chemical, biological, and psychological constraints on the one hand, and culture which is *Homo sapiens'* primary means of optimizing health and well-being, on the other (Harris 1994: 68).[35]

The constraints from nature bear upon the infrastructure most directly and powerfully, from where they are passed on to the structure and superstructure. Production and reproduction are "grounded in nature" and cannot be made to change through human wishes and desires without the expenditure of energy. The question is not whether thoughts are irrelevant for actions. The cultural materialist unit of analysis is the sociocultural system, which cannot exist without a symbolic and ideational sector, just as it cannot exist without an etic behavioral sector. The question is whether or not thoughts and actions are to be accorded equal weight. The cultural materialist answer is that they cannot be accorded equal weight.

The system is "asymmetrical" and infrastructural variables are considered to be more determinative in the evolution of sociocultural systems (Harris 1994: 70). Harris (2001a: 58) adds that

> thought changes nothing outside the head unless it is accompanied by the movement of the body or its parts. It seems reasonable, therefore, to search

for the beginnings of causal chains affecting socio-cultural evolution in the complex of energy-expending body activities that affect the balance between the size of each human populations, the amount of energy devoted to production, and the supply of life-sustaining resources. Cultural materialists contend that this balance is so vital to the survival and well-being of the individuals and groups who are its beneficiaries that all other culturally patterned thoughts and activities in which these individuals and groups engage are probably directly or indirectly determined by its specific character.[36]

It is in order to develop theories that "incorporate lawful regularities occurring in nature" that cultural materialism gives infrastructure, as the culture/nature interface, the highest analytical priority. As Harris (2001b: 57) adds,

> Since the aim of cultural materialism, in keeping with the orientation of science in general, is the discovery of the maximum amount of order in its field of inquiry, priority for theory building logically settles upon those sectors under direct restraint from the givens of nature.[37]

Cultural materialists assert that they subscribe to the principle formulated by Marx that "it is not the consciousness of men that determines their existence, but, on the contrary, their social existence determines their consciousness" (Marx 1959b: 44). The idea that behavior determines thought is difficult for many to grasp because people believe intuitively that they act out their own thoughts. For example, we think about going to the theater before we actually go there. Cultural materialists maintain that such plans and itineraries are not conjured up from thin air but merely "chart" the selection of "preexisting inventory of behavioral mazeways" which are culturally provided (Harris 2001a: 60).

THOUGHT, INFRASTRUCTURE, AND NEW INVENTIONS

Another idea that intuitively seems to refute the idea of the primacy of infrastructure over the mental emic superstructure is the process of how new inventions are made. It seems obvious that when new ways of doing things appear, or when new technologies develop, someone, somewhere must have first thought about those things. The cultural materialist principle that the behavioral infrastructure has primacy over the mental emic superstructure does not pertain to innovations that originate in the minds of individuals, but rather "how innovations assume a material social existence" (Harris 2001a: 59). Ideas in peoples' minds do not assume a material social existence until the appropriate infrastructural conditions are present.

For instance, as we have seen, one of the most momentous discoveries in human history, the invention of farming, was "known in thought" for millennia before the first farming community appeared. Ethnographic evidence from among surviving foraging peoples indicates that they are well acquainted with plant reproduction and in some cases they manipulate preferred wild species in order to increase outputs (Harris 2001a: 86; Sanderson 1999: 34). It is not knowing in thought, but rather the right infrastructural conditions that are more important in those thoughts assuming material expression. Moreover, once the appropriate material conditions are present, the same thoughts or innovations appear in the minds of people over and over again, as indicated by the recurrence of inventions such as ceramics, metallurgy, writing, calendars, and the domestication of plants and animals in different parts of the world (Harris 2001a: 59).

The transition to domestication was a global phenomenon (Sanderson 1999: 23–34). Moreover, there were dozens of regions/subregions where agriculture emerged independently in one of the most remarkable examples of world wide parallel evolution (Sanderson 1999: 33). Several different complexes of plants and animals were involved in the farming economies that evolved independently in different regions of the earth. The domestication of cereals (which is based upon the planting of seeds) that developed in the Near East was quite different from domestication of crops such as yams and manioc, which developed in Southeast Asia and South America and is based upon the planting of cuttings (Harris 2001a: 86). The idea that one group heard about distant peoples were planting seeds to obtain food led others to plant tuber cuttings is quite improbable.

The notion of independent inventions is further supported by the numerous patent disputes arising out of claims by different individuals regarding the invention of steamships, telephones, airplanes, photography, automobiles, and many other devices. As discussed in Chapter 7, Kroeber described many cases of independent inventions, such as the theory of natural selection by Charles Darwin and Alfred Wallace, the independent creation of calculus by Leibnitz and Newton, and the simultaneous independent rediscoveries of Mendel's principles of genetics. Kroeber (1952: 45) went on to conclude that "the history of inventions is a chain of parallel instances."

The principle of the primacy of infrastructure accounts for the similarities and differences in the societies around the world and the reasons for these similarities and differences:

> Given similar evolved infrastructural complexes in different societies one can expect convergence toward similar structural relationships and symbolic-ideational features. The reverse also holds: different infrastructures lead to different structures and different symbols and ideas (Harris 1999: 143).[38]

Indeed, as Lett (1987: 91) has noted, cultural materialists "have demonstrated incontrovertibly that sociocultural systems adjust themselves in patterned and predictable ways to ecological and demographic constraints." The implications of this are far reaching because it demonstrates beyond any doubt that sociocultural phenomena exhibit lawlike regularities and are amenable to scientific analysis.

There is an extensive body of archaeological, ethnographic, and historical evidence demonstrating the occurrence of divergent, convergent, and parallel evolution in sociocultural systems

in addition to the example of the agricultural revolution.

> Parallels and convergences in the evolution of New World and Old World political economies are difficult to dismiss as quirky stochastics effects (e.g., the independently evolved complexes surrounding ruling elites, use of preciosities consisting of rare metals and minerals, pyramids with hidden burial chambers, brother-sister marriage, human sacrifice, god-kings, astronomy, solar and lunar calendars, mathematics, etc.). Similarly, hundreds of studies based on the Human Relations Area Files or other large-scale comparative databases clearly demonstrate the nonrandom nature of sociocultural selection (Harris 1999: 145).[39]

Parallels and convergences do not mean that all cultures must evolve through same stages as envisioned by the nineteenth-century evolutionists, but rather they indicate "that sociocultural systems tend to develop along certain trajectories with greater probability than along others." Thus similarities and differences can be comprehended in terms of orderly, scientific processes. Such evidence stands in overwhelming opposition to the interpretivist/postmodernist claims that sociocultural phenomena are capricious and devoid of regularities and that a science of culture is impossible. That ideological position does not stand up against the overwhelming weight of ethnographic and archaeological evidence and is at odds with the conventions of science, historiography, as well as common sense.

BEEF AND PORK: MATERIALIST AND INTERPRETIVE VIEWS ON DIETARY TABOOS AND THE RATIONALITY AND IRRATIONALITY OF CULTURE

A look at some cultural materialist explanations and their contrasts with similar explanations generated under the auspices of other paradigms will help illustrate the points of contrast between the different theoretical approaches in American anthropology. Here we shall look at food taboos.

Cultural materialists treat dietary rules and behaviors in terms of a "comparative, ecological-historical frame" in which dietary practices are seen as the result of recurring causes. Moreover, these practices are construed as evolving along with the ecological system that gave rise to them (Harris 1997b: 385; Ross 1980b: 182). Harris's well-known and controversial paper, "The Cultural Ecology of India's Sacred Cattle" (1966), is a good example of this approach (also see Harris 1974, 1978a, 1978b, 1985, 1997b: 385–387; for contrary views see Diener et al., 1978; Heston 1971; Simoons 1979).

Interpretivists, on the other hand, treat dietary practices in the same manner they treat culture in general, in terms of systems of meanings and signification that are said to be subject to their own internal dynamics and independent of any forces extrinsic to the human mind. In this view, culture has total autonomy over material forces. People, it is reasoned, assign meaning to things, objects, plants, animals, and so on in their physical environment and then behave toward those things, objects, plants and animals according to the cultural meanings they themselves have imposed. Moreover, it is assumed that the valuations and signification humans impose on things have "no necessary connections with [the] physical properties [of the objects, things, etc.,] or the relations arising therefrom" (Sahlins 1976: 170). Thus, because meanings and signification are arbitrary, culture is considered to be arbitrary as well. Hopes for discovering laws of culture are therefore misplaced.

As with culture in general, interpretivists treat dietary practices as being arbitrary cultural developments as well, without any connection to material, environmental, or ecological conditions or circumstances. In other words, "valuations of edibility and inedibility, [are] themselves qualitative and in no way justifiable by biological, ecological, or economic advantage" (Sahlins 1976: 171). Some good examples of this approach include Douglas's (1966) explanation of the Israelite taboo on pork, Heston's (1971) interpre-

tation of India's sacred cattle complex, and Sahlins's interpretation on the American dietary preference for beef.

Here I shall examine Sahlins's (1976: 169) analysis of the American dietary preference for beef in terms of a symbolic cultural code, a cultural logic that he argues overrides material effectiveness, with no relation to the physical properties of cows or beef, nor to any biological, ecological, or economic conditions. Cultural logic in Sahlins's conception is irrational in the sense that is not based upon practical reason. I use Sahlins's example because it does not pertain to a far away and unknown culture, but to one close at hand. Just as the application of Lévi-Strauss's structural analysis to the cases close at hand reveals the flaws of that perspective much more explicitly, the case of beef eating Americans clearly reveals the defects in Sahlins's irrationalist interpretivist perspective.

Sahlins's explanation is an analogue of Mary Douglas's attempt to elucidate the abominations of Leviticus. Sahlins draws inspiration from Lévi-Strauss, although his viewpoint has the basic characteristics shared by all interpretive approaches, including the more recent varieties espoused by the Writing Culture group of postmodern interpretivists. In fact, Sahlins's formulations anticipate much of what was later claimed by interpretivists and postmodernists to be their own unique intellectual contributions.

Sahlins's anthropology sounds highly erudite and may appear fascinating in the same sense that Lévi-Strauss's pronouncements or the postmodernists' discourse about discourse have intellectual appeal to some. As we shall see, such theoretical approaches nevertheless comprise a form of ideological obscurantism that hinders and misdirects us from the important task of understanding what the world is really like.

Sahlins (1976: 171) begins with the ideological predilection of Americans toward beef and maintains that

the exploitation of the American environment, the mode of relation to the landscape, depends on the model of a meal that includes a central meat element with the peripheral support of carbohydrates and vegetables—while the centrality of the meat, which is also a notion of its "strength," evokes the masculine pole of a sexual code of food which must go back to the Indo-European identification of cattle or increasable wealth with virility. The indispensability of meat as "strength," and steak as the epitome of virile meats, remains a basic condition of American diet (note the training table of athletic teams, in football especially). Hence also a corresponding structure of agricultural production of feed grains, and in turn, a specific articulation to world markets—all of which would change overnight if we ate dogs.[40]

While material properties and ecological factors do not impinge upon culture in any way, in Sahlins's understanding, the cultural code itself does have determinative impact that extends from the realm of agricultural adaptation, to international trade, and world political relations. In other words, not only the U.S. beef industry, but U.S. agricultural practices, international trade, and American capitalism itself have been erected around what is essentially posited to be an irrational cultural custom, an ancient ideological predilection for the consumption of beef (Ross 1980b: 216). This is a sort of rendition of a Weberian "the American code of beef eating ethics."

Following this line of reasoning, the political and economic characteristics of U.S. capitalism would change if Americans began eating dogs instead of cows. Such is the power of culture over material relationships. In Sahlins's (1976: 173–174) view,

> The principal reason postulated in the American meat system is the relation of species to human society. . . . Let us take up in more detail the domesticated series cattle-pig-horses-dogs. All of these are in some measure integrated in American society, but clearly in different statuses, which correspond with degrees of edibility. The series is divisible, first, into two classes or edible (cattle-pigs) and inedible (horses-dogs), but then again, within each class, into higher and less preferable categories of

food (beef vs. pork) and more and less rigorous categories of tabu (dogs vs. horses). The entire set appears to be differentiated by participation as subject or object in the company of men. . . . To adopt the conventional incantations of structuralism, "every thing happens as if" the food system is inflected throughout by the principle of metonymy, such that as a whole it composes a sustained metaphor on cannibalism.[41]

Moreover, according to Sahlins (1976: 174),

> Dogs and horses participate in American society in the capacity of subjects. They have proper names, and indeed we are in the habit of conversing to them as we do not talk to pigs and cattle. Dogs and horses are thus deemed inedible, for, as the Red Queen said, "It isn't etiquette to cut anybody you've been introduced to." But as domestic cohabitants, dogs are closer to men [sic] than are horses, and their consumption is more unthinkable: they are "one of the family." Traditionally horses stand in a more menial, working relationship to people; if dogs are as kinsmen, horses are as servants and nonkin. Hence the consumption of horses is at least conceivable, if not general, whereas the notion of eating dogs understandably evokes some of the revulsion of the incest tabu. On the other hand, the edible animals such as pigs and cattle generally have the status of objects to human subjects, living their own lives apart, neither the direct complement nor the working instrument of human activities. Usually, then, they are anonymous, or if they do have names, as some milk cows do, these are mainly terms of reference in the conversation of men. Yet as barnyard animals and scavengers of human food, pigs are contiguous with human society, more so than cattle. Correspondingly, cut for cut, pork is a less prestigious meat than beef. Beef is the viand of higher social standing and greater social occasion. A roast of pork does not have the solemnity of prime rib of beef, nor does any part of the pig match the standing of steak.[42]

Thus, Sahlins invokes a culturally determined symbolic logic—"symbolic logic . . . organizes demand"—and states that "Edibility is inversely related to humanity," in order to explain American dietary system. Dogs live with us, they are our companions, and are almost members of the American family. Eating a dog is like cannibalism and is as unthinkable for an American as consuming the flesh of a human family member. Hence eating dogs is tabooed.

To emphasize the irrationality of American custom of keeping dogs as pet/kin, Sahlins observes that

[dogs] roam the streets of major American cities at will, taking their masters about on leashes and deposit their excrement at pleasure on curbs and sidewalks. A whole system of sanitation procedures had to be employed to get rid of the mess—which in the native thought, despite the respect owed the dogs themselves, is considered "pollution." (Nevertheless, a pedestrian excursion on the streets of New York makes the hazards of a midwestern cow pasture seem like an idyllic walk in the country.) Within the houses and apartments, dogs climb upon chairs designed for humans, sleep in people's beds, and sit at the table after their own fashion awaiting their share of the family meal. All this in the calm assurance that they themselves will never be sacrificed to necessity or deity, nor eaten even in the case of accidental death.[43]

On the other hand, cattle are less like people in the American cultural scheme, according to Sahlins. Americans do not live with their cattle under the same roof, they usually do not talk to them as they do to their dogs, and therefore cattle fall in the category of food object, and comprise the most highly preferred food item. Similarly, pigs as "barnyard animals" are more contiguous to human society and hence lower on the cultural list of preferred edible meats than beef. In this view, why any particular culture has a dietary preference is entirely adventitious (Ross 1980b: 182).

In Sahlins's idiographic research strategy the question of cross-cultural similarities and differences are irrelevant and inquiry in this area is a waste of time since each sociocultural pattern is treated as fortuitous, unique, or one of a kind. As such, cultures are incommensurable and attempts to investigate cross-cultural similarities or dif-

ferences are pointless. On this, the solipsist postmodernists would concur with Sahlins's position.

Sahlins labels America "the land of the sacred dog" and assumes that dogs occupy this status as a result of a cultural code, in the same way that India may be referred to as "the land of the sacred cow." Sahlins's (1976: 206) general conclusion is that meaning is the key, and all functional value is "relative to the given cultural scheme." Moreover, he boldly declares,

No cultural form can ever be read from a set of "material forces," as if the culture were the dependent variable of an inescapable practical logic. The positivist explanation of given cultural practices as necessary effects of some material circumstance—such as a particular technique of production, a degree of productivity or productive diversity, an insufficiency of protein or a scarcity of manure—all such scientist propositions are false (Sahlins 1976: 206).[44]

All the elements that would later go into the making of the postmodern/interpretive approach are specified here, including the irrationality of other cultures (rationality is ascribed to Western culture alone), the rejection of material causation, and the denigration of science and scientific knowledge as patently false.

Cultural materialists reject Sahlins's explanation as logically flawed and empirically spurious. First, consider his suggestion that Americans like beef because of an ancient Indo-European sexual code. Ross (1980b: 182) has pointed out that the same Indo-European ideological heritage that according to Sahlins makes beef the preferred food in the United States has resulted in the opposite case in India, where there is a taboo on the consumption of beef. Thus, ideology alone does not necessarily offer an explanation for the American dietary practice, as Sahlins would have us believe.

Second, beef did not dominate the American diet until relatively recent times and the change can be linked to alterations in material conditions of food production as a result of the integration of agriculture into a maturing capitalist economy and international trade (Ross 1980b: 182). Prior to these changes, pork dominated the American diet and ham comprised the valued centerpiece of the American dinner table—so much for Sahlins's treatment of beef as the epitome of virile meats and pigs as barnyard animals being on a lower scale of edibility. Only in the 1960s did the per capita consumption of beef exceed pork; thus the pig's contiguousness with human society seems to have had no effects on the consumption of pork throughout most of U.S. history (Ross 1980b: 191).

The cultural materialist explanation focuses upon ecological, demographic, and techno-economic conditions, all of which are to be found cross-culturally in association with other dietary customs. Such an analysis reveals that cultural habits are in fact shaped in a recurrent fashion by noncultural factors, cultural materialists would argue. Those who construe this as "ad hoc explanations" of specific cases (e.g., Herzfeld 2001: 180) have altogether misunderstood the basic theoretical and epistemological premises of the materialist paradigm.

Sahlins defines the edibility of the various animal species in terms of the cultural status assigned to various animals. He assumes that human/animal associations are random and entirely determined by symbolic factors. However, there are practical reasons why dogs are not an efficient source of animal protein and why cattle are not household pets that join their owners at the dinner table. As Ross (1980b: 183) has pointed out,

> It is ridiculous to maintain that such animals are not intrinsically suited to certain productive roles, which are optimally enacted in certain environments and for which these animals are usually enhanced through selective breeding by humans.[45]

Thus, there is nothing irrational about the fact that cattle, which happen to be animals most suited to utilize available natural fodder resources, are a source of food. Ruminant livestock

such as cattle, rather than dogs, are the most efficient means of exploiting the vast grasslands in the continental United States, which would otherwise be economically marginal. It is also not surprising that natural forage once constituted 70% of all cattle feed (Ross 1980b: 184). Thus for a country with vast areas of grasslands there was nothing impractical or irrational about using ruminants such as cattle over carnivores as a source of meat. It would be irrational to raise dogs as a source of meat when one has cattle, sheep, pigs, and poultry as alternate sources of animal protein and which thrive upon grains, rather than meat.

Carnivores like dogs are in general used as a source of meat in cultures that do not possess cheap alternative sources of meat from ruminants and omnivores (Harris 2001a: 255). Moreover, there is nothing unusual about the objectification of animals such as pigs, which were being reared and processed by means of a large-scale food production industry to feed the growing population of the United States in the nineteenth century. It is the same with cattle.

As for Sahlins's attempt to consider the American habit of keeping dogs as pets as the ascendancy of "cultural logic over material effectiveness," he neglects to consider the economic linkages between dog ownership and the pet food component of the meat industry in the United States and the power of advertising. Dog food has been one of the most profitable sectors of the meat industry. In the late 1970s, the annual sale of dog food alone was over two billion dollars.

Thus, Ross (1980b: 185) adds, "while it may initially seem clever, it is not especially edifying for Sahlins to promote the view of American culture as materially illogical simply by describing America as 'the land of the sacred dog'." It is the demand created for dogs by the massive pet food industry, Ross adds, that has made dogs a sacred cow in the United States. Finally, dogs can be "housetrained" cows cannot, and dogs have roles such as providing protection and companionship, which cows cannot fulfill. The relationship between humans and dogs in this respect goes back thousands of years. The dog food industry, of course, has capitalized upon these to maintain and expand its consumer market.

Sahlins suggestion that material conditions do not affect the status of pet dogs is not supported by evidence that suggests that there is a correlation between income levels and type of housing and dog ownership. Moreover, as Ross points out,

> Evidence that dog ownership is not simply the result of "correlations in a symbolic system," however, has been even more forcefully demonstrated in New York City where non-dog-owners (members of a distinct culture from that of a dog-owner? Surely not!) successfully lobbied for strict regulation of canine defecation. The consequences—which are beyond comprehension by structuralist logic—suggest that many household pets actually had been living in a tenuous relationship with their owners: In the weeks following passage of the new law, there was a staggering increase in dog abandonment. Such are the hazards in contemporary America of being treated no better than kinsmen (Ross 1980b: 185).[46]

As for the consumption of horse meat, Sahlins (1976: 173–174) notes that it is nonexistent in the United States because horses participate in American society, they are like servants (as opposed to dogs, who are kinfolk), they are shown affection, and, unlike cattle, people pet them and brush them. Sahlins (1976: 172) adds, regarding horses, that

> Americans have some reason to suspect they are edible. It is rumored that Frenchmen eat them. But the mention of it is usually enough to evoke the totemic sentiment that the French are to Americans as "frogs" are to people.[47]

By humorously and perhaps ethnocentrically attributing horse-eating to the presumed cultural eccentricities of the French, Sahlins overlooks the fact that horse meat became a part of the European diet as a response to a growing protein shortage exacerbated by the industrial revolution and a burgeoning class of urban proletariat. Horsemeat remains a source of cheap protein among the working class through much of Europe and is obtained from aged farm animals (Ross 1980b: 188). In the United States, horses raised for sport and as pets end up back in the food chain as dog and cat food.

Sahlins neglects to consider the fact that pet food made of horsemeat is also eaten by "people who are treated like dogs: old, ill, and desperately poor people" who are forced to seek cheap sources of animal protein (Harris 2001a: 256). Since interpretivists disregard the material conditions of life, it is easy for them to overlook the sad fact that not everyone in the richest industrial nation on earth can afford to eat steak, Indo-European cultural code or not!

Ross makes a case that the premium placed upon beef, pork, or dairy goods depends upon habits that develop in association with definite material conditions, such as human population density and margins for the intensification of agricultural production, among other factors. He notes, for example that the major beef-producing/consuming regions of the world are areas which possess (or possessed) sparsely populated grasslands and are relatively young nations, such as Uruguay, Paraguay, Argentina, New Zealand, and the United States.

Another factor in the maintenance of beef production has been the global capitalist division of labor that emerged by the late nineteenth century and which entailed huge investments in overseas grasslands, such as in Australia, Argentina, and the United States. British and Scottish capitalists, for example, invested 45 million dollars in ranching enterprises when the Great Plains was stripped of its bison herds (part of the U.S. government's policy to eradicate the subsistence base of the Plains Indians) and opened up in the 1880s (Ross 1980b: 189). American beef production remains dependent upon grasslands, which is now made accessible through "international capitalist **underdevelopment**," involving the conversion of arable lands in Third World nations into cattle pastures (Ross 1980b: 214).

Whether protein production centers on range fed cattle, swine, or dairy cows depends upon more than cultural codes, cultural materialists would say. Ross's study of the development of patterns of beef and pork consumption in the United States suggests that the preference for beef developed fairly recently and is largely attributable to ecological and demographic factors, new refrigeration technologies, railroads, and the development of monopoly capitalism linked to international trade. Demands for animal products, such as cow hides for shoe manufacturing, the need for the disposal of corn surpluses based on fluctuating prices, and the development of a nationwide and worldwide distribution network were all important factors in the development of the beef industry.

During the twentieth century, factors contributing to increased beef consumption in the United States included increasing concentrations of capital and capitalization of agriculture, the steady disappearance of small farms, active promotion of beef by supermarket chains affiliated with beef producers, and the mass availability of hamburgers through the fast food industry (Ross 1980b: 212–213). Ross links the reasons why the United States produces beef or pork at the prices it does to market prices and the agribusiness domination nationally, and capitalist underdevelopment abroad.

Cultural materialists have shown, therefore, that the significance of particular animal species as sources of protein is not primarily cultural but develops in association with patterns of land use, population pressure, and ecological and economic factors that repeatedly override the symbolic structures of the mind. As Harris (2001a: 255) points out,

> When the railroads began to cross the Great Plains, it became possible for mass-production meatpackers in Chicago to deliver cheap range-fed refrigerated beef to the Boston and New York markets. Beef acquired its preferential status be-

cause it was the principle target of a new capital-intensive agribusiness method of mass-producing fresh meat. Capital investment in beef exceeded capital investment in pork, not because cattle were a symbol of virility, but because pigs couldn't eat the free grass available in the Western rangelands. Steak acquired its special honorific status because it epitomizes the attempt to mass-produce meat that was tender and chewable as well as fresh. Moreover, the premium placed on tenderness was not merely an arbitrary preference, but one based on the prevalence of missing and rotted teeth in the mouths of urban consumers.[48]

To explain U.S. dietary practices as the consequence of an autonomous cultural code requires that one ignore the manner in which U.S. food production strategies have been linked from the time of European settlement to the larger mercantile system and influenced by global historical circumstances. Ross (1980b: 216–217) has observed that explanations which ignore agribusiness domination and capitalist underdevelopment nationally and globally represent an

> idealization of both culture and history, a detachment from time and space, which obscures both local and regional ecological process and the world-economic context in which cultures are embedded.[49]

Ross's (1980b: 188–189) analysis of ideologies and valuations associated with beef and pork consumption under changing material conditions in various places and times provide additional insights into the issue. By the sixteenth century in Europe, for example, demographic pressures on land led to the greater emphasis upon grain production over animal husbandry. Dairy goods became a primary source of protein, while beef consumption dwindled. Meat became generally scarce and expensive, and where it was eaten it was usually pork. The religious doctrine proscribing meat on certain days was increased so that in Pre-Commonwealth England nearly half the days of the year were meatless days.

Nor was such an ideological shift confined to Europe. A similar ideological development occurred in China. During the Han dynasty (207 B.C. to 220 A.D.), prior to major population increases, beef was prized. Human population growth and the absence of grasslands to maintain cattle made these animals too costly to eat. Cattle became more valuable for traction rather than as a source of meat. For this reason, in some instances the government prohibited the slaughter of oxen. By the time of the T'ang dynasty, in a development analogous to that in Europe, Chinese pharmacologists were maintaining that beef consumption was unhealthy. The vegetarian religion of Buddhism in China seems to have contributed to the unpopularity of beef, but did not have any effects on pork consumption (Ross 1980b: 188–189).

Sahlins's effort to reduce cultural practices to underlying codes is clearly at odds with historical, ethnographic, ecological, and economic realities. Empirical evidence and tangible material and historical circumstances play no roles in such interpretive accounts, nor does the issue of validation. This is a perennial problem of interpretive perspectives.

It comes as no surprise, therefore, to find present-day proponents of this kind of anthropology, such as the Geertzians and their Writing Culture emulators, exerting great energy in order to circumvent the problem of validation, as noted in the previous chapter. This they do by resorting to ultrarelativism, the notion of "multiple truths," and similar moves in order to justify their own intellectually indefensible aspiration to unaccountability. As we shall see in the following chapter, contemporary interpretivists repeatedly emphasize "local knowledge," local frames of reference, and morally condemn any suggestions about tests of correspondence between anthropological accounts and objective reality.

The energetic attempt to establish the idea that all truths are partial, committed, and incomplete is part of the same overall strategy to bypass the issue of accountability and validation in order to justify a perspective that cannot withstand challenge on the basis of logical and empirical criteria. Finally, there is the rhetoric of self-empowerment that assigns a negative moral value to rival research strategies, especially those strategies that seek to develop a scientific understanding of cross-cultural differences and similarities and the operation of sociocultural systems based upon public and replicable knowledge.

FROM COWS TO PIGS

In some cases ideological valuations regarding the consumption of particular animal species are supernaturally sanctioned, such as the taboo on cattle in India and the prohibition on pork in the ancient Middle East. Cultural materialists have assessed these taboos in terms of the same material variables specified in Ross' study. We shall now turn to the cultural materialist explanation for the taboo on pigs in the Middle East. This may be contrasted with Mary Douglas's symbolic explanation for the taboo, which was discussed in Chapter 13. The discussion that follows is based upon Harris (1991: 193–208).

During the early Neolithic in the Middle East, people raised sheep, goats, pigs, and cattle (see Simoons 1961: 13–46). These animals were grazed in the grasslands and forests that surrounded villages. As the early state-level societies arose and began to intensify production, human population densities began to increase as well. More and more of the grazing lands and forests surrounding farming village communities were converted to agricultural fields and planted to wheat, barley, and other crops in order to cope with increasing demands. Farmers in communities experiencing population pressure were now faced with the decision of either raising more animals or more cereal crops. The choice was to increase the production of plant foods over producing more animals.

The reason for this choice is simply that cereal crops fed to humans directly, as opposed to being fed to animals whose flesh is then consumed by people, is energetically more efficient (Harris 1997b: 192). However, domestic animals could not be dispensed with altogether. Domesticated animal species not only provided meat, but were also important as a source of milk, hair, wool, hide, manure for fertilizer, and draft power for plowing, threshing, and transport. The energetic constraints under which Neolithic farmers were operating made it too expensive for people to eat animals that contributed in such an important way to the subsistence and economic systems. Such agro-pastoral systems operate by capitalizing upon crop-livestock interaction. Thus, in areas of the Old World that were once zones of highest meat and grain production, the consumption of meat became a luxury for people, especially for the ordinary citizens.

Under the new circumstances, there was an incentive to keep the most useful animal species and eliminate those that were too costly to maintain. Eventually, eating the flesh of animals that were the most costly was forbidden altogether. The first of these animal species to be forbidden as a source of meat was the pig, as indicated by the dietary prohibitions among the ancient Israelites listed in the Old Testament, in the books of Moses, Leviticus (xi), and Deuteronomy (xiv).

Pigs were not always a hated animal species. The Middle East was among the earliest centers for the domestication of pigs. Pigs were eaten well into biblical times. In southwest Asia (a.k.a. Mesopotamia, Fertile Crescent, the Levant), the location where humans made the earliest transition to farming, pigs were prominent among the domesticated species and pig bones make up close to 30% of all mammal remains in the large archeological sites (Sanderson 1999: 24).

Of the various domesticated animal species pigs were raised mainly for meat. Pigs cannot be milked, made to pull plows, carry loads, or catch mice. However, they are especially efficient transformers of carbohydrates into meat protein and fat, and this seems to be the primary reason for which they were reared and are still reared in many parts of the world. A pig can produce

20 pounds of meat from every 100 pounds of feed it consumes, compared to roughly 7 pounds of meat produced by cattle from the equivalent amount of feed. In terms of the number of calories produced per number of calories of food consumed, pigs are three times more efficient than cattle and two times more so in comparison with poultry (Harris 1991: 196).

Given that animal flesh played a significant role in the redistributive feasts and sacrifices of the ancient Israelite elite, the taboo on the most efficient meat-producing animal is hard to comprehend. To explain this, cultural materialists have noted that

> Cultures tend to impose supernatural sanctions on the consumption of animal flesh when the ratio of communal benefits to costs associated with the use of a particular species deteriorates. Cheap and abundant species whose flesh can be eaten without danger to the rest of the system by which food is obtained seldom become the target of supernatural proscriptions. Animals that have high benefits and low costs at one time, but that become more costly later on, are the principle targets of supernatural sanctions. The most severe restrictions tend to develop when a nutritionally valuable species not only become more expensive but its continued use endangers the existing mode of subsistence (Harris 1991: 196–197).

In the ancient Middle East, changing ecological, socioeconomic, and demographic conditions made the pig just such an animal. Pigs became too costly to keep for several reasons. First, unlike ruminant species, such as sheep, goats, and cattle, pigs cannot digest cellulose and cannot be maintained on the byproducts of wheat and barley production, the main cereal crops grown in the ancient Middle East. Pigs require high-quality foods, such as tubers, roots, fruits, and nuts that are plentiful in forested environments, which once covered a large section of the Middle East.

Pigs were originally creatures of the forests. They thrive in forested environments, or areas with plenty of moisture and shade. These animals cannot sweat and they are therefore unable to tolerate direct sunshine and high temperatures without outside sources of moisture to regulate their body temperature. When these animals were first domesticated, the hilly flanks of the Taurus and Zagros mountains and other uplands regions of the Middle East were covered with forests, providing ideal environments for pigs. However, from around 7000 B.C., the expansion of farming and pastoral economies began to have a major environmental impact.

The rise of the state-level societies after 4000 B.C. was accompanied by increasing population growth and expansion and intensification of agro-pastoral production, which led to major decreases in forest cover and desertification. Millions of acres of forest cover were transformed into grasslands and deserts as a result of uncontrolled intensive use by humans.

In Mesopotamia, as noted previously, archaeological sites have yielded bones of domesticated pigs dating to the fifth and fourth millennia B.C. (Fagan 1997; Wenke 1990). There is evidence that pigs were eaten in pre-Dynastic Ur. There are also indications for the existence of specialists pig herders and pork butchers during the earliest Sumerian dynasties. After 2400 B.C., pork seems to have been tabooed and was no longer eaten (Harris 1991: 205). This shift coincides with ecological troubles and production failures that eventually led to the collapse of the Sumerian Empire.

The Israelites reached Palestine around 1200 B.C. and established control over mountainous territory not yet brought under cultivation. The forest cover in the Judean and Samaritan hills was removed and terraces were built for irrigation farming. Thus, environments suitable for raising pigs on natural forage were drastically reduced. To rear pigs under the changed ecological conditions required that their diet be supplemented with grain, bringing them into direct competition with humans (Harris 1991: 198). Adding to the costs of pig production under the altered conditions was the need to provide

them with artificial shade and moisture. Pigs did not fit into the pastoral and mixed farming economies that had evolved. Nomadic pastoralism entails long distance travel over arid grasslands and swimming across rivers, which pigs cannot do.

As for the mixed farming economies, these were based upon crop-livestock interactions in which ruminant species consumed straw and hay, the byproduct of cereals consumed by people, to produce manure for the grain fields, milk, meat, hair, wool, and hides for humans. Cattle, in addition, provided an important energy input into the production system in the form of traction (see Sidky 1996: 103–136 for an ethnographic analysis of such crop-livestock interactions). In comparison, pigs could not live on the byproducts of cereal crops and could not provide most of the products obtained from ruminant species; nor could they pull plows, or thresh grain, or carry loads. Moreover, there were the additional costs of having to provide these animals with shade and water and feeding them foods that humans could eat directly. Pigs had simply become too expensive to keep under the changed ecological conditions.

Nevertheless, seminomadic people occupying moister environments could raise pigs. Pigs thus remained a tempting source of meat and fat. Raising a few of these animals was still possible without posing a major threat to the subsistence system. However, rearing pigs in large numbers (i.e., intensive pig production) in environments in the process of deforestation would be very inefficient and extremely maladaptive. To prevent the harmless temptation of raising a few pigs for short-term benefits from becoming the harmful practice of rearing lots of pigs for long-term benefits, a total ban on eating or even handling pigs was thus a predictable outcome of the ecological and techno-economic circumstances (Harris 1991: 199; 2001a: 193).

In contrast to Mary Douglas's hypothesis, which is restricted to a single cultural context, the cultural materialist explanation accounts for why an animal that was once valuable acquired a hated ideological status not only among the ancient Israelites, but also among the Babylonians, Egyptians, and pre-Islamic Arabs (Harris 2001a: 194). Moreover, as implied by this explanation, where ecological and techno-economic conditions favor pigs, such as in Southeast Asia, Indonesia, Oceania, and temperate zones in China, pigs remain loved, as expected.

According to cultural materialists, pig hate in the regions noted above was linked to ecological, demographic, and techno-economic circumstances that recur cross-culturally in connection with dietary taboos (cf. Ross 1980b: 183). The same material factors that made the people of the ancient Middle East avid pig-haters made the people of China, Southeast Asia, and Melanesia great pig-lovers. The cultural materialist explanations for such dietary taboos places pigs in the context of and explains their status in terms of evolving sociocultural systems and the continuous interactions between ecological, demographic, and techno-economic factors as they change through time.

Critics have argued that the establishment of a religious prohibition on an animal that is ecologically destructive is "cultural overkill" (Alland 1975: 67). Why would the people of the ancient Middle East use these animals in the first place if raising them was too costly in the given context? The rebuttal is as follows:

> The distinction between a "taboo for use and a taboo for nonuse" is meaningless. In an ecological systems context, any taboo for nonuse is in some sense a taboo for use. In prohibiting one species, the taboo encourages the use of another. Thus proscription of the pig was prescription of the cow, sheep, and goat. What must be considered are the direct and indirect cost-benefits of the interdicted species in the system of production. . . . adaptation is an evolutionary process in which many major and minor changes take place simultaneously. Just as individuals are ambivalent and ambiguous about their own thought and emotions, so whole populations are ambivalent and ambiguous about aspects of the adaptive processes in which

they are participating. (Think of the pros and cons of offshore oil drilling and the debate about the taboo on abortion). It is not cultural overkill for divine laws to prohibit pork any more than it is cultural overkill to have divine laws prohibit homicide or bank robberies (Harris 2001a: 195).[50]

Harris (1991: 199) adds,

> When Jahweh prohibited homicide and incest, he did not say, "Let there be only a little bit of homicide" or "Let there be only a little bit of incest." Why, then, should he have said, "Thou shalt eat of the swine only in small amounts"?

The real question for Harris is why an animal that was once perfectly acceptable became unacceptable at a particular point in history.

> For five thousand years the Neolithic peoples of the Middle East thought that pigs were good to eat. Why did they change their minds? The answer surely has something to do with the fact that the entire ecosystem changed, and with it, the cultural and natural system of production and the role of the pig in that system (Harris 2001a: 195).[51]

Those who object to such an ecological cost/benefit analysis have pointed to some alternative explanations. Aside from Mary Douglas's explanation of the taboo on pigs, several others have been forwarded. One explanation is based on the idea that pigs are filthy creatures that wallow in and eat their own filth and are therefore unappetizing and so it stands to reason why these dirty creatures were forbidden. This explanation does not take into consideration that had people felt this way, pigs would never have been domesticated in the first place. Moreover, if this were the case, people in the many other parts of the world, where pigs are loved, would not readily consume pigs.

The reason pigs wallow in their own filth has more to do with how pigs are raised by humans than pig nature. Pigs cannot tolerate high temperatures and direct sunlight. They do not sweat and therefore cannot thermo-regulate without shade and moisture. Confined in out-door pens without any source of moisture to cool them, pigs are forced to rely upon their own feces and urine as a form of sunblock. Also, other domesticated species eat their own feces, for example chickens and cattle, so this is not an exclusive pig characteristic.

Another explanation, a pseudomedical one, for the taboo is that pigs harbor the parasite that causes trichinosis which can be transmitted to humans if pork is not properly cooked, and the ancients in their wisdom sought to prevent this by prohibiting the consumption of pork. There are problems with this position as well. If the issue were one of proper food preparation, one would expect a religious rule stating, "Thou shalt cook your pork well," rather than prohibiting this useful source of protein from being consumed altogether.

Similarly, if not properly cooked poultry can transmit disease. This is why "raw" chicken *shushi* is unknown. Yet no taboos were placed upon chickens. The disease or pseudomedical explanation is also unacceptable because pigs reared in hot climates rarely transmit trichinosis. Also, other animals, such as cattle, sheep, and goats, transmit diseases such as anthrax and brucellosis, which are more dangerous to humans than diseases transmitted by swine (Harris 1991: 200).

Another objection to the cultural materialist explanation of the Israelite taboo on pigs is that it leaves out the other creatures prohibited in the Old Testament. These too, however, are explained in terms of the cultural materialist cost/benefit analysis. First, most of the forbidden creatures were wild species that could only be acquired by hunting. For people dependent upon herding and farming, hunting animals that had not only become rare but could not be found in the local ecosystem was a bad cost/benefit proposition.

Animals with paws are mentioned but not identified by species. These would have included carnivores, such as wildcats, lions, foxes, and wolves. Hunting these creatures, which are skinny and hard to find and kill, is a low-benefit and high-cost way of acquiring meat protein.

Cats and dogs can be included in this category. Cats were domesticated in Egypt for rodent control. They are an inefficient source of meat. Similarly, dogs were domesticated to herd and hunt, roles in which they are more useful than as a source of meat (Harris 1991: 201).

Aquatic creatures without fins or scales were forbidden as well. These would have included eels, shellfish, whales, porpoises, sturgeons, lampreys, and catfish. None of these were likely to be found along the edge of the Sinai Desert and the hills of Judea, in the regions where the ancient Israelites lived. Among the category of birds forbidden by name, were the eagle, ossifrage, osprey, kite, falcon, raven, sea gull, hawk, owl, cormorant, ibis, and the like. These were either rare or of little nutritional value. Of the winged insects, those that go on all fours were forbidden. The insects exempted from the list are locusts, crickets, and grasshoppers. Locusts have a high benefit-to-cost ratio as an edible item, being large and meaty and occurring in great numbers, when they damage crops, and are easily gathered at a time when food is needed most.

Animals that chew cud but do not have cloven feet were forbidden as well. These included the camel, badger, and hare. Along with camels, rabbinical authorities also included horses and donkeys in their list (Harris 1991: 203). These are all large high-cost/high-benefit animals kept by the Israelites for carrying loads and traction. Horses were used by the elite and were necessary for military functions. Donkeys were the principle pack animals. None of these could be killed for food without incurring significant economic costs. Also forbidden were those creatures that possess cloven feet but do not chew cud, pigs being the sole example in this category (Harris 1991: 202). Thus, aside from those species whose roles in the ancient local ecosystems cannot be determined and a few that might have been included to "satisfy random prejudices," the list of forbidden species includes animals that are expensive or inconvenient sources of meat (Harris 1991: 203).

Harris points out that the food taboos often seem hard to comprehend because of the tendency by analysts to focus too narrowly upon particular cultures, which are treated apart from their broader ecological settings. This is a characteristic of the particularistic and relativistic approaches, which eschew nomothetic explanations and which are now in vogue in American cultural anthropology. Such perspectives, however, obscure important ecological relationships. For example, the taboo on pigs was not confined to the ancient Israelites, but was also found among their hated enemies, the Egyptians (Harris 1991: 204).

Moreover, the taboo was not confined to the edges of the Sinai Desert and the hills of Judea but was found over the entire pastoral zone of the Old World. This was a region that extended from North Africa, through the Middle East and Central Asia, including some adjoining river valleys as well (Harris 1991: 204). The existence of the taboo over this ecological zone suggests that the biblical taboos should be viewed as part of an adaptive response over a wide region to ecological changes brought on by intensification and depletion associated with the rise of the ancient states and empires (Harris 1991: 204).

With the rise of Islam, the pig taboo was incorporated into its religiously sanctioned dietary rules. However, the Israelite taboo on eating camel flesh was lifted. This is taken as another example in support of the ecological cost/benefit interpretation of animal taboos (Harris 1991: 206). The Arabs who supported Muhammad at the start of his mission lived in true desert oases and traveled across parched wastelands where only the camel could survive. While camels were too important to be consumed all the time, they were also "too valuable not to be eaten at all" in emergency situations arising in the context of caravan trade and military operations, when its meat could make a life or death difference (Harris 1991: 206). There is a similar edict concerning the consumption of wild pigs during life threatening emergencies.

Finally, once the religious principles were established they became elements of Jewish and Islamic cultures and since then have influenced subsequent generations of followers, who no longer live in the original Middle Eastern homes where these religions and taboos first appeared. The food taboos are thus perpetuated, but under conditions where they do not pose major subsistence costs. Cultural materialists maintain that if the costs change, the system of valuation associated with pigs is likely to change as well.

Cultural materialists admit that ecological cost-benefit analysis cannot account for all cultural practices, in all cases (Harris 1991: 207). Many such practices have no cost-benefits advantages or disadvantages at all. Nor do cultural materialists deny the existence of some feedback between conditions that shape ecological cost-benefits and religious beliefs (emic superstructure). However, they emphasize the causal priority of material costs and benefits over supernatural beliefs (Harris 1991: 208).

The cultural materialist explanation for the pig taboo involves interactions and feedbacks between infrastructural, structural, and superstructural components of the system in which the overall relationships is asymmetrical, as stipulated in the principle of the primacy of infrastructure (cf. Harris 1994: 70). The feedbacks are always there and ideas, beliefs, and values have a role in the operation and evolution of the sociocultural system, without which the infrastructural subsystem would evolve in a different direction altogether. It is a misrepresentation to describe this as "technological determinism" or to suggest that cultural materialists consider people's beliefs and values as being found directly in the nature of the technoenvironmental combination (e.g., Bloch 1983: 133). Similarly, it is a misrepresentation to assert that cultural materialists treat people as puppets (e.g., Salzman 2001: 130).

Cultural materialists are not interested in the beliefs and values individuals may or may not hold. As noted previously, people are often ambiguous about their own thoughts and emotions and may be ambivalent and unclear about the adaptive processes of which they are a part. Cultural materialists are concerned with cultural systems or macropatterns of behavior, not the behavior of particular individuals (Ehrenreich 1984: 648).

The Marxist anthropologist Maurice Bloch chides cultural materialists for rejecting Marx's dialects and argues that their explanations are ad hoc, meaning that they note that pigs are hated in the Middle East and then look for anything that will show that the belief makes economic sense. Similarly, Herzfeld (2001: 179) calls Harris's approach "after-the-fact rationalizations" and maintains that cultural materialist explanations "belongs to a category of folk explanation that is widespread in the West, where its legitimation as 'science,' has earned it considerable currency." He equates cultural materialist explanation with the pseudomedical explanation for the taboo on pork among Jews and Muslims (Herzfeld 2001: 180). We have already noted the differences between the cultural materialist explanation and pseudomedical explanations, which have nothing in common.

What Bloch and Herzfeld fail to consider is that the cultural materialist explanation for the pig taboo is not confined to the Middle East, as we have seen, but extends over a vast ecological zone. Moreover, cultural materialists have shown that such beliefs recur cross-culturally in association with analogous sets of material factors—ecological, demographic, and techno-

Pigs being prepared for a feast in the New Hybrides. Cultural materialists treat pig love, as in Melanesia, pig hate in the Middle East, as well as other dietary taboos, such as the prohibition on the consumption of beef in India and Nepal, in terms of infrastructural conditions, such as patterns of land use, population pressure, and ecological and economic factors.

A sacred cow in the middle of a busy street in Katmandu, Nepal. Hindu religion prohibits the consumption of beef. Cultural materialists have shown that the significance of particular animal species as sources of protein is related to ecological, demographic, and techno-economic conditions found cross-culturally in association with dietary customs (Photo by H. Sidky).

economic (cf. Ross 1980b: 183). Pig-love and pig-hate are both accounted for in terms of the same material conditions. There is nothing ad hoc about this.

Bloch (1983: 133) adds that cultural materialists do not specify "a general theory" of what kind of conditions will cause cows or pigs to acquire their ideological status and hence their theories are not falsifiable. This too is without any merit whatsoever. As noted previously, cultural materialists treat dietary rules and behaviors in terms of a "comparative, ecological-historical frame" in which dietary practices are construed as the result of recurring causes. This specifies not only why pigs are loved in some places and hated elsewhere but also why cows and dogs acquire particular ideological statuses. That "theory" is cultural adaptation in terms of the costs/benefits optimization required to meet

human biogram needs. The kind of responses whose costs and benefits underwrite cultural selection and cultural evolution are based upon the genetically given needs, aversions, and behavioral drives of *Homo sapiens* (Harris 1994: 68). The theory in question is falsifiable because it refers to pan-human biopsychological factors and cross-culturally recurring ecological, demographic, and techno-economic condition (cf. Harris 1994: 70).

CULTURAL MATERIALISM AND THE COLLAPSE OF THE SOVIET UNION

Just as the collapse of the Soviet Union has implication for the Marxist theory of society, it also has implications for all other research strategies based upon the works of Marx. For many Marxists, including Western anthropologists influenced by the works of Marx, the demise of the Soviet state was a source of embarrassment and has been accompanied by a noticeable waning of interest in Marxist ideology and Communist societies (Washburn 1998: 11).

Even if one attributes the failures of Communism/Marxism in Russia and Eastern Europe to misapplications of Marxism (and one has plenty of justifications for doing so), the fact remains that most of Marx's predictions have been failures (Harris 1999: 180). Dialectical forces did not negate capitalism, and the foretold crisis that would plunge it to its doom never transpired. The working classes did not experience greater wretchedness, workers of the capitalist world did not unite with their brothers and sisters in the Third World, and **class consciousness** did not override cultural, ethnic, religious, or gender barriers. People's democracies did not become saviors of the poor, but their brutal and savage persecutors. Finally, Communism did not replace capitalism; nor are there any indications that it will do so any time soon, despite Marx's confident proclamations.

This raises questions regarding the credibility of cultural materialism, a research strategy based upon aspects of Marx's work. Harris maintains that the events of 1990–1991 in the Soviet Union have different implications for cultural materialism because the principle of primacy of infrastructure actually explains the events leading to the collapse of the Soviet State. According to this principle, changes in the structural or symbolic–ideational components that are incompatible with the infrastructure will be selected against (Harris 1999: 180). Harris maintains that in the Soviet Union, political-economic (i.e., structural) and symbolic-ideational (superstructural) changes introduced in the name of Marxist materialism resulted in a stagnant, declining, or increasingly inefficient infrastructure. The Soviet political economy failed because it was incapable of accepting the demise of its smoke-stack-type infrastructure and because it inhibited infrastructural innovations for overcoming a deepening technological, demographic, environmental, and economic crisis.

By the 1980s, Harris points out, the Soviet Union was experiencing a serious energy crisis. There were frequent outages of power due to the breakdowns of out-of-date and poorly maintained electricity generating plants. Food production was plagued with similar problems. The output of grain had not increased over what it had been the previous decade despite massive investments. Transportation problems not only led to the losses of between 20 to 50% of grain, potato, sugar beet, and fruit crops before reaching consumers but also created delays and shortages, leading to rationing and hoarding. Per capita economic growth was nil or in the negative. On top of all these problems, there were environmental depletions and massive pollution.

The immense bureaucratic structure exercising central administrative control over the economy bogged down production. Production policies and regulations had many unintended consequences. Stringent quotas, for example, led to the manufacture of inferior quality goods, or outright fraud in production reports. Moreover, the pressure exerted by the central control for conformity to its numerous rules and regulations hampered technological innovations. The civilian economy had to operate with grossly inadequate telecommunication services and information processing technology (Harris 1999: 180–181).

The Soviet command structure designed to supervise and censor the dissemination of information was a barrier to the needed shift to high-tech industrial production based on the high-speed data storage and retrieval. Such a system hinges upon conditions such as freedom by individuals to exchange information and communication networks capable of managing the flow of information, none of which existed in the Soviet Union (Harris 1999: 183).

Finally, mismanagement, as well as uneven distribution of subsidies and goods and services, led to economic inequalities between the republics, which fueled the nationalist and separatist sentiments leading to the breakup of the Soviet State. Thus, according to Harris, the collapse of the Soviet Union was an example of selection against a political economy that was incompatible with the infrastructure (Harris 1999: 184).

If most of Marx's theories have failed as miserably as the Soviet political economy, what is left of Marx's paradigm worthy of retaining? Cultural materialists claim that Marx's work, stripped of all its decrepit and defunct theories, still leaves the principle of the primacy of infrastructure (Harris 1999: 187).

ASSESSMENT

Criticisms of cultural materialism come from three camps: (1) science oriented researchers; (2) symbolic anthropologists; and (3) postmodern interpretive writers. Here I shall examine all three.

Science oriented researchers have raised a number of issues regarding the theoretical and epistemological foundations of cultural materialism. For example, some have pointed out that "infrastructure" is a theoretical construct and cultural materialists never fail to discover infrastructural determinants. This being the case, it is charged, the principle of infrastructural determinism is unscientific because it can never be falsified as no conditions can be specified in which infrastructural factors do not exist.

This criticism stems from a misunderstanding of the nature of paradigms and theories. Paradigms define guidelines for the conduct of research. These include epistemological guidelines for gathering, testing, and validating knowledge, and theoretical guidelines that specify how to formulate and appraise theories (Harris 1994: 63). Epistemological and theoretical principles do not comprise a "scientific theory" and are therefore unfalsifiable (Magnarella 1999: 237). For this reason, paradigms cannot be assessed in terms of whether or not they are falsifiable, but rather in terms of their logical organization, in-

ternal coherence, and whether the theories they produce meet the scientific criteria of validation. The paradigm that produces many useful and empirically supported hypotheses in comparison with rival paradigms is the more appropriate way of understanding anthropological phenomena (Magnarella 1999: 237; see Sanderson 1999: 2–3).

A related criticism of cultural materialism is that "infrastructure" is an abstraction not an empirical object and thus cannot exert causal effects on empirical phenomena (O'Meara 1997: 406). This objection overlooks the fact that empirical science is founded upon the idea that empirical reality can only be known through observation and logical operations and therefore all knowable things, from subatomic particles to Trobriand kinship categories, are the outcomes of logical and observational operations (Harris 1997a: 412; Johnson 1995: 8). Thus, just because something is an abstraction does not mean it is unreal.

Another issue raised by critics is that the principle of infrastructural determinism is too vague or too broad to provide any useful insights. This criticism does not contest the principle of primacy of infrastructure. The principle holds true, as the vast body of evidence assembled by cultural materialists has demonstrated (Harris 1999, 2001a; Murphy and Margolis 1995a; Ross 1980a, b, c). To note a few examples, state-level societies appear only after the development of intensive forms of agriculture, large sedentary populations, a degree of social stratification, developed leadership with political power, and some extralocal trade (Gross 1992: 435). Or to mention another example, monotheistic ecclesiastical religions are always associated with state-level political economies (Lett 1997: 110; see also Swanson 1964).

What these critics contend is that although the primacy of infrastructure holds true "in broad outline," it does not tell us what is true in the specific case (Magnarella 1982: 140). It does not reveal "which changes" under precisely "what circumstances" arise from transformations in the infrastructure and which ones arise from alterations in the structure and superstructure (Lett 1997: 110). What is overlooked, however, is that the specificity demanded is an empirical problem, not one that can be prejudged on the basis of a research strategy. The cultural-materialist perspective specifies the existence of a chain of causality, which is ultimately rooted in infrastructural variables, without in any way stating a priori what holds true in any specific case. That requires empirical determination.

Another criticism, one generated from within the cultural materialist ranks, is aimed at the strict application of the principle of infrastructural determinism, which stipulates that every explanation of every sociocultural phenomenon must be unremittingly sought in the infrastructure until all possibilities are exhausted. For example, Ferguson (1995: 24–25) argues for a broader application of the principle, in which the answers to certain questions are regularly sought in the infrastructure, but answers to other kinds of questions are regularly sought in structural and superstructural conditions.

In other words, Ferguson maintains that causal regularities exist throughout the sociocultural system because of the presence of a hierarchy of progressively limiting constraints. Infrastructure is responsible for establishing the primary and main characteristics of each society, but it also provides multiple parameters for social organization. Structural phenomena must conform to infrastructural limitation but have a degree of latitude within those limitations for "autonomous" determinism. Ferguson attributes structure with primary determinism at all times, except for periods of major system change. Finally, in Ferguson's view, superstructure conforms to limitations imposed by the structure, but again with considerable autonomy.

Ferguson points out, however, that because of the existence of feedback loops throughout the system and because of multiple inputs from the infrastructure into structural processes, the range of autonomy is confined. The same is the case with superstructural processes (Ferguson 1995: 25). By drawing attention to the existence of causal relations throughout the system, Ferguson feels the exact nature of intrasystemic feedback would be clarified and areas of multiple possibilities identified. Such an application of the principle of infrastructural determinism, Ferguson argues, would also open the way for linkages with other scientific perspective in anthropology that focus upon processes above the level of infrastructure (Ferguson 1995: 26).

Ferguson's aims are desirable, but his corrective leads to a position very similar to the analytical framework espoused by Godelier (1975: 15) and other French Marxists, who also posited the existence of a hierarchy of functions and structural causality, which, only in the last analysis, were subject to infrastructural determinism. Through this strategy, French Marxists dispensed with Marx's general materialist strategy, which they labeled vulgar materialism, and shifted analysis to the level of structure and superstructure and intrasystemic dynamics, obscuring the determinative effects of demographic and techno-environmental factors. In other words, an approach analogous the one advocated by Ferguson led to a dematerialization of Marx by Godelier and others and, if not handled with great care and precision, might do likewise to the "materialism" in cultural materialism.

Ferguson has also pointed out that the primacy of infrastructural causality is most significant when one is dealing with broad, macro-evolutionary questions, involving centuries and millennia, whereas most anthropologists are concerned with historical changes involving decades, years, or even shorter intervals. Cultural materialists have acknowledged that their research perspective requires a broad diachronic framework and that sociocultural processes that operate in short-term timeframes appear to be dominated by structure and superstructure (Harris and Ross 1987b: 2–3). Ferguson suggests that the conception of a nested hierarchy of progressively limiting constraints, operating within infrastructural constraints, can adequately deal with short-term processes (Ferguson 1995: 31).

While the nested hierarchy of constraints may indeed allow conceptual treatment of short-term processes, it is vulnerable to the danger of dematerialization of cultural materialism. Also, we might note that there are infrastructurally determined transformations that are visible in narrow temporal frames. As Harris (1999: 150) has noted, cultural materialism remains highly relevant when looking at the vast day-to-day changes taking place in the economic organization, labor patterns, and ideology as the industrial infrastructure is transformed by computer technology.

Additional criticisms come from symbolic anthropologists who treat cultures as systems of meanings and signification subject to their own internal dynamics independent of forces extrinsic to the human mind or discourse. They criticize cultural materialism for neglecting the dimension of human values and meanings. Humans, interpretivists argue, are quintessentially meaning-seekers and symbol-users, and it is these characteristics that distinguish humans from other life forms (Gans 1985: 88; Lett 1987: 96).

These objections are based on the incorrect assumption that cultural materialism posits a simplistic and mechanical determinism and construes human thought as mere epiphenomena (e.g., Bloch 1983: 134; Murphy 1994: 57–58). To assert the primacy of infrastructure does not mean that structure and superstructure are passive bystanders. Cultural materialists maintain that structure and superstructure actively contribute to the continuity and change of infra-structures, but they do so within parameters set by "demo-techno-econo-environmental conditions" (Harris 1994: 70).

Jerry Moore (1997: 199–200) has observed that even if for the sake of argument one were to grant the primacy of infrastructure, this does not mean that other aspects of culture are "unin-

teresting." Moore goes on to pose the question: "Why should we give priority to etic research focused on infrastructure when as anthropologists we are interested in the rich diversity of human cultures?" Cultural materialists have never suggested that other aspects of cultures are uninteresting or impoverished. Both emic and etic factors play an essential part in cultural materialist theories. Cultural materialists note in the absence of superstructural instrumentalities the infrastructural subsystem would evolve along a radically different direction (Harris 1994: 70).

Particularistic and relativistic perspectives devoted to the "interesting" peculiarities of cultures for over half a century continue to be interested in those interesting aspects of culture. Unfortunately, from Boas to Geertz and the solipsist postmodernists, such anthropologists have not shed much light upon the operation of sociocultural systems and the causes of cross-cultural similarities and differences. Whole careers have been devoted to the "interesting" only to yield what amounts to clever stories, neat anecdotes, and a deceptive and spurious anthropology. Cultural materialists focus upon the infrastructure because they are concerned with the origins and operations of sociocultural systems, not whether the ideological-symbolic systems of, say, the Trobriand Islanders is more or less interesting than that of the Australian aborigines, or Euro-Americans, or any other groups in time and space.

Finally, there are objections to the cultural materialist approach from the postmodern interpretive and literary anthropological writers and those influenced by their views. These objections focus upon the paradigm's scientific epistemology. Postmodern critics consider science to be merely an ideological artifice of Euro-American culture, no more privileged or universally valid, than magic or religious beliefs, probably less so (Barrett 1996: 155). Science and scientific anthropology, in other words, are construed simply as the instrument and expression of the oppressive and corrupt Western, Euro-American worldview, nothing more (Herzfeld 2001: 2).

For postmodern anthropological writers, concepts such as ecology, economy, demography, and even the environment are treated as cultural constructs, and "not 'given' in any material sense" (Salzman 2001: 130). This is a reiteration of the old Boasian idea that cultural systems, as configurations of meaning and signification, are subject to their own internal dynamics independent of any external influences. Thus when one talks about the environment, for example, these writers would ask, Which "version of the environment" (Herzfeld 2001: 175)? The assumption is that because everything is culturally constructed, there are multiple realities, multiple versions of the natural environment, all equally valid (except, of course, scientific versions). One wonders why any sane individual would grant any sort of credibility to writers who cannot agree upon the nature of reality.

Postmodern interpretivists also object to scientific anthropology because its explanations impute rationality upon cultural customs such as food taboos, modes of subsistence, and religious configurations. This is objectionable from their moralistic perspective because rationality is construed to be an aspect of Western cultural worldview (Herzfeld 2001: 180). The Other is thus denied rationality. Herzfeld, following Milton (1996: 46), writes that such explanations fail to account for "irrational" cultural practices. He cites the example of megalithic statue building on Easter Island, a practice that contributed to deforestation and environmental degradation (see Young 1991), to make the point that universal rationality cannot explain such cases.

Herzfeld's understanding of the key issues and concepts relating to adaptation, adaptive choices, and the open-ended nature of cultural evolution appear as weak as his grasp of epistemological issues pertaining to science. There was nothing irrational about Easter Island statue building, which may have been a means of channeling communal labor (see Sahlins 1955). Humans make rational choices from among a number of possible alternatives, but this does not mean that a particular choice that is adaptive in the short run may not be maladaptive in the long run. This is why some sociocultural systems have been radically transformed and why others have collapsed and vanished altogether.

Sometimes the choice made from the range of alternatives is not the best possible one. The maladaptive nature of particular courses of action, such as loss of forest cover or depletion of resources, is often imperceptible to any single generation of people who grow up knowing only circumstances as they find them. To suggest that because people sometimes make maladaptive choices we can rule out rationality is the analogue of saying that because some species have become extinct, the idea that species evolve should be discarded. Moreover, to suggest that statue building by the people of Easter Island was irrational implies a comparison with some other standard and is as ethnocentric as attempting to impose one's own cultural categories upon the Other. The discourse and formulations of postmodern interpretivists are full of such contradictions and unsound reasoning.

As another example of the irrationality of the Other, Herzfeld mentions the Fore of New Guinea, a people who were being decimated by an encephalitic disease known as *kuru*, which first came to the full attention of Western scientists in the 1950s. The disease was purportedly spread through the practice of **mortuary cannibalism** involving the eating of a deceased individual's brain by his or her relatives (Herzfeld 2001: 180). The Fore irrationally continued this practice, Herzfeld points out, until they were forced to stop by the authorities. Again, irrational by whose standards? What is more problematic is that Herzfeld does not pause to consider that this case may involve "the myth of the cannibal Other" (cf. Pandian 1985) and that the idea of cannibalism has been part of the

Megalithic statues on Easter Island. Cultural constructionists erroneously construe this remarkable cultural tradition as a demonstration of the essential irrationality of cultural practices and the irrationality of the "Other" (Photo by H. Sidky).

discourse of colonial power about the "primitive" Other and should be assessed critically. Nor does he entertain the possibility that the evidence, at least in the case of the Fore, might be unreliable (see Arens 1998; Gardner 1999; Sidky 1997: 69).

These shortcomings in their argumentation notwithstanding, for the postmodern interpretivists, science represents a "master discourse," a culturally constructed illusion, or ideological device, of Western people, illegitimately applied to other cultures and environments. Anthropologists who assert that a scientific study of culture is possible are therefore imposing their own cul-

turally defined vision, or **master discourse,** upon those they study, transforming them into objects and depriving them of their subjecthood and humanity (Salzman 2001: 131).

Thus, for these writers, whose perspective excludes material causation and evolutionary holism, the attempt to assess scientifically the adaptive characteristics of cultural patterns and institutions becomes a ghastly immoral enterprise. This is because such endeavors "grants the analyst the right to sit in judgment on the cultures of the world, ranking them in a hierarchy of adherence to the principles of pure reason while remaining exempt from such judgment themselves" (Herzfeld 2001: 174). Again, we must remind ourselves that writers touting such views operate from an epistemological stance in which knowledge is defined according to moral criteria (see Sidky 2003: 382–430), and hence their orientation and credibility to discuss issues pertaining to science are comparable to those of the creationists and other defenders of supernaturalism.

Postmodern interpretivists vehemently oppose science and scientific perspectives and instead advocate approaches based upon local insights and the views of the social actors as individuals. In other words, they call for a focus upon the particulars of the particular as expressed in the voices of the Other. Anthropologists, these writers assert, should be listening to the voices or accounts that the people themselves provide for their own experiences (Salzman 2001: 130). To be authentic, anthropological narratives must be based upon and depict the native's version of reality. The problem with this position is, however, that no evidence whatsoever has been provided to support the view that nonscientific, subjective approaches committed to expressing the voices of the Other are any less biased, demeaning and patronizing, and distorted than scientific and rational approaches (see the discussion on emic research and the native's point of view in Chapter 12, the discussion of the uncomprehended symbol and the native's point of view in Chapter 13, and also the discussion in Chapter 15).

The objections from the postmodern/interpretive camp noted here touch upon the central theoretical debates in contemporary cultural anthropology. In the remainder of this book I shall undertake an assessment of the postmodern/interpretive point of view and the merits, or lack thereof, of some of its central assumptions, such as epistemological relativism, the idea of the cultural construction of reality, and science as folk knowledge.

Chapter 15

Postmodern Anthropology and Cultural Constructionism

During the 1980s, some anthropologists began to question the discipline's scientific goals and orientation. The call was for a new kind of anthropology, a "postmodern" anthropology. The postmodernists were attempting to respond to the vast global cultural transformations characteristic of the late twentieth century and sought to transform anthropology by switching epistemological focus away from field methods and toward how ethnographic texts were written. This was the movement spearheaded by the Writing Culture group. The postmodern twist was a symptom of what Geertz (1988: 71) described as "epistemological hypochondria," brought on by "grave inner uncertainties . . . concerning how one can know that anything one says about other forms of life is as a matter of fact so."

The tenets of this new anthropology were published in the mid-1980s in two books: *Anthropology as Cultural Critique: An Experimental Moment in the Human Sciences* (1986), by George Marcus and Michael Fischer, and *Writing Culture: The Poetics and Politics of Ethnography* (1986), a volume edited by James Clifford and George Marcus. The focal point of the debate generated

by the postmodernists was the area of the discipline that provides the basic data of cultural anthropology, i.e., ethnographic fieldwork.

The issues raised with respect to the problematic nature of ethnographic fieldwork are legitimate. It is indeed the case, as Geertz (1988: 10) has put it, that the fieldworker has the challenging task of "constructing texts ostensibly scientific out of experiences broadly biographical." As Appell (1989: 196) has noted in reference to this point,

> Ethnography includes not only logical arguments but narrative treatment of experienced reality. And all communicated experience inevitably lacks the rich detail of lived experience. The problem is not to acclaim that this slippage in conversion of experience to narrative must become the essence of ethnography, which it can't. It is to discover in what way and manner styles of ethnographic narrative distorts field experiences so that our skills in communicating cultural reality are not only improved but conform to the standards of a scientific community so that knowledge can be certified.[1]

Postmodernists have been concerned almost entirely with the slippage in the conversion of experience into narrative. Rather than striving to find solutions to the problem of slippage, they have opted for an entirely different set of criteria as to what constitutes anthropological knowledge. As Marcus and Fischer (1986: vii) declared,

For us, developments in contemporary anthropology reflects the central problem of representing social reality in a rapidly changing world. . . . Ethnography's concern is with description, and presents efforts to make ethnographic writing more sensitive to its broader political, historical, and philosophical implications place anthropology at the vortex of the debate about the problems of representing society in contemporary discourses.[2]

Marcus and Fischer (1986: 24) added that

the cultures of world peoples need constant *re*discovery as these people reinvent them in changing historical circumstances, especially at a time when confidence in metanarratives or paradigms [e.g., science] are lacking: . . . ours is an era of "postconditions"—postmodern, postcolonial, posttraditional. This continuing function of ethnography requires new narrative motifs, and a debate about what they might be is at the heart of the current trend of experiments with the past conventions of ethnographic realism.[3]

Several themes characterize the works of postmodern writers. First, they reject the rationalist tradition of the Enlightenment, science, modernity, and all things related to the Western worldview. Second, scientific anthropology, which is seen as a product of the West's modernist project, is condemned for all the sins of Western culture, ranging from the global domination of indigenous people, to colonialism, imperialism, slavery, environmental degradation, and so on (cf. Erickson and Murphy 1998: 26–27; Perry 2003: 184). Third, the domain of anthropological inquiry is restricted to a narrow dimension of culture—meaning/discourse. Meaning/discourse is not only treated as if it constitutes something self-contained, self-referential, and hermetically sealed, but also as if it constitutes culture as a whole.

Postmodern anthropologists draw inspiration for these views from a number of sources. Their condemnation of science is based upon the writings of irrationalist philosophers, such as Kuhn and Feyerabend (whose works were discussed in Chapter 2), and the works of French postmodern philosophers, the likes of Michel Foucault (1926–1984), Jacques Derrida, and others, whose works, while dissimilar in certain respects, share the following features: radical epistemological relativism, subjective and intuitive discourses immune to validation by empirical procedures, and the overt dismissal of the rationalist tradition of the Enlightenment (see Doherty et al., 1992; Hollinger 1994; Rosenau 1992; Smart 1993).

In addition, as Sokal and Bricmont (1998: 183) have pointed out, the works of these writers are characterized by

a fascination with obscure discourses . . . an excessive interest in subjective beliefs independently of their truth or falsity; and an emphasis on discourse and language as opposed to facts to which those discourses refer (or, worse, the rejection of the very idea that facts exist or that one may refer to them).[4]

Postmodern philosophers treat science simply as another narrative or social discourse, with no greater, and perhaps even less validity than other forms of knowledge (Barrett 1996: 155). As Norris (1997: 7) has pointed out, French postmodernists treat science as a textual or rhetorical construct, "a kind of writing" minus the slightest chance that it can get anything right.

The eviction of science and reason from their discourse, as Rosenau (1992: 129) has put it,

means for post-modernists, liberation from modernity's preoccupation with authority, efficiency, hierarchy, power, technology, commerce (the business ethic), administration, social engineering. . . . It means release from the modern science's concern for order, consistency, predictability (Rosenau 1992: 129).

The postmodernists' condemnation of anthropology as the "the child of imperialism," to use a phrase used long ago by Gough (1968), is influenced by the works of such writers as Talal Asad (1973) and Edward Said (1979), among others. Said charges anthropology of perpetuating "orientalism," a stereotypical cultural representation imposed by Euro-Americans upon people in the Middle East and Asia. For Said, anthropology is about orientalism, and orientalism is the science of colonialism/neocolonialism designed to objectify and demean "the Other."

Drawing inspiration from the works of writers such as Said and Asad, postmodern writers charge anthropology and its practitioners with a host of ethical and moral breaches (Jorgensen 1982; Nencel and Pels 1991; Scheper-Hughes 1995; Scholte 1972).

Having rejected the rationalist tradition of the Enlightenment, upon which science is based, postmodernists wish to reconfigure anthropology, its objectives, goals, and methodologies based upon an alternative position on knowledge. In this respect, postmodern anthropology and pseudoscience share a number of features in common, as indicated in Figure 15.1.

Marcus and Fischer (1986: 263) inaugurated their new vision of the field by declaring that anthropology is in "a crisis of representation." Clifford (1986: 2–3) confidently declared the demise of all grand anthropological paradigms. And Marcus (1986: 263) stated that "the larger theoretical project of twentieth-century social and cultural anthropology is in disarray." The message was that scientific paradigms had failed and were obsolete, and that anthropology was now a literary enterprise.

Not all anthropologists agree with this assessment of paradigmatic research in anthropology (Cerroni-Long 1999; D'Andrade 1995a, 1995b; Fox 1992, 1997; Gellner 1992; Harris 1999; Kuznar 1997; Lett 1997; Sidky 2003). Also to be questioned is the declaration that, "the larger theoretical project of twentieth-century social and cultural anthropology is in disarray." As Harris pointed out with good reasons,

A popular myth among interpretationist science-bashers is that positivist anthropology deservedly

collapsed because of its failure to produce a coherent body of scientific theories about society and culture. Marcus and Fischer for example assert that there is a crisis in anthropology and related fields because of the "disarray" in the "attempt to build general and comprehensive theories that would subsume all piecemeal research" (1986: 118). This implies that postmodernists have made a systematic study of the positivist corpus of theories that dealt with the parallel and convergent evolution of sociocultural systems. But they have not done this. It was only after World War II that nonbiological, positivist cultural and archaeological paradigms gained acceptance among anthropologists. In the ensuing years unprecedented strides have been made in solving the puzzles of sociocultural evolution through a genuinely cumulative and broadening corpus of sophisticated and powerful theories based on vastly improved and expanded research methods. The cumulative expansion of knowledge has been especially marked within archeology and at the interface between archaeology and cultural anthropology (see e.g., Johnson and Earle 1987). It is ironic, then, that at the very moment when anthropology is achieving its greatest scientific successes, anthropologists who have never tested the positivist theoretical corpus which they condemn hail the death of positivist anthropology and the birth of a "new" humanistic paradigm. Only those who know little about the history of anthropological theories could hail such a paradigm as "new," much less as a "reconfiguration of social thought" (Harris 1994: 73).[5]

While no evidence is provided that paradigms have collapsed or that "the larger theoretical project of twentieth-century social and cultural anthropology is in disarray," postmodernists gave the following reason for the collapse of anthropological paradigms at this time. Marcus and Fischer (1986: vii) observed that the discipline is in shambles because the "hopes for a natural science of society, [is] challenged by theories of interpretation that say that people must be treated differently from nature."

Closer inspection reveals that the arrival of a new event, "anthropology's experimental moment" being proclaimed by Marcus and Fischer, was simply the call for the adoption of some-

Distinguishing Characteristics	Postmodern Anthropology	Pseudoscience
Indifference to facts.	✔	✔
Sloppy research techniques, or "anything goes" approach to knowledge; appeal to private epistemologies.	✔	✔
Lack of interest in rules of valid evidence; avoid submitting premises to meaningful tests; forward proof-exempt hypotheses.	✔	✔
Dependence upon arbitrary cultural conventions rather than regularities in nature, or "the nature of nature."	✔	✔
Reliance on subjective validation; independent confirmation of the facts is absent.	✔	✔
Pretentious, ambiguous jargon used to generate an aura of authority and validity equal to that of science.	✔	✔
Appeals to emotion and sentiment; encourges a distrust of established facts and scholarly traditions.	✔	✔
Knowledge does not grow, new information is seldom produced, and nothing concrete is ever learned.	✔	✔
Persuasion through rhetoric, rather than valid evidence.	✔	✔
Explanations are by "scenario," or narratives.	✔	✔
Eschews rational standards and argues from logical fallacies. Operates on the basis of irrational, unobjective modes of thought.	✔	✔
Encourages people to believe anything they want. It offers specious arguments that any and all beliefs are equally valid.	✔	✔

Figure 15.1 Similarities between postmodern anthropology and pseudo-science. *Based in part on Coker (2001).*

thing akin to Max Weber's (1864–1920) *verstehen* argument, based on the assertion that "people must be treated differently from nature." In this view, which has not been new for a very long while, culture is construed as a web of symbols people carry inside their heads. Therefore, to comprehend this inner world the fieldworker cannot rely on theories or hypotheses but must instead attain the "insider's view" through intuition and empathy.

The *verstehen* argument is not only old, but it was also obliterated long ago:

Sympathetic identification . . . is neither sufficient nor essential to guarantee the discovery of truth in human studies. It is not sufficient because the mistakes people make when they think they have identified with others are notorious; it is not essential because it is possible to explain another person's behavior without identifying with him. It would be something of a nuisance if we tried to be schizophrenic while we studied schizophrenia. I conclude, therefore, that it is false to say that we understand the action of other human beings "only because they are known to us from the workings of our own human minds" (Frankel 1960: 95–96).

Nor is the postmodernists' ideological stance on knowledge new. Although couched in erudite and heavily jargon-laden discourses (which makes comprehension of these texts difficult for many readers), the alternative that postmodernists opt for is simply a cultural constructionist (truth by coherence) approach, i.e., that something becomes real only when it is assigned meaning because things do not exist apart from "the discourse that constitutes them" (e.g., Fabian 1989; Tedlock 1991; Tyler 1986a: 37; Veeser 1989).

On this point postmodern writers are treading very old territory, although they have considerably augmented the cultural constructionist position. As Fox (1997: 335) observes,

Thus, the argument goes, there are no absolute truths, since all knowledge is relative to the social condition of the knower: the Marxist sociology-of-knowledge position. In the latter-day version, however, the social condition of the knower has been expanded from social class, technically defined, to "gender" (an egregious solecism meaning, in essence, sex), ethnicity, race, religion, class (widely defined as position in the social dominance system), historical period, ideological position (which should be a product but has become a producer).[6]

Social theorists such as Weber, Marx, and Engels, among others, stressed that knowledge is something relative to class, background, and sociopolitical and economic factors (Fox 1997:

330). Postmodern writers go further by maintaining that these factors not only influence knowledge but that they also determine the truth of propositions. In these terms, the truth of Gregor Mendel's discoveries depended entirely upon the fact that he was a white European male, an Augustinian monk, and so on (cf. Fox 1997: 330). Had he been someone else, today we would have an entirely different field of genetics.

The great difficulty with this position is that Mendel was for the most part right, and the truth of his propositions would not have been any different had he had been, as Fox (1997: 330) puts it, "a black handicapped Spanish speaking lesbian atheist." In fact, there is a historical case in which someone tried to develop an alternative genetics, and it ended in disaster. That was Trofim D. Lysenko's (1898–1976) Marxist science of genetics that devastated Soviet agronomy (see Lecourt 1977; Medvedev 1969; Soifer 1994). Lysenko's science was based upon the assumption that genes operate differently in the Soviet Union than elsewhere in the world.

In the postmodernists' augmented version of cultural construction, objective reality (if even granted to exist) is beyond access. The idea that "representations" in the mind accurately reflect reality is in error (cf. Gross and Levitt 1994: 77). This is how the postmodernist Shweder (1991: 355–356) expresses the reality-doubting foundation of postmodernism:

Postmodern realists [sic] see no way across the gap between appearance-sensation-experience and reality, except though an irrepressible act of imaginative projection. Reality, according to postmodern theories, is not only just obscured from sight; it is intrinsically invisible, like a black hole.[7]

For the cultural constructionists, what we construe to be "reality" is constituted wholly by linguistic and cultural conventions and has little to do with nature, the physical universe, or the material conditions of life. In other words, the truth and falsity of assertions are determined in connection to particular cultures and depend entirely upon power relations, linguistic conventions, and the mutual agreement by members of particular discursive communities (the relativist fallacy). Power, language, and truth are closely linked in this formulation. For this reason, these writers allege, there can be no valid, universal or pan-human standards for distinguishing between different claims to knowledge. Hence, one must resort to irrepressible acts of "imaginative projection."

The postmodernists' epistemological relativism (a logically self-contradictory position that holds that relativism is absolute), serves to justify the complete disregard and disdain not only for disciplinary traditions, but also the established conventions of scholarship and rules of evidence. As Gellner (1988: 29) observes,

> The argument tends to be: because all knowledge is dubious, being theory-saturated/ethnocentric/paradigm dominated/interest-linked (please pick your preferred variant and cross out the others, or add your own) etc., therefore the anguish-ridden author, battling with the dragons, can put forward whatever he pleases.[8]

Logic, reason, empirical evidence, validation, and standards of proof and disproof are all rejected as "empty evocations," degraded, ridiculous, simple-minded (Tyler 1986a: 130; 1987: 207). As Sangren (1988: 414) perceptively pointed out,

> This amounts to a kind of desire for authority without responsibility. . . . Space is created for young scholars by ruling out the validity of earlier scholarship (and those who practice it); one is free to experiment and to criticize, delegitimate, demystify, deconstruct, explode, subvert, transgress, etc., any sort of "other," real or fabricated, that suits one's purposes, without bearing responsibility for defending one's positions; and an openly acknowledged freedom to engage in mystification and creative self-empowering fabrication unaccountable to any challenge of logic or facts is simultaneously and summarily appropriated for experimental writers and denied to totalizing "others."[9]

Postmodernists treat their cultural constructionist perspective as a private and "special"

epistemology for discovering special "truths" (O'Meara 1995: 427). This, of course, is a source of great concern for many anthropologists. As O'Meara (1995: 427) points out,

> I get nervous when people support their arguments by claiming a special "epistemology" for discovering "truths" about the world. The more private that epistemology and the more righteous those "truths" the more nervous I become. My unease peaks when "truth" starts appearing in quote marks—implying, I fear, that what is taken to be false by the pedestrian standards of observation and logical inference available to all may nevertheless be advanced as "true" by the supposedly loftier standard of "reflection" or some other form of revelation available only to a self-selected few.[10]

Postmodernists declare that ordinary epistemology is dead. This is because epistemology holds that the world abounds with meanings, opinions, myths, truths, and not all of these can be correct and therefore it is necessary to find a way to distinguish between these (Gellner 1992: 38). Thus, they resort to special epistemologies, the inner secrets of which are only known to the most culturally sensitive adherents of the movement (the fallacy of special pleading).

Denying the possibility that there are any logico-empirical operations that can be presented in favor of one set of ideas over another, postmodernists consider "truth" as something determined entirely by whose "voices" are heard and whose "voices" are silenced. Truth in other words is a coefficient of power and coercion (Foucault 1984: 75). If all truths are relative, each as valid as the next, then those who speak equally valid but suppressed truths are the powerless, the dissidents, poets, women, prophets, and madmen (Diggins 1992: 371).

Hence postmodern writers maintain that not only do the disempowered have a right to air their voices/narratives, but moreover that these narratives have equal, if not greater validity, in comparison with the hegemonic discourse embodied in the Western scientific tradition (Gross and Levitt 1994: 38).

It is the task of anthropology, postmodernists say, to write in a way as to provide space for "the voices" of those who have been silenced. As Marcus and Fischer (1986: 1–2) point out,

> These subjects, who must be spoken for, are generally located in the world dominated by Western colonialism or neocolonialism; thus, the rhetoric both exemplifies and reinforces Western domination. Moreover, the rhetoric itself is an exercise in power, in effect denying subjects the right to express contrary views, by obscuring from the reader recognition that they might view things *with equal validity,* quite differently from the writer.[11]

The objective is "the adequate representation of other voices or points of views across cultural boundaries" (Marcus and Fischer 1986: 2).

For the cultural constructionist, everything is interpretation, there are multiple realities and multiple truths, and all ways of knowing, or epistemologies, are of equal validity, legitimacy, and authority. Given the relativistic nature of knowledge, this implies that in the final analysis cultures are incommensurable and cross-cultural translation ultimately impossible.

The idea of incommensurability of culture is fashioned after the way postmodern gurus, such as Foucault and Derrida, construe language/knowledge/reality. Human existence is patterned around language, these writers argue, but language is structured by the prevailing power relations. "Truth," according to Foucault (1984: 74), "is linked in a circular relation with systems of power which produce and sustain it, and to the effects of power which it induces and which extends it." Each historical period has its own particular discourse and truth. Foucault's epistemological relativism is based upon the idea that knowledge is relative to structures of power (Foucault 1984: 75).

This view is highly exaggerated. Those who focus upon discourse and the cultural construction of knowledge/reality seldom go on to ask the more significant question of why each historical period has its own particular discourse. That question, as I have stated elsewhere (Sidky 2003), is, From where did the thoughts arise? People do not simply think up thoughts spontaneously but do so under particular historical conditions and institutional arrangements, as Marx (1959: 43) went to great effort to point out. Once we trace the "discourse" to its underlying sociopolitical and economic matrices, postmodernist claims that discourse and power are disembodied forces that impinge upon people and yet operate without any material constraints fall apart.

Derrida (1976: 46–48) takes a more drastic position on language and incommensurability of cultures, arguing that there is nothing beyond or outside language—language refers only to itself. He treats the concept of "reality" itself as a random and historically contingent construct of Western philosophy's logocentric metaphysics (Derrida 1976: 9). Logocentrism refers to the concern in Western philosophy with logic and reason, inherited from classical Greece.

What we construe as "reality," or our representations of what is "real," according to Derrida, is conceived and expressed through linguistic mediums. Therefore, all representations are texts and no one can go outside of the text (logical fallacy of argument from ignorance). In this formulation, reality is reduced to discourse, and the necessity of attending to the role of tangible, earthly circumstances magically vanishes from the intellectual horizon of the postmodern philosopher.

For Derrida, meaning and knowledge are products of and exist solely in language (we know the world only through existing linguistic categories), and language is an arbitrary and artificial creation; its categories refer to themselves and not to objects that exist outside language. In other words, the locus of knowledge is not the human mind but in writing and in texts, which are then interpreted. According to this view, if language has no referents or constraints outside itself, and if knowledge exists only in language, then knowledge and its truth postulates can change randomly just like linguistic meanings change randomly (Layton 1997: 200–201). Therefore, knowledge, which is an artifact of language, is as arbitrary as language itself (Layton 1997: 195; Perry 2003: 181–182).

Scientific knowledge is thus ruled to be merely another narrative or story, no different from any other, if not worse. While postmodernists revel in this alleged demonstration of the cultural origins of science as merely another narrative (Herzfeld 2001: x, 2, 5, 9, 10, 22), this portrayal is a misrepresentation of science and scientific knowledge (the genetic fallacy and the fallacy of style over substance). It is a sham because it dismisses a crucial piece of the equation, the empirical dimension of science (Sokal and Bricmont 1998: 197).

Science is not a narrative. One does not have to read Einstein, Darwin, Newton, or Galileo to learn physics, biology, mathematics, or astronomy (Sokal and Bricmont 1998: 196). The principles of aerodynamics work regardless of the language or languages in which it is conveyed, taught, and applied. Mendelian genetics works, and it works everywhere, despite its discovery by a white European Augustinian monk. In science it is the factual and theoretical formulations that matter, not the words used by writers of scientific texts.

As Reyna (1994: 562) has noted in regard to the suggestions that in scientific texts rhetorical ornamentation takes precedence over "factual substantiality" or "conceptual elegance,"

> The propositions of an induction may be offered with considerable rhetorical fanfare. However, the persuasive effect of these statements depends upon whether canons of inductive or deductive logic have been appropriately applied and not upon their rhetorical ornamentation. [Postmodernists have] confused the communication of scientific practices with the practice. Such a representation of science is a misrepresentation of it.[12]

Derrida's extreme linguistic determinism not only entails a radical constructionist view of reality, but it also implies that exact translation of one language into another is impossible. When we transpose familiar linguistic categories of Western discourse for "exotic" or alien categories so as to render them, we violate "native" life (cf. Layton 1997: 195). This happens the moment another culture is "shaped and reoriented by the glance of the foreigner" (Derrida 1976: 113). Anthropological efforts to reach across cultural barriers, or attain cross-cultural translation, are therefore exercises in futility.

If this view is correct, then every ethnographic and anthropological account produced through the twentieth century is pure rubbish and the whole anthropological enterprise is refuted. However, the notion of incommensurablity of cultures is highly problematic. First, this kind of skepticism about our inability to know anything beyond our linguistic prisons is logically flawed. As Abel (1976: 27) has put it in another context,

> It seems to me safe to deny the thorough-going skepticism of Gorgias, who argued that nothing existed; and if it did, it could not be apprehended; and if it could be apprehended, that apprehension could not be communicated. If he could tell us that, how can knowledge not be communicated.[13]

The same applies to Derrida's epistemological skepticism and claim to knowledge outside his linguistic prison. Yes, cross-cultural translation is difficult, but so is the effort to understand one's own culture. This does not justify a retreat into texts and fiction writing or the abandonment of method, and dismissal of empirical data and the requirements of verification and justification. As Abel (1976: 127) adds,

> There are problems in my ability to understand other cultures; but those problems are not different in kind from the problems in my ability to understand my own culture; or indeed, my own family; or even myself. These problems are not insurmountable. . . . [Some theorists say] that there is a difference between understanding why a leaf flies in the wind and why a man flies from a mob; and that, therefore, you can't study men as you do leaves. Of course that is true; but that is a truism. For you can't study ancient men as you do

contemporary men; or primitive men as you do civilized men; or men as you do women; or men as you do children; or men as you do apes; or men as you do leaves; or other men as you do yourself. But the requirement of the *justification* and optimum organization of knowledge remain constant.[14]

Competent anthropologists who have spent time doing fieldwork find the idea of incommensurability of cultures absurd. As Appell (1989: 196) has observed,

> The ability to communicate with others about a reality shared or to be shared does tend to predispose one against [the postmodernists'] argument. We do communicate, even with members of other cultures, and are able to construct a world that is accessible to other competent observers from both cultures.[15]

Referring to his own field experience, Roger Keesing (1994: 304) pointed out,

> I see no reason, in all the texts, to infer that the pragmatic way in which [the Other] finds his way through his world is qualitatively different from the way in which I find my way through mine, or that his culturally constructed senses of individuation and agency (or personhood or causality or whatever) are strikingly different than mine.[16]

Keesing (1994: 305) goes on to assert that the evocation of radical diversity of cultures or incommensurability of cultures posited by postmodernists is exaggerated out of "disciplinary vested interests," rather than being based on any sort of ethnographic evidence. In other words, postmodernists need "otherness." They need it for ideological reasons. As Keesing (1994: 302) put it,

> To show that conceptions of personhood, of emotions, of agency, of gender, of the body are culturally constructed demands that Difference be demonstrated and celebrated, that 'cultures' be put in separate compartments and characterized in essentialist terms.[17]

They need an "Other" who does not operate according to the logocentric Western *episteme* in order to show the historical situatedness of European cultural constructions.

The idea of the otherness of the Other is based upon the assumption that each culture creates distinctive and culturally specific human characteristics. In other words, human behavior and patterns of thought are the product of each individual culture, rather than "pan-human Culture." What this position disregards is humankind's common evolutionary heritage. Human *cultural universals* (Figure 15.2) clearly show what that common heritage is, what makes us all human, and what it means to be human (Brown 1991). To disregard the innumerable commonalities among people in all cultures is not only scientifically unfounded and a serious theoretical mistake, it is also highly immoral and unethical and verges upon racism. Cultural constructionists are unable to accommodate humankind's shared evolutionary heritage because their entire ideological facade hinges upon there being an "Other" who is radically different.

As to the issue of equivalent terms/words, we may note that languages may not have equivalent terms for a particular concept, phenomenon, or object, but this has not stopped us from comprehending other belief systems. Take, for instance, Christianity and Islam, conceptual systems that have spread well beyond their linguistic homes (Peoples and Bailey 1994: 56–57). Similarly, science (for example, the science of aerodynamics) has been taught and learned in diverse languages, and the application of its principles has resulted in the creation of heavier than air machines that fly (cf. Norris 1997: 248–264). There are no problems of cross-cultural translation or relative truths here.

For the postmodern writers, the problematic nature of cross-cultural translations means that those anthropologists who write clearly (appeal to complexity) as if they understand that which the natives understand (you may array everyone from Malinowski and Radcliffe-Brown onward) are deceiving themselves and their readers (Fabian 1983; Tedlock 1991; Veeser 1989; Wagner

age grading	etiquette	joking	postnatal care
athletics	faith healing	kin groups	pregnancy usages
bodily adornment	family	language	property rights
calendar	feasting	law	propitiation of
cleanliness training	fire making	luck superstition	supernatural beings
community	folklore	magic	puberty customs
organization	food taboos	marriage	religious rituals
cooking	funeral rites	mealtimes	residence rules
cooperative labor	games	medicine	sexual restrictions
cosmology	gestures	modesty	soul concepts
courtship	gift giving	mourning	status differentiation
dancing	government	music	surgery
decorative art	greetings	mythology	tool making
divination	hair styles	numerals	trade
division of labor	hospitality	obstetrics	visiting
dream interpretation	housing	penal sanctions	weaning
education	hygiene	personal names	weather control
eschatology	incest taboos	population policy	
ethics	inheritance rules		
ethnobotany			

Figure 15.2   Murdock's cultural universals: the common evolutionary heritage of humankind. *After Murdock (1945).*

1999: 89). Moral recriminations and senselessly bellicose discourses flow fast and furious and the entire philosophical foundation of modern scientific anthropology is called into question as an illegitimate and deceptive enterprise (e.g., Herzfeld 2001; Marcus 1994; Marcus and Fischer 1986).

Science and scientific knowledge are highly suspect because, if all knowledge is a cultural construct, then science cannot be what it claims to be, a universally applicable mode of generating reliable knowledge about the world and universe. The privileged position of science is attributed to the political superiority of the West, not because science works (the genetic fallacy). One must remember that in this equation power determines the truth and falsity of ideologies (Rosenau 1992: 6; Trouillot 1991: 120). As such, science is laden with and expresses prevailing Western assumptions of power and domination (Gross and Levitt 1994: 78). It is merely a mode of discourse that is a code of power reflecting "the particularistic values of currently politically

dominant cultures" (Herzfeld 2001: x, 2, 5, 9, 10, 22).

If science owes its prestige to the powerful position of the culture in which it originated, then anthropologists who strive to study other cultures scientifically are in fact engaged in a kind of intellectual imperialism. Some cultural constructionists assert that those who seek objective and scientific understanding of other cultures are "betraying their enduring entanglement with the logic of Enlightenment theories" and that scientific anthropology "is grounded in the politics of religious and economic domination" (Herzfeld 2001: 183, 184). Modern anthropology is thus an instrument and expression of the oppressive and decadent Western, Euro-American worldview (Herzfeld 2001: 2).

What is remarkable about this kind of moralism is that the oppressor of the Other, the enemy of humanity, and mystifier turns out to be (here is the surprising part) the anthropologist "in the office down the hall," who has doubts about an anthropology divorced from empirical truths (cf. D'Andrade 1995a: 408). Anthropologists who write clearly and demand that knowledge must be backed by compelling evidence are demonized, while somehow the soldiers, missionaries, traders, colonial officers, transnational corporations, and so on, the real harbingers of death and destruction for indigenous peoples, who systematically engaged in ethnocide and genocide, are conveniently pushed to the sidelines.

Cultural constructionists describe their perspective as the "rearrangement of the very principles of intellectual perspective," stemming from "a pragmatic understanding of epistemology" that has emerged out of a new intellectual awareness of the cultural origins of science and rationality (Herzfeld 2001: x, 2, 5, 9, 10, 22).

Having rejected the possibility that there are any means or standards by which knowledge can be evaluated or certified, how do cultural constructionists approach the problem of knowledge? Here they navigate entirely in terms of their own political and moral convictions. In other words, knowledge and "truth" are defined in accordance to *value judgments.* Such truths can only be attained, it might be noted, by private epistemologies and special powers with which these writers credit themselves and deny all others.

It seems, therefore, that although everything, including science, is "in, not above, historical and linguistics processes" (Clifford 1986: 2), the postmodernists are exempt from such constrictions (fallacy of special pleading). This entails a kind of "intellectual apartheid" that is played out in academic politics inside anthropology departments to the detriment of all concerned.

Beneath the erudite verbiage and lofty discourses, we discover, therefore, that the postmodernists' alternative to science is what philosophers call cheers or jeers, or the "Boo-Hooray theory of moral judgments" (Williams 2001: 91). Upon considering the demographics and constituency of the American anthropological community to which these writers belong, it becomes

evident that the value judgments in question represent the subjectively defined moral sensibilities emanating from a particular spectrum of upper middle class Euro-American culture (cf. D'Andrade 1995b: 4). This all makes for pretended or pseudomorality and pseudopolitics, not the real thing. Professing that somehow their own subjective views are above ideological and cultural biases on some moral ground, as these writers are prone to doing, is both logically inconsistent and presumptuousness, to say the least.

Such presumptuousness accounts for these writers' moral pretensions, which entail a lot of "sloganeerism," combined with a lot of self-righteousness and bellicose language. What a strange scholarly enterprise this is—an enterprise devoid of new knowledge because "truth" is already in hand (cf. Salzman 2001: 136). These writers want to "speak truth to evil" (Scheper-Hughes 1995), but it is a truth to which somehow they alone have access.

Judgments about what is good and evil say little about the institutions, structures, and so on in question; instead they dictate how we should respond emotionally to those institutions and structures. In other words, the issue is not about understanding the world but rather with advocating a particular view of the world that accords with some idiosyncratic and subjective political and moral agenda (D'Andrade 1995b: 4; Sahlins 1999).

Operating on the basis of their own moralistic sensibilities, these writers are highly inconsistent as to whose "voices" they hear. As Salzman (2001: 138) has pointed out,

> The postmodern view seems to be that no one has a right to criticize another culture, unless there is something done in that culture that we do not like! A well-known example is the feminist denunciation of gender rules and roles—in, for example, the Mediterranean, Africa, India, East Asia, all Muslim countries, and so forth, in total about 80 percent of humanity, not to mention all societies in human history until 1960—that do not conform to our Western idea of gender equality.

Muslim women may claim that they have taken the veil voluntarily as an act of faith, but Western feminists know that this is just *false consciousness,* that these women have been brainwashed to take on the ideas of the patriarchy, and that the veil is a manifestation of that oppression of these women. So the postmodern position seems to be: I stand for human rights; you are ethnocentric; he is racist. If postmodernists do not like what is done in some cultures, they are humanitarian; if someone else does not like what is done in some other culture, they are cultural imperialists.[18]

Bailey (1991: 109) has made an interesting point regarding such moralistic pretensions:

> Mostly this seems to me self-indulgent moralizing. It is the kind of conscience that makes speaking-socialists out of rich men's sons, venting oedipal anger into the public domain, beating one's breast for sins committed by the fathers, confessing without making restitution, foregrounding the "I" and making the "Other" nothing more than an instrument of catharsis.[19]

Guided by an overt rejection of the rationalist tradition of the Enlightenment, the agenda of the postmodern anthropologist is to embrace "local knowledge" and "local frames" of understanding, with the purpose of using marginal knowledge of marginal communities to critique, question, and destabilize "received values" of the dominant cultures (Herzfeld 2001: 5). Cultural constructionists have thus transmuted anthropology into a kind of morally charged advocacy. This is why these writers feel fully justified in making the pursuit of the voices of the Other, or the "native's point of view" the principle intellectual aspiration of their enterprise.

The cultural constructionists' treatment of the problem of knowledge as insurmountable and the fact that for them cultures are, in the final analysis, incommensurable, affects the type of intellectual activities in which they engage. Their domain of inquiry is highly circumscribed and centered upon the ethnographer himself/herself. The call is for "reflexivity" regarding the ethnographers' ap-

propriate role with respect to the people they study (Wagner 1999: 89).

From the point of view of these writers, scientific ethnographers were in error to assume that the monographs or texts they created were representations of something real in the world (pejoratively labeled "ethnographic realism"). Given their assumption that cultures are incommensurable, postmodern writers assert that rather than representing the lives of people from other cultures, scientific anthropological monographs really embody the ethnocentric cultural precepts and biases of the anthropologists themselves. Traditional ethnographies were therefore laden with the pretensions of objectivity, which obfuscated their true nature (Roth 1989).

Postmodern anthropologists want to do away with all of this and reject all efforts to generate objective accounts from the outsider's point of view. The ethnographer, they maintain, is "in, not above, historical and linguistics processes," caught in the very process through which the ethnographic text is generated. Therefore, the "axiomatic separation of theorizing scholar and ethnographic subject," espoused by scientific anthropologists, we are told, is no longer acceptable (Herzfeld 2001: 2, 10). For this reason, as Clifford (1986: 9–10) observes, anthropology "no longer speaks with automatic authority for others defined as unable to speak for themselves ('primitive,' 'pre-literate,' 'without a history')."

The observer and observed distinction is ousted because it implies the imposition of analytical categories, analytical judgments, a distinction between "our knowledge" and "their knowledge." It also implies that "the native's point of view," or "local knowledge," does not encompass the whole picture, and it clashes with the egalitarian view of knowledge espoused by the postmodernists. Those who insist upon such distinctions are said to be in fact engaged in a form of mental imperialism based upon the morally questionable ethnocentric assumption of a rationality transcending cultural boundaries (Herzfeld 2001: 10, 22, 174; Perry 2003: 127).

So what is the solution to the problem of knowledge confronting the ethnographer in the field? For the postmodernists, the answer lies in the careful scrutiny of how anthropologists create their texts (Marcus and Fischer 1986: 15–16).

As Clifford (1986: 2) points out, "We begin, not with participant-observation or with cultural texts (suitable for interpretation), but with writing, the making of texts." Experimentation with new writing techniques is called for (Marcus and Fischer 1986: 37) so as to "reposition anthropology with respect to its 'objects' of study" (Clifford 1986: 9–10). Clifford (1986: 13) goes on to say that there is a "general trend toward a *specification of discourse* in ethnography: who speaks? who writes? when and where? with or to whom? under what institutional and historical constraints?" "In this view of ethnography," Clifford (1986: 14) notes further, "the proper referent of any account is not a represented 'world'; now it is specific instances of discourse." As Marcus and Fischer (1986: 30) point out,

> Dialogue has become the imagery for expressing the way anthropologists (and by extension, their readers) must engage in an active communicative process with another culture. It is a two-way and two-dimensional exchange, interpretive processes being necessary both for communication internally within a cultural system and externally between systems of meaning.[20]

This kind of ethnography is a "text that presents two subjects in discursive exchange" (Rabinow 1986: 245).

> Many voices clamor for expression. Polyvocality was restrained and orchestrated in traditional ethnographies by giving to one voice a pervasive authorial function and to others the role of sources of "information" to be quoted or paraphrased. Once dialogism and polyphony are recognized as modes of textual production, monophonic authority is questioned, revealed to be characteristic of a science that has claimed to *represent* cultures (Clifford 1986: 15).[21]

Tyler (1986b: 127) writes that

because post-modern ethnography privileges "discourse" over "text," it foregrounds dialogue as opposed to monologue, and emphasizes the cooperative and collaborative nature of ethnographic situation in contrast to the ideology of the transcendental observer. In fact, it rejects the ideology of "observer-observed," their being nothing observed and no one who is observer. There is instead mutual, dialogical production of discourse, of a story of sorts. We better understand the ethnographic context as one of cooperative story making that, in one of its ideals forms, would result in a polyphonic text, none of whose participants have the final word in the form of a framing story or encompassing synthesis—a discourse on the discourse.[22]

By producing polyvocalic texts and paying attention to words and writing, postmodernists argue, they have eliminated the power imbalance between the ethnographer and informant that characterized traditional ethnographic research. This is treated as an exhilarating act of liberation. Gross and Levitt (1994: 74) have observed in this regard that

> the idea that close attention to the words, tropes [metaphors], and rhetorical postures of a culture gives one transmutative power over that culture finds acceptance for a number of reasons. First of all, it shifts the game of politics to the home turf of those who by inclination and training are clever with words, disposed to read texts with minute attention and to attend to the higher-order resonances of language. At the same time, it allows scholars of a certain stamp to construe the pursuit of the most arcane interests as a defiantly political act against the repressive strictures of society. This is exhilarating: it is radicalism without risk. It does not endanger careers but rather advances them. It is a radicalism that university administrators and even boards of governors have found easy to tolerate, since its calls to arms generally result in nothing more menacing than aphorisms lodged in obscure periodicals.[23]

Since for these writers everything begins and ends in circles of meaning embodied in texts written on paper, the key to liberation and social justice and equality for the oppressed lies in writing (non sequitur). The assumption is that "to be is to be written about, and to be subordinate or equal is to be written about as subordinate or equal. We can create a morally acceptable world just by writing appropriately" (Sapire 1989: 565). Thus, the undoubted fact that meaning or concepts can impose constraints upon the social world is transformed into to the indefensible idealist conclusion that the *only* constraints are conceptual ones (Gellner 1992: 64).

What is more problematic is that in the formulations of these anthropologists, domination in the real world is confused with domination on paper. Hence, their conclusion that subjectivism is a correlate of social justice and allowing the voice of the Other to be heard on paper (jargon-laden articles published in arcane journals) is an act of liberation that magically unshackles those who have been oppressed in the real world.

There is an inexcusable epistemological confusion here between entities of this world and written about entities of the ethnographic texts. Authority in texts may have something to do with the creation and perpetuation of power in society, but textual authority is not what postmodernists allege, "otherwise writers would be kings" (Sangren 1988: 411). As I have stated elsewhere, no matter how many hapless Others we liberate in our texts, liberation in the real world will not follow unless people's earthly circumstances and the structures that create and perpetuate injustice on the ground are eliminate (Sidky 2003).

So who really benefits from these "liberating" texts? Who is really liberated? While the postmodernists cause might seem to be a noble one (what anthropologist in his/her right mind would object to empowering the Other?), whose "voices" are really heard in these texts? Are there really multiple authors with authority shared? Is this really possible in any text written by an American professor in his or her university office in Chicago, New York, Texas, or sunny California?

Euro-American ethnographers employed by Euro-American universities usually write the texts. The texts are published by Euro-American presses, the passages are affected by reviewer input, publisher marketing strategies, editorial staffs, and so on, who control production and publication. Closer scrutiny suggests that this kind of writing is highly valuable, not to the Other, but to their authors in terms of tenure, publicity, lots of graduate students, courtship by elitist presses, and so forth.

This kind of scholarship has another characteristic. In their efforts to "write experimentally" to make discursive space for the voices of the other (which is merely patronizing the Other), clarity vanishes and the text is flooded with erudite jargon-laden passages, impenetrable language, bordering on, if not in fact, calculated and strategic ambiguity. This "smokescreen of jargon," to use Stanislav Andreski's (1972) phrase, gives the postmodernists' texts an illusionary aura of imperviousness by concealing the absence of substance.

A number of anthropologists have called attention to the postmodernists' impenetrable prose. Robert Murphy (1994: 56) called it a competitive game in which "obscure literary allusions and baroque rhetorical forms are weapons, a kind of egghead rap-talk." Carneiro (1995: 13) observes, "[It is] quite ironic that persons so concerned with 'meaning' as postmodern ethnographers claim to be, should show so little regard for the process of *conveying* meaning, namely, communication." Carneiro (1995: 14) adds that

> if literature is their forte, and the discovery of meaning their aim, why do post-modernist couch their discourse in language so elusive and obscure? I have a private theory about this . . . that postmodernists like Geertz and Tyler really don't *want* to be understood. In the guise of bringing enlightenment, they enjoy sowing the seeds of confusion. Deep down in their hearts, they relish being arcane and unfathomable. Why? Because they hold to the secret premise that *to appear abstruse it to be thought profound*.[24]

Thick descriptions and inscrutable rhetoric produces discourses that are unimpeachable. Magnarella (1993: 135) notes that postmodernism is "beyond truth" and is "immune to judgment." This is why postmodern texts are so valuable to their authors because they can say anything and never be wrong. If we think back to the discussion of the sources and foundation of knowledge in Chapter 2, this approximates religious ideology more so than scholarship. Carneiro (1995: 11) adds that

teasing subtexts from a main text is surely slippery business, but it's also a lot of fun. It's a game *anyone* can play, and *everyone* can win, because there are no rules. There is no correct interpretation, no right answer. Any answer is as good as any other.[25]

The end result of the exercise is that in spite of massive doses of creative energies spent in constructing polyvocalic texts, and in spite of the copious insertions of specialized terminologies, the author of the text is still there (it can't be any other way). And this leads to self-recrimination and guilt over a failed enterprise, which for the postmodernist seems to be a good thing (Gellner 1992: 29). And so they lash out with great vehemence at anyone who returns from the field with coherent accounts of another culture.

The postmodernists' emphasis upon "the voices" of the Other is another thorny subject. There are lots and lots of native voices (folk knowledge) and not all of them are saying the same thing. Moreover, not every voice encompasses the truth, the whole picture. So for whose voice does one make discursive space? Asking this question regarding members of our own communities reveals the preposterousness of this idea that somehow truth resides in "voices." Would you get the "truth" or the whole picture talking to your neighbor?, to your colleagues?, to the person on the street? Obviously not! Yes, some voices say important and valuable things, but not all the voices, all of the time. Certainly not voices over empirically grounded understandings of the world or scientific knowledge.

The following passage, written by a nonanthropologist, sheds some perspective on the subject of folk knowledge:

Certain kinds of folk knowledge are valid and priceless. Others are at best metaphors and codifiers. Ethnomedicine, yes; astrophysics, no. It is certainly true that all beliefs and all myths are worthy of respectful hearing. It is not true that all folk beliefs are equally valid—if we're talking not about the internal mindset, but about understanding the external reality (Sagan 1995: 252).[26]

Another twist in the cultural constructionist position is the kinds of texts that are actually produced in place of the ones writers of this persuasion claim they produce. Given that thought and reality are conflated in the discourse of the postmodernists, they insist that the ethnographer must tell us about himself or herself. The assumption is that

facts are inseparable from the observer who claims to discern them, and the culture which supplied the categories in terms of which they are described. This being so, he had better tell us about himself. He had better confess his culture. Real, self or culture-independent facts in any case being neither available nor accessible, there is not much else he can tell us. Even what he tells us about himself is suspect and tortuous. So he does tell us about himself with relish, and seldom gets much further; and, given the premises of the movement, it would be quite wrong of him if he did get much further. It would show that he failed to learn the deep doubts which are the movement's specialty (Gellner 1992: 25).[27]

Postmodernists dismiss the impersonal standards of observation and objectivity that exclude the ethnographer's "personal experiences," such as "participation and empathy" (Clifford 1986: 14–15) and require inclusion in the ethnographic texts the "states of serious confusion, violent feelings or acts, censorships, important failures, changes of course, and excessive pleasures are excluded from the published accounts" (Clifford 1986: 13).

Postmodernist juxtapose their point of view with what they call "the rhetoric of realism" of traditional ethnographies. Ruling the latter as false, postmodernists insist that ethnography is not, and cannot be a description of another culture. All that the postmodernists' ethnography can be is a subjective description of, or reflections upon, some aspect of the ethnographer's own experience, or self (Bailey 1991: 107–108) engaging the Other in dialogue. About all they can legitimately do, in plain English, is to "report their own experience" and tell stories about themselves (Wagner 1999: 89).

The results of this enterprise are the production of narratives, subjective, confessional, anecdotal accounts of the ethnographer's own experiences engaging in a dialogue with the "natives" in answer to questions such as "what were they to me," and "what was I to them," and the exercise of reflexivity over objectivity (Tedlock 1991).

This transforms anthropological inquiry into an activity comparable to poetry, the writing of fiction, and subjective musings or opinions in which truth becomes "a matter of convention, what people agree to be true" and "somewhat optional, unconstrained by nature, a matter of collective choice, man-made" (Bailey 1991: xviii). This perspective, as O'Meara (1995: 428) has pointed out, "throw[s] the gates wide open to distortion by answering every question according to how it serves our moral and political interests."

What all this amounts to really is that anecdotes are substituted for coherent analysis (cf. Dawes 2001: 113). This kind of anthropology entails the generation of cleverly and experimentally written stories, or story-telling, framed as "my adventures among the Other," or in the current jargon, "narrative ethnographies of the particular" (Abu-Lughod 1991: 150–151). This is "a retreat to ethnographic particularism," an unfortunate slippery path treaded long ago by Boas and his disciples. It led nowhere.

Stories are hopelessly bias ridden and serve ideological purposes. They do not enhance knowledge. As Dawes (2001: 114) has cogently pointed out,

> Information contained in a good story is particularly difficult to ignore. Even when we are making a conscious (and self-conscious) attempt to evaluate evidence in a logical and unbiased way, stories have an impact. A logical and unbiased evaluation is, for example, what jurists are typically instructed to attempt. Nevertheless, the story model of jury decision making has received substantial support, both from researchers observations and questioning people in real juries and from experimental work. . . . [The] problem with stories is that they are often *selected* to prove a point, rather than forming a basis of a statistical generalization (again a very dubious one) or causal inference. It is the generalization or inference that leads to the selection of the story in the first place—with the results that story provides absolutely no new information.[28]

For the postmodernists, however, stories or narratives are what anthropology is all about. Aware of the problematic epistemological aspects of story writing, they attempt to bypass these by resorting to the metaphor of ethnography as fiction. An ethnography is not simply a text, it is a thing that is constructed and artificial—it is a fiction. For these writers, fiction has a specific meaning. As Clifford (1986: 6) observes,

> To call ethnographies fictions may raise empiricist hackles. But the word as commonly used in recent textual theory has lost its connotation of falsehood, of something merely opposed to truth. It suggests the partiality of cultural and historical truths, the ways they are systematic and exclusive. Ethnographic writings can properly be called fictions in the sense of "something made up or fashioned." . . . But it is important to preserve the meaning not merely of making, but also of making up, of inventing things not actually real.[29]

Clifford (1986: 7) adds that

> the maker . . . of ethnographic text cannot avoid expressive tropes [metaphors], figures, and allegories that select and impose meaning as they translated it. In this view . . . *all constructed truths are*

made possible by powerful "lies" or exclusions and rhetoric. Even the best ethnographic texts—serious, true fictions—are systems, or economies of truth. Power and history work through them, in ways their authors cannot fully control (emphasis added).[30]

Despite the careful qualifications that ethnographic texts are not fictions in the sense of being false, Clifford's construal verges upon things that are untrue (i.e., "powerful lies").

Saying that ethnographies are fictions has implications with respect to the credibility of postmodernist writings. Therefore, those advocating this view provide qualifications such as, "Postmodern ethnography is fragmentary because it cannot be otherwise" (Tyler 1986b: 131). Or "Ethnographic truths are . . . inherently *partial*— committed and incomplete" (Clifford 1986: 7). Clifford (1989: 562) says, "*any* claim to authenticity must always be tactical, politically and historically contingent." In other words, these writers are saying that their ethnographies are stories that they have made up, the tales have little if any connection to what is the case, to facts, or to evidence, and that is the nature of anthropological research.

This trajectory has serious consequences in terms of the credibility and integrity of the discipline of anthropology. As Appell (1989: 198) has put it,

> The problem with the fictionalists and the interpretivists is that their program dissolves understanding and knowledge rather than expanding it. In denying the potentiality of shared knowledge, it obfuscates rather than clarifies. It encourages the growth of ethnocentrism rather than reducing it, and is therefore regressive, for the interpretive act is now egocentric, with the interpreter the focus. Yet the ego is to a large degree a construct of the individuals own culture, and its ethnocentric vision is unloosed when controls exercised by a scholarly anthropological community are dissolved. And, finally, the program trivializes and debases the hard, long task of developing skills of ethnographic observation and hypothesis test-

ing that minimize ethnocentric bias as much as possible.[31]

Anthropological knowledge is no longer knowledge but pseudomoralistic aphorisms emanating from the subjectively constituted values and sensibilities of a segment of upper-middle-class Euro-Americans.

This is highly liberating because cultural constructionist anthropology renders obsolete the question of the sources of our claims to knowledge and the thorny problem of validation of ethnographic accounts. As Clifford writes,

> The writing and reading of ethnography are overdetermined by forces ultimately beyond the control of either an author or an interpretive community. These contingencies—of language, rhetoric, power, and history—must now be openly confronted in the process of writing. They can no longer be evaded. But the confrontation raises thorny problems of verification: how are the truths of cultural accounts evaluated? Who has the authority to separate science from art? realism from fantasy? knowledge from ideology? Of course such separations will continue to be maintained, and redrawn; but their changing poetic and political grounds will be less easily ignored. *In cultural studies at least, we can no longer know the whole truth, even claim to approach it* (Clifford 1986: 25, emphasis added).[32]

Sorting out the real from unreal seems an insurmountable task, which is why there are no general agreements as to what constitutes an acceptable work of ethnography. As Clifford (1986: 10) adds, the "criteria for judging a good account have never been settled and are changing."

Here one encounters a paradoxical situation in the assertions of these writers. If criteria for judging between good accounts and bad accounts do not exist, then by implication all accounts are pretty much equally valid. This fits in with the "anything goes" approach to knowledge that is linked to the cultural constructionist view and the epistemological relativism it entails. Yet Clifford (1986: 24) disavows radical epistemological relativism:

> The authors of this volume do not suggest that one cultural account is as good as any other. If they espoused so trivial and self-refuting a relativism they would not have gone to the trouble of writing detailed, committed, critical studies.[33]

But the idea of polyvocality and declarations such as, "In cultural studies . . . we can no longer know the whole truth," "powerful lies" and so forth, betray Clifford's caveat. Clifford is compelled to take this view, because if he does not, if he acknowledges the possibility that one cultural account is as good as another, he vindicates traditional ethnographies at the expense of his own stance (Jarvie 1988: 428). Hence the flip-flop these writers engage in between a "theoretical free-for-all" and a puritanical anti-theory position (Gellner 1992: 27).

ASSESSMENT

In this chapter I have outlined the basic assumptions of postmodern interpretive anthropology. Throughout the discussion I have raised objections and noted the problematic aspects of this approach. The cultural constructionist perspective advocated by postmodernists challenges our disciplinary origins and traditions (Sidky 2003). For this challenge to be persuasive several questions must be answered: (1) Is all of reality culturally constructed in the manner these writers suggest? (2) Is objective reality unknowable? (3) Is science really another narrative, and hence useless as a means of acquiring objective knowledge? (4) Is the cultural constructionist perspective a better alternative to science? I maintain that the answer to all of these questions is an unqualified "No."

The cultural constructionist position is based upon the magnification of a reasonable doubt regarding how we know what we know into the entirely unreasonable position that no knowledge is possible so let us make-up what suits our private, subjective sensibilities (reduction to ab-

surdity). On the basis of this, proponents of this view feel justified to compose poems and stories about themselves and their adventures with the Other. They thus opt for private and special epistemologies, accessible only to the members of their movement (fallacy of special pleading).

The question that prudent thinkers must ask is this: Is there compelling evidence, or better yet, any evidence, that subjective epistemologies are superior in enhancing our understanding of humans, human behavior, and the operation of sociocultural systems? I maintain that there is no such evidence.

The fallacious nature of the cultural constructionists view becomes evident as soon as we assess it in the crucible of experience and extend it to *all* aspects of our day-to-day experiences and understandings:

> not only to the existence of atoms, electrons or genes, but also to the fact that blood circulates in our veins, that the Earth is (approximately) round, that at birth we emerge from our mother's womb. Indeed, even the most commonplace knowledge of our everyday lives—there is a glass of water in front of me on the table—depends entirely on the supposition that our perceptions do not *systematically* mislead us and that they are indeed produced by external objects that, in some way, resemble those perceptions (Sokal and Bricmont 1998: 53).[34]

As Abel (1976: 33) cogently puts it,

> The road that leads from my sense perceptions to my knowledge of a world outside myself is full of gaps, brambles, and obscurities. But it is the only road I have; if I refuse to travel on it because of its risks, I would not ever get outside of me. It is true that inference to the independent existences of external objects cannot be demonstrated. . . . *But our justification of such a belief is pragmatic: we survive and act successfully in the world by assuming it* (emphasis added).[35]

Applying the postmodernists' assertions to the epistemology of everyday life is the best antidote for their unreasonable excesses (Sokal and

Bricmont 1998: 92). These writers themselves do not extend their doubts about an objective reality and the hopelessness of understanding that reality to all their experiences. If this were the case, few cultural constructionists of this kind would be around, having been led by their doubts to step before moving cars and the like.

In day-to-day activities we explain "the coherence of our experiences" by supposing that the external world accords, at least in an approximate way, to the images perceived by our senses. Sokal and Bricmont (1998: 55) therefore raise the following question: If radical epistemological skepticism is problematic when applied to all aspects of our experiences and knowledge, why should we assume that it is valid when it comes to scientific knowledge? If I can get reliable knowledge of the world and would not deliberately step in front of a speeding motor vehicle, then why would my senses mislead me when I rely upon the systematic and rigorous procedures of scientific research? Cultural constructionists do not have a credible answer to this central epistemological question.

Practical rationality directs us in our daily experiences and this rationality is not qualitatively different from scientific rationality. As Sokal and Bricmont (1998: 56) point out,

> The scientific method is not radically different from the rational attitude in everyday life or in other domains of human knowledge. Historians, detectives, and plumbers—indeed, all human beings—use the same basic methods of induction, deduction, and assessment of evidence as do physicists or biochemists. Modern science tries to carry out these operations in a more careful and systematic way, by using controls and statistical testing, insisting on replication, and so forth. Moreover, scientific measurements are often much more precise than everyday observations; they allow us to discover hitherto unknown phenomena; and they often conflict with "common sense." But the conflict is at the level of conclusions, not the basic approach (Sokal and Bricmont 1998: 56).[36]

Therefore, while it is the case that propositions about objective reality cannot be proven absolutely, often they can be proven beyond reasonable doubt; unreasonable doubt will always remain (Sokal and Bricmont 1998: 57). Postmodern writers have groundlessly capitalized on the unreasonable doubt by extending it to all aspects of all knowledge. Yet there is overwhelming evidence that we can indeed acquire the kind of knowledge that these writers eschew. Their epistemophobia is unjustified.

The conformity between theory and experiment in thousands of cases, sometimes very precise conformity, proves that there is an external world/reality and that scientific approach has enabled us to understand that reality (Bernard 1995: 17; Sokal and Bricmont 1998: 57). Scientific knowledge in every field, including the study of humans, human origins, and the evolution and operation of sociocultural systems has grown and expanded.

There are no epistemological, theoretical, or methodological justifications for the cultural constructionist position. Therefore, as Cerroni-Long (1996: 52) has observed, "those anthropologists that go on telling stories or making poetry do so as personal choice, not because the study of culture requires it."

This being the case, prudent thinkers can rightly question the motives of those who opt for storytelling, rather than applying their intellectual abilities to real theoretical and methodological problems and the innumerable tangible issues facing human beings around the globe. Telling clever stories is intellectually and morally irresponsible. The fact that anthropologists have had little to contribute to the crisis in the Middle East post–September 11, except for some post hoc musings, should be a wake up call to those have made storytelling the agenda of the one discipline than can shed light on the complex global cultural conflicts.

Chapter 16

Conclusions: Anthropology in the Twenty-First Century

Anthropologists working during the closing decades of the twentieth century and the beginning of the twenty-first century found themselves confronted by a world that had been suddenly and dramatically transformed in unanticipated and very alarming ways. The changes included the end of the Cold War and its ideological partitions, economic and political globalization, reconfigurations of global power, and shifts in the focus of global politics to arenas pitting the West against non-Western societies.

There is hyperdiffusion, the Internet, transnational migrations, increasing disparities in wealth and access to limited and nonrenewable resources, satellite TVs and phones, the clash of conflicting value systems brought uncomfortably close by a world grown small, the simultaneous formation of a "global culture" and "desecularization" and "retribalization," and rising ethnic violence.

Finally, there is the specter of global terror networks, the Taliban phenomena in Afghanistan, the September 11 attacks on the United States, the crisis in the Middle East and the war against Iraq in 2003 and impending wars against others (cf.

Barber 1992; Fukuyama 1998; Huntington 1996; Rushdie 2001, 2002).

Barber (1992: 53) framed these events in terms of concurrent processes of tribalization and globalization:

A retribalization of large swaths of humankind by war and bloodshed: a threatened Lebanonization of national states in which culture is pitted against culture, people against people, tribe against tribe— a Jihad in the name of a hundred narrowly conceived faiths against every kind of interdependence, every kind of artificial social cooperation and civic mutuality. . . . [and] the onrush of economic and ecological forces that demand integration and uniformity and that mesmerize the world with fast music, fast computers, and fast food— with MTV, Macintosh, and McDonald's, pressing nations into one commercially homogenous global network: one McWorld tied together by technology, ecology, communications, and commerce. The planet is falling precipitantly apart AND coming reluctantly together at the very same moment. . . . The tendencies of what I am here calling the forces of Jihad and the forces of McWorld operate with equal strength in opposite directions, the one driven by parochial hatreds, the other by

413

universalizing markets, the one re-creating ancient subnational and ethnic borders from within, the other making national borders porous from without.[1]

The curious response by anthropologists confronted with these baffling transformations has been pessimism, self-doubt and a strategic reconfiguration of the nature of their intellectual enterprise. There has been a deliberate shift away from a concern with coming to terms with the world on empirical grounds and a move towards parochial concerns, retreat into ethnographic particularism, reflexivity, concerns for developing "critical politics" for the discipline, focus upon issues of "hybridity," "positionality," and "subjectivities" (Moore 1999: 8). Theory had acquired a new meaning. As Moore (1999: 9) puts it,

> Theory is now a diverse set of critical strategies which incorporates within itself a critique of its own locations, positions, and interests: that is, it is highly reflexive. This notion of theory—which is the legacy of a moment of high postmodern/deconstruction—*underpins multifarious intellectual projects across a range of disciplines.* It self-identifies as the *meta-critique of all critiques,* as a field of *nomadic critical operations* that undermines any attempt to *authenticate cultures, selves, histories.* This view of theory is itself a myth or rather only a moment in a larger critical strategy. It too can be critiqued, as it acknowledges, for its own pre-theoretical assumptions: its constituting concepts and values (emphasis added).[2]

Theory has become a sort of free-floating set of mental operations, something ephemeral in nature, ungrounded, eclectic. Theory has been transformed into acts of reflecting upon ourselves reflecting about ourselves, and venting of frustrations over the sorry state of world in these posttraditional, postcolonial times. This has led to disengagement with the world in concrete terms and to forays of mutual admiration of one another's erudite discourses about the predicament of culture, the evils of modernity, and anticipation over who will be the next to contrive the most politically correct and cross-culturally sen-

sitive moral sensibilities. As a result of this intellectual reconfiguration in anthropology, scientific epistemologies are declared to be entirely obsolete and inadequate for coming to terms with what has happened in the world.

It appears that the massive global changes (which demand new theoretical approaches, greater empirical understanding, and attention to what is the case) have redefined how anthropologists perceive reality itself. There is no novel breakthrough here, simply an ideological shift back to a kind of Hegelian ultraidealist position, which holds that reality is entirely culturally constructed, completely disassociated from an objective reality external to our consciousness. Only such a perspective can enable its proponents to conflate changes in sociocultural and political patterns with a change in the way reality itself is constituted so that it is no longer amenable to rational scientific analysis and comprehension.

One can only justify this view (i.e., that science is obsolete), however, if it is demonstrated that the way reality is constituted has in fact changed. As no one has provided such a demonstration, it seems that those anthropologists who have forsaken empirical understanding in anthropology in favor of eclectic and relativistic excursions and operations, and self-reflections, have done so out of personal choice.

Another point to consider is that the pursuit of reflexive, resonant narratives and proof-exempt discourses, "hybridity," "positionality," and "subjectivities," has not led to any substantial breakthroughs in our understanding of the world. It has not enhanced knowledge.

In terms of tangible outcomes, this escapade has led to the clouding of issues, the problem of knowledge has been made to appear desperately hopeless, and the intellectual integrity and credibility of anthropology as a discipline has been jeopardized.

The last two decades have been spent in the energetic pursuit of hybridities, positionalities, subjectivities, tropes, metaphors, and identities (constructed or otherwise) in the postconditions of the postcolonial and the posttraditional—a venture often working itself out into such politically correct research projects as explorations of the meaning of Nintendo games for upper-middle class Arab children in Egypt, or the effects of American TV soap operas on gender identities among the Bedouin.

Simultaneously there has been a spurning of culturally insensitive or politically incorrect topics such as violence and warfare. These verge on areas considered far too disrespectful and insensitive to delve into. Given this intellectual enterprise, anthropology's embarrassing silence regarding the pressing issues surrounding the September 11 attacks, the Taliban phenomenon, Al Qaeda, global terror networks, Islamist movements, and war-mongers in the West is hardly surprising.

This has been an unfortunate turn for the one discipline that by virtue of its subject matter and scientific perspective should be at the center of the clash of cultures that threatens to embroil the entire world in bloodshed, violence, rifts, and divisions. I have argued that the more complex life gets on earth, the greater our need for anthropological understandings that accord with the reality of the world. We need less epistemophobia, less flawed thinking, fewer explanations by "scenario" and "narrative," and a greater effort toward "thinking straight about the world," as Gilovich (1991: 6) has put it.

I have stated throughout this book that the problem of knowledge is not insoluble—the critical conceptual tools are already there for anyone who wishes to use them. It is hard work, but it can be done. Until someone devises a new epistemology—not ideologies of ambiguity or mystical hocus pocus of the sort emanating from Paris—the scientific approach remains the only means for thinking straight about the world.

In conclusion, what is the current status of science in anthropology? Salzman (2001: 11) has summed up the present circumstances:

> The scientific epistemological theory and the postmodern epistemological theory are alternative philosophical visions that have each been advocated and pursued by anthropologists throughout the 1990s. These different visions represent the major theoretical split among anthropologists at the turn of the millennium.[3]

Postmodern interpretive anthropology and its innumerable permutations are not the logical culminations of the discipline (McGee and Warms 2000: 519). The commitment to science and the efforts to develop increasingly more empirically accurate understandings of the world remain strong among many researchers. There is still hope for an anthropology that is about engaging the world and addressing tangible human problems, such as overpopulation, ethic violence, terrorism, and a host of other issues and concerns.

Glossary

Aboriginal   native, indigenous, original inhabitants of a particular territory, country, or continent.

Acculturation   cultural alterations due to the effects of direct contact between two previously separate societies.

Adaptation   process whereby organisms/populations adjust biologically or behaviorally to their physical/social environments that enhances their survival or reproductive success.

Ad hominem   logical fallacy entailing arguments that attack the character and personality of the proponent of an assertion, rather than the assertion itself.

Affinity   relationships based upon marriage. Contrasts with **Consanguinity.**

Age-Area Hypothesis   the assumption that the wider the distribution of a trait around a culture center the greater its age.

Anthropology   from two Greek words, *anthropos* for "human" and *logos* for study, the scientific study of humankind from a holistic and evolutionary perspective.

Animatism   Robert Marett's (1866–1943), term referring to the belief in an unpersonalized life force or vitalism in inanimate objects.

Animism   "the theory of souls," an idea forwarded by Edward B. Tylor referring to the belief in the existence of personalized spirits, such as souls, demonic beings, and other supernatural entities thought to inhabit nature and influence human affairs.

Anthropological Knowledge   a special and novel way of understanding humanity, comprising a holistic, pan-human, diachronic approach based upon the axiom that all generalizations about humankind, human behavior, and cultural systems must be shown to apply to many places and many times. It strives to provide a unified understanding of the human condition from a scientific perspective.

Antistructure   the characteristics of liminality in Victor Turner's (1920–1983) symbolic perspective.

Apollonian   a term used by Ruth Benedict (1887–1948), meaning peaceful/moderate, to refer to the psychological characteristics of the Zuñi.

Appeal to Authority (*argumentum ad verecundiam*) logical fallacy of citing prestigious individuals such as rock stars as experts, even though they do not have the appropriate qualifications, citing individuals whose expertise is in a different field, citing authorities out of context, or citing authorities in issues over which experts in the discipline disagree.

Appeal to Complexity logical fallacy in which it is asserted that the phenomenon in question is too complex for anyone to comprehend, therefore the opinion of the one making this argument is as valid as any other opinion.

Appeal to Emotion logical fallacy in which the validity of a proposition is established by appealing to people's emotions in the absence of evidence.

Appeal to Ignorance the logical fallacy that since no one can disprove the existence of a phenomenon, therefore that phenomenon exists.

Appeal to Mockery logical fallacy involving the substitution of ridicule in the place of evidence.

Appeal to Popularity (*argumentum ad populum*) logical fallacy that holds that since a lot of people agree with position A, then position A is true.

Applied Anthropology sometimes called the fifth subfield of the discipline, it entails the practical application of anthropological theories and knowledge from all the subfields of the discipline toward identifying and solving social problems in indigenous communities.

Argument from Ignorance (*argumentum ad ignorantiam*) absence of proof is taken as proof. No one can prove that the premise is false therefore it is true.

Archaeology or anthropological archaeology, the scientific study and reconstruction of recently extant and extinct cultures through the examination and interpretation of material remains and artifacts.

Archaeological Record the totality of scientific archaeological data about the nature and the evolution of sociocultural systems through time and space.

Armchair Anthropology pejorative term to refer to research based on data gleaned from travelogues, written accounts by missionaries, government officials, and other secondary sources; also, research without firsthand ethnographic fieldwork.

Artifact anything fashioned or altered by deliberate human action; also material traces of human behavior.

Asiatic Mode of Production Karl Marx's (1818–1883) concept exemplified by the precolonial social formations of India, Peru, and Mexico. In the Asiatic mode, the landing-holding village commune, partially organized on the basis of kinship, is the independent, self-sufficient unit of food and crafts production. The village commune is integrated into a wider political system governed by a king, to whom the village turns over its surplus production in the form of tribute. Asiatic mode of production follows an evolutionary trajectory different than those in Europe in which this mode of production is not replaced by a feudal mode but is instead undermined by capitalist modes of production.

Avunculate the relationship between ego and his mother's brother.

Avunculocality a postmarital residence rule stipulating that a married couple will reside with the groom's mother's brother.

Band an aggregated of twenty-five to fifty hunter-gatherers who camp together and jointly undertake socioeconomic activities. One of four culture types, the other three being tribe, chiefdom, and state.

Baraka in Islam, meaning inherent supernatural power, holiness, or blessing similar to the Polynesian concept of **Mana.**

Basic Law of Cultural Evolution   Leslie White's (1900–1975) premise that culture evolves, "as the amount of energy harnessed per capita per year is increased," represented by the formula $E \times T = C$, in which E stands for energy, T for the efficiency of technology, and C is culture.

Begging the Question   the logical fallacy that entails circular reasoning, in which the conclusion is already present in the premise. For example, the postmodernists' assertion "science is degraded because it is."

Beringia   a now submerged land bridge that linked Siberia and Alaska, which was exposed when sea levels dropped as a result of Pleistocene glaciations. The first American came to the northern hemisphere from Siberia by crossing Beringia.

Bilocality   a pattern of **Postmarital Residence** in which the couple lives with/near either the parents of the bride or the groom.

Binary Oppositions   double pairs of mutually exclusive, but complementary symbols. In Lévi-Strauss's view the human mind is structured and operates on the principle of binary oppositions (up-down, right-left, good/evil, light/dark, etc.).

Biological Determinism   the view that biology or race determines culture/behavior.

Boasian   pertaining to the research perspective established by Franz Boas (1858–1942).

Broad Spectrum Revolution   the incorporation of a wide range of previously untapped food resources by human populations in the Old World during the end of the Pleistocene.

Bullroar   small flat piece of decorated wood that makes a distinctive roaring sound when attached to a string and rapidly whirled around.

Cambridge School   early twentieth-century school of British social anthropologists known for the genealogical method of field investigation. Prominent members of this school included William H. R. Rivers (1864–1922) and Alfred C. Haddon (1855–1940). See also **Torres Straits Expedition.**

Capitalism   the political economy in which natural resources and the means of production are privately owned, wherein workers sell their labor in the wage market to make a living, and products are distributed within a market system. Production, distribution, and consumption are embedded in relationships of power.

Capitalist Mode of Production   system of production based upon wage labor in which the object of production is to acquire capital.

Capitalist World–Economic System   the global economic system that emerged during the period between 1450 to 1640, coinciding with European geographical expansions. The system went through several phases of development. From 1640 to 1760, it underwent a second phase of transformation, which may be characterized as a time of consolidation and solidification. The third phase, 1760 to 1917, coincided with mechanization (**Industrial Revolution**) and major global expansion of capitalism, which has defined many of the characteristics and dynamics of the capitalist world-economic system today, with its core- semiperiphery-periphery structure. Finally, the period from 1917 to present, the latest phase, has been one of "deepening" capitalist relations.

Carrying Capacity   the maximum number of people that can be supported in a given environment using a given technology without causing environmental degradation.

Cartesian   term referring to perspectives based upon the rationalist philosophy of René Descartes (1596–1650).

Cephalic Index   nineteenth-century formula referring to the ratio of the length and breadth of the head, which was thought to be a genetically determined indicator of intelligence.

Chiefdom   a type of sociopolitical organization that is intermediate between state-level and tribal societies, characterized by ranking and political integration based upon the centralized authority of a full-time ruler or chief. Chiefdoms possess a redistributive economy and a large sedentary population.

Churinga   among Australian aborigines, an elliptical object made of wood or stone covered with designs and symbols of supernatural significance.

Circular Reasoning   a type of reasoning in which X is employed to support Y and then Y is used to support X.

Civitas   Lewis Henry Morgan's (1818–1881) term for property-based societies.

Civilization   politically centralized, complex societies, with class differentiation, occupational specialization, monumental architecture, and standing armies. Also **State-Level Societies.**

Clan (sib)   a kin group whose members claim descent from a common ancestor but cannot specify all the linkages genealogically.

Class   one of several social strata whose members share similar socioeconomic characteristics and positions, usually defined in terms of differential access to the **Means of Production.**

Class Consciousness   the comprehension by a social class of its position and interests in society and its capacity to act with respect to those interests.

Classical Induction   a form of reasoning in which general conclusions are drawn from specific facts, or conclusions from the specific to the general. The central parameter for scientific knowledge, according to this view, is that all scientific propositions must be reducible to facts and that this method provides absolute truths. Classical induction is associated with Francis Bacon (1561–1626) and exemplified in modern times by the perspective of Franz Boas (1858–1942).

Classificatory Kinship Terminology   a system of kin reckoning in which members of an **Ego**'s nuclear family (lineal relatives) are classified along with more distant collateral kinfolk in each generation. An example of this form of kinship is the Iroquois system. The Iroquois child refers to his mother's sister with the term glossed as "mother," his father's brother as "father," mother's sister's sons and daughters are called by the same terms as brothers and sisters, and father's brothers sons and daughters are referred to as brother and sister. Mother's brother's sons and daughters and father's sister's sons and daughters are called cousins.

Cognitive Anthropology   theoretical perspective that developed out of anthropological studies of semantic domains and folk taxonomies, which focuses upon the relationship between culture and cognition.

Collective Consciousness   an idea espoused by the French sociologist Émile Durkheim (1858–1917), meaning shared thoughts and sentiments held by members of a group that appear as an ideological force that exists outside the individual members of society but which exercise a determinative influence upon their thoughts and behavior.

Colonialism   policy of nations striving to establish long-term socioeconomic, political, and military domination over other people and their lands, which includes the installation of administrative outposts and enclaves of their own citizens in the territories under control.

Communitas   Victor Turner's word for the condition of equality and solidarity that characterizes the relationships of individuals in the context of rituals.

Comparative Method   procedure for the analysis of classes of phenomena in search for causes of similarities and differences. Modern anthropologists employ the comparative method in two ways, conducting controlled comparisons and statistical cross-cultural comparisons. See **Cross-Cultural Comparison.**

Componential Analysis   method used to assemble and analyze folk taxonomies and ethnosemantic domains in cognitive anthropology.

Condensation   Victor Turner's idea that certain symbols are loaded with multiple and disparate meanings and can concurrently represent many ideas, relationships, and meanings.

Configurationalism   the investigation of unconscious underlying psychological patterns or configuarations that account for observable cultural patterns. Associated with the work of Ruth Benedict (1887–1948) and Edward Sapir (1884–1934).

Confusing Cause and Effect   logical fallacy in which a conclusion is reached without justification that variable A is the cause of variable B, because A and B occur together.

Consanguinity   "blood relationships," referring to kinship connections based upon descent in contrast to those based upon marriage. Contrasts with **Affinity.**

Consultant   see **Informant.**

Convergent Evolution   similar adaptations by distinct and unrelated cultures to similar environments.

Cosmology   beliefs pertaining to the nature of the world, universe, and the place of people in them.

Cosmogony   beliefs regarding the origins of the world/universe and everything in them.

Couvade   the phenomena in which a man simulates the pains of childbirth while his wife is in labor.

Covariations   relationships between related variables that vary concurrently.

Craniometry   the technique used to determine **Cephalix Index,** the ratio of the length and breadth of the head, which was thought to be a genetically determined indicator of intelligence.

Creation Myths   religiously validated cultural narratives dealing with the creation of people, the world, the universe, and everything in it.

Critical Theory   a neo-Marxist theoretical/advocacy perspective concerned with issues of emancipation and the construction of a truly democratic society. Associated with the **Frankfurt School.**

Cross-Cultural Comparison   approach in which conclusions about the operation of sociocultural systems are based upon the comparison of cultures around the world.

Cross-Cousin Marriage   marriage between **Ego** and the offspring of parental siblings of the opposite sex (i.e., children of ego's mother's brother and father's sister).

Culture   sets of learned and shared attitudes, beliefs, and values characteristic of a particular society.

Culture Area   a geographic location occupied by populations with similar characteristics, such as language, subsistence strategies, patterns of social organization, and artistic traditions.

Culture Climax   geographical location in which a culture type is expressed with the greatest intensity.

Culture Complex   or trait complex, a cluster of interlocked traits, such as beliefs, practices, and arrangements associated with, for example, **Totemism,** or a system of matrilineal descent.

Culture Core   Julian Steward's (1902–1972) concept referring to practices and institutional arrangements linked directly to the exploitation of the environment.

Culture and Personality   perspective pioneered by Ruth Benedict, which focuses on the relationship between culture and personality traits and draws upon Freudian psychology and learning psychology; or, field of anthropology concerned with the cross-cultural variations in personality characteristics and psychological traits.

Culture as Text   perspective viewing culture as made up of symbols in the form of words, writing, pictures, gestures, objects that embody meaning that the anthropologist can interpret.

Culture Type   Julian Steward's concept referring to societies with similar social structure, kinship, religion, etc., based on similarities in their **Culture Core.** Culture types include **Band, Tribe, Chiefdom,** and **State.**

Cultural Anthropology   the subfield of American anthropology that entails the first-hand scientific study and comparison of contemporary or recently extant human populations/societies.

Cultural Construction of Reality   based on the ultraidealist doctrine that "thought and reality are in actuality one and the same," that something becomes real only when it is assigned meaning because things do not exists apart from "the discourse that constitutes them." The idea of cultural construction of reality is the basis of the postmodernists' evocation of **Radical Plurality of Cultures** and ideas of **Multiple Realities** and **Multiple Truths.**

Cultural Critique   a political enterprise in which ethnographic knowledge is harnessed to criticize the received values of the anthropologist's own culture. Associated with anthropology as advocacy perspectives.

Cultural Determinism   the idea that culture comes from culture and its corollary, that culture can only be explained in terms of culture. A key element of Boasian anthropology and its present-day offshoots, such as interpretive anthropology.

Cultural Ecology   anthropological approach established by Julian Steward focusing upon the effects of the environment on labor patterns and their effects on the organization of other aspects of the culture.

Cultural Evolutionism   perspectives that seek to understand sociocultural similarities and differences in terms of the process of adaptation through time. There are two varieties of distinct evolutionary theories, the defunct nineteenth-century schemes and modern evolutionary/materialist/ecological perspectives.

Cultural Materialism   scientific anthropological research strategy that attempts to account for cross-cultural similarities and differences by focusing upon the material constraints upon human activity, such as the mode of production, the mode of reproduction, and ecological factors.

Cultural Relativism   the attitude or axiom that each culture must be evaluated in its own terms, and not in terms of the standards and values of the anthropologist's own society.

Cultural Universals   the set of shared human behavioral characteristics found in all cultures.

Culturology   Leslie White's (1900–1975) term for the scientific or nomothetic study of culture as a phenomenon in its own right.

Data   pertinent observations that form the basis for scientific research.

Deceptive Emotive Emphasis   logical fallacy which entails the use of words to convey feelings intended to emotionally sway an audience.

Deconstruction   the postmodernists' procedure of uncloaking hidden rhetorical devices, culturally entrenched metaphors, metaphysical assumptions, values, and hidden meanings that exist within texts.

Deduction   logical reasoning from the general to the particular, or reasoning which starts with a proposition and stipulates the consequences that follow from that proposition.

Deep Structure   Noam Chomsky's term for patterns of meaning intrinsic to the mind of the speaker.

Degenerationism   nineteenth-century theological perspective on the evolution of culture, which held that humans were created in a high state of morality and civilization and that the primitive savages around the world were merely the "outcasts of the human race," degenerates who had fallen from a state of "grace." Contrasts with **Progressionism.**

Demography   the statistical study of the characteristics of populations, such as size, density, sex and age ratios, and rates of fertility and mortality.

Dependent Variable   an element the value or behavior of which is affected by another variable.

Descent Group   a social unit the members of which claim descent from a common ancestor.

Descriptive Kinship Terminology System   a system of kin reckoning, such as that in English, in which collateral and lineal kin are kept separate.

Determinism   simple causality explanations (e.g., environmental, technological, biological).

Diachronic   pertaining to changes in cultural elements through time.

Dialectics   for Georg Wilhelm Friedrich Hegel (1770–1831), the rational cognitive progression, moving from perceptible information to ideas, arriving at the immutable principle or idea in sequential stages of thesis-antithesis-synthesis.

Dialectical Materialism   theoretical perspective associated with Karl Marx (1818–1883) and Friedrich Engels (1820–1895) in which social transformations are construed as being the result of inherent internal contradictions and conflicts arising out of opposing interests in sociocultural systems.

Dialogic Accounts   texts that represent the encounter between the ethnographer and the native informant, or ethnographic Other, in the form of a dialogue, with the voices of the Other given priority.

Diffusion   the distribution and spread of traits from one culture to another as a result of contact, imitation, or migration.

Diffusionism   theoretical perspective that places central importance upon to the transmission of traits between cultures as the mechanism of cultural evolution and culture change.

Diminishing Returns   in food production the point at which increase in effort is coupled with decrease in output.

Dionysian   a term used by Ruth Benedict, meaning highly competitive, individualistic, excessive, to refer the personality traits of the Kwakiutl.

Discourse   postmodernist jargon term meaning speech/talk embedded in power and through which knowledge is created and maintained.

Dogon   a people living in the territory south of the ancient city of Timbuktu, on the southern edge of the Sahara Desert, in Mali (former French Sudan), West Africa. The Dogon Sirius myth has been the subject of pseudoscientific claims regarding extraterrestrial visitations.

Dreamtime   or "dreaming," the spiritual worldview of Australian aborigines that all at once encompasses different human groups, human ancestors, plant and animal species, and the physical landscape, in the past, present, and future, whose relationships and interactions are symbolically defined.

Dreamtime Paths   aboriginal concept, sometimes also called "song lines," which refers to the routes taken by the totemic beings as they dotted the landscape with sacred sites.

Dysfunction   traits that are maladaptive or disrupt system equilibrium.

Ecology   the field of study pertaining to the interactions between animal and plant populations in the context of their habitat.

Ecological Anthropology   a theoretical perspective that treats human populations as components of ecosystems along with plant/animal populations and their interactions within a given habitat. The branch of sociocultural anthropology that focuses upon subsistence strategies, production, ownership, and the distribution of goods and services and the manner in which these activities affect the sociocultural system within the context of ecological, demographic, and cultural frameworks.

Ecological Niche   aspects of the particular environmental context to which an organism is adapted that both presents problems and possibilities for survival.

Ecosystem   the energy/material cycles that link living and nonliving components (biological communities and the physical environment in which they are found) within a system.

Egalitarian   societies characterized by near absence of private property, and lack of distinctions in power, privilege, and status among individuals. In such societies everyone has equal access to productive resources necessary for subsistence.

Ego   "I" from Latin, a term used to indicate the individual who is the focal point of a genealogy.

Emic Analysis   based upon rules, concepts, and categories meaningful to members of a particular culture. Contrasts with **Etic Analysis.**

Empiricism   the epistemological perspective that knowledge must be based upon experience or sensory data rather than reflection or imaginative speculation.

Enculturation   process by means of which cultural traditions are transmitted from one generation to the next.

Endogamy   marriage between individuals from the same social group (e.g., clan, class, caste). Contrasts with **Exogamy.**

Energy   the ability to do work.

Enlightenment   the historical period in Europe between the latter part of the seventeenth century to the end of the eighteenth century associated with significant scientific and philosophical developments.

Environmental Determinism   or environmentalism, the simplistic view that sociocultural phenomena are determined in a mechanistic way by the natural habitat.

Episteme   postmodern jargon term referring to the worldview of an age. Western *episteme* refers to the worldview associated with modernity, based upon Enlightenment philosophy centered upon science, reason, and logic.

Epistemology   the study of how we know what we know, or the study of the nature, sources, and limits of human knowledge.

Epistemological Relativism   the doctrine that all knowledge is relative, context dependent, situated, and culturally constructed.

Eskimo Kinship Terminology   a system of bilateral kinship in which the words referring to mother, father, brother, and sister are not applied to any relatives outside the nuclear family. Euro-Americans in the United States use this system.

Essentialism   the propensity to reify ideas and concepts as if they represent the essence or inherent qualities of the things to which they refer.

Ethnoscience   anthropological perspective aimed at describing cultures from the native's point of view. See **Cognitive Anthropology.**

Ethnosemantics   the study of lexical categories and their contrasts within domains, or the investigation of indigenous systems of classification.

Etic Analysis   based upon rules, concepts, and categories meaningful to the outsider observers' (scientific) point of view, contrasts with the insider's or **Emic Analysis.**

Ethnical Periods   stages of evolutionary development in nineteenth-century evolutionary schemes: savagery, barbarism, and civilization.

Ethnocentrism   value judgments rendered about other peoples/cultures on the basis of a belief in the superiority of one's own cultural standards and way of life.

Ethnocide   the deliberate destruction of a people's way of life, language, and sociocultural traditions.

Ethnographic Realism   postmodern pejorative jargon term referring to the assumption by traditional ethnographers that objective accounts of other cultures are possible and that ethnographic accounts represent something real in the world.

Ethnographic Record   the sum total of scientific information gathered by anthropologists.

Ethnography   systematic description of a particular people/culture through fieldwork. The word denotes the research process and the end product of that research, which is usually in the form of a written monograph.

Ethnography as Fiction   postmodern interpretivist jargon term applied to ethnographic writing. Used by Geertz, who maintains that anthropological writings "are fictions," things "made up," or "fashioned," or "merely 'as if' thought experiments." The postmodern interpretivists' usage of the term verges upon the definition of the word as false or unfactual. All ethnographic accounts are treated as fictions by interpretivists.

Ethnology   refers to the systematic comparison of cultures around the globe in order to answer particular questions and produce useful generalizations about humankind and human behavior.

Ethnosemantics   the investigation of indigenous systems of classification.

Equivocation   the logical fallacy that entails using the same term or concept in several different senses in the context of a single argument.

Exchange Value   from Marxist theory, the production of commodities for their exchange value in the market, in order to generate a profit and accumulate capital. See **Use Value.**

Exogamy   the practice of seeking marriage partners outside one's own local kin or status group. Contrasts with **Endogamy.**

Explanation   general abstract propositions (theories) and specific propositions (hypotheses) that represent how and why reality is constituted in the manner that it is constituted.

Explanatory   nomothetic perspectives that seek to specify general principles regarding classes of phenomena; perspectives that seek to identify general mechanisms in operation. Contrasts with **Explicatory.**

Explicatory   idiographic interpretive perspectives which strive to understand particular cases by placing them in their own unique contexts. Contrasts with **Explanatory.**

Externalism   a view of epistemic evaluation based upon the idea that we live in an external world/universe that exists independently of the beliefs people have about them and that these external conditions comprise the conditions of knowledge. Contrasts with **Internalism.**

Facts   confirmed observations (i.e., experiences of what occurs or has occurred).

Fallacy of Composition   logical error based on the view that what is true of the parts is true of the whole as well.

False Consciousness   premise by Marx and Engels, referring to the power of superordinate classes to distort people's consciousness, preventing them from becoming aware of the actual material conditions of their existence. Or, the symbolic manipulation by the ruling class of dominated classes in order to prevent them from becoming aware of the exploitative conditions under which they live.

Falsification   refutation of theories on the basis of experimentation or empirical observations.

Feedback   a form of causality in which the effects of an initial cause in return affect and modify or reinforce the initial cause. See **Positive Feedback** and **Negative Feedback.**

Fertile Crescent   an area encompassing Jordan, Syria, Iraq, part of Iran and Turkey, where the first farming communities appeared.

Fetishism   treating an object as if it embodies mysterious forces within it, or treating it as if it is a representation or the actual abode of a deity; giving something excessive adoration.

Feudalism   agrarian societies consisting of several stratified sociopolitical units integrated on the basis of a network of obligations under the authority of a higher ruling entity.

Fiction   see **Ethnography as Fiction.**

Fictive Kinship   extension of kin terms and associated attitudes to individuals who are not relatives either by descent or marriage.

Fieldwork   the main technique used by anthropologists for studying sociocultural phenomena.

Fission-Fusion   or flux, part of the adaptive strategy of hunting gathering bands in which group size and composition change with seasonal fluctuations in the availability of water and other resources, with a larger population breaking down into smaller units and later recombining.

Folk Knowledge   common knowledge, the "insider's point of view," the "native's voice,"

"the local frame of reference," culturally specific "theories" and "understandings" (mystical, poetic, intuitive, allegorical) about the way things "really are" that account for and explain human life, the world, universe, and everything in it.

Folk Taxonomy   hierarchically organized cognitive categories by means of which members of a culture classify objects.

Folklore   culturally specific, orally transmitted genres of narratives.

Foraging Societies   societies organized in bands of twenty-five to forty-five individuals whose mode of subsistence is based upon the collection of wild plants species and the hunting of animals. Also referred to as **Hunter-Gatherer Societies.**

Forces of Production   Marx's term for techno-economic factors, such as raw materials, tools, machinery, and other productive technologies.

Formalists   economic anthropologists subscribing to the view that all economies possess common abstract properties and therefore the concepts and principles of neoclassical economics applicable to Western market economies are pertinent as well to the study of non-Western economic systems. See **Formalist-Substantivist Debate.**

Formalist-Substantivist Debate   controversy over the difference between capitalist and noncapitalist economic systems and the appropriateness of neoclassical economic theory for the study of noncapitalist economies.

Fossil   the mineralized remains of ancient animals and plants.

Frankfurt School   an assemblage of theorists from a number of disciplines associated with the Institut für Sozialforschung (Institute for Social Research) in Frankfurt, Germany (refounded in New York as the New School for Social Research), who are the expositors of "critical theory," a neo-Marxist perspective geared toward emancipation, and the construction of a truly democratic society. Among the well-known Frankfurt theorists are Theodor W. Adorno (1903–1969), Max Horkheimer (1895–1973), Herbert Marcuse (1898–1979), Walter Benjamin (1892–1940), Erich Fromm (1900–1980), and Jürgen Habermas (b. 1929). During the 1980s, Habermas offered stout criticisms of postmodernism and its irrational and nihilistic social theories.

Functional Unity the premise that cultures are integrated wholes made up of many interrelated elements, in which changes in one element produces changes in other elements.

Functionalism theoretical approaches focusing upon the functions of institutions to fulfill individual biopsychological needs or ensure the maintenance and persistence of the social system. Also, label for the theoretical perspective developed by the British social anthropologist Bronislaw Malinowski (1884–1942).

Functionalist Fallacy the assertion that the reason for the existence of a cultural item is the function that it fulfills.

Gene Pool the totality of all the alleles in a breeding population.

Genetic Load the deleterious genes in a population's gene pool.

Genealogy an individual's conception of his/her ancestry.

Genealogical Method W. H. R. Rivers's (1864–1922) technique for collecting and organizing genealogical data that focused upon the social correlates of genealogical links and the taxonomical organization of kinship terms in order to determine the nature of kinship systems in descent based societies.

Generalized Exchange in Claude Lévi-Strauss's (b. 1908) work, exchange of women among several kinship groups that reinforces social bonds, in which, for example, men from group A marry women from group B, men of group B always take wives from group C, and men of group C always marry women from group A.

Genetic Fallacy the logical fallacy that the origins of a perspective is evidence for refuting that perspective.

Genocide the deliberate physical extermination of a people.

Genotype the actual genetic constitution of an organism. Contrasts with **Phenotype.**

Gens (singular, plural = **Gentes**) Morgan's term for a patrilineal clan, a group of consanguinally related individuals descended from a common ancestor.

Gestalt a term meaning patterned configuration. In psychology, the perspective that cultural elements must be understood in their social and experiential contexts.

Ghost Dance a nineteenth-century Native American revitalization movement.

Great Man Theory of History the view that the course and direction of human history has been shaped by the fortuitous appearance of individual geniuses.

Grue Paul Kay's term designating the blue-green wavelength of the color spectrum for which English does not have an equivalent term.

Hawaiian Kinship Terminology System a system of kinship reckoning in which all the members of the same sex and generation are referred to by the same term.

Hegemony the imposition of beliefs by one social group upon another leading to the acceptance and internalization of the values of the ruling class by the subordinates as part of the nature of things. A concept forwarded by the Italian Marxist Antonio Gramsci (1891–1937) elaborating upon Marx's idea of **False Consciousness.**

Heliocentric School extreme diffusionist perspective associated with Grafton Elliot Smith (1871–1937), which attributed the rise of world civilizations to an Egyptian cultural complex based upon sun worship.

Hermeneutic   from Greek for "interpretive," refers to the interpretation of culture treated as a literary text, linked to symbolic and interpretive anthropology. Also, understanding and classifying the meaning of human phenomena, acts, discourse, and institutions through sympathetic identification.

Heuristic   a concept that may be meaningless in itself, but which is useful in promoting or stimulating understanding, as in a mathematical model that can help us comprehend natural phenomena, but which itself is restricted and artificial in nature.

Heuristic Theory   abstract model that serves as a guide for the conduct of research.

Historical Particularism   the anti-scientific relativistic, idiographic anthropological perspective associated with Franz Boas, which stressed the uniqueness of each culture thought to be the outcome of chance historical developments.

Holistic   the comprehensive approach used by anthropologists to study humans in which all aspects of life, biological and cultural, are considered important in understanding human behavior and sociocultural evolution.

Homeostasis   the process by which systems maintain equilibrium.

Hominid   member of the Hominidae family that includes ancient and modern humans.

Homo sapiens   modern humans.

Horde   a defunct term used to describe the local groupings among Australian aborigines.

Human Relations Area Files (HRAF) anthropological data-retrieval system founded in 1949 at Yale University, in New Haven, Connecticut, which is employed to test hypotheses cross-culturally.

Human Variation   a subfield of physical anthropology that entails the study of biological and genetic variations in contemporary human populations around the world and the significance of these variations.

Humanism (Humanistic)   subjective, intuitive, idiosyncratic approach/epistemological orientation that focuses upon human interests, values, aesthetics, ethics, perceptions, and experiences and their interpretation.

Hunter–Gatherers   societies whose mode of production depends upon the collecting of wild plants and hunting of game animals. See **Foragers.**

Hydraulic States   nonindustrial states based on intensive irrigation agriculture, such as ancient Mesopotamia, Egypt, Peru, and Mesoamerica.

Hypothesis   a testable proposition about a set of expectations derived from a theory that should be found in the real world if the theory is valid.

Hypothesis Testing   determining if the expectations about phenomena suggested by the hypothesis are true in the real world.

Idealism   the perspective that systems of meaning or ideas are the basis of social forms.

Ideology   a systematic set of supernatural, religious, or political beliefs that legitimize the political and economic interests of the group or class subscribing to it.

Idiographic   a perspective focusing on the particular and the specific. Contrasts with **Nomothetic.**

Imperialism   the policy of creating and maintaining an empire through the political/military subjugation and domination of other nations/peoples and the appropriation and control of their territories and strategic resources.

Inbreeding Theories   perspectives that link the adoption of the incest taboo to the harmful genetic consequences of mating between closely related individuals.

Incest   sexual relationships among relatives with whom such relationships are forbidden by cultural rules or law.

Incest Taboo rule found in all cultures prohibiting mating or marriage between particular categories of relatives.

Incommensurability of Cultures related to the postmodernists' idea of the **Radical Plurality of Cultures** and the radical otherness of **the Other,** this view holds that cultures are unique, possess no points of commonality, they are therefore incommensurable, and cross-cultural translations are ultimately impossible.

Independent Invention nineteenth-century evolutionary concept relating to the development of similar cultural innovations due to the **Psychic Unity of Mankind,** as opposed to diffused traits.

Independent Variable a causal factor the value of which changes the values of dependent variables.

Indigenous original/native inhabitants of a region, country, or continent.

Inductive Method inference of propositions on the basis of specific observations.

Industrial Revolution the development of industrialized economy in Europe after 1750 involving a shift from farming to the production of industrial goods, the factory system, and urbanization.

Informant or "consultant," individual who provides information to the anthropologist conducting field research.

Infrastructure in cultural materialism, the mode of production and mode of reproduction that exert causal influence on sociocultural systems. In Marx's model of sociocultural systems, infrastructure refers to the techno-economic base.

Infrastructural Determinism or "primacy of infrastructure," the cultural materialist premise that the infrastructure exerts primary causal effects upon the structure and superstructure.

Inheritance of Acquired Characteristics Jean-Baptiste Lamarck's (1744–1892) theory that species evolve and changed through time as a result of adjustments to the effects of the environment in which they lived, and that the characteristics acquired in life by parents could be passed on to the next generation.

Intensification putting more people to work, doing the same thing, harder and for much longer periods relying on existing technologies and making more intensive use of existing resources.

Internalism a view of epistemic evaluation based on the axiom that reflection alone can tell us whether our beliefs are justified. Contrasts with **Externalism.**

Interpretive Anthropology the anthropological perspective associated with Clifford Geertz.

Intersubjectivity consensus between observers regarding the characteristics of a phenomenon under observation.

Inuit the term used by the Eskimo (now considered a pejorative term, like "Bushman" or "Abo") to refer to themselves.

Inversions Lévi-Strauss's concept referring to changes or "inversion" in the elements of myths, such as main protagonist's gender, or appearance, in the process of **Transformations.**

Iroquois Kinship Terminology System See **Classificatory Kinship Terminology.**

Irrigation (Hydraulic) Hypothesis a perspective stressing the role of large-scale canal construction/maintenance in the rise of the state, espoused by historian/sinologist Karl Wittfogel (1896–1988) and Julian Steward. See **Hydraulic States.**

Jargon highly specialized terminology associated with specific professions; specialized words used to mislead by overcomplicating issues.

Joking Relationship an institutionalized behavior of privileged familiarity between categories of relatives.

Key Informant   a knowledgeable member of a culture who provides the ethnographer with specialist data.

Kinship Terminology Systems   classifications of kin into labeled categories, or sets of terms used to designate genealogical connections between individuals.

Kula   Trobriand economic institution based upon trade partnerships that involves the circulation of ceremonial objects and other goods along a circular route linking numerous islands. The Kula is described in Bronislaw Malinowski's classic monograph *Argonauts of the Western Pacific* (1922).

Kulturkreis   meaning "culture circle," point of diffusion of traits, a central concept of the German Cultural Historical School associated with Fredrick Ratzel (1844–1904), Fritz Graebner (1877–1934), and Father Wilhelm Schmidt (1868–1954).

Kuru   a degenerative viral brain disease found among the Fore in the highlands of New Guinea thought to be transmitted through the consumption of brain tissue during mortuary rituals.

Large-Scale Societies   highly differentiated, complex societies that rely upon a broad and specialized system of exchange of commodities, ideas, and personnel.

Latent Functions   the underlying function or effect of a cultural institution or custom that is not perceived by members of the culture itself.

Least Plausible Hypothesis   the logical fallacy in which a probable scenario is discarded in favor of an improbable one.

Levels of Sociocultural Integration   Julian Steward's concept meaning the largest social grouping in a culture that can undertake collective action. Steward proposed family, tribe, and state. In current usage: **Band, Tribe, Chiefdom,** and **State.**

Lexemes   the labeled items within a semantic domain.

Lexicon   vocabulary.

Life Histories   details of the life of particular individuals as a cultural profile of their experiences related from their point of view. An ethnographic perspective developed by Boasian anthropologists.

Liminality   Victor Turner's word for limbo or statuslessness, when individuals are "betwixt and between all recognized fixed points in space-time of structural classification," or the period during which a person has left one status but has not entered another one.

Lineage   a group that traces descent unilineally to a common ancestor through known links.

Lineal relatives   relatives who are the direct descendants of ego's ancestor.

Linguistic Anthropology   subfield of anthropology dealing with the description of the structure of language, the relationship between languages, how languages change through time, and the relationship between language and culture.

Linguistic Relativity   the view that holds that language and culture are interrelated and that people's thoughts and perceptions of reality are powerfully influenced by the language they speak. See also **Sapir-Whorf Hypothesis.**

Logic   the study of valid reasoning that can tell us whether a conclusion is justified by its premises. Science is based upon formal rules of logic.

Logocentrism   postmodern jargon term referring to the concern in Western philosophy with logic and reason, inherited from classical Greece.

Lysenkoism   the bogus science of genetics developed in the Soviet Union by Trofim D. Lysenko (1898–1976).

Malthusian Theory   the proposition formulated by Thomas Malthus (1766–1834) that human populations increase faster than the rate of food production, resulting in shortages and starvation.

Mana   a Malayo-Polynesian word referring to a belief in the existence of a supernatural force found in particular objects and individuals that produces good luck, fortune, and health.

Manifest Functions   "official" explanations of the direct or obvious functions of cultural elements or institutions, as provided by members of the culture.

Market Exchange   refers to exchange based upon all-purpose money geared towards individual motives for profit and accumulation of wealth.

Master Discourse   postmodernists' jargon term for a form of knowledge believed to be universally valid and applicable to all cases. For example, science is construed as the master discourse of Western culture.

Material Forces of Production   in Marxist theory, meaning the objects and material instruments, machinery, tools, raw materials, arable land, and so on used in the process of production.

Materialism   the philosophical perspective based upon a material (physicalist) ontology in which causality is attributed to the physical properties of things, whether molecules, bacteria, brains, or cultures. It is associated with the view that all things can be explained in terms of their material attributes.

Matrilineal Descent   reckoning descent through female lines, which defines group membership and inheritance rights.

Matrilocal Residence   postmarital residence rule in which the groom lives with the bride's parents.

Mead-Freeman Controversy   a debate generated by the discrepancies between Margaret Mead's (1901–1978) ethnographic work in Samoa and findings by the Australian anthropologist Derek Freeman (1916–2001). This case, which antiscience critics have harnessed to their own cause, illustrates the ex-

tent to which anthropological accounts may be influenced by ideological and theoretical biases of individual fieldworkers.

Means of Production   Marxist term referring to the tools and technological information employed in the process of production.

Mechanical Materialism   see **Vulgar Materialism.**

Mendel, Gregor (1822–1884)   nineteenth-century Austrian Augustinian monk whose systematic experiments with garden peas led to the discovery of the basic laws of heredity. His findings were published in 1866, but their significance remained unacknowledged until the paper was re-discovered in 1900. The merger of Mendelian genetics and Darwinian natural selection in the 1930s and 1940s led to the development of the **Synthetic Theory of Evolution.**

Mesoamerica   the zone encompassing the territories of the Aztec and Mayan cultures in Central America.

Mesopotamia   the area which now makes up Jordan, Syria, and Iraq, also called **Near East,** where the first agricultural communities appeared. See also **Fertile Crescent.**

Mesolithic   "Middle Stone Age," a stage of Old World prehistory characterized by a diversification in subsistence strategies.

Metanarratives   See **Totalizing Metanarratives.**

Metaphor   expressions or figures of speech pertaining to one domain of experience applied to another domain. Called **Trope** in postmodern jargon.

Metaphysics   perspectives that strive to explain the world, universe and everything in them in terms of supernatural/nonmaterial principles (e.g., God/the gods/intelligent design).

Modal Personality   the central tendency of the personality traits characteristic of a society.

Mode of Production   Marx's concept referring to the manner in which techno-economic factors (forces of production) are organized in the context of the social relations established between those who control the means of production and producers in the process of work (relations of production).

Mode of Reproduction   practices and technologies that affect population size.

Model   a hypothetical description of reality based on an analogy, which facilitates analysis and explanation.

Moieties   from the French word *moitié* for "half," refers to descent groups comprising clans or phratries organized into two halves or social groups in which membership is based upon unilineal descent.

Monogenism   nineteenth-century view that all humans arose from a common stock and that the perceptible variations between contemporary human groups were due to environmental factors that had developed following a single act of creation. Associate with this perspective was the idea of the **Psychic Unity of Mankind,** namely that the human mind is the same everywhere.

Monumental   Architecture   large-scale public structures, such as pyramids, temples, and palaces constructed by means of a large-scale labor force at the disposal of central authorities in state-level societies.

Moral Career in Anthropology   a career strategy based upon gaining recognition for what one condemns.

Morpheme   smallest unit of meaning in speech.

Mortuary Rituals   rites associated with death and the disposal of the deceased's body.

Multiple Realities   postmodernist jargon term, an idea stemming from the position of **Epistemological Relativism** and the idea of the **Cultural Construction of Reality,** which holds that everything is culturally constructed, there are multiple realities, and

Multiple Truths, one as valid as the other, except for scientific truths.

Multiple   Truths   postmodernist jargon term based on the idea of **Multiple Realities,** which has become a charter for the notion of "anything goes" in the acquisition of knowledge, and the assertion that you have your truth and I have mine, each one is as valid as the next. This idea serves as the justification for rejecting empirical data and empirical verification.

Multilinear Evolution   theoretical view associated with Julian Steward in which evolutionary change is envisioned to occur along a number of pathways associated with particular environmental settings.

Multilocality   people with residence in one country and working in a different one.

Multiple Origin Theory   perspective on the evolution of modern humans and the relationships between modern and archaic *Homo sapiens.*

Multiple Outs   secondary rationalizations that explain away contradictions. It enables one to use the absence of evidence as evidence. Frequently employed in **Pseudoscience.** See also **Secondary Rationalizations.**

Multivocalic/Polyvocalic   something with multiple, open-ended, and ambiguous meanings.

Multivocality   Turner's term for the wide range of semantic meanings that characterize dominant symbols.

Mutation   the mechanism of evolutionary change due to a random transformation in the genetic code. Mutations in sex cells are the source of new alleles in a population's gene pool, and hence the basis of genetic variation.

Mysticism   the philosophical position that moral truths derive from contemplation. Also, the propensity toward things mysterious and obscure.

Mystification ideological practices that obscure the true nature of sociopolitical circumstances under a façade of commonsense reality.

Myth lore or narrative pertaining to the actions of supernatural beings and culture heroes relating to the creation of people, the world, universe, and everything in them.

Mythical Thought the term Lévi-Strauss uses to refer to the cognitive pattern underlying myth and magic wherein the logic of human thought is most apparent.

National Character Studies defunct approach focusing on personality characteristics thought to be shared by the people of a whole nation.

Natural Aversion Theory explanation for the incest taboo based on the premise that individuals raised together have a natural aversion towards sexual interactions (a phenomenon referred to as the **Westermarck Effect**) and that the incest taboo is a manifestation of this aversion.

Natural Selection the mechanism of biological evolution proposed by Charles Darwin. It refers to the process contributing to the survival and reproductive success of individuals/species in a given environment.

Near East the area which now makes up Jordan, Syria, and Iraq. Archaeological evidence indicates this area as the location of the first agricultural communities. See also **Fertile Crescent** and **Mesopotamia.**

Negative Feedback homeostatic processes operating to return system variables to initial values, or state of equilibrium. Contrasts with **Positive Feedback.** See also **Feedback.**

Neocolonialism exploitation of nonindustrial societies for labor and natural resources by indirect means, such as through multinational corporations.

Neoevolutionism label for the evolutionary perspective associated with Leslie White and his followers.

Neolithic John Lubbock/Lord Avebury's (1834–1913) term; a historical and evolutionary stage in the Old World associated with the transition from hunting gathering modes of subsistence to farming based upon the domestication of plant and animals and the introduction of polished stone tools around 10,000 years B.P.

Neolithic Revolution term first used by British archeologists V. Gordon Childe (1892–1957); refers to the development of agriculture and concomitant sociocultural transformations that took place in different places in the Old and New Worlds.

New Ethnography another name for Ethnoscience.

Newtonian related to Isaac Newton (1642–1727).

Nietzsche, Friedrich (1844–1900) an icon of the postmodern movement. Nietzsche was a highly influential German-Swiss philosopher. His important works include *The Birth of Tragedy* (1872), *Thus Spoke Zarathustra* (1883–1885), *Beyond Good and Evil* (1886), and *The Genealogy of Morals* (1887). He was deeply critical of Western religious and philosophical thought and morality. Among his most fervent admirers were Adolph Hitler and the Nazis, who idolized Nietzsche because of his distain for democracy and his notion of "will to power" and the moral relativism it entails. Mentally and emotionally disturbed for much of his life, Nietzsche became clinically insane before his death in 1900.

Nilhism nothingness, rejection of all doctrines, or the view that everything in the universe is transitory, impermanent, unreal.

Nomothetic approach geared toward producing generalizations or scientific laws. Contrasts with **Idiographic.**

Non Sequitur the logical error in which the conclusion does not follow from the premises.

Nuclear Incest sexual intercourse between any members of the nuclear family.

Objectivity   in science the requirements for objectively valid knowledge include (1) that propositions be validated in reference to publicly ascertainable evidence; (2) that statements must be testable/falsifiable by means of empirical evidence. There is also the addendum that all propositions that withstand this test are to be only provisionally accepted and are subject to review, modification, and even rejection. Science is a human enterprise and objectivity invariable means objectivity in relation to, and from the perspective of, human beings.

Objectified Thought   the term Lévi-Strauss uses to refer to the tangible manifestation of the underlying binary principles of the human mind in cultural products, such as myths, totemism, kinship systems, incest taboos, and cuisine.

Oceania   Pacific culture area consisting of Melanesia, Micronesia, Polynesia, and Australia.

Oedipus Complex   in psychoanalysis, the subconscious desires of a male child towards his mother and jealousy and hostility toward his father, associated with emotional conflicts and feelings of guilt. Called Electra complex in the case of daughters.

Ontology   premises about the nature of existence or the nature of reality.

Operationalizing   statement of the terms of a hypothesis/research procedure in such a manner that others are able to clearly understand those procedures and are able to apply the procedures themselves.

Organic Evolution   the process by which biological species adapt to their constantly changing environments.

Organic Analogy   the construal of cultural systems as organisms.

Orientalism   the stereotypical images and modes of analysis used by Europeans to describe or analyze the peoples and cultures of the Middle East and Asia.

Origin Myths   myths that deal with how humans or some aspect of the human condition originated.

Other   "The Other," or "the ethnographic Other," postmodern jargon terms used to refer to non-Western people emphasizing innate differences. It is linked to the idea of the radical plurality of cultures. The "otherness" of "the Other" and the notion of **Radical Plurality of Cultures** stem from the postmodernists' epistemological relativism, which holds that each culture produces a set of unique human characteristics and that human behavior and associated cognitive patterns are the product of each distinct culture, rather than "pan-human culture." Culture therefore produces an essential "otherness" or difference between humans. For this reason, postmodernists maintain that only those who have been enculturated in a particular cultural tradition can really understand it.

Overdetermination (Overdetermined)   a phenomenon having multiple causes.

Paleoanthropology   the scientific study of hominid fossil remains.

Paleolithic   also called the "Old Stone Age," earliest evolutionary stage in Old World prehistory, the interval between the appearance of **Oldowan** stone tools until roughly 10,000 B.P.

Paleoindians   the most ancient inhabitants of the Western Hemisphere.

Pan-Egyptian Theory   see **Heliocentric School.**

Pan-Human   pertaining to all humans, everywhere.

Paradigm   Thomas Kuhn's (1922–1996) concept for research strategy or intellectual framework that dominates and guides scientific inquiry during a particular time. See also **Research Strategy.**

Parallel Cousin   offspring of ego's mother's sister/father's brother.

Parallel Evolution   the development of similar adaptations by two or more sociocultural systems in response to similar causal forces.

Participant Observation   research technique developed during the course of the last century which involves the study of another culture over an extended time period during which anthropologists attempt to immerse themselves in the day-to-day activities of the group being studied so as to lessen the impact of their presence and to obtain a more in-depth view of the culture.

Pastoralism   a mode of subsistence and adaptive strategy based upon the herding of domestic livestock for food and necessary materials, found in Asia, Africa, and Europe, often in geographically marginal zones unsuitable for agriculture.

Patrilineal   tracing descent along the male line, which defines group membership and inheritance rights.

Patrimoieties   moieties with patrilineal descent.

Periphery   from **World Systems Theory,** the marginal areas in the global capitalist economy.

Personality   the totality of psychological traits, attitudes, values, and perceptions that account for the consistency of an individual's behavior.

Phenotype   the outward or observable appearance of an organism. Contrasts with **Genotype.**

Phoneme   basic unit of sound recognized as possessing a linguistic function.

Phratries   a group of clans or lineages whose members claim to be related, which forms a social unit for ritual and marriage purposes. In cases involving two clans, each is referred to as a **Moiety.**

Physical Anthropology   subfield of anthropology dealing with the scientific study of humans as a biological phenomena, the biological evolution of humans, their relationships with other primates, and the characteristics of present-day human populations.

Pleistocene Megafauna   extremely large animals, such as the woolly mammoth and other mammals, that vanished around the time of the last ice age circa 10,000 to 15,000 years ago.

Political Economy   a theoretical perspective building upon Marx's concept of "political economy," which stresses the role of political power, control, and authority in the organization of production, redistribution, and consumption, and an emphasis on the penetration of the global capitalist system into local systems.

Potlatch   redistributive feast by prestigious host involving ceremonial display and ostentatious gift-giving among the indigenous peoples of the Northwest Coast, such as the Kwakiutl.

Polygenism   nineteenth-century view that the different races of humankind arose as a consequence of separate acts of creation and each race belongs to a separate species.

Polyphony   multiple voices. See **Voices.**

Polytheism   belief in the existence of many gods. Contrasts with monotheism.

Popular Consensus   see **Folk Beliefs.**

Positivism   doctrine that scientific knowledge pertains only to empirical experience and is built up through the generation of propositional (testable) knowledge.

Possibilism   the view espoused by Boasian anthropologists that the environment sets limits upon what is possible but does not determine sociocultural phenomena. The concept was used to acknowledge the environment and at the same time justified the total disregard of environmental variables in the analysis of cultural phenomena.

Postmarital Residence Patterns   rules specifying where a new couple will reside after marriage (e.g., include patrilocality, matrilocality, avunculocality, and bilocality) that determine the nature of domestic units formed in a given society.

Positive Feedback   process that pushes the values of system variables beyond their initial condition, leading to disequilibrium or system change. Contrasts with **Negative Feedback.** See also **Feedback.**

Postmodern Anthropology   antiscience, subjective, literary perspective, which rejects the idea of universally valid objective knowledge and focuses upon culture as open-ended negotiated meanings and stresses the examination of how ethnographies are written.

Postmodernism   a style of architecture contrasted with "modern" architecture in being less geometric and functional and more fragmented, decentralized, eclectic, playful, extended to similar directions in the arts and humanities.

Prague School of Linguistics   a group of linguists associated with Nikolai Troubetzkoy (1890–1938) and Roman Jakobson (1896–1982) working in Prague in 1926.

Precapitalist Modes of Production   non-Western, small-scale economic systems based upon **Reciprocity** and **Redistribution** and embedded in institutions outside the market, such as kinship and personal ties. Precapitalist economic systems are dominated by production of items with **Use Value.**

Prelogical Thought   French philosopher Lucien Lévy-Bruhl's (1857–1939) construal of cognitive features of "primitive people," which is an analogue of the postmodernists' idea of the nonrational "ethnographic Other."

Primacy of Infrastructure   see **Infrastructural Determinism.**

Primitive   a pejorative term used during the nineteenth and early twentieth centuries to refer to people in small-scale societies, or aspects of the cultural traditions of those societies, such as "primitive religion," "primitive

economics," technology. Primitive society was treated as something distinct, requiring distinct theoretical formulations designed specifically for such social formations, for example, theories of primitive religion, theories of primitive social organization, theories of primitive economics.

Principle of Uncertainty   also called the "principle of indeterminacy," from physics, referring to the uncertainty in specifying the behavior of subatomic particles based on Werner Heisenberg's (1901–1976) findings: "The more precisely the position [of subatomic particles] is determined, the less precisely the momentum is known in this instant, and vice versa." Some postmodernists invoke this principle in a grotesquely uninformed and inane manner to cast doubt on all knowledge, scientific realism, causality, and to discredit science itself.

Primary States   complex, centralized polities that evolved independently out of local conditions in Mesopotamia, Egypt (North Africa), Subsaharan Africa, India, China, Mesoamerica, and South America. Also known as **Pristine States.**

Primatology   the scientific study of the evolution and behavior of non-human primates for clues regarding human evolution.

Pristine States   another word for **Primary States,** the first centralized polities that evolved out of local conditions independently of one another.

Probabilistic Induction   the view that inductive research can generate knowledge that is probable, but never absolutely certain, and that if knowledge can be reduced to the facts within a permissible range of probability, it has met the general requirement of legitimate scientific knowledge.

Progressionism   nineteenth-century perspective on human evolution that held that culture was the product of a gradual but cumulative and lawful natural progressive development and that the course of cultural evolution was in general upward from a primitive condition of savagery and barbarism to that of civilization. Contrasts with **Degenerationism.**

Proletariat   Marx's term for members of the working class in capitalist societies.

Prolonged Lactation   method of spacing births that entails breastfeeding an infant until the age of 3 or 4 and that has acted as a damper on population growth during most of human prehistory.

Pseudoscience   a perspective that imitates science, uses scientific-sounding jargon but that disregards scientific standards of proof and disproof, employs disingenuous and tendentious methods, and proposes hypotheses that are immune to validation and replication. Postmodern thought and pseudoscience have many features in common.

Psychic Unity of Mankind   or *Elementargedanken,* Adolf Bastian's (1826–1905) term to denote a basic set of elementary thought patterns common to all human minds, which produce similar responses to similar stimuli, although expressed with differing permutations in differing contexts.

Qualitative Research   strategies that stress description, interviewing, empathy, subjective understanding, and participant observation.

Quantitative Tesearch   strategies that stress the collection of quantifiable data for statistical analysis and hypothesis testing.

Radical Plurality of Cultures   postmodern view based upon the idea that each culture produces a set of unique and culturally particular human characteristics resulting in a degree of difference between cultures that is so profound and fundamental that cultures have no commonalties, no points of comparison (i.e., cultures are incommensurable).

Rapport   the personal relationship of empathy the fieldworker establishes with members of the culture he/she is studying.

Rationalism   the position that true knowledge derives from internal cognitive factors or innate ideas rather than sensory experience. Also, mode of thought based upon reason versus mysticism, faith.

Realism   a postmodern pejorative term for the epistemological position that ethnographic observations capture the way the world is (i.e., describe an aspect of reality).

Reciprocity   mutual exchange of gifts/goods/services that creates/solidifies social ties between the recipients who are obligated to reciprocate.

Redistribution   a type of exchange in which food and other goods flow to a central place and are then apportioned out during redistributive feasts under a political leader called a Big Man. An example of redistribution is the **Potlatch** ceremony among the Kwakiutl.

Reductionism   explanations of a level of complex phenomena according to a simpler level of phenomena, for example, explaining sociological phenomena in terms of individual psychological variables.

Reflexivity   postmodernists' jargon term meaning self-criticism and self-awareness in the context of research. Critical reflection upon one's own social/intellectual activities.

Reification   to reify, to mentally transform something that is not real into a "thing"; or the isolation of aspects of sociocultural phenomena theoretically and treating them as if they have an autonomous existence.

Relations of Production   Marx's term for the social relations established between those who control the means of production and the actual producers in the process of work.

Relativistic   the anthropological orientation that stresses the particularity and uniqueness of each culture.

Relativist Fallacy (subjectivist fallacy)   the logical fallacy that truth is relative to a particular culture, time, or individual.

Replication   the scientific requirement that results must be tested by different researchers in order to establish the validity of propositions.

Representation   relating to postmodernists' views on the ethnographer's authority to describe or represent another culture.

Research Strategy   abstract concepts, principles, and assumptions, also called a **Paradigm,** that allow the systematic generation of empirical propositions that function as a general theoretical guide for the explanation of empirical reality.

Restricted Exchange   Claude Lévi-Strauss's term referring to exchange of women in societies based upon **Moieties** (dual divisions based on descent), in which a man from group A takes a wife from group B, and a man from B marries a woman from group A. The exchange can take place among men of the same generation, or it can be completed in the next generation. Such exchange serves to solidify social ties, but not as powerfully as **Generalized Exchange.**

Revitalization Movements   religious-political movements, also called "messianic" or "millenarian movements," aimed at restoring cultural values and eradicating political domination by outsiders. The Ghost Dance among the Native Americans and the Boxer Rebellion are examples of revitalization movement.

Rites of Passage   Arnold van Gennep's (1873–1957) term for tripartite rituals held to mark the status changes of individuals at various phases in the life cycle. All such rites involve the stages of separation, marginality, and reincorporation.

Role Ambiguity   explanation for the incest taboo proposed by Bronislaw Malinowski (1884–1942) which stressed that the taboo came into place because marriages between parents and children or between siblings would create intense jealousies and sexual rivalries that would disrupt parental author-

ity that hinder the functioning of domestic groups.

Rorschach Ink-Blot Yest   a projective psychological test using standardized abstract patterns (ink blots) to provoke or elicit thoughts and ideas from subjects to reveal personality traits and conflicts.

Sacred and Profane   Durkheim's distinction between the supernatural and the mundane domains of human existence. The sacred is distinguished and differentiated from the profane by means of rituals, ritual behavior, recitations, sacred objects, emblems, and taboos.

Salvage Anthropology (Ethnography)   pejorative term used by postmodernists to refer to anthropological efforts directed at collecting information about cultures on the verge of extinction or undergoing radical alteration.

Sapir-Whorf Hypothesis   the principle that language determines thought and perceptions of reality, after the work of the linguistic anthropologists Edward Sapir and Benjamin Whorf (1897–1941).

Savagery, Barbarism, Civilization   fixed stages of sociocultural evolution in nineteenth-century anthropology through which all cultures were thought to pass, predicated upon assumptions of progression that placed European societies at the top of the scale of evolutionary development.

Science   the study of the world based upon empirical evidence, logic, and skeptical/critical thinking; the unremitting and systematic application of critical thinking and logic in the pursuit of propositional knowledge (Lett 1997). Or, a perspective based upon a particular set of epistemological tenets aimed at enhancing our understanding of the empirical world. Science is about critical judgment, the continual and unremitting criticism of premises and evidence. It involves (1) the generation of explanations for how and why experience/reality is constituted in the way that it is constituted and (2) the assessment of how well our understanding accords with that reality through systematic validation of those explanations (Reyna 1994: 556). Science is a systematic way of generating *self-correcting* knowledge (Kuznar 1997: 6). Contrasts with **Supernaturalism.**

Scientific Method the manner in which elements of the scientific research strategy are combined. It entails the definition of a problem, development of hypotheses, ascertaining the empirical implications of the hypotheses, gathering of relevant data by means of observation/experimentation, assessing the hypotheses in terms of these data, and rejecting or rephrasing the hypotheses accordingly.

Scientific Revolution a series of major advances in empirical knowledge and crucial methodological formulations in Europe mainly from 1590s onward, beginning with Nicolaus Copernicus (1473–1543) and culminating with Newton's *Principia* (1687), that led to the establishment of the scientific perspective as a superior way of acquiring knowledge about the world, universe, and everything in them.

Scientism the unscientific position that science provides absolute truths; science as revealed authority rather than as critical judgment.

Second Law of Thermodynamics also called the law of entropy, formulated by the German physicist Rudolf Julius Emanuel Clausius (1822–1888). It posits that all energy transformations entail the degradation of energy from highly concentrated forms to dispersed forms. The universe is winding down toward greater disorder or positive entropy. Living systems, however, are able to capture free energy from their surroundings and develop more internal differentiation and structural complexity, to become "more differentiated structurally and more specialized functionally," and attain "higher energy potentials." Higher forms are achieved through negative entropy.

Secondary Institutions Julian Steward's concept referring to practices and institutional arrangements outside the **Culture Core** and linked indirectly to the exploitation of the environment.

Secondary Rationalizations the process whereby contradictions in one's belief system are explained away. Also called **Multiple Outs.** Frequently employed in **Pseudoscience.**

Secondary States centralized polities that evolved under the impetus of other states.

Semantic Domains the categories that people in different cultures use to sort and classify information.

Semiperiphery from **World Systems Theory,** the intermediate structural position in the global capitalist economy between core and periphery.

Settlement Pattern Archeology reconstruction of the residential patterns of ancient human populations, focusing on clustering/dispersal and planning from which inferences can be made about social structure and socioeconomic activities.

Single Origin Theory a modern perspective on the evolutionary origins of *sapiens* populations.

Slavery circumstances in which human beings are owned by others as possessions; forced work by individuals whose labor and rights are the property of others.

Slippery Slope (*reductio ad absurdum*) the logical fallacy involving the demonstration of the unacceptability of a proposition by positing a chain of progressively more objectionable events that would follow from it.

Small-Scale Societies societies with localized social interactions and localized resource exploitation. Contrasts with **Large–Scale Societies.**

Social Darwinism   the doctrine espoused by Herbert Spencer (1820–1903) based on the application of the idea of "the survival of the fittest" to explain and justify socioeconomic inequalities, violence, and oppression.

Social Dramas   Victor Turner's concept referring to "aharmonic phases" in the social process, when conflict brings to the fore fundamental structural aspects of society that are not ordinarily visible.

Social Formations   Marxist concept referring to the totality of the hierarchical arrangements of subsystems, including economic practice, political practice, and ideological practice, that comprise a sociocultural system.

Societas   Morgan's term for societies based upon personal/kinship relations.

Social Structure   totality of the linkages between social roles.

Sociobiology   the scientific study of the evolution of behavior based on the application of Darwinian concepts to the study of the biological/genetic underpinnings of behavior.

Solipsism   the view that the only thing that can be known is the self and that the external world exists only in human imagination.

Special Pleading   logical fallacy involving the application of rules and principles upon others while declaring oneself exempt without providing evidence to justify the exemption.

State   autonomous centralized hierarchical polity, consisting of numerous communities and a large population, in which a central authority wields political and economic powers to conscript labor, extract taxes, and has monopoly over the use for physical force. See also **Civilization.**

Stratigraphy   the study of sequential, superimposed geological layers deposited by wind or water.

Straw Man Argument   logical fallacy involving an attack upon an opposing viewpoint that has been deliberately misrepresented, simplified, or caricaturized. Most of the postmodernists' criticisms of science are based upon strawman arguments.

Structural Linguistics   a perspective focusing upon the unconscious structure of language.

Structural Functionalism   the functionalist theoretical perspective developed by the British social anthropologist A. R. Radcliffe-Brown (1881–1955).

Structural Marxism   theoretical perspective developed by French anthropologists drawing upon anthropological findings and a particular interpretation of Marxist theory.

Structuralism   anthropological perspective developed by Claude Lévi-Strauss focusing upon the discovery of pan-human cognitive organizing principles underlying culture.

Style over Substance   logical fallacy that holds that the manner in which the argument is presented determines the truth of the propositions.

Subsistence   the means for procuring food/making a living.

Subsistence Economy   production and exchange intended for local consumption.

Subsistence Strategy   tools, techniques, knowledge, and practices used by members of a culture to meet their subsistence needs.

Subjective Understanding   in ethnography, attaining the "insider's view" of another culture. The ideal is for the fieldworker to gain a degree of familiarity with "native" values, logic, and beliefs that he/she can understand the world from the point of view of the participants of the culture being studied.

Substantivists   economic anthropologists who argued that neoclassical economic models applicable to capitalist economic systems are unsuitable for the analysis of noncapitalist societies. Substantivists advocated the analysis of the culturally distinct ways in which production, distribution, and consumption of goods and services takes place in each society. See **Formalist–Substantivist Debate.**

Sui Generis Durkheim's term meaning unique, a phenomena of its own kind, something that has it own individual attributes.

Sun Dance summer ritual among the Indians of the Great Plains involving fasting, dancing, and physical ordeal associated with visions and communion with the supernatural world.

Supernaturalism irrationalist perspectives based upon nonfalsifiable or falsified premises; examples include scientific creationism, "intelligent design," theories pertaining to extraterrestrial visitations as source for terrestrial civilizations, ESP, postmodernism, Talibism, and other fundamentalist politico-religious movements. Contrasts with **Science.**

Superorganic a metaphor meaning above biological, the view of culture as a phenomenon unique unto itself, distinct from biological phenomena. Renditions of this idea were forwarded by Herbert Spencer, Émile Durkheim, Leslie White, and Alfred Kroeber.

Superposition the principle that geological/archaeological strata are deposited progressively and, unless disturbed, the layers at the lower levels are older then those above them.

Surplus production of essential goods/services beyond the minimum needed to support the producers and channeled to central authorities in the form of taxes.

Surplus Value from Marx's labor theory of value, that commodification of labor allows the capitalist to buy the labor power of workers through wages for less than its full value, which then becomes the surplus value of commodities produced by means of that labor. Capitalist profit depends upon surplus value. Contrasts with **Use Value.**

Survivals Edward Tylor's term for nonfunctional cultural elements that have persisted from previous stages of evolutionary development.

Symbiotic Relationship symbiosis refers to circumstances in which two or more very different groups/organisms live in a close and mutually beneficial association with one another.

Symbol object, gesture, color, sound, and so on that suggests or evokes a meaning, concept, of feeling not intrinsic to the object, gestures, color, and so on itself. A symbol is a shared, agreed-upon meaning ascribed to phenomena.

Symbolic Anthropology a nonscientific, humanistic interpretive or **Hermeneutic** approach concerned with structures of signification and systems of meaning through which people live their lives. It is a perspective committed exclusively to an **Idiographic** and **Relativistic** orientation and focuses entirely upon the investigation of the emic domains of particular cultures. Now referred to as **Interpretive Anthropology.**

Synchronic pertaining to a single time period, non-historical perspective focusing on what is at hand at the present. Contrasts with **Diachronic.**

Synthetic Theory of Evolution the theoretical perspective based upon the merger in the 1930s and 1940s of Darwinian evolutionary theory and Mendelian genetics. See **Mendel.**

Systems Theory or "general systems theory" (GST), developed by Austrian-born theoretical biologist Ludwig von Bertalanffy (1901–1972). In anthropology, it entails the study of societies as comprising sets of interrelated parts and subsystems making up the totality, and the nature of the interrelationships between the parts and the whole. The causal relationships of a set of variables that influence one another comprise a system. Systems can be closed, in which there are no outside inputs of energy or matter, in contrast to open systems in which such inputs are involved. See also **Feedback.**

Taboo a supernaturally sanctioned prohibition.

Techno-Environmental Determinism the view that technology and environment are the main causal forces that exert determinative influence upon sociocultural systems.

Technological Determinism the simplistic view that sociocultural phenomena are determined in a mechanistic way by technological factors (e.g., Leslie White's formulations regarding the primacy of the role of technology as an energy capturing mechanism in the evolution of culture).

Teknonymy the custom of referring to an individual as the parent of his or her named offspring rather than by his or her actual name.

Teleology (Teleological) the principle that things have particular end goals (e.g., models that construe evolutionary development as the working out or unfolding of a preordained plan are teleological in nature).

Text postmodernists' jargon term meaning anything that can be read/interpreted in a creative manner and attributed with meaning. See **Culture as Text.**

Thematic Apperception Test a projective psychological test involving the use of cards with ambiguous pictures of human figures for which subjects are asked to construct a story as each card is presented. The subject's self-concepts and emotional tone are recorded for analysis.

Theory of Modes of Production the theoretical concept developed by the French writer Louis Althusser (1918–1990) based upon the specific case to which Marx had applied the idea of mode of production in *Das Kapital* (1885; 1894). Althusser maintained that by such an uncoupling of the concept of mode of production from the specific case of capitalism, it could be applied to any society, not just ones characterized by the capitalist political economy.

Thermodynamics the study of energy transformations. Leslie White viewed cultures as thermodynamic or energy capturing systems and posited that cultures evolve as the amount of energy increases per capita per year. See also **Second Law of Thermodynamics.**

Thesis-Antithesis-Synthesis Georg Wilhelm Friedrich Hegel's (1770–1831) construal of dialectical transformations. See **Dialectics.**

Thick Description the process of translating culture treated as text, espoused by Clifford Geertz.

Third World an imprecise term referring to economically underdeveloped and impoverished nations characterized by polarization between the rich and the poor, low standards of living, high demographic growth rates, and high degree of technological/economic dependence upon rich industrial societies, such as Japan, Western Europe, and the United States and Canada.

Three-Age-System scheme developed by Christian Thomsen (1788–1865) designating three successive stages of cultural evolution: Stone Age, Bronze Age, Iron Age.

Torres Straits Expedition the 1898 expedition to the Torres Straits by an interdisciplinary team headed by Alfred C. Haddon and included: Sidney H. Ray (linguist), W. H. R. Rivers (psychologist), C. S. Myers (musicologist), William McDougall (psychologists), Anthony Wilkin (archaeologist/ethnologist), and Charles Seligman (physician/ethnologist). It set the standards for subsequent field research.

Totalizing Metanarrative postmodern jargon term for the West's universalizing homogenized knowledge based upon science, reason, and rationality, which postmodernists construe as the culture-specific values of politically dominant Western countries inappropriately touted as universally valid.

Totem from the Ojibwa, meaning, "he is a relative of mine," a term referring to animal or plant species with which social groups appeared to stand in a certain ritual relationship.

Totemism   a special ritual relationship between humans and particular animal or plant species, sometimes claimed as ancestors.

Transformations   in Lévi-Strauss's work, myths possessing the same structure or formal arrangement of elements, but in which elements have been inverted (i.e., changes in the main protagonist's gender, or appearance, relationships between characters, etc., are transformations of one another). In such cases, the formal arrangement of the elements in the myth remain the same, and the myth still retains its referential meaning, which in the transformation can be read in another way.

Tribe   kinship-based society, with a common language/dialect and shared traditions, with subsistence economies usually based upon pastoralism or horticulture and lacking socioeconomic stratification or centralized political authority.

Trobriands   inhabitants of the Trobriand Islands situated to the northeast of New Guinea, made famous because of Bronislaw Malinowski's ethnographic work.

Trope   postmodern jargon term for metaphor. See **Metaphor.**

Truth by Coherence   truth based upon a set of ideas and propositions that are internally consistent with each other and also support one another.

Truth by Correspondence   the view that the truth of propositions about the world, the universe, and everything in them depends upon whether the propositions in question correspond to the way the world is, or the view that external facts comprise the conditions of knowledge.

Uncomprehended Symbols   meanings conveyed by symbols that are above the level of individual comprehension; symbolic meanings discerned by the anthropologist of which the participant in the culture are unaware.

Underdevelopment   the process whereby the penetration of the world capitalist system and capital investment into Third World countries and the siphoning off of local resources for the benefit of the wealthy nations and the world market has resulted in the dismantling of local production systems and the impoverishment of indigenous people (called "the development of underdevelopment") who are denied access to productive resources and made dependent upon outside forces.

Uniformitarianism   an important geological principle holding that natural processes have operated in a uniform manner through time and that the same processes at work in the past are at work at the present.

Unilineal Evolution   the view that cultural evolution follows the same fixed pathway and order from a stage of simple social and technological organization to one of complex social technological organization.

Universal Function   from functional anthropology, the premise that all of the elements of a culture fulfill or have particular functions.

Universal Grammar   Noam Chomsky's term referring to the basic features found in all human languages, believed to be based upon universal cognitive properties of the human mind or a genetic linguistic blueprint in the human mind.

Use Value   from Marxist theory, based upon a distinction between "capitalist production" and "simple commodity production," which was a characteristic of most of human history. In the latter form, a commodity is manufactured for its use value (i.e., benefit from having or using it) is sold, and the funds are used for the purchase of another use-value commodity that the manufacturer needs. This contrasts with capitalist production, in which commodities are produced for their **Exchange Value** for the generation of profits and accumulation of capital.

Ussher-Lightfoot Chronology a chronological framework devised by James Ussher (1581–1656), Archbishop of Armagh, Primate of Ireland, and Vice-Chancellor of Trinity College in Dublin, based on the Bible (working back through the patriarchs mentioned in the Bible to "Adam himself"), amended by Dr. John Lightfoot (1602–1675), vice-chancellor of Cambridge University. It held that the earth and everything in it were created instantaneously on October 23, 4004 B.C. at nine o'clock in the morning. According to some estimates, today up to quarter of the U.S. population believes in Ussher and Lightfoot's chronology.

Valid Argument an argument in which if premises are true, then so are the conclusions.

Validation the testing of explanatory propositions against empirical evidence to determine how well they fit the facts. Valid explanations are parsimonious and have higher correspondence (i.e., predictive power to correctly state that something does, will, or did occur in reality, relative to competing explanations) (Reyna 1994: 556).

Variable things/factors with changeable values.

Verstehen sociologist Max Weber's (1864–1920) perspective that culture is a web of symbols, meanings, and ideas that people carry inside their heads, the comprehension of which requires attaining the "insider's view" through intuition and empathy. It entails asking the question, "What did they think they were doing?"

Virilocality custom of women living near their husbands' relatives after marriage.

Voice/Voices "voices of the Other," a postmodern jargon term. It concerns the postmodernists' assertion that the only appropriate ethnographic representation is one that allows people to speak on their own behalf and is linked to their preoccupation with local knowledge, local frames, the native's point of view. See also **Folk Knowledge.**

Vulgar (Mechanical) Materialism pejorative label for materialists that do not subscribe to the dialectical method.

Westermarck Effect the phenomena noted by the anthropologist Edward Westermarck (1853–1936) that individuals raised together have a natural aversion toward sexual interactions and that the incest taboo was therefore a manifestation of this aversion. See also **Natural Aversion Theories.**

World Systems Theory a Marxist perspective that stresses the integrated nature of the world through the global capitalist economic system and the structural place of particular societies within that system.

Worldview the totality of precepts and beliefs, ritual attitudes, and religious ideas concerning the way the world is and the position of people and things in it, shared by members of a society and expressed in their myths, lore, rituals, and values.

Writing Culture School anthropological writers who took part in the School of American Research seminar in 1984, which led to the volume entitled *Writing Culture* (1986), edited by James Clifford and George Marcus, that codifies the central ideas of postmodern anthropology and its vehement antiscience, antitheory, antigeneralization stance.

Bibliography

Preface

Barrett, Stanley
1984 *The Rebirth of Anthropological Theory.* Toronto: University of Toronto Press.

Erickson, Paul, and Liam Murphy (eds.)
2001 *Readings for a History of Anthropological Theory.* Peterborough, Ontario: Broadview Press.

McGee, R. Jon, and Richard Warms
2000 *Anthropological Theory: An Introductory History.* Mountain View, CA: Mayfield.

Marcus, George
1992 Introduction. In *Rereading Cultural Anthropology.* G. Marcus (ed.). Durham, NC: Duke University Press, pp. vii–xiv.

Orlove, Benjamin
1980 Ecological Anthropology. *Annual Review of Anthropology* 9: 235–273.

Chapter 1

Angrosino, Michael
2002 *Doing Cultural Anthropology: Projects for Ethnographic Data Collection.* Prospect Heights, IL: Waveland.

Appadurai, Arjun
1991 Global Ethnoscapes: Notes and Queries for a Transnational Anthropology. In *Recapturing Anthropology: Working in the Present.* Richard Fox (ed.). Santa Fe, NM: School of American Research, pp. 191–210.

Barrett, Richard A.
1991 *Culture and Conduct: An Excursion in Anthropology.* Belmont, CA: Wadsworth.

Bates, Daniel G.
1998 *Human Adaptive Strategies: Ecology, Culture, and Politics.* Boston: Allyn and Bacon.

Bernard, H. Russell
1995   *Research Methods in Anthropology: Qualitative and Quantitative Approaches.* Walnut Creek, CA: AltaMira.

Bodley, John H.
1994   *Cultural Anthropology: Tribes, States, and the Global System.* Mountain View, CA: Mayfield.

Chagnon, Napoleon
1992   *Yanomamo.* New York: Holt, Rinehart and Winston.

Ellen, Roy (ed.)
1984   *Ethnographic Research: A Guide to General Conduct.* New York: Academic Press.

Ember, Carol R., and Melvin Ember
1990   *Cultural Anthropology.* Englewood Cliffs, NJ: Prentice Hall.

2001   *Cross-Cultural Research Methods.* Walnut Creek, CA: AltaMira.

Evans-Pritchard, Edward
1962   *Social Anthropology and Other Essays.* New York: Free Press.

Ferraro, Gary
1992   *Cultural Anthropology: An Applied Perspective.* St. Paul: West Publishing Co.

Fluehr-Lobban, Carolyn (ed.)
1991   *Ethics and the Profession of Anthropology.* Philadelphia: University of Pennsylvania Press.

Fowler, Don, and Donald Hardesty
1994   Introduction. In *Knowing Others: Perspectives on Ethnographic Careers.* D. Fowler and D. Hardesty (eds.). Washington: Smithsonian Institution Press, pp. 1–14.

Goodenough, Ward
1970   *Description and Comparison in Cultural Anthropology.* Chicago: Aldine.

Gross, Daniel
1992   *Discovering Anthropology.* Mountain View, CA: Mayfield.

Harris, Marvin
1994   Cultural Materialism Is Alive and Well and Won't Go Away Until Something Better Comes Along. In *Assessing Anthropology.* Robert Borofsky (ed.). New York: McGraw-Hill, pp. 62–76.

2001   *Cultural Materialism: The Struggle for a Science of Culture.* Walnut Creek, CA: AltaMira. (Original 1979.)

Hatch, E.
1983   *Culture and Morality: The Relativity of Values in Anthropology.* New York: Columbia University Press.

Howard, Michael C., and Janet Dunaif-Hattis
1992   *Anthropology: Understanding Human Adaptation.* New York: HarperCollins.

McGee, Jon, and Richard Warms
2000   *Anthropological Theory: An Introductory History.* Mountain View, CA: Mayfield.

Moran, Emilio
2000   *Human Adaptability: An Introduction to Ecological Anthropology.* Boulder, CO: Westview.

Murdock, George
1945   The common denominator of cultures. In *The Science of Man in the World Crisis.* Ralph Linton (ed.). New York: Columbia University Press, pp. 123–142.

1949   *Social Structure.* New York: Macmillan.

Peoples, James, and Garrick Bailey
1994   *Humanity: An Introduction to Cultural Anthropology.* Minneapolis/St. Paul: West Publishing.

Relethford, John
1990   *The Human Species: An Introduction to Biological Anthropology.* Mountain View, CA: Mayfield.

Salzmann, Zdenek
1993   *Language, Culture, & Society: An Introduction to Linguistic Anthropology.* Boulder, CO: Westview.

Scupin, Raymond
1992   *Cultural Anthropology: A Global Perspective.* Englewood Cliffs, NJ: Prentice Hall.

Sidky, H.
2003   *A Critique of Postmodern Anthropology: In Defense of Disciplinary Origins and Traditions.* Lewiston, NY: Mellen Press.

Spiro, Melford
1986   Cultural Relativism and the Future of Anthropology. *Cultural Anthropology* 1 (13): 259–289.

Spradley, James
1979   *The Ethnographic Interview.* New York: Holt, Rinehart and Winston.

1980   *Participant Observation.* New York: Holt, Rinehart and Winston.

Thomas, David Hurst
1998   *Archeology.* Fort Worth: Harcourt Brace College Publishers.

Wagner, Melinda
1999   The Study of Religion in American Society. In *Anthropology of Religion: A Handbook.* Stephen Glazier (ed.). Westport, CT: Praeger, pp. 85–101.

Washburn, Wilcomb
1998   *Against the Anthropological Grain.* New Brunswick, NJ: Transaction Publishers.

Wolcott, Harry
1995   *The Art of Fieldwork.* Walnut Creek, CA: AltaMira.

Chpater 2

Abel, Reuben
1976   *Man Is the Measure: A Cordial Invitation to the Central Problems of Philosophy.* New York: The Free Press.

Abu-Lughod, Lila
1991   Writing Against Culture. In *Recapturing Anthropology.* Richard Fox (ed.). Santa Fe, NM: School of American Research Washington Press, pp. 37-62.

Appell, G. N.
1989   Facts, Fiction, Fads, and Follies: But Where is the Evidence? *American Anthropologist* 91 (1): 195–198.

Barrett, Stanley
1996   *Anthropology: A Student's Guide to Theory and Method.* Toronto: University of Toronto Press.

Bell, James
1994   *Reconstructing Prehistory: Scientific Method in Archaeology.* Philadelphia: Temple University Press.

Bernard, H. Russell
1994   Method Belongs to All of Us. In *Assessing Anthropology.* Robert Borofsky (ed.). New York: McGraw-Hill, pp. 168–179.

1995   *Research Methods in Anthropology: Qualitative and Quantitative Approaches.* Walnut Creek, CA: AltaMira.

Brook, Andrew, and Robert Stainton
2000   *Knowledge and Mind: A Philosophical Introduction.* Cambridge, MA: MIT Press.

Coker, Rory
2001   *Distinguishing Science and Pseudoscience.* Austin Society to Oppose Pseudoscience Fact Sheet. Austin, TX.

Crapanzano, Vincent
1995   Comment on "Objectivity and Militancy: A Debate" by Roy D'Andrade and Nancy Scheper-Hughes. *Current Anthropology* 36 (3): 420–421.

Creel, Richard
2001   *Thinking Philosophically: An Introduction to Critical Reflection and Rational Dialogue.* Malden, MA: Blackwell.

D'Andrade, Roy
1995   What Do You Think You're Doing? *Anthropology Newsletter* 36 (7): 1, 4.

1999   Culture Is not Everything. In *Anthropological Theory in North America.* E. L. Cerroni-Long (ed.). Westport, CT: Bergin and Garvey, pp. 85–103.

Dawes, Robyn
2001   *Everyday Irrationality: How Pseudo-Scientists, Lunatics, and the Rest of Us Systematically Fail to Think Rationally.* Boulder, CO: Westview.

Fabian, Johannes
1989   *Time and the Other: How Anthropology Makes Its Objects.* New York: Columbia University Press.

Feder, Kenneth
1990   *Frauds, Myths, and Mysteries: Science and Pseudoscience in Archaeology.* Mountain View, CA: Mayfield.

Feyerabend, Paul
1963   Explanations, Predictions, Theories. In *Philosophy of Science: The Delaware Seminar.* Bernard Baumrin (ed.). New York: Interscience, pp. 2–39.

1975   *Against Method.* London: New Left Books.

Fox, Robin
1992   Anthropology and the "Teddy Bear" Picnic. *Society* (November–December): 47–55.

1997   State of the Art/Science in Anthropology. In *The Flight from Science and Reason.* P. Gross, N. Leavitt and M. Lewis (eds.). New York: New York Academy of Sciences. Distributed by Johns Hopkins University Press, pp. 327–345.

Futuyma, Douglas J.
1982   *Science on Trial: The Case for Evolution.* New York: Pantheon Books.

Gellner, Ernest
1992   *Postmodernism, Reason and Religion.* London: Routledge.

Geertz, Clifford
1988   *Works and Lives: The Anthropologist as Author.* Stanford: Stanford University Press.

Gilovich, Thomas
1991   *How We Know What Isn't So: The Fallibility of Human Reason in Everyday Life.* New York: The Free Press.

Greco, John
1999   What is Epistemology? In *The Blackwell Guide to Epistemology.* J. Greco and E. Sosa (eds.). Malden, MA: Blackwell, pp. 1–31.

Greco, John, and Ernest Sosa (eds.)
1999   *The Blackwell Guide to Epistemology.* Malden, MA: Blackwell.

Gross, Paul R., and Norman Levitt
1994   *Higher Superstition: The Academic Left and Its Quarrels with Science.* Baltimore: The Johns Hopkins University Press.

Hales, Steven (ed.)
2002   *Analytic Philosophy: Classic Readings.* Belmont, CA: Wadsworth.

Harris, Marvin
1994   Cultural Materialism Is Alive and Well and Won't Go Away Until Something Better Comes Along. In *Assessing Anthropology.* Robert Borofsky (ed.). New York: McGraw-Hill, pp. 62–76.

2001   *Cultural Materialism: The Struggle for a Science of Culture.* Walnut Creek, CA: AltaMira. (Original 1979.)

Hempel, Carl
1965   *Aspects of Scientific Explanation: And Other Essays in the Philosophy of Science.* New York: The Free Press.

Herzfeld, Michael
2001   *Anthropology: Theoretical Practice in Culture and Society.* Oxford: Blackwell.

Hospers, John
1988   *An Introduction to Philosophical Analysis.* Englewood Cliffs, NJ: Prentice Hall.

Johnson, Allen
1995   Explanation and Ground Truth: The Place of Cultural Materialism in Scientific Anthropology. In *Science, Materialism, and the Study of Culture.* Martin Murphy and Maxine Margolis (eds.). Gainesville: University of Florida Press, pp. 7–20.

Kuhn, Thomas S.
1970   *The Structure of Scientific Revolutions.* Chicago: University of Chicago Press. (Original 1962.)

Kuznar, Lawrence A.
1997   *Reclaiming a Scientific Anthropology.* Walnut Creek, CA: AltaMira.

Lakatos, Imre, and Alan Musgrave (eds.).
1970   *Criticism and the Growth of Knowledge.* Cambridge: Cambridge University Press.

Lett, James
1987   *The Human Enterprise: A Critical Introduction to Anthropological Theory.* Boulder, CO: Westview.

1997   *Science, Reason, and Anthropology: The Principles of Rational Inquiry.* Lanham, MD: Rowman and Littlefield.

1999   Science, Religion, and Anthropology. In *Anthropology of Religion: A Handbook.* Stephen Glazier (ed.). Westport, CT: Praeger. pp. 103–120.

Masterman, Margaret
1970   The Nature of a Paradigm. In *Criticism and the Growth of Knowledge.* Imre Lakatos and Alan Musgrave (eds.). Cambridge: Cambridge University Press, pp. 59–89.

Orans, Martin
1996   *Not Even Wrong: Margaret Mead, Derek Freeman, and the Samoans.* Novato, CA: Chandler and Sharp.

Rabinow, Paul
1986   Representations are Social Facts: Modernity and Postmodernity in Anthropology. In *Writing Culture: The Poetics and Politics of Ethnography.* James Clifford and George Marcus (eds.). Berkeley: University of California Press, pp. 234–261.

Reyna, S. P.
1994   Literary Anthropology and the Case against Science. *Man* 29: 555–581.

Rosaldo, Renato
1991   *Culture and Truth: The Remaking of Social Analysis.* Boston: Beacon Press.

Sagan, Carl
1993   *Broca's Brain: Reflections on the Romance of Science.* New York: Ballantine Books.

1995   *The Demon-Haunted World: Science as a Candle in the Dark.* New York: Random House.

2001   The Burden of Skepticism. In *Magic, Witchcraft, and Religion: An Anthropological Study of the Supernatural.* Arthur Lehmann and James Myers (eds.). Mountain View, CA: Mayfield, pp. 389–394.

Sidky, H.
1997   *Witchcraft, Lycanthropy, Drugs, and Disease: An Anthropological Study of the European Witch-Hunts.* New York: Peter Lang.

2003   *A Critique of Postmodern Anthropology: In Defense of Disciplinary Origins and Traditions.* Lewiston, NY: Mellen Press.

Sokal, Alan, and Jean Bricmont
1998   *Fashionable Nonsense: Postmodern Intellectuals' Abuse of Science.* New York: Picador.

Sosa, Ernest
1999   Skepticism and the Internal/External Divide. In *The Blackwell Guide to Epistemology.* J. Greco and E. Sosa (eds.). Malden, MA: Blackwell, pp. 145–157.

Sperber, Dan
1996   *Explaining Culture: A Naturalistic Approach.* Oxford: Blackwell.

Spiro, Melford
1986   Cultural Relativism and the Future of Anthropology. *Cultural Anthropology* 1 (13): 259–289.

Stove, David Charles
1982   *Popper and After: Four Modern Irrationalists.* Oxford: Pergamon Press.

Tedlock, Barbara
1991   From Participant Observation to the Observation of Participation: The Emergence of Narrative Ethnography. *Journal of Anthropological Research* 47 (1): 69–94.

Thomas, David Hurst
1998   *Archeology.* Fort Worth: Harcourt Brace.

Tiles, Mary, and Jim Tiles
1993   *An Introduction to Historical Epistemology: The Authority of Knowledge.* Oxford: Blackwell.

Toulmin, Stephen
1982   *The Return of Cosmology: Postmodern Science and the Theology of Nature.* Berkeley: University of California Press.

Tyler, Stephen
1986a   Post-Modern Anthropology. In *Discourse and the Social Life of Meaning.* Phyllis Chock and June Wyman (eds.). Washington, DC: Smithsonian Institution Press, pp. 23–49.

1986b   Post-Modern Ethnography: From Document of the Occult to Occult Document. In *Writing Culture: The Poetics and Politics of Ethnography.* James Clifford and George E. Marcus (eds.). Berkeley: University of California Press, pp. 122–140.

1987   *The Unspeakable.* Madison: University of Wisconsin Press.

Veeser, H. Aram
1989   *The New Historicism.* H. Aram Veeser (ed.). New York: Routledge.

Wagner, Melinda
1999   The Study of Religion in American Society. In *Anthropology of Religion: A Handbook.* Stephen Glazier (ed.). Westport, CT: Praeger, pp. 85–101.

Williams, Michael
2001   *Problems of Knowledge: A Critical Introduction to Epistemology.* Oxford: New York.

Chapter 3

Adams, William
1998   *The Philosophical Roots of Anthropology.* Stanford, CA: CSLI Publications.

Bastian, Adolf
1895   *Ethnische Elementargedanken in der Lehre vom Menschen.* Berlin: Weidmann.

Beattie, John
1964   *Other Cultures: Aims, Methods, and Achievements in Social Anthropology.* New York: The Free Press.

Bernard, Russell H.
1995   *Research Methods in Anthropology: Qualitative and Quantitative Approaches.* Walnut Creek, CA: AltaMira.

Bohannan, Paul, and Mark Glazer
1988   Introduction. In *High Points in Anthropology.* P. Bohannan, and M. Glazer (eds.). New York: Alfred Knopf, pp. xii–xxii.

Bowie, Fiona
2000   *The Anthropology of Religion: An Introduction.* Blackwell: Oxford.

Carneiro, Robert
1967a   Editor's Introduction. In *The Evolution of Society: Selections from Herbert Spencer's Principles of Sociology.* R. Carneiro (ed.). Chicago: University of Chicago Press, pp. ix–lvii.

1967b   On the Relationship Between Size and Complexity of Social Organization. *Southwestern Journal of Anthropology* 23: 234–243.

1973   Classical Evolution. In *Main Currents in Cultural Anthropology.* R. Naroll and F. Naroll (eds.). Englewood Cliffs, NJ: Prentice Hall, pp. 57–121.

Cavalli-Sforza, Luigi, P. Menozzi, and A. Piazza
1994   *The History and Geography of Human Genes.* Princeton, NJ: Princeton University Press.

Clark, G. A., and J. M. Lindley
1989   Modern Human Origins in the Levant and Western Asia: The Fossil and Archeological Evidence. *American Anthropologist* 91: 962–985.

Dole, Gertrude
1973   Foundations of Contemporary Evolutionism. In *Main Currents in Cultural Anthropology.* R. Naroll and F. Naroll (eds.). Englewood Cliffs, NJ: Prentice Hall, pp. 247–279.

Eggan, Fred
1954   Social Anthropology and the Method of Controlled Comparisons. *American Anthropologist* 56: 743–763.

Evans-Pritchard, E. E.
1965   *Theories of Primitive Religion.* Oxford: Clarendon Press.

Fagan, Brian
1972   *In the Beginning: An Introduction to Archaeology.* Boston: Little, Brown and Co.

Frazer, James George
1919–1927   *The Golden Bough: A Study in Magic and Religion.* London: Macmillan.

Gruber, Jacob
1973   Forerunners. In *Main Currents in Cultural Anthropology.* R. Naroll and F. Naroll (eds.). Englewood Cliffs, NJ: Prentice Hall, pp. 25–56.

Haddon, Alfred
1910   *A History of Anthropology.* New York: G. P. Putnam's Sons.

Harris, Marvin
2001   *The Rise of Anthropological Theory: A History of Theories of Culture.* Walnut Creek, CA: AltaMira Press. (Original 1968.)

Hatch, Elvin
1973   *Theories of Man and Culture.* New York: Columbia University Press.

Hays, H. R.
1964   *From Ape to Angel: An Informal History of Social Anthropology.* New York: Capricorn.

Hicks, David
2002   *Ritual and Belief: Readings in the Anthropology of Religion.* Boston: McGraw-Hill.

Honigmann, John J.
1976   *The Development of Anthropological Ideas.* Homewood, IL: The Dorsey Press.

Horai, Satoshi, K. Hayasaka, R. Kondo, K. Tsugane, and N. Takahata
1995   Recent African Origins of Modern Humans Revealed by Complete Sequences of Hominoid Mitochondrial DNA. *Proceedings of the National Academy of Sciences of the United States* 92 (2): 532–536.

Horton, Robin
2002   Neo-Tylorianism: Sound and Sense or Sinister Prejudice? In *Ritual and Belief: Readings in the Anthropology of Religion.* D. Hicks (ed.). Boston: McGraw-Hill, pp. 15–23.

Kahn, Joel
1995   *Culture, Multiculture, Postculture.* London: Sage.

Kaplan, David, and Robert Manners
1972   *Culture Theory.* Englewood Cliffs, NJ: Prentice Hall.

Kardiner, Abram and Edward Preble
1962   *They Studied Man.* London: Secker and Warburg.

Klein, Richard
1989   *The Human Career: Human Biological Origins.* Chicago: University of Chicago Press.

Koepping, Klaus-Peter
1982   *Adolf Bastian and the Psychic Unity of Mankind: The Foundations of Anthropology in Nineteenth Century Germany.* St. Lucia, Queensland: University of Queensland Press.

Kroeber, Alfred, and Clyde Kluckhohn
1963   *Culture: A Critical Review of Concepts and Definitions.* New York: Vintage. (Original 1952.)

Kuper, Adam
1999   *Anthropology and Anthropologists: The Modern British School.* London: Routledge.

Langness, L. L.
1993   *The Study of Culture.* Novato, CA: Chandler and Sharp.

Leacock, Eleanor
1963   Introduction. *Ancient Society.* L. H. Morgan. New York: Meridian Books, pp. i–xx.

Leopold, Joan
1980   *Culture in Comparative and Evolutionary Perspective: E. B. Tylor and the Making of Primitive Culture.* Berlin: Dietrich Reimer Verlag.

Lowie, Robert
1952   *Primitive Religion.* New York: Grosset and Dunlap. (Original 1924.)

1959   *The History of Ethnological Theory.* New York: Rinehart and Company. (Original 1937.)

Lubbock, Sir John
1865   *Pre-historic Times: As Illustrated by Ancient Remains, and the Manners and Customs of Modern Savages.* New York: D. Appleton.

1870   *The Origins of Civilisation: Mental and Social Condition of Savages.* New York: Appleton.

Lyell, Sir Charles
1830–1833   *Principles of Geology, Being An Attempt to Explain the Former Changes of the Earth's Surface, by Reference to Causes Now in Operation.* London: J. Murray.

1863   *The Geological Evidences of the Antiquity of Man: With Remarks on Theories of the Origin of Species by Variation.* London: J. Murray.

Magli, Ida
2001   *Cultural Anthropology: An Introduction.* London: McFarland.

Morgan, Lewis H.
1877   *Ancient Society: Researches in the Lines of Human Progress from Savagery, through Barbarism to Civilization.* New York: Henry Holt Co.

Morris, Brian
1988   *Anthropological Studies of Religion: An Introductory Text.* Cambridge: Cambridge University Press.

Murdock, George
1949   *Social Structure.* New York: Macmillan.

Murphree, Idus
1961   The Evolutionary Anthropologists: The Concepts of Progress and Culture in the Thought of John Lubbock, Edward B. Tylor, and Lewis H. Morgan. *Proceedings of the American Philosophical Society* 105: 265–300.

Murphy, Robert
1989   *Cultural and Social Anthropology: An Overture.* Englewood Cliffs, NJ: Prentice Hall.

Nadel, S.
1952   Witchcraft in Four African Societies: An Essay in Comparison. *American Anthropologist* 54: 18–29.

Naroll, R.
1973   Holocultural Theory Tests. In *Main Currents in Cultural Anthropology.* R. Naroll and F. Naroll (eds.). Englewood Cliffs, NJ: Prentice Hall, pp. 309–384.

Opler, Morris
1964   Cause, Process, and Dynamics in the Evolutionism of E. B. Tylor. *Southwestern Journal of Anthropology* 20: 123–144.

Pelto, Pretti, and Gretel Pelto
1979   *Anthropological Research: The Structure of Inquiry.* Cambridge: Cambridge University Press.

Radcliffe-Brown, Alfred R.
1977   *The Social Anthropology of Radcliffe-Brown.* Adam Kuper (ed.). London: Routledge and Kegan Paul.

Rambo, A. Terry
1991   The Study of Cultural Evolution. In *Profiles in Cultural Evolution: Papers from a Conference in Honor of Elman R. Service.* A. T. Rambo and K. Gillogly (eds.). Ann Arbor: The Museum of Anthropology, The University of Michigan, pp. 23–109.

Salzman, Philip
2001   *Understanding Culture: An Introduction to Anthropological Theory.* Prospects Heights, IL: Waveland.

Sanderson, Stephen
1990   *Social Evolutionism: A Critical History.* Oxford: Basil Blackwell.

1999   *Social Transformations: A General Theory of Historical Development.* Lanham, MD: Rowman and Littlefield.

Service, Elman

1971 *Primitive Social Organization: An Evolutionary Perspective.* New York: Random House.

1985 *A Century of Controversy: Ethnological Issues: From 1860 to 1960.* New York: Academic Press.

Slotkin, James

1965 *Readings in Early Anthropology.* Viking Fund Publications in Anthropology No. 40. New York: Wenner-Gren Foundation for Anthropological Research.

Smith, W. Robertson

1889. *Lectures on the Religion of the Semites.* Edinburgh: A. and C. Black.

Spencer, Herbert

1877–1897 *The Principles of Sociology.* New York: D. Appleton.

Stocking, George

1965 "Cultural Darwinism" and "Philosophical Idealism" in E. B. Tylor: A Special Plea for Historicism in the History of Anthropology. *Southwestern Journal of Anthropology* 21 (2): 130–147.

1968 Matthew Arnold, E. B. Tylor, and the Uses of Invention. In *Race, Culture, and Evolution: Essays in the History of Anthropology.* New York: Free Press, pp. 69–90.

1974 Some Problems in the Understanding of Nineteenth Century Cultural Evolutionism. In *Readings in the History of Anthropology.* Regna Darnell (ed.). New York: Harper and Row, pp. 407–425.

1987 *Victorian Anthropology.* New York: The Free Press.

Tylor, Edward

1861 *Anahuac: or, Mexico and the Mexicans, Ancient and Modern.* London: Longman.

1889 On a Method of Investigating the Development of Institutions: Applied to Laws of Marriage and Descent. *Journal of the Royal Anthropological Institute* 18: 245–269.

1916 *Anthropology: An Introduction to the Study of Man and Civilizations.* New York: D. Appleton. (Original 1881.)

1929 *Primitive Culture: Researches into the Development of Mythology, Philosophy, Religion, Language, Art, and Custom.* London: John Murray. 2 vols. (Original 1871.)

1964 *Researches into the Early History of Mankind and the Development of Civilization.* Chicago: University of Chicago Press. (Original 1865.)

Washburn, Wilcomb

1998 *Against the Anthropological Grain.* New Brunswick, NJ: Transaction Publishers.

Whately, Richard

1832 *Introductory Lectures on Political Economy: Delivered in Easter Term, MDCCCXXXI.* London: B. Fellowes.

White, Andrew

1955 *A History of the Warfare of Science with Theology in Christendom.* New York: Braziller. (Original 1895.)

White, Leslie

1987 "Diffusion vs. Evolution": An Anti-Evolutionist Fallacy. In *Leslie White: Ethnological Essays.* Beth Dillingham and Robert Carneiro (eds.). Albuquerque: University of New Mexico Press, pp. 41–57.

Wolpoff, Milford

1989 Multiregional Evolution: The Fossil Alternative to Eden. In *The Human Revolution: Behavioral and Biological Perspectives on the Origins of Modern Humans.* P. Mellars and C. Stringer (eds.). vol. 1. Edinburgh: Edinburgh University Press, pp. 62–108.

Chapter 4

Adams, William

1998 *The Philosophical Roots of Anthropology.* Stanford, CA: CSLI Publications.

Adams, Robert McC.
1966   *The Evolution of Urban Society: Early Mesopotamia and Prehispanic Mexico.* Chicago: Aldine.

Bachofen Johann
1861   *Das Mutterrecht.* Stuttgart: Krais and Hoffman.

Barrett, Stanley
1996   *Anthropology: A Student's Guide to Theory and Method.* Toronto: University of Toronto Press.

Bar-Yosef, O. and F. Valla
1990   The Natufian Culture and the Origin of the Neolithic in the Levant. *Current Anthropology* 31: 433–436.

Blanton, Richard, and S. Kowalewski, G. Feinman and J. Appel
1981   *Ancient Mesoamerica: A Comparison of Change in Three Regions.* New York: Cambridge University Press.

Bloch, Maurice
1983   *Marxism and Anthropology.* Oxford: Oxford University Press.

Carniero, Robert
1970   A Theory of the Origin of the State. *Science* 169: 733–738.

1987   Cross-Currents in the Theory of State Formation. *American Ethnologist* 14: 756–770.

Engels, Friedrich
1972   *The Origins of the Family, Private Property, and the State.* London: Lawrence and Wishart (Original 1884.)

Fiedel, Stuart
1987   *Prehistory of the Americas.* New York: Cambridge University Press.

Fortes, Meyer
1969   *Kinship and the Social Order: The Legacy of Lewis Henry Morgan.* Chicago: Aldine.

Fried, Morton
1967   *The Evolution of Political Society.* New York: Random House.

Futuyma, Douglas J.
1982   *Science on Trial: The Case for Evolution.* New York: Pantheon Books.

Godelier, Maurice
1977   *Perspectives in Marxist Anthropology.* Cambridge: Cambridge University Press.

Gross, Daniel
1992   *Discovering Anthropology.* Mountain View, CA: Mayfield.

Hallpike, C. R.
1988   *The Principles of Social Evolution.* Oxford: Clarendon.

Harris, Marvin
1997   *Culture, People, Nature: An Introduction to General Anthropology.* New York: Longman.

2001   *The Rise of Anthropological Theory: A History of Theories of Culture.* Walnut Creek, CA: AltaMira Press. (Original 1968.)

Hays, H. R.
1964   *From Ape to Angel: An Informal History of Social Anthropology.* New York: Capricorn.

Hoffecker, John, W. Powers, and T. Goebel
1993   The Colonization of Beringia and the Peopling of the New World. *Science* 259: 46–53.

Honigmann, John J.
1976   *The Development of Anthropological Ideas.* Homewood, IL: Dorsey.

Johnson, Allen and Timothy Earle
1987   *The Evolution of Human Societies.* Stanford: Stanford University Press.

Kahn, Joel
1995   *Culture, Multiculture, Postculture.* London: Sage.

Kang, Elizabeth
1979   Exogamy and Peace Relations of Social Units: A Cross-Cultural Test. *Ethnology* 18: 85–99.

Kirch, Patrick
1984   *The Evolution of the Polynesian Chiefdoms.* New York: Cambridge University Press.

1988 Circumscription Theory and Sociopolitical Evolution in Polynesia. *American Behavioral Scientist* 31: 416–427.

Krader, Lawrence
1968 *Formation of the State.* Engelwood Cliffs, NJ: Prentice Hall.

Kunza, Michael, and Richard Reanier
1994 Paleoindians in Beringia: Evidence from Arctic Alaska. *Science* 263: 660–662.

Leacock, Eleanor
1963 Introduction. *Ancient Society.* L. H. Morgan. New York: Meridian Books, pp. i–xx.

Leavitt, Gregory
1989 Disappearance of the Incest Taboo. *American Anthropologist* 91: 116–131.

1990 Sociobiological Explanations of Incest Avoidance: A Critical Review. *American Anthropologist* 92: 971–993.

1992 Inbreeding and Fitness: A Reply to Ulman. *American Anthropologist* 94: 448–449.

Magli, Ida
2001 *Cultural Anthropology: An Introduction.* London: McFarland.

Malefijt, Annemarie
1974 *Images of Man: A History of Anthropological Thought.* New York: Alfred Knopf.

Marcus, George, and Michael Fischer
1986 *Anthropology as Cultural Critique: An Experimental Moment in the Human Sciences.* Chicago: University of Chicago Press.

Morgan, Lewis H.
1851 *League of the Ho-de-no-sau-nee, or Iroquois.* New York: Sage & Bros.

1868 A Conjectural Solution to the Origin of the Classificatory System of Relationships. *Proceedings of the American Academy of Arts and Sciences* 7: 436–477.

1871 *Systems of Consanguinity and Affinity of the Human Family.* Washington, DC: Smithsonian Institution. (Original 1870.)

1877 *Ancient Society: Researches in the Lines of Human Progress from Savagery, through Barbarism to Civilization.* New York: Henry Holt Co.

Murphree, Idus
1961 The Evolutionary Anthropologists: The Concepts of Progress and Culture in the Thought of John Lubbock, Edward B. Tylor, and Lewis H. Morgan. *Proceedings of the American Philosophical Society* 105: 265–300.

Murphy, Robert
1989 *Cultural and Social Anthropology: An Overture.* Englewood Cliffs, NJ: Prentice Hall.

Opler, Morris
1964 Cause, Process, and Dynamics in the Evolutionism of E. B. Tylor. *Southwestern Journal of Anthropology* 20: 123–144.

Orlove, Benjamin
1980 Ecological Anthropology. *Annual Review of Anthropology* 9: 235–273.

Ottenheimer, Martin
1996 *Forbidden Relatives: The American Myth of Cousin Marriage.* Champaign, IL: University of Illinois Press.

Rambo, A. Terry
1991 The Study of Cultural Evolution. In *Profiles in Cultural Evolution: Papers from a Conference in Honor of Elman R. Service.* A. T. Rambo and K. Gillogly (eds.). Ann Arbor: The Museum of Anthropology, The University of Michigan, pp. 23–109.

Resek, Carl
1960 *Lewis Henry Morgan: American Scholar.* Chicago: University of Chicago Press.

Rivers, W. H. R.
1914 Kinship and Social Organization. *London School of Economics Monographs on Social Anthropology* No. 34. London: Athlone Press.

Salzman, Philip
2001 *Understanding Culture: An Introduction to Anthropological Theory.* Prospects Heights, IL: Waveland.

Sanderson, Stephen
1990   *Social Evolutionism: A Critical History.* Oxford: Basil Blackwell.

1999   *Social Transformations: A General Theory of Historical Development.* Lanham, MD: Rowman and Littlefield.

Service, Elman
1971   *Primitive Social Organization: An Evolutionary Perspective.* New York: Random House.

1975   *Origins of the State and Civilization.* New York: Norton.

1985   *A Century of Controversy: Ethnological Issues From 1860 to 1960.* Orlando: Academic Press.

Sidky, H.
1996   *Irrigation and State Formation in Hunza: The Anthropology of a Hydraulic State.* Lanham, MD: University Press of America.

Spencer, Charles
1990   On the Tempo and the Mode of State Formation: Neoevolutionism Reconsidered. *Journal of Anthropological Archaeology* 9: 1–30.

Steward, Julian
1955   The Development of Complex Societies. In *Theory of Culture Change: The Methodology of Multilinear Evolution.* Urbana: University of Illinois Press, pp. 178–209.

Thornhill, Nancy (ed.).
1993   *The Natural History of Inbreeding and Outbreeding.* Chicago: University of Chicago Press.

Tylor, Edward
1889   On the Method of Investigating the Development of Institutions Applied to Laws of Marriage and Descent. *Journal of the Royal Anthropological Institute of Great Britain and Ireland* 18: 245–272.

1929   *Primitive Culture: Researches into the Development of Mythology, Philosophy, Religion, Language, Art, and Custom.* London: John Murray. 2 vols. (Original 1871.)

White, Leslie
1948   Lewis Henry Morgan: Pioneer in the Theory of Social Evolution. In *An Introduction to the History of Sociology.* Harry E. Barnes (ed.). Chicago: University of Chicago Press, pp. 138–154.

1951   Lewis H. Morgan's Western Field Trips. *American Anthropologist* 53 (1): 11–18.

Zohary, Daniel, and M. Hopf
1988   *The Domestication of Plants in the Old World.* New York: Oxford University Press.

Chapter 5

Adams, William
1998   *The Philosophical Roots of Anthropology.* Stanford, CA: CSLI Publications.

Adams, Richard
1991   *Prehistoric Mesoamerica.* Norman: University of Oklahoma Press.

Barrett, Stanley
1996   *Anthropology: A Student's Guide to Theory and Method.* Toronto: University of Toronto Press.

Bar-Yosef, O., and F. Valla
1990   The Natufian Culture and the Origin of the Neolithic in the Levant. *Current Anthropology* 31: 433–436.

Bodley, John H.
1994   *Cultural Anthropology: Tribes, States, and the Global System.* Mountain View, CA: Mayfield.

Bogucki, Peter
1999   *The Origins of Human Society.* Malden, MA: Blackwell.

Bryan, Alan
1987   Points of Order. *Natural History* 6: 6–11.

Carneiro, Robert
1970   A Theory of the Origin of the State. *Science* 169: 733–738.

1987   Cross-Currents in the Theory of State Formation. *American Ethnologist* 14: 756–770.

1988 The Circumscription Theory: Challenge and Response. *American Behavioral Scientist* 31: 497–511.

Chang, K. C.
1986 *The Archeology of Ancient China.* New Haven: Yale University Press.

Clifford, James
1986 On Ethnographic Allegory. In *Writing Culture: The Poetics and Politics of Ethnography.* Berkeley: University of California Press, pp. 98–121.

1988 *The Predicament of Culture: Twentieth-Century Ethnography, Literature, and Art.* Cambridge, MA: Harvard University Press.

Cohen, Mark
1977 *The Food Crisis in Prehistory: Overpopulation and the Origins of Agriculture.* New Haven, CT: Yale University Press.

Connah, Graham
1987 *African Civilization.* Cambridge: Cambridge University Press.

Däniken, Erich von
1968 *Chariots of the Gods? Unsolved Mysteries of the Past.* Toronto: Bantam Books.

Eddington, Arthur Stanley
1942 *The Nature of the Physical World.* London: J. M. Dent & Sons. (Original 1928.)

Ember, Carol R., and Melvin Ember
2002 *Cultural Anthropology.* Englewood Cliffs, NJ: Prentice Hall.

Erickson, Paul, and Liam Murphy
1998 *A History of Anthropological Theory.* Peterborough, Ontario: Broadview Press.

Fagan, Brian
1997 *People of the Earth: An Introduction to World Prehistory.* New York: HarperCollins.

Fagan, Garrett, and Chris Hale
2001 The New Atlantis and the Dangers of Pseudohistory. *Skeptic* 9 (1): 78–87.

Fiedel, Stuart
1987 *Prehistory of the Americas.* New York: Cambridge University Press.

Gowlett, John
1984 *Ascent to Civilization: The Archaeology of Early Man.* New York: Alfred Knopf.

Graebner, Fritz
1911 *Methode der Ethnologie.* Heidelberg: C. Winter.

Griaule, Marcel
1965a *The Dogon.* London : Oxford University Press.

1965b *Conversations with Ogotemmêli: An Introduction to Dogon Religious Ideas.* London: Published for the International African Institute by the Oxford University Press.

Griaule, M., and G. Dieterlen
1976 A Sudanese Sirius System. In *The Sirius Mystery.* R. Temple. New York: St. Martin's Press, pp. 35–51.

Gross, Daniel
1992 *Discovering Anthropology.* Mountain View, CA: Mayfield.

Guidon, Niede, and G. Delibrias
1986 Carbon 14 Dates Point to Man in the Americas 32,000 Years Ago. *Nature* 321: 769–771.

Hancock, Graham
1995 *Fingerprints of the Gods.* New York: Doubleday.

Harlan, Jack
1978 The Origins of Cereal Agriculture in the Old World. In *Origins of Agriculture.* C. Reed. (ed.). The Hague: Mouton, pp. 357–383.

Harris, Marvin
1977 *Cannibals and Kings: The Origins of Cultures.* New York: Random House.

1997 *Culture, People, Nature: An Introduction to General Anthropology.* New York: Longman.

2001 *The Rise of Anthropological Theory: A History of Theories of Culture.* Walnut Creek, CA: AltaMira Press. (Original 1968.)

Hempel, Carl
1965 *Aspects of Scientific Explanation: And Other Essays in the Philosophy of Science.* New York: The Free Press.

Henry, Donald
1985 Preagricultural Sedentism: The Natufian Example In *Prehistoric Hunter-Gatherers: The Emergence of Cultural Complexity.* D. Price and J. Brown (eds.). New York: Academic Press, pp. 365–381.

Heyerdahl, Thor
1952 *American Indians in the Pacific: The Theory Behind the Kon-Tiki Expedition.* London: Allen and Unwin.

1989 *Easter Island: The Mystery Solved.* New York: Random House.

Higham, Charles
1988 *The Archaeology of Mainland Southeast Asia.* Cambridge: Cambridge University Press.

Hoffecker, John, W. Powers, and T. Goebel
1993 The Colonization of Beringia and the Peopling of the New World. *Science* 259: 46–53.

Hollyman, Stephenie
2001 *Dogon: Africa's People of the Cliffs.* New York: Harry N. Abrams.

Honigmann, John J.
1976 *The Development of Anthropological Ideas.* Homewood, IL: The Dorsey Press.

Howell, John
1987 Early Farming in Northwestern Europe. *Scientific American* 257 (5): 118–126.

Jackson, Michael
1989 *Paths Toward a Clearing: Radical Empiricism and Ethnographic Enquiry.* Bloomington: Indiana University Press.

Johnson, Gregory
1973 *Local Exchange and Early State Development in Southwestern Iran.* Anthropological Papers, no. 51. Ann Arbor: Museum of Anthropology, University of Michigan.

Jolly, Clifford, and Randall White
1995 *Physical Anthropology and Archaeology.* New York: McGraw-Hill, Inc.

Jones, Rhys
1989 East of Wallace's Line: Issues and Problems in the Colonization of the Australian Continent. In *The Human Revolution.* P. Mellars and C. Stringer (eds.). Princeton, NJ: Princeton University Press, pp. 742–782.

Lett, James
1997 *Science, Reason, and Anthropology: The Principles of Rational Inquiry.* Lanham, MD: Rowman and Littlefield.

1999 Science, Religion, and Anthropology. In *Anthropology of Religion: A Handbook.* Stephen Glazier (ed.). Westport, CT: Praeger, pp. 103–120.

Linton, Ralph
1936 *The Study of Man: An Introduction.* New York: Appleton-Century-Crofts.

Lowie, Robert
1959 *The History of Ethnological Theory.* New York: Rinehart and Company.

Lynch, Thomas
1990 Glacial-Age Man in South America? A Critical Review. *American Antiquity* 55 (1): 12–36.

Malefijt, Annemarie
1974 *Images of Man: A History of Anthropological Thought.* New York: Alfred Knopf.

McCorriston, Joy, and Frank Hole
1991 The Ecology of Seasonal Stress and the Origins of Agriculture in the Near East. *American Anthropologist* 93: 46–69.

McGee, R. Jon, and Richard Warms
2000 *Anthropological Theory: An Introductory History.* Mountain View, CA: Mayfield.

McIntosh, S. K., and R. McIntosh
1988 From Stone to Metal: New Perspectives on the Later Prehistory of West Africa. *Journal of World Prehistory* 2: 89–133.

Miller, Daniel
1985 Ideology and the Harrapan Civilization *Journal of Anthropological Archaeology* 4: 34–71.

Mooney, James
1973 *The Ghost-Dance Religion and Wounded Knee.* New York: Dover. (Original 1896.)

Moore, Andrew
1988 The Development of Neolithic Societies in the Near East. *Advances in World Archeology* 4: 1–69.

Murphy, Robert
1989 *Cultural and Social Anthropology: An Overture.* Englewood Cliffs, NJ: Prentice Hall.

Oppenheimer, Stephen
1999 *Eden the East: The Drowned Continent of Southeast Asia.* London: Phoenix.

Phillipson, David
1985 *African Archaeology.* New York: Cambridge University Press.

Possehl, Gregory
1990 Revolution in the Urban Revolution: The Emergence of Indus Urbanization. *Annual Review of Anthropology* 19: 261–282.

Rivers, William Halse
1906 *The Todas.* London: Macmillan.

1914 *The History of Melanesian Society.* Cambridge: Cambridge University Press.

Rowley-Conwy, Peter
1995 Abu Hureyra: The World's First Farmers. In *The Illustrated History of Humankind: Peoples of the Stone Age.* G. Burenhult (ed.). San Francisco: HarperCollins. vol. 2, p. 27.

Sagan, Carl
1993 *Broca's Brain: Reflections on the Romance of Science.* New York: Ballantine Books.

1995 *The Demon-Haunted World: Science as a Candle in the Dark.* New York: Random House.

Sanderson, Stephen
1999 *Social Transformations: A General Theory of Historical Development.* Lanham, MD: Rowman and Littlefield.

Schmidt, Wilhelm
1926–1955 *Der Ursprung der Gottesidee: Eine Historisch-Kritische und Positive Studie.* 12 vols. Münster i. W.: Aschendorffsche.

1939 *The Culture Historical Method of Ethnology: The Scientific Approach to the Racial Question.* New York: Fortuny's.

Schultz, Emily, and Robert Lavenda
1995 *Anthropology: A Perspective on the Human Condition.* Mountain View, CA: Mayfield.

Smith, Grafton Elliot
1927 The Diffusion of Culture. In *Culture: The Diffusion Controversy.* G. E. Smith, Bronislaw Malinowski, Herbert Spinden and Alexander Goldenweiser (eds.). New York: W. W. Norton, pp. 9–25.

1928 *In the Beginning: The Origin of Civilization.* New York: William Morrow.

Stiebing, William
1984 *Ancient Astronauts Cosmic Collisions and other Popular Theories about Man's Past.* New York: Prometheus Books.

Stoller, Paul
1986 The Reconstruction of Ethnography. In *Discourse and the Social Life of Meaning.* Phyllis P. Chock and June Wyman (eds.). Washington: Smithsonian Institution Press, pp. 51–74.

Temple, Robert
1976 *The Sirius Mystery.* New York: St. Martin's Press.

Trigger, Bruce
1982   The Rise of Civilization in Egypt. In *The Cambridge History of Africa,* Vol. 1. Cambridge: Cambridge University Press.

Wenke, Robert
1990   *Patterns of Prehistory: Humankind's First Three Million Years.* New York: Oxford University Press.

Whately, Richard
1832   *Introductory Lectures on Political Economy: Delivered in Easter Term, MDCCCXXXI.* London: B. Fellowes.

Wright, K.
1994   Ground Stone Tools and Hunter-Gatherer Subsistence in Southwest Asia: Implications for the Transition to Farming. *American Antiquity* 59: 238–263.

Chapter 6

Adams, William
1998   *The Philosophical Roots of Anthropology.* Stanford, CA: CSLI Publications.

Barrett, Richard
1991   *Culture and Conduct: An Excursion in Anthropology.* Belmont, CA: Wadsworth.

Barrett, Stanley
1984   *The Rebirth of Anthropological Theory.* Toronto: University of Toronto Press.

1996   *Anthropology: A Student's Guide to Theory and Method.* Toronto: University of Toronto Press.

Bell, James A.
1994   *Reconstructing Prehistory: Scientific Method in Archaeology.* Philadelphia: Temple University Press.

Benedict, Ruth
1943   Franz Boas: An Ethnologist. In *Franz Boas 1858–1942.* Menasha, WI: American Anthropological Association Memoir 61, pp. 27–34.

Boas, Franz
1885   *Baffin-land. Geographische Ergebnisse einer in den Jahren 1883 und 1884 ausgeführten Forschungsreise.* Gotha: J. Perthes.

1887   The Occurrence of Similar Inventions in Areas Widely Apart. *Science* 9: 485–486, 587–589.

1888   *The Central Eskimo.* Washington, DC: Government Printing Office.

1901   The Mind of Primitive Man. *Journal of American Folklore* 14: 1–11.

1911   *The Mind of Primitive Man.* New York: Macmillan.

1938   Methods of Research. In *General Anthropology.* Franz Boas (ed.). New York: D. C. Heath and Company, pp. 666–686.

1940   *Race, Language and Culture.* New York: Macmillan.

1966   *Kwakiutl Ethnography.* Chicago: University of Chicago Press.

Boserup, Ester
1965   *The Condition of Agricultural Growth: The Economics of Agrarian Change Under Population Pressure.* Chicago: Aldine.

Carneiro, Robert
1967   Editor's Introduction. In *The Evolution of Society: Selections from Herbert Spencer's Principles of Sociology.* R. Carneiro (ed.). Chicago: University of Chicago Press, pp. ix–lvii.

Cerroni-Long, E. L.
1999   Introduction: Anthropology at Century's End. In *Anthropological Theory in North America.* E. L. Cerroni-Long (ed.). Westport, CT: Bergin and Garvey, pp. 1–18.

Cohen, Joel
1995   Population Growth and the Earth's Human Carrying Capacity. *Science* 269: 341–346.

D'Andrade, Roy
1999 Culture is not Everything. In *Anthropological Theory in North America*. E. L. Cerroni-Long (ed.). Westport, CT: Bergin and Garvey, pp. 85–103.

Darnell, Regna
1998 *And Along Came Boas: Continuity and Revolution in Americanist Anthropology*. Amsterdam: John Benjamins.

Ellen, Roy
1986 *Environment, Subsistence and System: The Ecology of Small-Scale Social Formations*. Cambridge: Cambridge University Press.

Erickson, Paul, and Liam Murphy (eds.)
2001 *Readings for a History of Anthropological Theory*. Peterborough, Ontario: Broadview Press.

Gellner, Ernest
1982 Relativism and Universals. In *Rationality and Relativism*. Martin Hollis and Steven Lukes (eds.). Cambridge: MIT Press, pp. 181–200.

Gould, Stephen Jay
1996 *The Mismeasure of Man*. New York: Norton.

Graeber, Robert
1991 Population Pressure, Agricultural Origins, and Cultural Evolution: Constrained Mobility or Inhibited Expansion. *American Anthropologist* 93: 692–697.

1992 Population Pressure, Agricultural Origins, and Global Theory. *American Anthropologist* 94: 443–445.

Gruber, Jacob
1967 Horatio Hale and the Development of American Anthropology. *Proceedings of the American Ethnological Society* 2: xxiii–clxxx.

Harris, Marvin
1983 *Cultural Anthropology*. New York: Harper and Row.

1997 *Culture, People, Nature: An Introduction to General Anthropology*. New York: Longman.

1999 *Theories of Culture in Postmodern Times*. Walnut Creek, CA: AltaMira.

2001a *Cultural Materialism: The Struggle for a Science of Culture*. Walnut Creek, CA: AltaMira. (Original 1979.)

2001b *The Rise of Anthropological Theory: A History of Theories of Culture*. Walnut Creek, CA: AltaMira Press. (Original 1968.)

Hatch, Elvin
1973 *Theories of Man and Culture*. New York: Columbia University Press.

Hawkes, Kristen
1993 Why Hunter-Gatherers Work: An Ancient Version of the Problem of Public Good. *Current Anthropology* 34: 341–361.

Hinsley, Curtis
1983 Ethnographic Charisma and Scientific Routine: Cushing and Fewkes in the American Southwest, 1879–1893. In *Observers Observed: Essays on Ethnographic Fieldwork*. George Stocking (ed.). Madison: The University of Wisconsin Press, vol. 1, pp. 53–69.

Honigmann, John J.
1976 *The Development of Anthropological Ideas*. Homewood, IL: The Dorsey Press.

Hospers, John
1988 *An Introduction to Philosophical Analysis*. Englewood Cliffs, NJ: Prentice Hall.

Kaplan, David, and Robert Manners
1972 *Culture Theory*. Englewood Cliffs, NJ: Prentice Hall.

Keely, Lawrence
1988 Hunter-Gatherer Economic Complexity and "Population Pressure": A Cross-Cultural Analysis. *Journal of Anthropological Archaeology* 7: 373–411.

Keesing, Roger, and Felix Keesing
1971 *New Perspectives in Cultural Anthropology*. New York: Holt, Rinehart and Winston.

Kennedy, Kenneth
1973   Race and Culture. In *Main Currents in Cultural Anthropology*. R. Naroll and F. Naroll (eds.). Englewood Cliffs, NJ: Prentice Hall, pp. 123–155.

Kroeber, Alfred
1935   History and Science in Anthropology. *American Anthropologist* 35: 15–22.

Langness, L. L.
1993   *The Study of Culture*. Novato, CA: Chandler and Sharp.

Layton, Robert
1997   *An Introduction to Theory in Anthropology*. Cambridge: Cambridge University Press.

Lesser, Alexander
1981   Franz Boas. In *Totems and Teachers: Perspectives on the History of Anthropology*. Sydel Silverman (ed.). New York: Columbia University Press, pp. 1–33.

Lett, James
1987   *The Human Enterprise: A Critical Introduction to Anthropological Theory*. Boulder: Westview.

Lowie, Robert
1920   *Primitive Society*. New York: Boni and Liveright.

Magli, Ida
2001   *Cultural Anthropology: An Introduction*. London: McFarland.

McGee, R. Jon. and Richard Warms
2000   *Anthropological Theory: An Introductory History*. Mountain View, CA: Mayfield.

Mead, Margaret
1959   Apprenticeship under Boas. In *The Anthropology of Franz Boas: Essays on the Centennial of his Birth*. Walter Goldschmidt (ed.). Menasha, WI: American Anthropological Association, Memoir no. 89, pp. 29–45.

Miele, Frank
2001   The Shadow of Caliban: An Introduction to the Tempestuous History of Anthropology. *Skeptic* 9 (1): 22–35.

Milton, Kay
1996   *Environmentalism and Cultural Theory: Exploring the Role of Anthropology in Environmental Discourse*. London: Routledge.

Murdock, George
1949   *Social Structure*. New York: Macmillan.

Oswalt, Wendell H.
1972   *Other Peoples, Other Customs: World Ethnography and Its History*. New York: Holt, Rinehart and Winston.

Pelto, Pretti, and Gretel Pelto
1979   *Anthropological Research: The Structure of Inquiry*. Cambridge: Cambridge University Press.

Peoples, James, and Garrick Bailey
1994   *Humanity: An Introduction to Cultural Anthropology* Minneapolis/St. Paul: West Publishing.

Pfaffenberger, Bryan
1992   Social Anthropology of Technology. *Annual Review of Anthropology* 21: 491–516.

Radin, Paul
1939   The Mind of Primitive Man. *The New Republic* 98: 300–303.

Richards, Audrey I.
1932   *Hunger and Work in a Savage Tribe: A Functional Study of Nutrition Among the Southern Bantu*. London: Oxford University Press.

1939   *Land, Labour and Diet in Northern Rhodesia: An Economic Study of the Bemba Tribe*. London: Oxford University Press.

Rohner, Ronald P., and Evelyn C. Rohner
1969   Introduction: Franz Boas and the Development of North American Ethnography. In *The Ethnography of Franz Boas*. Ronald Rohner (ed.). Chicago: University of Chicago Press, pp. xiii–xxx.

1970   *The Kwakiutl: Indians of British Columbia*. New York: Holt, Rinehart and Winston.

Ross, Eric
1980   Preface. In *Beyond the Myths of Culture: Essays in Cultural Materialism*. Eric Ross (ed.). New York: Academic Press, pp xv–xvi.

Sanderson, Stephen
1990 *Social Evolutionism: A Critical History.* Oxford: Basil Blackwell.

Service, Elman
1985 *A Century of Controversy: Ethnological Issues From 1860 to 1960.* Orlando: Academic Press.

Smith, Marian
1959 Boas' Natural History Approach to Field Method. In *Anthropology of Franz Boas.* Walter Goldschmidt (ed.). Menasha, WI: American Anthropological Association Memoir No. 89, pp. 46–60.

Sparks, Corey, and Richard L. Jantz
2002 Reassessment of Human Cranial Plasticity: Boas Revisited. *Proceedings of the National Academy of Sciences* October 8, 10: 1073.

Sperber, Dan
1996 *Explaining Culture: A Naturalistic Approach.* Oxford: Blackwell.

Spiro, Melford
1986 Cultural Relativism and the Future of Anthropology. *Cultural Anthropology* 1 (13): 259–289.

Stocking, George, Jr.
1968 *Race, Culture, and Evolution.* New York: Free Press.

1974 Introduction: The Basic Assumptions of Boasian Anthropology. In *The Shaping of American Anthropology 1883–1911: A Franz Boas Reader.* George Stocking (ed.). New York: Basic Books, pp. 1–20.

Suttles, Wayne
1987 Affinal Ties, Subsistence, and Prestige Among the Coast Salish. (Original 1951.) In *Issues in Cultural Anthropology: Selected Readings.* D. McCurdy and J. Spradly (eds.). Prospect Heights, IL: Waveland, pp. 244–251.

Wax, Murray
1956 The Limitations of Boas' Anthropology. *American Anthropologist* 8: 63–74.

White, Leslie
1951 Lewis H. Morgan's Western Field Trips. *American Anthropologist* 53 (1): 11–18.

1963 *The Ethnology and Ethnography of Franz Boas.* Austin: Bulletin of the Texas Memorial Museum, no. 6.

1987a The Concept of Evolution in Cultural Anthropology [1959]. In *Leslie A. White: Ethnological Essays.* Beth Dillingham and Robert Carneiro (eds.). Albuquerque: University of New Mexico Press, pp. 129–147.

1987b Evolutionary Stages, Progress, and the Evaluation of Cultures [1947]. In *Leslie A. White: Ethnological Essays.* Beth Dillingham and Robert Carneiro (eds.). Albuquerque: University of New Mexico Press, pp. 59–83.

1987c Evolutionism in Cultural Anthropology: A Rejoinder [1947]. In *Leslie A. White: Ethnological Essays.* Beth Dillingham and Robert Carneiro (eds.). Albuquerque: University of New Mexico Press, pp. 85–96.

1987d Kroeber's *Configuration of Culture Growth* (1946). In *Leslie A. White: Ethnological Essays.* Beth Dillingham and Robert Carneiro (eds.). Albuquerque: University of New Mexico Press, pp. 199–214.

Williams, Michael
2001 *Problems of Knowledge: A Critical Introduction to Epistemology.* Oxford: New York.

Chapter 7

Adams, William
1998 *The Philosophical Roots of Anthropology.* Stanford, CA: CSLI Publications.

Aginsky, Bernard
1943 *Culture Element Distribution XXIV: Central Sierra.* Anthropological Records 8 (4) Berkeley: University of California Press.

Barnouw, Victor
1985 *Culture and Personality.* Homewood, IL: Dorsey.

Barrett, Richard
1991   *Culture and Conduct: An Excursion in Anthropology.* Belmont, CA: Wadsworth.

Barrett, Stanley R.
1996   *Anthropology: A Student's Guide to Theory and Method.* Toronto: University of Toronto Press.

Barry, Herbert, I. Child, and M. Bacon
1959   Relation of Child Training to Subsistence Economy. *American Anthropologist* 61: 51–63.

Barth, Fredrik
1956   Ecological Relationships of Ethnic Groups in Swat, North Pakistan. *American Anthropologist* 58: 1079–1089.

Benedict, Ruth
1923   *The Concept of the Guardian Spirit in North America.* Memoirs of the American Anthropological Association, 29.

1932   Configurations of Culture in North America. *American Anthropologist* 34: 1–27.

1934   *Patterns of Culture.* New York: Houghton Mifflin.

1938   Religion. In *General Anthropology.* Franz Boas (ed.). New York: D. C. Heath and Company, pp. 627–665.

1946   *The Chrysanthemum and the Sword.* Boston: Houghton Mifflin.

1948   Anthropology and the Humanists. *American Anthropologist* 30: 585–593.

1949   Child Rearing in Eastern European Countries. *American Journal of Orthopsychiatry* 19: 342–350.

Boas, Franz
1938   Methods of Research. In *General Anthropology.* Franz Boas (ed.). New York: D. C. Heath and Company, pp. 666–686.

Bohannan, Paul, and Mark Glazer
1988   Benjamin Lee Whorf: 1897–1941. In *High Points in Anthropology.* P. Bohannan and M. Glazer (eds.). New York: Alfred Knopf, pp. 149–151.

Bonvillain, Nancy
2000   *Language, Culture, and Communication: The Meaning of Messages.* Upper Saddle River, NJ: Prentice Hall.

Caudill, William, and Helen Weistein
1969   Maternal Care and Infant Behavior in Japan and America. *Psychiatry* 29: 244–266.

Clifford, James
1986a   Introduction: Partial Truths. In *Writing Culture: The Poetics and Politics of Ethnography.* James Clifford and George Marcus (eds.). Berkeley: University of California Press, pp. 1–26.

1986b   On Ethnographic Allegory. In *Writing Culture: The Poetics and Politics of Ethnography.* James Clifford and George Marcus (eds.). Berkeley: University of California Press, pp. 98–121.

D'Andrade, Roy
1995   *The Development of Cognitive Anthropology.* Cambridge: Cambridge University Press.

Darnell, Regna
1998   *And Along Came Boas: Continuity and Revolution in Americanist Anthropology.* Amsterdam: John Benjamins.

Derrida, Jaques
1976   *Of Grammatology.* Baltimore: Johns Hopkins University Press.

Driver, Harold
1937   *Culture Element Distribution VI: Southern Sierra Nevada.* Anthropological Records 1: 53–154. Berkeley: University of California Press.

1939   *Culture Element Distribution X: Northwest California.* Anthropological Records 1 (6): 297–433. Berkeley: University of California Press.

Drucker, Philip
1950   *Culture Element Distribution XXVI: Northwest Coast.* Anthropological Records 9 (3) Berkeley: University of California Press.

Du Bois, Cora
1944   *The People of Alor.* New York: Harper.

Edgerton, Robert
1965   Cultural vs Ecological Factors in the Expression of Values, Attitudes, and Personality Characteristics. *American Anthropologist* 68: 408–425.

Ellen, Roy
1986   *Environment, Subsistence and System: The Ecology of Small-Scale Social Formations.* Cambridge: Cambridge University Press.

Erickson, Paul A., and Liam D. Murphy
1998   *A History of Anthropological Theory.* Ontario: Broadview Press.

Erikson, Erik
1963   *Childhood and Society.* New York: Norton.

Freeman, Derek
1983   *Margaret Mead and Samoa: The Making and Unmaking of an Anthropological Myth.* Cambridge: Harvard University Press.

1998   *The Fateful Hoaxing of Margaret Mead: An Historical Analysis of Her Samoan Researches.* Boulder, CO: Westview.

Geertz, Clifford
1983   *Local Knowledge: Further Essays in Interpretive Anthropology.* New York: Basic Books.

Gibson, Ann J., and John H. Rowe
1961   A Bibliography of Alfred Louis Kroeber. *American Anthropologist* 63: 1060–1087.

Gordan, Joan (ed.).
1976   *Margaret Mead: The Complete Bibliography 1925–1975.* The Hague: Mouton.

Gold, Jerry
1983   Is Freeman Wrong about Mead? *Samoa News,* August 26, p. 14.

Goldschmidt, Walter
1965   Variation and Adaptability of Culture. *American Anthropologist* 67: 400–447.

Gorer, Geoffrey
1943   *Themes in Japanese Culture.* Transactions of the New York Academy of Sciences. Series II, 5.

Gorer, Geoffrey, and J. Rickman
1949   *The People of Great Russia.* London: Cresset.

Gross, Paul R., and Norman Levitt
1994   *Higher Superstition: The Academic Left and Its Quarrels with Science.* Baltimore: The Johns Hopkins University Press.

Hall, G. Stanley
1904   *Adolescence, Its Psychology and Its Relations to Physiology, Anthropology, Sociology, Sex, Crime, Religion and Education.* New York: Appleton.

Haring, Douglas
1949   *Personal Character and Cultural Milieu.* Syracuse, NY: Syracuse University Press.

Harris, Marvin
1983a   Margaret and the Giant-Killer. *The Sciences* 23 (4): 18–21.

1983b   The Sleep-crawling Question. *Psychology Today,* May: 24–27.

2001   *The Rise of Anthropological Theory: A History of Theories of Culture.* Walnut Creek, CA: AltaMira Press. (Original 1968.)

Hatch, Elvin
1973   *Theories of Man and Culture.* New York: Columbia University Press.

Herskovits, Melville
1955   *Cultural Anthropology.* New York: Alfred Knopf.

Herzfeld, Michael
2001   *Anthropology: Theoretical Practice in Culture and Society.* Oxford: Blackwell.

Holmes, Lowell D.
1987   *Quest for the Real Samoa: The Mead/Freeman Controversy & Beyond.* Massachusetts: Bergin & Garvey.

Honigmann, John J.
1976   *The Development of Anthropological Ideas.* Homewood, IL: The Dorsey Press.

Keesing, Roger M., and Felix Keesing
1971 *New Perspectives in Cultural Anthropology.* New York: Holt, Rinehart and Winston.

Klimek, Stanislaw
1935 *Culture Element Distributions I: The Structure of California Indian Culture.* University of California Publications in American Archaeology and Ethnology, 38: 12–70.

Kroeber, Alfred
1925 *Handbook of the Indians of California.* Washington: Bureau of American Ethnology, Bulletin 78.

1935 *The Prophet Dance of the Northwest and its Derivatives: The Source of the Ghost Dance.* American Anthropological Association, General Series in Anthropology. I.

1939 *Cultural and Natural Areas of Native North America.* University of California Publications in American Archaeology and Ethnology, vol. 38.

1944 *Configurations of Culture Growth.* Berkeley: University of California Press.

1952 *The Nature of Culture.* Chicago: University of Chicago Press.

1963 *An Anthropologist Looks at History.* Berkeley: University of California Press.

Langness, L. L.
1993 *The Study of Culture.* Novato, CA: Chandler and Sharp.

Layton, Robert
1997 *An Introduction to Theory in Anthropology.* Cambridge: Cambridge University Press.

Leaf, Murray J.
1979 *Man, Mind, and Science: A History of Anthropology.* New York: Columbia University Press.

Lowie, Robert
1920 *Primitive Society.* New York: Boni and Liveright.

Lucy, J. A.
1997 Linguistic Relativity. *Annual Review of Anthropology* 26: 291–312.

MacClancy, Jeremy
1996 Popularizing Anthropology. In *Popularizing Anthropology.* J. MacClancy and Chris McDonaugh (eds.). New York: Routledge, pp. 1–54.

Magli, Ida
2001 *Cultural Anthropology: An Introduction.* London: McFarland.

Malefijt, Annemarie
1974 *Images of Man: A History of Anthropological Thought.* New York: Alfred Knopf.

Malotki, E.
1983 *Hopi Time: A Linguistic Analysis of Temporal Concepts in the Hopi Language.* Berlin: Mouton.

Marcus, George, and Michael Fischer
1986 *Anthropology as Cultural Critique: An Experimental Moment in the Human Sciences.* Chicago: University of Chicago Press.

McNeill, David
1987 *Psycholinguistics: A New Approach.* New York: Harper and Row.

Mead, Margaret
1928 *Coming of Age in Samoa.* New York: Mentor. 1949 edition.

1930 *Growing Up in New Guinea.* New York: Blue Ribbon.

1935 *Sex and Temperament in Three Primitive Societies.* New York: Morrow.

1959 *An Anthropologist at Work: Writings of Ruth Benedict.* Boston: Houghton Mifflin.

1962 Retrospects and Prospects. In *Anthropology and Human Behavior.* T. Gladwin and W. C. Strutevant (eds.) Washington: Anthropological Society of Washington, pp. 40–65.

1977 An Anthropological Approach to Different Types of Communication and the Important Differences in Human Temperaments. In *Extrasensory Ecology: Parapsychology and Anthropology.* Joseph K. Long (ed.). Metuchen, NJ: Scarecrow Press, pp. 47–50.

2001 *Coming of Age in Samoa.* New York: Perennial. (Original 1928.)

Mead, Margaret, and Rhoda Métraux
1953 *The Study of Culture at a Distance.* Chicago: University of Chicago Press.

Mintz, Sidney
1981 Ruth Benedict. In *Totems and Teachers: Perspectives on the History of Anthropology.* Sydel Silverman (ed.). New York: Columbia University Press, pp. 141–168.

Moore, Jerry
1997 *Visions of Culture: An Introduction to Anthropological Theories and Theorists.* Walnut Creek, CA: AltaMira.

Murphy, Robert
1989 *Cultural and Social Anthropology: An Overture.* Englewood Cliffs, NJ: Prentice Hall.

Orans, Martin
1996 *Not Even Wrong: Margaret Mead, Derek Freeman, and the Samoans.* Novato, CA: Chandler and Sharp.

Peoples, James, and Garrick Bailey
1994 *Humanity: An Introduction to Cultural Anthropology.* Minneapolis/St. Paul: West Publishing.

Pinker, Steven
1994 *The Language Instinct.* New York: William Morrow.

Salzman, Philip
2001 *Understanding Culture: An Introduction to Anthropological Theory.* Prospects Heights, IL: Waveland.

Sanderson, Stephen
1990 *Social Evolutionism: A Critical History.* Oxford: Basil Blackwell.

Sapir, Edward
1917 Do We Need a Superorganic? *American Anthropologist* 19: 441–447.

1921 *Language: An Introduction to the Study of Speech.* New York: Harcourt, Brace and Co.

1929 The Status of Linguistics as a Science. *Language* 5: 207–214.

1932 Cultural Anthropology and Psychiatry. *Journal of Abnormal and Social Psychology* 27: 229–242.

1964 *Culture, Language and Personality: Selected Essays.* David Mandelbaum (ed.). Berkeley: University of California Press.

Schneider, David
1983 Schneider Replies. *Natural History* 92 (12): 4–6.

Service, Elman
1985 *A Century of Controversy: Ethnological Issues from 1860 to 1960.* Orlando: Academic Press.

Shankman, Paul
1996 The History of Samoan Sexual Conduct and the Mead-Freeman Controversy. *American Anthropologist* 98: 555–567.

2001 Requiem for a Controversy: Whatever Happened to Margaret Mead? *Skeptic* 9 (1): 48–55.

Shermer, Michael
2001 Spin-Doctoring the Yanomamo: Science as a Candle in the Darkness of the Anthropological Wars. *Skeptic* 9(1): 36–47.

Spier, Leslie
1921 *The Sun Dance of the Plains Indians.* Anthropological Papers 16. New York: American Museum of Natural History.

1935 *The Prophet Dance of the Northwest and its Derivatives: The Source of the Ghost Dance.* American Anthropological Association, General Series in Anthropology. I.

Steward, Julian
1941 *Culture Element Distributions: XIII, Nevada Shoshoni.* University of California Publications in Anthropological Records 4: 208–259.

1961 Alfred Louis Kroeber 1876–1960. *American Anthropologist* 63: 1038–1087.

Stocking, George, Jr.
1974   Introduction: The Basic Assumptions of Boasian Anthropology. In *The Shaping of American Anthropology 1883–1911: A Franz Boas Reader.* New York: Basic Books, pp. 1–20.

Suárez-Orozco, M., G. Spindler, and L. Spindler
1994   *The Making of Psychological Anthropology.* Fort Worth, TX: Harcourt Brace.

Tierney, Patrick
2000   *Darkness in El Dorado: How Scientists and Journalists Devastated the Amazon.* New York: W. W. Norton.

Vayda, Andrew P., and Roy Rappaport
1968   Ecology, Cultural and Non-Cultural. In J. Cliffton (ed.). *Introduction to Cultural Anthropology.* Boston: Houghton Mifflin, pp. 477–497.

Wallace, Anthony
1970   *Culture and Personality.* New York: Random House.

White, Leslie
1987   Introduction to Part I. In *Leslie White: Ethnological Essays.* Beth Dillingham and Robert Carneiro (eds.). Albuquerque: University of New Mexico Press, pp. 11–15.

Whiting, J. W. M., and I. L. Child
1953   *Child Training and Personality: A Cross-Cultural Study.* New Haven, CT: Yale University Press.

Whorf, Benjamin Lee
1941   The Relation of Habitual Thought and Behavior to Language. In *Issues in Cultural Anthropology: Selected Readings.* David McCurdy and James Spradley (eds.). Prospect Heights, IL: Waveland, 1987, pp. 51–67.

Wissler, Clark
1914   The Influence of the Horse in the Development of Plains Culture. *American Anthropologist* 16: 1–25.

1923   *Man and Culture.* New York: Thomas Crowell.

1926   *The Relation of Nature to Man in Aboriginal America.* New York: Oxford University Press.

1929   *An Introduction to Social Anthropology.* New York: Henry Holt.

1938   *The American Indian: An Introduction to the Anthropology of the New World.* New York: Oxford University Press.

Wolf, Eric R.
1981   Alfred L. Kroeber. In *Totems and Teachers: Perspectives on the History of Anthropology.* Sydel Silverman (ed.). New York: Columbia University Press, pp. 35–65.

Womack, Mari
1998   *Being Human: An Introduction to Cultural Anthropology.* Upper Saddle River, NJ: Prentice Hall.

Chapter 8

Asad, Talal
1986   The Concept of Cultural Translation in British Social Anthropology. In *Writing Culture: The Poetics and Politics of Ethnography.* James Clifford and George Marcus (eds.). Berkeley: University of California Press, pp. 141–164.

Barrett, Stanley
1996   *Anthropology: A Student's Guide to Theory and Method.* Toronto: University of Toronto Press.

Cheater, Angela
1989   *Social Anthropology: An Alternative Introduction.* London: Unwin Hyman.

Clifford, James
1986   Introduction: Partial Truths. In *Writing Culture: The Poetics and Politics of Ethnography.* James Clifford and George Marcus (eds.). Berkeley: University of California Press, pp. 1–26.

1988   *The Predicament of Culture: Twentieth-Century Ethnography, Literature, and Art.* Cambridge, MA: Harvard University Press.

Ellen, Roy
1986   *Environment, Subsistence and System: The Ecology of Small-Scale Social Formations.* Cambridge: Cambridge University Press.

Evans-Pritchard, Edward
1981   *A History of Anthropological Thought.* New York: Basic Books.

Firth, Raymond
1957   Introduction: Malinowski as Scientist and as Man. In *Man and Culture: An Evaluation of the Work of Bronislaw Malinowski.* Raymond Firth (ed.). London: Routledge and Kegan Paul, pp. 1–14.

1988   Malinowski in the History of Social Anthropology. In *Malinowski Between Two Worlds: The Polish Roots of an Anthropological Tradition.* Roy Ellen et al. (eds.). Cambridge: Cambridge University Press, pp. 12–42.

Gmelch, Geoge
1982   Baseball Magic. In *Anthropology for the Eighties.* J. Cole (ed.). New York: The Free Press, pp. 394–399.

Haddon, Alfred (ed.).
1901   *Reports of the Cambridge Anthropological Expedition to the Torres Straits.* Cambridge: Cambridge University Press, 1901–1935, vols. 1–7.

Hallpike, C. R.
1988   *The Principles of Social Evolution.* Oxford: Clarendon.

Harris, Marvin
1991   *Cultural Anthropology.* New York: Harper-Collins.

Hatch, Elvin
1973   *Theories of Man and Culture.* New York: Columbia University Press.

Hicks, David
1999   *Ritual and Belief: Readings in the Anthropology of Religion.* Boston: McGraw-Hill.

Irwin, Geoffrey
1983   Chieftainship, Kula and Trade in Massim Prehistory. In *The Kula: New Perspectives on Massim Exchange.* Jerry Leach and Edmund Leach (eds). Cambridge: Cambridge University Press, pp. 29–72.

Jarvie, I. C.
1964   *The Revolution in Anthropology.* London: Routledge & Kegan Paul.

1973   *Functionalism.* Minneapolis: Burgess.

Kaberry, Phyllis
1957   Malinowski's Contribution to Fieldwork Method and the Writing of Ethnography. In *Man and Culture: An Evaluation of the Work of Bronislaw Malinowski.* Raymond Firth (ed.). London: Routledge and Kegan Paul, pp. 71–91.

Kardiner, Abram, and Edward Preble
1962   *They Studied Man.* London: Secker and Warburg.

Kuper, Adam
1999   *Anthropology and Anthropologists: The Modern British School.* London: Routledge.

Leach, Edmund
1957   The Epistemological Background to Malinowski's Empiricism. In *Man and Culture: An Evaluation of the Work of Bronislaw Malinowski.* Raymond Firth (ed.). London: Routledge and Kegan Paul, pp. 119–137.

1966   On the "Founding Fathers," *Current Anthropology* 7 (5): 560–567.

1982   *Social Anthropology.* Oxford: Oxford University Press.

Malinowski, Bronislaw
1915   The Natives of Mailu: Preliminary Results of the Robert Young Research Work in British New Guinea. In *Malinowski Among the Magi: The Natives of Mailu.* Michael Young (ed.). London: Routledge (1988), pp. 77–331.

1916   Baloma: Spirits of the Dead in the Trobriand Islands. In *Magic, Science and Religion and Other Essays.* Garden City, NY: Doubleday (1954), pp. 149–274.

1922a   *Argonauts of the Western Pacific: An Account of Native Enterprise and Adventure in the Archipelagoes of Melanesian New Guinea.* London: George Routledge and Sons.

1922b   Ethnology and the Study of Society. *Economica* 2: 208–219.

1932   *The Sexual Life of Savages in North-Western Melanesia: An Ethnographic Account of Courtship, Marriage, and Family Life among the Natives of the Trobriand Islands, British New Guinea.* London: G. Routledge and Sons.

1934   Introduction. In *Law and Order in Polynesia: A Study of Primitive Legal Institutions.* By Ian Hogbin. London: Christophers, pp. xvii–lxxii.

1935   *Coral Gardens and their Magic: A Study of the Methods of Tilling the Soil and of Agricultural Rites in the Trobriand Islands.* 2 vols. New York: American Book Co.

1944   *A Scientific Theory of Culture and Other Essays.* Chapel Hill, NC: University of North Carolina Press.

1945   *The Dynamics of Culture Change: An Inquiry into Race Relations in Africa.* New Haven, CT: Yale University Press.

1948   *Magic, Science and Religion and Other Essays.* Garden City, NJ: Anchor.

1957   *Sex and Repression in Savage Society.* London: Kegan Paul. (Original 1927.)

1989   *A Diary in the Strict Sense of the Term by Bronislaw Malinowski.* Stanford: Stanford University Press.

Merton, Robert
1957   *Social Theory and Social Structure.* Glenco, IL: The Free Press.

Morris, Brian
1988   *Anthropological Studies of Religion: An Introductory Text.* Cambridge: Cambridge University Press.

Nadel, S. F.
1970   Malinowski on Magic and Religion. In *Man and Culture: An Evaluation of the Work of Bronislaw Malinowski.* R. Firth (ed.). London: Routledge and Kegan Paul, pp. 189–208.

Pratt, Mary Louise
1986   Fieldwork in Common Places. In *Writing Culture: The Poetics and Politics of Ethnography.* James Clifford and George Marcus (eds.). Berkeley: University of California Press, pp. 27–50.

Rabinow, Paul
1986   Representations are Social Facts: Modernity and Postmodernity in Anthropology. In *Writing Culture: The Poetics and Politics of Ethnography.* James Clifford and George Marcus (eds.). Berkeley: University of California Press, pp. 234–261.

Richards, A. I.
1943   Bronislaw Kasper Malinowski. *Man* 43 (1): 1–4.

Scoditti, G.
1983   Kula on Kitava. In *The Kula: New Perspectives on Massim Exchange.* Jerry Leach and Edmund Leach (eds.). Cambridge: Cambridge University Press, pp. 249–273.

Sperber, Dan
1996   *Explaining Culture: A Naturalistic Approach.* Oxford: Blackwell.

Spiro, Melford
1982   *Oedipus in the Trobriands.* Chicago: University of Chicago Press.

Stocking, George
1992   *The Ethnographer's Magic and Other Essays in the History of Anthropology.* Madison: University of Wisconsin Press.

Weiner, Annette.
1987   Introduction. In *The Sexual Lives of Savages in North-Western Melanesia.* Boston: Beacon Press, pp. xiii–xlix.

Chapter 9

Adams, William
1998   *The Philosophical Roots of Anthropology.* Stanford, CA: CSLI Publications.

Barrett, Stanley
1996   *Anthropology: A Student's Guide to Theory and Method.* Toronto: University of Toronto Press.

Durkheim, Émile
1915   *Elementary Forms of Religious Life.* New York: Allen and Unwin.

1938   *The Rules of Sociological Method.* New York: Free Press. (Original 1895.)

Eggan, Fred, and W. Lloyd Warner
1956   Alfred Reginald Radcliffe-Brown: 1881–1955. *American Anthropologist* 58: 544–547.

Ellen, Roy
1986   *Environment, Subsistence and System: The Ecology of Small-Scale Social Formations.* Cambridge: Cambridge University Press.

Evans-Pritchard, Edward
1981   *A History of Anthropological Thought.* New York: Basic Books.

Fox, Robin
1997   State of the Art/Science in Anthropology. In *The Flight from Science and Reason.* P. Gross, N. Leavitt and M. Lewis (eds.). New York: New York Academy of Sciences. Distributed by Johns Hopkins University Press, pp. 327–345.

Gray, Robert F.
1964   Introduction. *The Family Estate in Africa: Studies in the Role of Property in Family Structure and Lineage Continuity.* Robert F. Gray and P. H. Gulliver (eds.). London: Routledge and K. Paul, pp. 1–6.

Harris, Marvin
1997   Comment on "Causation and the Struggle for a Science of Culture" by Tim O'Meara. *Current Anthropology* 38: 410–415.

Hatch, Elvin
1973   *Theories of Man and Culture.* New York: Columbia University Press.

Jarvie, I. C.
1964   *The Revolution in Anthropology.* London: Routledge & Kegan Paul.

Kaplan, David, and Robert Manners
1972   *Culture Theory.* Englewood Cliffs, NJ: Prentice Hall.

Kuper, Adam
1999   *Anthropology and Anthropologists: The Modern British School.* London: Routledge.

Leach, Edmund
1954   *Political Systems of Highland Burma.* Boston: Beacon Press.

1970   *Claude Lévi-Strauss.* New York: Viking Press.

1982   *Social Anthropology.* Oxford: Oxford University Press.

Lévi-Strauss, Claude
1963   *Totemism.* Boston: Beacon Press. (Original 1962.)

Netting, Robert McC.
1977   *Cultural Ecology.* Menlo Park, CA: Cummings.

Radcliffe-Brown, Alfred R.
1913   Three Tribes of Western Australia. *Journal of the Royal Anthropological Institute* 43: 143–195.

1918   Notes on the Social Organization of Australian Tribes. *Journal of the Royal Anthropological Institute* 48: 222–253.

1933   *The Andaman Islanders.* Cambridge: Cambridge University Press. (Original 1922.)

1952   *Structure and Function in Primitive Society: Essays and Addresses.* E. Evans-Pritchard and F. Eggan (eds.). Glenco, IL: The Free Press.

1957   *A Natural Science of Society.* Glencoe, IL: The Free Press.

1958   *Method in Social Anthropology: Selected Essays.* M. N. Srinivas (ed.). Chicago: University of Chicago Press.

1977   *The Social Anthropology of Radcliffe-Brown.* Adam Kuper (ed.). London: Routledge and Kegan Paul.

Sahlins, Marshall
1976   *Culture and Practical Reason.* Chicago: University of Chicago Press.

Salzman, Philip
2001   *Understanding Culture: An Introduction to Anthropological Theory.* Prospects Heights, IL: Waveland.

Stocking, George
1984a   Dr. Durkheim and Mr. Brown: Comparative Sociology at Cambridge in 1910. In *Functionalism Historicized: Essays on British Social Anthropology.* George Stocking (ed.). Madison: University of Wisconsin Press, pp. 106–130.

1984b   Radcliffe-Brown and British Social Anthropology. In *Functionalism Historicized: Essays on British Social Anthropology.* George Stocking (ed.). Madison: University of Wisconsin Press, pp. 131–191.

Chapter 10

Adams, Richard
1975   *Energy and Structure: A Theory of Social Power.* Austin: University of Texas Press.

Adams, Robert McC.
1966   *The Evolution of Urban Society: Early Mesopotamia and Prehispanic Mexico.* Chicago: Aldine de Gruyter.

Adams, William
1998   *The Philosophical Roots of Anthropology.* Stanford, CA: CSLI Publications.

Baker, P.
1962   The Application of Ecological Theory to Anthropology. *American Anthropologist* 64: 15–21.

Barnes, Harry Elmer
1960   Forward. In *Essays in the Science of Culture.* G. Dole and R. Carneiro (eds.). New York: Thomas Crowell, pp. xi–xlvi.

Barrett, Stanley
1996   *Anthropology: A Student's Guide to Theory and Method.* Toronto: University of Toronto Press.

Bates, Marston
1953   Human Ecology. *Anthropology Today.* Chicago: University of Chicago Press.

Binford, Lewis
1962   Archaeology as Anthropology. *American Antiquity* 28: 217–225.

1968   Archaeological Perspectives. In *New Perspectives in Archaeology.* Sally Binford and Lewis Binford (eds.). Chicago: Aldine Publishing, pp. 5–32.

1972   *An Archeological Perspective.* New York: Seminar Press.

Bloch, Maurice
1983   *Marxism and Anthropology.* Oxford: Oxford University Press.

Boas, Franz
1887   The Occurrence of Similar Inventions in Areas Widely Apart. *Science* 9: 485–486, 587–589.

1966   *Kwakiutl Ethnography.* Chicago: University of Chicago Press.

Bodley, John
1975   *Victims of Progress.* Menlo Park, CA: Cummings.

1994   *Cultural Anthropology: Tribes, States, and the Global System.* Mountain View, CA: Mayfield.

Bogucki, Peter
1999   *The Origins of Human Society.* Malden, MA: Blackwell.

Butzer, Karl
1976   *Early Hydraulic Civilization in Egypt.* Chicago: University of Chicago Press.

Cardozo, Rebecca
1970   A Modern American Witch-Craze. In *Witchcraft and Sorcery: Selected Readings.* Max Marwick (ed.). Middlesex, England: Penguin, pp. 369–377.

Carneiro, Robert
1970   A Theory of the Origin of the State. *Science* 169: 733–788.

1981   Leslie White. In *Totems and Teachers: Perspectives on the History of Anthropology.* Sydel Silverman (ed.). New York: Columbia University Press, pp. 209–251.

1987   Cross-Currents in the Theory of State Formation. *American Ethnologist* 14: 756–770.

Cashdan, E.
1989   Hunters and Gatherers: Economic Behavior in Bands. In *Economic Anthropology.* S. Plattner (ed.). Stanford, CA: Stanford University Press, pp. 23–24.

Chang, K.
1986   *The Archeology of Ancient China.* New Haven, CT: Yale University Press.

Childe, V. Gordon
1950   *What Happened in History.* Middlesex: Penguin Books.

1951   *Social Evolution.* New York: H. Schuman.

Claessen, Henri, and Peter Skalník (eds.).
1982   *The Study of the State.* The Hague: Mouton.

Clemmer, Richard, L. Daniel Myers, and Mary E. Rudden (eds.).
1999   *Julian Steward and the Great Basin: The Making of an Anthropologist.* Salt Lake City: University of Utah Press.

Cohen, Mark
1977   *The Food Crisis in Prehistory: Overpopulation and the Origins of Agriculture.* New Haven, CT: Yale University Press.

Darnell, Regna
1998   *And Along Came Boas: Continuity and Revolution in Americanist Anthropology.* Amsterdam: John Benjamins.

Drucker, Philip
1965   *Cultures of the North Pacific Coast.* San Francisco: Chandler.

Ellen, Roy
1986   *Environment, Subsistence and System: The Ecology of Small-Scale Social Formations.* Cambridge: Cambridge University Press.

Ember, Carol R., and Melvin Ember
1990   *Cultural Anthropology.* Englewood Cliffs, NJ: Prentice Hall.

2002   *Cultural Anthropology.* Englewood Cliffs, NJ: Prentice Hall.

Evans-Pritchard, Edward
1981   *A History of Anthropological Thought.* New York: Basic Books.

Fagan, Brian
1999   *Archeology: A Brief Introduction.* Upper Saddle River, NJ: Prentice Hall.

Ferraro, Gary
1992   *Cultural Anthropology: An Applied Perspective.* St. Paul: West Publishing Co.

Fiedel, Stuart
1987   *Prehistory of the Americas.* New York: Cambridge University Press.

Flannery, Kent
1968   Archeological Systems Theory and Early Mesoamerica. In *Anthropological Archeology in the Americas.* Betty Meggers (ed.). Brooklyn, NY: Theo. Gaus' Sons, pp. 67–87.

Fox, R.
1968   *Encounter with Anthropology.* New York: Dell.

Fried, Morton
1967   *Evolution of Political Society: An Essay in Political Anthropology.* New York: McGraw-Hill.

Friedman, Jonathan
1974   The Place of Fetishism and the Problem of Materialist Interpretation. *Critique of Anthropology* 1: 26–62.

Geertz, Clifford
1963   *Agricultural Involution.* Berkeley: University of California Press.

Gellner, Ernest (ed.).
1980 *Soviet and Western Anthropology.* New York: Columbia University Press.

Goldenweiser, Alexander
1921 Four Phases of Anthropological Thought: An Outline. *Papers and Proceedings, American Sociological Society* 16: 50–69.

1924 Anthropological Theories of Political Origins. In *History of Political Theories.* C. E. Merriam and H. E. Barnes (eds.). New York: Macmillan, pp. 430–456.

Goldschmidt, Walter
1952 The Interrelations Between Cultural Factors and the Acquisition of New Technical Skills. In *The Progress of Underdeveloped Areas.* B. Hoselitz (ed.). Chicago: University of Chicago Press, pp. 135–151.

Gross, Daniel
1992 *Discovering Anthropology.* Mountain View, CA: Mayfield.

Haas, Jonathan
1982 *The Evolution of the Prehistoric State.* New York: Columbia University Press.

Hallpike, C. R.
1988 *The Principles of Social Evolution.* Oxford: Clarendon.

Harlan, Jack, J. de Wet, and A. Stemler (eds.).
1976 *Origins of African Plant Domestication.* The Hague: Mouton.

Harris, Marvin
1991 *Cannibals and Kings: The Origins of Cultures.* New York: Vintage. (Original 1977.)

2001a *Cultural Materialism: The Struggle for a Science of Culture.* Walnut Creek, CA: AltaMira. (Original 1979.)

2001b *The Rise of Anthropological Theory.* Walnut Creek, CA: AltaMira. (Original 1968.)

Hatch, Elvin
1973 *Theories of Man and Culture.* New York: Columbia University Press.

Henry, Donald
1989 *From Foraging to Agriculture: The Levant at the End of the Ice Age.* Philadelphia: University of Pennsylvania Press.

Herskovits, Melville
1933 Man, the Speaking Animal. *Sigma Xi Quarterly* 21: 67–82.

1941 Economics and Anthropology: A Rejoinder. *Journal of Political Economy* 49: 269–278.

Herzfeld, Michael
2001 *Anthropology: Theoretical Practice in Culture and Society.* Oxford: Blackwell.

Hyden, Brian
1981 Research and Development in the Stone Age: Technological Transitions Among Hunter-Gatherers. *Current Anthropology* 22: 510–548.

Ingold, Tim
1986 *Evolution and Social Life.* Cambridge: Cambridge University Press.

Joachim, M.
1996 Hunting and Gathering Societies. In *Encyclopedia of Cultural Anthropology.* David Levinson and Melvin Ember (eds.). New York: Henry Holt and Co. Vol. 2, pp. 624–629.

Johnson, Allen, and Timothy Earle
1987 *The Evolution of Human Societies: From Foraging Group to Agrarian State.* Stanford, CA: Stanford University Press.

Kaplan, David, and Robert Manners
1972 *Culture Theory.* Englewood Cliffs, NJ: Prentice Hall.

Kelly, Robert
1995 *The Foraging Spectrum: Diversity in Hunter-Gatherer Lifeways.* Washington: Smithsonian Institution Press.

Kent, Susan (ed.).
1996 *Cultural Diversity Among Twentieth-Century Foragers: An African Perspective.* Cambridge: Cambridge University Press.

Kirch, Patrick
1984   *The Evolution of Polynesian Chiefdoms.* New York: Cambridge University Press.

Kluckhohn, Clyde
1939   The Place of Theory in Anthropological Studies. *The Philosophy of Science* 6: 328–334.

Kottak, Conrad
2002   *Cultural Anthropology.* New York: Mc-Graw-Hill.

Kroeber, Alfred
1917   The Superorganic. *American Anthropologist* 19: 163–213.

1963   *An Anthropologist Looks at History.* Berkeley: University of California Press.

Lambeck, Michael
2001   Rappaport on Religion: A Social Anthropological Reading. In *Ecology of the Sacred: Engaging the Anthropology of Roy A. Rappaport.* E. Messer and M. Lambeck (eds.). Ann Arbor: University of Michigan Press, pp. 244–276.

Langness, L. L.
1993   *The Study of Culture.* Novato, CA: Chandler and Sharp

Laufer, Berthold
1918   Review of Culture and Ethnology by R. H. Lowie. *American Anthropologist* 20: 87–91.

Lee, Richard
1969   !Kung Bushman Subsistence: An Input-Output Analysis. In *Environment and Cultural Behavior.* A. P. Vayda (ed.). New York: Natural History Press, pp. 47–49.

1972   !Kung Spatial Organization: An Ecological and Historical Perspective. *Human Ecology* 1 (2): 125–148.

1979   *The !Kung San: Men, Women, and Work in a Foraging Society.* New York: Cambridge University Press.

1990   Primitive Communism and the Origin of Social Inequality. In *The Evolution of Political Systems: Sociopolitics of Small-Scale Sedentary Societies.* S. Upham (ed.). New York: Cambridge University Press, pp. 225–246.

1993   *The Dobe Ju/'hoansi.* Fort Worth: Harcourt Press.

Lee, Richard B., and R. Daly (eds.).
1999   *The Cambridge Encyclopedia of Hunters and Gatherers.* Cambridge: Cambridge University Press.

Lee, Richard, and Irven DeVore (eds.).
1968   *Man the Hunter.* Chicago: Aldine.

1978   *Kalahari Hunter-Gatherers.* Cambridge: Harvard University Press.

Lee, Richard, and Mathias Guenter
1991   Oxen or Onions? The Search for Trade and the Truth in the Kalahari. *Current Anthropology* 32: 593–601.

1995   Errors Corrected or Compounded: A Reply to Wilmsen. *Current Anthropology* 36: 298–305.

Lenkeit, Roberta
2001   *Introducing Cultural Anthropology.* Mountain View, CA: Mayfield.

Lett, James
1987   *The Human Enterprise: A Critical Introduction to Anthropological Theory.* Boulder, CO: Westview Press.

Lotka, Alfred
1922a   Contributions to the Energetics of Evolution. *Proceedings of the National Academy of Sciences* 8: 147–151.

1922b   Natural Selection as a Physical Principle. *Proceedings of the National Academy of Sciences* 8: 151–154.

1945   The Law of Evolution as a Maximal Principle. *Human Biology* 17: 167–194.

Lowie, Robert H.
1917   *Culture and Ethnology.* New York: Douglas McMurtrie.

1920   *Primitive Society.* New York: Boni and Liveright.

Manners, Robert
1973   Julian Haynes Steward: 1902–1972. *American Anthropologist* 75 (3): 886–903.

Marshall, L.
1960   !Kung Bushman Bands. *Africa* 30: 325–355.

Marx, Karl
1904   *A Contribution to the Critique of Political Economy.* Chicago: Charles Kerr. (Original 1859.)

McCorriston, Joy, and Frank Hole
1991   The Ecology of Seasonal Stress and the Origins of Agriculture. *American Anthropologist* 93: 46–69.

Medvedev, Z. A.
1969   *The Rise and Fall of T. D. Lysenko.* New York: Columbia University Press.

Meggers, Betty
1960   The Law of Cultural Evolution as a Practical Research Tool. In *Essays in the Science of Culture: In Honor of Leslie A. White.* Gertrude Dole and Robert Carneiro (eds.). New York: Thomas Y. Crowell, pp. 302–316.

Messer, Ellen
2001   Thinking and Engaging the Whole: The Anthropology of Roy A. Rappaport. In *Ecology of the Sacred: Engaging the Anthropology of Roy A. Rappaport.* E. Messer and M. Lambeck (eds.). Ann Arbor: University of Michigan Press, pp. 1–38.

Milton, Kay
1996   *Environmentalism and Cultural Theory: Exploring the Role of Anthropology in Environmental Discourse.* London: Routledge.

Moran, Emilio
1993   Ecosystem Ecology in Biology and Anthropology: A Critical Assessment. In *The Ecosystem Approach in Anthropology.* Emilio Moran (ed.). Ann Arbor: University of Michigan Press, pp. 3–40.

Morgan, Lewis H.
1851   *League of the Ho-de-no-sau-nee, or Iroquois.* New York: Sage & Bros.

1877   *Ancient Society: Researches in the Lines of Human Progress from Savagery, through Barbarism to Civilization.* New York: Henry Holt Co.

Murphy, Robert F.
1976   Introduction: A Quarter Century of American Anthropology. In *Selected Papers from the American Anthropologist 1946–1970.* Robert Murphy (ed.). Washington, DC: The American Anthropological Association, pp. 1–22.

1977   Introduction: The Anthropological Theories of Julian H. Steward. In *Evolution and Ecology: Essays on Social Transformation by Julian H. Steward.* Jane Steward and Robert Murphy (eds.). Urbana: University of Illinois Press, pp. 1–39.

1981   Julian Steward. In *Totems and Teachers: Perspectives on the History of Anthropology.* Sydel Silverman (ed.). New York: Columbia University Press, pp. 171–206.

Netting, Robert McC.
1968   *Hill Farmers of Nigeria: Cultural Ecology of the Kofyar of the Jos Plateau.* Seattle: University of Washington Press.

Odum, Eugene
1953   *Fundamentals of Ecology.* Philadelphia: Saunders.

Odum, Howard
1971   *Environment, Power, and Society.* New York: Wiley-Interscience.

Oliver, S. C.
1962   *Ecology and Cultural Continuity as Contributing Factors in the Social Organization of the Plains Indians.* University of California Publication in American Archaeology and Ethnology 48. Berkeley: University of California Press.

Opler, Morris
1961   Cultural Evolution, Southern Athapaskans, and Chronology in Theory. *Southwestern Journal of Anthropology* 20: 123–145.

Orlove, Benjamin
1980   Ecological Anthropology. *Annual Review of Anthropology* 9: 235–273.

Parsons, Elsie Clews
1920 Review of *Primitive Society* by R. H. Lowie. *The New Republic* 24: 245–246.

Pimentel, D., and M. Pimentel
1979 *Food, Energy, and Society*. London: Edward Arnold.

Price, Douglas, and James Brown (eds.).
1985 *Prehistoric Hunter-Gatherers*. New York: Academic Press.

Radcliffe-Brown, A. R.
1913 Three Tribes of Western Australia. *Journal of the Royal Anthropological Institute* 43: 143–195.

1918 Notes on the Social Organization of Australian Tribes. *Journal of the Royal Anthropological Institute* 48: 222–253.

Radin, Paul
1987 *The Method and Theory of Ethnology: An Essay in Criticism*. South Hadley, MA: Bergin and Garvey. (Original 1933.)

Rambo, A. Terry
1991a Energy and the Evolution of Culture: A Reassessment of White's Law. In *Profiles in Cultural Evolution: Papers from a Conference in Honor of Elman R. Service*. A. T. Rambo and K. Gillogly (eds.). Ann Arbor: The Museum of Anthropology, The University of Michigan, pp. 291–310.

1991b The Study of Cultural Evolution. In *Profiles in Cultural Evolution: Papers from a Conference in Honor of Elman R. Service*. A. T. Rambo and K. Gillogly (eds.). Ann Arbor: The Museum of Anthropology, The University of Michigan, pp. 23–109.

Rappaport, Roy
1984 *Pigs for the Ancestors*. New Haven: Yale University Press. (Original 1968.)

1993 Ecosystems, Populations and People. In *The Ecosystem Approach in Anthropology*. Emilio Moran (ed.). Ann Arbor: University of Michigan Press, pp. 41–72.

Rindos, David
1984 *The Origins of Agriculture: An Evolutionary Perspective*. New York: Academic Press.

Sahlins, Marshall
1958 *Social Stratification in Polynesia*. American Ethnological Society, Monograph 29. Seattle: Washington University Press.

1960 Evolution: Specific and General. In *Evolution and Culture*. Marshall Sahlins and Elman Service (eds.). Ann Arbor: University of Michigan Press, pp. 12–44.

1968 *Tribesmen*. Englewood Cliffs, NJ: Prentice Hall.

1972 *Stone Age Economics*. Chicago: Aldine.

1982 The Original Affluent Society. In *Anthropology for the Eighties*. J. Cole (ed.). New York: The Free Press, pp. 219–240.

1997 The Original Affluent Society. In *The Consumer Society*. Frank Ackerman and David Kiron (eds.). Washington, DC: Island Press, pp. 18–20.

Sahlins, Marshall, and E. Service (eds.).
1960 *Evolution and Culture*. Ann Arbor: University of Michigan Press.

Sanderson, Stephen
1990 *Social Evolutionism: A Critical History*. Oxford: Blackwell.

1999 *Social Transformations: A General Theory of Historical Development*. Lanham, MD: Rowman and Littlefield.

Sapir, Edward
1920a Review of *Primitive Society* by R. H. Lowie. *The Freeman* 1: 377–379.

1920b Review of *Primitive Society* by R. H. Lowie. *The Nation* 111: 46–47.

Schrire, C. (ed.).
1984 *Past and Present in Hunter Gatherer Studies*. Orlando, FL: Academic Press.

Service, Elman
1962   *Primitive Social Organization: An Evolutionary Perspective.* New York: Random House.

1971   *Cultural Evolutionism: Theory and Practice.* New York: Holt, Rinehart and Winston.

1975   *Origins of the State and Civilization: The Process of Cultural Evolution.* New York: Norton.

1976   Leslie Alvin White, 1900–1975. *American Anthropologist* 78: 612–617.

1979   *The Hunters.* Englewood Cliffs, NJ: Prentice Hall.

1985   *A Century of Controversy: Ethnological Issues from 1860 to 1960.* Orlando: Academic Press.

Sidky, H.
1996   *Irrigation and State Formation in Hunza.* Lanham, MD: University Press of America.

Steward, Julian
1936   The Economic and Social Basis of Primitive Bands. In *Essays in Honor of Alfred Louis Kroeber.* Cora DuBois (ed.). Berkeley: University of California Press, pp. 311–350.

1938   *Basin-Plateau Aboriginal Sociopolitical Groups.* Bureau of American Ethnology Bulletin 120.

1940   Native Cultures of Intermontane (Great Basin) Area. In *Essays in Historical Anthropology of North America.* Smithsonian Miscellaneous Collections 100: 445–502.

1941   *Culture Element Distributions: XIII, Nevada Shoshoni.* University of California Publications in Anthropological Records 4: 208–259.

1946–1950   *The Handbook of South American Indians.* Bureau of American Ethnology Bulletin 143, 7 vols. (1946–1959).

1949   Cultural Causality and Law: A Trial Formulation of the Development of Early Civilizations. *American Anthropologist* 51: 1–27.

1950   *Area Research: Theory and Practice.* Social Science Research Council Bulletin 63: 1–164.

1955   *Theory of Culture Change: The Methodology of Multilinear Evolution.* Chicago: University of Illinois Press.

1956   *The People of Puerto Rico: A Study in Social Anthropology.* Urbana: Illinois University Press.

1959   *Native Peoples of South America.* New York: McGraw-Hill (with Louis Faron).

1960a   *Alfred Louis Kroeber, 1876–1960.* Washington, DC: American Anthropological Society.

1960b   Review of *The Evolution of Culture* by Leslie A. White. *American Anthropologist* 62: 144–148.

1967   *Contemporary Change in Traditional Societies.* Urbana: University of Illinois Press. 3 vols.

1977a   The Concept and Method of Cultural Ecology. In *Evolution and Ecology: Essays on Social Transformation by Julian H. Steward.* Jane Steward and Robert Murphy (eds.). Urbana: University of Illinois Press, pp. 43–57. (Original 1955.)

1977b   Tappers and Trappers: Parallel Processes in Acculturation. In *Evolution and Ecology: Essays on Social Transformation by Julian H. Steward.* Jane Steward and Robert Murphy (eds.). Urbana: University of Illinois Press, pp. 151–179. (Original 1956.)

1977c   Wittfogel's Irrigation Hypothesis. In *Evolution and Ecology: Essays on Social Transformation by Julian H. Steward.* Jane Steward and Robert Murphy (eds.). Urbana: University of Illinois Press, pp. 87–99.

Stewart, Pamela, and A. Strathern
2001   Rappaport's Maring: The Challenge of Ethnography. In *Ecology of the Sacred: Engaging the Anthropology of Roy A. Rappaport.* E. Messer and M. Lambeck (eds.). Ann Arbor: University of Michigan Press, pp. 277–290.

Stiles, D.
1992   The Hunter-Gatherer "Revisionist" Debate. *Anthropology Today* 8 (2): 15.

Stocking, George, Jr.
1974 Introduction: The Basic Assumptions of Boasian Anthropology. In *The Shaping of American Anthropology 1883–1911: A Franz Boas Reader.* New York: Basic Books, pp. 1–20.

Sweet, Louise
1965 Camel Pastoralism in North Arabia and the Minimal Camping Unit. In *Man, Culture and Animals: The Role of Animals in Human Ecological Adjustments.* Leeds, A. & A.P. Vayda (eds.). American Assoc. Advancement of Science, publication no. 78, Washington DC, pp. 129–152.

1970 Camel Raiding of North Arabian Bedouin: A Mechanism of Ecological Adaptation. In *Peoples and Cultures of the Middle East.* L. Sweet (ed.). Garden City: Natural History Press, vol. 2, pp. 265–289.

Toumlin, S. E.
1981 Human Adaptation. In *The Philosophy of Evolution.* U. Jensen and R. Harré (eds.). Brighton: Harvester, pp. 176–195.

Trigger, Bruce
1998 *Sociocultural Evolution: Calculation and Contingency.* Oxford: Blackwell.

Turnbull, Colin
1961 *The Forest People: A Study of the Pygmies of the Congo.* New York: Simon and Schuster.

1968 The Importance of Flux in Two Hunting Societies. In *Man the Hunter.* R. Lee and I. DeVore (eds.). Chicago: Aldine, pp. 132–137.

Turner, Jonathan, M. Mulder, and L. Cosmides
1997 Looking Back: Historical and Theoretical Context of Present Practice. In *Human by Nature: Between Biology and the Social Sciences.* P. Weingart et al. (eds.). Mahwah, NJ: L. Erlbaum, pp. 17–64.

Tylor, Edward B.
1881 *Anthropology.* London: Macmillan.

Vayda, A. P., and B. J. McCay
1975 New Directions in Ecology and Ecological Anthropology. In *Annual Review of Anthropology.* B. J. Siegel, A. R. Beals, and S. A. Tyler (eds.), vol. 4. Palo Alto: Annual Reviews, pp. 293–306.

Vayda, Andrew P., and Roy Rappaport
1968 Ecology, Cultural and Non-Cultural. In *Introduction to Cultural Anthropology.* J. Cliffton (ed.). Boston: Houghton-Mifflin, pp. 477–497.

Wax, Murray
1956 The Limitations of Boas' Anthropology. *American Anthropologist* 8: 63–74.

White, Leslie (ed.)
1932a *The Acoma Indians.* Bureau of American Ethnology, 47th Annual Report, pp. 17–192.

1932b *The Pueblo of San Felipe.* American Anthropological Association. Memoir 38.

1934 *The Pueblo of Santo Domingo.* American Anthropological Association. Memoir 43.

1942 *The Pueblo of Santa Ana, New Mexico.* American Anthropological Association, Memoir 60.

1943 Energy and the Evolution of Culture. *American Anthropologist* 45: 335–356.

1948a Ikhnaton: The Great Man vs. the Culture Process. *Journal of the American Oriental Society* 68: 91–114. [In *The Science of Culture* 1949: 233–281.]

1948b Review of Graham Clark, *From Savagery to Civilization,* and V. Gordon Childe, *History. Antiquity* 22: 217–218.

1949 *The Science of Culture: A Study of Man and Civilization.* New York: Grove Press.

1959 *The Evolution of Culture: The Development of Civilization to the Fall of Rome.* New York: McGraw-Hill.

1962 *The Pueblo of Sia, New Mexico.* Bureau of American Ethnology, Bulletin 6.

1987a Evolutionism in Cultural Anthropology: A Rejoinder [1947]. In *Leslie A. White: Ethnological Essays.* Beth Dillingham and Robert Carneiro (eds.). Albuquerque: University of New Mexico Press, pp. 85–96.

1987b Introduction to Part I. In *Leslie White: Ethnological Essays.* Beth Dillingham and Robert Carneiro (eds.). Albuquerque: University of New Mexico Press, pp. 11–15.

1987c Evolutionary Stages, Progress, and the Evaluation of Cultures. In *Leslie White: Ethnological Essays.* Beth Dillingham and Robert Carneiro (eds.). Albuquerque: University of New Mexico Press, pp. 59–83.

1987d Review of Julian H. Steward's *Theory of Culture Change: The Methodology of Multilinear Evolution.* In *Leslie White: Ethnological Essays.* Beth Dillingham and Robert Carneiro (eds.). Albuquerque: University of New Mexico Press, pp. 123–128.

1987e Evolutionism and Anti-Evolutionism in American Ethnological Theory [1947]. In *Leslie White: Ethnological Essays.* Beth Dillingham and Robert Carneiro (eds.). Albuquerque: University of New Mexico Press, pp. 97–122.

1987f The Energy Theory of Cultural Development. In *Leslie White: Ethnological Essays.* Beth Dillingham and Robert Carneiro (eds.). Albuquerque: University of New Mexico Press, pp. 215–221.

1987g Individuality and Individualism: A Culturological Interpretation. In *Leslie White: Ethnological Essays.* Beth Dillingham and Robert Carneiro (eds.). Albuquerque: University of New Mexico Press, pp. 297–316.

White, Leslie (ed.).
1937 *Extracts from the European Travel Journals of Lewis H. Morgan.* Rochester Historical Society Publications XVI: 221–390.

1940 *Pioneers in American Anthropology: The Bandelier-Morgan Letters 1873–1883.* Albuquerque: The University of New Mexico Press, 2 vols.

Wilmsen, Edwin, and James Denbow
1990 Paradigmatic History of the San-Speaking People and Current Attempts at Revision. *Current Anthropology* 31: 489–524.

Winterhalder, Bruce
1984 Reconsidering the Ecosystem Concept. *Reviews in Anthropology* 12: 301–313.

Wittfogel, Karl
1957 *Oriental Despotism: A Comparative Study of Total Power.* New Haven, CT: Yale University Press.

Wolf, Eric
1964 *Anthropology.* Englewood Cliffs, NJ: Prentice Hall.

Woodburn, Richard
1968 An Introduction to Hadza Ecology. In *Man the Hunter.* R. Lee and I. DeVore (eds.). Chicago: Aldine, pp. 49–55.

Chapter 11

Aarne, Antti Amatus
1961 *The Types of the Folktale: A Classification and Bibliography.* Translated by Stith Thompson. Helsinki: Academia Scientarum Fennica.

Adams, William
1998 *The Philosophical Roots of Anthropology.* Stanford, CA: CSLI Publications.

Barnouw, Victor
1985 *Culture and Personality.* Homewood, IL: Doresy Press.

Barrett, Stanley
1984 *The Rebirth of Anthropological Theory.* Toronto: University of Toronto Press.

1996 *Anthropology: A Student's Guide to Theory and Method.* Toronto: University of Toronto Press.

Bidney, David
1967 *Theoretical Anthropology.* New York: Schocken Books. (Original 1953.)

Bischof, N.
1975 Comparative Ethology of Incest Avoidance In *Biosocial Anthropology.* R. Fox (ed.). London: Malaby Press, pp. 37–67.

Bittles, Alan et al.
1991   Reproductive Behavior and Health in Consanguineous Marriages. *Science* 2 (52): 789–794.

Bixler, Ray
1982   Comments on the Incidence and Purpose of Royal Sibling Incest. *American Anthropologist* 9: 580–582.

Bleakley, Alan
2000   *The Animalizing Imagination: Totemism, Textuality and Ecocriticism.* New York: St. Martin's Press.

Bodley, John H.
1994   *Cultural Anthropology: Tribes, States, and the Global System.* Mountain View, CA: Mayfield.

Bohannan, Paul and Mark Glazer (eds.).
1988   *High Points in Anthropology.* New York: Alfred Knopf.

Bourke, Colin, E. Bourke, and B. Edwards (eds.).
1998   *Aboriginal Australia: An Introductory Reader in Aboriginal Studies.* St. Lucia, Qld., Australia: University of Queensland Press.

Campbell, Bernard
1979   *Humankind Emerging.* Boston: Little, Brown.

Chomsky, Noam
1966   *Cartesian Linguistics.* New York: Harper and Row.

1972   *Language and the Mind.* New York: Harcourt.

Claus, Peter
1982   A Structuralist Appreciation of "Star Trek." In *Anthropology for the Eighties.* J. Cole (ed.). New York: The Free Press, pp. 417–429.

Cox, Marian
1893   *Cinderella.* London: Published for the Folklore Society by D. Nutt.

D'Andrade, Roy
1995   *The Development of Cognitive Anthropology.* Cambridge: Cambridge University Press.

Diamond, Stanley
1974   The Myth of Structuralism. In *The Unconscious in Culture: The Structuralism of Claude Lévi-Strauss.* Ino Rossi (ed.). New York: Dutton, pp. 292–335.

Douglas, Mary
1966   *Purity and Danger: An Analysis of Concepts of Pollution and Taboo.* New York: Praeger.

Dundes Alan (ed.).
1983   *Cinderella: A Casebook.* New York: Wildman Press.

Durkheim Émile
1915   *The Elementary Forms of the Religious Life.* London: Allen & Unwin,

Ember, Carol R., and Melvin Ember
1990   *Cultural Anthropology.* Englewood Cliffs, NJ: Prentice Hall.

Evans-Pritchard, E. E.
1965   *Theories of Primitive Religion.* Oxford: Oxford University Press.

Ferraro, Gary
1992   *Cultural Anthropology: An Applied Perspective.* St. Paul: West Publishing Co.

Fox, Robin
1967a   *Kinship and Marriage.* Baltimore: Penguin.

1967b   Totem and Taboo Reconsidered. In *The Structural Study of Myth and Totemism.* E. Leach (ed.). London: Tavistock, pp. 161–178.

Frazer, James George
1919–1927   *The Golden Bough: A Study in Magic and Religion.* London: Macmillan. 12 vols.

1968   *Totemism and Exogamy: A Treatise on Certain Early Forms of Superstition and Society.* London: Dawsons. (Original 1910.)

Freud, Sigmund
1920   *A General Introduction to Psychoanalysis.* New York: Boni and Liveright. (Original 1917.)

1938 Totem and Taboo: Resemblances Between the Psychic Life of Savages and Neurotics. In *The Basic Writings of Sigmund Freud*. A. Brill (ed.). New York: Modern Library, pp. 807–930. (Original 1911.)

1952 *Totem & Taboo*. New York. Norton

Gamst, Frederick
1980 Rethinking Leach's Structural Analysis of Color and Instructional Categories in Traffic Signals. In *Beyond the Myths of Culture: Essays in Cultural Materialism*. Eric Ross (ed.). New York: Academic Press, pp. 359–390.

Goldenweiser, Alexander
1910 Totemism: An Analytical Study. *Journal of American Folklore* 23: 178–298.

Gregor, Thomas
1985 *Anxious Pleasures*. Chicago: University of Chicago Press.

Gross, Daniel
1992 *Discovering Anthropology*. Mountain View, CA: Mayfield.

Haley, Michael, and R. Lunsford
1994 *Noam Chomsky*. New York: Twayne.

Harris, Marvin
1997 *Culture, People, Nature: An Introduction to General Anthropology*. New York: Longman.

2001a *Cultural Materialism: The Struggle for a Science of Culture*. Walnut Creek, CA: AltaMira. (Original 1979.)

2001b *The Rise of Anthropological Theory*. Walnut Creek, CA: AltaMira. (Original 1968.)

Hartung, John
1985 Review of *Incest: A Biosocial View*, by J. Shepher. *American Journal of Physical Anthropology* 67: 169–171.

Haviland, William A.
1993 *Cultural Anthropology*. Forth Worth: Harcourt.

Hénaff, Marcel
1998 *Claude Lévi-Strauss and the Making of Structural Anthropology*. Minneapolis: University of Minnesota Press.

Honigmann, John J.
1976 *The Development of Anthropological Ideas*. Homewood, IL: The Dorsey Press.

Hopkins, K.
1980 Brother–Sister Marriage in Roman Egypt. *Comparative Studies in Society and History* 22: 303–354.

Isaacs, Jennifer (ed.).
1980 *Australian Dreaming: 40,000 Years of Aboriginal History*. Sydney: Lansdowne Press.

Jenkins, Alan
1979 *The Social Theory of Claude Lévi-Strauss*. New York: St. Martins Press.

Kaffman, M.
1977 Sexual Standards and the Behavior of the Kibbutz Adolescent. *Journal of Orthopsychiatry* 47: 207–217.

Kaplan, David, and Robert Manners
1972 *Culture Theory*. Englewood Cliffs, NJ: Prentice Hall.

Keesing, Roger M., and Felix Keesing
1971 *New Perspectives in Cultural Anthropology*. New York: Holt, Rinehart and Winston.

Kroeber, Alfred
1920 Totem & Taboo: An Ethnologic Psychoanalysis. *American Anthropologist* 22: 48–55.

Kuper, Adam
1999 *Anthropology and Anthropologists: The Modern British School*. London: Routledge.

Langness, L. L.
1993 *The Study of Culture*. Novato, CA: Chandler and Sharp.

Layton, Robert
1997 *An Introduction to Theory in Anthropology*. Cambridge: Cambridge University Press.

Leach, Edmund
1970   *Claude Lévi-Strauss.* New York: Viking Press.

Leaf, Murray
1979   *Man, Mind, and Science: A History of Anthropology.* New York: Columbia University Press.

Leavitt, Gregory
1989   Disappearance of the Incest Taboo. *American Anthropologist* 91: 116–131.

1990   Sociobiological Explanations of Incest Avoidance: A Critical Review of the Evidential Claims. *American Anthropologist* 92: 971– 993.

Lett, James
1987   *The Human Enterprise: A Critical Introduction to Anthropological Theory.* Boulder, CO: Westview.

Lévi-Strauss, Calude
1963   *Totemism.* Boston Beacon Press. (Original 1962.)

1966   *The Savage Mind.* Chicago: University of Chicago Press.

1967   *Structural Anthropology.* New York: Anchor Books.

1969a   *Elementary Structures of Kinship.* Boston: Beacon Press. (Original 1949.)

1969b   *The Raw and the Cooked: Introduction to a Science of Mythology.* New York: Harper and Row. (Original 1964.)

1973   *From Honey to Ashes.* New York: Harper and Row. (Original 1967.)

1974   *Tristes Tropiques: An Anthropological Study of Primitive Societies in Brazil.* New York: Antheneum.

1978   *The Origins of Table Manners.* New York: Harper and Row. (Original 1968.)

1981   *The Naked Man.* New York: Harper and Row. (Original 1971.)

1985   *The View from Afar.* New York: Basic Books. (Original 1983.)

1987   *Anthropology and Myth, Lectures 1951– 1982.* Oxford: Basil Blackwell.

1988   *The Jealous Potter.* Chicago: University of Chicago Press. (Original 1985.)

1995   *Saudades do Brazil: A Photographic Memoir.* Seattle: University of Washington Press.

Lewis, Oscar
1955   Peasant Culture in India and Mexico: A Comparative Analysis. In *Village India: Studies in the Little Community.* M. Marriott (ed.). Chicago: University of Chicago Press, pp. 145–170.

Livingston, Frank
1982   Comment on Littlefield, Lieberman, and Reynolds. *Current Anthropology* 23: 651.

Long, John
1791   *Voyages and Travels of an Indian Interpreter and Trader.* New York: Johnson Reprint Corp. (1968).

Lowie, Robert
1920   *Primitive Society.* New York: Boni and Liveright.

1952   *Primitive Religion.* New York: Grosset and Dunlap. (Original 1924.)

Maher, John C., and Judy Groves
1997   *Introducing Chomsky.* New York: Totem Books.

Malefijt, Annemarie
1974   *Images of Man: A History of Anthropological Thought.* New York: Alfred Knopf.

Malinowski, Bronislaw
1927   *Sex and Repression in Savage Society.* London: Kegan Paul.

Mauss, Marcel
2000   *The Gift: The Form and Reason for Exchange in Archaic Societies.* New York: W. W. Norton. (Original 1924.)

McGee, R. Jon, and Richard Warms
2000   *Anthropological Theory: An Introductory History.* Mountain View, CA: Mayfield.

McLennan, John
1869   The Worship of Animals and Plants. *Fortune Review* 6: 407–427, 568–582.

Middleton, Russell
1962   Brother–Sister and Father–Daughter Marriages in Ancient Egypt. *American Sociological Review* 27: 603–611.

Moore, Jerry
1997   *Visions of Culture: An Introduction to Anthropological Theories and Theorists.* Walnut Creek, CA: AltaMira.

Morris, Brian
1988   *Anthropological Studies of Religion.* Cambridge: Cambridge University Press.

Murphy, Robert
1980   *The Dialectics of Social Life: Alarms and Excursions in Anthropological Theory.* New York: Columbia University Press.

Ortner, Sherry
1984   Theory in Anthropology Since the Sixties. *Comparative Studies in Society and History* 26 (1): 126–166.

Pandian, Jacob
1991   *Culture, Religion, and the Sacred Self.* Englewood Cliffs, NJ: Prentice Hall.

Parker, S.
1976   The Precultural Basis of the Incest Taboo: Toward a Biosocial Theory. *American Anthropologist* 78: 28–305.

Penner, Hans (ed.).
1988   *Teaching Lévi-Strauss.* Atlanta: Scholars Press.

Pusey, A. E.
1980   Inbreeding Avoidance in Chimpanzees. *Animal Behavior* 28: 543–552.

Radcliffe-Brown, Alfred R.
1952a   The Mother's Brother in South Africa. In *Structure and Function in Primitive Society: Essays and Addresses.* E. Evans-Pritchard and F. Eggan (eds.). Glenco, IL: The Free Press, pp. 15–31.

1952b   The Sociological Theory of Totemism. In *Structure and Function in Primitive Society: Essays and Addresses.* E. Evans-Pritchard and F. Eggan (eds.). Glenco, IL: The Free Press, pp. 117–132.

1977   The Comparative Method in Social Anthropology. In *The Social Anthropology of Radcliffe-Brown.* Adam Kuper (ed.). London: Routledge and Kegan Paul, pp. 53–69.

Segal, Robert (ed.).
1996   *Ritual and Myth: Robertson Smith, Frazer, Hooke, and Harrison.* New York: Garland.

1998   *The Myth and Ritual Theory: An Anthology.* Malden, MA: Blackwell.

Shepher, Joseph
1983   *Incest: A Biosocial Point of View.* New York: Academic Press.

Smith, William Robertson
1889   *Lectures on the Religion of the Semites.* Edinburgh: Adam and Charles Black.

Spencer, Baldwin, and F. J. Gillen
1904   *The Northern Tribes of Central Australia.* London: Macmillan.

Sperber, Dan
1996   *Explaining Culture: A Naturalistic Approach.* Oxford: Blackwell.

Staski, Edward, and Jonathan Marks
1992   *Evolutionary Anthropology: An Introduction to Physical Anthropology and Archaeology.* New York: Holt, Rinehart, and Winston.

Talmon, Yonina
1964   Mate Selection in Collective Settlements. *American Sociological Review* 29: 491–508.

Tonkinson, Robert
1991   *The Mardu Aborigines: Living the Dream in Australia's Desert.* Fort Worth: Holt, Rinehart and Winston.

Tylor, Edward
1889   On a Method of Investigating the Development of Institutions: Applied to Laws of Marriage and Descent. *Journal of the Royal Anthropological Institute* 18: 245–269.

Werner, Oswald
1973   Structural Anthropology. In *Main Currents in Cultural Anthropology*. Raoul Naroll and Frada Naroll (eds.). Englewood Cliffs, NJ: Prentice Hall, pp. 281–307.

Westermarck, Edward
1894   *The History of Human Marriage*. London: Macmillan.

Whelehan, P.
1985   Review of *Incest, a Biosocial View* by Joseph Shepher. *American Anthropologist* 87: 677–678.

White, Leslie
1949   *The Science of Culture: Study of Man and Civilization*. New York: Farrar, Straus and Cudahy.

Willner, Dorothy
1983   Definition and Violation: Incest and the Incest Taboo. *Man* 18: 134–159.

Wolf, Arthur
1966   Childhood Association, Sexual Attraction, and the Incest Taboo: A Chinese Case. *American Anthropologist* 68: 883–898.

1970   Adopt a Daughter-in-law, Marry a Sister: A Chinese Solution to the Problem of the Incest Taboo. *American Anthropologist* 70: 865–874.

1993   Westermarck Redivivus. *Annual Review of Anthropology* 22: 155–156.

1995   *Sexual Attraction and Childhood Association*. Stanford: Stanford University Press.

Chapter 12

Abu-Lughod, Lila
1991   Writing Against Culture. In *Recapturing Anthropology*. Richard Fox (ed.). Santa Fe, NM: School of American Research Press. Distributed by the University of Washington Press, pp. 37–62.

Barrett, Richard A.
1991   *Culture and Conduct: An Excursion in Anthropology*. Belmont, CA: Wadsworth.

Berlin, Brent
1992   *Ethnobiological Classification: Principles of Categorization of Plants and Animals in Traditional Societies*. Princeton, NJ: Princeton University Press.

Berlin, Brent, and Paul Kay
1969   *Basic Color Terms: Their Universality and Evolution*. Berkeley: University of California Press.

Bernard, Russell
1995   *Research Methods in Anthropology: Qualitative and Quantitative Methods*. Walnut Creek, CA: AltaMira.

Berreman, Gerald
1966   Anemic and Emetic Analyses in Social Anthropology. *American Anthropologist* 68: 405–413.

Bloch, Bernard, and George Trager
1942   *Outline of Linguistic Analysis*. Baltimore: Linguistic Society of America.

Boas, Franz
1943   Recent Anthropology. *Science* 98: 311–314, 334–337.

Bornstein, Marc
1973   The Psychophysiological Component of Cultural Difference in Color Naming and Illusions Susceptibility. *Behavior Science Notes* 8: 41–101.

Bria, Gina
1998   *The Art of Family: Rituals, Imagination, and Everyday Spirituality*. New York: Dell.

Burling, Robbins
1964   Cognition and Componential Analysis: God's Truth or Hocus Pocus? *American Anthropologist* 66 (1): 20–28.

Chomsky, Noam
1970   *Current Issues in Linguistic Theory*. The Hague: Mouton.

Clifford, James
1986   Introduction: Partial Truths. In *Writing Culture: The Poetics and Politics of Ethnography*. James Clifford and George Marcus (eds.). Berkeley: University of California Press, pp. 1–26.

Conklin, Harold
1955   Hanunóo Color Categories. *Southwestern Journal of Anthropology* 11: 339–344.

D'Andrade, Roy
1995   *The Development of Cognitive Anthropology.* Cambridge: Cambridge University Press.

1999   Culture Is Not Everything. In *Anthropological Theory in North America*. E. L. Cerroni-Long (ed.). Westport, CT: Bergin and Garvey, pp. 85–103.

Dolgin, Janet, David Kemnitzer, and David Schnieder
1977   "As People Express Their Lives, So They Are . . ." In *Symbolic Anthropology: A Reader in the Study of Symbols and Meanings*. Janet Dolgin, David Kemnitzer, and David Schnieder (eds.). New York: Columbia University Press, pp. 3–44.

Eastman, Carol
1990   *Aspects of Language and Culture.* Novato, CA: Chandler and Sharp.

Ellen, Roy, P. Parkes, and Alan Bicker (eds.).
2000   *Indigenous Environmental Knowledge and its Transformations: Critical Anthropological Perspectives.* Amsterdam: Harwood Academic.

Ember, Melvin
1978   Size of Color Lexicon: Interaction of Cultural and Biological Factors. *American Anthropologist* 80: 364–367.

Farber, Bernard
1981   *Conceptions of Kinship.* New York: Elsevier.

Fischer, John
1958   The Classification of Residence Censuses. *American Anthropologist* 60 (3): 508–517.

Frake, Charles
1961   The Diagnosis of Disease among the Subanun of Mindanao. *American Anthropologist* 63: 113–132.

1969   Notes on Queries in Ethnography. In *Cognitive Anthropology*. Stephen Tyler (ed.). New York: Holt, Rinehart and Winston, pp. 123–137.

1972   The Ethnographic Study of Cognitive Systems. In *Culture and Cognition: Rules, Maps, and Plans*. James Spradley (ed.). San Francisco: Chandler, pp. 191–205. (Original 1962.)

Geertz, Clifford
1973   *The Interpretation of Cultures: Selected Essays.* New York: Basic Books.

Gleason, Henry A.
1955   *An Introduction to Descriptive Linguistics.* New York: Holt, Rinehart, and Winston. (With the companion volume *Workbook in Descriptive Linguistics* [1955]. New York: Holt, Rinehart, and Winston.)

Goodenough, Ward
1956a   Componential Analysis and the Study of Meaning. *Language* 32: 195–216.

1956b   Residence Rules. *Southwestern Journal of Anthropology* 12 (1): 22–37.

1957   Cultural Anthropology and Linguistics. In *Report of the Seventh Annual Round Table Meeting on Linguistics and Language Study*. Paul Garvin (ed.). Washington: Georgetown University Monograph Series on Language and Linguistics No. 9, pp. 167–173.

1964   Introduction. In *Explorations in Cultural Anthropology*. Ward Goodenough (ed.). New York: McGraw-Hill, pp. 1–24.

1970   *Description and Comparison in Cultural Anthropology.* Chicago: Aldine.

Gross, Daniel
1992   *Discovering Anthropology.* Mountain View, CA: Mayfield.

Grenier, Louise
1998   *Working with Indigenous Knowledge: A Guide for Researchers.* Ottawa: International Development Research Centre.

Hamill, James, H. Sidky, and J. Subedi
2002   Birds for Words: Structure and Function in a Tibeto-Burman Folk Taxonomy. *Anthropological Linguistics* 44 (1): 65–85.

Harris, Marvin
1980   History and Ideological Significance of the Separation of Social and Cultural Anthropology. In *Beyond the Myths of Culture: Essays in Cultural Materialism*. Eric Ross (ed.). New York: Academic Press, pp. 391–407.

2001a   *Cultural Materialism: The Struggle for a Science of Culture*. Walnut Creek, CA: AltaMira.

2001b   *The Rise of Anthropological Theory*. Walnut Creek, CA: AltaMira.

Harris, Zellig
1951   *Methods in Structural Linguistics*. Chicago: University of Chicago Press.

Headland, Thomas N., Kenneth L. Pike, and Marvin Harris (eds.).
1990   *Emics and Etics: The Insider/Outsider Debate*. Newbury Park, CA: Sage Publications.

Honigmann, John J.
1976   *The Development of Anthropological Ideas*. Homewood, IL: The Dorsey Press.

Johnson, Allen, and Orna Johnson
2001   Introduction to the Updated Edition. In *Cutural Materialism: The Struggle for a Science of Culture*. M. Harris. Walnut Creek, CA: AltaMira, pp. vi–xiv.

Kaplan, David, and Robert Manners
1972   *Culture Theory*. Englewood Cliffs, NJ: Prentice Hall.

Kay, Paul
1975   Synchronic Variability and Diachronic Change in Basic Color Terms. *Language in Society* 4: 257–270.

Kay, Paul, and Chad McDaniel
1978   The Linguistic Significance of the Meanings of Basic Color Terms. *Language* 54: 610–646.

Kroeber, Alfred, and Clyde Kluckhohn
1963   *Culture: A Critical Review of Concepts and Definitions*. New York: Vintage. (Original 1952.)

Kroeber, Alfred, and Talcott Parsons
1958   The Concept of Culture and of Social Systems. *American Sociological Review* 23: 582–583.

Kronenfeld, David
1996   *Plastic Glasses and Church Fathers: Semantic Extension From the Ethnoscience Tradition*. New York: Oxford University Press.

Lounsbury, Floyd
1956   A Semantic Analysis of Pawnee Kinship Usage. *Language* 32: 158–194.

Malinowski, Bronislaw
1922   *Argonauts of the Western Pacific: An Account of Native Enterprise and Adventure in the Archipelagoes of Melanesian New Guinea*. London: George Routledge and Sons.

1944   *A Scientific Theory of Culture and Other Essays*. Chapel Hill, NC: University of North Carolina Press.

Oswalt, Wendell
1970   *Understanding Our Culture: An Anthropological View*. New York: Holt, Rinehart and Winston.

Parsons, Talcott
1964   *The Social System*. New York: The Free Press.

1968   *The Structure of Social Action: A Study in Social Theory and Special Reference to a Group of Recent European Writers*. New York: Free Press.

Pelto, Pertti, and Gretel Pelto
1979   *Anthropological Research: The Structure of Inquiry*. Cambridge: Cambridge University Press.

Perry, Richard
2003   *Five Concepts in Anthropological Thinking*. Upper Saddle River, NJ: Prentice Hall.

Pike, Kenneth
1947   *Phonemics: A Technique for Reducing Languages to Writing*. Ann Arbor: University of Michigan Press.

1954 *Language in Relation to a Unified Theory of the Structure of Human Behavior.* Glendale, CA: Summer Institute of Linguistics. Vol. 1.

Salzman, Philip
2001 *Understanding Culture: An Introduction to Anthropological Theory.* Prospects Heights, IL: Waveland.

Sapir, Edward
1949 The Unconscious Patterning of Behavior in Society. In *Selected Writings of Edward Sapir in Language, Culture, and Personality.* David Mandelbaum (ed.). Berkeley: University of California Press, pp. 544–559. (Original 1927.)

Schneider, David
1968 *American Kinship: A Cultural Account.* Englewood Cliffs, NJ: Prentice Hall.

Schneider, David, and Calvert Cottrell
1975 *The American Kin Universe: A Genealogical Study.* Chicago: Dept. of Anthropology, University of Chicago.

Spiro, Melford
1967 *Burmese Supernaturalism: A Study in the Explanation and Reduction of Suffering.* Englewood Cliffs, NJ: Prentice Hall.

1986 Cultural Relativism and the Future of Anthropology. *Cultural Anthropology* 1 (13): 259–289.

Spradley, James
1972 Foundations of Cultural Knowledge. In *Culture and Cognition: Rules, Maps, and Plans.* James Spradley (ed.). San Francisco: Chandler, pp. 3–38.

Spradley, James, and David McCurdy
1975 *Anthropology: The Cultural Perspective.* New York: John Wiley & Sons.

Sturtevant, William
1972 Studies in Ethnoscience. In *Culture and Cognition: Rules, Maps, and Plans.* James Spradley (ed.). San Francisco: Chandler, pp. 129–167.

Thompson, Evan
1995 *Colour Vision: A Study in Cognitive Science and the Philosophy of Perception.* London: Routledge.

Tonkinson, Robert
1991 *The Mardu Aborigines: Living the Dream in Australia's Desert.* Fort Worth: Holt, Rinehart and Winston.

Tyler, Stephen A.
1969 Introduction. In *Cognitive Anthropology.* Stephen Tyler (ed.). New York: Holt, Rinehart and Winston, pp. 1–23.

Wallace, Anthony
1972 Culture and Cognition. In *Culture and Cognition: Rules, Maps, and Plans.* James Spradley (ed.). San Francisco: Chandler, pp. 111–126.

White, Leslie
1987a Evolutionary Stages, Progress, and the Evaluation of Cultures. In *Leslie White: Ethnological Essays.* Beth Dillingham and Robert Carneiro (eds.). Albuquerque: University of New Mexico Press, pp. 59–83.

1987b Review of A. L. Kroeber and Clyde Kluckhohn, *Culture, A Critical Review of Concepts and Definitions.* In *Leslie A. White: Ethnological Essays.* Beth Dillingham and Robert Carneiro (eds.). Albuquerque: University of New Mexico Press, pp. 163–171. (Original 1952.)

Chapter 13

Barrett, Richard A.
1991 *Culture and Conduct: An Excursion in Anthropology.* Belmont, CA: Wadsworth.

Bernard, H. Russell
1995 *Research Methods in Anthropology: Qualitative and Quantitative Approaches.* Walnut Creek, CA: AltaMira.

Bohannan, Paul, and Mark Glazer
1988 Clifford Geertz. In *Highpoints in Anthropology.* P. Bohannan and M. Glazer (eds.). New York: Alfred Knopf, pp. 529-530.

Crapanzano, Vincent
1986 Hermes' Dilemma: The Masking of Subversion in Ethnographic Description. In *Writing Culture: The Poetics and Politics of Ethnography.* James Clifford and George Marcus (eds.). Berkeley: University of California Press, pp. 51-76.

Darnell, Regna
1984 Comment on Shankman: The Thick and the Thin. *Current Anthropology* 25 (3): 271.

D'Andrade, Roy
1995 *The Development of Cognitive Anthropology.* Cambridge: Cambridge University Press.

Dolgin, Janet, David Kemnitzer, and David Schnieder
1977 "As People Express Their Lives, So They Are . . ." In *Symbolic Anthropology: A Reader in the Study of Symbols and Meanings.* Janet Dolgin, David Kemnitzer, and David Schnieder (eds.). New York: Columbia University Press, pp. 3–44.

Douglas, Mary
1950 *Peoples of the Lake Nyasa Region.* London: Oxford University Press. (Published under her maiden name Mary Tew.)

1963 *The Lele of Kasai.* London: Oxford University Press.

1966 *Purity and Danger: An Analysis of Concepts of Pollution and Taboo.* New York: Praeger.

1972 Deciphering a Meal. *Daedalus* 101: 61–82.

1973 *Natural Symbols: Explorations in Cosmology.* London: Barrie and Jenkins.

Farrer, Claire
1984 Comment on Shankman: The Thick and the Thin. *Current Anthropology* 25 (3): 273–274.

Geertz, Clifford
1973 *The Interpretation of Cultures: Selected Essays.* New York: Basic Books.

1983 *Local Knowledge: Further Essays in Interpretive Anthropology.* New York: Basic Books.

1984 Distinguished Lecture: Anti Anti-Relativism. *American Anthropologist* 86 (2): 263– 278.

1988 Thick Description: Toward an Interpretive Theory of Culture. In *Highpoints in Anthropology.* P. Bohannan and M. Glazer (eds.). New York: Alfred Knopf, pp. 531–552.

Gennep, Arnold van
1960 *The Rites of Passage.* London: Routledge and Kegan Paul.

Gluckman, Max
1954 *Rituals of Rebellion in South-East Africa.* Manchester: Manchester University Press.

1956 *Custom and Conflict in Africa.* Glenco, IL: Free Press.

1965 *Politics, Law and Ritual in Tribal Society.* Chicago: Aldine.

Harris, Marvin
1991 *Cannibals and Kings: The Origins of Cultures.* New York: Vintage.

2001 *Cultural Materialism: The Struggle for a Science of Culture.* Walnut Creek, CA: AltaMira. (Original 1979.)

Herzfeld, Michael
2001 *Anthropology: Theoretical Practice in Culture and Society.* Oxford: Blackwell.

Kaplan, David, and Robert Manners
1972 *Culture Theory.* Englewood Cliffs, NJ: Prentice Hall.

Kottak, Conrad
2002 *Cultural Anthropology.* New York: McGraw-Hill.

Kuper, Adam
1999 *Anthropology and Anthropologists: The Modern British School.* London: Routledge.

Lett, James
1987 *The Human Enterprise: A Critical Introduction to Anthropological Theory.* Boulder, CO: Westview.

1997 *Science, Reason, and Anthropology: The Principles of Rational Inquiry.* Lanham, MD: Rowman and Littlefield.

Lévi-Strauss, Claude
1967 *Structural Anthropology.* New York: Basic Books. vol. 2.

1969 *The Raw and the Cooked: Introduction to a Science of Mythology.* New York: Harper and Row.

McGee, Jon, and Richard Warms
2000 *Anthropological Theory: An Introductory History.* Mountain View, CA: Mayfield.

Murphy, Robert
1979 *Cultural & Social Anthropology: An Overture.* Englewood Cliffs, NJ: Prentice Hall.

Nadel, Siegfried
1947 *The Nuba: An Anthropological Study of the Hill Tribes in Kordofan.* London: Oxford University Press.

1952 Witchcraft in four African Societies. An Essay in Comparison. *American Anthropologist* 54 (1): 18–29.

1954 *Nupe Religion.* London: Routledge and Kegan Paul.

1964 *The Theory of Social Structure.* Glencoe, IL: Free Press.

O'Meara, J. Tim
1989 Anthropology as Empirical Science. *American Anthropologist* 91 (2): 354–369.

Ortner, Sherry
1984 Theory in Anthropology Since the Sixties. *Comparative Studies in Society and History* 26 (1): 126–166.

Ortner, Sherry (ed.).
1999 *The Fate of Culture: Geertz and Beyond.* Berkeley: University of California Press.

Reyna, S. P.
1994 Literary Anthropology and the Case Against Science. *Man* 29: 555–581.

Ross, Eric
1980 Preface. In *Beyond the Myths of Culture: Essays in Cultural Materialism.* Eric Ross (ed.). New York: Academic Press, pp. xv–xvi.

Salzman, Philip
2001 *Understanding Culture: An Introduction to Anthropological Theory.* Prospects Heights, IL: Waveland.

Schneider, David
1968 *American Kinship: A Cultural Account.* Englewood Cliffs, NJ: Prentice Hall.

Shankman, Paul
1984 The Thick and the Thin: On the Interpretive Theoretical Program of Clifford Geertz. *Current Anthropology* 25 (3): 261–279.

Simoons, Frederick
1961 *Eat Not of This Flesh: Food Avoidances in the Old World.* Madison: University of Wisconsin Press.

Spiro, Melford
1968 Review of Purity and Danger: An Analysis of Concepts of Pollution and Taboo, by Mary Douglas. *American Anthropologist* 70 (2): 391–393.

1986 Cultural Relativism and the Future of Anthropology. *Cultural Anthropology* 1 (13): 259–289.

Turner, Victor
1957 *Schism and Continuity in an African Society.* Manchester: Manchester University Press.

1967 *The Forest of Symbols: Aspects of Ndembu Ritual.* Ithaca: Cornell University Press.

1968 *The Drums of Affliction: A Study of Religious Processes Among the Ndembu of Zambia.* Oxford: Clarendon.

1969 *The Ritual Process: Structure and Anti-Structure.* Chicago: Aldine.

1974 *Dramas, Fields, and Metaphors: Symbolic Action in Human Society.* Ithaca: Cornell University Press.

1977 Symbols in African Ritual. In *Symbolic Anthropology: A Reader in the Study of Symbols and Meanings.* Janet Dolgin, David Kemnitzer, and David Schnieder (eds.). New York: Columbia University Press, pp. 183–194.

1984   Liminality and the Performative Genres. In *Rite, Drama, Festival Spectacle: Rehearsals Toward a Theory of Cultural Performance.* J. MacAloon (ed.). Philadelphia: Institute for the Study of Human Issues, pp. 19–41.

White, Leslie
1949   The Symbol: The Origin and Basis of Human Behavior. In *The Science of Culture: A Study of Man and Civilization.* New York: Grove Press, pp. 22–39.

1962   Symboling: A Kind of Human Behavior. *Journal of Psychology* 53: 311–317.

1977   "Man, Culture, and Human Beings." In *Anthropology Full Circle.* Ino Rossi (ed.). New York: Praeger, pp. 246–251. (Original 1958.)

Wuthnow, Robert
1984   *Cultural Analysis: The Work of Peter L. Berger, Mary Douglas, Michel Foucault, and Jürgen Habermas.* London: Routledge & Kegan Paul.

Chapter 14

Adams, William
1998   *The Philosophical Roots of Anthropology.* Stanford, CA: CSLI Publications.

Alland, Alexander
1975   Adaptation. *Annual Review of Anthropology* 4: 59–73.

Althusser, Louis
1969   *For Marx.* London: Verso.

Althusser, Louis, and Etienne Balibar
1997   *Reading Capital.* London: Verso.

Applebaum, R. P.
1979   Born-Again Functionalism? A Reconsideration of Althusser's Structuralism. *Insurgent Sociologist* 9: 18–33.

Arens, William
1998   Why Man Has Been Left Off the Menu. *The Australian* (January 14): 35–36.

Bailey, Anne
1981   The Renewed Discussions of the Concept of the Asiatic Mode of Production. In *The Anthropology of Pre-Capitalist Societies.* Joel Kahn and Josep Llobera (eds.). Atlantic Highlands, NJ: Humanities Press, pp. 89–107.

Barrett, Stanley
1984   *The Rebirth of Anthropological Theory.* Toronto: University of Toronto Press.

1996   *Anthropology: A Student's Guide to Theory and Method.* Toronto: University of Toronto Press.

Binford, Lewis
1983   *In Pursuit of the Past.* London: Thames and Hudson.

Bloch, Maurice
1975   Introduction. In *Marxist Analysis and Social Anthropology.* M. Bloch (ed.). New York: John Wiley & Sons, pp. xi–xiv.

1983   *Marxism and Anthropology.* Oxford: Oxford University Press.

Boserup, Ester
1981   *Population and Technological Change.* Chicago: University of Chicago Press.

Carneiro, Robert
1970   A Theory of the Origin of the State. *Science* 169: 733–738.

1987   Cross-Currents in the Theory of State Formation. *American Ethnologist* 14: 756–770.

1988   The Circumscription Theory: Challenge and Response. *American Behavioral Scientist* 31: 497–511.

Cohen, Gerald Allan
2001   *Karl Marx's Theory of History: A Defence.* Princeton: Princeton University Press.

Cohen, Mark
1977   *The Food Crisis in Prehistory: Overpopulation and the Origins of Agriculture.* New Haven, CT: Yale University Press.

1995 The Osteological Paradox Reconsidered. *Current Anthropology* 35: 631–639.

Cook, Scott
1966 The "Anti-Market" Mentality: A Critique of the Substantive Approach to Economic Anthropology. *American Anthropologist* 68 (2): 323–345.

Cowgill, George
1975 On the Causes and Consequences of Ancient and Modern Populations. *American Anthropologist* 77: 505–525.

D'Andrade, Roy
1999 Culture Is Not Everything. In *Anthropological Theory in North America*. E. L. Cerroni-Long (ed.). Westport, CT: Bergin and Garvey, pp. 85–103.

Diamond, Stanley (ed.).
1979 *Toward a Marxist Anthropology: Problems and Perspectives*. The Hague: Mouton.

Diener, Paul
1978 The Dialectics of the Sacred Cow: Ecological Adaptation vs. Political Appropriation in the Origins of India's Cattle Complex. *Dialectical Anthropology* 3: 221–241.

Douglas, Mary
1966 *Purity and Danger: An Analysis of Concepts of Pollution and Taboo*. New York: Praeger.

Dunn, Stephen
1982 *The Fall and Rise of the Asiatic Mode of Production*. London: Routledge and Kegan Paul.

Ehrenreich, Jeffrey
1984 Comment on "Cultural Materialism: Food for Thought or Bum Steer?" by Drew Westen. *Current Anthropologist* 25 (5): 647–648.

Engels, Friedrich
1964 *Dialectics of Nature*. Moscow: Progress Publishers. (Original 1976.)

Fagan, Brian
1997 *People of the Earth: An Introduction to World Prehistory*. New York: HarperCollins.

Ferguson, R. Brian
1995 Infrastructural Determinism. In *Science, Materialism, and the Study of Culture*. Martin Murphy and Maxine Margolis (eds.). Gainesville: University Press of Florida, pp. 21–38.

Friedman, Jonathan
1974 The Place of Fetishism and the Problem of Materialist Interpretation. *Critique of Anthropology* 1: 26–62.

1975 Tribes States and Transformations. In *Marxist Analysis and Social Anthropology*. Maurice Bloch (ed.). London: Malaby Press, pp. 161–202.

1979 *System, Structure, and Contradiction in the Evolution of "Asiatic" Social Formations*. Copenhagen: National Museum of Denmark.

Gailey, Christine (ed.).
1992 *Dialectical Anthropology: Essays in Honor of Stanley Diamond*. Gainesville: University Press of Florida.

Gans, Eric
1985 *The End of Culture: Toward a Generative Anthropology*. Berkeley: University of California Press.

Gardner, Don
1999 Anthropophagy, Myth, and the Subtle Ways of Ethnocentrism. In *The Anthropology of Cannibalism*. L. Goldman (ed.). Westport, CT: Bergin and Garvey, pp. 27–50.

Gellner, Ernest
1992 *Postmodernism, Reason and Religion*. London: Routledge.

Giddens, Anthony
1979 *Central Problems in Social Theory: Action, Structure and Contradiction in Social Analysis*. London: Macmillan.

Godelier, Maurice
1975 Modes of Production, Kinship, and Demographic Structures. In *Marxist Analysis and Social Anthropology*. M. Bloch (ed.). New York: John Wiley & Sons, pp. 3–27.

1977 *Perspectives in Marxist Anthropology.* Cambridge: Cambridge University Press.

Goodenough, Ward
1964 Introduction. In *Explorations in Cultural Anthropology.* Ward Goodenough (ed.). New York: McGraw-Hill, pp. 1–24.

1970 *Description and Comparison in Cultural Anthropology.* Chicago: Aldine.

Gross, Daniel
1992 *Discovering Anthropology.* Mountain View, CA: Mayfield.

Gudeman, Stephen
1986 *Economics as Cultures: Models and Metaphors of Livelihood.* London: Routledge and Kegan Paul.

Handwerker, W.
1983 The First Demographic Transition: An Analysis of Subsistence Choices and Reproductive Consequences. *American Anthropologist* 85: 5–27.

Harris, Marvin
1966 The Cultural Ecology of India's Sacred Cattle. *Current Anthropology* 7: 51–66.

1974 *Cows, Pigs, Wars, and Witches.* New York: Random House.

1977 *Cannibals and Kings: The Origins of Cultures.* New York: Random House.

1978a Comment on "Ecology, Evolution, and the Search for Cultural Origins," by Paul Diener and Eugene E. Robkin. *Current Anthropology* 19: 515–517.

1978b India's Sacred Cow. *Human Nature* 1 (2): 28–36.

1981 *America Now: The Anthropology of a Changing Culture.* New York: Simon and Schuster.

1985 *Good to Eat: Riddles of Food and Culture.* New York: Simon and Schuster.

1989 *Our Kind: Who We Are, Where We Came From, and Where We Are Going.* New York: Harper and Row.

1991 *Cannibals and Kings: The Origins of Cultures.* New York: Vintage Books.

1994 Cultural Materialism Is Alive and Well and Won't Go Away Until Something Better Comes Along. In *Assessing Anthropology.* Robert Borofsky (ed.). New York: McGraw-Hill, pp. 62–76.

1997a Comment on "Causation and the Struggle for a Science of Culture" by Tim O'Meara. *Current Anthropology* 38: 410–415.

1997b *Culture, People, Nature: An Introduction to General Anthropology.* New York: Longman.

1999 *Theories of Culture in Postmodern Times.* Walnut Creek, CA: AltaMira.

2001a *Cultural Materialism: The Struggle for a Science of Culture.* Walnut Creek, CA: AltaMira. (Original 1979.)

2001b *The Rise of Anthropological Theory: A History of Theories of Culture.* Walnut Creek, CA: AltaMira Press. (Original 1968.)

Harris, Marvin, and Eric Ross (eds.).
1987a *Food and Evolution: Toward a Theory of Human Food Habits.* Philadelphia: Temple University Press.

Harris, Marvin, and Eric Ross
1987b *Death, Sex, and Fertility: Population Regulation in Pre-Industrial and Developing Societies.* New York: Columbia University Press.

Hassan, Fekri
1973 On Mechanisms of Population Growth during the Neolithic. *Current Anthropology* 14 (5): 535–542.

1981 *Demographic Archeology.* New York: Academic Press.

Hayden, Brian
1981 Research and Development in the Stone Age: Technological Transitions among Hunter-Gatherers. *Current Anthropology* 22: 519–548.

Headland, Thomas, Kenneth Pike, and Marvin Harris (eds.)
1990   *Emics and Etics: The Insider/Outsider Debate.* Newbury Park, CA: Sage Publications.

Herzfeld, Michael
2001   *Anthropology: Theoretical Practice in Culture and Society.* Oxford: Blackwell.

Heston, Alan
1971   An Approach to the Sacred Cow of India. *Current Anthropology* 12 (2): 191–209.

Jelliffe, D., and E. F. Jelliffe
1972   Lactation, Conception, and the Nutrition of the Nursing Mother and Child. *Journal of Pediatrics* 81: 829–833.

Johnson, Allen
1995   Explanation and Ground Truth: The Place of Cultural Materialism in Scientific Anthropology. In *Science, Materialism, and the Study of Culture.* Martin Murphy and Maxine Margolis (eds.). Gainesville: University Press of Florida, pp. 7–20.

Johnson, Allen, and T. Earle
1987   *The Evolution of Human Societies.* Stanford: Stanford University Press.

Johnson, Allen, and Orna Johnson
2001   Introduction to the Updated Edition. In *Cutural Materialism: The Struggle for a Science of Culture.* M. Harris. Walnut Creek, CA: AltaMira, pp. vi–xiv.

Kahn, Joel, and Josep Llobera
1981   Towards a New Marxism or a New Anthropology? In *The Anthropology of Pre-Capitalist Societies.* Joel Kahn and Josep Llobera (eds.). Atlantic Highlands, NJ: Humanities Press, pp. 263–329.

Kroeber, A. L.
1952   The Superorganic. In *The Nature of Culture.* A. L. Kroeber. Chicago: University of Chicago Press, pp. 22–51. (Originally published 1917.)

Layton, Robert
1997   *An Introduction to Theory in Anthropology.* Cambridge: Cambridge University Press.

Lett, James
1987   *The Human Enterprise: A Critical Introduction to Anthropological Theory.* Boulder, CO: Westview.

1997   *Science, Reason, and Anthropology: The Principles of Rational Inquiry.* Lanham, MD: Rowman and Littlefield.

Magnarella, Paul
1982   Cultural Materialism and the Problem of Probabilities. *American Anthropologist* 84: 138–142.

1999   Human Materialism: A Paradigm for Analyzing Sociocultural Systems and Understanding Human Behavior. In *Anthropological Theory in North America.* E. L. Cerroni-Long (ed.). Westport, CT: Bergin and Garvey, pp. 85–103.

Margolis, Maxine
1984   *Mothers and Such: Views of American Women and Why They Changed.* Berkeley: University of California Press.

2001   Introduction to the Updated Edition. In *The Rise of Anthropological Theory: A History of Theories of Culture.* M. Harris. Walnut Creek, CA: AltaMira, pp. vii–xiii.

Marx, Karl
1959a   Excerpt from Capital: A Critique of Political Economy. In *Basic Writings on Politics and Philosophy: Karl Marx and Friedrich Engels.* Lewis Feuer (ed.). New York: Anchor Books, pp. 133–146.

1959b   Excerpt from A Contribution to the Critique of Political Economy. In *Basic Writings on Politics and Philosophy: Karl Marx and Friedrich Engels.* Lewis Feuer (ed.). New York: Anchor Books, pp. 42–46.

1964   *Pre-Capitalist Economic Formations.* New York: International Publishers.

Marx, Karl, and Friedrich Engels
1959a   Excerpt from The German Ideology. In *Basic Writings on Politics and Philosophy: Karl Marx and Friedrich Engels.* Lewis Feuer (ed.). New York: Anchor Books, pp. 246–261.

1959b   Manifesto of the Communist Party. In *Basic Writings on Politics and Philosophy: Karl Marx and Friedrich Engels.* Lewis Feuer (ed.). New York: Anchor Books, pp. 1–41.

Milton, Kay
1996   *Environmentalism and Cultural Theory: Exploring the Role of Anthropology in Environmental Discourse.* London: Routledge.

Moore, Jerry
1997   *Visions of Culture: An Introduction to Anthropological Theories and Theorists.* Walnut Creek, CA: AltaMira.

Murphy, Martin, and Maxine Margolis (eds.).
1995a   An Introduction to Cultural Materialism. In *Science, Materialism, and the Study of Culture.* Martin Murphy and Maxine Margolis (eds.). Gainesville: University Press of Florida, pp. 1–4.

1995b   *Science, Materialism, and the Study of Culture.* Martin Murphy and Maxine Margolis (eds.). Gainesville: University Press of Florida.

Murphy, Robert
1980   *The Dialectics of Social Life: Alarms and Excursions in Anthropological Theory.* New York: Columbia University Press.

1994   The Dialectics of Deeds and Words. In *Assessing Anthropology.* Robert Borofsky (ed.). New York: McGraw-Hill, pp. 55–61.

Nag, Moni
1983   The Impact of Sociocultural Factors on Breastfeeding and Social Behavior. In *Determinants of Fertility in Developing Countries.* R. Bulatao et al. (eds.). New York: Academic Press, pp. 163–198.

O'Laughlin, Bridget
1975   Marxist Approaches in Anthropology. *Annual Review of Anthropology* 4: 341–370.

O'Meara, Tim
1997   Causation and the Struggle for a Science of Culture. *Current Anthropology* 38: 399–418.

Pandian, Jacob
1985   *Anthropology and the Western Tradition: Toward an Authentic Anthropology.* Prospect Heights, IL: Waveland.

Pike, Kenneth
1954   *Language in Relation to a Unified Theory of the Structure of Human Behavior.* Glendale, CA: Summer Institute of Linguistics.

Polanyi, Karl
1944   *The Great Transformation.* New York: Holt, Rinehart and Winston.

1968   Anthropology and Economic Theory. In Morton Fried (ed.). *Readings in Anthropology* (vol. 2). New York: Thomas Y. Crowell, pp. 215–238.

Rathje, William
1992   *Rubbish! The Archaeology of Garbage.* New York: HarperCollins.

Redding, Richard
1988   A General Explanation of Subsistence Change: From Hunting and Gathering to Food Production. *Journal of Anthropological Archaeology* 7: 56–97.

Rey, P. P.
1977   Contradictions de Classe dans le Sociétés Lignagères. *Dialectiques* 21: 116–133.

Ringer, Fritz
1997   *Max Weber's Methodology: The Unification of the Cultural and Social Sciences.* Cambridge, MA: Harvard University Press.

Ross, Eric
1980a   Introduction. In *Beyond the Myths of Culture: Essays in Cultural Materialism.* Eric Ross (ed.). New York: Academic Press, pp. xix–xxix.

1980b   Patterns of Diet and Forces of Production: An Economic and Ecological History of the Ascendancy of Beef in the United States Diet. In *Beyond the Myths of Culture: Essays in Cultural Materialism.* Eric Ross (ed.). New York: Academic Press, pp. 181–225.

1980c   Preface. In *Beyond the Myths of Culture: Essays in Cultural Materialism*. Eric Ross (ed.). New York: Academic Press, pp. xv–xvi.

Sahlins, Marshall
1955   Esoteric Efflorescence in Easter Island. *American Anthropologist* 57 (5): 1045–1052.

1972   *Stone Age Economics*. Chicago: Aldine.

1976   *Culture and Practical Reason*. Chicago: The University of Chicago Press.

Salzman, Philip
2001   *Understanding Culture: An Introduction to Anthropological Theory*. Prospects Heights, IL: Waveland.

Sanderson, Stephen
1990   *Social Evolutionism: A Critical History*. Oxford: Blackwell.

1999   *Social Transformations: A General Theory of Historical Development*. Lanham, MD: Rowman and Littlefield.

Sawer, Marian
1977   *Marxism and the Question of the Asiatic Mode of Production*. The Hague: Nijhoff.

Scupin, Raymond
1992   *Cultural Anthropology: A Global Perspective*. Englewood Cliffs, NJ: Prentice Hall.

Seddon David (ed.).
1978   *Relations of Production: Marxist Approaches to Economic Anthropology*. London: Cass.

Shannon, Thomas R.
1989   *An Introduction to the World-System*. Boulder, CO: Westview.

Sidky, H.
1996   *Irrigation and State Formation in Hunza: The Anthropology of a Hydraulic State*. Lanham, MD: University Press of America.

1997   *Witchcraft, Lycanthropy, Drugs and Disease: An Anthropological Study of the European Witch-Hunts*. New York: Peter Lang.

2003   *A Critique of Postmodern Anthropology: In Defense of Disciplinary Origins and Traditions*. Lewiston, New York: Mellen Press.

Sidky, M. H.
1987   Structural Domination and Control in the Capitalist World System: Prospects for Progressive Societal Transformation in the Third World. Thesis (Ph. D.), University of Pittsburgh.

Simoons, Frederick
1961   *Eat Not of This Flesh: Food Avoidances in the Old World*. Madison: University of Wisconsin Press.

1979   Questions in the Sacred-Cow Controversy. *Current Anthropology* 20 (3): 467–493.

Sokal, Alan, and Jean Bricmont
1998   *Fashionable Nonsense: Postmodern Intellectuals' Abuse of Science*. New York: Picador USA.

Sperber, Dan
1996   *Explaining Culture: A Naturalistic Approach*. Oxford: Blackwell.

Spooner, Brian (ed.).
1972   *Population Growth: Anthropological Implications*. Cambridge, MA: MIT Press.

Swanson, Guy E.
1964   *The Birth of the Gods: The Origin of Primitive Beliefs*. Ann Arbor: University of Michigan Press.

Tainter, Joseph A.
1988   *The Collapse of Complex Societies*. New York: Cambridge University Press.

Taylor, John
1979   *From Modernization to Modes of Production: A Critique of the Sociologies of Development and Underdevelopment*. Atlantic Highlands, NJ: Humanities Press.

Terray, Emmanuel
1972   *Marxism and "Primitive" Societies: Two Studies*. New York: Monthly Review Press.

Trigger, Bruce
1998   *Sociocultural Evolution: Calculation and Contingency*. Oxford: Blackwell.

Wallerstein, Immanuel
1979 *The Capitalist World-Economy.* Cambridge: Cambridge University Press.

Washburn, Wilcomb
1998 *Against the Anthropological Grain.* New Brunswick, NJ: Transaction Publishers.

Weber, Max
1930 *The Protestant Ethic and the Spirit of Capitalism.* London: Unwin.

Wenke, Robert
1990 *Patterns of Prehistory: Humankind's First Three Million Years.* New York: Oxford University Press.

Wessman, James
1981 *Anthropology and Marxism.* Cambridge, MA: Schenkman.

White, Benjamin
1982 Child Labour and Population Growth in Rural Asia. *Development and Change* 13: 587–610.

Wittfogel, Karl
1957 *Oriental Despotism: A Comparative Study of Total Power.* New Haven, CT: Yale University Press.

Wolf, Eric
1982 *Europe and the People Without History.* Berkeley: University of California Press.

Woolfson, Charles
1982 *The Labour Theory of Culture: A Re-Examination of Engels' Theory of Human Origins.* London: Routledge and Kegan Paul.

Young, Louise
1991 Easter Island: Scary Parable. *World Monitor* (August): 40–45.

Chapter 15

Abel, Reuben
1976 *Man Is the Measure: A Cordial Invitation to the Central Problems of Philosophy.* New York: The Free Press.

Abu-Lughod, Lila
1991 Writing Against Culture. In *Recapturing Anthropology.* Richard Fox (ed.). Santa Fe, NM: School of American Research Washington Press, pp. 37–62.

Andreski, Stanislav
1972 *Social Sciences as Sorcery.* New York: St. Martin's Press.

Appell, G. N.
1989 Facts, Fiction, Fads, and Follies: But Where is the Evidence? *American Anthropologist* 91 (1): 195–198.

Asad, Talal (ed.).
1973 *Anthropology and the Colonial Encounter.* London: Ithaca Press.

Bailey, F. G.
1991 *The Prevalence of Deceit.* Ithaca: Cornell University Press.

Barrett, Stanley
1996 *Anthropology: A Student's Guide to Theory and Method.* Toronto: University of Toronto Press.

1999 Forecasting Theory: Problems and Exemplars in the Twenty-First Century. In *Anthropological Theory in North America.* E. L. Cerroni-Long (ed.). Westport, CT: Bergin & Garvey, pp. 255–281.

Bartlett, F. C.
1923 *Psychology and Primitive Culture.* New York: Macmillan.

Bernard, H. Russell
1995 *Research Methods in Anthropology: Qualitative and Quantitative Approaches.* Walnut Creek, CA: AltaMira.

Brown, Donald
1991 *Human Universals.* Philadelphia: Temple University Press.

Carneiro, Robert
1995 Godzilla Meets New Age Anthropology: Facing the Post-Modernist Challenge to a Science of Culture. *Europa* 1: 3–31.

Cerroni-Long, E. L.
1996   Human Science. *Anthropology Newsletter* 37 (1): 50, 52.

1999   Introduction: Anthropology at Century's End. In *Anthropological Theory in North America.* E. L. Cerroni-Long (ed.). Westport, CT: Bergin & Garvey, pp. 1–18.

Clifford, James
1986   Introduction: Partial Truths. In *Writing Culture: The Poetics and Politics of Ethnography.* James Clifford and George Marcus (eds.). Berkeley: University of California Press, pp. 1–26.

1989   Comment on "Ethnography without Tears" by Paul A. Roth. *Current Anthropologist* 30 (5): 561–563.

Clifford, James, and George Marcus (eds.).
1986   *Writing Culture: The Poetics and Politics of Ethnography.* James Clifford and George Marcus (eds.). Berkeley: University of California Press.

Coker, Rory
2001   *Distinguishing Science and Pseudoscience.* Austin Society to Oppose Pseudoscience Fact Sheet. Austin, TX.

D'Andrade, Roy
1995a   Moral Models in Anthropology. *Current Anthropology* 36 (3): 399–408.

1995b   What Do You Think You're Doing? *Anthropology Newsletter* 36 (7): 1, 4.

Dawes, Robyn
2001   *Everyday Irrationality: How Pseudo-Scientists, Lunatics, and the Rest of Us Systematically Fail to Think Rationally.* Boulder, CO: Westview.

Derrida, Jaques
1976   *Of Grammatology.* Baltimore: Johns Hopkins University Press.

Diggins, John Patrick
1992   *The Rise and Fall of the American Left.* New York: W. W. Norton.

Doherty, Joe, Elspheth Graham, and Mo Malek
1992   Introduction: The Context and Language of Postmodernism. In *Postmodernism and the Social Sciences.* J. Doherty, E. Graham, and M. Malek (eds.). New York: St. Martin's Press, pp. 1–23.

Erickson, Paul, and Liam Murphy
1998   *A History of Anthropological Theory.* Peterborough, Ontario: Broadview Press.

Fabian, Johannes
1989   *Time and the Other: How Anthropology Makes Its Objects.* New York: Columbia University Press.

Foucault, Michel
1984   *The Foucault Reader.* New York: Pantheon.

Fox, Robin
1992   Anthropology and the "Teddy Bear" Picnic. *Society* (November–December): 47–55.

1997   State of the Art/Science in Anthropology. In *The Flight from Science and Reason.* P. Gross, N. Leavitt and M. Lewis (eds.). New York: New York Academy of Sciences. Distributed by Johns Hopkins University Press, pp. 327–345.

Frankel, Charles
1960   Philosophy and the Social Sciences. In *Both Human and Humane: The Humanities and Social Sciences in Graduate Education.* Charles E. Boewe and Roy F. Nichols (eds.). Philadelphia: University of Pennsylvania Press, pp. 94–117.

Geertz, Clifford
1988   *Works and Lives: The Anthropologist as Author.* Stanford: Stanford University Press.

Gellner, Ernest
1982   Relativism and Universals. In *Rationality and Relativism.* Martin Hollis and Steven Lukes (eds.). Cambridge: MIT Press, pp. 181–200.

1988   The Stakes in Anthropology. *American Scholar* 57: 17–30.

1992 *Postmodernism, Reason and Religion.* London: Routledge.

Gough, Kathleen
1968 Anthropology: Child of Imperialism. *Monthly Review* 19 (11): 12–27.

Gross, Paul R., and Norman Levitt
1994 *Higher Superstition: The Academic Left and Its Quarrels with Science.* Baltimore: The Johns Hopkins University Press.

Harris, Marvin
1994 Cultural Materialism Is Alive and Well and Won't Go Away Until Something Better Comes Along. In *Assessing Cultural Anthropology.* Robert Borofsky (ed.). New York: McGraw-Hill, pp. 62–76.

1999 *Theories of Culture in Postmodern Times.* Walnut Creek, CA: AltaMira.

Herzfeld, Michael
2001 *Anthropology: Theoretical Practice in Culture and Society.* Oxford: Blackwell.

Hollinger, Robert
1994 *Postmodernism and the Social Sciences: A Thematic Approach.* London: Sage.

Jarvie, I. C.
1988 Comment on Sangren's Rhetoric and the Authority of Ethnography: "Postmodernism" and the Social Reproduction of Texts. *Current Anthropology* 29 (3): 427–428.

Jorgensen, Joseph
1982 On Ethics in Anthropology. In *Anthropology for the Eighties.* J. Cole (ed.). New York: The Free Press, pp. 44–60.

Keesing, Roger
1994 Theories of Culture Revisited. In *Assessing Cultural Anthropology.* Robert Borofsky (ed.). New York: McGraw-Hill, pp. 301–312.

Kuznar, Lawrence A.
1997 *Reclaiming a Scientific Anthropology.* Walnut Creek, CA: AltaMira.

Layton, Robert
1997 *An Introduction to Theory in Anthropology.* Cambridge: Cambridge University Press.

Lecourt, Dominique
1977 *Proletarian Science?: The Case of Lysenko.* London: New Left Books.

Lett, James
1997 *Science, Reason, and Anthropology: The Principles of Rational Inquiry.* Lanham, MD: Rowman and Littlefield.

Magnarella, Paul J.
1993 *Human Materialism: A Model of Sociocultural Systems and a Strategy for Analysis.* Gainesville: University of Florida Press.

Marcus, George
1986 Afterword: Ethnographic Writing and Anthropological Careers. In *Writing Culture: The Poetics and Politics of Ethnography.* James Clifford and George Marcus (eds.). Berkeley: University of California Press, pp. 262–266.

1994 After the Critique of Ethnography: Faith, Hope, and Charity, but the Greatest of These Is Charity. In *Assessing Cultural Anthropology.* Robert Borofsky (ed.). New York: McGraw-Hill, pp. 40–54.

Marcus, George, and Michael Fischer
1986 *Anthropology as Cultural Critique: An Experimental Moment in the Human Sciences.* Chicago: University of Chicago Press.

Marx, Karl
1959 Excerpt from *A Contribution to the Critique of Political Economy.* In *Basic Writings on Politics and Philosophy: Karl Marx and Friedrich Engels.* Lewis Feuer (ed.). New York: Anchor Books, pp. 42–46.

Medvedev, Z. A.
1969 *The Rise and Fall of T. D. Lysenko.* New York: Columbia University Press.

Murdock, George
1945 The Common Denominator of Cultures. In *The Science of Man in the World Crisis.* Ralph Linton (ed.). New York: Columbia University Press, pp. 123–142.

Murphy, Robert
1994 The Dialectics of Deeds and Words. In *Assessing Cultural Anthropology.* Robert Borofsky (ed.). New York: McGraw-Hill, pp. 55–61.

Nencel, Lorraine, and Peter Pels
1991 Introduction: Critique and the Deconstruction of Anthropological Knowledge. In *Constructing Knowledge: Authority and Critique in Social Science.* L. Nencel and P. Pels (eds.). London: Sage, pp. 1–21.

Norris, Christopher
1997 *Against Relativism: Philosophy of Science, Deconstruction and Critical Theory.* Oxford: Blackwell.

O'Meara, Tim
1995 Comment on "Objectivity and Militancey: A Debate" by Roy D'Andrade and Nancy Scheper-Hughes. *Current Anthropology* 36 (3): 427–428.

Peoples, James, and Garrick Bailey
1994 *Humanity: An Introduction to Cultural Anthropology.* Minneapolis/St. Paul: West Publishing.

Perry, Richard
2003 *Five Concepts in Anthropological Thinking.* Upper Saddle River, NJ: Prentice Hall.

Rabinow, Paul
1986 Representations are Social Facts: Modernity and Postmodernity in Anthropology. In *Writing Culture: The Poetics and Politics of Ethnography.* James Clifford and George Marcus (eds.). Berkeley: University of California Press, pp. 234–261.

Reyna, S. P.
1994 Literary Anthropology and the Case Against Science. *Man* 29: 555–581.

Rosenau, Pauline
1992 *Post-Modernism and the Social Sciences.* Princeton, NJ: Princeton University Press.

Roth, Paul A.
1989 Ethnography without Tears. *Current Anthropology* 30 (5): 555–569.

Sagan, Carl
1995 *The Demon-Haunted World: Science as a Candle in the Dark.* New York: Random House.

Said, Edward
1979 *Orientalism.* New York: Vintage.

Sahlins, Marshall
1999 What Is Anthropological Enlightenment? *Annual Review of Anthropology* 28: i–xxiii.

Salzman, Philip
2001 *Understanding Culture: An Introduction to Anthropological Theory.* Prospects Heights, IL: Waveland.

Sangren, Steven P.
1988 Rhetoric and the Authority of Ethnography: "Postmodernism" and the Social Reproduction of Texts. *Current Anthropology* 29 (3): 405–435.

Sapire, David
1989 Comment on Ethnography without Tears by Paul Roth. *Current Anthropology* 30 (5): 564–565.

Scheper-Hughes, Nancy
1995 The Primacy of the Ethical: Propositions for a Militant Anthropology. *Current Anthropology* 36: 409–420.

Scholte, Bob
1972 Discontents in Anthropology. *Social Research* 38: 777–807.

Shweder, R.
1991 *Thinking Through Cultures.* Cambridge: Harvard University Press.

Sidky, H.
2003 *A Critique of Postmodern Anthropology: In Defense of Disciplinary Origins and Traditions.* Lewiston, NY: Mellen Press.

Soifer, Valerii
1994   *Lysenko and the Tragedy of Soviet Science.*
New Brunswick, NJ: Rutgers University Press.

Smart, Barry
1993   *Postmodernity.* London: Routledge.

Sokal, Alan, and Jean Bricmont
1998   *Fashionable Nonsense: Postmodern Intellectuals' Abuse of Science.* New York: Picador USA.

Tedlock, Barbara
1991   From Participant Observation to the Observation of Participation: The Emergence of Narrative Ethnography. *Journal of Anthropological Research* 47 (1): 69–94.

Trouillot, Michel-Rolph
1991   Anthropology and the Savage Slot: The Poetics and Politics of Otherness. In *Recapturing Anthropology: Working in the Present.* Richard Fox (ed.). Santa Fe, NM: School of American Research, pp. 17–44.

Tyler, Stephen A.
1986a   Post-Modern Anthropology. In *Discourse and the Social Life of Meaning.* Phyllis Chock and June Wyman (eds.). Washington, DC: Smithsonian Institution Press, pp. 23–49.

1986b   Post-Modern Ethnography: From Document of the Occult to Occult Document. In *Writing Culture: The Poetics and Politics of Ethnography.* James Clifford and George Marcus (eds.). Berkeley: University of California Press, pp. 122–140.

1987   *The Unspeakable.* Madison: University of Wisconsin Press.

Veeser, H. Aram (ed.).
1989   *The New Historicism.* New York: Routledge.

Wagner, Melinda
1999   The Study of Religion in American Society. In *Anthropology of Religion: A Handbook.* Stephen Glazier (ed.). Westport, CT: Praeger, pp. 85–101.

Williams, Michael
2001   *Problems of Knowledge: A Critical Introduction to Epistemology.* Oxford: New York.

Chapter 16

Barber, Benjamin R.
1992   Jihad vs. McWorld. *The Atlantic Monthly* March 269 (3): 53–65.

Fukuyama, Francis
1998   The End of History? In *The Geopolitics Reader.* G. Tuathail, S. Dalby, and P. Routledge (eds.). New York: Routledge, pp. 114–124.

Gilovich, Thomas
1991   *How We Know What Isn't So: The Fallibility of Human Reason in Everyday Life.* New York: The Free Press.

Huntington, Samuel P.
1996   *The Clash of Civilizations and the Remaking of World Order.* New York: Simon & Schuster.

McGee, Jon, and Richard Warms
2000   *Anthropological Theory: An Introductory History.* Mountain View, CA: Mayfield.

Moore, Henrietta
1999   Anthropological Theory at the Turn of the Century. In *Anthropological Theory Today.* Henrietta Moore (ed.). Cambridge, UK: Polity Press, pp. 1–23.

Rushdie, Salman
2001   America and Anti-Americans. *New York Times.* February 4.

2002   Yes, This Is About Islam. *New York Times.* November 2.

Salzman, Philip
2001   *Understanding Culture: An Introduction to Anthropological Theory.* Prospects Heights, IL: Waveland.

Credits

Chapter 1

1. From *Humanity: An Introduction to Cultural Anthropology* 3rd edition by Peoples/Bailey. © 1994. Reprinted with permission of Wadsworth, a division of Thomson Learning: www.thomson rights.com. Fax 800 730-2215.
2. From *Archaeology* 3rd edition by Thomas. © 1998. Reprinted with permission of Wadsworth, a division of Thomson Learning: www.thomsonrights.com. Fax 800 730-2215.
3. Rethelford, John (1990). *The Human Species: An Introduction to Biological Anthropology.* Mountain View, CA: Mayfield. Reproduced with permission of The McGraw-Hill Companies.
4. Reprinted by permission of Westview Press.
5. Harris, Marvin (1994). Cultural Materialism Is Alive and Well and Won't Go Away Until Something Better Comes Along. From Robert Borofsky (ed.), *Assessing Cultural Anthropology.* New York: McGraw-Hill. Reproduced with permission of The McGraw-Hill Companies.
6. From *Culture and Conduct: An Excursion in Anthropology* by Barrett. © 1991. Reprinted with permission of Wadsworth, a division of Thomson Learning: www.thomsonrights.com. Fax 800 730-2215.
7. From *Yanomamo: The Fierce People* 4th edition by Chagnon. © 1992. Reprinted with permission of Wadsworth, a division of Thomson Learning: www.thomsonrights.com. Fax 800 730-2215.
8. From Culture and Conduct: An Excursion in Anthropology by Barrett. © 1991. Reprinted with permission of Wadsworth, a division of Thomson Learning: www.thomsonrights.com. Fax 800 730-2215.

Chapter 2

1. Reprinted with the permission of The Free Press, a Division of Simon and Schuster Adult Publishing Group, from *How We Know What Isn't So: The Fallibility of Human Reason in Everyday Life* by Thomas Gilovich. Copyright 1991 by the Free Press.
2. Copyright © 1979 by the Estate of Carl Sagan. Originally printed in *Broca's Brain: Reflections on the Romance of Science* by Random House. Reprinted with permission from the Estate of Carl Sagan.
3. Reprinted by permission of Pergamon Press.
4. Martin Orans. 1996. *Not Even Wrong: Margaret Mead, Derek Free-*

man, and the Samoans. Novato, CA: Chandler and Sharp. Reprinted by permission of Chandler & Sharp Publishers, Inc.
5. Gross, Paul R., and Norman Levitt. *Higher Superstition: The Academic Left and Its Quarrels with Science.* pp. 58, 74. Copyright 1994 The John Hopkins University Press. Reprinted with permission of The Johns Hopkins University Press.
6. Bernard, H. Russell (1994). Method Belongs to All of Us. In *Assessing Anthropology.* Robert Borofsky (ed.). New York: McGraw-Hill. Reproduced with permission of The McGraw-Hill Companies.
7. Reprinted by permission of Simon & Schuster Inc.
8. Reproduced by permission of the American Anthropological Association from *American Anthropologist* volume 91:1, 1989. Not for sale or further reproduction.
9. Reprinted by permission of AltaMira Press, a division of Rowman & Littlefield, Inc.
10. Reprinted with the permission of The Free Press, a Division of Simon and Schuster Adult Publishing Group, from *How We Know What Isn't So: The Fallibility of Human Reason in Everyday Life* by Thomas Gilovich. Copyright 1991 by the Free Press.
11. Reprinted by permission of AltaMira Press, a division of Rowman & Littlefield Publishers, Inc.
12. Copyright © 1996 by Carl Sagan. Reprinted with permission from the Estate of Carl Sagan.
13. Reprinted by permission of AltaMira Press, a Division of Roman and Littlefield, Inc.
14. Reprinted by permission of Rowman & Littlefield Publishers, Inc.
15. From Vincent Crapanzano. 1995. "Comment on 'Objectivity and Militancy: A Debate' by Roy D'Andrade and Nancy Scheper-Hughes." *Current Anthropology,* 36(3), 420–421.
16. Reprinted by permission of Transaction Publishers. "Anthropology and the 'Teddy Bear' Picnic" by Robin Fox, *Society* (November-December), 1992. Copyright © 1992 by Transaction Publishers.
17. Reprinted by permission of AltaMira Press, a division of Rowman & Littlefield, Inc.
18. Reprinted by permission of Royal Anthropological Institute.

Chapter 3

1. Reprinted by permission of The American Philosophical Society.
2. Reprinted by permission of The American Philosophical Society.

3. From *Primitive Social Organization* by Elman Service. Copyright © 1971. Reproduced with the permission of The McGraw-Hill Companies.
4. Reprinted by permission of The University of Chicago Press.

Chapter 4
1. Reprinted by permission of The University of Chicago Press.
2. Reprinted by permission of The University of Chicago Press.
3. Reprinted by permission of The University of Chicago Press.
4. Reprinted by permission of University Press of America, Inc.

Chapter 5
1. From Linton, Ralph (1936/1964). *The Study of Man: An Introduction.* New York: Appleton-Century-Crofts. Reprinted with the permission of Ann Linton.
2. Reprinted by permission of Prentice Hall.
3. Copyright © 1979 by the Estate of Carl Sagan. Originally printed in *Broca's Brain: Reflections on the Romance of Science* by Random House. Reprinted with permission from the Estate of Carl Sagan.
4. Reprinted by permission of St. Martin's Press.
5. Copyright © 1979 by the Estate of Carl Sagan. Originally printed in *Broca's Brain: Reflections on the Romance of Science* by Random House. Reprinted with permission from the Estate of Carl Sagan.
6. Copyright © 1979 by the Estate of Carl Sagan. Originally printed in *Broca's Brain: Reflections on the Romance of Science* by Random House. Reprinted with permission from the Estate of Carl Sagan.
7. Copyright © 1979 by the Estate of Carl Sagan. Originally printed in *Broca's Brain: Reflections on the Romance of Science* by Random House. Reprinted with permission from the Estate of Carl Sagan.
8. From James Clifford and George Marcus (eds.). 1986. On Ethnographic Allegory. In *Writing Culture: The Poetics and Politics of Ethnography.* Berkeley: University of California Press. Copyright © 1986 The Regents of the University of California.
9. Copyright © 1979 by the Estate of Carl Sagan. Originally printed in *Broca's Brain: Reflections on the Romance of Science* by Random House. Reprinted with permission from the Estate of Carl Sagan.
10. Copyright © 1979 by the Estate of Carl Sagan. Originally printed in *Broca's Brain: Reflections on the Romance of Science* by Random House. Reprinted with permission from the Estate of Carl Sagan.
11. Reprinted by permission of *Skeptic* Magazine.

Chapter 6
1. Reprinted by permission of AltaMira Press.
2. Reprinted with the permission of The Free Press, a Division of Simon & Schuster Adult Publishing Group, from *Race, Language and Culture* by Franz Boas. Copyright © 1940 by Franz Boas. Copyright © renewed 1968 by Franziska Boas Michelson.
3. Reprinted by permission of University of New Mexico Press.
4. Reprinted by permission of Houghton Mifflin Company.
5. Reprinted with the permission of The Free Press, a Division of Simon & Schuster Adult Publishing Group, from *Race, Language and Culture* by Franz Boas. Copyright © 1940 by Franz Boas. Copyright © renewed 1968 by Franziska Boas Michelson.
6. Reprinted with the permission of The Free Press, a Division of Simon & Schuster Adult Publishing Group, from *Race, Language and Culture* by Franz Boas. Copyright © 1940 by Franz Boas. Copyright © renewed 1968 by Franziska Boas Michelson.
7. Reprinted with the permission of The Free Press, a Division of Simon & Schuster Adult Publishing Group, from *Race, Language and Culture* by Franz Boas. Copyright © 1940 by Franz Boas. Copyright © renewed 1968 by Franziska Boas Michelson.
8. Reprinted by permission of Houghton Mifflin Company.
9. Reprinted with the permission of The Free Press, a Division of Simon & Schuster Adult Publishing Group, from *Race, Language and Culture* by Franz Boas. Copyright © 1940 by Franz Boas. Copyright © renewed 1968 by Franziska Boas Michelson.
10. From *Humanity: An Introduction to Cultural Anthropology* 3rd edition by Peoples/Bailey. © 1994. Reprinted with permission of Wadsworth, a division of Thomson Learning: www.thomsonrights.com. Fax 800 730-2215.

11. Reprinted with the permission of The Free Press, a Division of Simon & Schuster Adult Publishing Group, from *Race, Language and Culture* by Franz Boas. Copyright © 1940 by Franz Boas. Copyright © renewed 1968 by Franziska Boas Michelson.
12. Reprinted with the permission of The Free Press, a Division of Simon & Schuster Adult Publishing Group, from *Race, Language and Culture* by Franz Boas. Copyright © 1940 by Franz Boas. Copyright © renewed 1968 by Franziska Boas Michelson.
13. Reprinted from Dan Sperber, 1996, *Explaining Culture: A Naturalist Approach.* Oxford: Blackwell.
14. Reprinted with the permission of The Free Press, a Division of Simon & Schuster Adult Publishing Group, from *Race, Language and Culture* by Franz Boas. Copyright © 1940 by Franz Boas. Copyright © renewed 1968 by Franziska Boas Michelson.
15. Reprinted with the permission of The Free Press, a Division of Simon & Schuster Adult Publishing Group, from *Race, Language and Culture* by Franz Boas. Copyright © 1940 by Franz Boas. Copyright © renewed 1968 by Franziska Boas Michelson.
16. Reprinted with the permission of The Free Press, a Division of Simon & Schuster Adult Publishing Group, from *Race, Language and Culture* by Franz Boas. Copyright © 1940 by Franz Boas. Copyright © renewed 1968 by Franziska Boas Michelson.
17. Reprinted by permission of Dr. David Kaplan.
18. Reprinted with the permission of The Free Press, a Division of Simon & Schuster Adult Publishing Group, from *Race, Language and Culture* by Franz Boas. Copyright © 1940 by Franz Boas. Copyright © renewed 1968 by Franziska Boas Michelson.
19. Reprinted with the permission of The Free Press, a Division of Simon & Schuster Adult Publishing Group, from *Race, Language and Culture* by Franz Boas. Copyright © 1940 by Franz Boas. Copyright © renewed 1968 by Franziska Boas Michelson.
20. Reprinted with the permission of The Free Press, a Division of Simon & Schuster Adult Publishing Group, from *Race, Language and Culture* by Franz Boas. Copyright © 1940 by Franz Boas. Copyright © renewed 1968 by Franziska Boas Michelson.
21. Reprinted by permission of University of New Mexico Press.
22. Reprinted by permission of Dr. David Kaplan.
23. Reprinted by permission of University of New Mexico Press.
24. Reprinted by permission of University of New Mexico Press.
25. Reprinted with the permission of The Free Press, a Division of Simon & Schuster Adult Publishing Group, from *Social Structure* by George Peter Murdock. Copyright © 1940 by The Macmillan Company. Copyright © renewed 1977 by George Peter Murdock.
26. Reprinted by permission of University of New Mexico Press.
27. Reprinted by permission of Basic Books.

Chapter 7
1. From Clark Wissler. 1926. *The Relation of Nature to Man in Aboriginal America.* New York: Oxford University Press.
2. From Clark Wissler. 1926. *The Relation of Nature to Man in Aboriginal America.* New York: Oxford University Press.
3. Reprinted by permission of Henry Holt and Company.
4. Reprinted by permission of University of Chicago Press.
5. Reprinted by permission of University of Chicago Press.
6. Reprinted by permission of University of Chicago Press.
7. Reprinted by permission of University of Chicago Press.
8. Reprinted by permission of University of Chicago Press.
9. Reprinted by permission of University of Chicago Press.
10. Reprinted by permission of University of Chicago Press.
11. Reprinted by permission of University of Chicago Press.
12. Reprinted by permission of University of Chicago Press.
13. Reprinted by permission of University of Chicago Press.
14. Reprinted by permission of University of Chicago Press.
15. Reprinted by permission of University of Chicago Press.
16. Reprinted by permission of University of Chicago Press.
17. Reprinted by permission of University of Chicago Press.
18. Reprinted by permission of University of Chicago Press.
19. Reprinted by permission of University of Chicago Press.
20. Reprinted by permission of University of Chicago Press.
21. From Alfred Kroeber, 1944, *Configurations of Culture Growth.* Copyright © University of California Press.
22. Reprinted by permission of University of Chicago Press.
23. Reprinted by permission of AltaMira Press.
24. From "The status of linguistics as a science," Edward Sapir, *Language* 5:207-14, 1929. Reprinted by permission of Linguistic Society of America.

25. From *Humanity: An Introduction to Cultural Anthropology* 3rd edition by Peoples/Bailey. © 1994. Reprinted with permission of Wadsworth, a division of Thomson Learning: www.thomson rights.com. Fax 800 730-2215.
26. Excerpts from *Patterns of Culture* by Ruth Benedict. Copyright 1934 by Ruth Benedict; copyright renewed © 1961 by Ruth Valentine. Reprinted by permission of Houghton Mifflin Co. All rights reserved.
27. Excerpts from *Patterns of Culture* by Ruth Benedict. Copyright 1934 by Ruth Benedict; copyright renewed © 1961 by Ruth Valentine. Reprinted by permission of Houghton Mifflin Co. All rights reserved.
28. Excerpts from *Patterns of Culture* by Ruth Benedict. Copyright 1934 by Ruth Benedict; copyright renewed © 1961 by Ruth Valentine. Reprinted by permission of Houghton Mifflin Co. All rights reserved.
29. Excerpts from *Patterns of Culture* by Ruth Benedict. Copyright 1934 by Ruth Benedict; copyright renewed © 1961 by Ruth Valentine. Reprinted by permission of Houghton Mifflin Co. All rights reserved.
30. Excerpts from *Patterns of Culture* by Ruth Benedict. Copyright 1934 by Ruth Benedict; copyright renewed © 1961 by Ruth Valentine. Reprinted by permission of Houghton Mifflin Co. All rights reserved.
31. Excerpts from *Patterns of Culture* by Ruth Benedict. Copyright 1934 by Ruth Benedict; copyright renewed © 1961 by Ruth Valentine. Repri nted by permission of Houghton Mifflin Co. All rights reserved.
32. Excerpt from *The Chrysanthemum and the Sword* by Ruth Benedict. Copyright 1946 by Ruth Benedict; copyright renewed © 1974 by Donald G. Freeman. Reprinted by permission of Houghton Mifflin Co. All rights reserved.
33. Excerpts from *Patterns of Culture* by Ruth Benedict. Copyright 1934 by Ruth Benedict; copyright renewed © 1961 by Ruth Valentine. Reprinted by permission of Houghton Mifflin Co. All rights reserved.
34. Excerpts from *Patterns of Culture* by Ruth Benedict. Copyright 1934 by Ruth Benedict; copyright renewed © 1961 by Ruth Valentine. Reprinted by permission of Houghton Mifflin Co. All rights reserved.
35. Excerpts from *Patterns of Culture* by Ruth Benedict. Copyright 1934 by Ruth Benedict; copyright renewed © 1961 by Ruth Valentine. Reprinted by permission of Houghton Mifflin Co. All rights reserved.
36. Reprinted by permission of AltaMira Press.
37. Excerpts from pp. 12-13, 169 (total 138 words) from *Coming of Age in Samoa* by Margaret Mead. Copyright © 1928, 1949, 1955, 1961, 1973 by Margaret Mead. Reprinted by permission of HarperCollins Publishers Inc.
38. Excerpts from pp. 12-13, 169 (total 138 words) from *Coming of Age in Samoa* by Margaret Mead. Copyright © 1928, 1949, 1955, 1961, 1973 by Margaret Mead. Reprinted by permission of HarperCollins Publishers Inc.
39. Martin Orans. 1996. *Not Even Wrong: Margaret Mead, Derek Freeman, and the Samoans.* Novato, CA: Chandler and Sharp. Reprinted by permission of Chandler & Sharp Publishers, Inc.
40. From George Marcus and Michael Fischer. 1986. *Anthropology as Cultural Critique: An Experimental Moment in the Human Sciences.* Chicago: University of Chicago Press. Copyright © 1986 The University of Chicago Press.
41. Martin Orans. 1996. *Not Even Wrong: Margaret Mead, Derek Freeman, and the Samoans.* Novato, CA: Chandler and Sharp. Reprinted by permission of Chandler & Sharp Publishers, Inc.
42. Martin Orans. 1996. *Not Even Wrong: Margaret Mead, Derek Freeman, and the Samoans.* Novato, CA: Chandler and Sharp. Reprinted by permission of Chandler & Sharp Publishers, Inc.
43. Martin Orans. 1996. *Not Even Wrong: Margaret Mead, Derek Freeman, and the Samoans.* Novato, CA: Chandler and Sharp. Reprinted by permission of Chandler & Sharp Publishers, Inc.
44. Martin Orans. 1996. *Not Even Wrong: Margaret Mead, Derek Freeman, and the Samoans.* Novato, CA: Chandler and Sharp. Reprinted by permission of Chandler & Sharp Publishers, Inc.

Chapter 8

1. Reprinted by permission of the Continuum International Publishing Group.
2. Reprinted by permission of Routledge.
3. From *Argonauts of the Western Pacific* by Bronislaw Malinowski, 1922. London: Routledge.
4. From *Argonauts of the Western Pacific* by Bronislaw Malinowski, 1922. London: Routledge.
5. From *Argonauts of the Western Pacific* by Bronislaw Malinowski, 1922. London: Routledge.
6. From *Argonauts of the Western Pacific* by Bronislaw Malinowski, 1922. London: Routledge.
7. From *Argonauts of the Western Pacific* by Bronislaw Malinowski, 1922. London: Routledge.
8. From *Argonauts of the Western Pacific* by Bronislaw Malinowski, 1922. London: Routledge.
9. From *Argonauts of the Western Pacific* by Bronislaw Malinowski, 1922. London: Routledge.
10. From *Argonauts of the Western Pacific* by Bronislaw Malinowski, 1922. London: Routledge.
11. From *Argonauts of the Western Pacific* by Bronislaw Malinowski, 1922. London: Routledge.
12. From Edmund Leach. 1966. "On the 'Founding Fathers'," *Current Anthropology,* 7(5), 560-567. Reprinted with permission of The University of Chicago Press.
13. Reprinted by permission of Kegan Paul.
14. From *A Scientific Theory of Culture and Other Essays* by Bronislaw Malinowski, with a preface by Huntington Cairns. Copyright © 1944 by the University of North Carolina Press; renewed 1972. Used by permission of the publisher.
15. From *A Scientific Theory of Culture and Other Essays* by Bronislaw Malinowski, with a preface by Huntington Cairns. Copyright © 1944 by the University of North Carolina Press; renewed 1972. Used by permission of the publisher.
16. From *A Scientific Theory of Culture and Other Essays* by Bronislaw Malinowski, with a preface by Huntington Cairns. Copyright © 1944 by the University of North Carolina Press; renewed 1972. Used by permission of the publisher.
17. From *A Scientific Theory of Culture and Other Essays* by Bronislaw Malinowski, with a preface by Huntington Cairns. Copyright © 1944 by the University of North Carolina Press; renewed 1972. Used by permission of the publisher.
18. From *A Scientific Theory of Culture and Other Essays* by Bronislaw Malinowski, with a preface by Huntington Cairns. Copyright © 1944 by the University of North Carolina Press; renewed 1972. Used by permission of the publisher.
19. From *A Scientific Theory of Culture and Other Essays* by Bronislaw Malinowski, with a preface by Huntington Cairns. Copyright © 1944 by the University of North Carolina Press; renewed 1972. Used by permission of the publisher.
20. From *A Scientific Theory of Culture and Other Essays* by Bronislaw Malinowski, with a preface by Huntington Cairns. Copyright © 1944 by the University of North Carolina Press; renewed 1972. Used by permission of the publisher.
21. From *A Scientific Theory of Culture and Other Essays* by Bronislaw Malinowski, with a preface by Huntington Cairns. Copyright © 1944 by the University of North Carolina Press; renewed 1972. Used by permission of the publisher.
22. From *A Scientific Theory of Culture and Other Essays* by Bronislaw Malinowski, with a preface by Huntington Cairns. Copyright © 1944 by the University of North Carolina Press; renewed 1972. Used by permission of the publisher.
23. From *Argonauts of the Western Pacific* by Bronislaw Malinowski, 1922. London: Routledge.
24. From *Argonauts of the Western Pacific* by Bronislaw Malinowski, 1922. London: Routledge.
25. From *Argonauts of the Western Pacific* by Bronislaw Malinowski, 1922. London: Routledge.
26. From *Argonauts of the Western Pacific* by Bronislaw Malinowski, 1922. London: Routledge.
27. From *Argonauts of the Western Pacific* by Bronislaw Malinowski, 1922. London: Routledge.
28. From *Argonauts of the Western Pacific* by Bronislaw Malinowski, 1922. London: Routledge.
29. From *Argonauts of the Western Pacific* by Bronislaw Malinowski, 1922. London: Routledge.
30. From *Argonauts of the Western Pacific* by Bronislaw Malinowski, 1922. London: Routledge.
31. Reprinted by permission of Beacon Press.
32. Reprinted by permission of Routledge.
33. From *A Scientific Theory of Culture and Other Essays* by Bronislaw Malinowski, with a preface by Huntington Cairns. Copyright ©

1944 by the University of North Carolina Press; renewed 1972. Used by permission of the publisher.

34. From *A Scientific Theory of Culture and Other Essays* by Bronislaw Malinowski, with a preface by Huntington Cairns. Copyright © 1944 by the University of North Carolina Press; renewed 1972. Used by permission of the publisher.

Chapter 9

1. Reprinted with the permission of The Free Press, a Division of Simon and Schuster Adult Publishing Group, from *Structure and Function in Primitive Society: Essays and Addresses* by Alfred R. Radcliffe-Brown. Copyright 1952 by the Free Press.
2. Reprinted with the permission of The Free Press, a Division of Simon and Schuster Adult Publishing Group, from *Structure and Function in Primitive Society: Essays and Addresses* by Alfred R. Radcliffe-Brown. Copyright 1952 by the Free Press.
3. Reprinted by permission of Routledge.
4. Reprinted with the permission of The Free Press, a Division of Simon and Schuster Adult Publishing Group, from *Structure and Function in Primitive Society: Essays and Addresses* by Alfred R. Radcliffe-Brown. Copyright 1952 by the Free Press.
5. From *The Social Anthropology of Radcliffe-Brown*, Adam Kuper (ed.), 1977. London: Routledge.
6. From *The Social Anthropology of Radcliffe-Brown*, Adam Kuper (ed.), 1977. London: Routledge.
7. From *The Social Anthropology of Radcliffe-Brown*, Adam Kuper (ed.), 1977. London: Routledge.
8. From *The Social Anthropology of Radcliffe-Brown*, Adam Kuper (ed.), 1977. London: Routledge.
9. Reprinted by permission of Simon & Schuster Inc.
10. Reprinted by permission of Simon & Schuster Inc.
11. Reprinted with the permission of The Free Press, a Division of Simon and Schuster Adult Publishing Group, from *Structure and Function in Primitive Society: Essays and Addresses* by Alfred R. Radcliffe-Brown. Copyright 1952 by the Free Press.
12. From *The Social Anthropology of Radcliffe-Brown*, Adam Kuper (ed.), 1977. London: Routledge.
13. From *The Social Anthropology of Radcliffe-Brown*, Adam Kuper (ed.), 1977. London: Routledge.
14. From *The Social Anthropology of Radcliffe-Brown*, Adam Kuper (ed.), 1977. London: Routledge.
15. Reprinted with the permission of The Free Press, a Division of Simon and Schuster Adult Publishing Group, from *Structure and Function in Primitive Society: Essays and Addresses* by Alfred R. Radcliffe-Brown. Copyright 1952 by the Free Press.
16. Reprinted with the permission of The Free Press, a Division of Simon and Schuster Adult Publishing Group, from *Structure and Function in Primitive Society: Essays and Addresses* by Alfred R. Radcliffe-Brown. Copyright 1952 by the Free Press.
17. Reprinted with the permission of The Free Press, a Division of Simon and Schuster Adult Publishing Group, from *Structure and Function in Primitive Society: Essays and Addresses* by Alfred R. Radcliffe-Brown. Copyright 1952 by the Free Press.
18. Reprinted with the permission of The Free Press, a Division of Simon and Schuster Adult Publishing Group, from *Structure and Function in Primitive Society: Essays and Addresses* by Alfred R. Radcliffe-Brown. Copyright 1952 by the Free Press.
19. Reprinted with the permission of Cambridge University Press.
20. Reprinted with the permission of The Free Press, a Division of Simon and Schuster Adult Publishing Group, from *Structure and Function in Primitive Society: Essays and Addresses* by Alfred R. Radcliffe-Brown. Copyright 1952 by the Free Press.
21. Reprinted with the permission of The Free Press, a Division of Simon and Schuster Adult Publishing Group, from *Structure and Function in Primitive Society: Essays and Addresses* by Alfred R. Radcliffe-Brown. Copyright 1952 by the Free Press.
22. Reprinted with the permission of The Free Press, a Division of Simon and Schuster Adult Publishing Group, from *Structure and Function in Primitive Society: Essays and Addresses* by Alfred R. Radcliffe-Brown. Copyright 1952 by the Free Press.
23. Reprinted with the permission of The Free Press, a Division of Simon and Schuster Adult Publishing Group, from *Structure and Function in Primitive Society: Essays and Addresses* by Alfred R. Radcliffe-Brown. Copyright 1952 by the Free Press.
24. Reprinted with the permission of The Free Press, a Division of Simon and Schuster Adult Publishing Group, from *Structure and Function in Primitive Society: Essays and Addresses* by Alfred R. Radcliffe-Brown. Copyright 1952 by the Free Press.
25. Reprinted with the permission of The Free Press, a Division of Simon and Schuster Adult Publishing Group, from *Structure and Function in Primitive Society: Essays and Addresses* by Alfred R. Radcliffe-Brown. Copyright 1952 by the Free Press.
26. Reprinted with the permission of The Free Press, a Division of Simon and Schuster Adult Publishing Group, from *Structure and Function in Primitive Society: Essays and Addresses* by Alfred R. Radcliffe-Brown. Copyright 1952 by the Free Press.
27. Reprinted by permission of Dr. David Kaplan.
28. Reprinted with the permission of The Free Press, a Division of Simon and Schuster Adult Publishing Group, from *Structure and Function in Primitive Society: Essays and Addresses* by Alfred R. Radcliffe-Brown. Copyright 1952 by the Free Press.

Chapter 10

1. Reprinted by permission of University of New Mexico Press.
2. Leslie White, 1959, *The Evolution of Culture*. Copyright © The McGraw-Hill Companies, Inc.
3. Reprinted by permission of University of New Mexico Press.
4. Reprinted by permission of University of New Mexico Press.
5. Reprinted by permission of University of New Mexico Press.
6. John Bodley, 1975/1990. *Victims of Progress*. Copyright © The McGraw-Hill Companies, Inc.
7. Reprinted by permission of University of New Mexico Press.
8. Reprinted by permission of University of New Mexico Press.
9. Reprinted by permission of University of New Mexico Press.
10. Reprinted by permission of University of New Mexico Press.
11. Reprinted by permission of University of New Mexico Press.
12. Reprinted by permission of University of New Mexico Press.
13. Reprinted by permission of University of New Mexico Press.
14. Reprinted by permission of University of New Mexico Press.
15. Reprinted by permission of University of New Mexico Press.
16. Reprinted by permission of the Estate of Professor Leslie White.
17. Reprinted by permission of the Estate of Professor Leslie White.
18. Leslie White, 1959, *The Evolution of Culture*. Copyright © The McGraw-Hill Companies, Inc.
19. Leslie White, 1959, *The Evolution of Culture*. Copyright © The McGraw-Hill Companies, Inc.
20. Leslie White, 1959, *The Evolution of Culture*. Copyright © The McGraw-Hill Companies, Inc.
21. Reproduced by permission of the American Anthropological Association from *American Anthropologist* volume 78, 1976. Not for sale or further reproduction.
22. Leslie White, 1959, *The Evolution of Culture*. Copyright © The McGraw-Hill Companies, Inc.
23. Reprinted by permission of AltaMira Press.
24. From Marshall Sahlins, 1960, Evolution: Specific and General. In *Evolution and Culture*. Marshall Sahlins and Elman Service (eds.). Ann Arbor: University of Michigan Press.
25. Reprinted by permission of AltaMira Press.
26. Reprinted by permission of AltaMira Press.
27. Reprinted by permission of University of Illinois Press.
28. Reprinted by permission of University of Illinois Press.
29. Reprinted by permission of University of Illinois Press.
30. Reprinted by permission of University of Illinois Press.
31. Reprinted by permission of University of Illinois Press.
32. Reprinted by permission of Mrs. Ann Rappaport.
33. Reprinted by permission of University of Illinois Press.
34. Reprinted by permission of University of Illinois Press.
35. Reprinted by permission of University of Illinois Press.
36. Reprinted by permission of University of Illinois Press.
37. Reprinted by permission of University of Illinois Press.
38. Reprinted by permission of Social Science Research Council.
39. Reprinted by permission of University of Illinois Press.
40. Reprinted by permission of University of Illinois Press.
41. Reprinted by permission of University of Illinois Press.
42. Reprinted by permission of University of Illinois Press.
43. Reprinted by permission of University of Illinois Press.
44. Reprinted by permission of University of Illinois Press.
45. Reprinted by permission of University of New Mexico Press.
46. Reprinted by permission of University of New Mexico Press.
47. Reprinted by permission of University of Illinois Press.
48. Reprinted by permission of University of Illinois Press.
49. Reprinted by permission of Blackwell Publishing.
50. Reprinted by permission of University of Toronto Press.

Chapter 11

1. Reprinted by permission of University of Toronto Press.
2. From *Claude Levi-Strauss* by Edmund Leach, copyright © 1970, 1974 by Edmund Leach. Used by permission of Viking Penguin, a division of Penguin Group (USA) Inc.
3. Reproduced with permission of PERSEUS BOOKS GROUP in the format Textbook via Copyright Clearance Center.
4. From *Claude Levi-Strauss* by Edmund Leach, copyright © 1970, 1974 by Edmund Leach. Used by permission of Viking Penguin, a division of Penguin Group (USA) Inc.
5. From *Claude Levi-Strauss* by Edmund Leach, copyright © 1970, 1974 by Edmund Leach. Used by permission of Viking Penguin, a division of Penguin Group (USA) Inc.
6. Reprinted from *Beyond the Myths of Culture: Essays in Cultural Materialism*, Eric Ross (ed.), Copyright © 1980, with permission from Elsevier.
7. From *Claude Levi-Strauss* by Edmund Leach, copyright © 1970, 1974 by Edmund Leach. Used by permission of Viking Penguin, a division of Penguin Group (USA) Inc.
8. Reproduced with permission of PERSEUS BOOKS GROUP in the format Textbook via Copyright Clearance Center.
9. Reprinted by permission of University of Chicago Press.
10. Reproduced with permission of PERSEUS BOOKS GROUP in the format Textbook via Copyright Clearance Center.
11. Reproduced with permission of PERSEUS BOOKS GROUP in the format Textbook via Copyright Clearance Center.
12. Reproduced with permission of PERSEUS BOOKS GROUP in the format Textbook via Copyright Clearance Center.
13. Reproduced with permission of PERSEUS BOOKS GROUP in the format Textbook via Copyright Clearance Center..
14. Reproduced with permission of PERSEUS BOOKS GROUP in the format Textbook via Copyright Clearance Center..
15. Reproduced with permission of PERSEUS BOOKS GROUP in the format Textbook via Copyright Clearance Center.
16. From *Claude Levi-Strauss* by Edmund Leach, copyright © 1970, 1974 by Edmund Leach. Used by permission of Viking Penguin, a division of Penguin Group (USA) Inc.
17. Reproduced with permission of PERSEUS BOOKS GROUP in the format Textbook via Copyright Clearance Center.
18. Reproduced with permission of PERSEUS BOOKS GROUP in the format Textbook via Copyright Clearance Center.
19. Reproduced with permission of PERSEUS BOOKS GROUP in the format Textbook via Copyright Clearance Center.
20. From *Claude Levi-Strauss* by Edmund Leach, copyright © 1970, 1974 by Edmund Leach. Used by permission of Viking Penguin, a division of Penguin Group (USA) Inc.
21. Reprinted by permission of AltaMira Press.
22. From E. E. Evans-Pritchard, *Theories of Primitive Religion*, 1965. Reprinted by permission of Oxford University Press.
23. Reprinted by permission of Dr. David Kaplan.
24. Reprinted with the permission of Cambridge University Press.
25. Reprinted by permission of University of Chicago Press.
26. From *Claude Levi-Strauss* by Edmund Leach, copyright © 1970, 1974 by Edmund Leach. Used by permission of Viking Penguin, a division of Penguin Group (USA) Inc.

Chapter 12

1. Reprinted (abstracted/excerpted) with permission from Franz Boas. 1943. Recent Anthropology. *Science*, 98, 311-314, 334-337.
2. From *Argonauts of the Western Pacific* by Bronislaw Malinowski, 1922. London: Routledge.
3. From Charles Frake (1972), The Ethnographic Study of Cognitive Systems. In *Culture and Cognition: Rules, Maps, and Plans.* James Spradley (ed.). San Francisco: Chandler.
4. From Charles Frake (1972), The Ethnographic Study of Cognitive Systems. In *Culture and Cognition: Rules, Maps, and Plans.* James Spradley (ed.). San Francisco: Chandler.
5. From *Cognitive Anthropology* by Tyler. Copyright 1969. Reprinted with permission of Wadsworth, a division of Thomson Learning.
6. Reprinted by permission of Georgetown University Press.
7. From Anthony Wallace (1972), Culture and Cognition. In *Culture and Cognition: Rules, Maps, and Plans.* James Spradley (ed.). San Francisco: Chandler.
8. Reprinted by permission of Georgetown University Press.
9. From James Spradley (1972), Foundations of Cultural Knowledge. In *Culture and Cognition: Rules, Maps, and Plans.* James Spradley (ed.). San Francisco: Chandler.
10. Ward Goodenough, 1964, *Explorations in Cultural Anthropology.* Copyright © The McGraw-Hill Companies, Inc.
11. From Anthony Wallace (1972), Culture and Cognition. In *Culture and Cognition: Rules, Maps, and Plans.* James Spradley (ed.). San Francisco: Chandler.
12. Reprinted by permission of the Summer Institute of Linguistics.
13. Reprinted by permission of the Summer Institute of Linguistics.
14. Reprinted by permission of the Summer Institute of Linguistics.
15. Reprinted by permission of Wiley Publishers.
16. Reprinted by permission of Wiley Publishers.
17. Reprinted by permission of Wiley Publishers.
18. From Charles Frake (1972), The Ethnographic Study of Cognitive Systems. In *Culture and Cognition: Rules, Maps, and Plans.* James Spradley (ed.). San Francisco: Chandler.
19. From *Cognitive Anthropology* by Tyler. Copyright 1969. Reprinted with permission of Wadsworth, a division of Thomson Learning.
20. Reprinted by permission of AltaMira Press.
21. From *Cognitive Anthropology* by Tyler. Copyright 1969. Reprinted with permission of Wadsworth, a division of Thomson Learning.
22. Reproduced by permission of the American Anthropological Association from *American Anthropologist* volume 66, 1964. Not for sale or further reproduction.
23. Reproduced by permission of the American Anthropological Association from *American Anthropologist* volume 66, 1964. Not for sale or further reproduction.
24. Reprinted with permission of Prentice-Hall.
25. Reprinted with permission of Ward Goodenough.
26. Reprinted with permission of Ward Goodenough.
27. Reprinted by permission of Dr. David Kaplan.
28. From William Sturtevant (1972), Studies in Ethnoscience. In *Culture and Cognition: Rules, Maps, and Plans.* James Spradley (ed.). San Francisco: Chandler.
29. Reprinted by permission of Harcourt Brace.
30. Reproduced by permission of the American Anthropological Association from *American Anthropologist* volume 68, 1966. Not for sale or further reproduction.

Chapter 13

1. Reprinted by permission of the Estate of Professor Leslie White.
2. From *Anthropology Full Circle* by Ino Rossi. Reprinted with the permission of Thomson Learning: www.thomsonrights.com <http://www.thomsonrights.com/>. Fax 800 730-2215. © 1991.
3. From *Culture and Conduct: An Excursion in Anthropology* by Barrett. © 1991. Reprinted with permission of Wadsworth, a division of Thomson Learning: www.thomsonrights.com. Fax 800 730-2215.
4. Reprinted from *Victor Turner: Dramas, Fields, and Metaphors: Symbolic Action in Human Society.* Copyright © 1974 by Cornell University. Used by permission of the publisher, Cornell University Press.
5. Reprinted from *Victor Turner: Dramas, Fields, and Metaphors: Symbolic Action in Human Society.* Copyright © 1974 by Cornell University. Used by permission of the publisher, Cornell University Press.
6. Reprinted from *Victor Turner: Dramas, Fields, and Metaphors: Symbolic Action in Human Society.* Copyright © 1974 by Cornell University. Used by permission of the publisher, Cornell University Press.
7. Reprinted from *Victor Turner: The Forest of Symbols: Aspects of Ndembu Ritual.* Copyright © 1967 by Cornell University. Used by permission of the publisher, Cornell University Press.
8. Reprinted from *Victor Turner: The Forest of Symbols: Aspects of Ndembu Ritual.* Copyright © 1967 by Cornell University. Used by permission of the publisher, Cornell University Press.
9. Reprinted from *Victor Turner: The Forest of Symbols: Aspects of Ndembu Ritual.* Copyright © 1967 by Cornell University. Used by permission of the publisher, Cornell University Press.
10. Reprinted from *Victor Turner: The Forest of Symbols: Aspects of Ndembu Ritual.* Copyright © 1967 by Cornell University. Used by permission of the publisher, Cornell University Press.
11. Reprinted from *Victor Turner: The Forest of Symbols: Aspects of Ndembu Ritual.* Copyright © 1967 by Cornell University. Used by permission of the publisher, Cornell University Press.
12. Reprinted from *Victor Turner: Dramas, Fields, and Metaphors: Symbolic Action in Human Society.* Copyright © 1974 by Cornell University. Used by permission of the publisher, Cornell University Press.

13. Reprinted with permission from *The Ritual Process: Structure and Anti-Structure* by Victor Turner, pp. 96–97, 130. Copyright © 1969 by Victor R. Turner. Renewed 1997 by Edith Turner. Published by Aldine de Gruyter, Hawthorne, New York.
14. Reprinted with permission from *The Ritual Process: Structure and Anti-Structure* by Victor Turner, pp. 96–97, 130. Copyright © 1969 by Victor R. Turner. Renewed 1997 by Edith Turner. Published by Aldine de Gruyter, Hawthorne, New York.
15. Reprinted with permission from *The Ritual Process: Structure and Anti-Structure* by Victor Turner, pp. 96–97, 130. Copyright © 1969 by Victor R. Turner. Renewed 1997 by Edith Turner. Published by Aldine de Gruyter, Hawthorne, New York.
16. Reprinted from *Victor Turner: The Forest of Symbols: Aspects of Ndembu Ritual.* Copyright © 1967 by Cornell University. Used by permission of the publisher, Cornell University Press.
17. Reprinted from *Victor Turner: The Forest of Symbols: Aspects of Ndembu Ritual.* Copyright © 1967 by Cornell University. Used by permission of the publisher, Cornell University Press.
18. Reprinted from *Victor Turner: The Forest of Symbols: Aspects of Ndembu Ritual.* Copyright © 1967 by Cornell University. Used by permission of the publisher, Cornell University Press.
19. Reprinted from *Victor Turner: The Forest of Symbols: Aspects of Ndembu Ritual.* Copyright © 1967 by Cornell University. Used by permission of the publisher, Cornell University Press.
20. Reprinted from *Victor Turner: The Forest of Symbols: Aspects of Ndembu Ritual.* Copyright © 1967 by Cornell University. Used by permission of the publisher, Cornell University Press.
21. From *Culture and Conduct: An Excursion in Anthropology* by Barrett. © 1991. Reprinted with permission of Wadsworth, a division of Thomson Learning: www.thomsonrights.com. Fax 800 730-2215.
22. Reprinted from *Victor Turner: The Forest of Symbols: Aspects of Ndembu Ritual.* Copyright © 1967 by Cornell University. Used by permission of the publisher, Cornell University Press.
23. Reprinted from *Victor Turner: The Forest of Symbols: Aspects of Ndembu Ritual.* Copyright © 1967 by Cornell University. Used by permission of the publisher, Cornell University Press.
24. Reprinted by permission of Routledge.
25. Reprinted by permission of Routledge.
26. Reprinted by permission of Routledge.
27. Reprinted by permission of Routledge.
28. Reprinted by permission of Routledge.
29. Reprinted by permission of Routledge.
30. Reprinted by permission of Routledge.
31. Reprinted by permission of Routledge.
32. "Deciphering a Meal" reprinted by permission of *Daedalus,* Journal of the American Academy of Arts and Sciences, from the issue entitled, "Myth, Symbol, and Culture," Winter 1972, Vol. 101, No. 1.
33. Reproduced by permission of the American Anthropological Association from *American Anthropologist* 70:2, 1968. Not for sale or further reproduction.
34. From *The Interpretation of Cultures* by Clifford Geertz. Copyright © 1973 by Basic Books. Reprinted by permission of Basic Books, Inc., Publishers.
35. From *The Interpretation of Cultures* by Clifford Geertz. Copyright © 1973 by Basic Books. Reprinted by permission of Basic Books, Inc., Publishers.
36. From *The Interpretation of Cultures* by Clifford Geertz. Copyright © 1973 by Basic Books. Reprinted by permission of Basic Books, Inc., Publishers.
37. Reprinted by permission of Basic Books.
38. From Paul Shankman. 1984. "The Thick and the Thin: On the Interpretive Theoretical Program of Clifford Geertz." *Current Anthropology,* 25(3), 261–279. Reprinted with permission of The University of Chicago Press.
39. From *The Interpretation of Cultures* by Clifford Geertz. Copyright © 1973 by Basic Books. Reprinted by permission of Basic Books, Inc., Publishers.
40. From *The Interpretation of Cultures* by Clifford Geertz. Copyright © 1973 by Basic Books. Reprinted by permission of Basic Books, Inc., Publishers.
41. From *The Interpretation of Cultures* by Clifford Geertz. Copyright © 1973 by Basic Books. Reprinted by permission of Basic Books, Inc., Publishers.
42. From *The Interpretation of Cultures* by Clifford Geertz. Copyright © 1973 by Basic Books. Reprinted by permission of Basic Books, Inc., Publishers.
43. Reproduced by permission of the American Anthropological Association from *Cultural Anthropology* volume 13:1, 1986. Not for sale or further reproduction.
44. From *The Interpretation of Cultures* by Clifford Geertz. Copyright © 1973 by Basic Books. Reprinted by permission of Basic Books, Inc., Publishers.
45. From *The Interpretation of Cultures* by Clifford Geertz. Copyright © 1973 by Basic Books. Reprinted by permission of Basic Books, Inc., Publishers.
46. From *The Interpretation of Cultures* by Clifford Geertz. Copyright © 1973 by Basic Books. Reprinted by permission of Basic Books, Inc., Publishers.
47. From *The Interpretation of Cultures* by Clifford Geertz. Copyright © 1973 by Basic Books. Reprinted by permission of Basic Books, Inc., Publishers.
48. From *The Interpretation of Cultures* by Clifford Geertz. Copyright © 1973 by Basic Books. Reprinted by permission of Basic Books, Inc., Publishers.
49. From *The Interpretation of Cultures* by Clifford Geertz. Copyright © 1973 by Basic Books. Reprinted by permission of Basic Books, Inc., Publishers.

Chapter 14
1. From Martin Murphy and Maxine Margolis (eds.). 1995. *Science, Materialism, and the Study of Culture.* Gainesville: University of Florida Press. Reprinted with permission of the University Press of Florida.
2. From Martin Murphy and Maxine Margolis (eds.). 1995. *Science, Materialism, and the Study of Culture.* Gainesville: University of Florida Press. Reprinted with permission of the University Press of Florida.
3. Reprinted by permission of AltaMira Press, a Division of Rowman & Littlefield Publishers, Inc.
4. Reprinted by permission of AltaMira Press.
5. Harris, Marvin (1994). Cultural Materialism Is Alive and Well and Won't Go Away Until Something Better Comes Along. From Robert Borofsky (ed.), *Assessing Cultural Anthropology.* New York: McGraw-Hill. Reproduced with permission of The McGraw-Hill Companies.
6. Reprinted by permission of Professor Lewis Feuer.
7. Reprinted by permission of Professor Lewis Feuer.
8. Reprinted by permission of Professor Lewis Feuer.
9. Reprinted by permission of Professor Lewis Feuer.
10. Reprinted by permission of Wiley Publishers.
11. Reprinted by permission of Professor Lewis Feuer.
12. From Maurice Bloch, *Marxism and Anthropology,* 1983. Reprinted by permission of Oxford University Press.
13. Copyright © 1998 by Alan Sokal and Jean Bricmont. From *Fashionable Nonsense: Postmodern Philosophers' Abuse of Science* by Alan Sokal and Jean Bricmont. Reprinted by permission of Picador.
14. Reprinted by permission of AltaMira Press.
15. Reprinted by permission of Professor Lewis Feuer.
16. Reprinted by permission of AltaMira Press.
17. Reprinted by permission of AltaMira Press.
18. Reprinted by permission of AltaMira Press.
19. Reprinted by permission of AltaMira Press.
20. Reprinted from *Beyond the Myths of Culture: Essays in Cultural Materialism,* Eric Ross (ed.), Copyright © 1980, with permission from Elsevier.
21. Reprinted by permission of AltaMira Press.
22. Reprinted by permission of AltaMira Press.
23. Reprinted by permission of AltaMira Press, a Division of Rowman & Littlefield Publishers, Inc.
24. Reprinted by permission of AltaMira Press, a Division of Rowman & Littlefield Publishers, Inc.
25. Reproduced with permission of PERSEUS BOOKS GROUP in the format Textbook via Copyright Clearance Center.
26. Harris, Marvin (1994). Cultural Materialism Is Alive and Well and Won't Go Away Until Something Better Comes Along. From Robert Borofsky (ed.), *Assessing Cultural Anthropology.* New York: McGraw-Hill. Reproduced with permission of The McGraw-Hill Companies.
27. Reprinted by permission of AltaMira Press.
28. From Martin Murphy and Maxine Margolis (eds.). 1995. *Science, Materialism, and the Study of Culture.* Gainesville: University of Florida Press. Reprinted with permission of the University Press of Florida.

29. Reprinted by permission of AltaMira Press.
30. Reprinted by permission of AltaMira Press.
31. Harris, Marvin (1994). Cultural Materialism Is Alive and Well and Won't Go Away Until Something Better Comes Along. From Robert Borofsky (ed.), *Assessing Cultural Anthropology*. New York: McGraw-Hill. Reproduced with permission of The McGraw-Hill Companies.
32. Harris, Marvin (1994). Cultural Materialism Is Alive and Well and Won't Go Away Until Something Better Comes Along. From Robert Borofsky (ed.), *Assessing Cultural Anthropology*. New York: McGraw-Hill. Reproduced with permission of The McGraw-Hill Companies.
33. From Martin Murphy and Maxine Margolis (eds.). 1995. *Science, Materialism, and the Study of Culture*. Gainesville: University of Florida Press. Reprinted with permission of the University Press of Florida.
34. Reprinted by permission of AltaMira Press.
35. Harris, Marvin (1994). Cultural Materialism Is Alive and Well and Won't Go Away Until Something Better Comes Along. From Robert Borofsky (ed.), *Assessing Cultural Anthropology*. New York: McGraw-Hill. Reproduced with permission of The McGraw-Hill Companies.
36. Reprinted by permission of AltaMira Press.
37. Reprinted by permission of AltaMira Press.
38. Reprinted by permission of AltaMira Press, a Division of Rowman & Littlefield Publishers, Inc.
39. Reprinted by permission of AltaMira Press, a Division of Rowman & Littlefield Publishers, Inc.
40. Reprinted by permission of University of Chicago Press.
41. Reprinted by permission of University of Chicago Press.
42. Reprinted by permission of University of Chicago Press.
43. Reprinted by permission of University of Chicago Press.
44. Reprinted by permission of University of Chicago Press.
45. Reprinted from *Beyond the Myths of Culture: Essays in Cultural Materialism*, Eric Ross (ed.), Copyright © 1980, with permission of Elsevier.
46. Reprinted from *Beyond the Myths of Culture: Essays in Cultural Materialism*, Eric Ross (ed.), Copyright © 1980, with permission of Elsevier.
47. Reprinted by permission of University of Chicago Press.
48. Reprinted by permission of AltaMira Press.
49. Reprinted from *Beyond the Myths of Culture: Essays in Cultural Materialism*, Eric Ross (ed.), Copyright © 1980, with permission of Elsevier.
50. Reprinted by permission of AltaMira Press.
51. Reprinted by permission of AltaMira Press.

Chapter 15

1. Reproduced by permission of the American Anthropological Association from *American Anthropologist* volume 91:1, 1989. Not for sale or further reproduction.
2. From George Marcus and Michael Fischer. 1986. *Anthropology as Cultural Critique: An Experimental Moment in the Human Sciences*. Chicago: University of Chicago Press. Copyright © 1986 The University of Chicago Press.
3. From George Marcus and Michael Fischer. 1986. *Anthropology as Cultural Critique: An Experimental Moment in the Human Sciences*. Chicago: University of Chicago Press. Copyright © 1986 The University of Chicago Press.
4. Copyright © 1998 by Alan Sokal and Jean Bricmont. From *Fashionable Nonsense: Postmodern Philosophers' Abuse of Science* by Alan Sokal and Jean Bricmont. Reprinted by permission of Picador.
5. Harris, Marvin (1994). Cultural Materialism Is Alive and Well and Won't Go Away Until Something Better Comes Along. From Robert Borofsky (ed.), *Assessing Cultural Anthropology*. New York: McGraw-Hill. Reproduced with permission of The McGraw-Hill Companies.
6. Reprinted by permission of The Johns Hopkins University Press.
7. From "Artful Realism" by Richard Shweder, originally published in *VIA*, Vol. 9, 1900. Reprinted by permission.
8. From Ernest Gellner (1982), Relativism and Universals. Martin Hollis and Steven Lukes (eds.), *Rationality and Relativism*. Cambridge, MA: The MIT Press, pp. 181–200.
9. From Steven P. Sangren. 1988. "Rhetoric and the Authority of Ethnography: 'Postmodernism' and the Social Reproduction of

Texts." *Current Anthropology*, 29(3), 405–435. Reprinted with permission of The University of Chicago Press.
10. From Tim O'Meara. 1995. "Comment on 'Objectivity and Militancy: A Debate' by Roy D'Andrade and Nancy Scheper-Hughes." *Current Anthropology*, 36(3), 427–428. Reprinted with permission of The University of Chicago Press.
11. From George Marcus and Michael Fischer. 1986. *Anthropology as Cultural Critique: An Experimental Moment in the Human Sciences*. Chicago: University of Chicago Press. Copyright © 1986 The University of Chicago Press.
12. Reprinted by permission of Royal Anthropological Institute.
13. Reprinted with the permission of The Free Press, a Division of Simon and Schuster Adult Publishing Group, from *Man Is the Measure: A Cordial Invitation to the Central Problems of Philosophy* by Reuben Abel. Copyright 1976 by the Free Press.
14. Reprinted with the permission of The Free Press, a Division of Simon and Schuster Adult Publishing Group, from *Man Is the Measure: A Cordial Invitation to the Central Problems of Philosophy* by Reuben Abel. Copyright 1976 by the Free Press.
15. Reproduced by permission of the American Anthropological Association from *American Anthropologist* volume 91:1, 1989. Not for sale or further reproduction.
16. Reprinted by permission of The McGraw-Hill Companies.
17. Reprinted by permission of The McGraw-Hill Companies.
18. Reprinted by permission of Waveland Press, Inc. from Philip Salzman, *Understanding Culture: An Introduction to Anthropological Theory* (Long Grove, IL: Waveland Press, Inc., 2001). All rights reserved.
19. Reprinted from F. G. Bailey, *The Prevalence of Deceit*. Copyright © 1991 by Cornell University. Used by permission of the publisher, Cornell University Press.
20. From George Marcus and Michael Fischer. 1986. *Anthropology as Cultural Critique: An Experimental Moment in the Human Sciences*. Chicago: University of Chicago Press. Copyright © 1986 The University of Chicago Press.
21. From James Clifford and George Marcus (eds.). 1986. On Ethnographic Allegory. In *Writing Culture: The Poetics and Politics of Ethnography*. Berkeley: University of California Press. Copyright © 1986 The Regents of the University of California.
22. From James Clifford and George Marcus (eds.). 1986. On Ethnographic Allegory. In *Writing Culture: The Poetics and Politics of Ethnography*. Berkeley: University of California Press. Copyright © 1986 The Regents of the University of California.
23. Gross, Paul R., and Norman Levitt. *Higher Superstition: The Academic Left and Its Quarrels with Science*. pp. 58, 74. Copyright 1994 The Johns Hopkins University Press. Reprinted with permission of The Johns Hopkins University Press.
24. Reprinted by permission of Robert Carneiro.
25. Reprinted by permission of Robert Carneiro.
26. Copyright © 1996 by Carl Sagan. Reprinted with permission from the Estate of Carl Sagan.
27. Reprinted by permission of Routledge.
28. Reprinted by permission of Westview Press.
29. From James Clifford and George Marcus (eds.). 1986. On Ethnographic Allegory. In *Writing Culture: The Poetics and Politics of Ethnography*. Berkeley: University of California Press. Copyright © 1986 The Regents of the University of California.
30. From James Clifford and George Marcus (eds.). 1986. On Ethnographic Allegory. In *Writing Culture: The Poetics and Politics of Ethnography*. Berkeley: University of California Press. Copyright © 1986 The Regents of the University of California.
31. Reproduced by permission of the American Anthropological Association from *American Anthropologist* volume 91:1, 1989. Not for sale or further reproduction.
32. From James Clifford and George Marcus (eds.). 1986. On Ethnographic Allegory. In *Writing Culture: The Poetics and Politics of Ethnography*. Berkeley: University of California Press. Copyright © 1986 The Regents of the University of California.
33. From James Clifford and George Marcus (eds.). 1986. On Ethnographic Allegory. In *Writing Culture: The Poetics and Politics of Ethnography*. Berkeley: University of California Press. Copyright © 1986 The Regents of the University of California.
34. Copyright © 1998 by Alan Sokal and Jean Bricmont. From *Fashionable Nonsense: Postmodern Philosophers' Abuse of Science* by Alan Sokal and Jean Bricmont. Reprinted by permission of Picador.
35. Reprinted with the permission of The Free Press, a Division of Simon and Schuster Adult Publishing Group, from *Man Is the

Measure: A Cordial Invitation to the Central Problems of Philosophy by Reuben Abel. Copyright 1976 by the Free Press.
36. Copyright © 1998 by Alan Sokal and Jean Bricmont. From *Fashionable Nonsense: Postmodern Philosophers' Abuse of Science* by Alan Sokal and Jean Bricmont. Reprinted by permission of Picador.

Chapter 16
1. Reprinted by permission of Benjamin Barber and The Atlantic Monthly.

2. Reprinted by permission of Polity Press.
3. Reprinted by permission of Waveland Press, Inc. from Philip Salzman, *Understanding Culture: An Introduction to Anthropological Theory* (Long Grove, IL: Waveland Press, Inc., 2001). All rights reserved.

Index